Commercial Law

Commercial Law

Other Titles in the Textbook Series

Constitutional and Administrative Law
Contract
Criminal Law
Employment Law
Environmental Law
Equity & Trust
Family Law
Land Law
Tort

Commercial Law

Sweet & Maxwell's Textbook Series

TENTH EDITION

Professor Robert Stokes

The Liverpool Law School

SWEET & MAXWELL

THOMSON REUTERS

Published in 2022 by Thomson Reuters
trading as Sweet & Maxwell.
Thomson Reuters is registered in England &Wales, Company No. 1679046.
Registered office and address for service:
5 Canada Square, Canary Wharf, London E14 5AQ.

For further information on our products and services, visit
www.sweetandmaxwell.co.uk

Typeset by Cheshire Typesetting Ltd, Cuddington, Cheshire

Printed in bound in Great Britain by CPI Group (UK) Ltd, Croydon, CR0 4YY

A CIP catalogue record for this book is available from the British Library.

Print ISBN: 978-0-414-10341-2
ProView ISBN: 978-0-414-10345-0
eBook ISBN: 978-0-414-10344-3
Print and ProView ISBN: 978-0-414-10342-9

FSC
www.fsc.org
MIX
Paper | Supporting responsible forestry
FSC® C013604

Guide to the Book

Table of Contents

Table of Contents

The Table of Contents provides you with an at a glance overview of the coverage for each chapter.

Table of Cases

The Table of Cases provides you with a handy list of all cases referred to througout this book.

Table of Cases

A v National Blood Authority (No.1); sub nom. **Hepatitis C Litigation (No.1)**, Re [2001] 3 All E.R. 289; [2001] Lloyd's Rep. Med. 187; (2001) 60 B.M.L.R. 1 QBD 9-009, 9-010, 9-015
Abouzaid v Mothercare UK (Ltd) [2001] C.L.Y. 920 9-015
Abraaj Investment Management Ltd v Bregawn Jersey Ltd; Abraaj Investment Management Ltd v Tuli [2010] EWHC 630 (Comm) 11-002
Abramova v Oxford Institute of Legal Practice [2011] EWHC 613 (QB); [2011] 14; 1982 S.L.T. 377; (1983) 80 L.S.G. 2516; (1983) 127 S.J. 508 (HL) 10-014
Alan Ramsay Sales & Marketing Ltd v Typhoo Tea Ltd [2016] EWHC 486 (Comm); [2016] 4 W.L.R. 59; [2016] E.C.C. 12 31-013
Albemarle Supply Co Ltd v Hind & Co [1928] 1 K.B. 307 (CA) 24-034
Aldridge v Johnson [1857] 26 L.J.Q.B. 296 3-019, 3-020, 8-005
Ali v Caton [2014] EWCA Civ 1313; [2015] P.I.Q.R. Q1 32-009
Allen v Simmons [1978] 1 W.L.R. 879; [1978]

Table of Statutes

1677 Statute of Frauds (c.3) 17-009, 21-038
1867 Policies of Assurance Act (c.144) 21-038
1872 Pawnbrokers Act (c.93) 18-001
1878–1882 Bills of Sale Acts 17-010, 17-015, 21-038
1889 Factors Act (c.45) 5-004
s.1(1) 5-011
s.2 5-004, 5-011, 5-012, 5-013, 5-014
(1) 5-010, 5-013
(3) 5-014
(4) 5-014
Pt III (ss.27–29) 5-030, 5-033, 7-009, 17-003, 18-001, 24-031, 24-033, 25-004
s.27 5-031, 5-033, 5-036, 7-009
(1) 5-030
(2) 5-030, 5-032
(3) 5-030, 5-033
(6) 7-009
s.29 5-033
(2) 5-032
1965 Hire Purchase Act (c.66) 18-001, 24-017
1967 Misrepresentation Act (c.7) 1-004, 16-024

Table of Statutes

The Table of Statutes provides you a handy list of all statutes referred to throughout this book.

Key Cases

All cases are highlighted making your research of the subject easier.

Remedies

6-005 There are two possible remedies:

Rescission

6-006 A misrepresentation by one party makes the contract voidable at the option of the other. This means that the latter can rescind the contract. This involves the parties being returned to their positions as they were before the contract, i.e. the return of the price to the buyer and the goods to the seller. If the innocent party is the buyer and he has not yet paid then he may simply refuse to do so and return the goods if he has already received them.

Rescission is an equitable remedy which means that it is not available if that would be unfair. Thus it is not available in the following situations:

(i) Where it is impossible to restore the parties to their pre-contract positions, e.g. if the purchaser had consumed the goods. In *Clarke v Dickinson*[17] Crompton J gave the grisly example of a butcher purchasing livestock being prevented from rescinding where he has already slaughtered the animal.

Key Extracts

Key extracts are boxed throughout to make them easily identifiable.

Ch.13). Also the Act limits the ability of the parties to the contract subsequently to remove or alter the third party's right, e.g. by varying the contract. Unless the contract otherwise provides, they cannot (s.2) do so without the third party's consent, if:

> **"(a) the third party has communicated his assent to the term to the promisor, [i.e. to the party who was contracted to perform the term in question], or**
> **(b) the promisor is aware that the third party has relied on the term, or**
> **(c) the promisor can reasonably be expected to have foreseen that the third party would rely on the term and the third party has in fact relied on it."**

When the third party seeks to enforce his right under the Act, the defendant is entitled to rely upon any defence (or set-off) which would have been available to the defendant if either (a) the other party to the contract had brought the claim, or (b) the third party had been a party to the contract.[3]

Paragraph Numbering

Paragraph numbering helps you move between sections and references with ease.

Bank Overdraft

17–021 This is an arrangement whereby the customer is allowed to overdraw (i.e. borrow) on his current account. Like a bank loan, it will fall within the third possibility (c) above. Unlike a bank loan, it will be flexible in a number of ways. First, the interest rate is liable to fluctuate over the period of the loan. Secondly, the debtor may not be required to pay it off at any particular rate but may be trusted to pay it off as and when he can. Thirdly, it may not be for a fixed sum but may simply allow the customer to overdraw up to a maximum amount. Lastly, it may not be restricted to one occasion. The customer is usually allowed, as he pays it off, to overdraw again and again—always subject to a maximum amount.

Bank's Revolving Credit

17–022 This is simply a version of a bank loan but has one feature of an overdraft—namely that the debtor, as his debt becomes reduced by his regular repayments, is automatically allowed to borrow again up to the original or an agreed figure. He can do this again and again.

Shop's Revolving Credit

Footnotes

Footnotes help minimise text distractions while providing access to relevant supplementary material.

(iv) the nature, attributes and rights of the advertiser.

The first feature, that of the characteristics of the product, includes availability; composition; method, place and date of manufacture; fitness for purpose; and quantity.[89] *Croydon LBC v Hogarth*[90] involved an advertising campaign which sent "invoices" marked as "paid" to businesses when in fact the "invoice" was actually a contract. The advertising campaign was held to be misleading under reg.3 since it led traders to believe that they already had a contract with the defendant business.

Where a trader engages in advertising which is contrary to reg.3, he is guilty of an offence

86 Directive 2006/114/EC which replaced Directive 84/450/EEC. See the discussion of the Control of Misleading Advertising Regulations 1988 at para.17-001, above.
87 SI 2008/1276. The Regulations came into effect on 26 May 2008.
88 reg.3(1).
89 See reg.3(4). These characteristics are broadly similar to the list previously to be found in s.2 of the Trade Descriptions Act 1968.
90 [2011] EWHC 1126 (QB).

General Reading

To help broaden our perspective we provide General Reading suggestions at the end of each chapter.

General Reading

- G. Battersby, "A reconsideration of 'property' and 'title' in the Sale of Goods Act" [2001] J.B.L. 1.
- H.L. Ho, "Some Reflections on 'Property' and 'Title' in the Sale of Goods Act" (1997) 56 C.L.J. 571.

The Time of the Transfer of Property

3–007 The rules as to what time that property passes are contained in ss.16–19 and they differ according to whether the contract is for the sale of specific or unascertained goods. Since the Consumer Rights Act 2015 adopts ss.16–19, the following discussion is relevant to both con-

Preface

It is often said that Commercial law never stands still and so the years following the publication of the previous edition of this text have proved. The judiciary has, as always, continued to develop commercial law and this edition incorporates a number of important decisions, many of which address fundamental questions such as the concept of "goods" (*The Software Incubator Ltd v Computer Associates (UK) Ltd*); "the meaning of defect" in product liability law (*Gee v DePuy*); and the scope of fiduciary duties (*Wood v Commercial First Business Ltd*) amongst others. I hope that this new edition continues to provide students of commercial law with a useful and accessible resource.

One matter which has not served to fundamentally modify the subject matter of this edition is the UK's withdrawal from the EU. The "snapshot" approach to preserving EU derived law through the combined effect of the European Union (Withdrawal) Act 2018 and the European Union (Withdrawal Agreement) Act 2020, outlined in Chapter One, has served to ensure welcome continuity and stability across the now separate legal systems.

However, it seems likely that greater, systematic, change may be just around the corner by virtue of the Brexit Freedoms Bill announced in January 2022. Whilst the draft text of the Bill has not yet been published, the Government has stated its intention to end the special domestic legal status of EU law: in essence, making it easier to remove or amend retained EU law with, it is argued, the effect of cutting £1 billion of red tape for businesses. Thus, more far-reaching reform, rendering much of what is said in Chapter One on the principal legislation implementing the UK's withdrawal from the EU obsolete, may come to fruition sooner rather than later.

Of course, having the power to more easily remove or amend laws stemming from the UK's previous membership of the EU is one thing; substantively changing the laws in those areas is another. It may be thought, given the breadth and complexity of the task, that reforms to the substance of retained EU Law would necessarily be a long-term process. Nonetheless, the new Prime Minister, Liz Truss, has committed to accelerate regulatory divergence from the European Union and remove or revise all retained EU Law by the end of 2023. Quite how practical such intentions are remains to be seen. Nor should it be forgotten that "retained EU law" is not synonymous with "bad law": indeed, I would argue that large parts of retained EU Law operate well! Nonetheless, it may well come to be that large areas of law covered by this textbook begin to look very different over the coming years.

Professor Rob Stokes
Liverpool
September 2022

Acknowledgments

Grateful acknowledgement is made for permission to reproduce from the following works:

Extracts from Queen's Bench Law Reports, Weekly Law Reports, Law Reports Appeal Cases, King's Bench Law Reports reproduced with the kind permission of The Incorporated Council of Law Reporting.

Extracts from the All England Law Reports reproduced by permission of RELX (UK) Limited, trading as LexisNexis.

Extracts from Lloyd's Reports reproduced by permission of Informa.

Extract from Medical Law Review: Goldberg, "Paying for bad blood: strict product liability after the hepatitis C litigation" [2002] Med. Law Rev. 165 reproduced by permission of Oxford University Press.

Whilst every care has been taken to establish and acknowledge copyright, and contact the copyright owners, the publishers tender their apologies for any accidental infringement. They would be pleased to come to a suitable arrangement with the rightful owners in each case.

Table of Contents

3. The Passing of Property and Risk

4. Perishing of Goods

5. Seller not the Owner

6. Misrepresentation

7. Terms of the Contract

8. The Supply of Goods and Services

9. Product Liability

11. Delivery and Payment

12. Seller's Remedies

13. Buyer's Remedies

16. Unfair Trading Practices

PART II—CONSUMER CREDIT

17. Introduction and Definition of Hire Purchase and Other Forms of Never-Never

21. Formation of a Consumer Credit Agreement

22. Creditor's Liability in Respect of Goods or Services Supplied

23. Enforcement by the Creditor or Owner

24. Termination of Hire Purchase Contracts

25. Termination of Credit Sale, Conditional Sale and Consumer Hire Agreements

PART III—AGENCY

26. The Law of Agency

27. The Creation of Agency

28. The Duties of an Agent

29. The Rights of an Agent Against His Principal

30. Contracts Made by Agents

31. Commercial Agents

32. Termination of Agency

Table of Cases

Financings v Stimson [1962] 1 W.L.R. 1184; [1962] 3 All E.R. 386 CA 21–002

Finlay v Kwik Hoo Tong. *See* James Finlay & Co Ltd v NV Kwik Hoo Tung Handel Maatschappij

First Energy (UK) Ltd v Hungarian International Bank Ltd [1993] 2 Lloyd's Rep. 194; [1993] B.C.C. 533; [1993] B.C.L.C. 1409; [1993] N.P.C. 34 CA (Civ Div) 27–008

Fisher v Bell [1961] 1 Q.B. 394; [1960] 3 W.L.R. 919; [1960] 3 All E.R. 731; (1961) 125 J.P. 101; (1960) 104 S.J. 981 DC 2–002

Flack v Pattinson [2002] EWCA Civ 1762 6–004

Foley v Classique Coaches Ltd [1934] 2 K.B. 1 CA 2–009

Formby Bros v Formby (1910) 102 L.T. 116 30–004

Forthright Finance Ltd v Carlyle Finance Ltd [1997] 4 All E.R. 90; [1997] C.C.L.R. 84 CA (Civ Div) 17–003

Forthright Finance Ltd v Ingate [1997] 4 All E.R. 99; [1997] C.C.L.R. 95 CA (Civ Div) 21–009

Forward Trust Ltd v Hornsby and Windermere Aquatic Ltd; sub nom. **Forward Trust Ltd v Hornsby and Windermere Aquatic Ltd, 1995 S.C.L.R. 574;** [1996] C.C.L.R. 18 Sh Ct 22–006

Foster v Biosil (2001) 59 B.M.L.R. 178 CC (Central London) 9–010, 9–011

Four Point Garage v Carter, *Times*, 19 November 1984 QBD 5–026

Fowler (LC) & Sons v St Stephen's College Board of Governors [1991] 3 N.Z.L.R. 304 30–005

Foxtons Ltd v Bicknell [2008] EWCA Civ 419; [2008] 2 E.G.L.R. 23; [2008] 24 E.G. 142; [2008] 17 E.G. 163 (C.S.); (2008) 105(18) L.S.G. 24; (2008) 152(17) S.J.L.B. 28; [2008] N.P.C. 52 29–004

Foxtons Ltd v O'Reardon [2011] EWHC 2946 QB 29–004

Foxtons Ltd v Thesleff [2005] EWCA Civ 514; [2005] 2 E.G.L.R. 29; [2005] 21 E.G. 140; [2005] 17 E.G. 122 (C.S.) 30–008

Fray v Voules, 120 E.R. 1125; (1859) 1 El. & El. 839 QB 28–002

Fred Drughorn Ltd v Rederiaktiebolaget Transatlantic; sub nom. **Rederi Aktienbolaget Transatlantic v Fred Drughorn Ltd** [1919] A.C. 203 HL 30–004

Freeman & Lockyer v Buckhurst Park Properties (Mangal) Ltd [1964] 2 Q.B. 480; [1964] 2 W.L.R. 618; [1964] 1 All E.R. 630; (1964) 108 S.J. 96 CA 27–002, 27–005

Frost v Aylesbury Dairy Co Ltd [1905] 1 K.B. 608 CA 7–023, 14–011

Fullwood v Hurley [1928] 1 K.B. 498 CA 28–007

FW Moore & Co Ltd v Landauer & Co; sub nom. **Arbitration Between Moore & Co Ltd and Landauer & Co** Re [1921] 2 K.B. 519; (1921) 6 Ll. L. Rep. 384 CA 7–013, 13–005

G Scammell and Nephew Ltd v HC&JG Ouston [1941] A.C. 251 HL 21–004

Galbraith & Grant Ltd v Block [1922] 2 K.B. 155 KBD 11–004

Gallie v Lee. *See* Saunders v Anglia Building Society (formerly Northampton Town and County Building Society)

Garnac Grain Co Inc v HMF Faure & Fairclough Ltd; sub nom. **Bunge Corp v HMF Faure & Fairclough Ltd** [1968] A.C. 1130; [1967] 3 W.L.R. 143; [1967] 2 All E.R. 353; [1967] 1 Lloyd's Rep. 495; (1967) 111 S.J. 434 26–004

Patel v Patel [2009] EWHC 3264 (QB); [2010] 1 All E.R. (Comm) 864; [2009] C.T.L.C. 249; [2010] Bus. L.R. D73 23–007

Payzu Ltd v Saunders [1919] 2 K.B. 581 CA 14–017

Peachdart Ltd, Re [1984] Ch. 131; [1983] 3 W.L.R. 878; [1983] 3 All E.R. 204; (1983) 1 B.C.C. 98920; (1984) 81 L.S.G. 204; (1983) 127 S.J. 839 Ch D 3–039

Pearson v Rose and Young; sub nom. **Pearson v Rose & Young (Little, Third Party, Marshall, Fourth Party)** [1951] 1 K.B. 275; [1950] 2 All E.R. 1027; 66 T.L.R. (Pt. 2) 886; (1950) 94 S.J. 778 CA 5–014, 5–015

Peekay Intermark Ltd v Australia & New Zealand Banking Group Ltd [2006] EWCA Civ 386; [2006] 2 Lloyd's Rep. 511; [2006] 1 C.L.C. 582 6–004

Pendragon v Coom unreported 22 March 2021 CC (Cardiff) 13–017

Pendragon Plc v Walon Ltd [2005] EWHC 1082 (QB) 11–003

PF (International) Ltd v Financial Conduct Authority [2018] UKUT 400 (TCC) 20–003

Pfeiffer Weinkellerei-Weineinkauf GmbH & Co v Arbuthnot Factors Ltd. *See* E Pfeiffer Weinkellerei-Weineinkauf GmbH & Co v Arbuthnot Factors Ltd

Pharmaceutical Society of Great Britain v Boots Cash Chemists (Southern) Ltd [1953] 1 Q.B. 401; [1953] 2 W.L.R. 427; [1953] 1 All E.R. 482; (1953) 117 J.P. 132; (1953) 97 S.J. 149 CA 2–002

Pharmapac (UK) Ltd v HBS Healthcare Ltd [2022] EWHC 23 (Comm) 7–006

Phillips v Brooks Ltd [1919] 2 K.B. 243 KBD 5–019, 5–020

Photo Production Ltd v Securicor Transport Ltd [1980] A.C. 827; [1980] 2 W.L.R. 283; [1980] 1 All E.R. 556; [1980] 1 Lloyd's Rep. 545; (1980) 124 S.J. 147 HL 10–014

Pignataro v Gilroy [1919] 1 K.B. 459 KBD 3–021, 3–023

Pilgrim Rock Ltd v Iwaniuk [2019] EWHC 203 (Ch); [2019] E.C.C. 8; [2019] C.T.L.C. 96 23–006

Pinnock Bros v Lewis & Peat Ltd [1923] 1 K.B. 690; (1923) 14 Ll. L. Rep. 277 KBD 7–013

PJ Pipe & Valve Co Ltd v Audco India Ltd [2005] EWHC 1904 (QB); [2006] Eu. L.R. 368 31–002, 31–007

Playboy Club London Ltd v Banca Nazionale del Lavoro SpA; sub nom. **Banca Nazionale del Lavoro SpA v Playboy Club London Ltd** [2018] UKSC 43; [2018] 1 W.L.R. 4041; [2019] 2 All E.R. 478; [2019] 1 All E.R. (Comm) 693; 179 Con. L.R. 17; [2018] P.N.L.R. 35; [2018] L.L.R. 657 30–003

Plevin v Paragon Personal Finance Ltd; Conlon v Black Horse Ltd; [2014] UKSC 61; [2014] 1 W.L.R. 4222; [2015] 1 All E.R. 625; [2015] 1 All E.R. (Comm) 1007; [2014] Bus. L.R. 1257; [2015] E.C.C. 2; [2015] Lloyd's Rep. I.R. 247 23–006, 23–008

Pool v Pool (1889) 58 L.J.P. 67 32–005

Porter v General Guarantee Corp [1982] R.T.R. 384 QBD 22–006

Poseidon Chartering BV v Marianne Zeeschip Vof (C-3/04) EU:C:2006:176; [2007] Bus. L.R. 446; [2006] 2 Lloyd's Rep. 105; [2006] E.C.R. I-2505 31–002

Prager v Blatspiel Stamp & Heacock Ltd [1924] 1 K.B. 566 KBD 27–011

Preist v Last [1903] 2 K.B. 148 CA 7–021

Presentaciones Musicales SA v Secunda [1994] Ch. 271; [1994] 2 W.L.R. 660;

Scotland v British Credit Trust Ltd [2014] EWCA Civ 790; [2015] 1 All E.R. 708; [2015] 1 All E.R. (Comm) 401; [2014] Bus. L.R. 1079; [2015] C.T.L.C. 25 21–009, 23–006

Scottish & Newcastle International Ltd v Othon Ghalanos Ltd [2008] UKHL 11; [2008] Bus. L.R. 583; [2008] 2 All E.R. 768; [2008] 2 All E.R. (Comm) 369; [2008] 1 Lloyd's Rep. 462; [2008] 1 C.L.C. 186; [2008] I.L.Pr. 30; (2008) 158 N.L.J. 334; (2008) 152(8) S.J.L.B. 32 11–011

Scruttons Ltd v Midland Silicones Ltd; sub nom. **Midland Silicones Ltd v Scruttons Ltd** [1962] A.C. 446; [1962] 2 W.L.R. 186; [1962] 1 All E.R. 1; [1961] 2 Lloyd's Rep. 365; (1962) 106 S.J. 34 HL 10–011

Scuderia Prestige Automobile Ltd v Malik [2021] EWHC 2744 (Ch) 1–010, 7–011

SEC v Chenery Corp (1943) 318 US 80 28–006

Secretary of State for Business, Innovation and Skills v PLT Anti-Marketing Ltd [2015] EWCA Civ 76; [2015] Bus. L.R. 959; [2015] E.C.C. 12; [2015] C.T.L.C. 8 16–008

Selectmove Ltd, Re [1995] 1 W.L.R. 474; [1995] 2 All E.R. 531; [1995] S.T.C. 406; [1994] B.C.C. 349; 66 T.C. 552 CA (Civ Div) 2–004

Septo Trading Inc v Tintrade Ltd [2021] EWCA Civ 718 7–004

Seton v Slade (1802) 7 Ves. Jr. 265 32–002

Shaw v Commissioner of Police of the Metropolis [1987] 1 W.L.R. 1332; [1987] 3 All E.R. 405; (1987) 84 L.S.G. 3011; (1987) 131 S.J. 1357 CA (Civ Div) 5–008

Shaw v Nine Regions Ltd [2009] EWHC 3514 (QB); [2010] C.T.L.C. 1 23–008

Shearman (t/a Charles Shearman Agencies) v Hunter Boot Ltd [2014] EWHC 47 (QB); [2014] 1 All E.R. (Comm) 689; [2014] 1 C.L.C. 240; [2014] E.C.C. 12 31–010

Shine v General Guarantee Corp [1988] 1 All E.R. 911; [1988] C.C.L.R. 14; (1987) 137 N.L.J. 946 CA (Civ Div); 7–018

Shipton Anderson & Co v Weil Bros & Co [1912] 1 K.B. 574 KBD 11–008

Shogun Finance Ltd v Hudson; sub nom. **Hudson v Shogun Finance Ltd** [2003] UKHL 62; [2004] 1 A.C. 919; [2003] 3 W.L.R. 1371; [2004] 1 All E.R. 215; [2004] 1 All E.R. (Comm) 332; [2004] 1 Lloyd's Rep. 532; [2004] R.T.R. 12; (2003) 100(46) L.S.G. 25; (2003) 153 N.L.J. 1790; (2003) 147 S.J.L.B. 1368 5–031

Short v Spackman (1831) 2 B & Ad. 962 30–010

Simmons v Potter [1975] R.T.R. 347; [1975] Crim. L.R. 354 DC 16–011

Sinclair Investments (UK) Ltd v Versailles Trade Finance Ltd (In Administration) [2011] EWCA Civ 347; [2012] Ch. 453; [2011] 3 W.L.R. 1153; [2011] 4 All E.R. 335; [2011] Bus. L.R. 1126; [2011] 2 B.C.L.C. 501; [2011] W.T.L.R. 1043; [2011] 2 P. & C.R. DG6 28–008

Siu Yin Kwan v Eastern Insurance Co Ltd [1994] 2 A.C. 199; [1994] 2 W.L.R. 370; [1994] 1 All E.R. 213; [1994] 1 Lloyd's Rep. 616; [1994] C.L.C. 31; (1994) 144 N.L.J. 87; (1994) 138 S.J.L.B. 26 PC (HK) 30–003, 30–004

Slater v Finning Ltd [1997] A.C. 473; [1996] 3 W.L.R. 190; [1996] 3 All E.R. 398; [1996] 2 Lloyd's Rep. 353; 1997 S.C. (H.L.) 8; 1996 S.L.T. 912; 1996 S.C.L.R. 863; [1996] C.L.C. 1236; (1996) 15 Tr. L.R. 458; (1996) 146 N.L.J. 1023; (1996) 140 S.J.L.B. 185 HL 7–021

Table of Statutes

2005 Mental Capacity Act (c.9) 32-008
s.1 32-008
(3) 32-008
s.4 32-008
s.7 2-008
s.9 32-008
s.13 32-008
Sch.4 32-008
para.1 32-008
2006 Consumer Credit Act (c.14) 18-001, 18-005, 18-011, 18-018, 18-019, 20-004, 21-034, 23-006
s.1 18-005
s.3 18-018
s.6 21-032
s.14(1) 23-012
s.16 23-017
2006 Companies Act (c.46) 3-040
s.51(1) 30-008
s.859A 3-039
s.860 3-039
2010 Bribery Act (c.23) 28-008
s.1 28-008
s.2 28-008
2011 Energy Act (c.16)
s.1 18-005
2013 Enterprise and Regulatory Reform Act (c.24) 16-022
s.26 16-022
2015 Consumer Rights Act (c.15) 1-002, 1-004, 1-005, 1-011, 1-013, 1-015, 1-016, 1-018, 1-019, 2-007, 2-009, 2-012, 3-001, 3-007, 3-029, 3-042, 4-001, 6-008, 7-001, 7-002, 7-004, 7-005, 7-007, 7-027, 7-032, 7-033, 7-034, 7-035, 8-001, 8-003, 8-007, 8-008, 8-009, 9-001, 9-002, 9-003, 9-004, 9-007, 9-009, 10-001, 10-011, 10-014, 10-015, 10-016, 10-026, 10-028, 10-029, 11-001, 11-004, 11-005, 11-007, 11-011, 13-001, 13-002, 13-005, 13-014, 13-017, 13-018, 13-021, 13-022, 13-023, 13-024, 14-002, 14-016, 14-020, 15-001, 16-015, 16-021, 16-024, 16-025, 17-005, 22-002, 22-009, 22-011, 22-012, 22-014, 22-017, 22-018, 23-010, 24-025, 24-026, 31-002
Pt 1 (ss.1-60) 10-027, 16-024
Pt 2 10-026, 10-027, 16-024
s.2 1-011
(2) 10-027
(3) 10-027
(4) 1-011
(5) 15-001
(6) 15-001
(9) 1-015, 7-034
Pt 1 Ch.2 (ss.3-32) 7-006, 8-003, 15-001
s.3 1-011, 8-008
s.4 3-001
(1) 1-011
s.5 1-011, 8-003
(1) 1-013
(2) 1-013
ss.5-8 1-011
s.6 1-018
s.7 1-016
s.8 8-003
s.9 7-027, 7-028, 7-034, 8-003, 8-005, 8-007, 8-008, 10-033, 13-020, 17-007, 22-009, 22-013
(1) 7-027
(2) 7-027
(3) 7-027
(5) 7-027
(7) 7-027
(c) 7-027
ss.9-11 22-002
ss.9-17 13-015

Table of Statutory Instruments

Part I

Sale of Goods

1

Introduction and Definition of Contract of Sale of Goods

What This Book is About

This book is about domestic commercial law. Commercial law is the body of rules applied to commercial transactions. These rules cover many diverse areas of law including the sale of goods; the law of agency; corporate law; banking law; and the regulation of consumer sales including trade descriptions law and consumer protection and the regulation of credit in consumer transactions. Given the vast scope of the term "commercial law", many have questioned whether commercial law should even be regarded as an area of law or whether it is merely an amalgamation of various distinct areas of law.[1] 1-001

This book is concerned primarily with three areas within commercial law: the sale of goods; the law of agency; and consumer credit. These areas form the core areas of law covered by undergraduate and analogous courses. This book is intended to offer a clear and concise doctrinal account of these areas of law whilst also offering an analytical approach in scrutinising and critiquing the law.

The sale of goods is the most common of type of commercial transaction. The term "sale of goods" embraces agreements which are apparently very different. For example, the sale of a newspaper for 30p from a stand in the street, the sale of industrial machinery for millions of pounds to a large company and the sale of aircraft to the government are all equally contracts (i.e. agreements) of sale of goods. Although this area of law developed through the law merchant it is now clear that there is an established divide between consumer and non-consumer cases. Issues such as remedies under sale of goods contracts, satisfactory quality and the passing of risk are now determined in no small part by the consumer status, or otherwise, of the buyer.

1 See, for example, the discussion in E. McKendrick, *Goode on Commercial Law*, 6th edn (London: Penguin, 2021), pp.8–9.

1-002 The bulk of the first part of this book is devoted to the contractual relationship between the buyer and seller, i.e. the rights and duties between them. A clue to these will often be found in the Sale of Goods Act 1979 and in some cases, the Consumer Rights Act 2015. Reference will constantly be made to sections of both Acts.

The second part of this book is concerned with the regulation of consumer credit, an area which has undergone considerable reform in recent years, driven no doubt, by the vast increase in the use of credit in recent times.

The third part of this book is devoted to the law of agency which is a fundamental aspect of commercial law. The role and importance of agency law within commercial law is considered below.

1-003 It must be remarked at the outset that it is principally between the buyer and seller that rights and obligations exist. These arise out of their bargain (i.e. their contract of sale). It is commonly thought, but wrongly so, that the buyer's best legal rights exist against the manufacturer. This common misconception is fostered and perhaps shared by a great many retailers. Of course, a manufacturer does enjoy the rights and incur the obligations of a seller but these exist as between himself and the person(s) to whom he sells his goods. Similarly, he has the rights and obligations of a buyer as against the person from whom he purchased his raw materials. A manufacturer does have some obligations which arise independently of his position as buyer or seller. Reference will be made to manufacturers as well as to auctioneers who also have liabilities (and rights) distinct from those of the seller and buyer.

One matter in particular will not figure too much in Pt I. This is where goods are taken on hire purchase, credit sale or conditional sale terms. These types of agreement will be considered in Pt II.

Historical Development of Sale of Goods Legislation

1-004 Before the definition of a contract of sale of goods is considered, something must be said of the history and sources of the law relating to sale of goods. The Sale of Goods Act 1979, only the second such Act to have been passed in this country, replaced the original Sale of Goods Act 1893. The original Act had been amended in the years before 1979 by such Acts as the Misrepresentation Act 1967, the Supply of Goods (Implied Terms) Act 1973, the Consumer Credit Act 1974 and the Unfair Contract Terms Act 1977. These amendments, though significant, were principally changes of detail and not substantial in extent. Thus the 1893 Act remained largely in the form in which it was originally enacted. The current Act, the Sale of Goods Act 1979, did not seek to make further changes in the law but was a consolidation measure which reproduced (with a few technical amendments) the provisions of the 1893

Act as amended. Thus the provisions of the 1979 Act are in large part the very same ones as those originally passed in 1893. Indeed, the majority of the section numbers are the same as they were in the 1893 Act. The 1979 Act has itself been amended, principally by the Sale and Supply of Goods Act 1994 and the Sale of Goods (Amendment) Act 1995. Most recently, the Consumer Rights Act 2015 has made further changes where a trader sells goods to a consumer. Nevertheless, it is still true to say that much of the law of sale of goods today is basically the common law, i.e. the law stated over the years by judges in the process of deciding cases before them. The 1893 Act was intended, not to effect radical changes in the law, but to codify it, i.e. to put the common law into one statute to which it was easy to refer.[2] The 1979 Act once again put the law into one statute by incorporating all the amendments which had been made in the original Act. However, decided cases still have to be referred to in two situations. The first is where the Act is silent or ambiguous on any given point and the second is where the court in a decided case has given a particular interpretation to a section of the Act (or to the same section in the original Act of 1893). In the case of a conflict between the pre-existing common law and any statute, the latter always prevails.

The Consumer Rights Act 2015

Recent years have borne witness to an increasing divergence between the law as it applies to business-to-consumer transactions and that which governs business-to-business transactions. This trend has been firmly entrenched by the enactment of the Consumer Rights Act 2015 which is an attempt to harmonise, simplify and consolidate key aspects of consumer law. Thus previously disparate (though largely equivalent in effect) statutory frameworks governing implied terms in consumer contracts of, for example, sale, hire purchase, and hire respectively, have been consolidated into a single Act. Nonetheless, the Sale of Goods Act 1979 remains a crucial piece of legislation. First, the Sale of Goods Act continues to regulate all sale of goods contracts made before 1 October 2015 when the relevant provisions of the Consumer Rights Act came into force. Secondly, the Sale of Goods Act continues to govern all sale of goods contracts which are outside of the ambit of the Consumer Rights Act. Thus a sale of goods between two businesses will be dealt with under the Sale of Goods Act and not by the Consumer Rights Act. The same is true for private sales (i.e. those where neither buyer nor seller is a trader). 1-005

The Sale of Goods Act remains a vital piece of legislation for a further reason: perhaps disappointingly for a piece of legislation which has simplification as an aim, the Consumer Rights Act does not address every aspect of consumer sales law. Thus even where a trader sells

2 See, M. Arden, "Time for an English Commercial Code?" (1997) 56 C.L.J. 516.

goods to a consumer after 1 October 2015, many aspects of the law which applies to that contract remain within the purview of Sale of Goods Act 1979 and indeed, the common law. These include important matters such as the capacity to enter into contracts for the sale of goods, provisions concerning the price to be paid and the sale of goods by a non-owner. Furthermore, in many situations the Consumer Rights Act 2015 either re-casts the position laid down previously by the Sale of Goods Act 1979 or expressly adopts the framework laid down in the 1979 Act. An example of the former is the obligation around the quality and fitness for purpose of the goods supplied. An example of the latter are the rules relating to the passing of property in sale of goods contracts.

Nonetheless, the Consumer Rights Act 2015 heralds a new era in consumer law and introduces a number of important developments. These will be explained in Part One, but in brief the Consumer Rights Act 2015 brings clarity to contracts for the supply of digital products, enhances the law relating to unfair contract terms in consumer contracts and consolidates consumer law enforcement powers. The impact of the Consumer Rights Act on existing legislation is substantial; it has replaced or modified a substantial number of important pieces of legislation including:

- The Sale of Goods Act 1979.
- Supply of Goods and Services Act 1982.
- The Unfair Contract Terms Act 1977.
- The Unfair Terms in Consumer Contracts Regulations 1999.

The Impact of Brexit

1-006 In June 2016 the UK held a referendum on its membership of the EU in which a majority voted in favour of the UK leaving the EU. In consequence, the European Union (Withdrawal) Act 2018 repealed the European Communities Act 1972 and took steps to facilitate the UK's withdrawal from the EU. The UK exited the EU on 31 January 2020 with a transition period ending on 31 December 2020. This transition period was labelled the "implementation period" (IP) by the European Union (Withdrawal Agreement) Act 2020 and the final day of the transition period was called "IP completion day". Throughout the implementation period, in general, EU law continued to apply in the UK (the European Communities Act being preserved by the 2020 Act for this purpose).

The 2018 Act[3] also made provision for the retention of EU law as follows:

- Section 2 ensured that EU-derived domestic legislation in effect immediately before IP day continues to have effect after IP completion day.
- Section 3 incorporated direct EU legislation operative immediately before IP completion day into domestic law;
- Section 4 saved rights, powers, liabilities etc available under s.2(1) of the European Communities Act 1972;
- Section 5 retained the principle of supremacy of EU law after IP completion day in "so far as relevant to the interpretation, disapplication or quashing of any enactment or rule of law passed or made before IP completion day" but not in respect of laws made after IP completion day.

Thus the 2018 Act created a new (far-reaching) category of law: "retained EU law". The effect of this is that most EU law applicable in the UK on IP completion day remains in effect until modified or withdrawn.[4] Needless to say, this is important and ensures that the established frameworks derived from the UK's membership of the EU continue and in so far as the subject matter of this textbook is concerned, generally do so substantively unchanged. This covers a wide range of areas of law, including, as we will see in the chapters that follow, consumer rights, product liability and unsafe goods, unfair trading, significant elements of consumer credit law and commercial agents.

Notwithstanding what has just been said, much of the retained EU law relevant to this textbook has been subject to minor amendments affecting wording (for example, references to "an EU obligation" have been amended to read "a retained EU obligation"). In some cases, amendments have been required that have a more substantial effect, for example, previous references to an importer into the EU within the Consumer Protection Act 1987 have been modified to refer instead to an importer into the UK. These will be highlighted where necessary in the chapters that follow.

The 2018 Act also made provision for the interpretation of retained EU law. Under s.6 domestic courts are no longer bound by decisions of the Court of Justice of the European Union (CJEU) that are made on or after 31 December 2020 (IP completion day). However, UK courts will have to interpret retained EU law in accordance with relevant decisions and principles laid down by the CJEU made prior to IP completion day. The exception to this is that the Supreme

3 As amended by the European Union (Withdrawal Agreement) Act 2020.

4 For a comprehensive discussion, see S. Whittaker, "Retaining European Union law in the United Kingdom" (2021) 137 L.Q.R. 477.

Court and the Court of Appeal can depart from CJEU decision made before IP completion day decisions where it appears correct to do so.[5]

1–007 It seems unlikely that we will see, in the short-term at least, vast swathes of the retained EU law discussed in this book, being fundamentally changed. First, the policy of the government in effecting Brexit has been, largely, one of ensuring continuity of laws applicable pre-and post the UK's withdrawal from the EU. This is evident in the approach of the European Union (Withdrawal) Act 2018 and the European Union (Withdrawal Agreement) Act 2020. Second, much of the EU-retained law considered in this book is generally considered to be working well. The law, of course, does not stand still and more substantial divergence between the UK legal position and that within the EU is starting to loom, specifically in areas where reform at UK or EU level (or both) is ongoing. A good example of this, product liability, is discussed in Ch.9. Even in these areas, however, it is not necessarily the case that significant divergence should be anticipated in the short-term—separate UK and EU proposals for reform to product liability law, for example, highlighted broadly comparable drivers for future reform. The same can be said for potential reforms to unfair trading laws as noted in Ch.16. It may be that the approaches taken share more similarities than they do differences. Nonetheless, the passage of time will ultimately start to render starker contrasts between the legal position in the UK and that in the EU with the predictable challenges (and increased costs) in consequence for businesses trading in both the UK and the EU.

The Role of Agency in Commercial Law

1–008 Given the broad areas of law which fall under the umbrella of "commercial law" it is not surprising that the relationship between agent and principal can play a significant role in many, if not all, of these areas. Moreover, this relationship is not merely predominant within the realm of business-to-business transactions. Consumers will from time-to-time have dealings with an agent, whether as principal or otherwise (though they may not realise it). For example, when purchasing a car an individual may act as principal where another (e.g. a car dealer) agrees to find a specific vehicle for his buyer. Equally, the consumer may be purchasing the car from an agent of a (possibly) undisclosed principal (i.e. the owner of the car). On the other hand, the car dealer may be advertised as an "Approved Agent of Vauxhall" when in law, that "agent" is buying and selling goods in his own right, i.e. there is no agency relationship and the contact of sale of goods will be between the customer and the dealer. It is clear that within commercial law countless transactions are conducted by agents. The role of agency, therefore, within commercial law should not be underestimated.

5 Initially, only the Supreme Court has this ability but it was extended to the Court of Appeal by the European Union (Withdrawal) Act 2018 (Relevant Court) (Retained EU Case Law) Regulations 2020 (SI 2020/1525).

Moreover, as will be seen throughout the text, many legal problems (and solutions) hinge upon agency law. For example, the ability of a purchaser to claim good title to goods bought from a non-owner will, in certain circumstances, depend upon whether the buyer purchased the goods from an agent. The passing of property in a sale of goods contract may well depend on the role of warehousemen acting as agent, whether for the buyer or for the seller.

The Sale of Goods Act 1979

Definition

Section 2(1) of the Sale of Goods Act defines a contract of sale of goods as: "a contract whereby the seller transfers or agrees to transfer the property in the goods to the buyer for a money consideration, called the price." Three elements in this definition require explanation, "property", "goods" and "money consideration". 1-009

"Property" means ownership. Selling is the most common method by which ownership is transferred from person to person. Sometimes the contract provides that ownership will be transferred at some later date. Such a contract is termed "an agreement to sell" but it is still a contract of sale within the definition because of the words in s.2(1), "agrees to transfer". Of course, a contract which lacks any agreement to transfer property (ownership) at all will fall outside the definition, e.g. a contract where one person simply agrees to borrow or hire another person's goods. This type of contract, i.e. where possession but not ownership is agreed to be transferred, is altogether different and is called a contract of bailment.

"Goods" is defined by s.61 to include "emblements, industrial growing crops and things attached to or forming part of the land which are agreed to be severed before sale or under the contract of sale". Thus, a contract to sell crops which are growing or to be grown—whether they mature within a year (e.g. wheat) or not (e.g. timber)—is a contract of sale of goods. The only exception to this is when the crops are sold along with the land on which they are growing or to be grown. In this case the crops are not "agreed to be severed before the sale or under the contract of sale".

Things, other than crops which are "attached to or form part of the land" are "goods" only if they are identifiable as being distinct from the land. *Morgan v Russell & Sons*[6] concerned the sale of some slag and cinders which were lying on a particular piece of ground. They were not in identifiable heaps but had melted into the soil. It was held that the slag and cinders were not distinct from the land itself and therefore were not "goods". 1-010

6 [1909] 1 K.B. 357.

Other things which are not "goods" are "things in action and money".[7] Things in action include cheques and stocks and shares. Although money is not normally "goods", a coin which is sold as a curio piece and not as currency, is regarded as goods: *Moss v Hancock*.[8] Apart from the exceptions mentioned, "goods" include "all chattels personal",[9] i.e. all tangible moveable things.

The third element of the definition is "money consideration". A contract of barter, i.e. where goods are exchanged for other goods, lacks this element and is not a contract of sale. However, where goods are exchanged for a combination of money and other goods, the contract is one of sale of goods. In this case there is a money consideration even though goods are also given. In *Dawson v Dutfield*,[10] two lorries worth £475 were to be paid for by a combination of two "trade-in" lorries worth £250 and the balance in cash. It was held that there was a contract of sale of goods and that the sellers could sue for the outstanding balance of the price.[11]

Whether there was a "money consideration" was in issue in *Esso v Commissioners of Customs and Excise*.[12] Esso devised a petrol sales promotion scheme whereby a World Cup coin was given away at Esso petrol stations with every four gallons of petrol purchased. Posters displayed at petrol stations read "Free World Cup Coins". "One coin given away with every four gallons of petrol". There could be no doubt that when a garage proprietor sold petrol to a customer he made a contract of sale (i.e. of the petrol) with the customer, since the customer agreed to pay a "money consideration", the price. Did the garage proprietor also make a contract of sale in relation to the World Cup coins? If he did, then Esso were liable to pay purchase tax (since abolished) in respect of all the World Cup coins they had produced. Esso advanced two arguments. First, they claimed that the garage proprietor made no contract at all with the customer in relation to the World Cup coins. The coins had small intrinsic value and therefore the offer in the posters could not have been intended to create a legally binding relationship (i.e. a contract) between the garage proprietor and the customer. The majority of their Lordships rejected this argument and held that it had been intended that a customer who accepted the offer by buying four gallons would thereby become entitled in law to have a World Cup coin. Esso's second argument succeeded. It was held that the contract in relation to the World Cup coins was not a contract of sale. There was not just one contract made between the garage proprietor and the customer. There were two. Beside the contract for the sale of the petrol there was a separate collateral contract relating to the World Cup coins. The posters amounted to an offer by the garage proprietor to supply a World Cup coin if the customer would buy four gallons of petrol. That offer was accepted by the customer making a contract to buy four gallons. The consideration which the customer gave for the garage proprietor's promise to supply a World Cup coin was the making

7 s.61.
8 [1899] 2 Q.B. 111.
9 s.61.
10 [1936] 2 All E.R. 232.
11 For a recent example, see *Scuderia Prestige Automobile Ltd v Malik* [2021] EWHC 2744 (Ch) where a trader acquired a Ferrari motor vehicle in exchange for a McLaren car, plus £35,000.
12 [1976] 1 W.L.R. 1.

of the contract to buy four gallons of petrol. The making of a contract to buy four gallons of petrol was not a "money consideration".[13]

The Consumer Rights Act 2015

As we noted above, the Consumer Rights Act 2015 applies not only to contracts of sale of goods but also to various other forms of supply contracts. Its scope is laid down by s.3 which lists four separate categories of supply contracts: sales contracts; contracts for the hire of goods; hire-purchase agreements; and contracts for transfer of goods. Each of these is given a statutory definition in ss.5–8 of the Act. A sales contract is defined in s.5 as a contract under which a trader transfers or agrees to transfer, ownership of goods to the consumer and the consumer pays, or agrees to pay, the price. Thus it is essentially the same definition as we discussed in relation to s.2 of the Sale of Goods Act with the core elements of "property", "goods", and "consideration" each being required. We can observe that that language used by the 2015 Act is slightly different to that under the Sale of Goods Act. The references to "property" and "money consideration" have been removed with the much less legalistic (and therefore more readily understandable to a lay audience) terms "ownership" and "price" being used instead. We have already noted that within the Sale of Goods Act "property" means "ownership". Similarly, under the Consumer Rights Act, "ownership" is defined as "the general property in goods, not merely a special property".[14] Thus the definitions are the same in both Acts. 1-011

There is, however, one fundamental difference between a sale of goods contract under the Sale of Goods Act and a sales contract under the Consumer Rights Act. The Consumer Rights Act applies only where a trader sells goods to a consumer. The same limitation applies to all supply contracts which fall under the ambit of the Act and the scope of the Consumer Rights Act is, therefore, both broader and narrower than that of the Sale of Goods Act. It is broader since it applies to supply contracts beyond only sales, but narrower since the status of the parties is crucial: the supplier must be a trader and the customer must be a consumer. The Consumer Rights Act defines trader and consumer in the following terms:[15]

> **"(2) *'Trader'* means a person acting for purposes relating to that person's trade, business, craft or profession, whether acting personally or through another person acting in the trader's name or on the trader's behalf.**

13 For a further discussion of this case and of contracts of barter, see paras 8-004 and 8-005, below.

14 CRA 2015 s.4(1).

15 CRA 2015 s.2.

(3) '*Consumer*' means an individual acting for purposes that are wholly or mainly outside that individual's trade, business, craft or profession."

The definition of "trader" is broad and will cover the full range of business activity, including that of sole traders, companies, and not-for-profit organisations. The definition of "consumer" is similarly broad. It may seem curious that an individual can still be labelled a "consumer" where they are acting for business purposes. To understand this extension of the definition, consider an example. An academic purchases a kettle to use at home. The kettle is used throughout the week, including one day every week when the academic works from home. Is the academic a "consumer" under the Consumer Rights Act? Since the kettle is primarily used for purposes not connected to the academic's profession, the answer is yes. Conversely, if the same academic purchases a home computer which is set up in his home office, and only ever used for work purposes, he will not be a "consumer" under the Act.[16] In the latter case, this does not necessarily mean that he will be left without recourse if, for example, the computer turns out to be defective. Any recourse, however, would not derive from the Consumer Rights Act and instead the provisions of the Sale of Goods Act would need to be considered.

Sale Distinguished From Other Transactions

1-012 One might expect, over a century after the original Sale of Goods Act was passed, that the classification of a contract for the sale of goods under s.2(1) is a settled and relatively straightforward exercise. The recent decision of the Supreme Court in *PST Energy 7 Shipping LLC v OW Bunker Malta Ltd (The Res Cogitans)*[17] reminds us that careful consideration of the contract is required. The dispute centred on the supply of shipping fuel called bunkers. OW Bunker contracted to supply bunkers to PST Energy's tanker (The Res Cogitans) with payment due within 60 days of the supply. The contract included a retention of title clause which reserved OW Bunkers' title until the goods had been paid in full. The contract provided that: (i) PST Energy was in possession of the bunkers solely as the bailee of the "seller" until full payment had been made, and that (ii) the buyer was not entitled to use the bunkers other than for the propulsion of The Res Cogitans.

The Supreme Court unanimously held that the contract was not one of sale falling within s.2 of the Sale of Goods Act. It was instead a sui generis supply contract since its "essential nature" was very different from that of a contract of sale of goods. The combined effect of the

16 Under s.2(4) of the Consumer Rights Act it is for the trader to prove that an individual was not acting for purposes wholly or mainly outside of their trade or profession.

17 [2016] UKSC 23.

reservation of title clause with the provision of 60 days' credit was that the agreement did not meet the requirements of s.2 of the Sale of Goods Act, i.e. it was understood by the parties that the goods (or at least a large proportion thereof) would likely be consumed before property could pass or payment had been made.[18] It was instead a contract of bailment with a licence to consume the bunkers prior to making payment.[19]

We have already examined the difference between sale and barter. More can be learned about the nature of a sale from a comparison of it with other contracts.

Contracts for labour and materials supplied

These contracts are not uncommon.[20] For example: a builder sub-contracts the job of putting the roof on a house which he is building. The sub-contract requires the sub-contractor to supply the tiles. This is not a contract of a sale of goods because its principal object is the provision of services: *Young & Marten v McManus Childs*.[21] 1-013

We have already highlighted that a fundamental element within a sale of goods is that the seller must transfer, or agree to transfer, property (ownership) in the goods to the buyer. This is made clear by the wording of s.2(1) of the Sale of Goods Act and s.5(1) of the Consumer Rights Act. This means that the transfer of ownership to the buyer should be the main object of the agreement. If the main purpose is something else (e.g. the provision of labour) then the agreement is not a contract of sale under the Sale of Goods Act nor a sales contract under the Consumer Rights Act.[22] This is so regardless of the fact that an incidental or ancillary object of the contract is the transfer of ownership in some goods. In *Robinson v Graves*[23] the Court of Appeal held that a contract whereby an artist agreed to paint a client's portrait for him was not a contract of sale of goods. Even though when finished, the canvas would be transferred to the buyer's ownership, the substance of the agreement was the provision by the artist of his skill and labour. If, on the other hand, the client selected from the artist's studio a finished painting and agreed to pay for it, that agreement would be a contract of sale of goods. In that case the artist would be agreeing, not to provide his skill and labour, but simply to part with the ownership of a finished canvas, the fruit of his past efforts. The substance of such an agreement is the transfer of ownership.

18 For an entertaining critique, see A. Tettenborn, "Of Bunkers and Retention of Title: When is a Sale not a Sale?" [2016] L.M.C.L.Q. 24.

19 For an unsuccessful attempt to extend the decision in *The Res Cogitans* to all-inclusive catering offered by holiday tour operators, see *Wood v TUI Travel Plc* [2017] EWCA Civ 11.

20 See, for example, *Wincanton Group Ltd v Garbe Logistics UK 1 SARL* [2011] EWHC 905 (Ch) where a contract for the supply and installation of warehouse racking was held not to be a sale of goods.

21 [1969] 1 A.C. 454.

22 Note, however, that if goods are to be produced or manufactured and then supplied to the consumer, there will be a sales contract under the Act, see CRA 2015 s.5(2).

23 [1935] 1 K.B. 597.

It is not always easy to decide what constitutes the substance of the contract, the provision of services or the transfer of ownership. It may be helpful to know that the courts have treated the following as contracts of sale—contracts: to make and supply ships' propellers according to a specification, *Cammell Laird v Manganese Bronze & Brass*[24]; to prepare and supply food in a restaurant, *Lockett v A. & M. Charles Ltd*[25]; and to compound and supply animal foodstuff according to a formula setting out the ingredients and their proportions, *Ashington Piggeries v Hill*.[26] A borderline case, *Samuels v Davis*[27] came before the Court of Appeal in 1943. It concerned a contract to provide a made-to-measure set of teeth and it arose because they did not fit. The Court sidestepped the question of whether it was a contract of sale or for services, by holding that, whichever it was, there was an implied term of the contract that the goods should be reasonably fit for the purpose for which they were intended. The seller was therefore liable.

Contracts to supply computer software

1-014 Here the contract may or may not involve the transfer of goods. Thus if the software is transferred by simply being downloaded on to the purchaser's machine from the internet or from a disk temporarily supplied by the software supplier, the contract is not one of sale of goods, since the program or software, not being tangible, does not amount to "goods", *St Albans DC v ICL*.[28] Nevertheless, if the program is intended by the parties to enable a computer to achieve specified functions, there will be an implied term at common law that the program is reasonably fit for this purpose. If, however, the software is supplied on a permanent medium, such as a disk, the contract will be one of sale of goods. It is then no different from a book (or video or audio cassette). In that case there will be the statutory implied terms that the goods will be of satisfactory quality and reasonably fit for their purpose. According to the St Albans judgment, the statutory implied obligations extend not only to the physical disk, book or video but also to its contents. Thus supplying an instructional manual containing wrong instructions would amount to a breach of these terms, as would supplying a disk with defective software.

Such an approach has been criticised for placing greater emphasis on the nature of the conveyance to the end user of the product than it does on the properties of the product being conveyed.[29] In *Beta Computers (Europe) Ltd v Adobe Systems (Europe) Ltd*[30] Lord Penrose

---

24 [1934] A.C. 402.

25 [1938] 4 All E.R. 170.

26 [1971] 2 W.L.R. 1051.

27 [1943] K.B. 526.

28 [1996] 4 All E.R. 481. For a discussion of the analogous situation under the Commercial Agents (Council Directive) Regulations 1993 see, para.31-002, above.

29 See the discussion in J. Adams, "Software and Digital Content" [2009] J.B.L. 396 at 398–399.

30 1996 S.L.T. 604. For commentary on this decision, see G. Gretton, "Software: binding the end-user" [1996] J.B.L. 524.

criticised the notion that where software is supplied on a permanent medium, such as a disk, the contract will be one of sale of goods and no different, for example, to a sale of a book:[31]

> **"This reasoning appears to me to be unattractive . . . . It appears to emphasise the role of the physical medium, and to relate the transaction in the medium to sale or hire of goods. It would have the somewhat odd result that the dominant characteristic of the complex product . . . would be subordinate to the medium by which it was transmitted to the user in analysing the true nature and effect of the contract".**

A further issue which has caused difficulty is the legal nature of the conveyance under which the software is supplied. This problem is based upon the situation when software is not sold, but rather is licensed.[32] In *Watford Electronics Ltd v Sanderson*[33] it was held that since the software had not been sold but had been supplied under licence, the Sale of Goods Act 1979 and therefore the statutory implied term as to quality, were inapplicable.[34] The Court was prepared, however, to import the same obligation through the common law.[35]

These two issues were considered in *Southwark LBC v IBM UK Ltd*[36] where IBM provided data management software to the claimants. The software provided was ultimately abandoned as being unfit for purpose. The terms of the contract made clear that the agreement granted merely a (perpetual) licence and that "title, copyright and all other proprietary rights" were retained. Consequently, the agreement was not subject to the implied terms as to quality and fitness under the Sale of Goods Act since there was no transfer of property in the software. Akenhead J suggested, obiter, that software supplied on compact disk should be regarded as "goods" within the meaning of the Act.[37] This was so for three reasons. First, although a compact disk has little intrinsic value, the Sale of Goods Act does not exclude any goods merely by reason of their value. Secondly, the fact that a compact disk is impressed with electrons simply gives it particular characteristics. Thirdly, the definition of "goods" is an inclusive rather than exclusive one.[38] 1-015

In the context of consumer supplies of digital content, the Consumer Rights Act has served to nullify these debates through the creation of a specific framework addressing digital

31 1996 S.L.T. 604 at 608–9.

32 In the majority of cases, this is correct.

33 [2001] 1 All E.R. (Comm) 696.

34 This view has received support, see for example, *Benjamin's Sale of Goods* but for a convincing argument to the contrary, see the discussion in S. Green and D. Saidov, "Software as Goods" [2007] J.B.L. 161 at 174–5.

35 This being less problematic than the finding that the contract would fall under the Supply of Goods and Services Act 1982 as a bailment under s.6(1).

36 [2011] EWHC 549.

37 [2011] EWHC 549 at [97].

38 [2011] EWHC 549 at [96].

content.[39] "Digital content" is defined in s.2(9) as meaning "data which are produced and supplied in digital form" although the Act will only apply where the consumer has paid a price for the content.[40] The only exception to this is where the digital content is provided free with goods or services or other digital content for which the consumer pays a price and which is not generally available to consumers for free, e.g. software supplied for free with a magazine.[41] The approach of the Consumer Rights Act to digital content will be considered in Ch.7.

Contracts of hire purchase

1–016 It is the hallmark of a contract of sale that seller and buyer each enter a commitment that there will be a transfer of ownership from the seller to the buyer. A hire-purchase agreement lacks this. Under a hire-purchase agreement the hirer undertakes to hire the goods for a specified period at a specified rent and he is given an option to buy the goods when he has paid all the specified rent. Since he has only an option and does not legally commit himself to buy the goods, the contract is not one of sale: *Helby v Matthews*.[42]

In reversing the decision of the Court of Appeal, Lord Macnaghten sitting in the House of Lords suggested that:[43]

> **"The contract. . .on the part of the dealer was a contract of hiring coupled with a conditional contract or undertaking to sell. On the part of the customer it was a contract of hiring only until the time came for making the last payment. It may be that at the inception of the transaction both parties expected that the agreement would run its full course, and that the piano would change hands in the end. But an expectation, however confident and however well-founded, does not amount to an agreement. . ."**

39 Ch.3 Pt 1 of the Consumer Rights Act. Defined in s.2(9).

40 CRA 2015 s.33(1). Note that reform continues at a European level concerning digital content: On the provision of "free" software in return for personal data see the Digital Content and Services Directive (Directive 2019/770/EU). As to tangible goods which come with a digital element, see the Sale of Goods Directive (Directive 2019/771/EU). Since the UK is no longer a Member State, it is not required to implement either Directive. Within the EU, the new directives apply to contracts entered into after 1 January 2022.

41 CRA 2015 s.33(2).

42 [1895] A.C. 471. A contract of hire with an "agreement to agree" whether or not to transfer property at its conclusion will not be regarded as hire purchase. In *Tanks and Vessels Industries Ltd v Devon Cider Company Ltd* [2009] EWHC 1360 (Ch) the court held that the parties had agreed to consider whether goods would be re-hired, purchased for their residual value or returned, at the end of the period of hire. Thus, it was not to be regarded as a contract of hire purchase.

43 [1895] A.C. 471 at 482.

Thus a contract of hire purchase is neither a contract for the sale of goods under the Sale of Goods Act 1979 nor a sales contract under the Consumer Rights Act 2015. It is, however, a contract for the supply of goods under the Consumer Rights Act and thus, for example, the statutory rights framework under the Act applies to hire purchase contracts.[44] Similarly, the Supply of Goods (Implied Terms) Act 1973 applies to give a non-consumer hirer certain basic protections where the Consumer Rights Act does not apply.

Consider the emergence in modern times of a new species of hire-purchase agreement: the "Lease Purchase" or "Personal Contract Purchase" commonly used within the motor industry to finance sales of new motor vehicles. Rent is payable throughout the agreement period and is calculated on the amount of depreciation likely on the vehicle. At the end of that period, the lessee has the option to purchase the vehicle for a sum calculated to be the capital/residual value of the vehicle. What is the economic objective of such a contract? Clearly it is distinct from that of a hire-purchase agreement, which is in effect a secured sale.[45] That much is self-evident from the nature of the instalment payments being calculated on the estimated depreciation of the vehicle (or goods) over the contract period. This however, may be contrasted with the payment structure of a typical modern hire-purchase agreement, where the option is frequently to buy the goods at the end of the contract period for only a nominal fee, which is certainly not representative of the estimated value of the goods at the end of the contract period. The courts have not yet had the opportunity to determine the legal classification of this new form of instalment contract. Since, however, the lessee has only an option and not a commitment to buy, it appears not to be a contract of sale of goods.

Contracts of agency

Sometimes X sells goods to Y who in turn sells them to Z. Sometimes however, Y acts as X's agent in selling to Z. In the former case Z buys his goods from Y and if they are not delivered or are defective Z can look to his seller, Y, and if necessary can sue him for breach of contract. In the latter case Z buys from X through X's agent Y; it is with X hat he has made his contract and if things go wrong, he can look to his seller, X, for a remedy. The answer to the question "who sold to Z?" depends upon whether Y was a buyer and reseller or whether he was merely an agent for X. The answer is not helped by the fact that people who are in fact buyers and resellers are often termed in the trade "agents". As previously noted, car dealers, for example, may be called "Vauxhall agents" but they are not necessarily agents for the manufacturer. They themselves buy new cars and resell them to members of the public. The true nature of the transaction can be ascertained only by examining the terms of the contract between X and Y. If 1-017

44 See the definition in Consumer Rights Act 2015 s.7.

45 Indeed, this fact is responsible for the number of cases involving the sale of goods by a non-owner. In many instances, a hirer under a hire-purchase agreement sells the goods due to the (mistaken) belief that he is entitled to do so.

it is clear that Y is buying the goods for himself, albeit with a commitment or intention to resell, then Y is a buyer and reseller.[46]

The problem can arise acutely in a situation where Y takes goods from X on "sale or return" terms. Is Y a buyer and reseller or is he X's agent? In either case he does not run the risk of being left with the goods; if he cannot find a purchaser he can return them to X. The answer is that he is X's agent if under the terms of his contract with X he has no right himself to buy the goods but can only sell to a third party; *Weiner v Harris*.[47] Contrariwise, if he has the right himself to buy the goods he is a buyer and the contract between X and Y will be one of sale of goods and not one of agency: *Weiner v Gill*.[48]

The problem can also arise where Y takes goods from X under a sale of goods contract which contains a retention of title clause, i.e. a clause stating that Y is not to become the owner unless and until he has paid for them and that if Y resells them before paying for them, X's ownership is to transfer from the goods to the proceeds of the resale received by Y. Suppose Y sells the goods to Z before he has paid X for them. Clearly, although he is not yet the owner of the goods, he has the authority of the owner, X, to resell them. In this situation is Y a buyer and reseller or is he merely X's agent for selling the goods to Z? This question will be important if Z wishes to sue his seller for breach of contract (e.g. if the goods are defective) or if Z fails to pay the price. Whom can Z sue and who can sue Z? To put it another way, who is the other party to the contract by which Z purchased the goods? Who is the seller who sold the goods to Z? The answer is twofold. First, as between X and Y, Y is acting as X's agent in selling to Z; secondly, as between Y and Z, Y is selling as principal: *Aluminium Industrie Vaasen BV v Romalpa Aluminium Ltd*.[49] Thus, although Y owes X the duties which an agent owes to his principal, it is Y who as seller can sue Z for the price and be sued by Z for the breach of the contract of sale.

Contracts of hire

1-018 Hiring, or bailment, is the transfer of possession of goods by the bailor to the bailee on condition that the goods shall be returned to the bailor under the terms of the contract. It is easily distinguishable from a sale of goods on the basis that the objective of a bailment is to transfer only physical possession of the goods. The objective of a sale of goods is to transfer the property within the goods.[50]

A contract of bailment can take the form of an instalment contract and can be regulated under s.15(1) of the Consumer Credit Act 1974 (as amended) which defines a "consumer hire agreement" as:

46 See generally, Pt.3, below.
47 [1910] 1 K.B. 285.
48 [1906] 2 K.B. 574.
49 [1976] 1 W.L.R. 676. For a fuller account see para.3-038, below.
50 See *Chapman Bros v Verco Bros & Co Ltd* (1933) C.L.R. 306.

> **"an agreement made by a person with an individual (the "hirer") for the bailment or (in Scotland) the hiring of goods to the hirer, being an agreement which:**
> **(a) is not a hire-purchase agreement, and**
> **(b) is capable of subsisting for more than three months".**

Where a contract to supply goods is properly regarded as a contract of hire and not of sale, the agreement will not fall under the Sale of Goods Act. It will be governed by either the Consumer Rights Act[51] (where a trader supplies goods on hire terms to a consumer) or otherwise, by the Supply of Goods and Services Act 1982. Thus the treatment of contracts of hire is generally analogous to those of sale of goods with the obvious exception concerning transfer of property.[52]

The Importance of the Definition

In consumer supplies where the Consumer Rights Act applies, many of the distinctions noted above are of limited significance since, in general terms, the Act governs different forms of consumer supply contracts in the same way. However, as we will see, this is not always true and there are some provisions in the Act which only apply to sales contracts and not to the broader category of supply contracts. A good example of this are the rules relating to delivery and risk laid down in s.28 and s.29. Thus understanding the concept of a sale of goods is very important. 1-019

Similarly, where the Consumer Rights Act does not apply, for example where there is a supply contract between two traders (or two consumers), the distinction between a sale of goods and other analogous supply contracts is crucial. Contracts other than contracts of sale of goods are not governed by the provisions of the Sale of Goods Act 1979. Although they will often be governed by some other Act of Parliament, none of them is governed by an Act which is as comprehensive as the Sale of Goods Act. Later in this book, some of these other Acts of Parliament are considered, including the Supply of Goods (Implied Terms) Act 1973 (Ch.22) and the Supply of Goods and Services Act 1982 (Ch.8). Another important statute, the Consumer Protection Act 1987, which deals with manufacturers' liability, is also considered later (Ch.9).

51 Under s.6, a contract of hire is defined as a contract, other than one of hire purchase, under which "the trader gives or agrees to give the consumer possession of the goods with the right to use them, subject to the terms of the contract, for a period determined in accordance with the contract."

52 See for example, s.17(1)(a) of the Consumer Rights Act: ". . .at the beginning of the period of hire the trader must have the right to transfer possession of the goods by way of hire for that period".

General Reading

P. Giliker, "Legislating on contracts for the supply of digital content and services: an EU/UK/ Irish divide?" [2021] J.B.L. 143.

D. Saidov, "Sales law post-Res Cogitans" [2019] J.B.L. 1.

2

Formation and Cancellation of the Contract

Formation of the Contract

A contract of sale is an agreement by which the seller and buyer undertake mutual obligations. At the very least the seller agrees that the buyer shall become the owner and the buyer agrees to pay the price. Often there are more obligations that just these. The number and extent of the obligations can be ascertained only by reference to the terms expressly agreed in the contract and to those extra terms which the law automatically implies into it. These will be discussed later.[1] At present we are concerned with what amounts to an enforceable agreement (i.e. a contract). If there is no contract or it is unenforceable, then neither the buyer nor the seller can complain that the other has broken it. 2-001

Time of Making the Contract

It is important to know exactly when a contract is made because until that time either party is free to back out. An agreement is made when one person makes an offer to another and that other person accepts it. Until there is an offer which is accepted, there is no contract. An offer is something which is clearly intended if accepted to form a binding agreement. Thus it has been held that the display of goods on the shelves of a self-service shop is not an offer: *Pharmaceutical Society of Great Britain v Boots Cash Chemists*.[2] The customer who takes them from the shelf therefore does not accept an offer. Rather, the offer is made by the customer when he takes the goods to the cash desk and it is accepted by the assistant at the cash desk. 2-002

1 See Ch.7.
2 [1952] 2 Q.B. 795.

At any time before that, either party can back out. In particular the customer can restore the goods to the shelf and will be under no obligation to pay for them.

Similarly, the display of goods in a shop window does not amount to an offer: *Fisher v Bell*.[3] The person who enters the shop and asks to buy the goods displayed in the window does not therefore accept an offer. He in fact makes an offer which the shopkeeper is free to accept or reject. The display of goods in the shop window or on the shelves of a supermarket is an invitation to treat, i.e. an invitation to members of the public to make an offer to buy. The acceptance of an invitation to treat does not make a contract.

The difference between an offer and an invitation to treat can most clearly be seen in auction sales. The auctioneer asks for bids. He may receive quite a lot of bids and will usually accept the highest. When the auctioneer asks for bids he is not making an offer but an invitation to treat. Each bid is a separate offer and a contract is not made until the auctioneer accepts one of them. Thus s.57(2) of the Sale of Goods Act reads:

> **"A sale by auction is complete when the auctioneer announces its completion by the fall of the hammer, or in other customary manner; and until the announcement is made any bidder may retract his bid."**

2-003 Another problem which has sometimes exercised the minds of academics is, "At exactly what stage is the contract concluded in the case of a purchase from an automated vending machine?" Is it when the purchaser puts his money in or is that merely an offer which the machine accepts? Some words of Lord Denning MR in *Thornton v Shoe Lane Parking*[4] are helpful in this context. The case actually involved a contract made between a motorist wishing to park his car and the proprietor of a car park with an automatic entrance barrier. His Lordship, however, also spoke about a machine which issues railway tickets and his comments would appear to apply equally to a machine selling goods. Referring to the customer, he said:[5]

> **"He was committed at the very moment when he put his money into the machine. The contract was concluded at that time. It can be translated into offer and acceptance in this way: the offer is made when the proprietor of the machine holds it out as being ready to receive the money. The acceptance takes place when the customer puts his money into the slot."**

It seems then that the display of goods in an automatic vending machine—unlike that in a shop window or on the shelves of a supermarket—is not merely an invitation to treat but is an offer.

3 [1961] 1 Q.B. 394.
4 [1971] 2 Q.B. 163.
5 [1971] 2 Q.B. 163 at 169.

Once an offer can be identified there is not usually any difficulty in ascertaining whether it has been accepted. The general rule is that an acceptance takes effect when it is actually communicated to the offeror: *Entores v Miles Far East Co*;[6] and *Brinkibon Ltd v Stahag Stahl*.[7] There are, however, two or three exceptions to this. First, in circumstances where the post is expected to be used as the means of communication between the seller and buyer, an acceptance takes effect when it is posted. Thus there is still a contract even if the letter of acceptance is lost in the post: *Household, Fire & Carriage Insurance Company v Grant*.[8] Secondly, where the offeror expressly or implicitly waives the need for acceptance to be communicated to him, the acceptance will take effect when the acceptor does whatever act is necessary to indicate his acceptance. The vending machine situation provides a good example of this. The contract is complete when the customer puts his money in the slot. He is certainly not expected to telephone or to write a letter to the proprietor of the machine.

Even if the offeror waives the need for communication to him, there must always be some act to indicate acceptance. The offeror cannot say "if you do nothing you will thereby accept my offer!" In *Felthouse v Bindley*[9] the offeror wrote to his nephew offering to buy the latter's horse. In the letter he said, "If I hear no more about him, I consider the horse mine". The nephew sent no reply and the court held that no contract was made. A contract is an agreement. It follows that one person cannot impose a contract upon another. If, on the other hand, the person to whom an offer is made says, for example, "If you do not hear from me within a week, you can assume that I have accepted your offer", then that will amount to an acceptance unless he communicates otherwise within the week. In *Re Selectmove Ltd*,[10] Gibson LJ said:[11] 2-004

> **"Where the offeree himself indicates that an offer is to be taken as accepted if he does not indicate to the contrary by an ascertainable time, he is undertaking to speak if he does not want an agreement to be concluded. I see no reason in principle why that should not be an exceptional circumstance such that the offer can be accepted by silence".**

There may be a third exception to the general rule that an acceptance takes effect when it is actually communicated to the offeror. In *Brinkibon Ltd v Stahag Stahl*[12] the House of Lords confirmed the decision in *Entores v Miles Far East Co*,[13] that normally in the case of a telephone

6 [1955] 2 Q.B. 327.
7 [1983] 2 A.C. 34.
8 (1879) 48 L.J.Q.B. 577.
9 [1863] 1 New Rep. 401.
10 [1995] 1 W.L.R. 474.
11 [1995] 1 W.L.R. 474 at 478.
12 [1983] 2 A.C. 34.
13 [1955] 2 Q.B. 327.

conversation or a telex communication the postal exception does not apply and therefore the acceptance takes effect when (and where) it is actually communicated to the offeror. Their Lordships did, however, state that a different result might apply to a telex message which was not a direct communication in office hours between the acceptor and the offeror, e.g. if it was sent at night or was sent or received through telex machines operated by third persons. In such a case the acceptance could take effect upon dispatch or upon communication to the machine at the receiving end of the telex link or upon actual communication to the offeror. A court would have to decide that issue by reference to the intention of the parties, to sound business practice and to its own judgment as to where the risk should lie.

Sales Via the Internet

2–005 Doubtless, the advertising of goods (or indeed services) will normally amount to no more than an invitation to treat. Someone responding to such an advertisement and submitting an order via an email may then be making what is in law an offer. If so, the advertiser is free to accept or not. Assuming that the advertiser accepts by email, there will presumably be the same uncertainty as to when the contract is made, as was expressed in the *Brinkibon* case about the position where the parties were not in direct telex communication in office hours. It would seem absurd, however, for the result to be that the contract is not made until the offeror decides to log on and check his emails (perhaps a week more or later?). In one widely publicised instance in 1999 Argos, a catalogue shopping company, advertised on its website a television set for £3 instead of £300.[14] Apparently many orders for these televisions were placed via the internet before the company realised its mistake. For those people who had not received any confirmation of their order, it seems reasonably clear that there was no contract. Apparently, however, some had received confirmation by email. This was, arguably, an acceptance. This unfortunate incident gave rise to no reported decision.[15] It seems probable however, the contract was unenforceable by any of the buyers since they surely must have known that the bargain (a television for £3) was not intended by the seller and the law does not allow one party to snatch a bargain which he knows is not intended by the other, *Hartog v Colin and Shields*.[16]

14 See, for example *http://news.bbc.co.uk/1/hi/business/the_economy/441740.stm* [Accessed 19 April 2022]. In 2002 Kodak mistakenly advertised a digital camera at £100, and not the intended price of £329. It is questionable whether the contractual intent argument would be applicable in this situation. However, it appeared that the customers who had placed orders had received confirmation emails, and in any event, Kodak honoured the orders. See *http://news.bbc.co.uk/1/hi/sci/tech/1795624.stm* [Accessed 19 April 2022].

15 See generally, D. Capps, "Electronic Mail and the Postal Rule" [2004] I.C.C.L.R. 207.

16 [1939] 3 All E.R. 566. The same principle should also apply to the situation in March 2012 whereby Tesco erroneously advertised an Apple iPad for £49 instead of the actual price of £559. See *http://www.bbc.co.uk/news/technology-17357383* [Accessed 19 April 2022].

Unsolicited Goods and Services

Goods are sometimes sent without prior request.[17] The recipient might become worried if successive letters then come threatening that action will be taken to obtain the price. Clearly, the recipient who does nothing does not enter into a contract to buy the goods and therefore is not bound to pay. In spite of the lack of any right to payment, some unscrupulous firms have in the past found it profitable to market their wares by sending them out unsolicited. This had two undesirable results. One was that some members of the public were unaware that they need not pay and gave in to the pressure of successive threatening letters. The other was that the goods, if they were not purchased by the recipient, still belonged to the sender. Therefore the recipient did not dare to throw them away and was in effect forced to give them house room. The Unsolicited Goods and Services Act 1971 tackled both of these social problems. Section 2 makes it a criminal offence to make demand for a payment for unsolicited goods without reasonable cause to believe that there is a right to it. Section 1 provided that after six months unsolicited goods were deemed to be an unconditional gift to the recipient. 2-006

Section 1 of the 1971 Act has since been repealed and replaced in order to bring it into line with art.9 of the Distance Selling Directive.[18] That was achieved initially by the Consumer Protection (Distance Selling) Regulations 2000[19] and the current law is to be found in the Consumer Protection from Unfair Trading Regulations 2008.[20] Regulation 27M deals with inertia selling by way of reference to the Blacklist of prohibited practices listed in Sch.1 to the 2008 Regulations. It is a criminal offence for a trader to demand "immediate or deferred payment for or the return or safekeeping of products supplied by the trader, but not solicited by the consumer".[21] In addition to any criminal sanctions[22] where a trader engages in inertia selling the consumer is not obligated to pay for the products supplied and may "use, deal with or dispose of the goods as if they were an unconditional gift to him".[23] Thus the old requirement under s.1 of the Unsolicited Goods and Services Act 1971, namely that unsolicited goods will become an unconditional gift after six months, is no longer valid: under the Regulations, there is no such time limit.

---

17 This is called inertia selling.

18 97/7/EC.

19 SI 2000/2334, as amended. The Regulations came into force on 31 October 2000.

20 SI 2008/1277, as amended by the Consumer Contracts (Information, Cancellation and Additional Charges) Regulations 2013 (SI 2013/3134 with effect from 13 June 2014. For an account of the Consumer Protection (Distance Selling) Regulations 2000 which applied prior to 13 June 2014, the reader may be directed to the 8th edn of this text.

21 Consumer Protection from Unfair Trading Regulations 2008 Sch.1 para.29.

22 See reg.12. The 2008 Regulations are discussed in Ch.16.

23 Though only as between the sender and the recipient, i.e. third party rights are unaffected, see reg.27M(4).

Form of the Contract

2–007 The law on this is very easy and is contained in s.4 of the Sale of Goods Act:

> **". . .a contract of sale may be made in writing (either with or without seal), or by word of mouth, or partly in writing and partly by word of mouth, or may be implied from the conduct of the parties."**

In this respect contracts of sale of goods are different from contracts for the sale of land. Whereas there are no particular formalities for the former, a contract for the sale of land can only be made in writing incorporating all the terms on which the parties have expressly agreed and signed by or on behalf of each party.[24] The distinction between goods and land is therefore important.[25] The distinction between consumer sales and other sales of goods (e.g. trader to trader sales, private sales and all sales entered into before 1 October 2015) is not: s.4 applies to those sales in exactly the same way since the Consumer Rights Act 2015 does not address issues around the form of the contract. Another area upon which the Consumer Rights Act is silent is the capacity of the parties to enter into the contract and again, the provisions of the Sale of Goods Act apply.

Capacity

2–008 Certain persons lack the legal capacity to make a contract. Thus contracts are not generally binding on the following people: persons who at the time of making the contract were either minors or so insane or drunk as not to know what they were doing. Such a person can enforce the contract against the other party but cannot generally himself be sued. An exception to this, however, is found in s.3 of the Sale of Goods Act:

> **"(1) Capacity to buy and sell is regulated by the general law concerning capacity to contract and to transfer and acquire property.**
>
> **(2) Where necessaries are sold and delivered to a minor or to a person who by reason of . . . drunkenness is incompetent to contract, he must pay a reasonable price for them.[26]"**
>
> **(3) In subsection (2) above 'necessaries' means goods suitable to the condition in life of the minor or other person concerned and to his actual requirements at the time of the sale and delivery."**

24 Law of Property (Miscellaneous Provisions) Act 1989 s.2.

25 See para.1-008, above.

26 s.3(2) used to provide for the situation where necessaries are supplied to someone who is incompetent to contract by reason of mental incapacity. That situation is now dealt with similarly by the Mental Capacity Act 2005 s.7.

In one case a minor undergraduate bought 11 fancy waistcoats: *Nash v Inman*.[27] It was held that the tailor could not sue for any money because the goods were not necessaries; the minor was already well supplied with waistcoats. The result of this decision was that not only was the minor under no obligation to pay for the waistcoats but also, apparently, he could keep them! Now, however, the law is different. Section 3 of the Minors' Contracts Act 1987 empowers the court, where it would be "just and equitable" (i.e. fair) to do so, to require the minor to return property which he has acquired under a contract which is unenforceable against him.[28]

Not surprisingly some traders are reluctant to deal with minors on any basis other than that the minor pays cash before taking the goods away. On the other hand, to refuse to give credit can be to turn away valuable business. Thus sometimes a trader will agree to give credit to a minor providing an adult (usually a parent) signs a document guaranteeing the minor's debt. Until 1987, however, a guarantee was no safeguard because the legal nature of a guarantee is that it is subsidiary to, and dependent upon, the contract which is guaranteed. If the latter was void, then the trader had no recourse against the guarantor: *Coutts & Co v Browne-Lecky*.[29] If, on the other hand, the adult had signed a contract, not of guarantee but of indemnity, that contract could be enforced against the adult even if the minor's contract was void: *Yeoman Credit Ltd v Latter*.[30] Thus the difference between a contract of guarantee and one of indemnity was vital. Now, however, where a contract is unenforceable against someone merely because he is a minor, a contract of guarantee is enforceable against the guarantor.[31]

The Price

The Amount

This is dealt with (for all sales of goods) under the Sale of Goods Act 1979.[32] Section 8 provides: 2-009

> **"(1) The price in a contract of sale may be fixed by the contract, or may be left to be fixed in a manner agreed by the contract, or may be determined by the course of dealing between the parties.**

27 [1908] 2 K.B. 1.

28 The Family Law Reform Act 1969 reduced the age of majority to 18 so that only people under that age enjoy the privileged status of minor.

29 [1947] K.B. 104.

30 [1961] 1 W.L.R. 828.

31 Minors' Contracts Act 1987 s.2.

32 The Consumer Rights Act is silent on questions of price.

> **(2) Where the price is not determined as mentioned in sub-section (1) above the buyer must pay a reasonable price.**
> **(3) What is a reasonable price is a question of fact dependent on the circumstances of each particular case."**

The price is normally a basic part of the agreement and normally it will be expressly agreed. It might appear from s.8(2) that, if no price is agreed and there is no method of ascertaining it, a reasonable price is automatically payable. This is not necessarily so. The price is so basic that, if the parties have expressly left it over for later agreement, the court may well conclude that the parties did not intend to make, and have not made, a contract. This was the conclusion of the House of Lords in *May & Butcher v R*[33] where an agreement for the purchase of government tentage provided that the price, the manner of delivery and dates of payment were to be agreed upon from time to time. If the contract had simply failed to mention these items, they could have been resolved by applying the provisions of the Sale of Goods Act. Equally, if the contract had provided for the price to be fixed by the seller (or buyer), that would have been binding. However, the contract expressly left the price and other items over for later agreement. That being so, and the items being so basic, their Lordships held that the parties had not intended to make a contract but simply had agreed to agree. There was therefore no contract.

If, however, a relatively minor matter is left over for later agreement it does not necessarily follow that there is no contract. It is perfectly possible in law for parties to make an interim agreement for the sale of goods which requires further negotiation to iron out the less important details of the transaction: *Pagnan S.p.A. v Feed Products*.[34] All the circumstances must be examined to see whether they intended to make a binding contract, albeit one with some details outstanding. In *Foley v Classique Coaches Ltd*[35] the defendants bought some land from the claimant and it was a condition of the purchase that the defendants agreed to buy petrol (for their coach business) only from the claimant. The agreement provided for the price of the petrol "to be agreed by the parties from time to time" and, failing agreement, to be settled by arbitration. It was held there that the parties had made a binding contract, albeit with the price still outstanding.

Clearly if there is no contract, as in *May & Butcher v R*,[36] no price is payable and s.8 is irrelevant. If there is a contract the price is ascertained by the relevant method in s.8 (in *Foley's* case by arbitration, the manner agreed in the contract).

33 [1934] 2 K.B. 17.
34 [1987] 2 Lloyd's Rep. 601.
35 [1934] 2 K.B. 1.
36 [1934] 2 K.B. 17.

Valuation

Valuation by a third party is one method the parties can stipulate for ascertainment of the price. Section 9 provides that where he cannot or does not make the valuation, the contract is avoided. In that case there is no obligation on the seller to deliver the goods and none on the buyer to pay. Section 9 has one exception to this: 2-010

> **". . .if the goods or any part of them have been delivered to and appropriated by the buyer he must pay a reasonable price for them."**

Section 9(2) provides that where the valuation is prevented by the fault of one of the parties, the other may maintain an action for damages against the party at fault. Where the valuer makes the valuation, then, unless the valuer was acting fraudulently in connivance with one of the parties, the valuation will be binding as between the parties. If, however, the valuation was arrived at negligently, the victim (i.e. the buyer or seller, depending upon whether the valuation was too high or too low) will have a claim in negligence against the valuer: *Arenson v Casson*.[37]

Deposits

It is not uncommon for the buyer to pay part of the price at the time of making the contract to buy. This payment could be either a deposit or mere part payment. The effect of a deposit or mere part payment is a matter of agreement between the parties. In the absence of any agreement to the contrary, a deposit is generally forfeited by the buyer if the sale falls through because of his fault. A mere part payment, however, is returnable. A deposit is, in the words of Lord Macnaghten in *Soper v Arnold* "a guarantee that the purchaser means business".[38] It is a security for the completion of the purchase. 2-011

As so often, the law endeavours to discover the intention of the parties. It examines all the circumstances to see whether they intended the money to be a deposit or merely a payment on account. If the parties actually use the word "deposit", then unless there is evidence to the contrary it will be assumed that that is what they meant: *Elson v Prices Tailors Ltd*.[39]

Of course, if the seller has a claim against the buyer either for the price or for damages[40] he will in making his claim have to bring into account any money already received—whether as deposit or merely as a part payment. The seller cannot expect on the one hand to be fully compensated for the sale falling through and on the other to be allowed in addition to retain a deposit already received.

37 [1975] 3 W.L.R. 815.
38 [1889] 14 App.Cas. 429 at 435.
39 [1963] 1 W.L.R. 287.
40 See Ch.12.

The Consumer Contracts (Information, Cancellation and Additional Charges) Regulations 2013

2-012 The Consumer Contracts (Information, Cancellation and Additional Charges) Regulations 2013[41] incorporate into domestic law various elements of the Consumer Rights Directive[42] with effect from 13 June 2014. Broadly put, the regulations put in place harmonised rules relating to the provision of pre-contract information and cancellation rights in "distance contracts" and "off-premises supply contracts". In so doing the regulations replace the two separate legislative schemes designed to protect consumers when entering into non-face-to-face contracts with traders, the Consumer Protection (Distance Selling) Regulations 2000,[43] and the Cancellation of Contracts made in a Consumer's Home or Place of Work etc Regulations 2008.[44] These regulations continue to govern distance and off-premises (doorstep) sales for contracts entered into before the Consumer Contracts (Information, Cancellation and Additional Charges) Regulations 2013 took effect.[45]

The regulations apply to a very wide range of contracts between traders and consumers as defined in reg.4.[46] The definition is identical to that under the Consumer Rights Act 2015, thus a "trader" is defined as "a person acting for purposes relating to his trade, business, craft or professional". Conversely, a "consumer" is an individual "acting for purposes which are wholly or mainly outside that individual's trade, business, craft or profession".[47]

The regulations impose requirements around, in particular, information to be provided and cancellation rights in "distance contracts" and "off-premises contracts", however, provision (albeit limited) is also made for "on-premises contracts". Each of these has a technical meaning laid down in reg.5.

2-013 A contract is a "distance contract" if:[48]

1. it concerns goods, services or digital content,

---

41 SI 2013/3134.

42 Directive 2011/83/EU.

43 SI 2000/2334.

44 SI 2008/1816.

45 For an account of each the reader is directed to the 8th edn of this text.

46 The regulations do not extend to certain, specified contracts as detailed in reg.6. For example, the regulations do not apply to contracts concluded by means of automatic vending machines or automated commercial premises; contracts under which goods are sold by way of execution or otherwise by authority of law. Neither do the regulations apply to gambling contracts, contracts for the rental of accommodation for residential purposes, etc. See reg.6 for the complete list of excluded contracts.

47 reg.4.

48 See the definition of a "distance contract" under the Consumer Rights Directive art.2(9).

2. it is between a trader (i.e. a supplier acting for commercial or professional purposes) and a consumer (i.e. a natural person wholly or mainly acting for purposes outside his business),

3. it is concluded under an organised distance sales or service provision scheme run by the trader, and

4. the trader makes exclusive use of distance communication up to, and at the moment, when the contract is made.

Distance communication is any means of communication not involving the simultaneous presence of the consumer and the supplier (or the supplier's representative)—e.g. internet, telephone, mail order, letter, fax, e-mail, television. A transaction where initial contact is made by distance communication but where the contract is made face-to-face is not a "distance contract".

The expression "an organised distance sales or service provision scheme" is obscure. What about a telephone enquiry by a consumer as a result of consulting Yellow Pages which leads to a contract being made during that telephone conversation? The fact that the supplier, e.g. a department store, has placed an advertisement in such a telephone directory does not in itself show that the supplier has a "distance sales scheme". On the other hand if it advertises its telephone number and runs a "home delivery service" then it does run such a scheme. The requirement for an "organised distance sales . . . scheme" will certainly exclude the regulations from applying to a supplier who does not normally indulge in distance sales but who does, for example, on a one-off occasion agree to take an order from a customer by telephone.

An "off-premises contract" on the other hand has a somewhat convoluted definition. Regulation 5 states:

> **"'off-premises contract' means a contract between a trader and a consumer which is any of these—**
>
> **(a) a contract concluded in the simultaneous physical presence of the trader and the consumer, in a place which is not the business premises of the trader;**
>
> **(b) a contract for which an offer was made by the consumer in the simultaneous physical presence of the trader and the consumer, in a place which is not the business premises of the trader;**
>
> **(c) a contract concluded on the business premises of the trader or through any means of distance communication immediately after the consumer was personally and individually addressed in a place which is not the business premises of the trader in the simultaneous physical presence of the trader and the consumer;**

(d) a contract concluded during an excursion organised by the trader with the aim or effect of promoting and selling goods or services to the consumer".

2-014 Fundamentally, these various iterations all relate to the practice of door-to-door salesmen and associated trading practices.

Finally, an "on-premises contract" means "a contract between a trader and a consumer which is neither a distance contract nor an off-premises contract".

Pre-contract Information in On-premises Contracts

2-015 The regulations make provision for "on-premises contracts". However, as we will see, the information which must be provided is notably less than that required for "distance contracts" and "off premises contracts".[49] Furthermore, the obligation does not extend to what the regulations deem "day-to-day" transactions which are performed immediately at the time the contract is entered into.[50] This is important, since otherwise simple transactions, such as purchasing groceries in a supermarket would become a very complicated matter indeed since the information which must be given is substantial:[51]

(a) the main characteristics of the goods, services or digital content, to the extent appropriate to the medium of communication and to the goods, services or digital content;

(b) the identity of the trader (such as the trader's trading name), the geographical address at which the trader is established and the trader's telephone number;

(c) the total price of the goods, services or digital content inclusive of taxes, or where the nature of the goods, services or digital content is such that the price cannot reasonably be calculated in advance, the manner in which the price is to be calculated;

(d) where applicable, all additional delivery charges or, where those charges cannot reasonably be calculated in advance, the fact that such additional charges may be payable;

(e) where applicable, the arrangements for payment, delivery, performance, and the time by which the trader undertakes to deliver the goods, to perform the service or to supply the digital content;

49 reg.9(1).

50 reg.9(2).

51 See Sch.1 to the Regulations.

(f) where applicable, the trader's complaint handling policy;

(g) in the case of a sales contract, a reminder that the trader is under a legal duty to supply goods that are in conformity with the contract;

(h) where applicable, the existence and the conditions of after-sales services and commercial guarantees;

(i) the duration of the contract, where applicable, or, if the contract is of indeterminate duration or is to be extended automatically, the conditions for terminating the contract;

(j) where applicable, the functionality, including applicable technical protection measures, of digital content; and

(k) where applicable, any relevant compatibility of digital content with hardware and software that the trader is aware of or can reasonably be expected to have been aware of.

This information must be given (or made available) to the consumer prior to the conclusion of the on-premises contract in a clear and comprehensible manner (unless the information is already apparent from the context of the transaction itself).[52]

Pre-contract Information in Distance and Off-premises Contracts

Where the contract is an "off-premises contract" or a "distance contract" the information which must be provided is laid down by Sch.2 and is even more extensive than listed above for "on-premises" contracts. As with the information to be provided prior to the conclusion of an "on-premises" contract, the information must be provided in a clear and comprehensible manner.[53] Furthermore, where the contract is cancellable (see below) the trader must give the consumer a standardised cancellation form as provided in Sch.3. In respect to off-premises contracts, the information, plus any cancellation form, must be legible and given to the consumer on paper unless the consumer agrees to another durable medium. This is modified in the case of distance contracts where some allowance is permitted in order to reflect the variety 2-016

52 Under ss.11(4) and 12 of the Consumer Rights Act, any information provided is treated as a term of the contract, see below, paras 7-029–7-030.

53 See reg.10 (off-premises contracts) and reg.13 (distance contracts).

of distance communication methods. Regulation 13(1) provides that the information must be given "in a way appropriate to the means of distance communication used".[54]

The information to be provided is both extensive and highly technical:[55]

(a) the main characteristics of the goods, services or digital content, to the extent appropriate to the medium of communication and to the goods, services or digital content;

(b) the identity of the trader (such as the trader's trading name);

(c) the geographical address at which the trader is established and, where available, the trader's telephone number, fax number and e-mail address, to enable the consumer to contact the trader quickly and communicate efficiently;

(d) where the trader is acting on behalf of another trader, the geographical address and identity of that other trader;

(e) if different from the address provided in accordance with paragraph (c), the geographical address of the place of business of the trader, and, where the trader acts on behalf of another trader, the geographical address of the place of business of that other trader, where the consumer can address any complaints;

(f) the total price of the goods, services or digital content inclusive of taxes, or where the nature of the goods, services or digital content is such that the price cannot reasonably be calculated in advance, the manner in which the price is to be calculated;

(g) where applicable, all additional delivery charges and any other costs or, where those charges cannot reasonably be calculated in advance, the fact that such additional charges may be payable;

(h) in the case of a contract of indeterminate duration or a contract containing a subscription, the total costs per billing period or (where such contracts are charged at a fixed rate) the total monthly costs;

---

54 If the information is provided on a durable medium, unsurprisingly, it must be legible (reg.13(2)). See also reg.13(4) which serves to prioritise certain information where the means of distance communication is such that it provides limited space (or time) for what is a substantial list of information required. The information prioritised is, as one would expect, matters such as the main characteristics of the goods or services, the identity of the trader, the price, etc. The other information may be provided in another way.

55 In the case of a public auction, the information listed in paras (b)–(e) may be replaced with the equivalent details for the auctioneer.

(i) the cost of using the means of distance communication for the conclusion of the contract where that cost is calculated other than at the basic rate;

(j) the arrangements for payment, delivery, performance, and the time by which the trader undertakes to deliver the goods, to perform the services or to supply the digital content;

(k) where applicable, the trader's complaint handling policy;

(l) where a right to cancel exists, the conditions, time limit and procedures for exercising that right in accordance with regs 27–38;

(m) where applicable, that the consumer will have to bear the cost of returning the goods in case of cancellation and, for distance contracts, if the goods, by their nature, cannot normally be returned by post, the cost of returning the goods;

(n) that, if the consumer exercises the right to cancel after having made a request in accordance with reg.36(1), the consumer is to be liable to pay the trader reasonable costs in accordance with reg.36(4);

(o) where under regs 28, 36 or 37 there is no right to cancel or the right to cancel may be lost, the information that the consumer will not benefit from a right to cancel, or the circumstances under which the consumer loses the right to cancel;

(p) in the case of a sales contract, a reminder that the trader is under a legal duty to supply goods that are in conformity with the contract;

(q) where applicable, the existence and the conditions of after-sale customer assistance, after-sales services and commercial guarantees;

(r) the existence of relevant codes of conduct, as defined in reg.5(3)(b) of the Consumer Protection from Unfair Trading Regulations 2008, and how copies of them can be obtained, where applicable;

(s) the duration of the contract, where applicable, or, if the contract is of indeterminate duration or is to be extended automatically, the conditions for terminating the contract;

(t) where applicable, the minimum duration of the consumer's obligations under the contract;

(u) where applicable, the existence and the conditions of deposits or other financial guarantees to be paid or provided by the consumer at the request of the trader;

(v) where applicable, the functionality, including applicable technical protection measures, of digital content;

(w) where applicable, any relevant compatibility of digital content with hardware and software that the trader is aware of or can reasonably be expected to have been aware of; and

(x) where applicable, the possibility of having recourse to an out-of-court complaint and redress mechanism, to which the trader is subject, and the methods for having access to it.

In either a "distance contract" or an "off-premises" contract, if the trader does not provide the information concerning additional costs and charges (items (g), (h), and (m) above) he will be unable to impose those charges on the consumer. Two final points should be made regarding "distance" contracts under the regulations. First, reg.16 requires that the trader must give the consumer confirmation of the contract on a durable medium. The confirmation must be given within a reasonable time and not later than the time of delivery where goods are being supplied or when performance commences in the case of any service supplied under the contract.[56] Secondly, where a distance contract is "concluded by electronic means" (such as internet sales) reg.14 lists certain additional requirements. In particular, where the contract places the consumer under an obligation to pay, the trader must make the consumer aware of:

- The main characteristics of the goods or services.
- The total price of the goods or services (including the cost per billing period for contracts including a subscription (or, where relevant, the means by which the price will be calculated).
- Where applicable, any additional delivery charges (or other costs).
- The duration of the contract or for contracts of no fixed duration, the means of terminating the contract and the minimum duration of the contract.

This information must be provided directly before the consumer places the order and must be given in a clear and prominent manner. Furthermore, the regulations make special provision for distance contracts concluded by electronic means:

56 See also, the provision made for intangible supplies of digital content in reg.16(3).

- The trader must ensure that the consumer, when placing the order, explicitly acknowledges that the order implies an obligation to pay.[57]

- If placing an order entails activating a button or a similar function, the trader must ensure that the button or similar function is labelled in an easily legible manner only with the words "order with obligation to pay" or a corresponding unambiguous formulation indicating that placing the order entails an obligation to pay the trader.[58]

- The trader must ensure that any trading website through which the contract is concluded indicates clearly and legibly, at the latest at the beginning of the ordering process, whether any delivery restrictions apply and which means of payment are accepted.[59]

Cancellation Rights

The general rule is that, once a contract is made, neither party is free to back out. To that rule there is an exception created by the Consumer Contracts (Information, Cancellation and Additional Charges) Regulations 2013 which harmonise the previously separate legislative frameworks governing cancellation rights in "off-premises contracts" and "distance contracts".[60] These regulations came into force on 13 June 2014 and, broadly speaking, give a cooling-off (cancellation) period of 14 days to a consumer who enters into a contract to buy goods (or services) as a result of doorstep canvassing or who enters into a distance contract. This cancellation right is however, limited in a number of respects. First, the cancellation provisions do not apply where, the contract is either outside of the scope of the regulations[61] or:[62] 2-017

(a) for the supply of a medicinal product by administration by a prescriber or under a prescription or directions given by a prescriber;

(b) for the supply of a product by a health care professional under arrangements for the supply of services as part of the health service, where the product is one that, at least in some circumstances is available under such arrangements free or on prescription;

57 reg.14(3). Where this requirement is not met, the consumer will not be bound by the order.

58 reg.14(4). As with reg.14(3), where this requirement is not met, the consumer will not be bound by the order.

59 reg.14(6).

60 SI 2013/3134. The 2013 Regulations replace the Consumer Protection (Distance Selling) Regulations 2000 and the Cancellation of Contracts made in a Consumer's Home or Place of Work etc Regulations 2008. The old regulations continue to have application in respect of distance and off-premises contracts entered into before 13 June 2014. For discussion of the old law, the reader may be directed to the 8th edn of this text.

61 See reg.6.

62 See reg.27.

(c) for passenger transport services; or

(d) an off-premises contract where the payment to be made by the consumer is not more than £42.[63]

Similarly, reg.28 excludes any cancellation rights where there is a contract:

- For the supply of goods or services (other than supply of water, gas, electricity or district heating) for which the price is dependent on fluctuations in the financial market which cannot be controlled by the trader and which may occur within the cancellation period.

- For the supply of goods that are made to the consumer's specifications or are clearly personalised.

- For the supply of goods which are liable to deteriorate or expire rapidly.

- For the supply of alcoholic beverages where:
  (i) their price has been agreed at the time of the conclusion of the sales contract,

  (ii) delivery of them can only take place after 30 days, and

  (iii) their value is dependent on fluctuations in the market which cannot be controlled by the trader.

- Where the consumer has specifically requested a visit from the trader for the purpose of carrying out urgent repairs or maintenance.[64]

- For the supply of a newspaper, periodical or magazine with the exception of subscription contracts for the supply of such publications.

- Concluded at a public auction.

- For the supply of accommodation, transport of goods, vehicle rental services, catering or services related to leisure activities, if the contract provides for a specific date or period of performance.

---

63 Note that this limitation applies to off-premises contracts only—there is no equivalent limitation on distance contracts.

64 Though note reg.28(2).

To this list we must also add situations where the cancellation right is prima facie available but will be lost in certain circumstances. These situations are also detailed in reg.28 and include the following:

(a) in the case of a contract for the supply of sealed goods which are not suitable for return due to health protection or hygiene reasons, if they become unsealed after delivery;

(b) in the case of a contract for the supply of sealed audio or sealed video recordings or sealed computer software, if the goods become unsealed after delivery; and

(c) in the case of any sales contract, if the goods become mixed inseparably (according to their nature) with other items after delivery.

Where a contract remains cancellable despite the foregoing provisions, reg.29 provides that a consumer has the right to cancel without incurring any liability, at any time within the cancellation period, without giving any reason to the trader. This right is exercisable by the consumer informing the trader of their decision to cancel the contract.[65] The cancellation period is specified by reg.30. Accordingly, the standard cancellation period is 14 days, however, the period commences at different times depending on the nature of the contract. The position can be summarised as follows:

- If the contract is a sales contract, the cancellation period ends at the end of 14 days after the day on which the goods come into the physical possession of either the consumer, or a person (excluding the carrier) identified by the consumer to take possession of them.[66]

- If the contract is a service contract, the cancellation period ends at the end of 14 days after the day on which the contract is entered into.

- If the contract is a contract for the supply of digital content which is not supplied on a tangible medium, the cancellation period ends at the end of 14 days after the day on which the contract is entered into.

Regulation 30 does not apply, however, where the trader is in breach of the requirement to provide the consumer with the necessary information detailing the right of cancellation. In this case, the cancellation period is extended in accordance with reg.31. Where the trader does

65 Any clear statement will be effective, however, the consumer may use a model cancellation form if they wish, see reg.32(3). Where the decision is not effected face-to-face, as will often be the case (for obvious reasons) provided that the consumer sends their communication within the 14-day cancellation period, it will be effective.

66 reg.30(3). Note, however, the special provisions for certain sales contracts under regs 30(4)–(6).

comply with the information requirement within 12 months,[67] the cancellation period ends 14 days after the consumer receives the required information. Where, however, the trader does not provide the necessary information within that 12-month period, the cancellation period will end 12 months after the day on which it would have ended under reg.30. In effect, therefore, where a trader does not provide the requisite information, a consumer's cancellation period can be extended by up to 12 months.

Effect of Cancellation

2-018 Broadly speaking, the consumer is entitled to be repaid any money he has already paid before cancellation and must return any goods he has received.[68] There are certain exceptions to what has just been said. First, in regard to delivery charges, reg.34 provides that the trader must reimburse such charges, but only where the where the consumer has expressly chosen a kind of delivery costing more than the least expensive common and generally acceptable kind of delivery offered by the trader. In this case, the trader must only reimburse the consumer to the amount the consumer would have paid had he chosen the least expensive and generally acceptable form of delivery. A good example of this would be, in most cases, express (next-day) delivery. Where the consumer expressly chooses this form of delivery and pays for the privilege, the trader will not be obligated to reimburse the full amount. Instead, the trader must, under reg.34(3) reimburse for (in most cases) standard delivery. Any reimbursement must be made without undue delay and within the time frame specified by reg.34. Broadly, this will be the earlier of 14 days from either the date the consumer can evidence having returned the goods, or the day on which the trader receives the goods.[69]

It is possible for the trader to make a deduction from any reimbursement where the value of the goods supplied under a cancelled contract has been diminished "as a result of handling of the goods by the consumer beyond what is necessary to establish the nature, characteristics and functioning of the goods". This would extend to for example, items of clothing which have been worn by the consumer prior to their decision to cancel the sales contract. In such a situation, the trader can recover a sum equivalent to the loss in value caused by the consumer's actions, up to the full contract price for the goods.[70]

This leaves the matter of what happens to the goods where a sales contract[71] has been cancelled under reg.29. Regulation 35(1) provides that it is the trader's responsibility to collect the goods if:

67 Note that the 12-month time frame runs from day 1 of the 14-day period mentioned in reg.30.

68 See reg.33 and reg.34.

69 reg.34(4) and (5). See also, reg.34(6).

70 reg.34(9) and (10).

71 See reg.36 for special rules regarding the supply of services within the cancellation period. Similarly, see reg.37 for similar rules relating to the supply of digital content within the cancellation period.

> **"(a) the trader has offered to collect them, or**
> **(b) in the case of an off-premises contract, the goods were delivered to the consumer's home when the contract was entered into and could not, by their nature, normally be returned by post."**

Where it is not the trader's responsibility, the consumer must return the goods without undue delay and no later than 14 days after the day when the consumer cancelled the contract. The consumer can return the goods either by sending them to the trader or by handing the goods over to a person authorised by the trader to receive them.[72] In general, the consumer will bear the direct costs of returning the goods to the trader. However, this will not be the case where the trader did not inform the consumer, prior to entering the contract, that such costs would be the responsibility of the consumer.[73]

72 reg.35(2).

73 reg.35(5). Regulation 35 also provides that the consumer will not be responsible for the costs of returning the goods where the trader has agreed to bear those costs. See also reg.35(8) regarding the costs where the trader collects the goods.

3

The Passing of Property and Risk

Introduction

A contract of sale is made in order to transfer ownership from the seller to the buyer. This transfer of ownership is called by the Sale of Goods Act "the Transfer of Property". It often takes place on the very instant that the contract is made. However, it can occur at almost any time from the making of the contract onwards—perhaps months or years later. Until it does so, the goods remain the property of the seller. The word "property" as used in the Sale of Goods Act is generally taken to mean ownership[1] and is defined by s.61 as "the general property in the goods". Indeed, the Consumer Rights Act 2015 defines "ownership" as "the general property in goods, not merely a special property" and adopts the framework dealing with the transfer of property laid down by the Sale of Goods Act.[2] We will look at that framework shortly, however, it must be appreciated at the outset that when considering the passing of property from the seller to the buyer, we are dealing with something different from the physical handing over, (i.e. delivery) of the goods. The transfer of ownership and the transfer of physical possession often do not occur simultaneously. Thus, sometimes a seller will find himself still in the possession of goods after the ownership in them has passed to the buyer. Equally, it is possible for goods to be delivered to the buyer some time before property in the goods passes to him. 3-001

1 The curious approach of the Sale of Goods Act in distinguishing concepts of "property" and "title" in Pt III has been subject to much academic thought. See for example, P.S. Atiyah, J. Adams, H. MacQueen Atiyah, *The Sale of Goods,* 12th edn (Harlow: Longman, 2010), pp.305–310; H.L. Ho, "Some Reflections on "Property" and "Title" in the Sale of Goods Act" (1997) 56 C.L.J. 571; and T.Y. Lin, "Does Ownership Matter in the Sale of Goods" [2011] J.B.L. 749. For a compelling analysis of the relationship between "property" and "title" within the Sale of Goods Act, see G. Battersby, "A reconsideration of 'property' and 'title' in the Sale of Goods Act" [2001] J.B.L. 1.

2 CRA 2015 s.4. Note, however, the recent Law Commission Proposals which would serve to disapply the SGA provisions in respect of *some* consumer sales contracts. See below, para.3–042.

Contrary to common belief, the buyer's right to obtain possession of the goods does not depend upon him being the owner. Unless the parties agree otherwise, he has the right to take delivery upon payment of the price and to do so irrespective of whether property has passed to him. Why then does it matter at what point in time the property passes? The answer is that four important things depend upon the passing of property.

(i) Unless the parties agree a different time for payment, the seller can sue for the price only after property has passed—s.49.[3]

(ii) Unless and until the buyer has the ownership in the goods he cannot transfer that ownership on to any further person. This rule is subject to a number of exceptions.[4]

(iii) In the event of either the seller or the buyer becoming bankrupt (or, in the case of a company, going into liquidation), the rights of the other party over the goods may well depend upon whether property has passed to the buyer.

(iv) Risk, prima facie, passes with property where the Sale of Goods Act applies—s.20. The risk of accidental damage is borne (unless otherwise agreed) by the owner. This rule is of questionable merit. It would seem sensible to link risk with possession rather than with ownership, because the person in possession of the goods is in the best position to see that they come to no harm. As we will see, where the Consumer Rights Act 2015 applies, risk and ownership have been decoupled with the result that risk, prima facie, passes on possession.[5]

Classification of the Contract

3–002 We cannot pinpoint the exact time that property passes without first classifying the contract. It will be one of two types, being either (i) for the sale of specific goods, or (ii) for the sale of unascertained goods.

3 See para.12-003, below.
4 See Ch.5, below.
5 CRA 2015 s.29.

Specific Goods

These are defined in s.61 as "goods identified and agreed upon at the time a contract of sale is made and includes an undivided share, specified as a fraction or percentage, of goods identified and agreed as aforesaid". If, at the time the contract is made, it is possible to point out the particular goods upon which the parties have agreed, then those goods are clearly "identified and agreed upon" and therefore specific. For example second-hand car deals are usually contracts for the sale of specific goods. At the time of the contract the parties know which particular car is being sold and bought. They have "identified and agreed upon" a particular car. Similarly, most contracts made in supermarkets are purchases of specific goods. At the time of the contract (i.e. at the cash desk) the parties have identified and agreed upon the goods (i.e. those brought by the customer to the cash desk).[6] 3-003

Kursell v Timber Operators[7] concerned the sale of timber which at the time the contract was made was still growing in a Latvian forest. The buyer was to fell and remove the trees himself. The trees which he was entitled to fell and remove (i.e. which he was buying) were described in the contract as "all trunks and branches of trees, but not seedlings and young trees of less than six inches diameter at a height of four feet from the ground". They were to be measured at the time of felling and the buyer was given 15 years in which to do the felling. Until the time for felling, it therefore could not be said which trees were within the contract. They were not "identified" at the time the contract was made. It was held that they were not, therefore, specific goods.

An agreement to sell some unspecified goods out of a larger specified quantity, as in *Kursell v Timber Operators,* is not a contract for the sale of specific goods. The goods actually being sold must be identified. Contracts to sell the following are therefore not contracts for the sale of specific goods: "a bottle of port from the seller's stock"; or, "12 of the seller's stock of 13 bottles of port". This description does not tell us which out of the 13 are being sold. *Re Wait*[8] involved a contract to sell 500 tons of wheat out of the cargo of 1,000 tons in the ship Challenger. The 500 tons were not specific goods because, in the words of Lord Hanworth MR, "There was no ascertainment or identification of the 500 tons out of the cargo in bulk".[9] Even if the 500 tons were subsequently separated from the bulk of the cargo, and thereby identified, this would not make them "specific goods". The relevant time is when the contract is made. Only if they are at that time identified and agreed upon will they be specific goods. This is clear from the definition in s.61.

6 Contrast the position of groceries bought online via the website of the same supermarket, though care is needed as to identifying when the contract is made and the effect of a trader including a term which states that the consumer's offer is only accepted on dispatch of the goods to the consumer. For a comprehensive discussion of such terms, see *Consumer sales contracts: transfer of ownership* (2021, Law Com. No. 398, Ch.5).

7 [1927] 1 K.B.298.

8 [1927] 1 Ch. 606.

9 [1927] 1 Ch. 606 at 617.

3-004 Suppose a seller with just 12 bottles of port in stock agrees to sell 12 bottles of port to a particular buyer. Even this may not be a contract for the sale of specific goods. Even if the seller has every intention of supplying the buyer with the 12 bottles currently in stock, it still may not be a contract for the sale of specific goods. In order to determine whether it is, the terms of the contract must be examined and, if necessary, construed (i.e. interpreted). If the terms are such as to leave the seller free, if he should wish to do so, to obtain more wine of the same description for delivery to the buyer, then the contract goods have not been identified and agreed upon at the date of the contract and the contract is not one for the sale of specific goods: *Re London Wine Co (Shippers)*.[10] There is a difference between a contract to sell "12 bottles of port" and one to sell "the 12 bottles of port which I now have in stock". The former is not a contract for the sale of specific goods, whereas, if the seller has just 12 bottles of port in stock, the latter is a contract for the sale of specific goods.[11]

The words in the definition of specific goods referring to "an undivided share, specified as a fraction or percentage, of goods identified and agreed as aforesaid" deal with the position where what is sold is a share in goods which are identified. A typical example would be the sale of "a 10 per cent share in the race horse White Rum". The horse, White Rum, is identified and agreed upon at the time of the contract. Provided (a) that it is an undivided share that is being sold (e.g. not the right back leg!), and (b) that the share is expressed as a fraction or percentage, the contract will still be one for the sale of specific goods.

Unascertained Goods

3-005 The Sale of Goods Act does not give a definition of unascertained goods. If the contract is not for the sale of specific goods however, then it must be for the sale of unascertained goods, i.e. goods which are not identified and agreed upon at the time of contracting. This was the position in both *Kursell v Timber Operators*[12] and *Re Wait*.[13] However, within the category of unascertained goods the Sale of Goods Act distinguishes between two types:

(i) A specified quantity of unascertained goods out of an identified bulk, e.g. "500 tons of wheat from the cargo of 1000 tons on the Challenger."

(ii) Purely generic unascertained goods, e.g. "500 tons of wheat".

In the former the seller can fulfil his contract only by delivery of 500 tons from the specified cargo, whereas in the latter he can fulfil his contract by supplying 500 tons from any source.

10 [1986] P.C.C. 121.

11 Consequently goods purchased online will generally be sales of unascertained goods, irrespective of whether the online seller has only one such item in stock at the time of contracting.

12 [1927] 1 K.B.298.

13 [1927] 1 Ch. 606.

This difference, however, does not alter the fact that both are contracts for the sale of unascertained goods.

Having been told that there can be a contract for either the sale of specific goods or for the sale of unascertained goods, one might ask, "Is there not a third category? Can there not be a contract for the sale of ascertained goods?" The answer is that there is no third category. If at the time the contract is made, the goods are ascertained (i.e. identified and agreed upon), then the contract is one for the sale of specific goods. If they become ascertained only after the contract was made, the contract at the time of its creation was for the sale of unascertained goods. The time for classification is when the contract is made. Therefore there are only two possible categories of contract, for the sale of specific goods and for the sale of unascertained goods. The word "ascertained" is used in the Sale of Goods Act to mean goods which become identified and agreed upon only after the contract is made.

Future Goods

Section 5(1) reads: 3-006

> **"The goods which form the subject of a contract of sale may be either existing goods, owned or possessed by the seller, or goods to be manufactured or acquired by him after the making of the contract of sale, in this Act called future goods."**

The problem here is to decide into which category future goods fall. Are they specific or are they unascertained? Examples of future goods are:

- 275 tons of barley to be grown by the seller (see *Sainsbury v Street*[14]).
- A limited edition Porsche 911 to be acquired by the seller (see *Hughes v Pendragon Sabre Ltd*[15]).
- Animal feedstuff to be made according to a specification supplied by the buyer (see *Ashington Piggeries v Hill*[16]).
- A ship to be built by the seller to a specification (*McDougall v Aeromarine of Emsworth*[17]).

Although these particular examples each contain a contract for the sale of unascertained goods, it is not true that all future goods automatically fall into that category. For example,

14 [1972] 1 W.L.R. 834.
15 [2016] EWCA Civ 18.
16 [1971] 2 W.L.R.1051.
17 [1958] 1 W.L.R.1126.

X may agree to sell Y "the Morris car, registration ABC 123, at present in the ownership of Q and to be acquired from him by X". This is a contract for the sale of specific goods. In *Varley v Whipp*[18] the contract was for the sale of a specified second-hand reaping machine which at the time of the contract the seller did not own but still had to acquire. The court nevertheless regarded the reaping machine as specific goods.

The Time of the Transfer of Property

3-007 The rules as to what time that property passes are contained in ss.16–19 and they differ according to whether the contract is for the sale of specific or unascertained goods. Since the Consumer Rights Act 2015 adopts ss.16–19, the following discussion is relevant to both consumer sales contracts and non-consumer sale of goods contracts.

Specific Goods

3-008 Section 17 says that property in specific goods passes to the buyer at such time as the parties intend it to be transferred.[19] It also says that the intention of the parties can be determined by reference to the terms of the contract, the conduct of the parties and the circumstances of the case.[20] If the contract expressly states when property is to pass then that is fine and the matter is one of contractual construction.[21] Often, however, it does not do so. The seller is concerned about being paid and the buyer about getting hold of the goods.[22] It is not unusual therefore for the contract expressly to deal with the time for payment and the time for delivery but to be silent about the time of the transfer of property. In such a case, one must still examine all the circumstances of the case in order to discern the parties' original intention as to the passing of property. For example, a clue may be obtained from the time that the parties have stipulated

18 [1900] 1 Q.B. 513.

19 s.17(1).

20 s.17(2).

21 As was the case in *Re Anchor Line Ltd* [1937] 1 Ch. 1 where the Court of Appeal held that property had not passed under rule 1 of s.18 as the written contract established an intention that property was not to pass until the full price had been paid. See also, *Gregor Fisken Ltd v Carl* [2021] EWCA Civ 792 at [72]–[80] where the Court of Appeal held that property in a classic motor vehicle passed on completion and that this intention was evident for both the vehicle and its gearbox (which had been separated from the vehicle).

22 This is certainly accurate in the majority of consumer sales, although still reflects the state of mind of the contracting parties in sales generally. See the observations of Lord Wright in *Smyth & Co Ltd v Bailey Son & Co Ltd* [1940] 3 All E.R. 60 at 67.

for delivery and/or payment. In *Ward v Bignall*,[23] Diplock LJ said ". . .in modern times very little is needed to give rise to the inference that property in specific goods is to pass only on delivery or payment".[24]

One is attempting to discover the intention of the parties at the time the contract was made. If their intention subsequently changes, that is irrelevant and the property will pass in accordance with their intention at the time of making the contract. In *Dennant v Skinner*[25] the buyer had a van knocked down to him at auction. Shortly after this he paid for it by cheque and on request signed a statement that property in the van was not to pass to him until the cheque cleared. The court in attempting to discover the intention of the parties ignored the signed statement because it had been made after the making of the contract.[26]

Often even the diligent searcher will fail to discover when the parties intended property to pass. In this case property passes according to whichever of the rules in s.18 is relevant (see below).[27]

Unascertained Goods

Section 16 says: 3-009

> **"Subject to section 20A below where there is a contract for the sale of unascertained goods no property in the goods is transferred to the buyer unless and until the goods are ascertained."**

This is no more than common sense. Until the parties have identified the goods which the buyer is to have, no property can pass from the seller to the buyer for the simple reason that it is impossible to tell in which goods the property is passing. So, in a case where the seller was to build a yacht for the buyer and they agreed that on payment of the first instalment the vessel and all materials used in its construction should become the absolute property of the buyer, the court held that no property passed on payment of the first instalment because at that time the boat's construction had not commenced and the materials to be used had not yet been identified.[28] A similar contract was involved in *Re Blyth Shipbuilding and Dry Dock Co*[29] but in that case the vessel was already in course of construction when the first instalment was paid. It was held that property in the incomplete ship passed on payment of the first instalment but

23 [1967] 1 Q.B. 534.

24 [1967] 1 Q.B. 534 at 545. See also, *Michael Gerson (Leasing) Ltd v Wilkinson* [2001] Q.B. 514 at 531.

25 [1948] 2 K.B. 164.

26 Note, however, that subsequent conduct may provide evidence of intention at the time of contracting. See *The Filiatra Legacy* [1991] 2 Lloyd's Rep 337 and *Tanks and Vessels Industries Limited v Devon Cider Co Ltd* [2009] EWHC 1360 (Ch) [50] (ascertained goods).

27 This is what happened in *Dennant v Skinner*.

28 *McDougall v Aeromarine of Emsworth* [1958] 1 W.L.R.1126.

29 [1926] Ch. 494.

that no property passed at that time in some materials which were lying in the ship yard and might be used in the ship's construction. The reason was that it was not at that time ascertained that those materials were definitely to be used.

Suppose a seller, S, has contracted with A in Aylesbury to sell him 60kg of potatoes and with B in Bristol to sell him 25kg and with C in Cardiff to sell him 15kg. Suppose also that the seller dispatches a lorry carrying 100kg of potatoes to make delivery to A, B and C in that order. Until the lorry has unloaded both A's and B's deliveries, the potatoes are all mixed up and C's 15kg are unascertained. As soon as A's and B's deliveries have both been made, C's 15kg become ascertained through exhaustion, since it is then possible to say that all the potatoes left on the lorry are destined for C. Now suppose that before the lorry is dispatched, C sells his 15kg to B and arranges with S that the lorry shall drop 40kg to B in Bristol. In that case B's 40kg become ascertained through exhaustion as soon as A's 60kg have been unloaded. That is so even though B's 40kg may not have been subdivided or allocated as between separate contracts by which he bought them: *Karlshamns Oliefabiker v Eastport Navigation Corporation, The Elafi*.[30]

3-010 No property can pass in goods until they are ascertained. There is one exception to this. It is that there are special rules, introduced in 1995 and stated in s.20A, which apply to a contract to sell a specified quantity of unascertained goods out of a specified bulk and these rules provide for a special kind of proprietary interest to pass even before the goods have become ascertained. These special rules are dealt with later. So now we leave that exception aside for the moment and consider the ordinary rules which govern the passing of property in both contracts for the sale of specific goods and contracts for the sale of unascertained goods.

Although, apart from the exception just mentioned, no property can pass until the goods have become ascertained, it does not follow that the property will necessarily pass as soon as the goods are ascertained. Property passes when the parties intend it to—s.17. Section 17 applies to ascertained goods in exactly the same way as it does to specific goods. If the intention of the parties is not apparent, then property passes according to the relevant rule in s.18, i.e. in the case of a contract for the sale of unascertained goods, usually rule 5.

Rules in s.18

3-011 Section 17 is the governing section and the rules in s.18 are to be consulted only if the parties have not evinced their intention as to when property is to pass. This is clear from the opening words of s.18:

> **"Unless a different intention appears, the following are rules for ascertaining the intention of the parties as to the time at which the property in the goods is to pass to the buyer."**

30 [1982] 1 All E.R. 208.

Rule 1

> **"Rule 1: Where there is an unconditional contract for the sale of specific goods in a deliverable state the property in the goods passes to the buyer when the contract is made, and it is immaterial whether the time of payment or the time of delivery, or both, be postponed."** 3-012

The essence of this is that if the goods are identified and agreed upon and ready to be handed over, the parties are taken to have intended the buyer to become the owner immediately, i.e. at the very instant that the contract is made. In *Dennant v Skinner*[31] a van was auctioned and knocked down to a Mr King. Hallet J quoted rule 1 and continued:[32]

> **"Accordingly, upon the fall of the hammer the property of this car passed to King unless that prima facie rule is excluded from applying because of a different intention appearing or because there was some condition in the contract which prevented the rule from applying".**

He held that therefore the van became King's immediately.

It is not completely settled what the meaning in rule 1 of "an unconditional contract" actually is. This could refer to a contract without any conditions whatsoever. Such an interpretation, however, would be absurd, since any contract of sale must have a condition somewhere at its core. It is difficult to imagine one without at least two conditions, namely, that the buyer will pay the price and that the seller will deliver the goods. The words "unconditional contract" therefore do not mean a contract without conditions in the sense just referred to, i.e. important terms of the contract (see Ch.7). It seems sensible therefore to assume that they mean a contract which contains no condition preventing rule 1 from applying. An example of such a condition would be if, to the buyer's knowledge at the time the contract was made, the seller was not the owner of the goods. In that case ownership will not pass to the buyer before the seller has himself succeeded in acquiring that ownership. This was precisely the position in the case, referred to earlier, of *Varley v Whipp*, where at the time of the contract the seller still had to acquire the second-hand reaping machine which he was agreeing to sell. It was held that the contract was not "unconditional" and that therefore rule 1 did not apply.

The words "deliverable state" are defined in s.61(5) as, goods "in such a state that the buyer would under the contract be bound to take delivery of them". Thus if the goods require anything to be done to them in order for them to be ready for delivery or in order to make them comply with the contract, they will not be in a deliverable state. In *Underwood v Burgh Castle*

31 [1948] 2 K.B. 164.
32 [1948] 2 K.B. 164 at 171.

Brick & Cement Syndicate[33] the contract was to sell a 30-ton condensing machine which at the time of the contract was standing bolted to a concrete emplacement in which it had become embedded because of its weight. It was an expensive and time-consuming task to remove it. In the contract the sellers had agreed to do this and to deliver the machine f.o.r. (free on rail) which meant that they undertook to see that the machine was conveyed to and loaded upon the train. The Court of Appeal had two reasons for deciding that rule 1 did not apply. First, the parties had, by making an f.o.r. agreement, indicated their intention that property should pass when the goods were loaded on to the rail. Secondly, the machine was not at the time of the contract in a deliverable state, since it still had to be removed from the concrete emplacement.

3–013 We now come to the closing words of rule 1, "it is immaterial whether the time of payment or the time of delivery, or both, be postponed". From these, it is clear that a buyer can be the owner of the goods even though he has not paid for them and even though they remain in the seller's possession. As we shall see in Ch.12, the seller usually has the right to retain possession of the goods until the buyer pays. This does not alter the fact that if rule 1 applies, the buyer becomes the owner at the instant the contract is made. As Hallet J explained in *Dennant v Skinner*, "the passing of property and the right to possession are two different things. Here, in my judgment, the property had passed on the fall of the hammer, but still the (seller) had a right to retain possession of the goods until payment was made."[34]

In other words, what occurs after the contract is made, in relation either to the possession of the goods or to the payment of the price, can have no bearing upon the operation of rule 1. However, what might affect it is if at the time of the making of the contract the parties make an agreement about delivery and/or payment, i.e. that they be postponed. Such an agreement could easily give rise to the inference that they intended property to be similarly postponed (see *Underwood v Burgh Castle Brick & Cement Syndicate*, above). In that situation none of the rules in s.18 would apply since those rules are only relevant "unless a different intention appears".

Rule 2

3–014 **"Rule 2: Where there is a contract for the sale of specific goods and the seller is bound to do something to the goods for the purpose of putting them into a deliverable state, the property does not pass until the thing is done and the buyer has notice that it has been done."**

Rule 2 is therefore concerned with the situation where, unlike in rule 1, there is a conditional contract—the condition relating to the seller[35] doing something to render the goods in a deliverable state. One example of an act which renders the goods in a deliverable state is

33 [1922] 1 K.B. 343.

34 [1948] 2 K.B. 164 at 172.

35 Similarly to rule 3, only acts to be done by the seller.

that of topping up casks of turpentine (where the agreement between the parties required this topping up).[36] The key issue here is whether the goods meet the "state in which they are to be delivered by the terms of the contract".[37]

One unanswered question here is what "notice" means. Suppose the seller puts a letter in the post informing the buyer that the goods are in a deliverable state. Does property pass when the letter is posted or when it arrives? "Notice" probably means actual knowledge in which case the property passes when the letter arrives. So, if the letter is lost, property does not pass until the buyer actually discovers that the goods are in a deliverable state. The Act is also silent on the issue of whether it is the seller who should give notice to the buyer.[38]

Rule 3

"Rule 3: Where there is a contract for the sale of specific goods in a deliverable state but the seller is bound to weigh, measure, test, or do some other act or thing with reference to the goods for the purpose of ascertaining the price, the property does not pass until the act or thing is done and the buyer has notice that it has been done." 3-015

It is important here to note that rule 3 applies only if it is the seller who is to do the weighing, measuring, testing, etc. In *Nanka-Bruce v Commonwealth Trust Ltd*,[39] it was agreed that the buyer would pay 59s. per 60lb. The buyer was going to resell the goods and it was recognised that the buyer's sub-purchaser would test the weight and thus ascertain the precise sum to be paid to the seller. The Privy Council held that property passed from the seller before the sub-purchaser had tested the goods for weight. Thus, where specific goods are to be weighed or tested, etc. by some person other than the seller, property will pass under rule 1 or rule 2 unless the parties have agreed otherwise.

Rule 4

"Rule 4: When goods are delivered to the buyer on approval or on sale or return or other similar terms the property in the goods passes to the buyer: 3-016

36 *Rugg v Minett* (1809) 11 East 210.

37 *Underwood v Burgh Castle Brick & Cement Syndicate* [1922] 1 K.B. 343 at 345, per Bankes LJ.

38 It would appear likely that provided the buyer has notice, it is not relevant who provided that notice. Consider the similar concept of "assent" for the purposes of rule 5 which specifies buyer and seller.

39 [1926] A.C. 77.

> **(a) when he signifies his approval or acceptance to the seller or does any other act adopting the transaction**
> **(b) if he does not signify his approval or acceptance to the seller but retains the goods without giving notice of rejection, then, if a time has been fixed for the return of the goods, on the expiration of that time, and, if no time has been fixed, on the expiration of a reasonable time."**

It is sometimes difficult to know whether the purchaser has done an act adopting the transaction. He will have done such an act if he does something which substantially impedes his ability to return the goods at the end of the period (whether that be a stipulated period or a reasonable length of time). Thus he "adopts" the transaction when he resells the goods or when he pledges them with a pawnbroker (*Kirkham v Attenborough*[40]). What is the position, though, where the buyer resells the goods on sale or return terms? Passages from the judgments from *Genn v Winkel*[41] are particularly helpful here. Fletcher Moulton LJ said:

> **". . .a person who receives goods on sale or return and at once passes them on to someone else under a like contract is entitled to demand them from that third person just as soon as the original owner of the goods has the right to demand them from him, and, therefore, I do not see that he has lessened or impeded his power of returning the goods when the owner of the goods has a right to demand them back, but I am clear that, if he allows a period to elapse before he hands them to a third person on sale or return, he has done an act which limits and impedes his power of returning the goods as soon as the owner of the goods demands them. For instance, if fourteen days be a reasonable time in such a contract in this particular trade, and if he waits seven days before entrusting the goods to a third person on sale or return, that third person has a right to keep them as against him for fourteen days, whereas the original owner of the goods has a right to the return of them within seven days from that date, and I think that that is clearly an act inconsistent with anything but his having adopted the transaction."**

40 [1897] 1 Q.B. 201.
41 (1911) 28 T.L.R. 483.

Buckley LJ said:

> **"If A delivers goods to B on sale or return and B having received them immediately delivers them to C on sale or return, the reasonable time in the one case must, I think, be co-extensive with that in the other case, and if that reasonable time elapses and C brings back the goods to B and B takes them back to A, everybody is acting within his rights, and it appears to me that the property never passes. That is not the point for decision in this case, and those are not the facts here, but that is a first step towards explaining the reason why I arrive at my conclusion. If under like circumstances A delivers goods to B and B delivers them to C, in each case on sale or return, and the reasonable time be, let us say, fourteen days, and C after four days sells the goods or elects to buy the goods, the result will be, I think, that the property will have passed, because C will have done an act which renders it impossible for B to return the goods to A."**

Two further points need to be made about rule 4. First, if the cause of the purchaser being unable to return the goods within the approval period is something which occurs entirely without his fault and beyond his control (e.g. if the goods are stolen or accidentally destroyed) he can offer that as an excuse and property will not pass: *Re Ferrier*.[42]

Secondly, as with all the rules in s.18, rule 4 is irrelevant if the parties when making the contract express their intentions as to when property should pass. Thus in *Weiner v Gill*[43] although jewellery sold on approval was subsequently resold by the buyer, the court held that property had not passed because of an express statement in the original contract that property was not to pass until the seller was paid.

Rule 5

> **"(1) Where there is a contract for the sale of unascertained or future goods by description, and goods of that description and in a deliverable state are unconditionally appropriated to the contract, either by the seller with the assent of the buyer or by the buyer with the assent of the seller, the property in the goods then passes to the buyer; and the assent may be express or** 3-017

42 [1944] Ch. 295.

43 [1906] 2 K.B. 574.

> **implied, and may be given either before or after the appropriation is made.**
>
> **(2) Where, in pursuance of the contract, the seller delivers the goods to the buyer or to a carrier or other bailee or custodier (whether named by the buyer or not) for the purpose of transmission to the buyer, and does not reserve the right of disposal, he is to be taken to have unconditionally appropriated the goods to the contract."**

There are many contracts for the sale of unascertained goods where the parties do not express their intention as to when property shall pass. Rule 5(1) applies to these contracts. It contains two basic requirements for property to pass. First, goods complying with the contract must be unconditionally appropriated to the contract by one of the parties. Secondly, the other party must give his assent.

The requirement that the goods must be in a deliverable state has recently been considered by the Court of Appeal in *Kulkarni v Manor Credit (Davenham) Ltd*.[44] The court held that, in the context of a sale of a new car, the requirement that the goods be in a deliverable state required the registration plates to have been fitted to the car. This was so since without the registration plates the (consumer) buyer would not be bound to take delivery of the goods.[45]

The issue of unconditional appropriation tends to be more complex. Take an example: Mrs Jones telephones her coal merchant asking him to deliver six bags of coal. He agrees. Next day the merchant, his lorry loaded with 200 bags of coal, sets out to make deliveries. He arrives at Mrs Jones's door with 150 bags left on the lorry. He knocks at the door. She unlocks the coal house door for him. He goes to his lorry where he drags six bags to the edge of the lorry's platform. He takes one of them, brings it to the coal house and empties it there. He repeats this with each of the other five bags. At what time does the property in the coal pass to Mrs Jones? It is not when the merchant set out on his round because at that time Mrs Jones' coal was as yet unascertained—*McDougall v Aeromarine of Emsworth* (above). For the same reason, it did not pass when the merchant drew up outside her house.

3–018 Rule 5(1) tells us that property passes when it is unconditionally appropriated by one party with the other's assent.[46] In *Carlos Federspiel & Co v Charles Twigg & Co*[47] Pearson J had to consider what amounted to an "unconditional appropriation". He said:[48]

44 [2010] EWCA Civ. 69.

45 [2010] EWCA Civ. 69 at [25].

46 For a straightforward illustration of unconditional appropriation, see the example given by Moses J in *R. (On the Application of Valpak) v Environment Agency* [2002] EWHC 1510 [33] (purchase of bottled beer from a public house).

47 [1957] 1 Lloyd's Rep. 240.

48 [1957] 1 Lloyd's Rep. 240 at 255.

> **"A mere setting apart or selection of the seller of the goods which he expects to use in performance of the contract is not enough. If that is all, he can change his mind and use those goods in performance of some other contract and use some other goods in performance of this contract."**

Thus, in our example, property did not pass when the merchant moved the six bags towards the edge of the lorry's platform. Pearson J went on:[49]

> **"To constitute an appropriation of the goods to the contract, the parties must have had, or be reasonably supposed to have had, an intention to attach the contract irrevocably to those goods."**

It would seem then that in our example there was an unconditional appropriation of the contents of each bag as it was emptied into Mrs Jones' coal house. Pearson J was considering a contract where the seller had agreed to dispatch goods f.o.b. (free on board) a ship, i.e. the seller undertook to convey the goods to the ship and to load them.

He had got as far as packaging and labelling them at his premises prior to taking them to the ship. Pearson J held that property had not passed under rule 5(1) for two reasons. First, s.18 was irrelevant since the parties by making an f.o.b. contract had indicated their intention that property was to pass as and when the goods were loaded on to the ship (see *Underwood v Burgh Castle Brick & Cement Syndicate*, above). Secondly, the goods had been merely set aside and not unconditionally appropriated.

The approach of Pearson J in *Carlos Federspiel & Co v Charles Twigg & Co* may be contrasted with that in *Aldridge v Johnson*.[50] Here there was a contract for the sale of a specified quantity of barley from a bulk held by the seller. It was agreed that the buyer was to provide sacks, into which the seller would load the barley. Having filled some of the sacks, the seller then stopped and emptied all of the sacks, i.e. returning the barley to the general bulk. Shortly after this, the seller became bankrupt. The court held that the buyer was entitled to that quantity of barley which had been placed into the sacks by the seller prior to bankruptcy. The act of filling the sacks constituted the act of appropriation necessary for property to pass. It is difficult to reconcile the decisions in the Federspiel case and *Aldridge v Johnson*. Certainly, in a physical sense, the act of placing the barley into the sacks was not the "final and decisive" act as required under Pearson J's approach. 3–019

Re London Wine Co (Shippers)[51] also illustrates the principle that for an appropriation there has to be an apparent intention to attach the goods irrevocably to the contract. The selling company dealt in wine and maintained considerable stocks. It contracted to sell wine on terms

49 [1957] 1 Lloyd's Rep. 240.
50 [1857] 26 L.J.Q.B. 296.
51 [1986] P.C.C. 121.

that after the contract the wine would be stored for the purchaser by the vendor. The company issued each purchaser with a document confirming that the purchaser was the sole owner of the wine he had purchased. In one instance a contract was made to sell to one purchaser a quantity of a given type of wine which exactly equalled the seller's stock of it. In another instance several contracts with different purchasers exhausted the seller's stock of another type of wine. Each purchaser was given a document stating him to be the owner of the quantity he had purchased of the wine in question. It was held, nevertheless, that in neither instance was there an appropriation. Where there were several purchasers of the same type of wine, it was impossible to say who owned which of the bottles of wine in the seller's stock. Even where there was only one purchaser, there was nothing to identify the particular cases of wine in stock as the subject-matter of the purchaser's contract. It was quite open to the selling company, if it wished, to obtain more wine of the same description for delivery to the purchaser. Thus no property passed in any of the wine remaining in the seller's stock.

The decision in *Re London Wine Co (Shippers)* was distinguished in *Re Ellis Son & Vidler*,[52] where again wine was sold on terms that after the sale it would be stored for the purchasers by the vendor. In this case, however, there was to be, and was, a segregation of the wine within the seller's warehouse, so that upon a contract being made, wine of the appropriate year and description was segregated from the general trading stock of the seller and kept together with other wine bought by customers and stored for them by the seller. Within the segregated part of the warehouse, wine of any particular year and description was kept together but was not further allocated to the different customers who had bought wine of that year and description. When later (perhaps years later) a customer asked for delivery of, say, a case of his Chateau Plonk 1976, that request would be fulfilled by the seller taking and delivering any case from the quantity of the Chateau Plonk 1976 stored in the segregated part of the warehouse. The judge dealt with this situation in a combination of two novel ways. First, he held that since the contract contemplated no immediate delivery of the goods but merely segregation in the hands of the seller for retention purposes, the wine became sufficiently ascertained when that segregation occurred. That was so, even though the cases of wine were not at that stage allocated to each individual customer. Secondly, he held that property passed when the parties intended it to, namely when the wine was set aside for storage. Since at that time the cases of wine in storage were not allocated as between different purchasers, the nature of the property right which passed to the buyer was unusual. Thus each set of cases of identical wine which was held by the seller, not mingled with the trading stock, but segregated and in store for a group of customers, was the property of that group of customers, each holding the wine as tenant in common. This means that each customer had an undivided share in the set of cases, a share proportionate to the number of cases he had bought. The key distinctions between this case and *Re London Wine* were, first, that in this case there was to be a segregation of the wine by the seller for storage purposes, and secondly, that the London Wine Company, unlike the seller in the present case, was free to sell its stock and satisfy its customers from any other available source. The ruling in

52 [1994] 1 W.L.R. 1181.

the present case anticipated the rules relating to a specified quantity of unascertained goods out of an identified bulk which were shortly afterwards introduced by s.20A.[53]

When goods have to be dispatched by a carrier (e.g. the Post Office) rule 5(2) is often helpful.[54] Thus the goods will normally be unconditionally appropriated when handed over to the carrier.[55] However, there are two limitations to this. First, there is no unconditional appropriation where the seller reserves the right of disposal—see s.19 (below). The other limitation is that property cannot pass in unascertained goods—see s.16 (above). To put it another way, goods are not appropriated unless it is clear which goods are appropriated. This is neatly illustrated by *Healy v Howlett*.[56] The seller contracted to sell 20 boxes of mackerel f.o.r. (free on rail). He dispatched by rail all at the same time 190 boxes to go to various customers. He did not label the boxes to go to particular destinations but left it to the rail company to allot the appropriate number of boxes to the various destinations. Ridley J held that putting the 190 boxes on the rail was not in this case an unconditional appropriation because it was impossible to say which of them was appropriated to any given buyer. They therefore were still unascertained goods. Hence, property could not pass until the railway company made the allotments. 3-020

The problem of when an unconditional appropriation can occur can arise in a very different situation; when the buyer has to collect the goods, not from the seller, but from a third person. There is an unconditional appropriation when the goods are identified and the third person acknowledges that he now holds them for the buyer: *Wardars (Import & Exports) v W. Norwood*.[57] This case concerned the sale of 600 cartons of frozen kidneys out of a bulk of 1,500 cartons stored for the seller at a cold store. The buyer's carrier went to the cold store with a delivery order. He found that 600 cartons had been set aside ready for him. He handed his delivery order to an official who thereupon gave instructions for loading to commence. The Court of Appeal held that there was an unconditional appropriation when the delivery order was accepted and loading was allowed to commence.

Under rule 5(1) an unconditional appropriation will not pass property unless the other party assents.[58] This assent could sometimes be difficult to establish but fortunately rule 5 allows it to be implied and to be given in advance. Thus, in our earlier example, Mrs Jones's assent can be inferred from the fact that she unlocked the coal house door. Similarly, in *Aldridge v Johnson*[59] where the buyer supplied bags for the seller to put the goods (barley) into, it was held that property passed when the seller filled the bags. An easy and neat

53 See paras 3-030–3-036 below.

54 Indeed, *Kulkarni v Manor Credit (Davenham) Ltd* [2010] EWCA Civ. 69 would suggest that rule 5(2) and not rule 5(1) is the default setting for contracts for unascertained consumer goods to be delivered after the contract is made. See the comments of Rix LJ at [43].

55 Delivery being a straight forward example of an appropriation to the contract.

56 [1917] 86 L.J.K.B. 337.

57 [1968] 2 Q.B. 663.

58 In *Kulkarni v Manor Credit (Davenham) Ltd* [2010] EWCA Civ. 69 at [34] Rix LJ cited the old case of *Mucklow (Assignees of Royland) v Mangles* (1808) 1 Taunt 318 in suggesting that where assent was given on the basis of a misrepresentation, i.e. by a seller who knows that he will not pass property in the goods, that assent is not valid.

59 [1857] 26 L.J.Q.B. 296.

example of assent can also be found in the case of a purchase of petrol at a garage. If a petrol pump attendant puts the petrol into the customer's car, that is clearly an unconditional appropriation to which the buyer's assent is clearly implied: *Edwards v Ddin*.[60] At a self-service garage it is the motorist who unconditionally appropriates the petrol by pouring it into his tank, the assent of the seller being equally clearly implied. Thus at a self-serve station, as in the case of a non-self-service one, property in the petrol passes to the buyer when it is poured into his tank: *R v McHugh*.[61]

3–021 On the other hand, assent is sometimes given only after the unconditional appropriation is made. In that case the property passes not upon appropriation but when the other party's assent is subsequently given. This was the position in *Pignataro v Gilroy*[62] where the sale concerned some unascertained bags of rice which the buyer was to collect. The sellers got the rice for collection and were requested by the buyer for a delivery order enabling him to collect the rice. They sent him a delivery order but he failed to come and collect the rice. He did nothing. The buyer's assent to the appropriation made by the sellers was inferred from his failure to object after receiving the delivery order. Therefore property passed to him when, after a reasonable length of time, he had failed to object.

"Rule 5: (3) Where there is a contract for the sale of a specified quantity of unascertained goods in a deliverable state forming part of a bulk which is identified either in the contract or by subsequent agreement between the parties and the bulk is reduced to (or to less than) that quantity, then, if the buyer under that contract is the only buyer to whom goods are then due out of the bulk,

(a) the remaining goods are to be taken as appropriated to that contract at the time when the bulk is so reduced; and

(b) the property in those goods then passes to that buyer.

(4) Paragraph (3) above applies also (with the necessary modifications) where a bulk is reduced to (or to less than) the aggregate of the quantities due to a single buyer under separate contracts relating to that bulk and he is the only buyer to whom goods are then due out of that bulk."

Rules 5(3) and (4) were added to the section by the Sale of Goods (Amendment) Act 1995. They give statutory authority to the decision in *Karlshamns Oliefabiker v Eastport Navigation Corporation, The Elafi*,[63] explained at para.3-009 above. The principle involved is one of ascertainment and appropriation by exhaustion. Where the buyer agrees to buy goods out of a specified bulk, e.g. "50 tonnes out of the 110 tonnes of potatoes currently in the seller's

60 [1976] 1 W.L.R. 942.
61 [1977] R.T.R. 1.
62 [1919] 1 K.B. 459.
63 [1982] 1 All E.R. 208.

Bedford warehouse", the complete property in the remaining potatoes at the warehouse passes to the buyer at the moment that the 100 tonnes is reduced to 50 tonnes (or less). At least that is so provided that (a) the goods are in a deliverable state, (b) the buyer is the only buyer remaining entitled to potatoes from that warehouse, (c) the buyer has assented to the appropriation, and (d) the parties have not made an agreement for property to pass at some later stage. In the absence of some particular evidence to the contrary, the buyer's assent is likely to be implied from the mere fact that he agreed to buy from the specific bulk, since he must have meant to leave the seller free to deal with the remaining 60 tonnes and that automatically must involve the buyer assenting to the remaining ones being thereby appropriated to him. It makes no difference if it is under more than one contract that the buyer is entitled to the whole of the remaining quantity of the outstanding bulk: rule 5(4). Of course, if the 110 tonnes have become reduced to less than 50 tonnes, then, whilst property in whatever tonnage is left will at some stage pass to the buyer, the buyer may well have a claim against the seller for breach of contract for delivery of less than the contract quantity. Nor can the seller within the terms of the contract make up the shortfall from another source.

On the question of what proprietary interest the buyer gets in the bulk before property passes under rule 5(3) and (4), see paras 3-030–3-036 below.

Section 19

Section 19 provides that, if the seller reserves a right of disposal of the goods until certain conditions are fulfilled, property does not pass until those conditions are fulfilled. Thus if a seller entrusts identified and appropriated goods to a carrier with instructions that they be conveyed to the buyer but not handed over until the buyer has paid, property in the goods will remain with the seller until the buyer pays for them. 3-022

It is quite common in an import or export sale for the seller to arrange the carriage of the goods by ship to the buyer and also to arrange for their insurance en route. Such contracts are termed c.i.f. because the cost (i.e. the price paid by the buyer to the seller) includes the insurance and freight. In this case the bill of lading (i.e. the document given by the shipowner acknowledging that he has received the goods) will usually indicate that the goods are held according to the seller's instructions. The seller will normally send by air to the buyer some documents: one will be the bill of lading transferred to the buyer allowing him to collect the goods at their port of destination; another will be a bill of exchange which the buyer will normally sign and return thereby undertaking to pay for the goods on the date specified on the bill of exchange. If the buyer finds that the bill of lading is not in order, i.e. it indicates that the contract has not been complied with, he can refuse to accept it and will therefore refuse to sign the bill of exchange. In such a case no property passes to the buyer—s.19. Also, s.19 requires the buyer to return the bill of lading to the seller. If on the other hand the buyer finds the bill of lading in order he will retain it and will sign and return the bill of exchange. When he does this, property will pass. This, of course, does not preclude the buyer from refusing to accept the goods if when they arrive they do not comply with the contract. If he does that, then property will pass back to the seller: *Kwei Tek Chao v British Traders*.[64]

Transfer of Risk in Non-consumer Cases

Section 20

3–023 Unless the parties agree otherwise, risk passes with property—s.20(1). Thus if the goods are damaged or stolen, this loss falls on the seller if it occurs before property has passed; otherwise it falls on the buyer. This is so irrespective of whose possession the goods were in at the time. This is illustrated by *Pignataro v Gilroy* where we have seen that property passed to the buyer under s.18 r.5. The buyer failed to collect them and they were stolen from the seller's warehouse. It was held that the buyer must bear this loss because property had passed to him before the goods were stolen.

The basic rule that risk passes with property is subject to three limitations; they are s.20(2) and (3) and the fact that s.20(1) only applies unless otherwise agreed.

Section 20(2)

3–024 **"But where delivery has been delayed through the fault of either buyer or seller the goods are at the risk of the party at fault as regards any loss which might not have occurred but for such fault."**

This was applied in *Demby Hamilton v Baden*[65] where the buyer was supposed to take delivery of some apple juice in weekly loads. The buyer held up delivery and the juice went bad as a result. It was held that the buyer must bear the loss.

64 [1954] 2 Q.B. 459.
65 [1949] 1 All E.R. 435.

Section 20(3)

"Nothing in this section shall affect the duties or liabilities of either seller or buyer as a bailee or custodier of the goods of the goods of the other party." 3-025

This means that the person in possession must take reasonable care of the goods even if the ownership is with the other party. Thus if the goods are damaged or stolen because of his negligence he will have to bear the loss even though at the time he was not the owner. To put it another way, the risk which under s.20 passes with property (i.e. which falls upon the owner) does not include the risk of loss or damage due to the other party's negligence.

"Unless otherwise agreed"

The parties can agree when risk shall pass. They can select a time before or after the passing of property. In order for their agreement to have any effect it must be part of the contract. It may be remembered that in *Healy v Howlett*[66] no property passed in the mackerel put by the sellers on to the rail because the consignment was not allotted as to the various destinations. After putting them on the rail the sellers sent the buyers an invoice stating "At sole risk of purchaser after putting fish on rail here". Ridley J said, "I do not see how those words form part of the contract". He therefore ignored them. The mackerel went bad before the railway had allotted particular boxes to particular destinations. Therefore, since property had not passed, the loss fell on the seller. 3-026

An agreement that the passing of risk shall not be simultaneous with the passing of property can be inferred from the circumstances. An example of this is the difficult case of *Sterns v Vickers*.[67] The sellers owned 200,000 gallons of white spirit stored for them by an independent person, X, in his tanks. They sold to the buyers 120,000 out of the 200,000 gallons and gave the buyers the benefit of free storage at X's for a given period, i.e. down to 31 January. It was agreed that the buyers would make their own arrangement for storage thereafter. The sellers gave the buyers a delivery note to enable them to collect the spirit from X. However, the buyers chose to keep it at X's and did not come to remove it for some months by which time it had deteriorated. Clearly, the property had not passed because, until collected, the 120,000 gallons out of the 200,000 tank remained unascertained. In spite of this, the Court of Appeal held that the parties intended risk to pass when the buyers accepted the delivery note. The buyers therefore had to bear the cost of the deterioration. There are three things to note about this case. First, the agreement that risk should pass independently from property was not express but inferred by the court from the circumstances of the case. Secondly, that agreement

66 [1917] 86 L.J.K.B. 337.
67 [1923] 1 K.B. 78.

resulted in risk passing before property. Thirdly, it resulted in the risk passing in unascertained goods.

The last point is not without difficulty. Which goods were at the buyer's risk? Clearly no more than 120,000 gallons. If, say, 100,000 out of the 200,000 gallons had deteriorated, it would have been difficult to allocate the loss as between seller and buyer. Presumably it would be done pro rata, i.e. the buyer would bear

$$\frac{120,000}{200,000} = 3/5 \text{ of the loss}$$

3-027 This is possible where, as in *Sterns v Vickers*, the contract is for the sale of unascertained goods out of a specified bulk. One can identify the bulk, calculate the total loss and make the buyer bear a proportion according to his share of the bulk. This could not be done for the sale of purely generic goods. In that case until the goods are ascertained it is impossible for risk to pass. Not only would it be impossible to identify the goods which were at the buyer's risk but it would also be impossible to identify any goods which were pro rata at his risk.

There is now a fourth point which can be made about the case. It is that if the facts had arisen after 1995, there would have to be a qualification to the statement that property had not passed to the buyer. The qualification is that, under the law as it now is, the buyer (assuming that he had paid for the goods) would have acquired an undivided share of 60 per cent of the 200,000 gallons and thus when all of the gallons deteriorated, he would have had to bear the loss in so far as it affected his 60 per cent. In other words the net result would still be the same if the facts of *Sterns v Vickers* occurred again today.[68]

Let us now turn to a less difficult decision where the rule in s.20 may be affected, i.e. where the seller undertakes to deliver the goods. The seller does not have to agree to this and if he does, that will not normally affect the operation of s.20. Thus the risk of loss or damage (other than that caused by late delivery or the seller's negligence) will pass at the same time as the passing of property. If on the other hand the seller agrees to deliver "at his own risk" this will alter the operation of s.20. Its effect will be that even if property passes earlier to the buyer, the goods will remain at the seller's risk until their arrival. However, even in this case, unless the parties agree otherwise, the buyer must bear the "risk of deterioration necessarily incident to the course of transit".[69] Thus where the seller agrees to deliver the goods "at his own risk" the buyer will bear the risk of any unavoidable deterioration in the goods in transit but the seller will have to bear the risk of them being stolen from his lorry en route.

68 As to the buyer getting an undivided share in an identified bulk, see paras 3-030–3-036 below.
69 s.33.

Effect of Loss Falling on One Party

If because risk had passed to him the buyer has to bear some loss, it follows that he is not excused from carrying out the contract. Thus if he refuses to accept the goods or to pay because they have deteriorated, he is in breach of contract. The seller will have all the usual seller's remedies.[70] If, because risk had not passed to the buyer, the seller has to bear the loss, it does not necessarily excuse him from performing the contract. It will do so only if it frustrates the contract (renders it impossible to carry it out).[71] Unless the contract is frustrated, the seller will still have to carry out the contract and if he delivers goods which do not comply with it, he will be in breach of contract. 3-028

Transfer of Risk in Consumer Cases

The general rule of when risk is to pass under a contract for the sale of goods detailed above is no longer valid in consumer cases. Indeed, this was the case even prior to the enactment of the Consumer Rights Act 2015: The Sale and Supply of Goods to Consumers Regulations 2002[72] inserted s.20(4) into the Sale of Goods Act with the effect that where the buyer dealt as a consumer, the goods remained at the seller's risk until they are delivered to the consumer. This position has been adapted slightly under the Consumer Rights Act. Section 29(2) states that: 3-029

> **"The goods remain at the trader's risk until they come into the physical possession of—**
> **(a) the consumer, or**
> **(b) a person identified by the consumer to take possession of the goods."**

Thus, where there is a sales contract under the Consumer Rights Act 2015, the question of whether property has passed from trader to consumer is irrelevant to whether the goods are at the risk of the consumer buyer. The question to be asked under the new rule is simply that of whether the goods have been delivered to the consumer or a person nominated by the consumer to take physical possession of the goods. Until such time, they are to remain at the risk of the seller, irrespective of whether property has passed under either s.17 (contractual intention) or s.18 (rules for ascertaining intention). This is so unless the consumer elects to appoint

70 See the discussion of remedies available to the seller in Ch.12.
71 See Ch.4.
72 SI 2002/3045 (now revoked).

a carrier to deliver the goods other than one which the trader has offered to the consumer. In this situation, risk in the goods will pass on delivery of the goods to the nominated carrier.[73]

The abolition of the res perit domino (risk passes with property) rule for buyers who deal as consumers is a very sensible change in direction for the law and certainly constitutes a more accurate reflection of when consumers would themselves expect to be liable for any loss or deterioration of the goods. Take for example the situation where a consumer purchases groceries online and those groceries deteriorate in transit: it is clear that the risk of those goods deteriorating in transit will be borne by the seller unless the consumer has specified a particular carrier other than one which the trader customarily offers.

In our example, the old position of s.20(1) would require the parties to ascertain exactly when property passed. This would likely be a sale of unascertained goods since they would not be identified and agreed upon at the time of making the contract and in the absence of any contractual intention, property would pass when the requirements of s.18 r.5 were met. This would hinge on the interpretation of the final and decisive act theory of appropriation and could, in practice, be anytime after contracting up to actual delivery depending on business practice and the nature of the goods in question.[74] That these uncertainties have been removed from consumer sales is to be commended.[75]

Unascertained Goods From an Identified Bulk

3–030 Until 1995 there was no statutory provision dealing expressly with the situation where the subject matter of the contract was a specified quantity from an identified source, e.g. "nine bottles of the seller's current stock of 1992 Chateau Plonk", or "400 of the 1,000 tonnes of wheat currently in the Wally's Warehouse at Woodford". Since such a contract is for the sale of unascertained goods, it followed (by virtue of the rule in s.16) that no property could pass to the buyer until his nine bottles or his 400 tonnes had become ascertained. This was less than ideal in a situation where the buyer had paid the price and the seller had become insolvent before the particular goods to be supplied to the buyer had become identified. This was because in that situation the goods remained the property of the seller and hence became the property of the seller's trustee in bankruptcy and the buyer became simply an unsecured creditor.

73 CRA 2015 s.29(3).

74 Consider for example, the practice of many online supermarkets to bag purchased groceries and pack the filled bags into crates to be delivered to the customer. What would the act of unconditional appropriation be in such a case?

75 Further support for the reform comes from the expectation that a seller can reasonably be expected to insure his interest in the goods, whereas a consumer cannot.

The injustice of this situation is well illustrated by the decision in *Re Wait*.[76] We have already seen that Lord Hanworth MR identified a contract to sell 500 tons of wheat out of the cargo of 1,000 tons in the ship Challenger as being a contract for the sale of unascertained goods. As the 500 tonnes had not been appropriated to the contract at the time of the seller's bankruptcy, property could not pass and the seller's trustee in bankruptcy was able to claim the entire cargo, irrespective of the fact that the buyer had paid the price for the goods. The buyer's claim of an equitable assignment over the 500 tonnes was rejected by the Court of Appeal.[77] Atkin LJ said that:

> **"It would have been futile in a Code intended for commercial men to have created an elaborate structure of rules dealing with rights at law, if at the same time it was intended to leave, subsisting with the legal rights equitable rights inconsistent with, more extensive, and coming into existence earlier than the rights so carefully set out in the various sections of the Code".[78]**

If any equitable assignment could not have survived the enactment of the Sale of Goods Act 1893, as suggested by Atkin LJ, then where the rules as to the passing of property within the Act were not satisfied, the pre-paying buyer was left as an unsecured creditor. This argument was applied by the Privy Council in *Re Goldcorp Exchange Ltd*[79] where gold bullion was purchased and stored on behalf of customers. The Privy Council held that where the gold bullion of each customer was pooled (i.e. stored in bulk and not segregated) there was a sale of generic goods, and thus no property had passed to the buyer under the Sale of Goods Act as the gold remained unascertained and unappropriated.[80] This approach led to the unfortunate situation where, in the case of a seller's insolvency, a certificate or document of title purporting to establish ownership of goods forming part of a bulk was ineffective. The Sale of Goods Act did not allow property to pass in unascertained goods and no equitable interest could be

76 [1927] 1 Ch. 606.

77 See *Tailby v Offical Receiver* (1888) 13 App Cas 523. For an alternative approach to the proper interpretation of *Re Wait*, see S. Eaton and R. Friel, "Protecting Prepaying Buyers of Unascertained Goods: Why 'Pay Before You Go' May be Bad for You" *Common Law World Review* 36(1) 50. In the context of future goods, see *Hughes v Pendragon Sabre Ltd* [2016] EWCA Civ 18 at [42].

78 [1927] 1 Ch. 606, at 635–6.

79 [1995] 1 A.C. 74.

80 See also *Re Stapylton Fletcher* [1994] 1 W.L.R. 1181 where the approach of Atkin LJ was approved. In many cases on similar facts the identification of a contractual bulk could not be established. This is obviously not merely an issue of physical identification, but requires the seller to be contractually obliged to supply goods from a specified bulk. Where no bulk can be identified, clearly no equitable interest could be recognised even if (contrary to the now accepted view) such an interest could survive the Sale of Goods Act 1893. See further, S. Worthington, "Sorting out ownership interests in a bulk: gifts, sales and trusts" [1999] J.B.L. 1. The identification of a contractual bulk remains problematic: see, for example, *Quadra Commodities S.A. v XL Insurance Co SE* [2022] EWHC 431 (Comm) at [110]–[112].

established over the bulk following the enactment of the Sale of Goods Act 1893.[81] It was to remedy this defect in the law that the Sale of Goods (Amendment) Act 1995 was passed.[82]

3–031 This Act created a qualification to the rule in s.16 of the Sale of Goods Act. It did this by inserting into the Sale of Goods Act a new section, s.20A. Section 20A(1) states:

> **"This section applies to a contract for the sale of a specified quantity of unascertained goods if the following conditions are met:**
>
> **(a) the goods or some of them form part of a bulk which is identified either in the contract or by subsequent agreement between the parties; and**
>
> **(b) the buyer has paid the price for some or all of the goods which are the subject of the contract and which form part of the bulk."**

This section applies to any contract for the sale of a specified quantity of goods which is part of an identified bulk. Its effect is that as soon as the buyer pays the price (or part of it), the buyer immediately acquires property in an undivided share in the bulk, becoming thereby an owner in common of the bulk.[83] The buyer's share is "such share as the quantity of the goods paid for and due to the buyer out of the bulk bears to the quantity of goods in the bulk". So, if the buyer has agreed to buy "400 tonnes out of the 1,000 tonnes of wheat in Wally's Woodford Warehouse", and he has paid for his 400 tonnes, then provided that there are 1,000 tonnes of wheat in the warehouse, the buyer will own an undivided share of 40 per cent of the 1,000 tonnes. If the seller should subsequently remove 200 tonnes from the bulk (e.g. to supply a second buyer), then the bulk is reduced by that amount. In that case the first buyer's undivided share will automatically become a larger proportion of the reduced bulk, i.e. it will then amount to 50 per cent of the now remaining 800 tonnes. Thus, although no property in the buyer's particular 400 tonnes can be transferred to the buyer until his particular 400 tonnes have been identified, he does acquire a proprietary right in the form of this undivided share in the bulk.

This cannot occur before payment and in any case the effect of s.20A is subject to contrary agreement by the parties. The parties can by agreement decide that s.20A will not apply at all (i.e. that the buyer will not get an undivided share in the bulk) or that the property in the undivided share will pass at some point of time after payment.[84] They cannot agree to it passing at any earlier stage.

---

81 On the issue of documents of title and goods stored in a bulk, see C. Proctor, "Documents Of Title—Or Are They?" (1995) 8 J.I.F.B.L. 382.

82 For an excellent account of the pre-1995 Act difficulties, see I. Davies, "Continuing dilemmas with passing of property in part of a bulk" [1991] J.B.L. 111.

83 By virtue of s.20A(2).

84 See, for example, *Quadra Commodities S.A. v XL Insurance Co SE* [2022] EWHC 431 (Comm) at [112].

Of course, in the example given above the seller could remove all of the rest of the bulk, i.e. so that only 400 tonnes were left. In that case the buyer would cease to have an undivided share, but would then have complete property in the bulk by virtue of s.18 rule 5(3).[85]

Insufficient Quantity in the Bulk

What is the position if the bulk becomes reduced to less than the quantity to which the buyer is entitled? This could happen in several different ways. 3-032

The seller makes contracts under which the total quantity contracted to be sold out of the bulk is greater than the total quantity in the specified bulk

Suppose the seller has 1,000 tonnes of wheat in the warehouse. Suppose that he agrees to sell 500 tonnes of the bulk to A, 400 tonnes of it to B and 300 tonnes of it to C. Suppose also that each of A, B and C have paid the seller in full. Suppose also that the contracts are made and the payments are made in that order, i.e. A first, B second and C third. In that situation, while the bulk is still undivided, it is an obvious matter of common sense that A, B and C cannot each have an undivided share in a bulk of 1,200 tonnes, since the bulk contains only 1,000 tonnes. The result therefore has to be one of the two following: 3-033

(i) the seller can and does give C only that which the seller has still got, namely an undivided share in one tenth of the bulk of 1,000 tonnes; or

(ii) C is introduced as an extra purchaser having an undivided share of three-twelfths of the bulk, thereby diluting A's and B's undivided shares to five-twelfths and four-twelfths respectively.

The second of those two solutions cannot apply because of the rule that the seller cannot give that which he does not have; he can give only that which he has got. This rule is known by its Latin: nemo dat quod non habet (no one can give that which he does not have) and is fully explained in Ch.5. Since, immediately prior to the sale to C, the seller has only an undivided share in one-tenth of the bulk of 1,000 tonnes, that is all C can get. Thus A's and B's shares remain undiluted and C gets an undivided share in one-tenth of the bulk of 1,000 tonnes. Suppose now, however, that the seller delivers to C, pursuant to the seller's contract with C, 300 tonnes out of the bulk. If at the time of that delivery C takes in good faith, unaware of A's and B's contracts, C will obtain complete property in the 300 tonnes delivered. This is because

85 See para.3-021, above.

of s.24 of the Sale of Goods Act, which creates an exception to the rule that the seller cannot pass property (i.e. ownership) which he does not have. Section 24 applies where a person, having sold goods, continues in possession and then delivers the goods under any sale or other disposition to another person who takes them in good faith and without notice of the previous sale.[86] When in these circumstances C obtains property in the 300 tonnes that are delivered to him, A's and B's rights are reduced to undivided shares in the reduced bulk of 700 tonnes, shares of five ninths and four ninths respectively. That is the effect of s.20A(4) which provides that where the aggregate of the undivided shares of buyers in a bulk would exceed the whole of the bulk, the undivided share of each buyer is reduced proportionately so that the aggregate of the undivided shares is equal to the whole bulk. If the next thing that happens is that the seller becomes bankrupt, A and B will be entitled to take the remaining 700 tonnes and divide it between themselves in proportions of five to four. This will of course leave each of them with a shortfall and to that extent they will become unsecured creditors of the seller.

Of course it could have happened that, shortly before becoming insolvent, the seller delivered out of the remaining bulk of 700 tonnes to one or other of A or B. Suppose then that, before becoming insolvent and bankrupt, the seller delivered to B 400 tonnes from the bulk pursuant to B's contract. In that case complete property in the 400 tonnes will have at that point passed to B, by virtue of s.18 rule 5(1). At the moment of delivery to B, A will have become the only buyer entitled to the remaining bulk which at a mere 300 tonnes was less than he contracted to buy. Thus at that moment complete property in the remaining 300 tonnes will have passed to A. So far as his shortfall of 200 tonnes is concerned, his only claim is as an unsecured creditor against the seller. Thus the effect of delivery to B is to transfer to A the full effect of the shortfall. At least, this is so unless there was an express contractual agreement to the contrary between A and B. This is because s.20B provides that each owner in common of the bulk (here A, B and C) is deemed to have consented to delivery out of the bulk to any other owner in common of the bulk.

The seller delivers goods out of the bulk to another buyer in pursuance of a contract other than one to supply goods from that particular bulk.

3-034 Suppose that the bulk is 1,000 tonnes and that A is the only buyer to whom the seller has contracted to sell goods (500 tonnes) from that particular bulk and suppose that A has paid for them. In that case a delivery to another buyer (X) of 100 tonnes will simply reduce the bulk to 900 tonnes and A will then have an undivided share of five ninths of the 900 tonnes remaining. Now, however, suppose that the quantity sold and delivered to X is 600 tonnes out of the bulk. The effect of this delivery is to reduce the remainder of the bulk to 400 tonnes. Obviously, complete property in the remaining 400 tonnes will pass to A. The sale and supply of 600 tonnes to X appears to have reduced A's rights by 100 tonnes. How can A's proprietary rights

86 s.24 is dealt more fully at para.5-021, below.

in 100 tonnes be given to X? The answer lies again in s.24 that, despite the fact that the seller does not have a right to any more than 500 of the 1,000 tonnes, he can nevertheless pass to X good title to goods already sold to A. This occurs, by virtue of s.24, provided that X takes in good faith and is unaware of A's contract.

The bulk is destroyed, reduced or damaged by accident or act of God

Suppose that there are 1,000 tonnes in the bulk and that A has contracted to buy, but has not yet paid for, 500 tonnes of them. In that case A will have acquired no property, not even an undivided share in the goods. That being so, no risk will have passed to A, unless the parties have agreed otherwise or else the seller can establish that delivery has been delayed through A's own fault.[87] A's contract will become frustrated at common law if the contract has become impossible, e.g. if the bulk is totally lost in an act of God, such as an accidental fire.[88] 3-035

Now, suppose that A has paid for his 500 tonnes before the fire occurs and suppose that there is no other buyer with an interest in the 1,000 bulk. A and B each had an undivided share of 50 per cent in the 1,000 tonnes. Normally, risk passes with property. So, assuming that the whole of the 1,000 tonnes are lost, each of A and B loses his entire interest in the bulk.[89] The position is different, however, if the fire destroys only part of the bulk. According to the Law Commission Report whose recommendations the Sale of Goods (Amendment) Act 1995 was passed to implement, "the risk of partial destruction of the goods rests with the seller (in the absence of agreement to the contrary) so long as the quantity destroyed is within the quantity retained by the seller". In other words, in any case of destruction of any of the bulk, it is assumed that the share in the goods retained by the seller is destroyed first. Only when that has all been destroyed do the various buyers with undivided shares begin each to suffer a loss proportionate according to the size of their respective undivided shares. Of course it is possible that none of the damaged goods are destroyed but that some or all of them are damaged. In that case the same principle applies. The damage is taken to have occurred first to the share of the goods retained by the seller. Of course if the damage is to all of the bulk equally, then the seller and the buyer(s) will bear the loss in proportion of their respective shares. So if the buyer has agreed to buy (and has paid for) 120,000 gallons out of a bulk of 200,000 gallons and the whole bulk is damaged equally, the buyer will have to bear 60 per cent and the seller 40 per cent of that loss.[90]

---

87 See s.20 at para.3-024, above.

88 For more explanation of frustration see para.4-007, below.

89 For a discussion of the uncertainty surrounding the question of whether risk passes with co-ownership under s.20A, see N. McKay, "The passing of risk and s.20A Sale of Goods Act 1979" [2010] Cov.L.J. 17.

90 See *Sterns v Vickers*, para.3-026, above, for a case where similar facts arose before the advent of the new law on undivided shares.

Limits to the New Rules

3-036 For the rules in s.20A to apply, the agreement must be for a specified quantity of goods forming part of an identified bulk. This section, whereby the buyer may acquire an undivided share in the bulk, applies only where the parties agree that the goods are to come from that bulk. It is not enough that each of the parties had in mind this particular source for the goods if they have not actually pre-agreed it. If they have agreed simply that the seller will supply "500 tonnes of wheat", then the contract can be fulfilled by the seller supplying wheat from any other source, even though they may both have assumed that this particular source would be used. Section 20A applies only where the particular bulk is identified either by the contract or else by subsequent agreement between the parties. Even then, the section will not apply unless that identified source amounts to a "bulk" which means:

> **"a mass or collection of goods of the same kind which**
> **(a) is contained within a confined space or area, and**
> **(b) is such that any goods in the bulk are interchangeable with any other goods therein of the same number or quantity."[91]**

Section 20A will still not apply unless the agreement is for a "specified quantity" (e.g. 500 tonnes, 40 cases, nine bottles) of goods from the bulk. Thus a contract for the sale of "500 tonnes of the 1,000 tonnes of wheat in the seller's warehouse at Woodford" is one for unascertained goods and s.20A will apply to it. On the other hand, a contract to purchase a percentage or a fraction (e.g. 10 per cent or one-half) of the bulk is an example of a contract for the purchase of specific goods and s.20A will not apply to it. Thus a contract for the sale of "half of the 1,000 tonnes of wheat currently in the seller's warehouse at Woodford" is a contract for the sale of specific goods. Although the Act still has no provision for such a contract (beyond stating that it is a contract for specific goods), it is nevertheless still presumably intended by the parties that the buyer will acquire an undivided share in the bulk. The property in that undivided share will pass when the parties intend it to. If it turns out that the bulk is greater than the 1,000 tonnes, then the buyer will either gain or lose in comparison with his expectations. If it turns out to be less, presumably he may have a claim for misrepresentation or breach of contract, since the seller had informed and/or promised him that the bulk comprised 1,000 tonnes. It may be that the example of "half of a bulk of 1,000 tonnes of wheat" is unrealistic because the parties would be much more likely to state "500 tonnes out of the bulk of 1,000 tonnes". The percentage or fraction approach is more likely to be adopted by parties who are selling and buying part of an item which is indivisible, e.g. a racehorse.

91 s.61.

Retention of Title Clauses[92]

In business it is not uncommon for a seller (X) to sell large quantities of a commodity to a buyer (Y Ltd) in the knowledge that Y Ltd will be able to pay for them only out of the proceeds of reselling them. It may be that Y Ltd is only a buyer and reseller, i.e. only a link in the chain of distribution. Alternatively it could be that Y Ltd is a manufacturer and that the commodity he buys from X is part of his raw materials. In either case the problem for X is the same, namely what is X's position if Y Ltd having taken delivery then becomes insolvent and goes into liquidation before paying for the goods? Has X got property rights over the goods entitling him to recover the goods (or their value) in priority to any other creditors of Y Ltd, or, on the other hand, is he merely an unsecured creditor having only a right to sue for the price? The latter will be the case if property has passed to Y Ltd. In that situation X, being an unsecured creditor, is likely to obtain no more than a small percentage of the price he is owed. In the absence of a contrary statement in the contract between X and Y Ltd, property will normally have passed by virtue of ss.16–18 of the Sale of Goods Act.[93] However, a provision in the contract to the effect that property does not pass until Y Ltd has paid the price, will not entirely meet X's needs. Y Ltd has got to be allowed to sell the goods; otherwise Y Ltd may never be able to pay X. How can X protect himself against the possibility that Y Ltd, having sold the goods, might then go into liquidation before paying X? The way to do so was demonstrated by the Dutch sellers in *Aluminium Industrie Vaasen BV v Romalpa Aluminium Ltd*.[94] 3-037

The Romalpa Case

The contract was for the sale by a Dutch company of aluminium foil some of which the buyers (an English company) were to use in their manufacturing process. At the time of manufacture the foil would obviously become mixed with other materials. The buyers took delivery of the foil but never made full payment. Later they became insolvent and a receiver was appointed. At that time the buyers still had some of the foil which had not yet been taken into the manufacturing process (i.e. unmixed foil). They had also sold some of the foil, some unmixed and some mixed (manufactured). The Dutch sellers now relied upon a clause (cl.13) in their contract of sale with the buyers and claimed therefore to have proprietary rights entitling them to have priority over the buyer's other creditors. This claim, however, was limited to unmixed foil and the proceeds of the sale of unmixed foil. Clause 13 was in two parts. The first part dealt with unmixed foil and stated that ownership in the foil would transfer to the buyers only when they had paid all that was owing to the sellers. The second part dealt with mixed foil and stated that the ownership of the sellers would transfer from the foil used in the manufacture to the finished 3-038

92 See generally, C.G.J. Morse, "Retention of title in English private international law" [1993] J.B.L. 168.

93 See paras 3-008–3-021, above.

94 [1976] 1 W.L.R. 676.

products and that these would remain the property of the sellers until full payment had been made to them. Furthermore the buyers were to keep the finished goods as "fiduciary" for the sellers. The second part of cl.13 also authorised the buyers to sell these goods on the condition that they would, if requested, transfer to the sellers the benefit of those sales.

Foil (mixed or unmixed) which had been sold by the buyers clearly now belonged to whoever had bought it, since the Dutch sellers had expressly authorised the buyers to sell it. Any unmixed foil unsold by the buyers clearly still belonged to the Dutch sellers by virtue of the first part of cl.13. Ownership passes when (and not before) the parties intend it to. In relation to the unmixed foil which the buyers had sold, the Court of Appeal held that the Dutch sellers were entitled to receive from the buyers the proceeds of the sales by the buyers. The Dutch sellers were entitled to those proceeds of sale in priority to the buyers' other creditors (secured and unsecured). This was because of the right of an owner (here, the Dutch sellers) to "trace". This is a right to follow, and take, the proceeds of a sale where the owner's goods are disposed of by someone in a fiduciary relationship with the owner. It was held that cl.13 clearly imposed that fiduciary relationship upon the buyers.

In relation to the unmixed goods the clause worked by a combination of two things. First, it reserved title to the sellers and secondly it imposed a fiduciary duty upon the buyers which enabled the sellers to trace into the proceeds of sale.

Mixed Goods[95]

3-039 What would be the position with mixed goods? The answer is that the clause would, because it states, give the sellers property rights over the mixed (manufactured) goods. This, however, is not because title in the mixed goods is reserved to the sellers. It is possible to reserve title only in goods in which one has got title to start with, i.e. the unmixed goods. In *Re Peachdart*[96] the sellers of leather which the buyers then made into handbags could reserve title in the leather which they supplied but could not reserve title in the handbags which were newly created goods. When made into handbags, the leather ceased to exist as separate goods and became absorbed into the handbags. The contract of sale of the leather stated that the ownership in any mixed goods (i.e. handbags) should also be and remain with the sellers. The ownership which the sellers were thus given in the handbags was not, however, reserved to the sellers but was granted to them by those who would otherwise have been the owners, namely the buyers of the leather. This property right was therefore a charge created by the buyers of the leather. It was void because any charge created by a company is void unless registered: Companies Act 1948.[97] It seems then that a *Romalpa* clause will, if properly worded, work in the case of unmixed goods and the proceeds of sale of unmixed goods, but that in the case of mixed goods

95 See D. Webb, "Title and Transformation: who owns manufactured goods?" [2000] J.B.L. 513.

96 [1983] 3 All E.R. 204.

97 Now see, Companies Act 2006 s.859A.

(and their proceeds of sale) will work only if it is registered as a charge created by the buying company.

Where the goods subject to a retention of title clause are used by the buyer in a manufacturing process, it is a question of fact whether or not, like the leather in *Re Peachdart*, they have lost their identity and therefore cease to be the property of the seller. Grapes made into wine, olives into oil, wheat into bread, all clearly do thereby lose their identity. The following have been held similarly to have lost their identity: resin used to make chipboard (*Re Bond Worth*[98]); and Acrilan made into yarn and then into carpet (*Borden UK v Scottish Timber Products Ltd*[99]). In *Hendy Lennox Ltd v Grahame Puttick Ltd*[100] a diesel engine in which the seller had reserved title was used by the buyer as a major component of a diesel generating set which the buyer made. The engine remained unchanged and readily identifiable by a serial number and could be disconnected relatively easily from the generator in a matter of hours by undoing bolts and other connections. Distinguishing *Re Peachdart* and the other cases above, the judge held that the engine's incorporation did not preclude the seller from being entitled to retake the engine upon the buyer's liquidation. The engine had remained an engine, albeit connected to other things.[101]

Unmixed Goods

In *Clough Mill Ltd v Martin*[102] the Court of Appeal confirmed that the seller can, by virtue of the terms of the contract, effectively retain title in unmixed goods which the buyer has not resold. 3–040
Such a clause does not require registration under the Companies Act because the buyer is not creating a charge over his (the buyer's) assets. Rather the goods do not become the buyer's assets until the buyer has paid. Thus if the buyer goes into liquidation before fully paying for the goods, any of the goods which have not been resold by the buyer and which remain unmixed will belong to the seller. The seller, not the buyer's other creditors, will be entitled to take those goods. Assuming that the seller can resell them elsewhere for the same price as the buyer had agreed to pay, the seller will suffer no loss. If the seller is able to sell the goods elsewhere for more than the buyer had agreed to buy, the seller will in fact make a profit (i.e. will be better off than if the buyer had fully paid the seller before going into liquidation).

It is possible that before going into liquidation the buyer had paid part of the price to the seller. Clearly if the seller has been able to sell the goods elsewhere for the same price as the buyer had agreed to pay (or a greater price) the seller must refund the buyer's part payment. That part payment will then be available for the buyer's other creditors. If, however, the seller has been able to resell the goods elsewhere only at a loss (i.e. for less than the buyer

98 [1980] Ch. 228.
99 [1981] Ch. 25.
100 [1984] 1 W.L.R. 485.
101 See generally, A. Hicks, "When goods sold become a new species" [1993] J.B.L. 485.
102 [1985] 1 W.L.R. 111.

had agreed to pay) the seller is entitled to deduct that loss from the refund. The loss (i.e. the amount to be deducted) is the difference between the price the buyer had agreed to pay and the lower price which the seller is able to get on a resale elsewhere. Suppose the buyer had agreed to pay £2,000 and at the time of liquidation had paid only £1,000. Assuming that the seller had retained title to the goods, the seller must refund the £1,000 unless the seller is unable to resell the goods elsewhere for at least £2,000. If the seller was only able to sell the goods elsewhere for £1,800, then the seller must refund £800.

Now, suppose that the buyer had agreed to pay £2,000 (for the goods, a load of timber) and had actually paid the £2,000 but that the contract reserved title to the seller until the buyer had satisfied all his liabilities towards the seller (i.e. under not only this contract but also other contracts there might be between them). Suppose also that at the time the timber was delivered and through to the time of the buyer's liquidation the buyer owed £500 to the seller under another contract. In *Armour v Thyssen*[103] the House of Lords upheld the validity of "all liabilities" retention clauses. Thus the retention of title clause would entitle the seller to take and resell such of the timber he had supplied under this contract as remained unsold and unmixed in the buyer's possession. The seller would then be entitled to deduct from the £2,000 refund, not only any loss on reselling the timber but also the £500 just mentioned. If, on the other hand, the seller were able to sell the goods for more than £2,000, say £2,200, the extra value would belong to the seller (see obiter dicta in *Armour v Thyssen*). In this respect "all liabilities" clauses are no different from other retention of title clauses. Thus, in the example just given, if the seller resells the goods for £2,000 or for a higher sum, the seller will still be refunding the same net figure of £1,500.

Proceeds of Sale of Unmixed Goods

3-041 In the Romalpa case, not only was the seller entitled, as owner, to the unmixed goods which the buyer had not sold, but the seller was also entitled to the proceeds of sale which the buyer had received from sub-sales of unmixed goods. This was because the terms of the contract between seller and buyer made it clear that the buyer in reselling the goods was doing so, not for his own account, but as agent for, and on account of, the seller. This is not, however, the normal effect of a clause authorising the buyer to sub-sell the goods. The normal effect of such an authorisation is that the buyer is sub-selling for his own account. In *Pfeiffer GmbH v Arbuthnot Factors*[104] there was a clause retaining title for the seller and nevertheless authorising the buyer to make sub-sales. The contract required the buyer to pass on to the seller all the buyer's rights under the sub-sales contracts. However, it required this to be done only up to the amount of the buyer's outstanding indebtedness to the seller. It was held that this did not entitle the seller to take from the buyer the proceeds of the sub-sales of his (the seller's) property; instead it merely created a charge in favour of the seller which was void because it was not

103 [1991] A.C. 339.
104 [1988] 1 W.L.R. 150.

registered under the Companies Act. In order, without being registered, to entitle the seller to take the proceeds of sale in priority to the buyer's other creditors, the contract should, it seems:

(1) reserve the seller's title to the goods themselves (i.e. until either the buyer has paid or else the goods are sold by the buyer or lose their identity in the buyer's manufacturing process), and

(2) expressly state one or more of the following things:

(a) that the buyer is (until title passes) in possession of the goods as bailee of the seller;

(b) that the buyer, in having possession of the goods and in selling them, is in a "fiduciary" relationship with the seller;

(c) that the buyer in selling them, does so on account of, and as agent for, the seller; and

(3) not provide that the buyer's duty to account to the seller for the proceeds of sub-sales is limited to the buyer's outstanding indebtedness to the seller.

These provisions would give the seller a kind of property right over, and thereby give the seller entitlement to, all the proceeds of the sub-sales of unmixed goods (except those sub-sales made after title has already passed to the buyer). To make commercial sense of this arrangement, the contract would also need to contain a provision placing a duty on the seller to account to the buyer for any amount by which the proceeds of sub-sales of unmixed goods exceed the amount of the buyer's indebtedness to the seller.

Proposed Reform for Consumer Sales Contracts

In April 2021 the Law Commission published its final report (together with a draft Bill) on the rules governing the transfer of ownership in consumer sales contracts.[105] The Report builds on its previous work in this area where it was noted that the statutory rules around the transfer of property within the Sale of Goods Act were complex, technical, and capable of causing confusion 3-042

105 *Consumer sales contracts: transfer of ownership* (2021, Law Com. No. 398).

when applied to consumer sales contracts (and particularly in the context of internet sales).[106] Accordingly, the Report recommends new rules, introduced via amendment to the Consumer Rights Act 2015, framed in updated, consumer-focused, language, with the effect that:

- where the actual goods to be used to fulfil the contract are selected when the sales contract is made, ownership transfers to the consumer when the contract is made;
- where the actual goods to be used to fulfil the contract are not selected at the time the contract is made because the goods are to be made to a specification agreed between the parties, ownership will pass when the manufacture or production for the consumer has been completed;
- in other cases where the actual goods to be supplied are not selected when the sales contract is made, ownership transfers to the consumer when the trader identifies the goods to fulfil the contract. The proposed Bill provides for various methods through which this could happen including, amongst other things, the physical labelling or setting aside of the goods (where intended to be permanent) or the communication by the trader to the consumer of a unique identifier with ownership passing on which ever specified event occurs first.[107]

It will be recalled that earlier it was said that the Consumer Rights Act 2015 adopted the rules laid down by ss16–20B of the Sale of Goods Act 1979 as to when ownership passes in a sales contract. The proposed Bill modifies this and disapplies the SGA rules, however, the proposed reforms do not go so far as to offer a single system of rules as to when property passes in consumer sales. In particular, conditional sales are specifically excluded[108] and thus would remain subject to the SGA provisions as too would consumer contracts for the sale of an undivided share of goods (specified otherwise than as a fraction or percentage) or for the sale of an undivided share of goods forming part of a bulk.

It remains to be seen whether the draft Bill is ultimately implemented: it is notable that the Law Commission has suggested that "there may not be sufficient justification for implementation of the final draft Bill as a standalone measure at the present time".[109]

106 See, *Consumer Prepayments on Retailer Insolvency* (2016, Law Com. No. 368).

107 See the proposed s.18B under the draft Bill for the complete list.

108 Note that the Bill deals only with sales contracts, so analogous supply contracts such as hire purchase are also unaffected.

109 Consumer sales contracts: transfer of ownership (2021, Law Com. No. 398) at para.1.16.

General Reading

G. Battersby, "A reconsideration of 'property' and 'title' in the Sale of Goods Act" [2001] J.B.L. 1.

T. Burns, "Better Late than Never: The Reform of the Law on the Sale of Goods Forming Part of a Bulk" (1996) 59 M.L.R. 260.

I. Davies, "Continuing Dilemmas with Passing of Property in Part of a Bulk" [1991] J.B.L. 111.

A. Hicks, "When goods sold become a new species" [1993] J.B.L. 485.

H.L. Ho, "Some Reflections on 'Property' and 'Title' in the Sale of Goods Act" (1997) 56 C.L.J. 571.

G. McCormack, "Reservation of title—past, present and future" [1994] *Conveyancer and Property Lawyer* 129.

C.G.J. Morse, "Retention of title in English private international law" [1993] J.B.L. 168.

D.M. Sassoon, "Deterioration of Goods in Transit" [1962] J.B.L. 352.

D.M. Sassoon, "Damage resulting from natural decay under insurance, carriage and sale contracts" (1965) 28 M.L.R. 180.

L.S. Sealey, "'Risk' in the law of sale" (1972) 31 C.L.J. 225.

D. Webb, "Title and Transformation: who owns manufactured goods?" [2000] J.B.L. 513.

4

Perishing of Goods

In the last chapter we considered the problem of who is to bear the loss when the goods perish. We now face a different problem—namely, what effect does the perishing of the goods have upon the contract? In other words, must both parties still carry out the contract and, if not, to what extent is either party excused? To answer these questions, we must look to the Sale of Goods Act and the common law.[1] 4–001

Goods Perishing Before the Contract is Made

Section 6 provides: 4–002

> **"Where there is a contract for the sale of specific goods, and the goods without the knowledge of the seller have perished at the time when the contract is made, the contract is void."**

If the parties have made an agreement about goods which do not exist, it is an agreement about nothing. Thus in *Couturier v Hastie*[2] a contract to sell a cargo of corn was held to be void because, unknown to the seller, the ship's master had already sold it in Tunisia, as it had begun to ferment en route. At the time of the contract the cargo no longer existed.

1 The Consumer Rights Act 2015 is silent on these issues so the position is the same for both consumer and non-consumer sales.

2 (1856) 5 H.L.Cas. 673.

The words "void contract" are a contradiction in terms; a void contract is no contract at all. Thus neither party is under any obligation to carry it out. In *Couturier v Hastie*, where the seller was suing the buyer for the price, the action therefore failed. It follows that if the buyer had paid he could have recovered that money.

One must not be misled by the apparent simplicity of s.6 and *Couturier v Hastie*. There are in fact some considerable difficulties.

"Perish"

4-003 The meaning of this word as used in the Sale of Goods Act is in doubt. In *Horn v Minister of Food*,[3] Morris J considered that potatoes which had become seriously rotten had not "perished" because they were still potatoes, albeit worthless ones. From this it appears that they would have to become unrecognisable as potatoes before they could have been said to have perished. This view seems a little extreme and in *Asfar v Blundell*[4] it was held that dates, which were under water for two days and became impregnated with sewage, had perished—i.e. in a commercial sense. They could no longer be bought and sold as dates. Whichever of these two cases correctly reflects the meaning of "perish", one thing seems clear—goods which have deteriorated to some slight extent but not sufficiently to change their commercial character, have not "perished".

It was held in *Barrow, Lane & Ballard v Phillips*[5] where goods had disappeared (presumably stolen) that they had perished within the meaning of s.6. The case involved the sale of a specific lot of 700 bags of nuts lying in the seller's warehouse. Unknown to the parties, 109 of the bags had already disappeared. Wright J applied s.6 and held that the contract was void. Had it been severable, i.e. if it had been for the sale of separate lots to be separately paid for, then presumably the contract would have been void only as to those lots which were not complete at the time of the contract. In that case the seller would have had to deliver and the buyer to pay for the lots remaining complete. The decision in *Barrow, Lane & Ballard v Phillips* clearly indicates that if only some of the goods have perished that is sufficient to make the contract void.

There remains one further point about the word "perish". Goods that never existed cannot perish. It follows that if A agrees to sell specific goods to B which both A and B believe to exist but which never have existed, s.6 cannot apply. However, the contract would still be void, because at common law a contract is void if it is made on a false assumption that its subject-matter is in existence. Section 6, like many other sections of the Act, is no more than an attempt to put into an Act of Parliament a rule of the common law. It was not intended to oust or restrict any of the common law rules.[6] Thus in our example where no goods perished because none ever

3 [1948] 65 T.L.R. 106.

4 [1896] 1 Q.B. 123.

5 [1929] 1 K.B. 574.

6 s.62(2).

existed, the contract is void at common law. The reason is that right from the start the contract is impossible to carry out. It is an agreement built upon a non-existent foundation.

"Unascertained Goods"

Section 6 applies only to specific goods.[7] However, again the common law may declare void a contract which does not fall within s.6. A contract for the sale of unascertained goods may or may not be void because of the fact that certain goods have perished or do not exist at the time of the contract. It will be void if that fact makes it impossible right from the outset to carry out the contract. It is important to remember the distinction explained in the last chapter between purely generic unascertained goods (e.g. "500 tonnes of wheat") and unascertained goods from an identified bulk (e.g. "500 tonnes of wheat out of the 1,000 tonnes in the vessel Neptune"). In the case of purely generic goods, if the particular goods which the seller had in mind to supply had in fact perished at the time of the contract, this would not make it impossible for him to perform the contract. He could fulfil the contract by supplying wheat from any source; the contract is therefore not void. On the other hand, if he has to supply goods from a particular source and at the time of the making of the contract that source has ceased to exist (e.g. the Neptune has sunk) the contract is void at common law. 4-004

Contrary Agreement

Both s.6 and the common law rule making contracts void apply only in the absence of any agreement of the parties to the contrary. It is a matter of examining the contract to see whether the parties intended it to remain valid even if the goods were not in existence or had perished. For example, the buyer may have agreed to buy a spes (i.e. a chance). He may have agreed that if the goods were in existence he would acquire the ownership of them and if they were not in existence he would get nothing, but that in either event he would pay the price. If that were the agreement made by the parties the contract would be valid, even if the goods were not in existence, and the buyer would be liable to pay the price. In *Couturier v Hastie*,[8] the House of Lords said that it was a matter of construing the contract and it was only after doing so that their Lordships held that the buyer had not agreed to buy a spes and that the contract was therefore void. It will be relatively seldom that a buyer will agree to buy a spes. He will certainly be most unlikely to agree a very high price if he is to run the risk of getting absolutely nothing for his money. 4-005

A different possible interpretation of a contract is that not the buyer but the seller has undertaken to accept the risk that the goods might not exist, i.e. he has undertaken as part of

7 The definition of "specific goods" under s.61(1) of the Sale of Goods Act 1979 was considered in the previous chapter.

8 (1856) 5 H.L.Cas. 673.

the contract that the goods do in fact exist. In this case, if it turns out that the goods do not exist at the time of the contract, the seller will be liable in damages to the buyer for breach of his contractual undertaking. This is exactly what happened in the Australian case of *McRae v Commonwealth Disposals Commission*.[9] The Disposals Commission agreed to sell a wreck on the Jourmand Reef off the coast of Papua. The buyer subsequently discovered that the wreck had never existed and that, indeed, neither had the reef! The Australian court construed the agreement and concluded that the contract was not void, because the sellers had impliedly warranted that the wreck existed at the spot specified. The sellers were therefore liable in damages to the buyer.

To sum up: a contract is void if, at the time the contract is made and unknown to the parties, goods have perished or do not exist, thereby rendering it impossible for the contract to be performed. This, however, is subject to the qualification that the contract will not be void if the parties expressly or impliedly agreed otherwise.

Goods Perishing After the Contract is Made

4-006 Section 7 provides:

> **"Where there is an agreement to sell specific goods, and subsequently the goods, without any fault on the part of the seller or buyer, perish before the risk passes to the buyer, the agreement is avoided."**

Like s.6, this section is only part of a wider principle of common law. The principle here relates to frustration of contract. It applies when, through no fault of either party, events take an unexpected turn making it impossible to carry out the contract as originally conceived. In such circumstances the contract is frustrated or (in the terminology of s.7) avoided. This can occur not only if the goods subsequently perish but also, for example, if after the contract is made, it becomes illegal to carry it out. It happened in *Avery v Bowden*[10] where there was a contract to bring goods from Russia. Before the ship was due to be loaded, the Crimean War broke out, making it illegal to trade with Russia (the enemy). It was held that no claim could be brought against the defendant for failing to load because the contract had been frustrated by illegality before the time for loading.

9 (1951) 84 C.L.R. 377.

10 (1856) L.J.Q.B. 3.

It can be seen that in the event of specific goods perishing, the contract may be avoided by s.7 but if in any other case the contract becomes impossible or illegal to perform, it will be frustrated at common law.

Again, there are some difficulties:

The Time of Perishing

Both s.7 and the common law doctrine of frustration are concerned with events occurring after the contract was made. If the goods had already perished at the time the contract was made then s.6 is the appropriate section. If s.6 applies, the contract is void. Where the events occur after the contract was made and the contract is avoided or frustrated the effect is not the same (see below). 4-007

"Perish"

The word "perish" presumably means the same as in s.6. Indeed, one of the cases quoted above, *Horn v Minister of Health*,[11] was a case on s.7. 4-008

The point was made in relation to s.6 that goods cannot perish if they have never been in existence. Thus a contract for the sale of future goods (e.g. a crop to be grown on a specific farm) will not be avoided by s.7 if the goods do not materialise. Nevertheless such a contract may be frustrated at common law. In *Howell v Coupland*,[12] the seller agreed to sell 200 tons of the potato crop on a specific piece of land, which would normally have produced easily that amount. However, the crop failed due to blight. The Court held that the seller was not liable for non-delivery of the goods because the contract had been made on the assumption that the crop would materialise. The crop failure was an unexpected turn of events rendering it impossible to perform the contract which was therefore frustrated.

"Unascertained Goods"

Again like s.6, s.7 applies only to specific goods. However, a contract for the sale of unascertained goods can be frustrated at common law if it subsequently becomes impossible to perform because of an unexpected turn of events, as in *Howell v Coupland*. As with s.6, it is important to remember the difference between unascertained goods out of a specific bulk (e.g. *Howell v Coupland*) and purely generic goods. In his judgment in *Howell v Coupland*, Blackburn J said:[13] 4-009

11 [1948] 65 T.L.R. 106.
12 (1876) 1 Q.B.D. 258 (CA).
13 (1873–74) 9 Q.B. 462 at 466.

> **"Had the contract been simply for so many tons of potatoes of a particular quality then, although each party might have had in his mind when he made the contract this particular crop of potatoes, if they had all perished, the defendant would still have been bound to deliver the quantity contracted for."**

Thus a great deal turns on the exact terms of the contract—whether it stipulates "200 tonnes of potatoes to be grown on Blackacre" or simply "200 tonnes of potatoes". The failure of the crop of Blackacre will only render it impossible to perform the contract in the first example, whereas in the latter case the contract can be fulfilled by supplying potatoes from any source.

The Passing of Risk and Property

4-010 Once risk has passed to the buyer the contract cannot be avoided by s.7. Equally, a contract for the sale of unascertained goods out of a specific bulk will not be frustrated by the perishing of the bulk if it occurs after risk has passed to the buyer. All of this should be easily understood when it is realised that the effect of the contract being avoided or frustrated is generally that the parties are no longer required to carry out the contract; they are excused. So, for example, the buyer is under no obligation to pay. If this were to be the position when goods perish after the risk has passed to the buyer, it would be a contradiction in terms. In such a case the only way to make some sense of the rule that the buyer must bear the loss is still to make him pay whilst allowing him to take whatever remains of the goods. That is exactly the legal position. The contract in such a case is most certainly not frustrated or avoided.

Neither will the contract be avoided or frustrated if at the time the goods perish, property has already passed to the buyer. Section 7, on its wording, applies only to agreements to sell. An agreement to sell becomes a sale when property passes to the buyer. The common law doctrine of frustration applies only where the main purpose of the contract has become impossible to achieve: *Herne Bay Steam Boat Co v Hutton*.[14] The main purpose of a contract of sale of goods is that the buyer should become the owner of the goods: *Rowland v Divall*.[15] That purpose is achieved the instant that property passes to the buyer. The contract cannot be frustrated by the goods perishing after that moment.

Effect of the Contract being Frustrated or Avoided

4-011 The main effect is that the parties are excused from further performance of the contract. The seller need not deliver the goods and the buyer need not pay for them. The law is putting into

14 [1903] 2 K.B. 683.

15 [1923] 2 K.B. 500. See further, para.7-008, below.

effect what it reasonably presumes to have been the intention of the parties. It presumes, although the parties did not anticipate the contract becoming impossible or illegal to perform, that nevertheless, if they had thought about it, they would have stated that further performance was to be excused.

Thus, if the parties did actually turn their minds to the possibility that such things might happen (e.g. that the goods might perish) and provided in the contract for that eventuality, then the effect of the event occurring will be whatever is stated in their contract. In this case it is not in fact accurate to say that the contract is avoided or frustrated; the contract remains and its provisions apply. Indeed, s.7 applies only in the absence of contrary agreement.

Usually it is reasonable to presume that (if the parties had considered the eventuality that the contract would become impossible or illegal to perform), they would have intended all further performance to be excused. However, the law will not excuse all further performance of the contract if that, on the facts of the particular case, is an unreasonable presumption of what the parties would have intended. *Sainsbury v Street*[16] is a more recent case with facts similar to those in *Howell v Coupland*.[17] The contract was an agreement to sell 275 tons of barley to be grown by the seller on his farm. In the event the crop was an unexpectedly poor one and amounted to only 140 tons. Clearly, following the decision in *Howell v Coupland*, the seller was excused his obligation to deliver 275 tons. The question was whether he was entirely excused from performance for he had not offered to supply the reduced amount of 140 tons but instead sold it to someone else. MacKenna J held that there was an implied term that in such a case the seller was not completely excused from all performance but that the buyer had the option of accepting delivery of the reduced quantity, at a pro rata price. Therefore the seller was liable in damages for non-delivery of 140 tons. So it can be seen that the parties will usually be excused further performance of the contract, either partly or entirely, according to what is a reasonable presumption of what the parties would have intended.

A problem can arise for the buyer if, before the contract is frustrated or avoided, he has paid all or part of the price. Can he recover his money? The answer differs according to whether the contract was avoided by s.7 or frustrated at common law. In the former case there is an "all or nothing" rule. The buyer is entitled to the return of his money in full provided he has suffered a total failure of consideration, i.e. has received no benefit under the contract: *Fibrosa Spolka Akcyjna v Fairburn Lawson Combe Barbour Ltd*.[18] This will be the position provided the goods perished before any had been delivered to the buyer. If, however, he had any benefit under the contract, i.e. some use of the goods, before the goods perished, then he will be unable to recover any of the money he has paid. It will, of course, seldom happen that after the buyer has had some benefit, the contract is avoided by s.7 because usually by the time goods are delivered to the buyer, risk will have passed to him; s.7 applies only where the goods perish before the risk passes to the buyer. 4-012

16 [1972] 1 W.L.R. 834.
17 (1876) 1 Q.B.D. 258.
18 [1943] A.C 32.

On the other hand, if the contract is frustrated at common law (as occurred in *Howell v Coupland*) the position as to the return of the price to the buyer is now regulated by the Law Reform (Frustrated Contracts) Act 1943 (which does not apply to contracts avoided by s.7). The position under this Act is that the buyer can recover his money but the court can deduct, from that, a sum towards expenses incurred by the seller in performing the contact. Furthermore the 1943 Act empowers the court to order the buyer to pay a reasonable sum for any benefit he has received under the contract. This will occur if, for example, the buyer has had some use of the goods and subsequently they perished, thereby frustrating the contract. It should be emphasised again that this last situation will occur only very seldom, because usually by the time the buyer gets possession of the goods, risk will have passed to him and, if the goods perish after risk has passed to the buyer, that will not frustrate the contract. If the contract is not frustrated, the buyer will not be entitled to the return of any money and will have to pay any money outstanding.

Effect of s.20A

4–013 Section 20A was introduced into the Sale of Goods Act in 1995. As was explained in the last chapter, it gives a proprietary interest to someone who buys and pays for goods which are agreed to be part of an identified bulk. Such a buyer has an undivided share in the bulk. We saw that, as between the seller and buyer, this has the effect that any destruction of the goods is taken to destroy the seller's share of the bulk first. What, however, is the position where more than the seller's share of the goods is destroyed? In that case some of the buyer's share of the goods is then taken to be destroyed and thus, if the whole bulk is destroyed, the whole of the buyer's as well as the whole of the seller's shares are destroyed. Section 20A imposes on the buyer the risk of any loss which would prevent the seller being able to carry out the contract. Let us return to the example where the contract is for the sale of "400 tonnes out of the 1,000 tonnes of wheat stored in Wally's Woodford Warehouse". Let us also assume that the buyer has paid for his 400 tonnes and that the seller has not contracted to sell any of the 1,000 tonnes to anyone else. In those circumstances, if, say, 700 tonnes of the bulk are destroyed by lightening, then it is assumed that 600 of those tonnes were the seller's and that the buyer has thus lost only 100 tonnes. That does of course render it impossible for the seller to fulfil his contract to supply the buyer with 400 tonnes from the stock in the warehouse. Nevertheless, the contract is not frustrated because, if it were, that would make nonsense of providing that the buyer must bear the loss of the 100 tonnes. Thus the buyer is not entitled to the return of any of the price though he is of course entitled to take delivery of the remaining 300 tonnes.

5

Seller not the Owner

Introduction

A person not having the authority to do so sells or otherwise disposes of goods which do not belong to him. This may involve an element of roguery but the knotty question which often comes before the courts is "who is the owner?" Is it the original owner or is it the innocent purchaser? Whichever of these two is the loser usually suffers a considerable loss. If it is the buyer he will have to give up the goods (or their value) for which he has already paid good money. It is true that whichever is the loser will have a remedy against the unauthorised seller. However, if the latter is a rogue he is likely to have disappeared and if he can be found will probably be penniless. 5-001

There is, then, a problem of ownership. One should remember that the law uses three words all meaning the same thing, "ownership", "property" and "title". In choosing between the original owner and the innocent purchaser, the law has to choose between upholding the sanctity of property and giving effect to a commercial transaction. There is no obvious answer. The law's solution is to have a general principle in favour of the original owner with a number of exceptions in favour of the innocent purchaser. The goods will therefore be regarded as belonging to the original owner unless one of the exceptions applies.

The General Principle: Nemo Dat Non Quod Habet

Nemo Dat

5-002 The general principle is in s.21(1):

> **"Subject to this Act, where goods are sold by a person who is not their owner, and who does not sell them under the authority or with the consent of the owner, the buyer acquires no better title to the goods than the seller had, unless the owner of the goods is by his conduct precluded from denying the seller's authority to sell."**

This rule that someone without title cannot without authority transfer title is illustrated by the decision in *Greenwood v Bennett*.[1] Bennett, the original owner of a Jaguar car, entrusted it to one Searle for some repairs to be carried out. Searle was a rogue and used it for his own purposes. He had a crash and damaged it extensively. Entirely without authority he sold it for £75 to Harper, a garage proprietor who was unaware that Searle was not the owner. Harper spent some £226 on repairing it and sold it to a finance company. The court held that the car still belonged to Bennett. Searle did not have title and therefore could not transfer it to Harper. For the same reason Harper did not transfer title to the finance company. There was one further point: Harper carried out work in good faith believing the car to be his; because of this Bennett recovered a car worth more than it would otherwise have been. It was held that Bennett must compensate Harper for the work by paying him £226.

A Claim for Conversion

5-003 An owner who wishes to bring a claim to recover possession of his goods from someone who has refused to return them can bring a claim for conversion.[2] If the owner wishes to bring a claim against someone who has wrongfully sold the owner's goods, his claim will again be for conversion. Suppose the goods are sold by X to Y who in turn sells them to Z. Suppose the goods belong to O and that X sold them wrongfully and without authority. We have just seen that the general rule is that since X is not the owner he cannot confer ownership on Y, who similarly cannot confer ownership on Z. If Z refuses to return the goods to O, O has a claim against Z for conversion of the goods. Alternatively, O may choose to bring his claim for conversion

1 [1972] 3 W.L.R. 691.

2 Torts (Interference with Goods) Act 1977.

against X or Y. Where O brings his claim against Z, Z will naturally wish to claim against Y who sold to him. He can do this. He can claim the return of the price he paid to Y. This claim is based upon a breach of contract by Y in that Y did not have any right to sell the goods and failed to confer any ownership upon his buyer, Z.[3] The fact that Y may have been quite innocent and genuinely believed at the time that the goods were his to sell gives him no defence either to a claim by Z for breach of contract or to a claim by O for conversion. Y can also reclaim from X the price Y paid to X.

Now suppose that Y had improved the goods (just as Harper did in *Greenwood v Bennett*). The Torts (Interference With Goods) Act 1977, passed after the decision in *Greenwood v Bennett*, provides a mechanism by which the innocent improver is to be reimbursed. If O sues Y for conversion (i.e. for selling O's goods to Z), then O will obtain judgment against Y for damages equal to the value of the goods on the date of the sale to Z, less the deduction of an improvement allowance. That allowance is the proportion of the value of the goods which is attributable to the improvement by Y. If O does not sue Y but instead sues Z for conversion, then Z gets the benefit of the improvement allowance. The judgment obtained by O against Z will not normally be an order to Z to return the goods. Such an order will be granted only where damages would not be an adequate remedy (e.g. if the goods were unique or virtually so). O may, however, obtain judgment against Z in the alternative, i.e. judgment ordering Z either to return the goods or to pay damages equal to their value. Z is thereby given the option. In either case Z gets the benefit of the improvement allowance. In the latter case it is deducted from the damages he has to pay O. Where he returns the goods to O, O must pay Z the improvement allowance. In our example, this allowance relates to improvements performed by Y. Thus in a claim by Z against Y, Y is entitled to deduct the improvement allowance when returning Z the price paid by Z.

In all of this it has been assumed that the general rule applies and that X, not being the owner, could not confer ownership on Y who in turn could not confer ownership on Z. It now remains to examine those exceptional circumstances where the original owner may lose his ownership, i.e. where title may be conferred by someone who himself has no title.

Exceptions to the Nemo Dat Principle

Sale by Agent

Section 21(1) begins by stating that "where goods are sold by a person who is not their owner, and who does not sell them under the authority or with the consent of the owner" good title is not passed. The common law rules of agency are preserved by s.62(2).[4] Thus where an agent 5-004

3 See para.7-008, below.

4 Unless the common law rules are inconsistent with the provisions of the Sale of Goods Act.

sells goods on behalf of the owner (his principal) and that sale is within the common law rules of an agent's authority, good title will pass to the buyer, even where the agent's actual authority has been exceeded. The law of agency will be covered in Part Three of this book. However, in summary, an agent may pass good title even though he has exceeded his actual authority in the following ways: apparent authority;[5] usual authority;[6] or necessity.[7]

There are obviously similarities between the common law agency exception under s.21(1) and the mercantile agency exception under s.2 of the Factors Act. As will be seen shortly, a mercantile agent will always be an agent under the common law. The reverse however is not necessarily true.[8]

Estoppel

5-005 When an estoppel is raised, the original owner is estopped (precluded) from asserting that the sale was unauthorised. Thus if an estoppel is raised the unauthorised sale takes effect as if it was authorised—i.e. it transfers ownership to the buyer in the ordinary way (see s.21(1) above).

An estoppel is raised when the original owner by his statements or conduct leads the innocent purchaser to believe that the unauthorised seller in fact has the right to sell the goods. More accurately, for the innocent purchaser to obtain a good title by estoppel, all the following requirements must be fulfilled:

(i) The original owner must have made a representation (by statement or conduct) that the seller was entitled to sell the goods.

(ii) The representation must have been made intentionally or negligently.

(iii) The representation must have misled the innocent purchaser.

(iv) The innocent purchaser must have bought (and not merely agreed to buy) the goods.

---

5 Where the principal clothes the agent with the appearance of authority to sell the goods. This must, similarly to a representation in estoppel, generally, go beyond merely allowing an agent to have possession of the goods or documents of title.

6 Thus, where the sale is in the ordinary course of the agent's business, good title can pass to the innocent third party purchaser even though there is no actual or apparent authority: *Watteau v Fenwick* [1893] 1 Q.B. 346, see para.27-009, below.

7 This is still possible in the context of sale of goods, where, for example, the goods are perishable and sold by a carrier acting as agent: *Springer v Great Western Railway Co* [1921] 1 K.B. 257, see para.27-011, below.

8 A common law agent may for example not be acting in the course of a business or indeed receive any payment or consideration for their service. This will take the sale or disposition outside the Factors Act 1889, but such an agent may still pass good title to the buyer under the common law rules of agency (though not, obviously, via the concept of usual authority).

One problem with the first requirement is what conduct by the original owner will amount to a representation that the seller has the right to sell the goods. A case where a plea of estoppel succeeded and the innocent purchaser therefore obtained a good title was *Eastern Distributors v Goldring*.[9] The facts, however, can be appreciated only with knowledge of the role of the finance company in a modern hire-purchase transaction.[10] Briefly, the customer sees at a trader's premises the item he wishes to acquire. He asks for credit and, at the trader's suggestion, he fills in a finance company's hire-purchase proposal form, which is in fact an offer made by the customer and addressed to the finance company to acquire the item from the finance company on hire-purchase terms. The customer will leave the completed form with the trader. The trader himself will then fill in another form offering to sell the same item to the finance company. He will then send both forms to the finance company which will either accept or reject both offers. If it accepts, it thereby agrees to purchase the item for cash from the trader and at the same time agrees to transfer it on hire-purchase terms to the customer.

In *Eastern Distributors v Goldring*, the customer wished to raise a loan on his van. He and the motor trader got together to deceive the finance company. They each filled in their respective forms as if the van belonged to the trader and as if the customer wished to acquire the van on hire-purchase terms. Everything appeared in order to the finance company, which accepted the forms believing the trader to be the owner to be the owner of the van. Thus it bought the van from the trader and transferred it on hire-purchase to the customer. The customer did not pay his instalments under the hire-purchase agreement and sold the van to X, an innocent purchaser. The finance company discovered the fraud and the question arose as to who was the owner. The customer was the original owner and, provided he had not in the interim lost his ownership, he transferred that ownership to X. However, the court upheld the finance company's claim that the customer had by the doctrine of estoppel lost his ownership to the finance company. He had submitted through the trader a form offering to acquire the van on hire-purchase terms. Thereby he had represented to the finance company that the van was not his but that it belonged to the trader. This was an intentional deception. Since the customer was therefore stopped from asserting his ownership, the finance company obtained good title when it bought the van from the dealer. It still had that ownership because under a hire-purchase agreement property does not pass until the customer has paid all of his instalments.[11] Thus the car did not belong to the customer who therefore could not transfer ownership to X. 5-006

In *Goldring*'s case, the customer had done something clearly conveying to the finance company that he did not own the van and that so far as he was concerned the seller (the trader) had every right to sell it. An act which does not clearly convey that fact is not sufficient to raise an estoppel. So, if the owner of goods merely allows another person to have possession of them, (e.g. at a left luggage office) that act will not raise an estoppel for it does not convey to others that he considers the person in possession to have the right to dispose of them. If O lends his car to Q who then sells it to P, but is unauthorised to do so, O is still the owner and he can

9 [1957] 2 Q.B. 600.

10 For a full explanation, see para.17-011, below.

11 See para.1-014, above and Ch.18, below.

assert that ownership. In *Central Newbury Car Auctions v Unity Finance*[12] a customer wished to acquire a car on hire-purchase. He and the motor trader filled in the usual forms. Before the finance company's reply was received, the trader allowed the customer to take delivery of the car (together with its registration document). The customer sold the car to X. The finance company rejected the offers. It was held that the car still belonged to the trader. His allowing the customer to have possession of the car did not amount to a representation that the customer had the right to sell it. His giving him possession also of the registration document made no difference since a registration document is not in the eyes of the law a document of title.[13]

The same principle has been developed in respect of possession, not of the goods, but of a document of title. In *Mercantile Bank of India Ltd v Central Bank of India Ltd*[14] railway receipts were pledged with the Central Bank of India (i.e. used to raise finance). The receipts were then released in order for the pledgor to secure the goods. Instead of doing this however, he used the receipts to raise a further loan, this time with the Mercantile Bank of India. The argument of estoppel against the Central Bank failed with the Privy Council stating that possession of the railway receipts "no more conveyed a representation that the merchants were entitled to dispose of the property than the actual possession of the goods themselves would have done".[15] This line of authority[16] restricts the possibility of successfully raising estoppel as a defence against conversion but does demonstrate a pragmatic approach to protecting the original owner's title to the goods. This must be correct: were the courts to allow a defence of estoppel purely through the act of (carelessly) allowing another person to have possession of the goods, the impact upon the nemo dat principle would be substantial and would be applicable in a broad range of cases.

5–007 An estoppel will not be raised unless the representation was intentional or negligent. In *Eastern Distributors v Goldring*[17] the original owner (the customer) clearly intended to make the deception. In *Mercantile Credit Co v Hamblin*[18] the customer had no such intention. Like the customer in the former case, Mrs Hamblin wished to raise a loan on her vehicle. She went to a motor trader who told her that this could be done. He agreed that he would enquire as to what terms could be obtained from a finance company and would then telephone Mrs Hamblin to see if they were acceptable. He got her to sign a proposal form of a particular finance company. She believed this to be an application to the finance company for a loan on the security of her car. In fact it was the usual proposal form to acquire the car on hire-purchase terms. Placing

---

12 [1957] 1 Q.B. 371.

13 In his dissenting judgment, Denning LJ suggested that the log book was best evidence of title and adopted the dictum of Ashurst J in *Lickbarrow v Mason* (1787) 2 Term Rep 63 whereby wherever the owner enables the rogue to dispose of the goods with the appearance of ownership (and occasion the loss), the original owner should be estopped.

14 [1938] A.C. 287.

15 [1938] A.C. 287 at 303, per Lord Wright.

16 *Johnson v Credit Lyonnais Co* (1877) 3 CPD 32; *Mercantile Bank of India Ltd v Central Bank of India Ltd* [1938] A.C. 287; *Jerome v Bentley* [1952] 2 All E.R. 114; and *Central Newbury Car Auctions v Unity Finance* [1957] 1 Q.B. 371.

17 [1957] 2 Q.B. 600.

18 [1965] 2 Q.B. 242.

her confidence and trust in him she was guided by the trader and signed the form in blank and agreed with the trader that, if he succeeded in obtaining terms acceptable to her, he would then be able to fill in the details on the form and send it to the finance company. However, the trader subsequently filled in the form without having reported back to her and thereby without her authority. He also filled in the usual trader's form offering to sell the car to the finance company and sent both forms off to the finance company. The finance company accepted the proposals. Who now owned the car? Mrs Hamblin had not intended to make it appear that the car belonged to the trader. The court held that she was not negligent. She knew nothing of financial matters and had acted quite reasonably in placing her trust and confidence in a motor trader who had a good reputation in the area. In the absence of intention or negligence, no estoppel could be raised against her. The car was therefore still hers.

The question of negligence was discussed in *Moorgate Mercantile v Twitchings.*[19] Moorgate Mercantile were a finance company which owned a car. They let it on hire-purchase terms to a customer. Before completing his instalments, the customer without authority sold the car to Twitchings, a car dealer. Moorgate Mercantile and Twitchings were both members of H.P. Information Ltd (H.P.I). H.P.I. was an organisation which operated a register where finance companies could register their hire-purchase agreements so that any other member (e.g. a car dealer) could, before buying a second-hand car, check with H.P.I. to see if the car was the subject of a registered hire-purchase agreement. On this occasion Moorgate Mercantile had carelessly failed to register their hire-purchase agreement with the result that Twitchings was told by H.P.I. that there was no hire-purchase agreement registered in connection with this particular car. Twitchings claimed that Moorgate Mercantile were estopped from denying that their hire-purchase customer was the owner of the car. This claim failed. Moorgate Mercantile had not made any representation to Twitchings. The only statement to Twitchings had been made by H.P.I., namely that there was no registered hire-purchase agreement relating to the car in question. That statement had been true and had in any case not been made by Moorgate Mercantile, since H.P.I. was not an agent of Moorgate Mercantile for the purpose of making such a statement. As to negligence it was true that Moorgate Mercantile had been careless in failing to register their hire-purchase agreement. However, carelessness did not amount to negligence unless the carelessness was a breach of a legal duty to take care. Moorgate Mercantile were under no legal duty to join H.P.I. and, having joined, were under no legal duty to take care to register their hire-purchase agreements.[20] Thus in the absence of either a deliberate misleading by Moorgate Mercantile or negligence on their part, no estoppel could be raised against them. Moorgate Mercantile therefore succeeded in their claim against Twitchings for conversion of the car.[21] Moorgate Mercantile was distinguished by the court in

---

19 [1976] 3 W.L.R. 66.

20 Thus in *Industrial and Corporate Finance Ltd v Wyder Group Ltd* (2008) 152 S.J.L.B. 31 estoppel was not available as a defence to the finance company's conversion claim.

21 Since 1995 H.P.I., now run by Equifax, has offered a service to traders and to ordinary members of the public enabling them, on payment of a small fee, to have a search of the H.P.I. register carried out and also to be given a guarantee of compensation if the information is incorrect or incomplete. The H.P.I. report will cover not

Chatfields-Martin Walter Ltd v Lombard North Central Plc.[22] In this case the finance company prematurely deleted the HPI records indicating the existence of outstanding finance agreements on a motor vehicle. This constituted a representation that the finance agreements had been settled and consequently the finance company was estopped from asserting their title to the goods.

An estoppel can be raised only if the representation misled the innocent purchaser. In *Farquharson Bros v King*[23] a timber firm owned some timber which was in the possession of a dock company. The firm told the dock company to deal with the timber according to the instructions of a clerk of the firm. The clerk, a rogue, instructed the dock company to hold the timber to the order of "Brown" (which was the clerk under an assumed name). In his assumed name of Brown he sold the timber to an innocent purchaser. To whom did the timber belong? The House of Lords held that it still belonged to the timber firm. The statement made by the timber firm to the dock company had not come to the attention of the innocent purchaser; it therefore could not have misled him. The only thing which misled the purchaser was Brown's roguery. No estoppel could be raised against the timber firm.

5-008 Where an innocent purchaser is able to rely upon an estoppel, property in the goods passes to him in the normal way, i.e. as if his seller himself has good title to give. Thus he will obtain good title if, and when, according to the terms of the contract of purchase, property in the goods is to pass to him. To put it another way, someone who has "bought" goods (i.e. to whom property has passed under his contract of purchase) can rely upon an estoppel. Someone who has only agreed to buy (i.e. to whom property has not yet passed) cannot do so: *Shaw v Commissioner of Police for the Metropolis.*[24] In this case the innocent purchaser had agreed to buy a car from, as he later discovered, someone who did not own it, on terms that property in the car would pass to him upon payment of the price. It was held that since he had not paid the price, no property in the goods could have passed to him. Therefore he could not claim a good title by raising an estoppel against the true owner.

It will be evident from the above discussion that instances where there has been a successful plea of estoppel in an action for conversion are few and far between. The clear requirement of a representation beyond simply allowing a non-owner to have possession of the goods (or documents of title)[25] and the very restrictive requirements of estoppel through negligence severely limit the ability of the doctrine to pass good title to the third party.[26]

just existing finance agreements relating to the vehicle but also whether it has ever been: stolen, an insurance "write-off" or the subject of a number plate change. For an account of the interrelated provisions of the law in this area, see P. Dobson, "Risks in Buying a Used Car" (1996) 140 S.J. 1180. See also para.5-030 and *Barber v N.W.S. Bank* at para.7-009, below.

22 [2014] EWHC 1222 (QB).

23 [1902] A.C. 325.

24 [1987] 1 W.L.R. 1332.

25 i.e. a representation which misleads the third party as to the actual ownership of the goods.

26 See the comments of Lord Wright in *Mercantile Bank of India Ltd v Central Bank of India Ltd* [1938] A.C. 287 at 302.

Owner's Signature on Document Intended to Have Legal Effect

Quite apart from the doctrine of estoppel, there may be another alternative basis on which the owner may be precluded from denying the seller's authority to sell namely where the owner has signed a document clearly conveying the implication that the seller is entitled or authorised to sell the goods. There is a rule that normally a person is bound by his signature: *Saunders v Anglia Building Society*.[27] This rule is not confined to someone signing a fully completed document. It applies also to someone signing a document with blanks for the particular transaction not filled in but agreeing to, or authorising, another to fill in those blanks later: *United Dominions Trust v Western*.[28] Thus in *Mercantile Credit v Hamblin*,[29] if Mrs Hamblin had authorised or agreed to the trader filling in the proposal form, the result of the case would have been different. Mrs Hamblin would have been precluded from denying the trader's authority to sell the car. This would have been not because of the doctrine of estoppel (which would have required either a deliberate misleading or negligence by her), but because of her signature on a document which, as was apparent on its face, was intended to have legal effect and which she had authorised the trader to complete. 5-009

There are two particular exceptions to this rule, i.e. where the signer will not be bound by his signature. The first is where he can plead non est factum. This plea will succeed where he can show two things: (i) that he was radically mistaken about the nature or effect of the document; and (ii) that he was not careless in signing it (*Saunders v Anglian Building Society*[30]). The mistake in *Mercantile Credit v Hamblin*[31] would not have been sufficiently radical to justify a plea of non est factum. The hire-purchase proposal (i.e. involving the sale of the car by Mrs Hamblin on hire-purchase terms) was not radically different in substance from a loan on the security of the car.

The second exception could arise in a *Mercantile Credit v Hamblin* type of situation. It would arise if the motor trader were the agent of the finance company in dealing with the customer. At common law the dealer is not normally the agent either of the finance company or of the customer. However, s.56 of the Consumer Credit Act 1974 now makes him in most cases the statutory agent of the finance company.[32] The customer cannot be bound to the finance company by his signature on a document which the finance company's agent knows does not reflect the customer's intention.

27 [1971] A.C. 1004.
28 [1976] Q.B. 513.
29 [1965] 2 Q.B. 242, see para.5-007, above.
30 [1971] A.C. 1004.
31 [1965] 2 Q.B. 242.
32 See para.21-009, below.

Mercantile Agents

5-010 The Factors Act 1889 s. 2(1) provides:

> **"Where a mercantile agent is, with the consent of the owner, in possession of goods or of documents of title to goods, any sale, pledge or other disposition of the goods, made by him when acting in the ordinary course of business of a mercantile agent, shall, subject to the provisions of this Act be as valid as if he were expressly authorised by the owner of the goods to make the same; provided that the person taking under the disposition acts in good faith, and has not at the time of the disposition notice that the person making the disposition has not authority to make the same."**

There are six requirements to be fulfilled in order for an unauthorised sale by a mercantile agent to confer good title upon an innocent purchaser.

The seller must be a mercantile agent, i.e. a factor

5-011 Broadly, a mercantile agent is an independent agent acting in a way of business to whom someone else entrusts his goods and upon whom is conferred authority of a type referred to in the Factors Act 1889 s.1(1). That section provides:

> **"The expression 'mercantile agent' shall mean a mercantile agent having in the customary course of his business as such agent authority either to sell goods, or to consign goods for the purposes of sale, or to buy goods, or to raise money on the security of goods."**

This statutory definition is not complete. In order to be a mercantile agent, an agent must have not merely the customary authority referred to in the statute but also three further characteristics. First, he must be independent from the person (his principal) for whom he is agent. A "mere servant or shopman" or "caretaker" is therefore not a mercantile agent.[33] Secondly, he must be acting as agent in a way of business. This "business" characteristic does not require that he should regularly carry on business as agent but simply that on the occasion in question he was acting as a business proposition. In *Lowther v Harris*[34] an agent was entrusted with a tapestry with a view to selling it. He was instructed not actually to conclude a sale without

33 Nor does the Act apply where the mercantile agent is selling goods in his own right, i.e. is the legal owner: *Fadallah v Pollak* [2013] EWHC 3159.

34 [1927] 1 K.B. 393.

having first referred back to his principal; he was to receive commission if a sale was concluded. In fact, he sold the tapestry to an innocent purchaser without having first referred back to his principal. Wright J held that the agent who had no general occupation as agent, who normally bought and sold goods on his own account and who was the agent for only the one principal, was nevertheless a mercantile agent. Therefore, since all the requirements in s.2 of the Factors Act were fulfilled, the innocent purchaser had good title to the tapestry.

The third characteristic referred to above is that the agent must be authorised to deal with the goods in his own name without disclosing his agency. In *Rolls Razor Co v Cox*[35] the court had to consider the status of some travelling salesmen. Lord Denning MR said:[36]

> **"The usual characteristics of a factor are these. He is an agent entrusted with the possession of goods of several principals, or sometimes only one principal, for the purpose of sale in his own name without disclosing the name of his principal and he is remunerated by a commission. These salesmen lacked one of those characteristics. They did not sell in their own names but in the name and on behalf of their principals, the Company. They are agents pure and simple and not factors."**

Before leaving the question of who is a mercantile agent, it should be said that someone who is not an agent cannot be a mercantile agent.[37] It can be difficult sometimes when someone takes goods on "sale or return" terms to decide whether he was acting as an agent or as principal.[38]

The mercantile agent must be in possession of the goods or documents of title; and he must have the possession at the time he sells, pledges or otherwise disposes of the goods

An example of a document of title is a bill of lading (i.e. the document given by a shipowner acknowledging that he has received goods which have been shipped). A motor vehicle's registration document is not, however, a document of title.[39] Thus, a mercantile agent in possession of the registration book but not of the vehicle itself can not confer good title under s.2 of the Factors Act: *Beverley Acceptances v Oakley*.[40] 5-012

35 [1967] 1 Q.B. 552.

36 [1967] 1 Q.B. 552 at 568.

37 Equally, it is not necessarily true that someone who is an agent will be a mercantile agent under the definition of s.1(1) and the common law.

38 See Ch.1.

39 *Central Newbury Car Auctions v Unity Finance* [1957] 1 Q.B. 371. On the role of the vehicle registration document, see, I. Davies "Registration Documents and Certification of Title of Motor Vehicles" [2001] J.B.L. 489. See also the comments of Rix LJ in *Kulkarni v Manor Credit (Davenham) Ltd* [2010] EWCA Civ. 69 at [38].

40 [1982] R.T.R. 417.

A mercantile agent in possession of the vehicle itself might well be able to confer good title on an innocent purchaser, but the sale to the latter must occur whilst the mercantile agent is still in possession. Imagine a mercantile agent who obtains possession of the goods (perhaps by borrowing them from the owner) and who shows them to X, an innocent prospective purchaser. The mercantile agent then will not confer good title on X under s.2 of the Factors Act if he does not make the contract of sale with X until after he has returned the goods to their true owner.[41]

The mercantile agent must be in possession of the goods or documents of title in his capacity as a mercantile agent

5-013 The car owner who leaves his car with a garage for repairs to be carried out does not consent to the garage having possession in its capacity as a mercantile agent (i.e. as a dealer). Therefore the garage cannot confer good title under s.2 of the Factors Act. A case which illustrates this point neatly is *Staffs Motor Guarantee Ltd v British Wagon Ltd*[42] where a lorry was sold to the defendant finance company for the purposes of letting the vehicle back to the dealer under a hire-purchase agreement. During this time possession of the lorry remained with the dealer who then sold the lorry on to a third party. When the dealer failed to make the payments due under the hire-purchase agreement, the finance company sought to recover the vehicle. The third party sought to rely upon, inter alia, s.2(1) of the Factors Act. The court rejected this argument stating that at the time of the disposition to the third party, the dealer was in possession of the lorry not as a mercantile agent but as a hirer under the hire-purchase agreement. This was sufficient to reject the s.2 defence.[43]

The mercantile agent must be in possession of the goods or documents of title with the consent of the owner.

5-014 The consent is presumed in the absence of evidence to the contrary and withdrawal of consent is of no effect until that withdrawal is brought to the notice of the person taking the goods.[44] The fact that consent was obtained by a trick or by fraud is irrelevant so long as the consent was given to the agent in his capacity as a mercantile agent. For the consent to be operative it must be such as to clothe the agent with apparent authority to sell the goods. This would occur in the case of a second-hand car only if the owner consented to the dealer having possession of not only the car but also of the registration book and the ignition key. Two cases illustrate the point. In *Pearson v Rose and Young*[45] the owner left his car with a dealer with instructions for the latter not to sell it but to see what offers could be obtained for it. The owner did not intend to leave the registration document but showed it to the dealer who arranged a

41 *Beverley Acceptances v Oakley* [1982] R.T.R. 417.
42 [1934] 2 K.B. 305.
43 Contrast the approach under s.24 of the Sale of Goods Act 1979.
44 Factors Act s.2(3) and 2(4).
45 [1951] 1 K.B. 275.

trick whereby the owner was called away on an imaginary emergency thereby forgetting the registration document. The dealer sold the car. The dealer was in possession of the car with consent and in his capacity as a mercantile agent, since the possession was with a view to an eventual sale, but he was not in possession of the registration document with the consent of the owner. As regards the registration document, it was not a case of obtaining consent by a trick; he had obtained the possession by a trick but he had obtained no consent at all to the possession.

This case was followed in *Stadium Finance v Robbins*[46] where the owner left his car with a dealer with instructions to see what offers could be obtained for it. He retained the ignition key though he accidentally left the registration document locked in the glove compartment. The dealer supplied his own key, found the registration document and sold the car. It was held that the owner had not clothed the dealer with apparent authority since he had retained the ignition key and not consented to the dealer having possession of the registration document. In each of these cases, therefore, the innocent purchaser acquired no title to the car which still belonged to the original owner. This was extremely harsh on the innocent purchaser who bought goods in good faith from a mercantile agent and who could not reasonably have suspected that anything was wrong.

Sometimes the ownership of goods is split. This occurs for example when goods are pledged as security for a loan. The pledgor gives the pledgee (the lender) some rights but does not part with all rights of ownership. The pledgor and pledgee together combine to constitute "the owner". Someone in possession with the consent of both can be said to be in possession "with consent of the owner". *Lloyds Bank v Bank of America*[47] involved dealings not with goods but with documents of title. The owner, a mercantile agent, pledged bills of lading with Lloyds Bank. Lloyds Bank released the bills back to him so that he could sell them and thereby obtain the money to pay off the loan from the bank. However, instead of selling them, he pledged them, without authority from Lloyds, with the Bank of America. It was held that all the requirements of s.2 of the Factors Act were complied with including the requirement that the mercantile agent be in possession of goods or of the documents of title with the consent of "the owner". Therefore the Bank of America took its title entirely free from the interest of Lloyds Bank. Thus Lloyds Bank lost its security.

The mercantile agent in disposing of the goods must have been acting in the ordinary course of business of a mercantile agent.

Arguably, selling a second-hand car without an ignition key or registration document would not be acting in the ordinary course of business.[48] This was taken one step further in 5-015

46 [1962] 2 Q.B. 664.

47 [1938] 2 K.B. 147.

48 This was the view adopted in both the *Pearson* case and the *Stadium Finance* case, although has been questioned by Chapman J in *Astley Industrial Trust Ltd v Miller* [1968] 2 All E.R. 36. What if the car, minus the registration document, was sold at a price which reflected the absence of the document? Logically, this ought to be within the ordinary course of business, although such a disposition would presumably be strong evidence to suggest that the third party purchaser was not bona fides and without notice.

Stadium Finance v Robbins[49] where it was held that this requirement was not complied with. Willmer LJ said:[50]

> **"A sale involving delivery to the hirer of the car without its registration book would not in my judgment be in the ordinary course of business. Following Pearson's case, I think the same applies to a sale involving delivery. . .of a registration book obtained by larceny or fraud or other unlawful means."**

On the other hand, the agent does not have to have been acting within the ordinary course of his own particular business or even within the normal course of business of his particular type of trade. It is sufficient that he was acting within the ordinary course of business of mercantile agents generally. The mercantile agent in *Oppenheimer v Attenborough*[51] was a diamond broker. Without authority he pledged the diamonds entrusted to him. Although diamond brokers do not ordinarily have authority to pledge diamonds in their possession it was held that the broker had acted in the ordinary course of business of a mercantile agent. The test for the disposition therefore is objective, i.e. whether it is in the ordinary course of business for mercantile agents generally. The pledgee therefore obtained good title to the diamonds.

The principle, that the disposition of a car where its logbook is obtained through a trick will be outside the usual course of business, is difficult to reconcile with the approach taken in *Oppenheimer v Attenborough*. The basis for the decision in *Oppenheimer* was the issue of how the disposition appeared to the third-party purchaser, hence the need for an objective approach to the ordinary course of business of mercantile agents generally. This seems to be in conflict with the approach of the court in *Pearson* and *Stadium Finance*, where the presence of the logbook (obtained through a trick) was ignored for the purposes of ascertaining whether the disposition was in the ordinary course of business. This approach is perhaps difficult to support. In the case of a mercantile agent who obtains possession of the registration document to a vehicle through a trick or who supplies his own ignition key in order to sell the vehicle, it is difficult to see why such a sale would not be in the ordinary course of business for a mercantile agent. Certainly, from the third party's point of view there would not necessarily be anything out of the ordinary regarding the disposition. As noted above, the impact of these two decisions is extremely harsh on the innocent purchaser.

---

49 [1962] 2 Q.B. 664.

50 [1962] 2 Q.B. 664 at 675.

51 [1908] 1 K.B. 221.

The person taking the goods must have taken them in good faith without notice of the agent's lack of authority

The burden of proof lies on him to prove that he was in good faith, etc.[52] He will find it difficult to do this in circumstances where he is "put upon notice". An example can be found in the judgment of Lord Alverstone CJ in *Oppenheimer v Attenborough*:[53] 5-016

> **"there may be particular agents, such for instance as auctioneers, by whom a pledge would be such a departure from the ordinary course of their business as to put the pledgee upon notice."**

We have already seen the difficulties caused by the disposition of motor vehicles without, for example, its logbook or registration key on the question of whether the disposition was in the ordinary course of business for a mercantile agent. It may be suggested that where such a disposition occurs a more logical approach would be to regard the lack of a registration book (or ignition key) as a matter which goes towards the bona fides, or lack thereof, of the third-party purchaser.

Market Overt

Until 1995 there was a statutory rule in s.22(1) of the Sale of Goods Act that a sale by a trader in a market overt (i.e. a shop in the City of London or an open market) passed good title to an innocent purchaser even if the trader did not have title to the goods. This in effect, allowed stolen goods to be sold to an innocent third party purchaser who would gain good title to the goods to the detriment of the original owner.[54] The rule was abolished, quite rightly, by the Sale of Goods (Amendment) Act 1994 which repealed s.22(1) of the Sale of Goods Act.[55] 5-017

Sale Under a Voidable Title

Section 23 of the Sale of Goods Act provides: 5-018

52 *Heap v Motorists Advisory Agency* [1923] 1 K.B. 577.

53 [1908] 1 K.B. 221 at 226.

54 Interestingly, the Twelfth Report of the Law Reform Committee (1966) Cmnd. 2958 recommended amending this exception so as to broaden the scope of the provision to all retail sales. This was, unsurprisingly given the ability of the exception to confer good title in stolen goods onto a bona fide third party purchaser, never acted upon.

55 See generally, the Consultation Paper, "Transfer of Title: ss.21–26 of the Sale of Goods Act 1979" (1994).

> **"Where the seller of goods has a voidable title to them, but his title has not been avoided at the time of the sale, the buyer acquires a good title to the goods, provided he buys them in good faith and without notice of the seller's defect of title."**

A voidable title is less than perfect and yet s.23 allows a seller with a voidable title to confer a perfect title upon an innocent purchaser. A void title on the other hand is no title at all and an innocent purchaser who buys from someone with a void title can derive no benefit from s.23 (although, of course, he might acquire good title by virtue of some other exception to the nemo dat principle).

What is a voidable title and how it differs from a void title can best be shown by an example: A owns some goods which he sells to B who in turn sells them to C. If the first contract (i.e. between A and B) is valid then title passes from A to B. If it is void for any reason, then it is no contract at all and no ownership passes to B. If it is voidable then it is initially valid but can be avoided (set aside) later. Under a voidable contract ownership passes to B in the normal way but will pass back to A if and when the contract is later avoided. The most common example of a voidable contract is one where a party has by making a misrepresentation induced the other party to enter the contract. This gives the latter (the innocent party) the right subsequently to avoid the contract.[56] In our example, if B has induced A to sell him the goods by making a misrepresentation, then B will acquire only a voidable title. A will have the right to set the contract aside and to demand the return of the goods. If however, B sells the goods to C before A finds out that he has been duped, then C (provided he was innocent) will get a perfect title by virtue of s.23 and A will therefore be unable to recover the goods.

5-019 Although a misrepresentation by B can render the contract between A and B voidable, there can be present some factor which renders that contract completely void. The difficulties have arisen mainly in cases where B has misrepresented to A his (B's) identity. In these cases, the contract between A and B is void if the two following characteristics are both present:

(i) The buyer's identity was a vital factor for the seller (A) in deciding to make the contract.

(ii) The seller when making the contract was intending to deal with someone other than B.

In *Cundy v Lindsay*[57] the seller, Lindsay, received a letter from a rogue called Blenkarn from an address at 37, Wood Street, Cheapside. The letter ordered some goods and was signed by Blenkarn in such a way that the signature looked like "Blenkiron & Co". Lindsay knew of a reputable firm Blenkiron & Co who traded from 123, Wood Street. Without checking Blenkiron's address, Lindsay despatched the goods to "Messrs.Blenkiron & Co, 37, Wood Street". Blenkarn

56 See Ch.6.
57 (1878) 3 App. Cas. 459.

received the goods but never paid for them and sold them to Cundy who knew nothing of his fraud. The House of Lords held that the contract between Lindsay and Blenkarn was void and that therefore the goods still belonged to Lindsay.

Cundy v Lindsay involved a transaction conducted through the post. In a contract made between parties face-to-face, the seller will find it difficult to prove that to him the identity of the buyer was a vital factor in deciding to make the contract. In the absence of strong evidence to the contrary, the law presumes that in face-to-face agreements the seller is prepared to deal with the person in front of him whoever that may be. This is particularly so in the case of a shopkeeper. In *Phillips v Brooks*[58] a rogue called North entered a jeweller's shop, selected some items including a ring and asked to pay by cheque and to take the ring with him. The shopkeeper agreed to this after the rogue identified himself as Sir George Bullough. The rogue took the ring to Brooks, a firm of pawnbrokers, and pledged it with them for £350. The cheque given to the jeweller proved worthless and he sued the pawnbroker to recover the ring. It was held that the contract between the jeweller and the rogue was not void but merely voidable. Since it had not been set aside before the pawnbroker took the ring, the pawnbroker acquired good title to the ring. Of course, he did not get complete ownership for he did not buy the ring but the limited title he got was perfectly valid and he could enforce that against the jeweller.

Phillips v Brooks was followed by the Court of Appeal in *Lewis v Averay*.[59] Lewis advertised 5-020
his car for sale. A rogue responded to the advertisement. He told Lewis that he was Richard Green, a well-known film actor (which was untrue). They agreed on a price of £450 and after seeing "proof" of the buyer's identity as Richard Green (a pass for Pinewood Studios), Lewis agreed to accept a cheque. The rogue took the car and registration documents. The cheque was worthless. The rogue posed as Mr Lewis in selling the car to Averay, an innocent purchaser. The Court held that there was a contract between Lewis and the rogue and that therefore Averay now had perfect title to the car. Lord Denning MR said:[60]

> **"When a dealing is had between a seller like Mr Lewis and a person who is actually there present before him, then the presumption in law is that there is a contract, even though there is a fraudulent impersonation by the buyer representing himself as a different man than he is. There is a contract made with the very person there who is present in person. It is liable no doubt to be avoided for fraud but it is still a good contract. . ."**

In both the last cases, the innocent purchaser (the pawnbroker in *Phillips v Brooks*[61] and Mr Averay in *Lewis v Averay*[62]) acquired the goods before the contract between the original

58 [1919] 2 K.B. 243.
59 [1972] 1 Q.B. 198.
60 [1972] 1 Q.B. 198 at 207.
61 [1919] 2 K.B. 243.
62 [1972] 1 Q.B. 198.

owner and the rogue had been avoided. If, before the innocent purchaser bought the goods, the original owner had avoided his contract with the rogue, ownership in the goods would have reverted to the original owner. If this had happened the rogue could not have conferred title upon the innocent purchaser (unless under some other exception to the nemo dat principle) for the rogue would no longer have a voidable title.

The normal method of the original owner to "avoid" the contract is for him to inform the rogue that he does so. However, it is often impossible to locate the rogue. In this case the contract is avoided as soon as the original owner has done all that he reasonably can. *Car and Universal Finance v Caldwell*[63] was another case where a rogue bought a car and by fraud induced the seller to accept a cheque which proved to be worthless. On discovering the truth the seller immediately informed the police and the Automobile Association. It was held that this operated to avoid the contract. After this, but before the car or rogue had been traced, the rogue sold the car to an innocent purchaser. Since, at the time the rogue sold the car, his title had been avoided, it was held that the purchaser acquired no title under s.23.[64]

Although entirely pragmatic, it may be questioned why, as a matter of principle, communication of the seller's intention to avoid the contract, communicated only to a third party, i.e. the police, should have the effect of avoiding a contract. This rule is obviously designed to assist the original owner who having been deceived by a rogue is desperate to avoid the contract and reclaim the goods. Nevertheless, it is rather harsh on an innocent third party purchaser as their legal claim to goods bought in good faith depends upon (i) the speed with which the rogue sells the car on; and (ii) the speed with which the original owner takes steps to avoid the contract. This is particularly true in the (common) case where the original owner accepts a cheque as payment for the goods.[65]

Seller in Possession

5-021 Two provisions in two different statutes are almost identical, s.24 of the Sale of Goods Act and s.8 of the Factors Act 1889. Section 8 provides:

> **"Where a person, having sold goods, continues, or is, in possession of the goods or of the documents of title to the goods, the delivery or transfer by that person, or by a mercantile agent acting for him, of the goods or documents of title under any sale, pledge, or other disposition thereof, or under any agreement for sale, pledge or other disposition thereof, to any person receiving the same in good faith**

63 [1965] 1 Q.B. 535.

64 It is for the innocent third party purchaser to show that his purchase was made before the original owner avoided the contract: *Thomas v Heelas* [1988] C & F.L.R. 211.

65 The Twelfth Report of the Law Reform Committee (1966) Cmnd. 2958 called for actual communication to be required in order for the original owner to avoid the contract, see para.16.

and without notice of the previous sale, shall have the same effect as if the person making the delivery or transfer were expressly authorised by the owner of the goods to make the same."

This relates to the situation where A sells or agrees to sell goods to B and then later sells them to C. To whom do the goods belong? If under the contract between A and B property had not yet passed to B (see Ch.3), then A was still the owner when he sold to C. Still being the owner, A could pass that ownership to C. One has to examine the two contracts, B's and C's, and find out under which of them property was to pass first. If it is C's then C will be the owner.

Usually (i.e. in the case of a sale of specific goods in a deliverable state, see Ch.3), property will have passed first to B (i.e. at the time that he made his contract). In this case, following the nemo dat principle, B is now the owner; they were B's goods at the time A sold them to C and therefore A could not, without B's authority, confer title upon C. The result would be different, however, if C could show that C's contract with A fell within one of the exceptions to the nemo dat principle.

The statutory provisions in s.8 of the Factors Act and s.24 of the Sale of Goods Act constitute one of those exceptions and were designed specifically to help someone in C's position. In order for C to acquire good title under these provisions, a number of requirements must be fulfilled:

The seller must have been in possession of the goods or documents of title

The point here is that the first purchaser can safeguard himself by taking immediate delivery and not leaving the goods or documents of title with the seller. The seller's possession does not have to be a "personal possession". If they were in the possession of a warehouseman (or other agent) holding them on behalf of the seller, that is sufficient. In *City Fur Manufacturing Co v Fureenbond*[66] A owned some skins which were stored for him at an independent warehouse. A sold them to B who did not collect them. Later, A pledged them to C. On A's instructions the warehouseman handed them over to C who therefore acquired good title to the goods under s.25(1) of the Sale of Goods Act 1893 (now s.24 of the Sale of Goods Act 1979). 5-022

The nature of the seller's possession is immaterial. So if A sells to B who then decides to leave them for A to repair, A is a person who "having sold goods continues or is in possession of the goods": *Pacific Motor Auctions v Motor Credits*.[67] If A sells and delivers them to an innocent purchaser, the latter will acquire good title. It does not matter that A was at the time in possession in his capacity, not as a seller, but as a repairer. The decision of the Privy Council in *Pacific Motor Auctions v Motor Credits* necessitated the rejection of the previously accepted

66 [1937] 1 All E.R. 799.

67 [1965] A.C. 867.

approach. Under the principle in *Staffs Motor Guarantee Ltd v British Wagon Ltd*[68] it had been generally accepted that the question of capacity was vital to a successful defence based on s.24, i.e. that mere physical possession was in itself, insufficient and that it must be established that the seller was in possession as a seller.[69] The decision in Pacific Motor Auctions removed such considerations and was followed by the Court of Appeal in *Worcester Works Finance v Cooden Engineering*.[70] This position should be contrasted, however, with the situation where the seller was not in possession of the goods at the time of the sale to the first purchaser, but subsequently acquired possession of the goods as bailee of the first purchaser. In this situation, where the seller re-sells the goods to an innocent third party purchaser, s.24 is of no application.[71]

The subsequent purchaser must be "in good faith and without notice of the previous sale"

5–023 In *Worcester Works Finance v Cooden Engineering*[72] all the requirements of the section were fulfilled. X sold a car to Y (a car dealer) who in turn sold it to Z (a finance company). The reason for the sale by Y to Z was that Z at the same time accepted a hire-purchase proposal relating to the same car from M, a customer of Y's. Y (the car dealer) was fraudulent and two things occurred which ought not to have done. First, the cheque which Y had given X when Y took delivery of the car from X was dishonoured. Secondly, Y never gave possession of the car to his customer (M) as he should have done after the finance company (Z) had accepted the hire-purchase proposal. After Y's cheque to X was dishonoured, X (with Y's acquiescence) repossessed the car from Y's premises. At the time of this repossession by X the car clearly belonged to Z. This was because X had sold it to Y who had sold it to Z. It was held, however, that Y, in allowing X to repossess the car, was within the section. Having sold the car to Z, Y was a seller in possession of it. Since he had not delivered it to his customer (M) he had "continued" in possession (albeit wrongfully). His allowing X to repossess the car amounted to a "delivery or transfer" of it under a "disposition". This was because it amounted to a transfer back to X of property in the car (because Y's cheque had not been met) in return for X waiving any right to enforce payment from Y. At the time of the repossession, X was unaware of Y's sale to Z and thus, by repossessing the car with Y's acquiescence, X obtained ownership of it by virtue of s.25(1) of the 1893 Act (i.e. s.24 of the Sale of Goods Act 1979).

68 [1934] 2 K.B. 305.

69 This was approved by the Court of Appeal in *Eastern Distributors v Goldring* [1957] 2 Q.B. 600.

70 [1972] 1 Q.B. 210.

71 *Fadallah v Pollak* [2013] EWHC 3159 (QB).

72 [1972] 1 Q.B. 210.

Buyer in Possession

There is normally no problem because a buyer in possession of goods will usually in fact be the owner of them, i.e. property will have passed to him (see Ch.3). Being the owner, if he sells the goods he will be able to pass on that ownership to his purchaser. If he himself has not paid for them, then the person who sold him the goods will be able to sue him for the price but will have lost any chance of recovering the goods. 5-024

However, it is possible in some circumstances for the buyer to take delivery of the goods before property has passed to him. This is most likely where he agrees with the seller that property shall not pass to him until he has paid for them. This occurred in *Weiner v Gill*.[73] In this situation he cannot confer good title on the sub-purchaser unless that sale falls under an exception to the nemo dat principle.

The most likely exception is that contained in two almost identical statutory provisions, s.25 of the Sale of Goods Act and s.9 of the Factors Act 1889. The latter reads:

> **"Where a person, having bought or agreed to buy goods, obtains with the consent of the seller, possession of the goods or the documents of title to the goods, the delivery or transfer, by that person, or by a mercantile agent acting for him, of the goods or documents of title, under any sale, pledge, or other disposition thereof, to any person receiving the same in good faith and without notice of any lien or other right of the original seller in respect of the goods, shall have the same effect as if the person making the delivery or transfer were a mercantile agent in possession of the goods or documents of title with the consent of the owner".**

The requirements for the operation of this exception to the nemo dat principle are as follows:

The person selling (pledging, etc.) must be someone who has "bought or agreed to buy"

Someone who has taken only an option to buy has not "bought or agreed to buy". This excludes someone who has taken the goods on "sale or return" terms: *Edwards v Vaughan*.[74] For the same reason, someone hiring goods under a hire-purchase agreement is also excluded. Therefore if the hirer sells the goods, s.25 of the Sale of Goods Act and s.9 of the Factors Act will not operate to give his purchaser a good title. This is apparent from *Helby v Matthews*,[75] where someone 5-025

73 [1906] 2 K.B. 574, see para.3-015, above.

74 [1910] 26 T.L.R. 545.

75 [1895] A.C. 471.

who was hiring a piano on hire-purchase terms, sold it to an innocent purchaser. The House of Lords held that the hirer had not "bought or agreed to buy" the piano which therefore still belonged to the person from whom it had been hired. In the light of this decision it is easy to understand why hire-purchase has become popular with traders and finance companies as a means of supplying goods on credit.[76]

It has been held that a buyer under a conditional sale agreement is someone who "bought or agreed to buy": *Lee v Butler*.[77] However, that position has been radically altered by the Consumer Credit Act 1974. A buyer under a conditional sale agreement which is a consumer credit agreement within the meaning of the Act is for the purposes of s.25 of the Sale of Goods Act and s.9 of the Factors Act, not someone who has "bought or agreed to buy".[78]

We have already seen that someone with a voidable title can nevertheless transfer to an innocent purchaser a perfect title, provided he does so before his title is avoided. However, if the transaction falls within s.25 (or s.9 of the Factors Act), he can pass on a good title even after his voidable title has been avoided: *Newtons of Wembley v Williams*.[79] The reason is that, even though his title has been avoided, he is still someone who has "bought or agreed to buy" the goods. In *Newtons of Wembley v Williams* a rogue bought a car and persuaded the seller to accept a cheque. When the cheque was dishonoured the seller did all he could to trace the rogue and car and he informed the police. After this incident occurred but before the rogue was traced, the rogue took the car along to a market in Warren Street (where dealers commonly sold cars) and he sold it to an innocent purchaser. The Court of Appeal held that the innocent purchaser acquired good title under s.9 of the Factors Act.

The person selling the goods must have been a buyer "in possession", i.e. he must have obtained "with the consent of the seller, possession of the goods or documents of title to the goods"

5-026 Two principles derive from *Cahn v Pockett's Bristol Channel Steam Packet Co.*[80] First, it is sufficient that he obtains possession with the seller's consent and it is immaterial whether that consent is later withdrawn. Secondly, it is immaterial whether or not he had obtained possession before he made the contract with the innocent purchaser; it is sufficient that the possession was obtained before he transferred or delivered the goods or documents of title to the innocent purchaser. The facts were that B agreed to buy goods from S. S sent to B a bill of lading together with a bill of exchange.[81] B did not, as he should have done, sign and return the bill of

76 For full discussion of the distinction between hire-purchase and sale, see para.17-002, below.
77 [1893] 2 Q.B. 318, see Ch.18.
78 Consumer Credit Act 1974 Sch.4 and Sale of Goods Act s.25(2).
79 [1965] 1 Q.B. 560.
80 [1899] 1 Q.B. 643.
81 See Ch.3, para.3-022, above.

exchange. This meant that property did not pass to B.[82] However, B had already agreed to sell the goods to Cahn and, on receiving the documents from S, he transferred the bill of lading (the document of title to the goods) to Cahn. It was held that Cahn acquired good title to the goods by operation of s.25 of the Sale of Goods Act.

The question of whether the person selling had been a buyer "in possession" arose in *Four Point Garages Ltd v Carter*.[83] An innocent purchaser, Mr Carter, agreed to buy a new Ford Escort XR3i from X, a car dealer. X, who did not have one in stock, contracted to buy one from Four Point Garage. Under the terms of the contract, property in the car was not to transfer to X until he had paid Four Point Garage. Mr Carter paid X for the car. At X's request Four Point Garage delivered the car direct to Mr Carter, who believed that he would be taking delivery from X. X became insolvent without ever paying Four Point Garage. The latter claimed that the car was still theirs since X had never paid and property had therefore never passed to X. It was held, however, that Mr Carter had obtained good title under s.25. When Four Point Garage, at X's request, delivered direct to Mr Carter, it was exactly the same as if X had taken delivery from Four Point Garage and himself delivered the car to Mr Carter. In other words, X was deemed to have been a buyer "in possession" and deemed to have delivered the car to the innocent purchaser.

There must be a delivery or transfer of the goods or documents of title to the innocent sub-purchaser

Where documents of title are involved it will usually turn out that the buyer transfers to his sub-purchaser the same document of title which he received from his seller. This occurred in *Cahn v Pockett's*. The requirement is equally complied with if he receives a document of title from his seller and then transfers to the innocent sub-purchaser a different document of title relating to the same goods: *Mount v Jay*.[84] 5-027

The buyer in possession must have acted in the normal course of business of a mercantile agent

This may seem a little absurd since the buyer in possession may well not be a mercantile agent. It is, however, implicit in the closing words of both s.9 of the Factors Act and s.25 of the Sale of Goods Act. This was held to be so by the Court of Appeal in *Newtons of Wembley v Williams*.[85] The sale in that case (see above) was in fact in the ordinary course of business of a mercantile agent, since car dealers did commonly sell cars in Warren Street. 5-028

82 See s.19, considered at para.3-022, above
83 *The Times*, 19 November 1984.
84 [1960] 1 Q.B. 159.
85 [1965] 1 Q.B. 560.

The sub-purchaser must be bona fide and unaware that the original seller has any rights in respect of the goods

5-029 The seller's lien and other rights will be explained in Ch.12.

If any one of the above requirements is not fulfilled, the sub-purchaser will not acquire good title by virtue of the two sections under consideration. However, it is always possible that the person who sold him the goods later acquires the title to them. This can happen if, for example, the sub-purchaser bought the goods from someone who was hiring them on hire-purchase terms. Normally under a hire-purchase agreement as soon as the hirer pays off all moneys due under the agreement, the goods become the hirer's property. Thus if the hirer subsequently pays off all the remaining instalments, ownership will pass to the hirer and straight on to the purchaser from the hirer. This process is known as "feeding the title". It means that the purchaser from the hirer does eventually acquire good title, albeit somewhat delayed: *Butterworth v Kingsway Motors*.[86]

We have seen that s.25 of the Sale of Goods Act and s.9 of the Factors Act typically apply where a seller lets his buyer take possession but retains property (title to the goods) until the buyer pays the price. There is then a risk that the buyer, before he has paid and therefore before he has acquired title, sells and delivers the goods to a sub-purchaser who is unaware that he is buying from someone who has no title. The theory behind the sections is that, if an owner of goods agrees to sell them to someone and retains title but nevertheless lets the buyer have possession, that owner must bear the consequences (i.e. loss of title) if the buyer then sells and delivers the goods to the innocent sub-purchaser. Thus the sections give good title to the innocent sub-purchaser. Typically then they operate to defeat the title of the unpaid seller (let us call him C) who has entrusted his goods to a buyer who, without paying C, has in turn sold them to an innocent purchaser. In *National Mutual General Insurance Association Ltd v Jones*[87] the issue was whether the sections could operate to defeat the title of someone much earlier in the chain of events than C. Thieves had stolen a car and sold it to A who sold it to C (a car dealer), who sold it to D (another car dealer), who sold it to Jones. Jones claimed to have good title by virtue of the two sections, thereby defeating the title of the owner from whom the thieves had stolen the car. The House of Lords rejected this argument and held that the two sections could defeat the title only of an owner who entrusted possession of his goods to a buyer. Therefore, the two sections could not take title away from the original owner from whom the goods had been stolen.

86 [1954] 1 W.L.R. 1286, see para.7-008, below.

87 [1988] 2 W.L.R. 952.

Disposition of Motor Vehicles Under the Hire Purchase Act 1964 Pt III[88]

Part III is all that remains of the 1964 Act, the rest having been repealed. Section 27(1) of the Hire Purchase Act 1964 lays down the scope of the exception and provides as follows: 5-030

> **"This section applies where a motor vehicle has been bailed or (in Scotland) hired under a hire-purchase agreement, or has been agreed to be sold under a conditional sale agreement, and, before the property in the vehicle has become vested in the debtor, he disposes of the vehicle to another person."**

The section continues:

> **"(2) Where the disposition referred to in subsection (1) above is to a private purchaser, and he is a purchaser of the motor vehicle in good faith, without notice of the hire-purchase or conditional sale agreement (the 'relevant agreement') that disposition shall have effect as if the creditor's title to the vehicle has been vested in the debtor immediately before that disposition.**
>
> **. . .**
>
> **(3) Where the person to whom the disposition referred to in subsection (1) above is made (the 'original purchaser') is a trade or finance purchaser, then if the person who is the first private purchaser of the motor vehicle after that disposition (the 'first private purchaser') is a purchaser of the vehicle in good faith without notice of the relevant agreement, the disposition of the vehicle to the first private purchaser shall have effect as if the title of the creditor to the vehicle had been vested in the debtor immediately before he disposed of it to the original purchaser."**

This provision is drafted in complex (and extensive) language, despite the fact that it is of application only in very limited circumstances. Nevertheless, the intent behind the exception is relatively straightforward. We have just seen that a hirer under a hire-purchase agreement is not someone who has "bought or agreed to buy" for the purposes of s.25 of the Sale of Goods Act. This meant that an innocent purchaser could buy a car from such a hirer only to discover at some later date that the car did not belong to him after all. The owner could reclaim the car and was entitled to come along and seize it. Part III of the 1964 Act was designed to protect the

88 See generally, I. Davies "Wrongful Dispositions of Motor Vehicles—a legal quagmire" [1995] J.B.L. 36.

innocent purchaser in this situation.[89] The purchaser acquires good title providing the following requirements are fulfilled:

The seller must be someone who is hiring the vehicle under a hire-purchase agreement or buying it under a conditional sale agreement

5-031 The nature of these two types of agreement has already been explained in Ch.1. *Kulkarni v Manor Credit (Davenham) Ltd*[90] is a useful reminder of the fact that if the seller sells the vehicle on to an innocent third-party purchaser before becoming a hirer under a hire purchase agreement, s.27 is of no application.

In *Shogun Finance v Hudson*[91] a rogue took possession of a Mitsubishi Shogun under hire purchase terms using a stolen driving licence as proof of identity and address. The rogue then sold the vehicle on to an innocent third-party purchaser, Mr Hudson, and disappeared. The finance company, as legal owner of the vehicle, sued Mr Hudson in conversion. The House of Lords, upholding the decision of the Court of Appeal held that the contract was void for mistake as the finance company intended to deal with the person named on the hire-purchase documents, and not with the rogue. As the rogue was therefore not "someone who is hiring the goods under a hire-purchase agreement" the s.27 of the Hire Purchase Act did not apply. In order for a subsequent purchaser without notice to gain title under this provision, that purchaser must be dealing with the individual named on the hire-purchase documents. This would appear to represent a significant restriction on the ambit of the section as it removes from the scope of s.27 any situation where a rogue impersonates another in order to gain possession of a vehicle on either hire-purchase or conditional sale terms.[92]

The purchaser must be a private purchaser

5-032 Section 29(2) creates a statutory definition of a trade purchaser in the following terms:

89 In *Eastern Distributors v Goldring* [1957] 2 Q.B. 600 at 614, Devlin J summed up the problem in saying: "It is very hard on the defendant. . .his fate is a common one when hire purchase agreements are concerned and is now one of the regular ways in which unsuspecting buyers are deceived by what they take to be ownership".

90 [2010] EWCA 69. For commentary, see L. Merrett, "Is possession nine tenths of the law in the sale of goods?" [2010] C.L.J. 236. See further, para.5-012, above.

91 [2003] 3 W.L.R. 1371.

92 For commentary on the injustice of this decision upon the subsequent purchaser, see C. Elliot, "No Justice for Innocent Purchasers of Dishonestly obtained Goods: Shogun Finance v Hudson" [2004] J.B.L. 381.

> **"In this Part of this Act, 'trade or finance purchaser' means a purchaser who, at the time of the disposition made to him, carries on a business which consists, wholly or partly—**
> **(a) of purchasing motor vehicles for the purpose of offering or exposing them for sale, or**
> **(b) of providing finance by purchasing motor vehicles for the purpose of bailing or (in Scotland) hiring them under hire-purchase agreements or agreeing to sell them under conditional sale agreements and 'private purchaser' means a purchaser who, at the time of the disposition made to him, does not carry on any such business."**

Put simply, a private purchaser is someone who is not a dealer (or finance house) carrying on a business in the motor trade. Dealers do not need the same protection since they know the importance of checking to see whether the seller is the owner of the car.[93] Thus a car dealer does not obtain the protection and that is so even if he is buying the vehicle for his own private purposes and not for his business purposes: *Stevenson v Beverley Bentinck*.[94]

The operation of this distinction can be seen in the recent decision of the Court of Appeal in *GE Capital Bank Ltd v Rushton*.[95] GE Capital Bank lent money to a car dealer, T&T Motors, for the purposes of purchasing stock. The title in the cars was to remain vested in GE Capital until the loan was repaid in full. T&T Motors ultimately sold the cars purchased under this stocking plan to Rushton, who was not a car dealer but admitted to buying the cars with a view to resale and profit. Rushton then sold one of the vehicles, a Volkswagen Golf, to Jenkins. Upon discovering the sale of the vehicles GE Capital, who had not been repaid the loan, sued Rushton and Jenkins in conversion. The Court of Appeal held that Rushton was trade purchaser under s. 27(2) on the basis that:[96]

> **". . .he clearly had decided to purchase them as a business venture with a view to selling them at a profit. In those circumstances purchasing the vehicles from T & T was no less a step in carrying on a business of purchasing motor vehicles for the purpose of offering**

93 See previous discussion of H.P.I. Ltd. This is accurate despite the availability of such a service to members of the general public.

94 [1976] 1 W.L.R. 483.

95 [2006] 1 W.L.R. 899. For commentary, see J. Chuah, "Definition of private purchaser under section 27 Hire Purchase Act 1964" (2006) F. & C.L. February, 6–7.

96 At [40], per Moore-Bick LJ. Curiously, the earlier decision in *Beverley Bentinck* appears not to have been considered, although authorities under equivalent provisions in the Money Lenders Act (ss.2 and 6); the Trade Descriptions Act (s.1(1)); the Unfair Contract Terms Act (s.12(1)); and the Sale of Goods Act (s.14(2)) were considered.

or exposing them for sale than it would have been if he had already prepared a showroom or forecourt to receive them."

5-033 Accordingly Rushton was liable in conversion to the true owner, GE Capital Bank. Jenkins was not liable in respect of the Volkswagen Golf as s.27 had conferred good title upon him.[97]

Thus, it is possible for Pt III of the 1964 Act to operate even though the hirer sells the car to a dealer. Although the Act gives no protection to a dealer, it will give protection to the first private purchaser providing that he was bona fide, etc.[98] So if the dealer sells the car to an innocent private purchaser, the latter will acquire good title, as indeed did Jenkins in *GE Capital Bank Ltd v Rushton*.

An interesting case on the meaning of trade or finance purchaser under s.29 of the HPA is *Welcome Financial Services Ltd v Nine Regions Ltd*.[99] Welcome Financial Services supplied a Ford KA on hire purchase terms to a consumer who then proceeded, almost immediately, to use the vehicle as security for a loan with Nine Regions Ltd. The consumer signed a bill of sale[100] which transferred property in the vehicle to Nine Regions Ltd and entered into a loan agreement. When the consumer defaulted on that loan Nine Regions seized the car and it was sold at auction. The court held that Nine Regions was not a private purchaser because it had purchased the vehicle with the intention of selling it in the event of the customer defaulting on the loan. Consequently, Nine Regions could not rely on the protection offered by s.27 HPA.

The goods involved must be a motor vehicle

5-034 Thus the decision would be the same today, if the facts of *Helby v Matthews*[101] (a piano) were again to come before the courts.

The private purchaser must be bona fide and unaware of any relevant hire-purchase or conditional sale agreement

5-035 In *Barker v Bell*[102] the private purchaser of a motor car believed what he was told by the vendor, namely that the latter had bought the car under a hire-purchase agreement from B finance company. The vendor showed him a receipt from B finance company across which was written "final payment". In fact, unknown to the purchaser, the vendor was hiring the car under a

97 Although he was liable for conversion of the other vehicles under the stocking plan by virtue of him having assisted Rushton in the removal and storage of the vehicles.

98 By virtue of s.27(3).

99 [2010] EWHC B3 (Mercantile), [2012] C.C.L.R. 3.

100 See generally, G.S. McBain, "Repealing the Bills of Sale Acts" [2011] J.B.L. 475.

101 [1895] A.C. 471.

102 [1971] 1 W.L.R. 983.

hire-purchase agreement with A finance company. It was held that the purchaser was unaware of any relevant hire-purchase agreement. Lord Denning MR said:[103]

> **". . .a purchaser is only affected by notice if he has actual notice that the car is on hire purchase. He is not affected merely by being told that it was previously on hire purchase which has now been paid off."**

The purchaser therefore obtained good title to the car.

The test of the private purchaser's bona fides and unawareness of the hire-purchase agreement is a subjective one. It is not one of whether the private purchaser ought to have been suspicious or less gullible. It is purely a subjective question of honesty. Good faith is equated with honesty and bad faith with dishonesty. Also, the relevant time to apply the test is when the private purchaser makes his purchase. Thus a private purchaser who had suspicions that the motor vehicle was the subject of a hire-purchase agreement but whose suspicions had at the time of the purchase been laid to rest was a purchaser in good faith without notice of the hire-purchase agreement, who therefore obtained good title: *Dodds v Yorkshire Bank Finance Ltd*.[104]

The transaction under which the private purchaser buys the goods must be an ordinary sale, or hire-purchase or conditional sale agreement

Thus where the private purchaser takes the motor vehicle in settlement of a debt, s.27 will not offer any protection: *VFS Financial Services Ltd v JF Plant Tyres Ltd*.[105] Similarly, the 1964 Act gives no protection in the event of a pledge. 5-036

Having looked at the requirements, it remains to point out that there are no financial limits on the operation of the 1964 Act. It is immaterial for how much the car was being hired or bought or how much credit was involved. Equally it is immaterial whether the hirer or buyer was a body corporate.[106]

The 1964 Act, then, gives protection to a bona fide private purchaser who buys a motor vehicle unaware that the seller is hiring or buying it under a hire-purchase or conditional sale agreement. For example, O supplies a car to P on hire-purchase terms and P, before he has finished paying off his instalments, sells the car to a bona fide purchaser, Q, who is unaware of

103 [1971] 1 W.L.R. 983 at 986.

104 [1992] C.C.L.R. 92.

105 [2013] EWHC 346. This should be contrasted with a sale on part-exchange terms, where the Act would apply to protect the private purchaser.

106 Contrast the approach of the Consumer Credit Act 1974 (which regulates both hire-purchase and conditional sale agreements) prior to the amendments introduced by the Consumer Credit Act 2006.

the hire-purchase agreement. The Act gives good title to Q, but only as against O. Thus, if O were not the owner but had, for example stolen the car (or bought it from someone who had stolen it) then the true owner (i.e. from whom the car was stolen) will still have good title (i.e. unless one of the other exceptions to the nemo dat principle applies).

Finally, it is now possible for a buyer (whether a trade purchaser or a private purchaser) to have a check carried out to discover whether a motor vehicle is subject to an existing finance agreement, has ever been an insurance "write-off" or has been stolen.[107]

Sale Under a Common Law or Statutory Power

5-037 Certain persons are given the right by common law or statute in certain circumstances to sell the goods of another. Examples are a pawnbroker selling the pledgor's goods when the loan is not repaid and an innkeeper selling the guest's property when the bill is not paid. When a sale is made under a common law or statutory power the purchaser acquires good title to the goods.[108]

It is also to be noted that under the Torts (Interference with Goods) Act 1977 a person such as a repairer, improver, valuer or storer has the right to sell uncollected goods. He must first serve upon the bailor (i.e. the person who left the goods for repair, treatment or valuation, etc.) a notice containing certain details of the intended sale. If after expiry of the notice the goods remain uncollected and the right of sale is duly exercised, the purchaser will obtain good title as against the bailor. However, if the bailor was not the owner but had, for example, stolen them before leaving them for repair or treatment, etc. then the true owner will still have good title (i.e. unless one of the other exceptions to the nemo dat principle applies).

Sale Under a Court Order

5-038 The High Court has power in certain circumstances to order the sale of goods. If it exercises this power, the purchaser acquires good title, notwithstanding any claim by the original owner.[109]

Effect of Writ of Execution

5-039 When judgment is given in court for a sum of damages, the defendant usually pays up. If he does not, the successful claimant can enforce the judgment by causing a writ of control (formerly a writ of execution) to be issued. It is then the enforcement officer's duty to carry it out. He has the legal right to seize enough of the defendant's goods to satisfy the judgment. He has

107 See para.5-005, above.

108 Sale of Goods Act s.21(2)(a).

109 Sale of Goods Act, s.21(2)(b).

this right in relation to goods which the defendant owns at the time the enforcement officer receives the writ. Anyone who after that time purchases goods from the defendant therefore runs the risk of having them seized. However, the Courts Act 2003 protects the purchaser from this provided that when he bought the goods he was bona fide and unaware of any writ of execution relating to the defendant.[110]

General Reading

I. Davies "Registration Documents and Certification of Title of Motor Vehicles" [2001] J.B.L. 489.

I. Davies "Wrongful Dispositions of Motor Vehicles—a legal quagmire" [1995] J.B.L. 36.

I. Davies, "Transferability and Sale of Goods" (1987) 7 Legal Studies 1.

C. Elliot, "No Justice for Innocent Purchasers of Dishonestly obtained Goods: Shogun Finance v Hudson" [2004] J.B.L. 381 at 381–387.

QC, "Sale of a Motor Vehicle by Hire-Purchaser" (1954) 17 M.L.R. 238.

L. Merrett, "The Importance of Delivery and Possession in the Passing of Title" [2008] C.L.J. 376.

L.A. Rutherford and L.A. Todd, "Section 25(1) of the Sale of Goods Act 1893: The reluctance to create a mercantile agency" [1979] C.L.J. 346.

P.J. Schofield, "The notionally absent registration book" [1963] J.B.L. 344.

A. Tettenborn, "Transfer of chattels by non-owners: still an open problem" [2018] C.L.J. 151.

110 See Sch.7, para 8.

6

Misrepresentation

General Introduction

The seller who makes a false statement in connection with the supply of goods can find he is liable in one or more ways. These include the following: First, the seller may be liable to a conviction under the Consumer Protection from Unfair Trading Regulations 2008 which implement the Unfair Commercial Practices Directive 2005 (and replace, inter alia, the Trade Descriptions Act 1968). Secondly, he may be liable to his purchaser under the new scheme of private redress introduced by the Consumer Protection from Unfair Trading Regulations 2008. These will be considered in Ch.16. Thirdly, he may be liable to his purchaser for a breach of a term of his contract—a matter to be considered in the next chapter. Fourthly, the purchaser may have a remedy for misrepresentation. 6–001

What Amounts to an Actionable Misrepresentation?

A misrepresentation is a false statement of fact made by one party (or his agent) which is intended to and does induce the other party to enter the contract. A statement may be made in writing, orally or even by conduct, for example, by making the goods tell a lie about themselves as in the case where the seller patched up a crack in the barrel of a cannon so as to make it appear unfractured: *Horsfall v Thomas*.[1] When considering whether a misrepresentation has 6–002

1 (1862) 1 H. & C. 90.

been made and if it has, its nature, the role of the court is to determine what a reasonable person would have understood as being represented, whether from the express words used or as being inferred from the words and conduct of the representor.[2] This includes an analysis of the characteristics of the representee. For example, whether the representee is a consumer or an experienced business organisation.[3]

A mere statement of opinion, provided the opinion is genuinely held, is not a statement of fact: *Bisset v Wilkinson*.[4] However, a statement of opinion by someone in a position to know the facts will be regarded as a statement of fact. In *Smith v Land & House Property Corporation*[5] the seller of some premises described them as "let to Mr Frederick Fleck (a most desirable tenant)". In fact it had been only with difficulty that the seller had managed to get rent from Mr Fleck, who was still in arrears. It was held that the seller made a misrepresentation.

A mere trader's puff is not a statement of fact. Thus the car dealer who describes a second-hand vehicle as "a beautiful looking car" makes no misrepresentation. However, the distinction between a trader's puff and a statement having legal significance is a fine one. The car dealer who tells his purchaser "It's a good little bus. I would stake my life on it", will not be able to claim either that it was a mere trader's puff or that it was a mere statement of opinion. After all, the dealer is in a position to know whether the car has any serious defects.

6–003 The statement need not be made fraudulently. Although the remedies available may be less extensive, a statement made innocently can nevertheless amount to a misrepresentation, as in *Leaf v International Galleries*[6] where the sellers innocently stated that a painting was by Constable, a statement which they genuinely believed.

A statement is not an actionable misrepresentation unless it induces the other party to enter the contract. It does not have to be the only thing which persuaded him to do so but it does have to have been a factor in influencing him. If he placed no reliance at all upon it, he cannot complain of a misrepresentation. In *J.E.B. Fasteners Ltd v Marks Bloom*[7] it was said that the misrepresentation must play a real and substantial, but not necessarily a decisive, part in causing the other party to enter into the contract.[8]

Thus in *Horsfall v Thomas*,[9] above, the purchaser lost his case because he had not bothered to examine the canon before purchasing it and therefore was unaware of the misrepresentation.[10] Equally, if the purchaser, though aware of the statement, chooses to

2 *MCI WorldCom International Inc v Primus Telecommunications Inc* [2004] EWCA Civ. 957 at [30]; *Raiffeisen Zentralbank Österreich AG v The Royal Bank of Scotland Plc* 2010 EWHC 1392 (Comm) at [83].

3 *Raiffeisen Zentralbank Österreich AG v The Royal Bank of Scotland Plc* [2010] EWHC 1392 (Comm) at [81]. See also, *Springwell Navigation Corporation v JP Morgan Chase Bank* [2010] EWCA Civ. 1221 at [121].

4 [1927] A.C. 177.

5 (1884) 28 Ch D. 7.

6 [1950] 2 K.B. 86.

7 [1983] 1 All E.R. 583.

8 [1983] 1 All E.R. 583 at 590. This formulation was echoed in *Spice Girls Ltd v Aprilia World Service BV* [2002] EWCA Civ. 15 at [70] where the Court of Appeal suggested that the misrepresentation must be a "material inducement".

9 (1862) 1 H & C 90.

10 See also, *Ex parte Biggs* (1859) 28 L.J.Ch. 50 and *Renault UK Ltd v FleetPro Technical Services Ltd* [2007] EWHC 2541 (QB) (a misrepresentation made to a computer system). Consider the approach of

place no reliance upon it, he cannot subsequently complain of it. This would be the position if a potential purchaser, on being told that a car was mechanically sound, nevertheless insisted, before buying, on having his own mechanic examine it. Where, however, the buyer does not insist upon having an independent examination of the goods, the fact that he had the opportunity to discover the truth (i.e. discover the misrepresentation) will not necessarily prevent a remedy for misrepresentation where it would be unreasonable to expect an individual to make such an inspection.[11] In *Redgrave v Hurd*[12] Baggallay LJ stated: "the mere fact that he does not avail himself of the opportunity of testing the accuracy of the representation made to him will not enable the opposing party to succeed on that ground". The justification for this principle is straightforward. Where a person makes a statement intending it to be relied on, he cannot subsequently complain when it is, in fact, relied upon.

It is also clear that where a buyer places reliance on a misrepresentation, the fact that he had been given information casting doubt over the validity of the representation made by the seller will not necessarily prevent the buyer's action from succeeding. In *Flack v Pattinson*[13] the claimant (Flack) brought an action for misrepresentation arguing that Pattinson, acting as agent for Queensgate Industries Limited, had made a material misrepresentation which induced him to purchase a vintage racing car. Pattinson had told the claimant that the car in question was "Innes Ireland's 2.5 Grand Prix car". This was, in fact, not true as although the car had been owned by Innes Ireland, it had only been raced by Innes Ireland with a 1.5 litre engine. A motor engineer with knowledge of the car had informed Flack that the car "had always been a Formula 2 car, and not a Formula 1 car, i.e. it was a 1.5 litre car". Despite this warning, Flack nevertheless purchased the car for £180,000. At first instance, the court held that Flack was entitled to recover damages for misrepresentation since Pattinson had either known his statement to be untrue, or should have known it to be untrue. The defendant appealed, arguing that given the warning made to Flack, the misrepresentation made by Pattinson could not have been relied upon. The Court of Appeal rejected this argument, citing Lord Blackburn in *Smith v Chadwick*:[14] 6-004

> **"I think that if it is proved that the defendants with a view to induce the plaintiff to enter into a contract made a statement to the plaintiff of such a nature as would be likely to induce a person to enter into a contract, and it is proved that the plaintiff did enter into the contract, it is a fair inference of fact that he was induced to do so by the statement."**

s.14(2) (implied term as to satisfactory quality) in respect of pre-contractual examinations discussed in Ch.7 below.

11 See *Smith v Eric S Bush* [1990] 1 A.C. 831 where the House of Lords held that it was unreasonable to expect the purchasers of a private property to commission an independent survey of the property (having relied upon a valuation commissioned by the lender (mortgage company)).

12 (1881) 20 Ch D. 1 at 23.

13 [2002] EWCA Civ. 1762, affirming [2001] All E.R. (D) 301 (December).

14 (1884) 9 App. Cas. 187 at 196.

Since the claimant could raise evidence that he wished to purchase a 2.5 litre (formula 1) car and not a 1.5 litre (formula 2) car,[15] the fact that a warning had been given by a third party was not sufficient to dissuade the court from finding that he had relied upon Pattinson's misrepresentation. Where, however, the claimant would have discovered the true state of affairs on reading the contract, he will not be able to claim that he was induced into entering that contract by a previous misrepresentation: *Peekay Intermark Ltd, Harish Pawani v Australia and New Zealand Banking Group Ltd.*[16]

Remedies

6–005 There are two possible remedies:

Rescission

6–006 A misrepresentation by one party makes the contract voidable at the option of the other. This means that the latter can rescind the contract. This involves the parties being returned to their positions as they were before the contract, i.e. the return of the price to the buyer and the goods to the seller. If the innocent party is the buyer and he has not yet paid then he may simply refuse to do so and return the goods if he has already received them.

Rescission is an equitable remedy which means that it is not available if that would be unfair. Thus it is not available in the following situations:

(i) Where it is impossible to restore the parties to their pre-contract positions, e.g. if the purchaser had consumed the goods. In *Clarke v Dickinson*[17] Crompton J gave the grisly example of a butcher purchasing livestock being prevented from rescinding where he has already slaughtered the animal.

(ii) Where it would involve upsetting the rights of an innocent third party, e.g. if the purchaser has sold the goods to an innocent sub-purchaser.[18]

(iii) Where there has been a lapse of more than a reasonable length of time from the time the contract was made. Thus in *Leaf v International Galleries*, above, the purchaser

15 Flack already owned a Formula 2 racing car.
16 [2006] EWCA Civ. 386.
17 (1858) 120 E.R. 463.
18 See Ch.5.

was unable to rescind the contract some five years after it was made. (In the case of a fraudulent misrepresentation, the purchaser is allowed a reasonable length of time from when he discovers it to be untrue.)

(iv) Where the innocent party has affirmed the contract, i.e. indicated his intention of continuing with it in spite of the misrepresentation. In *Long v Lloyd*[19] the seller had claimed that the lorry was capable of 40 mph and 11 mpg. On the first run the purchaser discovered a number of faults; the dynamo did not work and the lorry consumed petrol at the rate of 5 mpg. He telephoned the seller and complained. The seller offered to meet half the cost of repairing the dynamo. The buyer accepted that offer. When the lorry broke down again, the purchaser indicated that he was rescinding the contract. It was held that he could not, since by accepting the seller's offer on the telephone he had accepted the goods and thereby affirmed the contract.

Affirmation, which defeats the buyer's right to rescission for misrepresentation, is similar to "acceptance", which defeats the buyer's right to reject the goods and regard the contract as repudiated for breach of condition.[20]

Damages

Damages may be claimed on their own or in addition to rescission. Unlike rescission, damages are not available for all misrepresentations and the state of mind of the person who made the misrepresentations is important.[21] 6-007

(i) A fraudulent misrepresentation is one made (a) without belief in its truth, or (b) with such a degree of recklessness as amounts to dishonesty (careless whether it be true or false). For a fraudulent misrepresentation, damages are available in deceit: *Derry v Peek*.[22]

(ii) A negligent misrepresentation is one made by someone who believes it to be true but has no reasonable grounds for so believing, e.g. a car dealer who claims that a car of a type not manufactured before 1990 as having been made in 1989. Damages are available for a negligent misrepresentation.[23]

19 [1958] 1 W.L.R. 753.

20 See para.13-006, below.

21 For a critique of damages available for misrepresentation see J. Poole and J. Devenney, "Reforming Damages for Misrepresentation: the Case for Coherent Aims and Principles" [2007] J.B.L. 269.

22 [1889] 14 App. Cas. 337.

23 Misrepresentation Act 1967 s.2(1).

(iii) A completely innocent misrepresentation is one made by someone who genuinely and on reasonable grounds believes it to be true. Damages are not normally available for this sort of misrepresentation, although the court does have a discretion to award damages instead of (but not in addition to) rescission.[24]

The burden of proof is upon the defendant to prove that he had reasonable grounds for believing his statement. Otherwise it will be presumed to have been a negligent one.[25]

In *Howard Marine & Dredging Co Ltd v Ogden*[26] the owner of a vessel which a customer was considering hiring told the customer that its payload was 1,600 tons, whereas its payload was in fact only 1,055 tons (so stated in the ship's documents). After the contract was made, the hirer bought a claim for damages for misrepresentation. The owner claimed to have had reasonable grounds to believe the truth of his misrepresentation because the Lloyd's Register had (in a rare mistake) wrongly stated the payload as 1,800 tons. It was held that in showing that he relied upon the figures in Lloyd's Register and had disregarded the figure in the ship's documents, he had failed to prove that he had reasonable grounds to believe the truth of his representation. The hirer therefore won his claim for damages.

Exclusion

6-008 The ability of one party to exclude liability for misrepresentation is addressed in s.3 of the Misrepresentation Act 1967 which has recently been amended by the Consumer Rights Act 2015. Outside of trader to consumer contracts falling within the Consumer Rights Act, any provision in a contract which would have the effect of excluding, or restricting liability for a misrepresentation is ineffective, except to the extent that the clause is shown to satisfy the requirement of reasonableness.[27] The requirement of reasonableness is set out in s.11 of the Unfair Contract Terms Act.[28] Within a trader to consumer contract falling within the Consumer Rights Act, any attempt to exclude or restrict liability for a misrepresentation will be effective only where it is not unfair under s.62 of the Consumer Rights Act 2015. Statutory control of exemption clauses and unfair terms is dealt with in Ch.10.

24 Misrepresentation Act 1967 s.2(2).
25 Misrepresentation Act 1967 s.2(1).
26 [1978] Q.B. 574.
27 Misrepresentation Act 1967 s.3 as amended by the Unfair Contract Terms Act 1977 and the Consumer Rights Act 2015.
28 See paras 10-016–10-018 below.

Additional or Alternative Defendant

We are in this chapter considering misrepresentations made to the buyer by his seller (or the seller's agent). It follows that the remedies we have discussed are those which the buyer has against the seller. Normally the seller will be the only person against whom the buyer will be entitled to make a claim. However, there is an exception, created by s.75 of the Consumer Credit Act 1974. So, where the buyer bought the goods under a credit agreement of a certain type he will be able to bring against the creditor a claim similar to that which he can bring against the seller. The most common type of situation where this will occur is where the buyer uses his credit card to buy an item costing over £100. The credit card company is the person who provides the credit (i.e. is the creditor) and therefore the buyer may be able to bring a claim against the credit card company for a misrepresentation by the seller. The circumstances in which s.75 of the Consumer Credit Act applies will be more fully considered in Ch.22. 6–009

Section 56 of the Consumer Credit Act also can operate to entitle a buyer in some cases to sue the creditor (e.g. a credit card company) in respect of a misrepresentation by the seller. Section 56 is more fully considered in Ch.21.

General Reading

P. Atiyah and G. Treitel, "Misrepresentation Act 1967" (1967) 20 M.L.R. 369.

H. Beale, "Damages in Lieu of Rescission for Misrepresentation" (1995) 111 L.Q.R. 385.

R. Halson, "Rescission for misrepresentation" (1997) 5 R.L.R 89.

J. Poole and J. Devenney, "Reforming damages for misrepresentation: the case for coherent aims and principles" [2007] J.B.L. 269.

We are in this chapter considering [illegible] the buyer by the seller (or the seller's agent). It follows that the [illegible] discussed the [illegible] the buyer has against the seller. Normally the seller will be the only person against whom the buyer will be entitled to make a claim. [illegible] of the Consumer Credit Act 1974 [illegible] where the buyer bought the goods under a credit agreement [illegible] he will be able to bring against the [illegible] the same claim as he can bring against the seller. The most common type of [illegible] will be [illegible] where the buyer uses his credit card [illegible] costing over £100. [illegible] provides the credit [illegible] and [illegible] claim against the credit card company [illegible] the seller. [illegible] of the Consumer Credit Act [illegible] in Ch.22 [illegible]

[illegible]

[illegible]

7

Terms of the Contract

Introduction

Contracts of sale vary enormously. At one extreme one may find a written contract containing 7-001
many detailed clauses setting out the terms of the contract. At the other extreme, the parties may have expressly agreed only as to which goods were being sold and how much the price was. In the latter case the parties have left much unsaid, e.g. as to delivery, payment, the transfer of ownership, the quality of the goods, etc. Many provisions of the Sale of Goods Act were designed to remedy such deficiencies in the contract and the same can be said for the Consumer Rights Act 2015.

Freedom of Contract

The original Sale of Goods Act of 1893 was intended not to dictate to the parties what the terms 7-002
of their bargain should be, but only to provide solutions to problems and questions unforeseen and unconsidered by the parties. Thus most of the sections of the Act originally applied only in the absence of contrary agreement by the parties. The Act was based upon the notion of freedom of contract, i.e. that the parties were free to make their contract upon whatever terms they pleased. In relation to exemption clauses, however, the Unfair Contract Terms Act 1977 and more recently, the Consumer Rights Act 2015, have made a large inroad into this notion. Thus in consumer sales and all other sale of goods contracts, the ability of the parties to contract out of the legislative framework is limited. Section 55(1) of the Sale of Goods Act 1979 now reads as follows:

> **"Where a right, duty or liability would arise under a contract of sale of goods by implication of law, it may (subject to the Unfair Contract Terms Act 1977) be negatived or varied by express agreement, or by the course of dealing between the parties, or by such usage as binds both parties to the contract."**

Similarly, s.38 of the Consumer Rights Act prevents any attempt to exclude or restrict the trader's liability for a number of the rights prescribed by the Act, including those as to the quality of the goods, compliance with any description, etc. The relevant provisions of the Unfair Contract Terms Act 1977 and the Consumer Rights Act 2015 will be considered in Ch.10. The latter is capable of applying to other terms as well as exemption clauses and therefore represents a particularly significant inroad into the doctrine of freedom of contract. In the present chapter we shall consider terms other than exemption clauses.

Rights of Third Parties

7-003 As a general rule only the buyer and the seller can sue or be sued on a contract of sale. This results from two aspects of the privity of contract doctrine. First, the contract can be enforced only against someone who is party to it. Secondly, only someone who is a party to the contract can enforce it. The Contracts (Rights of Third Parties) Act 1999, however, created an exception to the latter.[1] Section 1 provides:

> **"(1) Subject to the provisions of this Act, a person who is not a party to a contract (a "third party") may in his own right enforce a term of the contract if—**
>
> **(a) the contract expressly provides that he may, or**
>
> **(b) subject to subsection (2), the term purports to confer a benefit on him.**
>
> **(2) Subsection (1)(b) does not apply if on a proper construction of the contract it appears that the parties did not intend the term to be enforceable by the third party.**
>
> **(3) The third party must be expressly identified in the contract by name, as a member of a class or as answering a particular description but need not be in existence when the contract is entered into.**
>
> **(4) . . . ."**

1 For a discussion of the effect of the 1999 Act, see M. Dean, "Removing a Blot on the Landscape" [2000] J.B.L. 143.

Suppose X buys an item, informing the retailer that it is a gift for Y (whom he names[2]) and arranging that the retailer will send it to Y at her address. If the item proves to be defective can Y rely on this provision to enable her to claim against the retailer under the terms in the contract governing the quality of the goods? The answer is not easy. The effect of the 1999 Act is to enable Y to enforce a term which purports to confer a benefit upon her. Arguably the only term which purports to confer a benefit on Y is the term as to delivery, thereby giving her a right to sue the retailer if the item is not delivered. Much depends on the circumstances presented. Will the courts read the situation as one where there was a term of the contract that Y was to have the benefit of all the terms in the contract which give rights to the buyer? A similar situation arises where M buys a wedding present for P & Q from the shop where P & Q have informed M that they have arranged their wedding present list.

Where the 1999 Act gives a third party a right to enforce a contract term, that right is subject to any other relevant terms of the contract such as a clause expressly limiting such a claim—although no term will be effective to exclude or limit a right to sue for death or personal injury caused by negligence. Where the third party's right exists, the judicial remedies available to the third party for breach of contractual term are the same as if the third party had been a party to the contract, e.g. damages and/or rejection of the goods and return of the price (see Ch.13). Also the Act limits the ability of the parties to the contract subsequently to remove or alter the third party's right, e.g. by varying the contract. Unless the contract otherwise provides, they cannot (s.2) do so without the third party's consent, if:

> **"(a) the third party has communicated his assent to the term to the promisor, [i.e. to the party who was contracted to perform the term in question], or**
>
> **(b) the promisor is aware that the third party has relied on the term, or**
>
> **(c) the promisor can reasonably be expected to have foreseen that the third party would rely on the term and the third party has in fact relied on it."**

When the third party seeks to enforce his right under the Act, the defendant is entitled to rely upon any defence (or set-off) which would have been available to the defendant if either (a) the other party to the contract had brought the claim, or (b) the third party had been a party to the contract.[3]

---

2 The word "expressly" in s.1(3) prevents any process of construction or implication: *Avraamides v Colwill* [2006] EWCA Civ. 1533 at [19].

3 For a third party's right to rely on an exemption clause, see para.10-011, below.

Express Terms

7-004 Although the parties are free to agree what terms they choose, they will not be bound by any term which is not properly incorporated in the contract. In the case of terms in a written contract signed by both parties, there will be no doubt that the terms have been properly incorporated.[4] Often, however, the terms will not be in a signed contract. It is perfectly possible for the parties to incorporate terms by agreeing to them either orally or in writing whether or not signed. Chapter 10 deals with the position where one of the terms is an exclusion clause. In that case, the party whom the clause favours (usually the seller) will not be found to have incorporated it in the contract unless either it was in a contractual document signed by the other party or else reasonable steps had been taken to bring it to the attention of the other party. This rule applies not only to exclusion clauses but also to any clause which is particularly onerous or unusual and unlikely to be known to the other party: *Interfoto Picture Library v Stiletto Visual Programmes*.[5] In that case an advertising agency telephoned a transparency library with whom the agency had never previously dealt. The agency asked to hire some transparencies of the 1950s. Accordingly the library sent 47 transparencies with a delivery note clearly requiring that they be returned by 19 March. The delivery note included nine conditions, printed in four columns, which the agency never read. Condition 2 stated that a charge of £5 plus VAT per transparency was payable for each day that they were late being returned. After the agency returned the transparencies 14 days late, the library claimed over £3,500 under this condition. The court refused to allow the claim, holding that the clause (imposing an exorbitant charge) was particularly onerous and unusual and the library had not taken all reasonable steps to bring it to the attention of the agency. Presumably the library should have at least highlighted it in some way such as printing it in red, on the front of the delivery note, perhaps with a large red hand pointing to it. As Bingham LJ put it, ". . .the more outlandish the clause, the greater the notice which the other party, if he is to be bound, must in all fairness be given".[6]

As a general rule, if sufficient notice is given and the clause is therefore incorporated, the court will enforce it. That is unless it is: (i) a clause made unenforceable by the Consumer Rights Act 2015 (see Ch.10); (ii) an exclusion clause made unenforceable by the Unfair Contract Terms Act 1977 (also see Ch.10); or (iii) a penalty clause.[7]

Terms which are not expressly agreed between the parties but are inserted by law into the contract are called implied terms. It should be noted, however, that the Consumer Rights Act has not adopted this terminology and instead refers to terms which are to be treated as being included within the contract. This is equivalent to "implied terms" under the Sale of Goods Act and is intended to make the law more comprehensible to consumers. The Consumer Rights

4 On the issue of apparent conflict between a seller's general terms and a term specifically agreed between the parties, see *Septo Trading v Tintrade* [2021] EWCA Civ 718.

5 [1988] 2 W.L.R. 615.

6 [1988] 2 W.L.R. 615 at 624.

7 Curiously, the clause in *Interfoto Picture Library v Stiletto Visual Programmes* was almost certainly a penalty clause and unenforceable even if it had been properly incorporated (see para.14-009, below).

Act also avoids the traditional classification of terms as being either a condition or a warranty. The consequences of a breach of a statutory right laid down by the Consumer Rights Act is dealt with by the Act itself, which creates a bespoke framework of remedies. This will be discussed in Ch.13.

Warranties and Conditions

The law classifies breaches of contract into two categories, first, breaches of a less serious nature which entitle the innocent party only to damages, and secondly, more serious breaches which give him also the option to regard the contract as repudiated. The difference is that with the first type, the innocent party, though entitled to damages, must still perform his part of the bargain, whereas with a repudiatory breach he may, in addition to claiming damages, regard himself as discharged from his obligations under the contract. The former and less serious type is a breach of warranty and the latter is a breach of condition. 7–005

As noted above, the Consumer Rights Act avoids this legalistic terminology and instead creates a bespoke framework of remedies depending on which statutory provision has been breached. Nonetheless, it remains important to know which terms are conditions and which merely warranties since the classification remains operative under the Sale of Goods Act and at common law. With the terms implied by ss.12–15 of the Sale of Goods Act it is easy because the Act makes it clear. With terms expressly agreed by the parties it is not always so easy. It is a matter of construing (interpreting) the contract—conditions being those terms which "go to the root" of the contract or are "of the essence" of it. In *Wallis & Wells v Pratt and Haynes*,[8] Fletcher Moulton LJ said that conditions "go so directly to the very substance of the contract or, in other words, are so essential to its very nature that their non-performance may fairly be considered by the other party as a substantial failure to perform the contract at all". Warranties "are other obligations which, though they must be performed, are not so vital that a failure to perform them goes to the substance of the contract". Section 61(1) of the Sale of Goods Act defines a warranty as:

> **". . .an agreement with reference to goods which are the subject of a contract of sale, but collateral to the main purpose of such contract, the breach of which gives rise to a claim for damages, but not to a right to reject the goods and treat the contract as repudiated."**

The neat classification, just explained, of contract terms into two categories, conditions and warranties, has begun to crumble in recent years. So far as the effect of the breach of condition is concerned, the position, with one exception, remains unaltered. If the seller commits any breach (even a minor one) of a term which is clearly a condition, the buyer will be

8 [1911] A.C. 394.

entitled not only to damages but also to reject the goods and treat himself as discharged from his obligations. The exception was created by the Sale and Supply of Goods Act 1994 which inserted s.15A into the Sale of Goods Act. It applies to non-consumer sales where the following circumstances are all present:

(i) the condition broken is one relating to description, quality or sample implied by ss.13, 14 or 15 of the Sale of Goods Act; and

(ii) the breach is so slight that it would be unreasonable for the buyer to reject the goods.

This limitation on the right to reject is further explained in Ch.13.

Where there is a breach of any term which is not a condition, that breach could be either repudiatory (i.e. equivalent in effect to a breach of condition) or a mere breach of warranty (i.e. giving rise only to a claim to damages). It is a matter of looking at the extent of the actual breach which has occurred. If that breach "goes to the root of the contract" or deprives the other party of "substantially the whole benefit of the contract", then it entitles the latter to treat the contract as repudiated and himself as discharged from it. This approach was clearly adopted by the Court of Appeal in *Cehave v Bremner (The Hansa Nord)*[9] and approved by the House of Lords in *Reardon Smith Line v Hansen-Tangen*.[10] In *Cehave*, a written contract for the sale of fruit pellets contained the express term "Shipment to be in good condition". On shipment some (about a third) of the pellets were not in "good" condition. However, although they were worth less on the open market than if they had been in "good" condition, they were still fit the purpose for which the buyer wanted them (making into cattle food) and were still so upon arrival. It was held that there was no breach of the condition implied by the Sale of Goods Act as to merchantable quality, because the pellets were still saleable, albeit at a reduced price. Also the express term was not a "condition" in the contract. Therefore, since the sellers' breach had not been serious enough to go to the root of the contract, the buyers were entitled only to damages. It seems that an express stipulation will not easily be construed by the court as a "condition". It will be a condition only if either there is an earlier case establishing that such a clause is a condition (i.e. "of the essence") or else it was clearly intended by the parties when they made the contract that any breach of that term would entitle the other party to repudiate the contract and reject the goods.

Stipulations as to Time

7-006 There is a presumption that the time of the payment is not "of the essence" (s.10), although the parties could expressly agree otherwise. However, a stipulated time for delivery is likely to be more important and therefore in an ordinary commercial transaction a delivery date is

9 [1976] Q.B. 44.
10 [1976] W.L.R. 989.

normally "of the essence": *Hartley v Hymans*.[11] Similarly, if a date is specified for shipment by the seller, that will be "of the essence". So, if a delivery or shipment date is not met, the buyer, as well as claiming damages, can if he wishes regard the contract as repudiated, i.e. reject the goods and reclaim any money paid. Of course, if delivery is late the buyer may accept late delivery, thereby waiving his right to treat the contract as repudiated. If he does, he loses his right to reject the goods but still has a right to damages—s.11(4).[12]

In *Rickards v Oppenheim*[13] the seller contracted to build a car for the buyer, the car to be built by 20 March. It was not ready by that date. The buyer did not repudiate the contract but pressed for early delivery. When at the end of June it still was not finished, the buyer informed the seller that if it was not ready in another four weeks he would then regard the contract as repudiated. It was held that the buyer had acted within his rights. By his waiver he had lost the right to regard the contract as repudiated on 20 March but in the circumstances it was a condition of his waiver that delivery should take place as soon as possible. He could therefore revive his right by giving reasonable notice. At the end of four weeks, the car was still not ready. Therefore the buyer was under no obligation to buy it.

Suppose that under a contract, the seller is to deliver the goods to a ship and that the buyer is to nominate the ship so that delivery can be made. Then, if there is a stipulation as to the time by which the buyer must make his nomination, that stipulation as to time relates to delivery and will be "of the essence": *Bunge Corporation v Tradax*.[14] Thus, if the buyer is late in making his nomination, the seller is entitled, if he wishes, to regard the contract as repudiated (i.e. entitled to refuse to supply the goods).

Implied Terms and Statutory Rights

The expression "buyer beware" is not entirely reflected in the law. It is true that in the law relating to misrepresentation, the seller cannot be liable for failing to disclose defects in the goods but only for any actual statements made by him or his agents. Similarly, the new rights to redress under the Consumer Protection from Unfair Trading Regulations 2008 do not extend to misleading omissions. However, legislation has for a long time existed to ensure 7-007

11 [1920] 3 K.B. 479. For a recent example, see *Pharmapac (UK) Ltd v HBS Healthcare Ltd* [2022] EWHC 23 (Comm) (time was of the essence in a contract for the supply of personal protective equipment at the start of the Covid-19 pandemic notwithstanding the fact that the contract did not expressly state as such).

12 Note that s.11(4) does not apply where the contract falls under Ch.2 of Pt I of the Consumer Rights Act where the specific framework of remedies applies instead. See further, Ch.13, below. For a useful summary of fundamental principles around when time will be of the essence, see *Alegrow S.A. v Yayla Agro Gida San Ve Nak A.S.* [2020] EWHC 1845 (Comm).

13 [1950] 1 K.B. 616.

14 [1981] 1 W.L.R. 711.

that the buyer receives certain basic benefits from the transaction. Until the enactment of the Consumer Rights Act, ss.12–15 of the Sale of Goods Act applied to both consumer sales and sale of goods contracts generally (though not necessarily with the same effect). However, following the enactment of the Consumer Rights Act, the dichotomy between consumer and non-consumer sales is stark. Where a trader sells goods to a consumer, the Consumer Rights Act applies and gives the consumer a wide range of rights and protections. In contrast, for other sale of goods transactions, e.g. a sale between two traders, the Sale of Goods Act applies and whilst it does offer some protection for the buyer, they are considerably less than under the Consumer Rights Act. The remainder of this chapter will discuss those two statutory frameworks and the various statutory rights (Consumer Rights Act) and implied terms (Sale of Goods Act) which impact on sale of goods law. Despite the additional protections offered by the Consumer Rights Act, it will be seen that what might be termed the core of the framework is heavily based on the implied terms framework under the Sale of Goods Act. This means that the common law decisions under the Sale of Goods Act may well be relevant to our understanding of the equivalent statutory right under the Consumer Rights Act. Caution must be exercised when reading the earlier decisions however. First, many of those cases were disputes between two commercial parties, and therefore the application of the law to a consumer sale could well be different. For this reason, we may see over the coming years common law interpretations specific to the Consumer Rights Act. Secondly, it must be noted that under the original Sale of Goods Act 1893 the wording of some of these sections was different. The Supply of Goods (Implied Terms) Act made some slight changes and, in relation to the implied condition as to merchantable (now satisfactory) quality, the Sale and Supply of Goods Act 1994 made more significant changes. Thus some of the cases which will be discussed in the next few pages were decided on sections which were not absolutely identical with the current provisions. However, because the changes were not substantial, this does not significantly diminish the authority of those cases, except (and it will be indicated) in relation to some cases on merchantable quality. The current wording of the sections will be used in this book.

In spite of this the words "buyer beware" still carry a very real warning in one type of purchase and that is what is colloquially called a private sale. The reason, as will be seen, is that the implied terms as to quality (in s.14) apply only where the goods are sold in the course of a business.

Implied Terms Under the Sale of Goods Act

Title—s.12

7-008 Section 12(1) and (2) reads:

"(1) In a contract of sale, other than one to which subsection (3) below applies, there is an implied term on the part of the seller that in the case of a sale he has a right to sell the goods, and in the case of an agreement to sell he will have such a right at the time when the property is to pass.

(2) In a contract of sale, other than one to which subsection (3) below applies, there is also an implied term that:

(a) the goods are free, and will remain free until the time when the property is to pass, from any charge or encumbrance not disclosed or known to the buyer before the contract is made, and

(b) the buyer will enjoy quiet possession of the goods except so far as it may be disturbed by the owner or other person entitled to the benefit of any charge or encumbrance so disclosed or known."

Section 12(5A) makes it clear that the term in s.12(1) is a condition and that the term in s.12(2) is a warranty. Most important is the implied condition that the seller has a right to sell the goods. This condition is commonly broken by someone selling goods which are not his. Chapter 5 was devoted to the question of who then owns the goods, the purchaser or the original owner. If the purchaser does so, then he has no quarrel with his seller. If, however, the original owner still owns them, the purchaser has an action against his seller for breach of the implied condition; he can claim for damages and/or return of the price.

Rowland v Divall[15] has attracted considerable criticism. Three months after buying and taking delivery of a car, the purchaser discovered that it had not belonged to the seller and still belonged to its original owner. It was returned to the latter and the purchaser brought an action against the seller under s.12. It was held that he was entitled to the return of the price, on the ground that he had suffered a "total failure of consideration". The whole object for a buyer in making a purchase is to obtain legal ownership of the goods. If he does not obtain that, then he suffers a total failure of consideration and is entitled to the return of the price. Thus, in effect, the buyer had over three months' free use of the car.

If the buyer does obtain ownership, then he does not suffer a total failure of consideration. It can happen that at the time of the sale the seller is not the owner (and thus in breach of the condition in s.12) but that he subsequently obtains that ownership, e.g. by buying the goods from their owner. This "feeds" the purchaser's title.[16] Thus good title is conferred upon the purchaser but at a date later than it should have been. If this occurs, the buyer can no longer claim to have suffered a total failure of consideration. The goods will be his, he will not be able to reject them[17] and his only claim will be for damages. However, at any time before the 7-009

15 [1923] 2 K.B. 500.

16 See para.5-029, above.

17 This is because he will have "accepted" them, s.35, see para.13-006, below.

purchaser's title is fed (i.e. before the seller obtains ownership) the buyer is entitled by virtue of the seller's breach of condition to regard the contract as repudiated, to reject the goods and thus to reclaim the price on a total failure of consideration. These principles were applied in *Butterworth v Kingsway Motors*.[18] Miss A acquired a car on hire-purchase terms. Before completing her payments and therefore before the car was hers, she sold it to B. B sold it to C, who sold it to Kingsway Motors, who in turn sold it to Butterworth. In all this time Miss A still had not completed her payments. It followed that each seller was liable to his buyer for breach of the condition in s.12. After using the car for 11 months, Butterworth discovered that he was not the owner. He thereupon immediately wrote to Kingsway Motors informing them of the situation and claiming the return of his purchase price. A week later Miss A completed her payments under her hire-purchase agreement and in doing so fed title down the line of purchasers. The process of feeding stopped at Kingsway Motors who thus became owners of the car. Ownership did not pass to Butterworth who by his letter had already indicated that he regarded his contract as repudiated. It was held that Butterworth had suffered a total failure of consideration and was entitled therefore to the return from Kingsway Motors of his purchase price. However, neither Kingsway Motors nor C nor B had suffered a total failure of consideration because their title had been fed. Once they had "accepted" the goods (see para.13-006 below) and their title had been fed, they lost the right to reject the goods for breach of condition. Kingsway Motors, C and B obtained only damages from their respective sellers. Kingsway Motors' damages were assessed as the difference between the value of the car when ownership should have passed to them (i.e. when they bought it) and its lower value when ownership actually passed to them (i.e. when title was fed). C obtained the same sum from B and B from Miss A.

Butterworth v Kingsway Motors involved a motor vehicle and was decided before the enactment of the Hire Purchase Act 1964 Pt III. We have seen (para.5-030 above) that by virtue of s.27 of the 1964 Act where someone, who has possession of a motor vehicle under a hire-purchase or conditional sale agreement, sells the vehicle before making all the payments under the agreement (i.e. before acquiring property in the vehicle), the first private purchaser (provided he was innocent and bona fide) will become the owner. Thus, if the facts of *Butterworth v Kingsway Motors* were to arise again today, Butterworth would acquire title to the car provided that the first private purchaser (either B, C or Butterworth himself) was innocent and bona fide. Would that prevent Butterworth being entitled to reject the car? The answer depends upon whether on the one hand B or C was the innocent bona fide first private purchaser or whether on the other hand B and C were trade purchasers and Mr Butterworth was himself the first private purchaser. If it were the former, then Kingsway Motors would have good title (acquired from C) and therefore Kingsway Motors would not be in breach of the term that they had the right to sell the car. If it were Mr Butterworth who was the first private purchaser, then Kingsway Motors would still be in breach of the term as to title and Mr Butterworth's right to reject the car for breach of condition would be unaffected by the 1964 Act. This was held in *Barber v NWS Bank*,[19] relying upon s.27(6) of the 1964 Act which provides that ". . .nothing

18 [1954] 1 W.L.R. 1286.

19 [1996] C.C.L.R. 30.

in this section shall exonerate [the] trade or finance purchaser who becomes a purchaser of the vehicle and is not a person claiming under the first private purchaser, from any liability (whether civil or criminal) to which he would be subject apart from this section".

It can happen that the ownership of one person is subject to certain rights which someone else has over the goods. This could occur where someone has a lien over the goods, i.e. a right to retain possession of them until a debt is paid. For example, when goods are entrusted to a repairer for repair, he has a lien over them to compel payment of his repair bill. The owner can still sell the goods even though they are in the possession of the repairer who is exercising his lien. In this case the seller will not be in breach of the terms implied by s.12, provided that before the contract was made he disclosed to the buyer the existence of the lien.

It can happen that there is some doubt about someone's title to goods, e.g. a finder's title. A finder does have title to the goods (a "possessory" title) but it is subject to the title of the original owner. The latter, if he ever turns up, can therefore reclaim the goods. A finder who sells goods without first disclosing that he only has a finder's title is in breach of the condition in s.12. However, if he has disclosed that fact so as to indicate that he is transferring to the purchaser only his own possessory title, then he will not be in breach of the condition—s.12(3). 7-010

Section 12(3) applies to a contract where it appears from the contract or is to be inferred from the circumstances that the parties intended that the seller should transfer only a limited title (whether it be the limited title of the seller himself or of some third person from whom the seller would obtain it). In such a contract there is no implied condition that the seller has or will have a right to sell the goods. There are, however, implied warranties of quiet possession, etc. The seller will be in breach of these if all charges and encumbrances (e.g. liens) known to him were not made known to the buyer before the contract was made.

So far it may have appeared that the condition in s.12 will be broken only if the seller turns out not to be the owner, anything less serious being merely a breach of one of the warranties. There is, however, some overlap between the warranties and the condition in s.12. The condition is broken if for any reason (undisclosed to the buyer) the seller does not have the right to sell the goods. The sellers in *Niblett Ltd v Confectioners' Materials Co*[20] agreed to sell tins of condensed milk. They supplied tins labelled "Nissly Brand". This infringed the Nestlé trade mark. Nestlé Co could have obtained an injunction restraining the sale of those tins and they required the buyers not to resell them without first removing the labels. The buyers claimed damages from the sellers. It was held that the sellers were in breach of both the condition that they had the right to sell the goods and also of the warranty of quiet possession.

Niblett's case was considered in *Microbeads v Vinhurst Road Markings*.[21] Shortly after the sale of some road marking machines, a company unconnected with the contract of sale obtained a patent relating to road marking machines. This entitled them to bring a patent action against the buyers to enforce the patent. The buyers sued the sellers under s.12 claiming a breach of the condition as to title and a breach of the warranty of quiet possession. It was held that there had been no breach of the condition as to title because that condition related to the

20 [1921] 3 K.B. 387.

21 [1975] 1 W.L.R. 218.

time of the sale. At that time no patent had been obtained; the buyers could use the machines undisturbed; and the sellers thus had the right to pass the ownership in the machines and to confer undisturbed possession upon the buyers. The warranty as to quiet possession, however, relates to the future. It states that the buyer "will enjoy quiet possession". The sellers were liable to the buyer in damages for breach of warranty.

Description—s.13[22]

7-011 Section 13 reads:

> **"(1) Where there is a contract for the sale of goods by description, there is an implied term that the goods will correspond with the description.**
>
> **(1A) As regards England and Wales and Northern Ireland, the term implied by subsection (1) above is a condition.**
>
> **(2) If the sale is by sample as well as by description it is not sufficient that the bulk of the goods corresponds with the sample if the goods do not also correspond with the description.**
>
> **(3) A sale of goods is not prevented from being a sale by description by reason only that, being exposed for sale or hire, they are selected by the buyer."**

The condition is implied only where there is a sale by description. Clearly, goods are sold by description where the purchaser has not seen the goods but is relying on the description alone.[23] Equally, in the words of Lord Wright in *Grant v Australian Knitting Mills*:[24]

> **"there is a sale by description even though the buyer is buying something displayed before him on the counter; a thing is sold by description, though it is specific, so long as it is sold not merely as the specific thing but as a thing corresponding to a description."**

In that case the sale of woollen underwear across the counter was held to be a sale by description. The essence of a sale by description is that in deciding to buy the buyer placed some (but not necessarily exclusive) reliance upon the description. In *Beale v Taylor*[25] the buyer saw an advertisement for a "Herald, convertible, white, 1961". He answered the advertisement,

22 See generally, J.D. Feltham "The Sale by Description of Specific Goods" [1969] J.B.L. 16.

23 Note that a photograph of the goods can form part of the description. See *Local Boy'z Ltd v Malu NV* [2021] EWHC 2439 (Comm).

24 [1936] A.C. 85.

25 [1967] 1 W.L.R. 1193.

inspected the car and bought it. Although the buyer had inspected the car, he had relied not purely on his own assessment of its value, but to some extent on the description. The seller was held liable under s.13, since the car consisted of the rear half of a 1961 car and the front half of an earlier model. This seemingly straightforward matter can be complicated by the nature of the goods themselves as demonstrated in *Brewer v Mann*[26] where a historic Bentley motor vehicle was supplied on hire purchase terms. The claimant argued that the vehicle did not conform to the description "1930 Bentley Speed Six" since the bodywork had been changed and the engine was a Bentley engine modified to Speed Six specification and not an original Speed Six engine. At first instance, the court held that the supplier was liable for non-conformity with the description since only a small section of the original chassis remained. This was rejected by the Court of Appeal. The description "1930 Bentley Speed Six" did not require the vehicle to be an original Speed Six car. Thus changes to the bodywork and engine would not necessarily constitute a breach of description.[27] The identity of a historic vehicle was to be ascertained in accordance with the custom of the classic car trade and the engine of a Speed Six Bentley was not necessarily key to its description.

In most cases the mere fact that a description was given (e.g. "good condition" or "1996 model") will be sufficient and convincing evidence that the sale was by description. It will be obvious that the buyer has relied, at least to some extent, upon the description. If in fact, however, it is clear that there was no reliance at all upon the description, the sale will not be a sale by description. In *Harlingdon & Leinster Enterprises Ltd v Christopher Hull Fine Art*,[28] an art dealer contacted another art dealer informing him that he had two paintings by Gabriele Munter (an artist of the German expressionist school). The later visited the former (the seller) and inspected the paintings. The seller, as the buyer knew, had no expertise in, or knowledge of, the German expressionist school. Hence, the buyer placed no reliance upon the seller's attribution but relied solely upon his own judgement and assessment. It was held that, since it was not within the reasonable contemplation of the parties that the buyer was relying upon the seller's attribution, there was no sale by description.[29] 7-012

A sale in a supermarket is usually a sale by description. The reason that the buyer selects a packet labelled, say, "cocoa" from the shelf is that she wants cocoa and is relying on the description "cocoa" accurately to identify the packet and its contents. It is a sale by description even though it is the customer who decides which particular goods to select from the display—s.13(3).[30] Occasionally, goods, e.g. vegetables, are displayed without any label or notice describing them. It would seem that such goods are not sold by description.

26 [2010] EWHC 2444 (QB).

27 *Brewer v Mann* [2012] EWCA Civ. 246. Contrast the position where a vehicle is modified to take the appearance of a different (more valuable) model and then described as such: *Scuderia Prestige Automobile Ltd v Malik* [2021] EWHC 2744 (Ch).

28 [1991] 1 Q.B. 564. For case commentary, see J.N. Robson and P. Adams, "Consumer Sales" [1990] J.B.L. 433.

29 See generally, J. Ulph, "Markets and Responsibilities: Forgeries and the Sale of Goods Act 1979" [2011] J.B.L. 261.

30 Traditionally, whether such a sale constituted a "sale by description", i.e. where the buyer had inspected (and/or selected the goods prior to the sale) had been doubted. See *Morelli v Fitch & Gibbons* [1928] 2 K.B. 636 and *Grant v Australian Knitting Mills* [1936] A.C. 85.

A sale by sample will often be a sale also by description. Section 13(2) embodies a principle illustrated by *Nichol v Godts*.[31] The buyer bought by sample "foreign refined rape oil". It was held that the goods must correspond not only with the sample but must also be "foreign refined rape oil".

7–013 In order to determine whether the goods correspond with the contractual description it may be necessary to determine the exact scope and meaning of the description. Obviously, the more detailed it is, the more stringent is the seller's obligation to supply goods corresponding with it. A contract to supply "staves" is one thing, but a contract to supply "staves, half an inch thick" is altogether more onerous. If in the latter case the seller supplies staves between half an inch and nine-sixteenths of an inch thick, he is in breach of the condition as to description: *Arcos v Ronaasen*.[32] If the seller wants a margin, he must stipulate for it in the contractual description.

The fact that the goods are of defective quality is usually irrelevant in deciding whether they correspond with their description. *Pinnock Bros v Lewis & Peat*[33] involved a contract for the sale of "copra cake" which was to be used to feed cattle. The goods actually supplied consisted of copra cake combined with a quantity of castor oil, the latter being poisonous to cattle. The sellers were in breach of the condition as to description. However, this was not because the goods were unfit for use but rather because they included goods of a different description. *Ashington Piggeries v Hill*[34] involved a contract for the sale of "Norwegian herring meal fair average quality for the season, expected to analyse. . ." which was to be used to feed mink. The sellers supplied Norwegian herring meal, i.e. Norwegian herrings plus preservative. The herrings and preservative had reacted together and produced a chemical which was poisonous to mink. Here, the sellers were not in breach of the condition as to description since, unlike Pinnock's case, there was no addition of goods outside the contractual description. The key to s.13 was said to be "identification" not "quality". Hence the expression "fair average quality for the season" was not held to be part of the contractual description, since it did not "identify" the goods sold. Goods which are useless or unsuitable for any normal purpose will still correspond with their description (here "Norwegian herring meal") if it accurately identified them. A balloon, though punctured, is nevertheless accurately identified and described as a "balloon".

Re Moore and Landauer[35] is now a controversial decision. The sellers had agreed to sell a quantity of tinned pears which were to be packed in cases containing 30 tins each. They had delivered the correct total quantity of tins but half of them were packed in cases of 24 tins each. It was held that the contract requirement that they be packed in cases of 30 was part of the contract description. Therefore the buyers were entitled to refuse to accept delivery because the sellers had committed a breach of condition (i.e. of s.13) and the buyers were entitled to do so even if they would have suffered no loss by having the tins packed in cases of 24 instead

31 (1854) 10 Exch. 191.
32 [1933] A.C. 470.
33 [1923] 1 K.B. 690.
34 [1971] 2 W.L.R. 1051.
35 [1921] 2 K.B. 519.

of cases of 30. The correctness of the decision in *Re Moore and Landauer* has, however, been doubted by Lord Wilberforce in *Reardon Smith Line v Hansen Tangen*.[36] Because s.13 is an implied condition, anything which is regarded by the court as part of the contract description automatically becomes "of the essence" and, if not complied with, has until recently automatically given the buyer the right to reject the goods for breach of condition, no matter how slight the breach was. The modern trend has therefore been to regard as part of the contract description only those contract words which help in "identifying" the goods. Other expressions in the contract (such as "fair average quality for the season" or "packed in cases of 30") can then be regarded not as part of the contract description but as express terms of the contract in their own right. Unless the contract clearly indicates otherwise, these express terms (not being stipulations as to the time of delivery) will then normally be warranties and not conditions. Thus if the seller is in breach of one of them, the buyer will not be entitled to reject the goods unless the seller's breach is such as to deprive the buyer of substantially the whole benefit of the contract: *Cehave v Bremer*.[37] Of course, if there is a defect of quality, a buyer who wishes to reject the goods may still be able to do so, i.e. if he can show that there has been a breach of one of the conditions implied by s.14. Even then, however, a buyer who is a non-consumer will not be entitled to reject the goods if the breach was so slight as to make rejection unreasonable.[38]

It is clear from the wording of s.13(1) that the implied term as to description is of application to all sales and not restricted to those which are "in the course of business". Thus in *Varley v Whipp*[39] a non-trade seller was liable under s.13 where a second-hand reaping machine was described, wholly inaccurately, as being little used. The implied term as to quality was inapplicable, due to the status of the seller but the court held that the misdescription breached s.13. Thus the relationship between s.13 and s.14 will frequently be of great practical importance.[40]

Quality—s.14

There are two conditions which may be implied by s.14—as to satisfactory quality (s.14(2)) and as to fitness for purpose (s.14(3)). Before considering in what circumstances these conditions will be implied, note should be made of s.14(1) which reads: 7-014

> **"Except as provided by this section and section 15 below and subject to any other enactment, there is no implied term about the quality or fitness for any particular purpose of goods supplied under a contract of sale."**

36 [1976] W.L.R. 989.

37 [1976] Q.B. 44, para.7-005, above.

38 See para.13-005, below.

39 [1900] 1 Q.B. 513.

40 See generally, the discussion above and *Ashington Piggeries v Hill* [1971] 2 W.L.R. 1051.

The two conditions implied by s.14 extend not only to the goods actually bought but also to goods "supplied under" the contract, e.g. a returnable bottle: *Geddling v Marsh*.[41] They also extend to the instructions. It would, for example, be no defence for the seller to say that his farm fertiliser was perfectly safe and effective when applied in the right concentration (at the right time of year) if the instructions supplied with the fertiliser stated in error the wrong concentration, whether too weak to be effective or so strong as to kill the crops. The law does not consider just the goods. It asks whether the goods with their instructions were of satisfactory quality and reasonably fit for their purpose: *Wormell v R.H.M. Agriculture (East)*.[42] In the case of a book, video cassette or computer disk containing a software program, the two conditions extend, apparently, not just to the physical book, disk or video but also to the contents.[43]

Satisfactory Quality—s.14(2)

7-015 Section 14(2), (2A), (2B) and (2C) read:

"(2) Where the seller sells goods in the course of a business, there is an implied term that the goods supplied under the contract are of satisfactory quality.

(2A) For the purposes of this Act, goods are of satisfactory quality if they meet the standard that a reasonable person would regard as satisfactory, taking account of any description of the goods, the price (if relevant) and all the other relevant circumstances.

(2B) For the purposes of this Act, the quality of goods includes their state and condition and the following (among others) are in appropriate cases aspects of the quality of goods—

- **(a) fitness for all the purposes for which goods of the kind in question are commonly supplied,**
- **(b) appearance and finish,**
- **(c) freedom from minor defects,**
- **(d) safety, and**
- **(e) durability.**

(2C) The term implied by subsection (2) above does not extend to any matter making the quality of goods unsatisfactory—

- **(a) which is specifically drawn to the buyer's attention before the contract is made,**
- **(b) where the buyer examines the goods before the contract is made, which that examination ought to reveal, or**

41 [1920] 1 K.B. 668.

42 [1987] 1 W.L.R. 1091.

43 See *St Albans DC v ICL* [1994] T.L.R. 579, discussed at para.1-012, above.

> **(c) in the case of a contract for sale by sample, which would have been apparent on a reasonable examination of the sample."**

The implied term as to satisfactory quality is a condition. It is implied only if the goods are sold "in the course of a business". These words were new in s.14 by virtue of the Supply of Goods (Implied Terms) Act 1973. Someone can sell "in the course of business" without being a dealer in, or a regular seller of, goods of the description sold. The phrase is simply there to distinguish between a sale made in the course of a seller's business and a purely private sale outside the confines of any business. Of course a butcher selling meat or a baker selling bread are each selling in the course of their business. Equally, the baker sells his bread van in the course of a business when he part-exchanges it for a new one. The solicitor who sells off old office furniture or a computer no longer wanted for the practice similarly is selling in the course of a business. This meaning of the phrase was established in *Stevenson v Rogers*,[44] in which a sale of his fishing boat by a fisherman was held to be a sale in the course of a business. This case casts doubt upon an earlier decision, *R & B Customs Brokers v U.D.T.*,[45] giving the phrase a much narrower meaning in the Unfair Contract Terms Act 1977. It seems clear, however, that a similar phrase in the (now repealed) Trade Descriptions Act 1968 does indeed have a narrower meaning.[46] Section 61(1) of the Sale of Goods Act states that:

> **"'business' includes a profession and the activities of any government department (including a Northern Ireland department), or local or public authority."**

Thus someone buying goods from the local council does have the benefit of the implied condition that they shall be of satisfactory quality. Suppose that the seller is a private seller not selling in the course of a business, but that he gets an agent to make the sale for him. Suppose also that the agent is acting in the course of a business. In that case the seller is treated as if he were selling in the course of a business, unless either the buyer knew that he was not doing so or else reasonable steps had been taken to bring that fact to the buyer's attention before the contract was made: s.14(5) and *Boyter v Thomson*.[47]

There are three exceptions in s.14(2). First, the buyer cannot complain of defects which had been specifically drawn to his attention, although naturally the condition will still apply in 7-016

44 [1999] 1 All E.R. 613. For commentary, see I. Brown, "Sale of Goods in the Course of Business" (1999) 115 L.Q.R. 384.

45 [1988] 1 W.L.R. 321. *R & B Customs Brokers* was nevertheless followed and applied by the Court of Appeal in *Feldaroll v Hermes Leasing (London) Ltd* [2004] EWCA Civ. 747, [2004] C.C.L.R. 8. See further, para.10-027, below.

46 See para.16-017, below.

47 [1995] 2 A.C. 628.

relation to other defects rendering the goods of unsatisfactory quality. The second exception applies "where the buyer examines the goods before the contract is made". So, if the buyer does, he cannot complain of defects which he ought thereby to have discerned. In *Thornett & Fehr v Beers*[48] the buyers of some barrels of glue had examined only the outside. It was held that a normal examination would have involved looking inside and that they could not complain of defects in the glue which an inspection would have revealed. This decision may not be the same today, because the wording of s.14(2C)(b) now refers to defects which "that examination ought to reveal" and not to any examination which ought to have been made. One could not say (it is arguable) that the examination actually made in *Thornett* (i.e. of the outside of the barrel) ought to have revealed defects apparent only on an examination which was not made (i.e. of the inside). Nevertheless, the buyer's legal position may be better if he made no examination than if he made merely a superficial examination. This is not the case, however, where there is a sale by sample. The third exception prevents any liability under s.14(2) in respect of any defect which would have been apparent on a reasonable examination of the sample, i.e. even if no such examination was carried out.

Returning to the second exception, suppose the buyer examines the goods, discovers a defect but decides nevertheless to buy, taking the view that the defect is one that can be easily remedied. If it is easily remedied, then clearly the buyer cannot complain of the defect in question. If it turns out to be incapable of being remedied, the result may well be different. If at the time of making the contract the buyer was unaware and could not reasonably have been aware of the gravity of the defect, then the court would probably hold that the condition as to satisfactory quality was implied. In *R & B Customs Co Ltd v United Dominions Trust Ltd*[49] the buyer had discovered that the car had a leak but did not discover until after the contract the gravity of the leak or that it was incurable. Neill LJ said:[50]

> **"I am not at present persuaded, however, that the condition in section 14(2) is excluded if at the time the contract is made the buyer is reasonably of the opinion that the defect can be, and will be, rectified at no cost to himself."**

The Court of Appeal side-stepped having to decide that issue, by holding that the buyer was entitled anyway to rely on s.14(3) (para.7–021 below); the car was not reasonably fit for the particular purposes (driving upon the roads in England, in English weather) for which the buyer had informed the seller that he wanted it.

7–017 Beyond these exceptions, it is clear that liability under s.14(2) is strict, i.e. it is not relevant whether at the time of the contract the defect was such that it could have been detected or prevented.[51]

48 [1919] 1 K.B. 486.

49 [1988] 1 W.L.R. 321.

50 [1988] 1 W.L.R. 321 at 333.

51 See for example, the decision of the Court of Appeal in *Randall v Newson (or Newsom)* (1877) 2 QBD 102.

Prior to 1994 the implied term in s.14(2) was an implied condition that the goods would be of merchantable quality. The Sale and Supply of Goods Act 1994 amended s.14(2). It replaced the word merchantable with the word satisfactory and introduced a new definition set out in ss.14(2A) and (2B). According to that definition it is important to assess the quality of the goods against the description applied to them. Clearly, goods sold as "mink food" will not be of satisfactory quality if it is poisonous to mink. That is so even if it is perfectly wholesome for other animals. What, however, is the position if it sold as "animal food"? Under the previous law, there was clear authority that the goods did not have to be fit for all the purposes for which goods of that kind were commonly bought; it was sufficient if they were fit for one or more of those purposes: *Aswan Engineering Establishment v Lupdine*.[52] Now, however, s.14(2B)(a) seems to require the goods to be fit for all the purposes for which goods of that kind are commonly bought. Thus if the goods are sold as "animal food" and animal food is commonly bought to feed mink, then if the food is poisonous to mink, it would appear that it is not of satisfactory quality.

The definition also states that the price can be relevant. This appears to be no change from the previous law relating to merchantable quality. The relevance of the price was discussed in *Brown v Craiks*[53] which involved the sale of industrial fabric. The buyer found it unsuitable for making into dresses. It was, however, perfectly suitable for other industrial purposes and could be sold for such, albeit at a slightly lower price. The House of Lords held that it was of merchantable quality because it was saleable without any substantial reduction of the price. Their Lordships said that if it had been saleable only at a "throw away" price, that would indicate that it was not of merchantable quality.

The word satisfactory in the definition indicates that the goods are not necessarily required to be of the very best quality but that the level of quality demanded depends upon the circumstances of the case, including the price. In this respect the law has not changed. For example, second-hand goods can hardly be expected to be in perfect condition. In *Bartlett v Sydney Marcus*[54] the seller, a car dealer, told the buyer that the car had a defective clutch and that if he bought it as it was he could have it for £550 but that if the seller were to repair it first, the price would be £575. The buyer opted to take the car as it was. About a month later the buyer had the clutch repaired at a cost of £45 and claimed this sum from the seller, alleging that the car was not of merchantable quality and not reasonably fit for the purposes of being driven on the road. The claim failed. "A buyer should realise that, when he buys a second-hand car, defects may appear sooner rather than later." The car came up to the standard required. On the other hand major defects in a second-hand car might well mean that it is not of satisfactory quality.[55] A second-hand car which is not safe to be driven on the road (for example because the brakes are in such a state that they would fail if the driver had to carry out an emergency 7-018

52 [1987] 1 W.L.R. 1.

53 [1970] 1 W.L.R. 752.

54 [1965] 1 W.L.R. 1013.

55 See *Crowther v Shannon* [1975] 1 W.L.R. 30, discussed at para.7-023, below.

stop) is clearly not of satisfactory quality: *Lee v York Coach and Marine*[56] (unless of course the car was only sold for scrap).

In *Clegg v Andersson (t/a Nordic Marine)*[57] Clegg agreed to buy a yacht with a keel "in accordance with the manufacturer's standard specification" at a price of £236,000. Following delivery of the yacht in August 2000, the seller informed Clegg that the keel was substantially heavier than detailed within the manufacturer's specification. During August 2000 and March 2001 Clegg and Andersson corresponded on issues arising from the overweight keel before Clegg sought to reject the yacht for breach of s.14(2).[58] The Court of Appeal held that the yacht was not of satisfactory quality "because of the overweight keel, the adverse effect it had on rig safety and the need for more than minimal remedial work".[59] Hale LJ emphasised the manner in which the objective test of s.14(2) should be implemented in stating that:[60]

> **"The test is whether a reasonable person would think the goods satisfactory, taking into account their description, the price (if relevant) and all other relevant circumstances: see s 14(2A). The question, as the joint Report of the Law Commission and the Scottish Law Commission explained, is 'not whether the reasonable person would find the goods acceptable; it is an objective comparison of the state of the goods with the standard which a reasonable person would find acceptable.'"**

The application of that test to the facts of Clegg is relatively straightforward. As her Ladyship said:[61]

> **"If a reasonable person had been told in September 2000 that the seller himself had realised that a very large quantity of lead would have to be removed in some as yet unspecified way from the keel of a brand new boat costing nearly a quarter of a million pounds with as yet unspecified consequences for its safety and performance he or she would have had little difficulty in concluding that the boat could not be of satisfactory quality."**

56 [1977] R.T.R. 35.

57 [2003] EWCA Civ. 320. See further, F.M.B. Reynolds, "Loss of the Right to Reject" (2003) (119) L.Q.R. 544.

58 At first instance it was also contended that the yacht was in breach of s.13(1), though this matter was not pursued in the Court of Appeal.

59 [2003] EWCA Civ. 320 at [49].

60 [2003] EWCA Civ. 320 at [72], citing *Sale and Supply of Goods* (1987, Law Com. No.160) at para.3.25.

61 [2003] EWCA Civ. 320 at [73].

In *Rogers v Parish (Scarborough) Ltd*[62] the Court of Appeal gave an authoritative ruling on how the old definition of merchantable quality applied in the case of a motor vehicle. It seems very likely that this ruling will be held to be equally applicable to the new definition of satisfactory quality. The old definition referred, as the new one does in s.14(2B), to the purposes for which goods of that kind are commonly bought. In *Rogers v Parish* it was held that in the case of motor vehicles those purposes include not merely the purpose of driving it from place to place but of doing so with the appropriate degree of comfort, ease of handling and pride in the vehicle's outward and interior appearance. The appropriate degree varies with the price, the description and other relevant factors. The relative weight to be attached to the different characteristics of the vehicle depends upon which market it is to be aimed at. On a vehicle sold as new, the performance and finish to be expected are those of a model of average standard with no mileage. No less is to be expected of a vehicle sold with a manufacturer's warranty. This authoritative ruling made it clear that defects in appearance, if of sufficient degree, could render a vehicle unmerchantable. That is true also of the new definition of satisfactory quality (see s.14(2B)(b)). The merest blemish on a Rolls Royce might render it unsatisfactory whereas it might not on a humbler car (see s.14(2B)(c)). The concept of satisfactory quality is one of degree. Deficiencies which are unacceptable on a car sold as new might be acceptable on a second-hand car. Nevertheless, the general approach laid down in *Rogers v Parish (Scarborough) Ltd* applies equally to second-hand vehicles (*Business Applications Specialists Ltd v Nationwide Credit Corp Ltd*[63]) and, as noted earlier, sufficiently serious defects can render even a second-hand car of unsatisfactory quality. Thus in *Shine v General Guarantee Finance Co Ltd*[64] a 20-month-old Fiat was held to be unmerchantable because, unknown to the buyer, it had eight months earlier been totally submerged in water for over 24 hours and had consequently been treated as a "write-off" by its insurer. The car would equally be of unsatisfactory quality under the new definition.

In *Lowe v W Machell Joinery Ltd*[65] the Court of Appeal considered the implied term as to quality in the context of a bespoke staircase. Notwithstanding the fact that the staircase complied with the buyer's specifications, a majority of the Court held that the staircase was not of satisfactory quality (nor fit for purpose under s.14(3)).[66] This was so since the staircase could not lawfully be used due to non-compliance with building regulations and was not affected by fact that the defect could easily be remedied at no cost to either party.[67] This, the court acknowledged, placed the suppliers in a difficult position since if they had amended the specification so as to supply a staircase which was compliant with the building regulations, they would have been supplying goods which were not in conformity with the contract and thereby been in breach of s.13(1).[68] 7-019

62 [1987] Q.B. 933.

63 [1988] C.C.L.R. 135.

64 [1988] C.C.L.R. 14.

65 [2011] EWCA Civ. 794.

66 See para.7-021, below.

67 [2011] EWCA Civ. 794 at [50].

68 The supplier can guard against this situation by (i) entering into a written contract (which was not the case in *Machell*), and (ii) by warning their customer on receipt of the specification that it would lead to goods which were in breach of the building regulations.

The issue of minor defects and motor vehicles was recently litigated in *Egan v Motor Services (Bath) Ltd*[69] where an Audi TT displayed "a tendency to 'veer', 'deviate' or 'drift' to the nearside".[70] This was put down to camber sensitivity rather than an inherent abnormality. Nevertheless, tests on the rear wheels of the vehicle showed that the wheel alignment was outside the manufacturer's specifications. This, it was argued, was sufficient to constitute a breach of satisfactory quality, under s.14(2B)(c)—freedom from minor defects. This argument was rejected by the Court of Appeal. Smith LJ stated:

> **"However, it seems to me unlikely that a buyer will be entitled to reject goods simply because he can point to a minor defect. He must also persuade the judge that a reasonable person would think that the minor defect was of sufficient consequence to make the goods unsatisfactory. Of course, if a car is not handling correctly, one would expect any reasonable person to say that it is not of satisfactory quality. That the judge recognised. But, the mere fact that a setting is outside the manufacturer's specification will not necessarily render the vehicle objectively unsatisfactory".**

This decision reinforces the point that the factors listed within s.14(2B) are merely indicative of issues which will raise the question of whether goods are of satisfactory quality. The test for whether goods are of satisfactory quality, however, is that laid down in s.14(2A): whether the defect is such that a reasonable person would conclude that the goods were not of satisfactory quality. Nevertheless, it is perhaps surprising that the goods, operating outside the manufacturer's specifications, were held to be of satisfactory quality. This is particularly so if one considers the general approach laid down in *Rogers v Parish*. The car in *Egan* was brand new, relatively expensive and a prestige model. Moreover, the closing words of Smith LJ are telling: "This case was about abnormal handling. The judge held that the handling was not abnormal and that was fatal to the appellant's case". It may be suggested that where a car is found to have abnormal steering rather than merely "camber sensitivity" the car would obviously be of unsatisfactory quality, but not due to a minor defect. Abnormal steering would most likely constitute unsatisfactory quality with reference to fitness for purpose[71] safety[72] and durability.[73]

7-020 It is of interest to speculate whether the decision in *Aswan Engineering Establishment v Lupdine*[74] would be the same under the new definition of satisfactory quality. In that case some heavy-duty buckets (which were suitable for most purposes for which such buckets were normally bought or used) collapsed when left by the buyer for several days stacked in extreme

69 [2007] EWCA Civ. 1002.

70 Such was the finding of fact at first instance, discussed in the Court of Appeal.

71 s.14(2B)(a).

72 s.14(2B)(d).

73 s.14(2B)(e)—such abnormality would likely cause excessive tire wear.

74 [1987] 1 W.L.R. 1.

heat such that the contents reached 70°C (156° Fahrenheit). It was held that they were of merchantable quality because the definition did not require the goods to be suitable for all the purposes for which such goods were commonly bought. It seems highly likely that the same result would be achieved under the new definition but by a slightly different line of reasoning, namely that the definition of satisfactory quality does not require that the goods be fit for extreme or outlandish purposes but just for such uses as such goods are commonly supplied, i.e. normally used. Leaving the buckets stacked in such extreme temperatures could well be held to be an extreme, abnormal use.

Where goods are to be despatched to the buyer by carrier, it is reasonable to expect the goods to be of such a quality as to be able to withstand a normal journey—*Mash & Murrell v Joseph Emmanuel*.[75] More generally, it is now clear that durability is part of the definition of satisfactory quality—s.14(2B)(e).[76] It may be accurate to say that the goods must be of satisfactory quality for a reasonable period after delivery so long as they remain in the same apparent state as that in which they were delivered, apart from normal wear and tear. That would bring s.14(2) into line with the implied condition as to fitness for purpose (see para.7-021 below).

Fitness for Purpose—s.14(3)

Section 14(3) reads:[77] 7-021

> **"(3) Where the seller sells goods in the course of a business and the buyer, expressly or by implication, makes known (a) to the seller or (b). . .any particular purpose for which the goods are being bought, there is an implied term that the goods supplied under the contract are reasonably fit for that purpose, whether or not that is a purpose for which goods are commonly supplied, except where the circumstances show that the buyer does not rely, or that it is unreasonable for him to rely, on the skill or judgment of the seller. . ."**

This is a condition and, like the one in s.14(2), is implied only where the goods are sold in the course of a business. Further, the buyer must have made known to the seller the particular purpose for which he was buying the goods. With goods having only one normal use the mere fact of purchase will, by implication, make it known that this is what the buyer wants them for, e.g. a hot-water bottle, as in *Priest v Last*.[78]

75 [1961] 1 W.L.R. 862.

76 See, for example, *Dana UK Axle Ltd v Freudenberg FST GmbH* [2021] EWHC 1751 (TCC) at [170].

77 For an explanation of the omitted words, see para.21-021,below.

78 [1903] 2 K.B. 148.

Someone who buys goods having more than one common use or someone who wants goods for an abnormal purpose will not benefit from s.14(3) unless the seller was expressly informed of the particular purpose for which they were required. In *Griffiths v Peter Conway*[79] the purchaser of a tweed coat contracted dermatitis from wearing it. Someone with normally sensitive skin would not have been affected but the purchaser had abnormally sensitive skin. Not having made that fact known to the seller, she lost the case. This decision was approved in *Slater v Finning*,[80] where a boat owner had bought and had installed in his boat engine a new part, a camshaft. It failed while at sea as did two further replacement camshafts. The expert evidence was that the cause of the failures was excessive torsional resonance excited by some cause external to the engine and the camshaft. It was held that the camshaft was fit for the purpose for which the seller had been informed that it was required, namely use as a component part of the engine in the buyer's boat, i.e. an ordinary boat, the sellers not having been informed of any special characteristic of the boat. There is no breach of the implied condition where the failure of the goods arises from some idiosyncrasy not made known to the seller, in the buyer or in the circumstances of the planned use of the goods. That is so even if the buyer is himself unaware of that abnormal feature or idiosyncrasy.

7-022 If the buyer does not rely, or it is unreasonable for him to rely, on the seller's skill or judgement, he will have no claim under s.14(3). However, the courts seem quite ready to infer the necessary reliance. Lord Wright, in *Grant v Australian Knitting Mills* said:[81]

> **"...thus to take a case like that in question of a purchase from a retailer the reliance will be in general inferred from the fact that a buyer goes to the shop in confidence that the tradesman has selected his stock with skill and judgment."**

On the other hand, if the buyer asks for an article by its trade or brand name and does so in such a way as to exclude any discussion of its suitability, then he is not relying on the seller's skill or judgement: *Baldry v Marshall*.[82]

Sometimes there will be partial reliance, the buyer relying in some respects upon the seller's skill and judgement and in others upon his own. Should the goods prove unfit for their purpose, the buyer will have a claim only if their unfitness relates to the sphere of reliance placed upon the seller. In *Cammell Laird v Manganese Bronze & Brass*[83] the sellers were to supply a particular ship's propellers which they were to make according to a specification supplied by the buyer. The seller's skill and judgement were relied upon as to matters not within the buyer's specification. This included ensuring that adequate materials were used and that the specification was embodied in the propellers. It also included other matters not provided

79 [1939] 1 All E.R. 685.
80 [1997] A.C. 473.
81 [1936] A.C. 85 at 99.
82 [1925] 1 K.B. 260.
83 [1934] A.C. 402.

for in the specification. In fact the propellers were unfit for their purpose because they were not thick enough, a matter not included in the buyer's specification. The sellers were liable.

In *Teheran-Europe v S.T. Belton*[84] tractors were purchased for the purpose of exporting and reselling in Persia. They in fact infringed Persian regulations and the buyer was fined by a Persian criminal court. He sued the seller. It was held that since the buyer knew much more about Persia than the seller, he must have been relying on his own judgement as to whether the tractors were suitable for the Persian market. The buyer lost. 7-023

The words "reasonably fit" do not require the goods to be of the very best quality. The quality to be expected will depend upon all the circumstances of the sale. Second-hand goods cannot be expected to be perfect. Minor defects must, for example, be expected to materialise in a second-hand car.[85] However, major defects existing at the time of the sale are another matter. In *Crowther v Shannon*[86] a car dealer sold for £390 an eight-year-old Jaguar car with 82,000 miles on the milometer. Three weeks and 2,300 miles later, the engine seized up. It needed replacing. It was held that the fact the engine seized up after only three weeks was evidence that at the time of the sale the car was not reasonably fit for the purpose of being driven on the road. The seller was liable for breach of the condition of fitness for purpose.

Although the words "reasonably fit" do not require the goods to be of the very best quality, they do impose upon the seller an absolute obligation. It is of no defence that he acted reasonably if in fact the goods are not reasonably fit for their purpose. In *Frost v Aylesbury Dairy*[87] milk was sold containing typhoid germs. It was no defence that the sellers had taken all reasonable precautions as to hygiene.[88]

It is at the time of delivery that the goods must be of reasonable fitness for the purpose for which the buyer indicated he wanted them. They must also continue to be so for a reasonable time after delivery. In *Lambert v Lewis*[89] Lord Diplock said that the condition of fitness for purpose was a continuing obligation "that the goods will continue to be fit for that purpose for a reasonable time after delivery, so long as they remain in the same apparent state as that in which they were delivered, apart from normal wear and tear." In that case a farmer had bought from a dealer a towing coupling for his Land Rover. He continued to use the coupling after it had become apparent to him that the locking mechanism of the coupling was broken. Subsequently, due to defective design (i.e. not the broken locking mechanism), the coupling failed while in use and a road accident occurred as a result of the trailer becoming detached from the Land Rover. Clearly, the farmer had been supplied with a coupling which was not reasonably fit for the purpose for which he had indicated he wanted it. Nevertheless, he was 7-024

84 [1968] 2 Q.B. 545.

85 See *Bartlett v Sydney Marcus*, above.

86 [1975] 1 W.L.R. 30.

87 [1905] 1 K.B. 608.

88 Similarly, it is no defence to show that levels of a prohibited additive were (i) undetectable at the time of the contract, and (ii) were not hazardous to health: *Hazlewood Grocery Ltd v Lion Foods Ltd* [2007] All E.R. (D) 433 (Jul) (sale of chilli-powder with a banned food dye. The court was also prepared to find that the chilli-powder was not of satisfactory quality).

89 [1982] A.C. 225.

unable, on the basis of that breach of condition, to claim from the seller any of the damage and losses which the farmer suffered in the accident. Once it had become apparent to the farmer that the locking mechanism was broken, that brought to an end the seller's obligation that the coupling continue to be reasonably fit for its purpose.

The operation of s.14(3) is well illustrated by the recent case of *BSS Group Plc v Makers (UK) Ltd (t/a Allied Services)*[90] where incompatible components were used in plumbing work, the failure of which led to a flood. The Court of Appeal applied *Jewson Ltd v Boyhan*[91] and identified the relevant questions as (i) whether the buyer made known to the vendor the purpose for which the goods were bought; (ii) whether they were reasonably fit for that purpose; and (iii) if they were not reasonably fit for that purpose, whether the supplier demonstrated either (a) that the buyer did not rely upon its skill and judgement, or (b) any reliance was unreasonable. The court found that the buyer had impliedly communicated the fact that the components were to be used together and that the components were not fit for that purpose due to their incompatibility. Although each component was sound, the seller "had to exercise its skill and judgment in assessing whether they both worked together".[92] Finally, the seller could not establish that the buyer had not relied (or had unreasonably relied) on the seller's skill and judgement in supplying compatible components.

Relationship Between s.14(2) and 14(3)

7-025 The relationship between the implied terms as to quality and fitness for purpose has recently been considered by the Court of Appeal. In *Jewson Ltd v Boyhan* (as *Personal Representative of Thomas Michael Kelly*)[93] Kelly purchased 12 electric boilers from Jewson, a builders' merchant to be installed in a property Kelly was developing. Prior to the sale, Kelly met with the sellers and also representatives from Amptec, the manufacturers of the boiler in question. At the meeting, the Amptec representative produced promotional literature, detailing the nature and performance of the boiler, including, inter alia, its efficiency and its ability to provide "affordable warmth". Following the installation of the boilers, all of which worked satisfactorily, Kelly refused to pay, arguing that the sellers had breached s.14(2) and 14(3) as the energy efficiency rating of the boilers was such that the flats were unsaleable. At first instance, the Court held that the boilers were not of satisfactory quality:[94]

---

90 [2011] EWCA Civ. 809 (in reference to the equivalent provision, s.4(2A) of the Supply of Goods and Services Act 1982).

91 *Jewson Ltd v Boyhan* [2003] EWCA Civ. 1030 at [15], per Clarke LJ.

92 *BSS Group Plc v Makers (UK) Ltd (t/a Allied Services)* [2011] EWCA Civ. 809 at [39].

93 [2003] EWCA Civ. 1030. For commentary, see C. Twigg-Flesner, "The Relationship between Satisfactory Quality and Fitness for Purpose" (2004) 63 C.L.J. 22.

94 *Jewson Ltd v Kelly* [2002] EWHC 2515 at [82]. For commentary on the first instance decision, see "Sale of Goods—Satisfactory Quality and Fitness for Purpose" *Consumer Law Today* 26(1) 1.

> **"The fact that the boilers intrinsically worked satisfactorily was not sufficient for them to be of satisfactory quality since a reasonable person would have said that a new form of electric boiler claiming to provide efficient low-cost heating in residential dwellings ought to be capable of being shown to meet such a claim within the tests or procedures then prevailing or if not why not."**

The Court of Appeal reversed this decision, however, finding that since an objective assessment of the quality of the goods would lead the conclusion that the boilers were of satisfactory quality, there was no breach of s.14(2). Furthermore, since Kelly had not communicated any requirement to Jewson Ltd of boilers which would receive high energy efficiency rating, there was no breach of s.14(3). In fact neither Kelly nor Jewson Ltd were aware of the SAP tests (the government energy efficiency tests). Sedley LJ explained that:[95]

> **"Section 14(2) is directed principally to the sale of substandard goods. This means that the Court's principal concern is to look at their intrinsic quality, using the tests indicated in subss.(2A), (2B) and (2C). Of these, it can be seen that the tests postulated in paras (a) and (d) of subs.(2B), and perhaps others too, may well require regard to be had to extrinsic factors. These will typically have to do with the predictable use of the goods. But the issue is still their quality".**

This does not mean that s.14(2) is restricted to matters of intrinsic quality since, as we have already noted, s.14(2) enables the court to consider "all other relevant circumstances".[96] Nonetheless, Jewson makes clear that "factors peculiar to the purposes of the particular buyer", i.e. the need for a boiler with a high energy efficiency rating, was a matter for s.14(3), and therefore requires communication to the seller in order that the seller may exercise reasonable skill and judgement in assessing whether the proposed goods would be suitable for that specific purpose.[97]

Sample—s.15

Section 15 provides: 7-026

95 [2003] EWCA Civ. 1030 at [77].

96 *Webster Thompson Ltd v J.G. Pears (Newark) Ltd* [2009] EWHC 1070 (Comm) at [38].

97 See *Provimi France SAS v Stour Bay Co Ltd* [2022] EWHC 218 (Comm) for a thorough discussion of s.14(2) and s.14(3) and their relationship at [306]–[332].

> **"(1) A contract of sale is a contract for sale by sample where there is an express or implied term to that effect in the contract.**
> **(2) In the case of a contract for sale by sample there is an implied term—**
> **(a) that the bulk will correspond with the sample in quality;**
> **(b) . . .**
> **(c) that the goods will be free from any defect, making their quality unsatisfactory, which would not be apparent on reasonable examination of the sample."**

Section 15 applies only if there is a term of the contract that it is a contract of sale by sample. In the case of a written contract the sale will be by sample only if that is included in the writing. Merely exhibiting a sample during the negotiations will not make it a sale by sample unless the parties agree that it is a sale by sample. In *Drummond v Van Ingen*,[98] Lord Macnaghten explained the function of a sample:[99]

> **"The office of a sample is to present to the eye the real meaning and intention of the parties with regard to the subject-matter of the contract which, owing to the imperfection of language, it may be difficult or impossible to express in words. The sample speaks for itself."**

The term in s.15(2) is a condition. Under s.15(2)(a) it is no defence that the bulk can easily be made to correspond with the sample. In *E & S Ruben v Faire Bros*[100] Linatex was sold which was crinkly, whereas the sample was soft. The seller was liable even though, by a simple process of warming, the bulk could have been made soft.

The buyer cannot complain under s.15(2)(c) of defects which he could reasonably have discovered on an examination of the sample. This is similar to the position under s.14(2) above.

98 [1887] App. Cas. 284.

99 [1887] App. Cas. 284 at 297.

100 [1949] 1 K.B. 254.

Statutory Rights Under the Consumer Rights Act[101]

Satisfactory Quality—s.9

Section 9 mirrors, to a very large extent, the equivalent provision laid down in s.14(2) of the Sale of Goods Act. Under s.9(1) every contract for the supply of goods, including sales contracts, is treated as including a term that the quality of the goods is satisfactory. The concept of satisfactory quality is then further defined in, again, much the same way as under s.14(2) of the Sale of Goods Act. Thus s.9 states: 7-027

> **"(2) The quality of goods is satisfactory if they meet the standard that a reasonable person would consider satisfactory, taking account of—**
> **(a) any description of the goods,**
> **(b) the price or other consideration for the goods (if relevant), and**
> **(c) all the other relevant circumstances.**
>
> **(3) The quality of goods includes their state and condition; and the following aspects (among others) are in appropriate cases aspects of the quality of goods—**
> **(a) fitness for all the purposes for which goods of that kind are usually supplied;**
> **(b) appearance and finish;**
> **(c) freedom from minor defects;**
> **(d) safety;**
> **(e) durability."**

Given the extensive similarity between the wording of the obligation as to satisfactory quality under both statutory frameworks, much of the discussion around s.14(2) above is of equal application to s.9. As with all of the implied terms which have been re-enacted under the Consumer Rights Act 2015 it may well be that, over time, the judiciary will develop jurisprudence specific to the consumer context of the 2015 Act. However, at the time of writing

101 Note that reform continues at a European level concerning the supply of goods and digital content to consumers: In particular, see the Sale of Goods Directive (Directive 2019/771/EU). Since the UK is no longer a Member State, it is not required to implement the Directive. Within the EU, the new directives apply to contracts entered into after 1 January 2022. There are some differences between the CRA 2015 and the new Directive and thus divergence between the UK framework and that in the EU. For example, the Directive extends the reverse burden of proof to 12 months from delivery whereas in the UK, the period is only 6 months. See also, the Digital Content and Services Directive (Directive 2019/770/EU), noted at para.7-034, below.

much of the common law under s.14(2) of the Sale of Goods Act ought to be instructive to our understanding of s.9 of the Consumer Rights Act.[102]

One element which does serve to distinguish the concept of satisfactory under s.9 from the non-consumer equivalent in s.14(2) is s.9(5) which reads:

> **"The relevant circumstances mentioned in subsection (2)(c) include any public statement about the specific characteristics of the goods made by the trader, the producer or any representative of the trader or the producer."**

This is a re-enactment of the modification first introduced by the Sale and Supply of Goods to Consumer Regulations 2002 which inserted s.14(2D) into the Sale of Goods Act.[103] The provision is designed to ensure that any public statements made by the manufacturer (or representative) are to be taken into account when assessing whether the goods are of satisfactory quality.[104] Thus, where s.9 applies the objective assessment of the quality of the goods undertaken in s.9(2) will be made through recourse to any applicable public statements concerning the goods, in addition to the factors within s.9(3). This ensures that a consumer will be able to claim a remedy where the trader is in breach of s.9 where the goods do not match up to, for example, promotional material released by the manufacturer. Therefore, if a manufacturer of LCD televisions advertises a new model with specific qualities (such as the quality of the screen or colour reproduction) these advertising statements will be considered as part of what the reasonable man is entitled to expect in the purchased product. This is so irrespective of the mode of advertising used by the manufacturer, i.e. whether through television or the internet, etc. It is also now irrelevant whether the statement is made (or repeated) by the trader to the consumer, i.e. the consumer will be entitled to pursue remedies as to quality against the trader using public statements made only by the manufacturer (e.g. on the manufacturer's internet site).

Given the possible impact of this extension to the definition of satisfactory quality, it is not surprising that certain statutory limitations have also been copied over from s.14(2) and incorporated into s.9. Section 9(7) prevents public statements from being considered under s.9(2) in three separate circumstances:

---

102 In *Van Gordon v Volkswagen Financial Services (UK) Ltd (t/a Audi Finance)* (Unreported, Nottingham County Court, 30 April 2019) the court had little difficulty in finding an Audi vehicle with a persistent rattle to be of unsatisfactory quality given its £55,000 price and nature as a 'prestige' vehicle although no decisions on the equivalent term in earlier legislation were cited. Note however, that caution should be exercised and particularly so in the context of decided cases under s.14(2) SGA, for example, where the status of the buyer as a non-consumer was operative.

103 As originally enacted, s.14(2D) applied only where the buyer dealt as a consumer. This wording is unnecessary in the current iteration since s.9 only applies where a trader supplies goods to a consumer. Section 14(2D) has been repealed by the Consumer Rights Act.

104 On s.14(2D), see C. Willet, M. Morgan-Taylor and A. Naidoo, "The Sale and Supply of Goods to Consumers Regulations" [2004] J.B.L. 94.

> **"(a) when the contract was made, the trader was not, and could not reasonably have been, aware of the statement,**
> **(b) before the contract was made, the statement had been publicly withdrawn or, to the extent that it contained anything which was incorrect or misleading, it had been publicly corrected, or**
> **(c) the consumer's decision to contract for the goods could not have been influenced by the statement."**

Thus where a trader is not (and could not reasonably have been) aware of a public statement made by the manufacturer, the statement will not be considered under s.9(2). The question of when a trader could reasonably be expected to be aware of the statement could raise some interesting disputes in the future, though the trader would presumably be expected to be aware of statements made through the manufacturer's official internet site and official literature relating to the product, etc. Paragraph (c) will presumably prevent liability for trade puffs as well as in situations where the buyer was unaware of the public statement. The latter provides no difficulty, though the former once again raises the fine distinction on occasion between trade puffs and statements intended to convey factual information to the end-user.[105]

Fitness for Purpose—s.10

Section 10 reads: 7-028

> **"(1) Subsection (3) applies to a contract to supply goods if before the contract is made the consumer makes known to the trader (expressly or by implication) any particular purpose for which the consumer is contracting for the goods.**
> **(2) . . .**
> **(3) The contract is to be treated as including a term that the goods are reasonably fit for that purpose, whether or not that is a purpose for which goods of that kind are usually supplied.**
> **(4) Subsection (3) does not apply if the circumstances show that the consumer does not rely, or it is unreasonable for the consumer to rely, on the skill or judgment of the trader or credit-broker."**

105 See for example the discussion of this point in relation to trade puffs, representations and contractual terms in Ch.6. See also, C. Willet, M. Morgan-Taylor and A. Naidoo, "The Sale and Supply of Goods to Consumers Regulations" [2004] J.B.L. 94 at 97–98.

Thus, as with the implied term as to quality under s.9, s.10 re-enacts the implied condition as to fitness under s.14(3) of the Sale of Goods Act previously discussed above. The essential features to establish liability are therefore the same: a particular purpose must be made known to the trader (whether expressly or through implication) and the goods must not be reasonably fit for that purpose. It follows therefore that the questions to be asked remain those expressed by the Court in *BSS Group Plc v Makers (UK) Ltd (t/a Allied Services)*[106] in the context of s.14(3):

(i) whether the consumer made known to the trader the purpose for which the goods were bought;

(ii) whether the goods were reasonably fit for that purpose; and

(iii) if they were not reasonably fit for that purpose, whether the trader demonstrated either (a) that the consumer did not rely upon its skill and judgement, or (b) any reliance was unreasonable.

Description—s.11

7-029 Section 11 reads:

> **"(1) Every contract to supply goods by description is to be treated as including a term that the goods will match the description.**
>
> **(2) If the supply is by sample as well as by description, it is not sufficient that the bulk of the goods matches the sample if the goods do not also match the description.**
>
> **(3) A supply of goods is not prevented from being a supply by description just because—**
>
> **(a) the goods are exposed for supply, and**
>
> **(b) they are selected by the consumer."**

This mirrors, albeit with slightly modified language and a revised layout, the position under the equivalent term in the Sale of Goods Act (s.13). Thus the general discussion above regarding the application of s.13 is of relevance to the application of s.11 here. In particular, the fundamental distinction as to quality and description ought to apply in precisely the same fashion under s.11 of the Consumer Rights Act as it does to s.13 of the Sale of Goods Act.[107]

Section 11 does, however, extend beyond s.13 in one substantive aspect. Section 11(4) provides that where the trader provides certain information regarding the main characteristics of

106 [2011] EWCA Civ. 809 (in reference to the equivalent provision, s.4(2A) of the Supply of Goods and Services Act 1982).

107 See para.7-013 above.

the goods as required by the Consumer Contracts (Information, Cancellation and Additional Charges) Regulations 2013,[108] that information will be treated as a term of the contract. Section 11(5) makes it clear that any change to that information is not effective unless "expressly agreed between the consumer and the trader." This addition is necessary in order to ensure that the Consumer Rights Directive is properly implemented, however, concerns have been expressed as to the extensive overlap between the terms to be treated as included within contracts under s.11(1) and s.11(4).[109]

Pre-contract Information—s.12

Section 12 of the Consumer Rights Act provides another deviation from the implied terms framework under the Sale of Goods Act. We have noted that where the information regarding the main characteristics of the goods is provided (as required by the Consumer Contracts (Information, Cancellation and Additional Charges) Regulations 2013, that information will be regarded as a term of the contract by virtue of s.11(4). Where information is provided under regs 9, 10 or 13 of the 2013 Regulations, and is not concerned with the main characteristics of the goods, that information will also be regarded as a term of the contract.[110] This will extend, for example, to information around delivery (including charges) and the geographical location of the trader. Section 12(3) makes it clear that any change to that information is not effective unless "expressly agreed between the consumer and the trader." 7-030

Sample—s.13

Where there is a contract for the supply of goods by sample, s.13 provides that: 7-031

> **"(a) the goods will match the sample except to the extent that any differences between the sample and the goods are brought to the consumer's attention before the contract is made, and**
>
> **(b) the goods will be free from any defect that makes their quality unsatisfactory and that would not be apparent on a reasonable examination of the sample."**

In as much, it corresponds to s.15 of the Sale of Goods Act discussed above. In this context, a sample refers to a representative part of the whole goods in question. Thus if a consumer purchases home furnishings such as curtains, laminate flooring, carpet, etc. using a sample,

108 See in para.(a) of Sch.1 or Sch.2. For a general account of the 2013 Regulations, see Ch.2, above.

109 See, for example, R. Canavan, C. Twigg-Flesner and H. MacQueen, *Atiyah and Adam's Sale of Goods*, 13th edn (Harlow: Pearson, 2016), p.504.

110 s.11(2).

they will be protected where the goods supplied fails to conform to the sample, unless the differences are brought to the attention of the consumer before the contract is made. This provision should be distinguished from s.14(2) of the Consumer Rights Act which is concerned with an analogous scenario: that where a consumer purchases goods having seen or examined a demonstration model. Here, the consumer will view the entire contract goods, as opposed to a mere sample.

Conformity with Model Seen—s.14

7-032 Section 14(2) requires that every contract to supply goods by reference to a model seen or examined prior to the contract is to be treated as including a term that "the goods will match the model except to the extent that any differences between the model and the goods are brought to the consumer's attention before the consumer enters into the contract." This is, strictly speaking, a new statutory right provided for by the Consumer Rights Act since it has no direct equivalent under the Sale of Goods Act (though it is likely that the Sale of Goods Act framework of implied terms would have protected a consumer where the goods supplied did not correspond with a model examined pre-contract). Nonetheless, s.14(2) offers a very clear guide to consumers that if, for example, they purchase goods having viewed a model on the shop-floor, if the goods supplied do not match the model they will be -protected. This will cover a great number of sales (in particular, for example, retail sales of larger electronic items such as televisions will often be sold through demonstration models on the shop-floor). Likewise, supplies of new motor vehicles will often involve a consumer inspecting a demonstrator model prior to placing an order for a vehicle. If, for example, the demonstrator model is a particularly high specification, this must be made clear to the consumer prior to contract if the vehicle they will order is not so highly specified.

Right to Supply—s.17

7-033 Section 17 requires the trader to have the right to sell the goods at the time when ownership is to pass.[111] The provision corresponds to s.12(1) of the Sale of Goods Act 1979, discussed above where we noted its significance to contracts of sale of goods which have the passing of ownership at their heart. Section 17 also replicates the implied terms from s.12(2) of the 1979 Act, i.e. that the goods are free from any charge or encumbrance not disclosed or known to the consumer before entering into the contract and the consumer will enjoy quiet possession of the goods.

111 As with the other statutory rights laid down by the CRA 2015 it also extends to non-sale supply contracts. For obvious reasons, s.17(1) does not extend to contracts of hire where there is never an intention to pass ownership in goods. See further, CRA 2015 s.17(3).

Digital Content[112]

In Ch.1 we noted the difficulties surrounding the definition of a contract of sale of goods and products such as computer software. It will be recalled that the judiciary developed a distinction between the sale of software through tangible media, such as DVD disks and intangible supplies, such as downloads. Only the former would constitute a sale of goods under s.2 of the Sale of Goods Act due to the definition of "goods" in the Act. One consequence of this arrangement was uncertainty as to the legal nature of a buyer's rights as to, for example, the quality and fitness for purpose of the software. Whilst it was generally accepted that the common law would have implied terms equivalent to those found in the Sale of Goods Act, a much clearer solution has now been provided by the Consumer Rights Act. In essence, where a trader supplies digital content to a consumer, the consumer has the benefit of various terms which will be included as a term of the contract. Digital content is afforded a broad definition in s.2(9) and means "data which are produced and supplied in digital form". The scope of the protection offered by the Act is, however, limited to supplies of digital content where the consumer has paid a price, thus excluding free downloads for example.[113] Where the digital content is generally not supplied free of charge but is supplied for free with other goods, services or digital content, the consumer will be protected by the Act.[114] 7-034

The terms to be treated as being included within a contract for the supply of digital content to a consumer are modelled very closely on those we have already discussed in relation to the sale of goods. Thus digital content must be of satisfactory quality[115] and fit for purpose.[116] Similarly, the digital content must match the description given and the supply contract must include, as terms, any pre-contract information required by the Consumer Contracts (Information, Cancellation and Additional Charges) Regulations 2013. The trader must also have the right to supply the digital content.[117] These terms have, where necessary been modified to better reflect the digital nature of the product being supplied. For example, the term as to satisfactory quality does not include appearance and finish as a specified factor to be considered when assessing the standard the digital content must reach. Similarly, whereas s.9 precludes from the term of satisfactory quality any defect which ought to be revealed on a reasonable examination of the goods, the equivalent term applicable to supplies of digital content refers instead to an examination of any trial digital content. The Act also makes provision for two matters specific to digital content. First, s.39 ensures that a

112 Note that reform continues at a European level concerning digital content: On the provision of "free" software in return for personal data see the Digital Content and Services Directive (Directive 2019/770/EU). Since the UK is no longer a Member State, it is not required to implement the new Directive. Within the EU, the new directives apply to contracts entered into after 1 January 2022.

113 s.33(1).

114 s.33(2).

115 s.34.

116 s.35.

117 s.41.

consumer benefits from the terms as to satisfactory quality, fitness for purpose, and description where "there is a contract to supply digital content and the consumer's access to the content on a device requires its transmission to the device under arrangements initiated by the trader". This provision ensures that the Act applies to digital content which is supplied via the internet (and satellite transmission), i.e. movie streaming services accessed via internet-ready televisions.

Secondly, s.40 ensures that the (common) practice whereby digital content is modified after the contract has been completed (e.g. software updates) is included within the ambit of the Act. Thus, where software, for example, is updated to offer new features (or perhaps ensure greater protection against viruses and malware) the modified version of the software must also comply with the requirements of satisfactory quality, fitness for purpose and description.[118]

Remedies

7-035 Remedies for a breach of contract will be considered in Ch.13. It should be emphasised at this stage, however, that the Consumer Rights Act 2015 adopts a very different approach to that of the Sale of Goods Act 1979. Under the 1979 Act, the position is relatively straightforward: for breach by the seller of any term of the contract, the buyer can sue for damages. In the case of a breach of condition the buyer normally has the additional right to reject the goods and recover the price. The buyer however may lose the right to reject the goods either by waiver of that right or by "acceptance" of the goods.[119] Under the Consumer Rights Act, however, the traditional rules relating to conditions, warranties and acceptance are discarded. Instead, the Act creates a bespoke framework which dictates the available remedies where the trader fails to comply with the various statutory rights provided for (including special provision for digital content). This, together with buyer's remedies under the Sale of Goods Act will be explained in Ch.13.

General Reading

O. Bray and B. Kerry, "Digital Content Under the Consumer Rights Act 2015" [2015] Entertainment Law Review 271.

118 Note the effect of s.40(3) regarding the time frame for claims in this context.

119 "Acceptance" has a technical meaning. See below, para.13–005.

M.G. Bridge, "Sale of Goods in Scotland—a second tender: J&H Ritchie Ltd v Lloyd Ltd" [2007] J.B.L. 814.

M.G. Bridge, "The Sale and Supply of Goods Act 1994" [1995] J.B.L. 398.

B. Davenport, "United Kingdom: Changes in the Quality Terms Implied into Contracts for the Sale and Supply of Goods" (1995) 3 J.I.B.F.L. 140.

W.C.H. Ervine, "Satisfactory Quality: what does it mean?" [2004] J.B.L. 684.

P. Giliker, "The Consumer Rights Act 2015—a bastion of European consumer rights?" (2017) 37 Legal Studies 78.

P. Mitchell, "The Development of Quality Obligations in Sale of Goods" (2001) 117 L.Q.R. 645.

A. Samuels, "The Consumer Rights Act 2015" [2016] J.B.L. 159.

8

The Supply of Goods and Services

In Ch.1 we noted a range of supply contracts which, although not contracts of sale of goods, were in certain aspects, similar. These include contracts of barter, contracts for work and materials supplied, contracts for hire, and contracts for services. Historically, a great deal turned on the classification of the contract, i.e. whether it was one of sale of goods in which case the Sale of Goods Act applied, or whether it was not, in which case the 1979 Act did not apply. Following the enactment of the Consumer Rights Act much of that significance has been eroded. This is so because the Consumer Rights Act unified, to a large extent, the rights of a consumer in sale and supply contracts. The Act also addresses the rights laid down within contracts for services. Prior to the enactment of the Consumer Rights Act, however, the position of the customer under those analogous contracts was governed by the Supply of Goods and Services Act 1982. This chapter will examine that Act, which is now of relevance to supply contracts which fall outside of the Consumer Rights Act and will highlight the position for consumer supplies under the Consumer Rights Act. 8-001

The Supply of Goods and Services Act 1982

This Act is mainly concerned with certain types of contract which are not contracts of sale of goods. Nevertheless, some of these contracts are closely related to sale of goods contracts and much of the law in the Act is modelled on parts of the Sale of Goods Act. The Act consists of three sets of implied terms. Each set is implied in a defined category of contracts. The extent to which the parties can contract out of these terms will be explained in Ch.10.[1] 8-002

1 At para.10-025, below.

Contracts for the Transfer of Goods

8-003 We are concerned here with contracts which are not contracts of sale of goods or hire purchase but where, nevertheless, one person transfers, or agrees to transfer, ownership in goods to another. The main kinds of contracts which fall into this are contracts of exchange or barter (which are not contracts of sale of goods because they lack a money consideration) and contracts (e.g. of repair) where, although some goods are supplied, the substance of contract is the provision of services. Prior to the enactment of the Consumer Rights Act, such contracts were subject to statutory control through the Supply of Goods and Services Act 1982.[2] However, for contracts entered into on or after 1 October 2015 the Consumer Rights Act now applies instead where a trader supplies goods to a consumer.[3] In this situation, the statutory rights are the same as those we discussed in Ch.7 for sales contracts. Thus, for example, a contract of barter is to be treated as including terms as to satisfactory quality (s.9), fitness (s.10), description (s.11), pre-contract information (s.12), sample (s.13), model (s.14), and supply including freedom from encumbrances and quiet possession (s.17). Only where the Consumer Rights Act does not apply will the Supply of Goods and Services Act be relevant. Thus for example, where a trader exchanges goods with another trader, the contract will fall under the Supply of Goods and Services Act. Section 1(1) of that Act provides the broad ambit of the first set of implied terms by defining the concept of a "contract for the transfer of goods" as a "contract under which one person transfers or agrees to transfer to another the property in goods, other than an excepted contract and other than a contract to which Chapter 2 of Part 1 of the Consumer Rights Act 2015 applies". There are four categories of excepted contract: The first two are contracts of sale of goods and hire-purchase contracts. The reason for these exceptions is that both categories are governed by its own set of statutory implied terms.[4] The two other excepted contracts are, first, where the property is transferred under a deed (covenant) gratuitously made, and secondly, any contract intended to operate by way of mortgage, pledge, charge or any other security.[5]

The 1982 Act implies terms as to: title, freedom from encumbrances and quiet possession (s.2); description (s.3); satisfactory quality and fitness for purpose (s.4);[6] and sample (s.5).

2 See generally, B. Davenport, "United Kingdom: Changes in the Quality Terms Implied into Contracts for the Sale and Supply of Goods" (1995) 3 J.I.B.F.L. 140.

3 CRA 2015 s.8.

4 The relevant statutory provisions are as follows: in the case of sale of goods contracts, ss.12–15 of the Sale of Goods Act 1979 and in the case of hire-purchase agreements, ss.8–11 of the Supply of Goods (Implied Terms) Act 1973.

5 Until 6 April 2005 there was a further category of excepted contracts, namely where property in goods was obtained in exchange for trading stamps. This was repealed by the Regulatory Reform (Trading Stamps) Order (SI 2005/871) and such contracts are now governed by the 1982 Act. Where, however, a combination of cash and trading stamps are used, the Sale of Goods Act 1979 will apply.

6 See generally, B. Davenport, "United Kingdom: Changes in the Quality Terms Implied into Contracts for the Sale and Supply of Goods" (1995) 3 J.I.B.F.L. 140.

These terms relate to the goods supplied, are implied in identical circumstances and are identical in effect as the terms implied by ss.12–15 of the Sale of Goods Act.

Even though the implied terms in ss.2–5 of the 1982 Act are identical to those in ss.12–15 of the Sale of Goods Act[7], it still may be necessary to distinguish between on the one hand a contract governed by ss.2–5 of the 1982 Act and on the other a contract of sale of goods. Two particular reasons spring to mind. First, the doctrine of "acceptance" (see para.13-006 below) applies only to sale of goods contracts which fall under the Sale of Goods Act. The result is that a customer under, say, a contract of barter may have longer in which to reject the goods for a breach of condition than a buyer under a sale of goods contract. In this respect all non-sale of goods contracts falling outside of the Consumer Rights Act are the same, i.e. the question whether the customer has lost his right to reject the goods for breach of condition is not determined by whether he has "accepted" the goods but by whether he has affirmed the contract.[8]

The second reason for distinguishing between sale of goods contracts and others is that the Sale of Goods Act applies only to contracts of sale of goods and the Supply of Goods and Services Act 1982 does not contain provisions corresponding to any other than ss.12–15 of the Sale of Goods Act. Similarly, the Consumer Rights Act does, in a small number of respects, treat sales contracts under s.5 differently from other forms of supply contracts such as barter, etc. falling under s.8. So, for example, there are no statutory rules relating to the passing of property and risk under a contract of barter. It is therefore a matter of common law and there is not much English case law on the matter. Consider now some different types of contract.

Collateral Contracts Which are not Contracts of Sale of Goods

It will be remembered that if there is no money consideration, a contract will not be a sale of goods contract. Hence, in *Esso v Commissioners of Customs and Excise*,[9] although there was a contract of sale of goods in relation to the petrol, the collateral contract relating to the World Cup coin was not a contract of sale of goods. It is difficult, perhaps, to imagine a dispute about title, description, quality or sample arising in relation to a World Cup coin. Consider, however, the situation where an electrical wholesaler advertises that with every refrigerator sold to a trader in November a free electric toaster will be supplied. According to the reasoning in the Esso case, the advertisement is an offer (i.e. to supply a toaster). A trader can accept that offer during November by entering a contract to buy a refrigerator from the wholesaler. The 8-004

7 Note also, that the new s.5A, inserted by the Sale and Supply of Goods Act 1994, duplicates the modification of remedies in non-consumer cases (minor breach of condition to be treated as a breach of warranty) as found in the Sale of Goods Act s.15A. See Ch.13, at para.13-005.

8 This point does not apply to contracts governed by Ch.2 of Pt I of the Consumer Rights Act 2015 since that Act instead creates a bespoke framework of remedies. For a discussion of the doctrine of affirmation in relation to hire-purchase agreements, see para.22-017, below.

9 [1976] 1 W.L.R. 1. See para.1-008, above.

consideration given by the trader for the toaster is not money but is the entering of the contract to buy the refrigerator. The result is that if the toaster is not of satisfactory quality the trader's claim is under s.4 of the Supply of Goods and Services Act, however if the refrigerator is not of satisfactory quality then his claim is under s.14 of the Sale of Goods Act. In the latter case the buyer could exercise his right to reject the refrigerator for breach of condition and then recover the price on a total failure of consideration. He would still presumably be entitled to retain the toaster which he obtained under a separate collateral contract. Although, if the toaster and not the fridge had been of less than satisfactory quality, then there would be no point in rejecting the toaster for breach of condition, since under the contract (i.e. the one relating to the toaster) no price was payable by the trader and therefore none would be recoverable. Nevertheless, the trader could of course sue for damages.

Contracts of Barter or Exchange

8-005 Where goods are swapped for other goods, then there is no contract of sale of goods since there is no money consideration. What, however, about the situation where goods are swapped for a combination of money and other goods? This problem typically occurs where goods are part-exchanged or "traded in". For example, a customer buying a new car with a cash price of £5,000 might get the garage to allow him £500 part-exchange allowance on his old car. In this case there is still a contract of sale of the new car because of the existing money consideration (of £4,500): *Dawson v Dutfield*.[10] The position is still the same even if the part-exchange allowance is for most or nearly all of the price—say, in our example, £4,800—because there is still a money consideration, albeit a small one.[11] Thus, if the new car proves not to match the description by which it was sold or not to be of satisfactory quality, the customer's claim is founded on ss.9 or 11 of the Consumer Rights Act (where the customer is a consumer) or ss.13 or 14 of the Sale of Goods Act (where the customer is not a consumer).

Consider now the traded-in car. At first sight it appears that there is no money consideration given by the garage for the traded-in car. However, it is usual in the car trade for a value to be agreed for the traded-in car as well as for the new car, i.e. the trade-in allowance is a precise stated figure (e.g. £500). In this case it may be correct to regard the traded-in car, not as being exchanged or bartered towards the new car, but as sold for £500 which sum the customer uses towards payment for his new car. Looked at in this way, the whole transaction between the garage and the customer is not a sale of a new car and a part-exchange (or barter) of the old but represents a sale of each. In *Aldridge v Johnson*[12] barley valued at £215 was sold in return for £23 and bullocks valued at £192. The court considered that, each set of goods having been allocated a price, there were mutual sales. It seems to follow that if X agrees to swap his coat

10 [1936] 2 All E.R. 232. See para.1-008, above.

11 *Aldridge v Johnson* [1857] 26 L.J.Q.B. 296.

12 *Aldridge v Johnson* [1857] 26 L.J.Q.B. 296.

for Y's jacket, there is a contract of barter but if in making the contract they allocate a value or price of say, £20 to each item, there would be mutual sales.

Contracts Where Payment for Goods is Made by Cheque, Trading Check, Credit Card or Other Voucher

Are these contracts of sale of goods or are they contracts under which the customer gives no money consideration? Clearly, where the payment is by cheque, the contract is one of sale of goods. Indeed, s.38 of the Sale of Goods Act expressly contemplates this possibility. If the cheque bounces (i.e. is dishonoured), the seller will be able to sue for the price because acceptance of payment by cheque will have been conditional (i.e. upon the cheque being honoured). 8-006

Where a trading check is used to pay for goods, the contract is also one of sale of goods: *Davies v Commissioners of Customs and Excise*.[13] With a trading check, although the buyer does not actually hand over any cash, he does hand over something having an agreed cash value (i.e. agreed between himself and the seller). Just as it is sale of goods when a customer trades in a car in part exchange for another, so it is a sale of goods when a retailer supplies goods in return for a trading check. In each case the seller (i.e. the customer trading in his car and the retailer providing the goods in return for the trading check) receives no actual cash, but he receives something having an agreed cash value. The same can be said where payment is made by means of a credit (or charge) card. The seller, in accepting payment by the card, is taking something having an agreed cash value. Therefore, provided that the commodity being bought is goods (as opposed to services) the contract between seller and buyer is one of sale of goods. This is so despite the fact that the contract is in one respect different from that where payment is made by cheque. Where payment is made by means of a credit (or charge) card, that is an absolute, not a conditional, payment: *Re Charge Card Services Ltd*.[14] Thus if the card company fails to pay the seller, e.g. because the card company is insolvent, the seller is not entitled to recover payment from the card holder.[15]

Where a voucher, other than a trading check or credit card, is used (e.g. a book-token) there is no case law telling us into which category the contract falls. Where the voucher is used together with cash to buy goods, clearly there is a sale of goods contract. Where the voucher alone is used, presumably the same reasoning used in the last paragraph will apply. Thus, where, as in the case of a book-token, the voucher is used as having an agreed cash value (i.e. as a cash equivalent), the contract is one of sale of goods. Shop gift vouchers would come into this category also.

13 [1975] 1 W.L.R. 204.

14 [1988] 3 W.L.R. 723.

15 Accounts of how trading checks and credit cards work are given at paras 17-024 and 21-017, below.

Contracts for Work with Materials Supplied

8-007 Where the main purpose or "substance" of the contract is the provision of services then it is not a sale of goods contract even though there is to be a transfer of ownership in some goods. Two examples are construction contracts (where the customer will become the owner of the bricks and tiles, etc. used) and repair contracts (where the customer will become owner of any spare parts used). Where the customer is not a consumer, the first set of implied terms in the 1982 Act (ss.2–5) will apply in relation to the goods supplied under the contract. Suppose an electrician is called in to repair a computer in a shop and suppose that shortly afterwards the computer breaks down again. This could be due to (i) faulty replacement parts fitted by the electrician, (ii) failure to exercise due car and skill by the electrician, or (iii) some other reason, such as failure of some other part in the computer. Only if it is the first of these will the customer have a claim under the first set of implied terms in the 1982 Act. If his claim relates not to the goods but to the quality of service provided, then the relevant law is that contained in the third set of implied terms in the 1982 Act. Where the customer is a consumer, the Consumer Rights Act applies but the same distinction is relevant. Where the computer breaks down after a repair using faulty replacement parts the consumer will be able to rely on s.9 of the Consumer Rights Act. Where the claim relates to the quality of service provided, the consumer will be able to claim under s.49 of the Consumer Rights Act.[16]

Contracts of Hire

8-008 A contract of hire is a contract of bailment. Under it, the hirer (the bailee) obtains possession but not property (i.e. not ownership). Since there is no transfer or agreement to transfer property (ownership) to the hirer, there is no contract of sale of goods under the Sale of Goods Act. The Consumer Rights Act, however, does apply to contracts of hire since they fall under the definition of a supply contract in s.3. The Consumer Rights Act defines a contract of hire as a contract, other than a hire purchase agreement if:

> **". . . under it the trader gives or agrees to give the consumer possession of the goods with the right to use them, subject to the terms of the contract, for a period determined in accordance with the contract."**

16 See para.8-009, below.

The statutory rights are almost identical as those considered in Ch.7 for sales contracts. Thus a contract of hire is to be treated as including terms as to satisfactory quality (s.9), fitness (s.10), description (s.11), pre-contract information (s.12), sample (s.13), and model (s.14). The distinction between the statutory rights in hire agreements and other supply contracts under the Consumer Rights Act is with regard to the right to supply under s.17. Since a contract of hire is not intended to transfer ownership in the goods, this statutory term is modified in hire contracts. Thus s.17(1)(a) provides that:

> **". . .in the case of a contract for the hire of goods, that at the beginning of the period of hire the trader must have the right to transfer possession of the goods by way of hire for that period".**

Similarly, s.17(3) provides that a contract of hire is to be treated as including a term that the hirer will enjoy quiet possession of the goods for the period of hire. The exception to this is where that possession may be disturbed by the owner or a third party entitled to disturb the hirer's quiet possession due to a disclosed encumbrance or charge.

Where the Consumer Rights Act does not apply (e.g. where the contract of hire was entered into before 1 October 2015 or it is a contract between two traders for example) we must turn again to the Supply of Goods and Services Act. Under the 1982 Act the first set of implied terms discussed above are inapplicable since there is no transfer of property. Nonetheless, ss.6–10 of the Supply of Goods and Services Act 1982 apply to contracts of hire other than hire-purchase agreements.[17] The intention behind them is to imply in hire contracts, terms similar to those implied in sale of goods contracts by ss.12–15 of the Sale of Goods Act. In fact the implied terms as to description,[18] satisfactory quality and fitness for purpose[19] and sample[20] are identical in effect to the corresponding Sale of Goods Act provisions. The only difference is that which reflects the fact that no property is intended to transfer within a contract of hire. Thus, rather than replicating the implied condition as to the right to sell, s.7 of the 1982 Act contains (i) a condition as to title, namely that the bailor has (or, in the case of an agreement to bail in the future, will have) a right to transfer possession to the bailee (hirer) for the period of the hire, and (ii) a warranty of quiet possession during the period of hire except in so far as the bailee's (hirer's) possession may be disturbed by someone entitled to the benefit of any charge or encumbrance disclosed or known to the bailee (hirer) before the contract.

17 s.6(3) makes clear that an agreement to hire goods falls under the Act regardless of whether services are also to be supplied and that the consideration can take any form, i.e. monetary or otherwise.

18 s.8.

19 s.9.

20 s.10.

Contracts for Services

8–009 As with the types of contract previously mentioned, the dichotomy between the Consumer Rights Act and the Supply of Goods and Services Act is again operative with regard to contracts for services with the Consumer Rights Act largely reflecting the position under the 1982 Act. It is clear that these terms are implied not only in contracts where the supply of service is the substance of the contract but also in contracts of hire and sale of goods where, although the substance of the contract is the hire or transfer of ownership of goods, there is nevertheless an undertaking by the seller that he will provide a service (e.g. of installing the goods).[21] These terms are implied by the Supply of Goods and Services Act 1982 ss.13–15:

> **"13. In a contract for the supply of a service where the supplier is acting in the course of a business, there is an implied term that the supplier will carry out the service with reasonable care and skill.**
>
> **14(1). Where, under a contract for the supply of a service by a supplier acting in the course of a business, the time for the service to be carried out is not fixed by the contract, left to be fixed in a manner agreed by the contract or determined by the course of dealing between the parties, there is an implied term that the supplier will carry out the service within a reasonable time.**
>
> **(2) What is a reasonable time is a question of fact.**
>
> **15(1). Where, under a contract for the supply of a service, the consideration for the service is not determined by the contract, left to be determined in a manner agreed by the contract or determined by the course of dealing between the parties, there is an implied term that the party contracting with the supplier will pay a reasonable charge.**
>
> **(2) What is a reasonable charge is a question of fact."**

These terms, with minor modifications to language and presentation are re-enacted by the Consumer Rights Act. Thus s.49 of the Consumer Rights Act dictates that where a trader supplies a service to a consumer, the trader must perform the service with reasonable care and skill. Similarly, s.51 contains equivalent provisions to those noted above concerning the price to be paid in the absence of any agreement between the parties. The Consumer Rights Act does,

21 s.12(3). See, for example, *Abramova v Oxford Institute of Legal Practice* [2011] EWHC 613 (QB) where a claim for negligent teaching was rejected. Note that under the Consumer Rights Act, express provision is made for the situation where the trader contracts to both supply and install goods. Under s.15 goods will not conform to the supply contract where they have been incorrectly installed by the trader. The consequences of this are explained in Ch.13 below.

however, extend the terms with contracts for the supply of services to consumers. Under s.50, "anything that is said or written to the consumer" which is taken into account by the consumer when deciding to enter into the contract or is taken into account by the consumer when making any decision about the service after entering into the contract, will be treated as a term of the contract. Moreover, information provided by the trader to the consumer concerning the main characteristics of the service as required by the Consumer Contracts (Information, Cancellation and Additional Charges) Regulations 2013[22] will also be treated as a term of the contract.

By way of exception, however, these terms are not implied in any contract of employment or apprenticeship.[23] Moreover, the Secretary of State has power by statutory instrument to exclude one or more of the terms in the third set of the Supply of Goods and Services Act from applying to specified services.[24] Three such exclusion orders have so far been made, excluding s.13 from applying to:

(i) the services of an advocate in court or before any tribunal, inquiry or arbitrator and in carrying out preliminary work directly affecting the conduct of the hearing;

(ii) the services rendered to a company by a director of a company in his capacity as such[25];

(iii) the services rendered to a building society by a director of the society, or those rendered to an industrial or provident society by a management committee member, in his capacity as such[26]; and

(iv) the services of an arbitrator or umpire in his capacity as such.[27]

The first of these was to prevent s.13 sweeping away the immunity form an action in negligence conferred upon advocates (notably solicitors) by the decision in *Rondel v Worsley*.[28] The exclusion order was not necessary in order to preserve the immunity of barristers because a barrister does not have a contractual relationship with his client and therefore s.13 would not apply to him anyway. The immunity for advocates has since been removed by the decision in *Arthur J.S. Hall & Co v Simons*.[29]

22 SI 2013/3134.
23 SGSA s.12(2); CRA 2015 s.48(2).
24 The same power exists in relation to the Consumer Rights Act, see s.48(5).
25 Supply of Services (Exclusion of Implied Terms) Order (SI 1982/1771).
26 Supply of Services (Exclusion of Implied Terms) Order (SI 1983/902).
27 Supply of Services (Exclusion of Implied Terms) Order (SI 1985/1).
28 [1969] 1 A.C. 191.
29 [2002] 1 A.C. 615. The immunity of expert witnesses in relation to evidence given in court or views expressed in anticipation of legal proceedings has recently been removed by the Supreme Court in *Jones v Kaney* [2011] UKSC 13.

The third set of terms does not apply to contracts of employment. The exclusion of s.13 from applying to the services of a director is thus necessary in order to prevent it discriminating unfairly against non-employed directors. If s.13 had applied to directors it would have imposed on them an objective standard of care. That would have been a rather higher standard of care than the law in fact imposes upon directors.

9

Product Liability

9-001 A manufacturer of a defective product may be found liable on any one of a number of grounds. There are five principal grounds which this chapter shall consider. It is important to realise that each ground has both advantages and disadvantages and moreover, multiple grounds may be applicable on the facts. For example, broadly speaking, in a case of a defective product that injures the consumer purchaser, both the implied terms of the Sale of Goods Act and the provisions of Pt I of the Consumer Protection Act 1987 may well apply. In such a situation the buyer will be able to pursue either the manufacturer (under the Consumer Protection Act) or the retailer (under the Sale of Goods Act or the Consumer Rights Act).[1]

The Contract of Sale

9-002 Like any other seller of goods, a manufacturer can be liable for a breach of a term of his contract of sale. This liability benefits only the immediate purchaser from the manufacturer, because liability for breach of contract exists only between parties to the same contract. In the case of direct marketing the immediate purchaser may be the actual consumer. Where goods are marketed via wholesaler and retailer, the person who buys the goods from the retailer cannot complain that the manufacturer was in breach of his contract of sale with the wholesaler. He can of course sue upon his own contract of sale, i.e. sue the retailer. The protection offered through ss.12–15 of the Sale of Goods Act, and their counterparts in the Consumer Rights Act, are often seen, and correctly so, as important safeguards for the consumer. Nevertheless one

1 See, for example, *Ide v ATB Sales Ltd* [2007] EWHC 1667 where the Consumer Protection Act was used rather than the seemingly more straightforward claim under s.14(2) of the Sale of Goods Act. See para.9-011, below.

must remember that, although they enhance the purchaser's contractual rights against his seller, they do not confer upon him any rights against other persons. Indeed, if X buys goods and passes them as a gift to Y, those implied terms are of no benefit at all to Y, unless the contract purports to confer that benefit upon him thereby enabling him to rely on the Contracts (Rights of Third Parties) Act 1999.[2]

There is another way, assignment, by which Y can be given the benefit of the purchaser's (X's) rights against the seller. The most effective way of doing this is for X to comply with the provisions of s.136 of the Law of Property Act 1925, i.e. to give Y a written notice, signed by X, unconditionally assigning to Y all X's rights as buyer under the contract of sale.[3] X can do this at the time of giving goods to Y or at any later stage. Of course in transferring his rights to Y, X is losing them himself. The consent of the seller is not needed for such an assignment. However, X cannot assign his burdens under the contract without the seller's consent (i.e. the obligation to pay).

Collateral Contract or Guarantee

9-003 Where goods are marketed indirectly and the manufacturer therefore does not sell directly to the consumer, it can nevertheless happen that the manufacturer makes a collateral contract with the consumer. The classic case of this was *Carlill v Carbolic Smoke Ball Co*[4] where the defendants published an advertisement claiming that their product was a cure and preventative of any number of illnesses. In particular, the company promised in the advertisement to pay £100 to anyone who contracted influenza after using a carbolic smoke ball as instructed for a specified period. Mrs Carlill saw the advertisement, purchased a smoke ball, used it as instructed for the specified period and nevertheless caught "flu". Although she had not bought the smoke ball from the company, it was held that there was a contract between her and the company, albeit not a contract of sale. A contract is a bargain and the bargain was that the company made her the promise in the advertisement and she in return bought one of their smoke balls from a retailer. The company made her an offer in the advertisement which she accepted by buying a smoke ball from the retailer.

It can be seen then that manufacturers' "guarantees" (or "warranties") often form the basis of a contract between manufacturer and customer similar to that in *Carlill v Carbolic Smoke Ball Co.*[5] It is true that often they do not specify a sum of money and sometimes may contain

2 See para.7-003, above.
3 See, for example, N. Curwen, "The problems of transferring carriage rights: an equitable solution" [1992] J.B.L. 245.
4 [1893] 1 Q.B. 256.
5 [1893] 1 Q.B. 256.

many qualifications. Nevertheless, if a guarantee promise (e.g. "The goods are warranted to be in perfect condition on leaving the factory") is broken, then the manufacturer is liable, subject to the qualifications in the guarantee. An example of such a qualification might occur where a manufacturer promises to refund the purchase price "provided the goods are first returned carriage paid to manufacturer".

Sometimes a guarantee does more than qualify the benefits which it gives. It may take away or qualify other rights of the consumer which are quite independent of the guarantee. In particular it may claim to restrict or remove the consumer's ability to bring an action for negligence.[6] This may be achieved by some clause in the guarantee such as "Apart from his obligations under the terms of this guarantee, the manufacturer shall not be liable for any loss however arising". This type of guarantee was in the past commonly created by the manufacturer supplying with the goods a reply paid postcard which the purchaser was asked to fill in and post, thereby accepting the terms. Prior to the enactment of the Consumer Rights Act 2015, a clause in the manufacturer's or distributor's guarantee which attempted to exclude or restrict the manufacturer's or distributor's liability to the consumer was of no effect.[7] The Law Commission concluded that this additional protection was superfluous for two reasons.[8] First, the breadth of the other provisions within UCTA were such that such attempts to restrict liability would potentially be caught in any event and secondly, the liability for manufacturers under Pt I of the Consumer Protection Act offered satisfactory protection for consumers.[9] Consequently, the Consumer Rights Act 2015 does not preserve the specific protection offered to consumers by UCTA s.5 but under s.30 of the Consumer Rights Act consumer guarantees must:

(i) be written in plain, intelligible language;

(ii) include the name and address of the guarantor;

(iii) state that the consumer has statutory rights regarding the goods which are not affected by the guarantee;

(iv) state the duration and territorial scope of the guarantee; and

(v) be made available to the consumer in writing, and within a reasonable time.

---

6 See para.9-005, below.

7 By virtue of UCTA s.5.

8 Law Commission Report No. 292 (2005) Cmnd. 6464, paras 3.48–3.49.

9 It is not possible to contract out of liability under Pt I. In effect, s.5 would be relied on only where the damage caused by the defective product was for less than £275 and thereby not recoverable under the CPA. See below, para.9-013.

9–004 The general principles of exclusion clauses, together with UCTA and the Consumer Rights Act will be considered in Ch.10. Section 30 also confirms that guarantees freely given, have contractual effect, thus removing any question mark as to the validity of such guarantees at common law.[10] Consequently any guarantee offered by, for example, the manufacturer, will be legally enforceable. Section 30(2) defines "consumer guarantee" in the following terms:

> **"'Guarantee' here means an undertaking to the consumer given without extra charge by a person acting in the course of the person's business (the 'guarantor') that, if the goods do not meet the specifications set out in the guarantee statement or in any associated advertising—**
>
> **(a) the consumer will be reimbursed for the price paid for the goods, or**
>
> **(b) the goods will be repaired, replaced or handled in any way."**

Note, therefore, that the protection offered by s.30 extends only to guarantees freely given. It is of no application to extended warranties where consideration will be provided.[11]

Negligence

9–005 *Donoghue v Stevenson*[12] was a landmark in legal development. The House of Lords established the principle that a consumer who suffers damage because of a manufacturer's negligence can sue the latter for damages and can do so irrespective of whether the consumer bought the goods. Mrs Donoghue and a friend went into a café. The friend bought for Mrs Donoghue a bottle of ginger beer, manufactured by Stevenson. Mrs Donoghue drank some. When the remainder was poured out, she noticed that the bottle contained two half-decomposing snails. She suffered some shock as well as some gastro-enteritis.

From the consumer's point of view, there is a considerable drawback to an action in negligence; he has to prove that the manufacturer (or one or more of his employees) was negligent. This involves showing that reasonable care was not taken in the manufacture. This can be difficult because the consumer has no means of knowing what goes on (or went on) in the factory. Sometimes it may seem obvious that there must have been negligence, as in the case of the

---

10 CRA 2015 s.30(3). This replicates the position under reg.15(1) of the Sale and Supply of Goods to Consumers Regulations 2002 (SI 2002/3045) which implemented the European Directive on Consumer Guarantees (Directive 99/44/EC). The Regulations were revoked by the Consumer Rights Act 2015.

11 See C. Willett et al, "The Sale and Supply of Goods to Consumers Regulations" [2004] J.B.L. 94 at 115–116.

12 [1932] A.C. 562.

purchaser of a bath bun who found a stone in the middle of it.[13] In such a case, the facts may be said to speak for themselves—res ipsa loquitur. Then it is up to the manufacturer to prove that there was no negligence, i.e. that all reasonable care was taken. In *Chaproniere v Mason*[14] the manufacturer brought evidence to show that he had a safe system of operations such as to prevent alien matter entering the food. The court held that this did not show an absence of negligence since someone must have been careless in not following the proper system. The manufacturer was therefore liable.

A similar situation arose in *Daniels v White*[15] where some carbolic acid got into a bottle of lemonade. The manufacturer brought evidence that he had a safe system of operating and adequate supervision to ensure that the system was followed. Here it was held that this showed that all reasonable care had been taken. The manufacturer was therefore not liable. However, the reasoning behind the decision in *Daniels v White* seems questionable. If there was in operation a good system to prevent alien matter entering the lemonade, then an employee must have been very negligent if the alien matter entered the product despite "the system". An employer is answerable for the negligence of his employees. Therefore in *Daniels v White*[16] it would seem that the employer (the defendant) ought to have been held liable. The decision has been criticised and in *Hill v James Crowe*[17] MacKenna J refused to follow it.

It should be pointed out that an action in negligence is not restricted to shock and personal injuries but may also include damage to property or even sometimes purely financial loss. 9–006

It should also be pointed out that *Donoghue v Stevenson*[18] established a principle of wider application than it may so far have appeared. Anyone (whether he is a manufacturer or not) who ought to appreciate that his acts or omissions may well cause harm to another may be liable to that other for any damage caused by his negligence in carrying on those activities.

Suppose a manufacturer of catapults sells some to a wholesaler, who sells some to a retailer who in turn sells one to a young boy. Suppose also that, because it has a latent defect, the catapult is not of satisfactory quality and that it breaks in use and injures the boy's eye as a result. The boy will no doubt succeed in his claim for breach of contract against the retailer, as will the retailer succeed against the wholesaler and the wholesaler against the manufacturer: *Godley v Perry*.[19] The retailer's claim against the wholesaler is a claim for indemnity. This simply means that retailer is entitled to claim from the wholesaler (as damages for breach of contract) the whole amount which the retailer is himself liable to pay his buyer. That is the amount of the retailer's loss arising from the wholesaler's breach of contract. On the same reasoning the wholesaler is entitled to indemnity from the manufacturer. In this way, liability is passed back up the chain of distribution. What if there is a blockage in the process? This could happen if, for

13 *Chaproniere v Mason* (1905) 21 T.L.R. 633.
14 (1905) 21 T.L.R. 633.
15 [1938] 160 L.T. 128.
16 [1938] 160 L.T. 128.
17 [1978] I.C.R. 298.
18 [1932] A.C. 562.
19 [1960] 1 W.L.R. 9.

example, the wholesaler has gone out of business or if in the contract between the wholesaler and the retailer there is a valid exemption clause which prevents the wholesaler being liable to the retailer. In this case, the retailer is liable to his buyer, the boy, but now has no contract under which he can recover indemnity. We have already seen that if the defect was due to the negligence of the manufacturer, the boy could himself have sued the manufacturer directly for negligence. That, however, is not much use to the retailer if the boy has chosen instead to sue the retailer for breach of contract. In *Lambert v Lewis*[20] Lord Diplock suggested that in that case someone down the chain of distribution who suffers economic loss (i.e. because he has to pay out damages for breach of contract), might well be able to claim indemnity direct from the negligent manufacturer under the principle in *Donoghue v Stevenson*.[21]

Product Liability

9-007 From the customer's point of view, the drawback to the implied terms in the Sale of Goods Act and the statutory rights in the Consumer Rights Act is that only the buyer can sue the seller. If someone other than the buyer was injured by the goods, neither Act gives him any rights—other than in the exceptional case where the Contracts (Rights of Third Parties) Act 1999 applies.[22] A claim in negligence, on the other hand, can be brought by any consumer. The drawback to this claim is that the defendant (usually the manufacturer) must be shown to have been negligent. Part I of the Consumer Protection Act 1987 implemented the Product Liability Directive[23] and gives the consumer an additional right to make a claim which is free of both these drawbacks. Under this Act, anyone who is injured by a defective product can sue the manufacturer, irrespective of whether the manufacturer was negligent. Damage caused to non-business property can be claimed if it exceeds £275 in value. In giving this right, the Act does not remove or alter any other rights of the consumer, e.g. under the Sale of Goods Act; the Consumer Rights Act; or the law of negligence.

Basis of the Claim—s.2

9-008 To succeed under Pt I of the Consumer Protection Act, the claimant must establish four things, namely that:

20 [1982] A.C. 225.
21 [1932] A.C. 562.
22 See para.7-003, above.
23 85/374/EEC.

(a) a product contained a defect;

(b) the claimant suffered damage;

(c) the damage was caused by the defect; and

(d) the defendant was, producer, own-brander or importer into the UK (or, sometimes, supplier of the product).

Meaning of "Defect"

A product is defective "if the safety of the product is not such as persons generally are entitled to expect".[24] Safety includes safety in the context of risks of damage to property as well as in the context of death or personal injury. Thus new furniture would be defective if it contained live woodworm, even though the presence of the woodworm posed no threat of personal injury. Safety is a relative, not an absolute concept. A sharp kitchen knife cannot be made absolutely safe if it is to be any use as a kitchen knife. If, however, it were marketed as a child's toy or the blade were such that when used to peel potatoes it disintegrated into splinters, then it would not be as safe as people generally were entitled to expect. Thus s.3(2) provides that in determining whether a product is defective all the circumstances are to be taken into account, including: 9–009

> **"(a) the manner in which, and purposes for which, the product has been marketed, its get-up, the use of any mark in relation to the product and any instructions for, or warnings with respect to, doing or refraining from doing anything with or in relation to the product;[25]**
>
> **(b) what might reasonably be expected to be done with or in relation to the product; and**
>
> **(c) the time when the product was supplied by its producer to another.**

24 s.3(1). The fundamental distinction therefore, is that between dangerous goods and those which are merely shoddy. Part I of the CPA operates only in respect to the former category.

25 As to the relationship between "defect" and warnings supplied with the product, see *Worsley v Tambrands Ltd* [2000] P.I.Q.R. 95. In *Worsley* the court held that there was no liability (under either CPA or the common law) since the producer had done what the consumer was "entitled to expect: (1) they had a clearly legible warning on the outside of the box directing the user to the leaflet; (2) the leaflet was legible, literate, and unambiguous and contained all the material necessary to convey both the warning signs and the action required if any of them were present . . .", at 103.

As in the knife example earlier, the marketing and/or labelling will affect the use as to which the product is likely to be put. Something advertised as a toy is likely to be used by children. If something is advertised and sold as a hover-mower, is it reasonable to expect it to be used as a hedge-trimmer? If not, then it is not defective just because it is dangerous when used in that way.

Public expectations as to safety are to be judged as at the time the producer supplied the product in question. A producer is not required to meet expectations of safety which arise after he has supplied the product. Suppose manufacturer A has for some years produced a razor which will not normally cut the user unless it is slid sideways across the skin. Suppose that in May 2001 manufacturer B markets a razor which is equally efficient but which will not normally cut the user, even when slid sideways. Imagine that a razor supplied by manufacturer A in February 2000 is bought from a retailer in June 2001 and when used in July 2001 cuts the user's face when slid sideways across it. The fact that manufacturer B produced a safer razor after the razor in question had been supplied by manufacturer A is not enough to enable us to say that manufacturer A's razor was defective. If, however, another user is cut by a razor which manufacturer A supplied after May 2001, this user can point to the safer design of manufacturer B's razor as evidence that the razor which cut him was not as safe as persons were (at the time manufacturer A supplied it) entitled to expect.

The courts have considered the definition of "defective": *A v National Blood Authority (No.1)*[26] concerned the claims of 114 claimants for recovery of damages arising out of their infection with Hepatitis C due to transfusions with contaminated blood. Leaving aside the issue of whether the state of the art defence applied to the facts, Burton J had to determine whether the infected blood was defective under the Directive.[27] This issue was answered in the affirmative:[28]

> **"The blood products in this case were non-standard products, and were unsafe by virtue of the harmful characteristics which they had and which the standard products did not have".[29]**

Therefore the presence of Hepatitis C within the blood constituted a defect since:

> **". . .the public at large was entitled to expect that the blood transfused to them would be free from infection. There were no warnings and no material publicity, certainly none officially initiated by or for**

26 [2001] 3 All E.R. 289.

27 Burton J dealt with the issue of "defect" under art.6 of the Directive and not its equivalent, s.3 of the Act. See the comments at [2] of the judgment.

28 [2001] 3 All E.R. 289 at [79].

29 "A *non-standard* product is one which is different, obviously because it is deficient or inferior in terms of safety, from the standard product: and where it is the harmful characteristic or characteristics present in the non-standard product, but not in the standard product, which has or have caused the material injury or damage", at [36].

> **the benefit of the defendants, and the knowledge of the medical profession, not materially or at all shared with the consumer, is of no relevance. It is not material to consider whether any steps or any further steps could have been taken to avoid or palliate the risk that the blood would be infected."**

This was so despite the facts (i) that the defendant was unaware of the risk, and (ii) that the medical profession was aware of the risk, since the issue was one of the legitimate expectations of the public.[30] 9-010

In the recent case of *Wilkes v Depuy International Ltd*[31] the court was required to determine whether an artificial hip which fractured after only three years was defective under the Consumer Protection Act. In rejecting the claim, Hickinbottom J took a very different approach to that of Burton J in A and was critical of the "rigid categorisation" achieved through the standard/non-standard product dichotomy[32] and the use of the phrase "legitimate expectations" to describe the standard expected.[33] Indeed, Hickinbottom J suggested that:

> **"on the particular facts of a specific case, the assessment may be difficult in practice; but it is conceptually simple. In my view, the courts should guard against either over-complicating, or over-analysing, the exercise."**

Thus, in the view of the court, when considering the question of whether the product is defective, it is clear that:[34]

(i) "Defect" is concerned with the condition of product itself and not on the acts and omissions of those involved in the manufacture of the product (thus distinguishing liability under the Act from claims in negligence).

(ii) The key issue is safety, not efficacy or fitness for purpose (thus distinguishing liability under the Act from contractual claims) and that "safety" is an inherently relative concept. Thus, in the context of medical products, there will inevitably be a risk of damage.

(iii) The level of safety expected by a particular patient is not relevant, nor is the level of safety which the general public think the product ought to provide. Likewise, actual

30 As ascertained by the court. See *B (A Child) v McDonald's Restaurants Ltd* [2002] EWHC 490.

31 [2016] EWHC 3096 (QB).

32 [2016] EWHC 3096 (QB), "the categorisation of defects into "standard"/"non-standard", as a classification, is unnecessary and undesirable" at [94].

33 [2016] EWHC 3096 (QB), "a test of what persons generally are 'entitled to expect' requires no gloss, and does not benefit from being re-described" at [71].

34 [2016] EWHC 3096 (QB) at [63]–[65].

> expectations of an actual or notional individual or group of individuals is not relevant, rather it is the level of safety which people are entitled to expect.

The question that follows is, therefore, what factors are relevant in determining the meaning of "defect". There are, obviously, those factors specifically noted in the non-exhaustive list in s.3(2) of the Act but one of the more controversial aspects of Burton J's judgment in *A v National Blood Authority* was his approach in finding the following factors to be irrelevant:[35]

(i) The avoidability of the harmful characteristic.

(ii) The impracticality, cost or difficulty of taking such measures.

(iii) The benefit to society or utility of the product.[36]

The approach of Burton J on this issue has been subject to considerable criticism. One frequent criticism stems from the use of "consumer expectation" particularly where the product is particularly complicated since it is highly likely that the public at large will have no expectations whatsoever. A further criticism is in Burton J's failure to accept the relevance of the cost-benefit analysis. As Goldberg puts it:[37]

> **"There is a strong argument in favour of such an approach, particularly in the context of medicinal products including whole blood and other blood products. It is arguable that all medicinal products carry a risk of adverse reactions, even in a minority of consumers, and that these consumers are not necessarily entitled to expect that the products will be risk-free. Despite the emphasis on consumer expectation in Burton J.'s judgment, there is an inherent logic in addressing the problems of defective medicinal products, including blood and blood products, by weighing the risks against the anticipated benefits and against the 'costs' of not using the product, such as the risk of disease."**

On this point in Wilkes, Hickinbottom J again took a different approach in stating that a risk-benefit approach was not only permissible, but "inherent in the relative nature of 'safety'":[38]

35 [2001] 3 All E.R. 289 at [68].

36 These points essentially form a cost-benefit analysis.

37 R. Goldberg, "Paying for bad blood: strict product liability after the hepatitis C litigation" [2002] Med. Law Rev. 165 at 174.

38 [2016] EWHC 3096 (QB) at [82]. Note also the comments, obiter, at [83] regarding the relevancy of costs.

> **"Given that. . .a [medical] product will inevitably have some risks attached. . .any assessment of its safety will necessarily require the risks involved in use of that product to be balanced against its potential benefits including its potential utility. As such a product will almost always involve design compromises, the effect of eliminating or reducing a particular risk can only be seen in the context of any adverse consequences of doing so, in the form of increased risks of a different sort or reduced benefit and utility."**

In *Gee and others v DePuy International Ltd*[39] the court again considered the concept of "defect" within s.3. The claimants (312 in total) had each undergone hip replacement surgery and suffered an adverse reaction to fragments of metal debris generated by their artificial hip. The court held that the artificial hip joints were not defective under the Act and applied the flexible approach to defining "defect" articulated in *Wilkes*, preferring that to the approach in *A v National Blood Authority*. Mrs Justice Andrews emphasised that "safety is inherently and necessarily a relative concept, because no product, and particularly a medicinal product, if effective, can be absolutely safe".[40] In the case of artificial hip joints, it was understood that such products will shed debris in the course of their normal operation and that such debris can cause an immunological reaction. Thus, the claimants' argument that the artificial hip joints had a propensity to shed debris, causing harm, and were therefore defective was flawed. What was crucial was whether the "incidence of that harm, either in nature or degree, is abnormal" and if it was, if such abnormality resulted in the product falling below the standard of safety persons generally are entitled to expect.[41] The court concluded that the claimants had not established that the artificial hip joints had an abnormal potential for damage since the available data did not show that the product had a materially worse failure rate than comparator products.[42]

It remains to be seen how the judiciary will approach the concept of "defect" in future cases, although the clarity brought by the decision in *Wilkes* and *Gee* is certainly welcome. Nonetheless, recent decisions have, however, demonstrated related difficulties faced by claimants in establishing that the product concerned was defective under s.3. In *Foster v Biosil*[43] the claimant sought damages under the Act when a breast implant ruptured within seven months following a double mastectomy. The court held that in order to succeed the claimant had to be show that (i) the goods were defective, and (ii) how the defect had occurred. Since there was scientific evidence showing that implants rarely ruptured, the claimant failed to show that the

39 [2018] EWHC 1208 (QB).

40 [2018] EWHC 1208 (QB) at [110].

41 [2018] EWHC 1208 (QB) at [112].

42 See the Scottish decision in *Hastings v Finsbury Orthopaedics Ltd* [2021] CSIH 6 where the approach taken followed that in *Wilkes* and *Gee*.

43 (2001) 59 B.M.L.R. 178.

goods were defective under s.3(1). Similarly, in *Richardson v LRC Products Ltd*[44] the claimant, Mrs Richardson, became pregnant after a condom failed and sued the manufacturer under Pt 1 of the Consumer Protection Act. Despite considerable (conflicting) scientific evidence, the judge was unable to identify any reason for the condom failing and thus the question was whether the condom failing, in itself, led to the conclusion that the product was defective under s.3. Kennedy J held that the condom was not defective simply by reason of the fact that it had fractured and failed. In so finding, he was persuaded by evidence that condoms do suffer from "inexplicable failures" and that the condoms had been manufactured to standards in excess of the relevant British Standard.[45] Whilst this last point is, by itself, not determinative, it is clear that the decision makes the distinctions between what people actually expect as to the safety of products and what persons generally are entitled to expect. In the case of the condom, Kennedy J accepted that "the user's expectation is that a condom will not fail" but found that they were not entitled to this expectation. This was so, since, "there are no claims made by the defendants that one will never fail and no-one has ever supposed that any method of contraception intended to defeat nature will be 100 per cent effective".[46] Accordingly, Mrs Richardson's claim failed.

9–011 There are indications, albeit only tentative, that the courts are starting to alleviate some of the difficulties faced by claimants relying upon the Consumer Protection Act. In *Ide v ATB Sales Ltd*[47] the claimant sought damages for personal injury when the handlebar on his mountain bike fractured injuring his head and causing significant brain damage. The defendant importer argued that the claimant had somehow lost control of the bike and that the handlebar was fractured as a result of this, rather than any defect within the product itself. The court was, however, satisfied that on the balance of the evidence produced, the handlebar was defective within s.3(1).[48] This was so despite the fact that the bicycle was manufactured to British standards.[49] Moreover, there is no requirement for the claimant to show how the defect occurred as was suggested in *Foster v Biosil*.[50] In *Baker v KTM Sportmotorcycle UK Ltd*[51] the Court of Appeal

44 [2000] P.I.Q.R. 164.

45 [2000] P.I.Q.R. 164 at 170–171.

46 [2000] P.I.Q.R. 164 at 170.

47 [2007] EWHC 1667 (QB).

48 Contrast *Hufford v Samsung Electronics (UK) Ltd* [2014] EWHC 2956 (TCC) where a refrigerator caught fire. The claimant failed to prove that the product was defective in light of scientific evidence, accepted by the court, that the fire originated outside of the product.

49 This argument was advanced by the defendants as evidence that the bike met the test under s.3(1), i.e. that the bike was as safe as persons generally are entitled to expect. This submission was acknowledged (at [15]) but not considered in the judgment. Interestingly, in *Wilkes v DePuy International Ltd* [2016] EWHC 3096 (QB) it was suggested that compliance with relevant regulatory standards may be evidence, "and in an appropriate case, powerful evidence", of the standard of safety the general public are entitled to expect, at [101]. In *Gee and others v DePuy International Ltd* [2018] EWHC 1208 (QB) on the other hand, regulatory approval was "of limited assistance" at [489].

50 [2007] EWHC 1667 at [80]. See the comments of Hickinbottom J in *Wilkes v DePuy International Ltd* [2016] EWHC 3096 (QB) at [73].

51 [2017] EWCA Civ 378.

followed *Ide v ATB Sales Ltd* in holding that there was no need for the claimant to establish a specific design or manufacturing defect nor prove how the defect was caused. What matters is that the claimant proves that the product was defective.[52]

Similarly, in *Boston Scientific Medizintechnik GmbH v AOK Sachsen-Anhalt*[53] the European Court of Justice has also taken a pro-consumer approach to questions around the definition of "defect" and causation under the Product Liability Directive.[54] The court ruled that, in the context of medical products (pace-makers) where a group or series of products were identified as potentially defective, "it is possible to classify as defective all the products in that group or series, without there being any need to show that the product in question is defective".[55] The court justified this approach on the basis of the level of safety the general public is entitled to expect from a pacemaker, including the objective characteristics of the product (i.e. to fulfil a life-saving function) and the requirements of the group intended to use the product, (i.e. -particularly vulnerable patients). In the specific context of medical devices of that kind which are implanted into the human body, this is a welcome decision since how might a claimant otherwise prove that their specific pacemaker was defective? Where it is recognised that a batch of pacemakers is defective in that some products within that batch may fail without warning, it is surely correct that the costs of replacing those devices (i.e. surgery) should be met by the manufacturer.[56] The decision is not one which has broader, or indeed, general application to product liability law where the general principle that it is for the injured party to prove a defect is obviously correct.

Meaning of "product"

The definition of product is very wide. Thus there is liability for defects in virtually anything which might conceivably be considered a product, including goods,[57] electricity, gas and vapours. There is an exception in the case of land. 9-012

Liability is imposed for defective goods, not for defective land. "Goods" include "things comprised in land by virtue of being attached to it".[58] A building is land. A builder will therefore not be liable under the Act for damage caused by a defect in the building because it was badly built, e.g. because the foundations were inadequate, though he might be liable under some

52 Similarly, in *Al-Iqra v DSG Retail Ltd* [2019] EWHC 429 (QB) court was able to infer, in the absence of misuse, that a heater was defective where it had been established that it was the cause of a fire.

53 C-503/13.

54 1999/34/EC.

55 C-503/13 at [41].

56 Note the comments of the CJEU regarding the need to fairly apportion the risks inherent with modern technologies at [42].

57 s.1(2) provides that "'product' means any goods or electricity and . . .includes a product which is comprised in another product, whether by virtue of being a component part or raw material or otherwise".

58 s.45.

other legal provision.[59] A brick or tile used in the construction of a building is a thing comprised in land by virtue of being attached to it. Therefore, if a tile, because it is defective, breaks and falls on to a passer-by, the manufacturer of the tile will be liable under the Act.

Under the Act as originally enacted, agricultural produce and game were excluded from liability under the Act unless it had undergone an "industrial process" giving it "essential characteristics". These expressions were not defined in the Act. Presumably the freezing or canning of peas or the turning of meat into sausages would amount to such an industrial process. In that case, the industrial processor was regarded as the producer and could be liable to anyone injured by a defect in the peas or sausages. That is so even if the defect (e.g. salmonella) was present in the produce before it reached the industrial processor. These provisions making the industrial processor liable as producer remain. However, in accordance with an amendment to the Product Liability Directive[60] and with effect from 4 December 2000, the immunity (i.e. of farmers) from liability in respect of primary agricultural produce and game has been removed. This was done by the Consumer Protection Act 1987 (Product Liability) (Modification) Order 2000.[61]

Damage—s.5

9–013 Under Pt I of the 1987 Act damages can be claimed for death or personal injuries and also for the loss of, or damage to, property (including land) which is:[62]

(a) of a description of property ordinarily intended for private use, occupation or consumption; and

(b) intended by the person suffering the loss or damage mainly for his own private use, occupation or consumption.

Damage to business property cannot be claimed under the Act.[63] Furthermore, the claimant cannot claim even for his private (non-business) property loss or damage unless it exceeds £275. This is to prevent trivial claims for property damage.[64] If, however, the amount of the

59 e.g. negligence or the Defective Premises Act 1972.
60 1999/34/EC.
61 SI 2000/2771.
62 s.5(3).
63 See, for example, *Renfrew Golf Club v Motocaddy Ltd* [2016] CSIH 57 (no liability under Pt I of the Act for damage to the clubhouse of a private members' golf club since the clubhouse could not be said to be property ordinarily intended for private use).
64 s.5(4).

damage done to the claimant's private property exceeds £275, then the whole amount is recoverable, including the first £275.[65]

A claim under Pt I of the Consumer Protection Act cannot be made for any damage to the defective product itself.[66] Thus if a defective toaster catches fire damaging the house and contents, one adds up the value of the damage done (but not including either the toaster itself or any property used mainly for business purposes, e.g. a word-processor). If the value exceeds £275, then it can be claimed under the Act. If the defect had been a component of the toaster, say the heating element, the result would still be the same unless the heating element had not been supplied as part of the toaster (e.g. had been bought as a replacement later). If the defective element had not been supplied with the toaster, then the value of the damage done to the toaster (but not to the element) could be included in the claim.[67] The rule is that one cannot claim for damage to the defective product itself or to any product which was supplied with the defective product comprised within it.

Where a defective product is used as a component by another manufacturer, there will be two defective products and two producers. Under the Act the claimant can sue either. Whichever he sues, he cannot include a claim for damage done to the component or to the larger item which was supplied with the component comprised in it.

The defendant—s.2

Under the 1987 Act a claim can be brought against the producer,[68] the own-brander[69] or the importer.[70] The producer is the manufacturer. In the case of products (like salt, oil or coal) which are won or abstracted, the person who wins or abstracts them is the producer. In the case of other products (e.g. agricultural produce) which are not manufactured, the producer is the farmer or the person who carries out an industrial process (e.g. freezing) which gives them essential characteristics. 9–014

An own-brander is liable if he has own-branded the goods in such a way as to hold himself out as being the producer. If Superstores own-brands the coffee it sells, it can avoid liability by labelling it with a statement such as "Made for Superstores by Coffee Fellers Inc".

Following the withdrawal of the UK from the EU, the only importer liable under the Act is the person who imported the product into the UK.[71] Prior to then an importer was defined as

65 Someone suffering property damage not exceeding £275 may, or course, be able to claim for it in negligence or under the implied terms of the Sale of Goods Act.

66 s.5(2).

67 In this case, of course, the claim would not itself be against the toaster manufacturer but against the manufacturer of the heating element.

68 s.2(2)(a).

69 s.2(2)(b).

70 s.2(2)(c).

71 Prior to the withdrawal of the UK from the EU, this referred to the person importing into the EU. See the Product Safety and Metrology etc. (Amendment etc.) (EU Exit) Regulations 2019/696, Sch.3, para.3.

the person who imported the product into the EU. Thus, before the UK's withdrawal from the EU, if a product was made in France and brought to England, there was no importer to sue, only a French producer. Now, the claimant can sue the UK importer.[72]

Where there is a long chain of distribution, the claimant may find it difficult to identify who was the producer or importer into the UK. He may ask anyone who has supplied the product in question, e.g. the retailer, wholesaler or distributor, to identify the producer, own-brander or importer into the UK.[73] If the supplier fails to make the identification and also fails to identify the person who supplied the product to him, the supplier is liable as if he had himself been the producer.

Defences—s.4

9–015 Section 4 provides the following defences:

1. The defect is due to compliance with any statutory requirement including any retained EU obligation.[74]

2. The defendant did not supply the product, e.g. it was stolen from his premises.

3. The defendant supplied the product otherwise than in the course of business and the defendant did not produce it (or own-brand it or import it into the UK) with a view to profit. This lets off grandad who makes grandson John a toy and gives it to him for Christmas. Similarly a tourist returning from Japan with a gift for a friend in Britain will not be liable either as supplier or as importer.

4. The defect did not exist in the product at the time it was supplied by the defendant (i.e. the producer, own-brander or importer). Thus the defendant would not be liable if chocolates he had made and supplied were poisoned by saboteurs at the retailer's premises.

72 Indeed, since the Regulation on Jurisdiction and the Recognition and Enforcement of Judgments in Civil and Commercial Matters (Recast) (Regulation 1215/2012/EU) which enabled the enforcement of UK judgments in all EU states (including Denmark) ceased to apply at the end of the transitional period following the UK's withdrawal from the EU pursuing the UK importer will much more straightforward route. The UK's application to join the Lugano Convention (which would have applied a similar framework to Regulation 1215/2012/EU) was rejected by the European Commission in July 2021.

73 s.2(3).

74 Prior to the withdrawal of the UK from the EU, this referred to any EU obligation. See the Product Safety and Metrology etc. (Amendment etc.) (EU Exit) Regulations 2019/696, Sch.3, para.4.

5. A component manufacturer is not liable where the defect is attributable to instructions given by the manufacturer of the larger product. In such circumstances, the defence will not, of course, be available to the producer of the larger product.

6. The "developmental risks" defence is available where the defendant shows "that the state of scientific and technical knowledge at the relevant time was not such that a producer of products of the same description as the product in question might be expected to have discovered the defect if it had existed in his products while they were under his control".[75] In short, a producer relying on this defence needs to show that the defect was not discoverable at the time he supplied the product. Suppose that in 2001 a pair of gloves supplied by the manufacturer in 1993 is proved to have caused arthritis to the wearer because the gloves were made with polyester. To succeed under the Consumer Protection Act, the claimant would have to establish that in 1993 people generally were entitled to expect the gloves not to carry the risk of causing arthritis.[76] If the claimant can establish that, then the manufacturer will have a defence if he can show that in 1993, given the then state of scientific and technical knowledge, the risk of the polyester causing arthritis was not discoverable. Establishing the defence might be very important to the manufacturer if over the years he has supplied a lot of such gloves and a lot of wearers have suffered arthritis because of them.

Whichever of these six defences in s.4 is raised, the burden of establishing it rests upon the defendant.

The same is true of the defence of contributory negligence.[77] With this defence the defendant is saying that the claimant has failed to take reasonable care and has thereby been partly responsible for his own injuries, loss or damage. This could apply where the claimant has made an unreasonable use of the product. In fact an unreasonable use of the product might allow the defendant three different arguments in his own defence. So suppose an adult sniffs glue, making himself very ill and subsequently sues the glue manufacturer. The latter could argue:

(i) That there was no defect in the glue, i.e. it was as safe as persons generally were entitled to expect. This argument would be especially strong if there were no commercially viable way of producing glue without the risk of toxic fumes, and if the container had carried a clear warning of the risks.

(ii) That the claimant's illness was caused not by the alleged defects in the product but entirely by his own decision to sniff the glue.

75 This defence was rejected in *A v National Blood Authority (No.1)*, considered above, since the risk was known. It was immaterial that the contamination was undetectable by the producer. See also, *Abouzaid v Mothercare UK (Ltd)* [2001] C.L.Y. 920.

76 See para.9-009, above.

77 s.6(1).

(iii) That the claimant by his own failure to take reasonable care for his own safety contributed to his own illness.

In this example it is difficult to know which of these arguments would find favour with a court. If either of the first two did so, the defendant would not be liable. If only the third found favour, the damages awarded would be a reduced proportion of what would be awarded for such an illness in the absence of contributory negligence.

Exclusion of Liability and Limitation

9-016 No exclusion or limitation of liability clause can exclude or limit the liability imposed by Pt I of the Consumer Protection Act.[78]

The rules on limitation are an entirely different matter. These are rules laid down by law which allow a claim to be brought only if legal proceedings are commenced before the expiry of a deadline. There are two such rules which apply to claims for product liability under the Consumer Protection Act:[79]

1. Proceedings must be commenced within three years of when the injury or damage occurred or, if the injury, etc, was not discovered until later, within three years of when the claimant became aware of the injury or damage.

2. No proceedings may be commenced more than 10 years after the producer supplied the product. If the own-brander or importer is being sued, then the 10 years run from when he supplied the product.

The 10 years begin to run the moment that the particular product in question was supplied by its producer (own-brander or importer). If those 10 years have expired, it is immaterial that the defendant continued, or even is still continuing, to manufacture and supply identical goods.

Part II of the Consumer Protection Act 1987

9-017 Part II has four functions. First, it empowers the Secretary of State to make safety regulations governing the making and supplying of goods, e.g. regulations designed to secure that goods

78 s.7.

79 See Sch.1 which amends the Limitation Act 1980.

are safe, that appropriate information is supplied with them and that inappropriate information is not supplied. Thus, for example, regulations may govern the composition or design of goods, may require goods to conform to a certain standard (e.g. a British Institute Standard) and may require a warning or instructions to be given with the goods. Some regulations made under earlier Acts continue to be effective under the 1987 Act. They relate to such things as children's nightdresses, carrycot stands, electric blankets, prams and pushchairs, cosmetics, colour coding of electrical appliances, and upholstered furniture. The regulations will sometimes affect only a manufacturer (e.g. where they govern design or composition). Other regulations may affect any supplier, whether manufacturer, wholesaler or retailer (e.g. regulations requiring information to be supplied with the goods). It is a criminal offence to infringe the regulations.

Secondly, Pt II enables quick action to be taken against the marketing of unsafe goods. Section 13 gives the Secretary of State powers to issue two types of instruction:

(i) a "prohibition notice" can be issued to prevent the trader upon whom it is served from supplying any specified type of goods which the Secretary of State considers unsafe; and

(ii) a "notice to warn" can require the trader upon whom it is served to take specified steps to warn consumers about unsafe goods which that trader supplies or has already supplied.

A "notice to warn" might well be served, for example, upon a car manufacturer if it appears that a certain model had a dangerous design fault. The notice will specify what steps the manufacturer must take. It may require him to publish a warning in the newspaper or it could, for example, require him to write individually to all purchasers of that model. Failure by a trader to comply with a prohibition notice or notice to warn is a criminal offence.

A prohibition notice can in practice be made only when the fact that there are dangerous goods on the market has come to the attention of the Secretary of State. It has sometimes been the case, however, that unsafe imported goods have been in the shops and bought in considerable quantities before the Secretary of State has learnt of their presence in the country. Hence each enforcement authority (i.e. local trading standards department) now has power to serve a "suspension notice" upon a trader where it has reasonable grounds to think that legal safety requirements have been infringed.[80] The notice will prohibit the trader from supplying specified goods for up to six months. If it turns out that there had been no infringement of the law in relation to the goods in question, the trader may be entitled to compensation from the enforcement authority.[81] In order to catch suspect goods at the ports, customs officers have power to seize and detain goods for up to two working days in

80 s.14.
81 s.14(7).

order to enable local trading standards officers to examine them to determine whether they infringe legal safety requirements.[82]

9-018 The third aspect of Pt II is that s.10 made it an offence for a trader to supply consumer goods which fail to comply with a general safety requirement. This offence was, however, rendered virtually redundant by the General Product Safety Regulations 1994 and repealed by the General Product Safety Regulations 2005.[83]

The fourth aspect of Pt II of the Consumer Protection Act relates to civil liability. The Act entitles a consumer to bring an action for damages against any trader in respect of damage or loss suffered by the consumer because of an infringement by the trader of safety regulations.[84] Thus a child whose nightdress catches fire because when supplied it did not comply with the safety regulations will be able to claim compensation for her burns from the manufacturer. This is so even if she did not buy it direct from the manufacturer (or, indeed, even if she did not buy it). She does not have to prove any negligence on the part of the manufacturer. However, it has been held that breaches of safety regulations which would fall under Pt I of the Consumer Protection Act 1987 will not be actionable under s.41: *Wilson v Beko Plc*.[85] Civil liability under the Act cannot be excluded or restricted by any exemption clause.

Criminal and civil liability under Pt II of the Consumer Protection Act attaches only to persons who are acting "in the course of carrying on a business". The defendant in *Southwark London Borough v Charlesworth*[86] was a shoe-repairer who also carried on a secondary business as a seller of second-hand goods. At his shop he sold an electric fire which infringed safety regulations.[87] The fire had come from his home and the money from the sale of the fire did not go through the books of the business. Nevertheless, there was no differentiation in the shop between the fire and other goods he was selling in his secondary line of business. That being so, the court held that the sale took place in the course of business. The result might have been different if there had been a notice attached to the goods making it clear that these goods had nothing to do with the defendant's business as a dealer in second-hand goods but had come from his home and that the sale of the goods was to be a private transaction.

82 s.31.

83 reg.46(2).

84 s.41.

85 [2019] EWHC 3362 (QB). This is so since under the Product Liability Directive it is not possible to extend strict liability for damage caused by defective products beyond that provided for in the Directive.

86 (1983) 147 J.P. 470.

87 In force under the Consumer Protection Act 1961.

The General Product Safety Regulations 2005

These Regulations[88] revoked and replaced the General Product Safety Regulations 1994 which implemented the Directive on General Product Safety.[89] They create criminal offences which are concerned with the marketing of unsafe products. The Regulations potentially apply if a product: 9-019

(i) is placed on the market by a producer; or

(ii) is supplied by a distributor.

For this purpose, placing on the market includes offering or agreeing to place on the market or exposing or possessing a product to place on the market. Supplying includes offering or agreeing to supply or exposing or possessing a product to be supplied.

Scope of the Regulations

The Regulations apply to the situation where a producer, in the course of a commercial activity, places on the market any product intended for consumers or likely to be used by consumers. They also impose requirements of care on a distributor of such a product. 9-020

- By reg.5, the producer commits an offence if he "places a product on the market" which is not a "safe" product.
- By reg.8, a distributor commits an offence if he does not act with due care in order to help ensure compliance with reg.5.

The latter requires, for example, that a distributor does not supply any products "which he knows, or should have presumed, on the basis of the information in his possession and as a professional, are dangerous".[90] The Regulations do not apply to any product which is used exclusively in the context of a commercial activity, e.g. a machine tool supplied to be used in a factory, or a computer to be used by a firm's secretary. Of course, if that same computer were instead sold direct to the secretary for her private use at home, then the Regulations would apply. "'Commercial activity' includes a business and a trade". This expression does not expressly include a profession. Apparently, for example, if that same computer were supplied

88 The General Product Safety Regulations 2005 (SI 2005/1803) implementing Directive 2001/95/EC. The regulations came into force, for the most part, on 1 October 2005.

89 92/59/EC.

90 reg.8(1)(a).

for use in the parish office of a church, that would still be within the Regulations, since presumably the church could not be said to be a business or a trade.

There is only a very short list of products excluded from the Regulations. Second-hand goods, demonstration models and reconditioned goods are all included. The only products excluded are:

- second-hand antiques;
- products supplied for repair or reconditioning before use, provided the supplier clearly informs the customer to that effect; and
- any product where there is retained EU law that makes specific provision governing all aspects of the safety of the product.[91]

Meaning of "Safe"

9-021 Safety is defined in terms of risk to persons, not property. A safe product "means any product which, under normal or reasonably foreseeable conditions of use, including duration, does not present any risk or only the minimum of risk compatible with the product's use, considered as acceptable and consistent with a high level of protection for the safety and health of persons".[92] Few products will be considered totally safe. It is enough, however, if three requirements are satisfied: (i) the risks presented are the minimum risk compatible with the product's use; (ii) those risks are "acceptable"; and (iii) those risks are consistent with a high level of protection for the safety and health of persons. The following factors, in particular, are to be taken into account:

- The characteristics and composition of the product, its packaging and instructions for assembly and maintenance.
- Its effect on other products, where it is reasonably foreseeable that it will be used with other products.

91 With the exception of Regulation (EC) No 765/2008 which deals with conformity marking (i.e. CE marks) and related market surveillance rules. The Regulation was incorporated into domestic law by the EU (Withdrawal) Act 2018 thus retaining largely the same framework. Most goods that previously required CE marking now fall under the UKCA (UK Conformity Assessed) mark where they are placed on the market in England, Wales, and Scotland. Note that a grace period is currently in effect until 1 January 2023 whereby most goods can still use the CE mark. In Northern Ireland the position is different and in general, continues to align with the EU framework where manufactured goods are placed on the market. See *https://www.gov.uk/guidance/placing-manufactured-goods-on-the-market-in-northern*-ireland [Accessed 25 April 2022].

92 See the definition of "safe product" under reg.2.

- Its presentation, labelling, any instructions for use and disposal and any other information provided by the producer.
- The categories of consumers at serious risk when using the product, especially children.

Obviously articles such as toys that are likely to be used by children will have to be safe for that group of consumers. The reference to instructions for disposal leaves open the possibility of a product being found to be unsafe because of the risks it poses when it is to be disposed of, i.e. after its useful life is over. This could well catch products which contain toxic chemicals. The reference to a product being used with other products might well apply, for example, to a shelf support bracket. Clearly such a bracket is only likely to be used together with other products, i.e. the shelf and the items to be placed on the shelf. The strength of the bracket will in that situation clearly be a feature of its safety.

The giving of information is a key feature. Thus reg.7 requires a producer to provide information to enable consumers to assess the risks inherent in it throughout the normal or reasonably foreseeable period of its use, where those risks are not immediately apparent without adequate warnings. It also requires producers to take measures, commensurate with the characteristics of the product, to enable consumers to be informed of the risks and to enable the producer, if necessary, to withdraw the product. In the case of many products, this in effect requires the producer to use a batch number system, so that different batches of the product can be identified from a mark or number on the product itself. It may also require sample testing of the marketed products, the investigation of complaints and keeping of distributors informed of risks which materialise after marketing.

In relation to many products there are published standards. Sometimes these are embodied in safety regulations; they may be technical specifications; or they may be national voluntary standards or contained in codes of good practice, etc. There is no absolute defence in respect of a product which complies with safety regulations. There is in that case, however, a presumption, until the contrary is proved, that the product is safe.[93] So far as concerns other types of standards, these are things to be taken into account in determining the safety which consumers may reasonably expect and hence whether the risks presented by the product are acceptable.

Who is Liable?

Primarily, it is the "producer" as defined in reg.2. There are, however, various people who may be regarded as the producer and thus liable. They are: the manufacturer provided that the manufacturer is established in the UK; any own-brander in the UK;[94] anyone reconditioning 9-022

93 See reg.6.

94 Where, for example, someone who presents himself as the manufacturer by affixing to the product his name, trade mark or other distinctive mark.

the product; and in cases where the manufacturer is not based in the UK, the manufacturer's established representative in the UK or the importer of the product into the UK.[95] As seen above, a distributor also can be liable, e.g. for failing to act with due care to help ensure compliance.[96]

Defences

9–023 The defence of due diligence is available to anyone charged with an offence under the Regulations.[97] The defence is commonly found in consumer protection legislation and was, for example, also a defence to someone charged with an offence under s.10 of the Consumer Protection Act[98] or under safety regulations. It is imperative that the defendant took all reasonable steps and exercised all due diligence to avoid committing the offence.[99] An importer or wholesaler will not be able to rely on this defence if he has taken no steps to require his supplier to supply goods which correspond with the relevant legal requirements. This may mean not only placing specific contractual obligations upon his supplier but also making tests on more than infrequent random samples of the goods supplied: *Riley v Webb*[100] and *Rotherham MBC v Raysun*.[101]

The amount of care required before the defendant can be said to have taken all reasonable steps and exercised all due diligence will be a question of fact in each case. In a situation where the defendant had imported goods from a source (e.g. the German wine industry) where there is known to be a thorough system of verification and testing to see the correct standard has been reached, he may not be expected to sample at all: *Hurley v Martinez*.[102] When considering whether he should sample, the degree of risk to be guarded against is an important factor. Thus, it is noticeable that in cases (such as *Rotherham MBC v Raysun*[103]) where the defendant is relying on the defence of due diligence to a consumer safety charge, the court is much more likely to demand a thorough sampling system than it is in cases (such as *Hurley v Martinez*[104]) where the defendant is relying on the same defence to a misleading statement charge. In *Hurley v Martinez*, the defendant was charged over a misstatement of the alcoholic strength (as 8 per cent instead of 7.2 per cent) on German wine.

95 In cases where the manufacturer is not himself established, and has no representative established in the UK.

96 Prior to the withdrawal of the UK from the EU, the references here to the UK were all instead to the EU, e.g. the manufacturer's representative established in the EU. See the Product Safety and Metrology etc. (Amendment etc.) (EU Exit) Regulations 2019/696, Sch.9, para.2.

97 See reg.29.

98 Now repealed by the General Product Safety Regulations 2005, see reg.46(2).

99 See generally, D. Parry, "Judicial approaches to due diligence" [1995] Crim. L.R. 695.

100 [1987] C.C.L.R. 65.

101 [1989] C.C.L.R. 1.

102 [1991] C.C.L.R. 1.

103 [1989] C.C.L.R. 1.

104 [1991] C.C.L.R. 1.

Of course, taking steps to ensure that goods comply with a British Standards specification is not capable of being sufficient to satisfy the defence of due diligence, unless compliance with the British Standards specification will automatically involve compliance with the provisions (e.g. of the Toys (Safety) Regulations 1989) under which the proceedings are brought: *Balding v Lew Ways Ltd*.[105]

By way of exception, a distributor who is charged with an offence, under the Regulations, of failing to act with due care to help ensure compliance with the requirement that the product is safe, will not be able to rely upon the defence of due diligence unless, within the limits of his activities, he has participated in monitoring the safety of the products placed on the market, in particular by passing on information on product risks and co-operating in any action taken to avoid those risks. Thus, for example, a car dealer who failed to recall a model identified as being within a defective batch would not be able to rely upon the defence.

Prohibition Notices, Notices to Warn, Suspension Notices

Prohibition notices, notices to warn and suspension notices are all notices which can be issued under the terms of the General Product Safety Regulations 2005.[106] One available power is that of the requirement to mark and warn under regs 12 and 13. In order to comply with this the warning must be "suitable, clearly worded and easily comprehensible".[107] 9-024

The enforcement authorities also have the ability to serve a "suspension notice". This notice is available where the authority has "reasonable grounds for suspecting that a requirement of these Regulations has been contravened in relation to a product" and allows for a period of time as is necessary to "organise appropriate safety evaluations, checks and controls". During this time, the following actions are prohibited:[108]

(a) placing the product on the market, offering to place it on the market, agreeing to place it on the market or exposing it for placing on the market, or

(b) supplying the product, offering to supply it, agreeing to supply it or exposing it for supply.

105 *The Times*, 19 March 1995.

106 Unlike the 1994 version, the current General Product Safety Regulations contain built-in enforcement provisions in Pt 3.

107 reg.12(2).

108 reg.11(1). Under reg.11(2) the notice may also require that the authority be kept informed of the whereabouts of the product.

Where the enforcement authority has reasonable grounds for believing that a product is a dangerous product (i.e. not a safe product)[109] they have the ability to issue a withdrawal notice which makes the same prohibition as the "suspension notice" previously discussed but is permanent, rather than temporary.[110] This notice can be served in respect of a product already on the market, but where it is served in respect of such a product:[111]

> **"a withdrawal notice may only be served by an enforcement authority where the action being undertaken by the producer or the distributor concerned in fulfilment of his obligations under these Regulations is unsatisfactory or insufficient to prevent the risks concerned to the health and safety of persons."**

9–025 This notice is, therefore, designed to be employed only where the producer or distributor is either unwilling or unable to take the steps necessary to ensure compliance with the general safety requirement. This limitation on the availability of a "withdrawal notice" is not applicable, however, where the product poses a serious risk and requires (in the view of the enforcement authority) urgent action.[112]

In the event of a product being deemed unsafe which has already gone to market, the enforcement authorities have the power to issue a "recall notice" under reg.15. The content of this notice is governed by reg.15(2), which provides that the notice may require:

> **"(a) the recall to be effected in accordance with a code of practice applicable to the product concerned, or**
> **(b) the recipient of the recall notice to—**
> **(i) contact consumers who have purchased the product in order to inform them of the recall, where and to the extent it is practicable to do so,**
> **(ii) publish a notice in such form and such manner as is likely to bring to the attention of purchasers of the product the risk the product poses and the fact of the recall, or**
> **(iii) make arrangements for the collection or return of the product from consumers who have purchased it or for its disposal,**
> **and may impose such additional requirements on the recipient of the notice as are reasonable and practicable with a view to achieving the return of the product from consumers to the person specified in the notice or its disposal."**

109 See the definitions of both in reg.2.
110 reg.14(1).
111 reg.14(3).
112 reg.14(4).

This list is therefore not exhaustive and is subject to reg.15(3) which provides that "the enforcement authority shall take into consideration the need to encourage distributors, users and consumers to contribute to its implementation" when deciding what the notice may contain.

Such a notice is available only where the product is dangerous and the requirements of reg.15(4) are satisfied. Regulation 15(4) requires that (a) any other action possible under the regulations would be insufficient; (b) action taken by the producer or distributor is unsatisfactory or insufficient; and (c) a period of seven days notice has been given.[113] 9-026

The sanctions for breach of these offences are stated in reg.20. Any person in breach of the general safety requirement under reg.5 is liable on conviction on indictment to imprisonment for a term not exceeding 12 months or to a fine not exceeding £20,000 (or to both). The same liability falls on any distributor in breach of reg.8(1)(a). A person in breach of reg.7(1) or reg.7(3) shall be guilty of an offence and liable on summary conviction to imprisonment for a term not exceeding three months or to a fine not exceeding level 5 on the standard scale (£5,000 at present) or to both. A person in breach of requirements relating to any of the safety notices (i.e. to mark; warn, etc.) is guilty of an offence and liable on conviction on indictment to imprisonment for a term of up to 12 months or to a fine not exceeding £20,000 (or to both).[114]

Proposals for Reform

It will have been observed from the discussion above that the impact of the UK's withdrawal from the EU has been limited, since the European Union (Withdrawal) Act 2018 served to retain EU-derived legislation dealing with product safety in domestic UK law. It seems likely however, that this harmony will not last much longer with reform having been proposed at both domestic and EU levels. On the EU side, the European Commission has adopted a proposal for a new general product safety regulation.[115] The proposal is wide-ranging and would, if enacted, repeal the current General Product Safety Directive which was implemented in the UK by the General Product Safety Regulations 2005 discussed above. In particular, the proposal aims to address product safety risks introduced by new technologies and online marketplaces. Further, the Commission has recently consulted on its proposal to reform the Product Liability Directive which was implemented in the UK by Part I of the Consumer Protection Act 1987 also discussed above.[116] The consultation builds on challenges identified by the Commission in its 2018 evaluation of the Directive[117] and considers in particular the position of intangible products, barriers 9-027

113 Under reg.15(5), paras (b) and (c) are not necessary where the product poses serious risk and requires urgent action.

114 On summary conviction this is reduced to imprisonment for a term of up to three months or to a fine not exceeding the statutory maximum (or to both).

115 COM (2021) 346 final.

116 The consultation closed on 10 January 2022. Draft legislation is anticipated before the end of 2022.

117 *Evaluation of Council Directive 85/374/EEC on the approximation of laws, regulations and administrative provisions of the Member States concerning liability for defective products: final report* (2018).

to civil liability, the position of online market places, and specific problems posed by the growth of artificial intelligence. Thus, it seems likely that there will be some significant changes to the EU landscape around product safety and civil liability for unsafe products.

On the domestic front, the Office for Product Safety and Standards[118] has consulted on potential changes to the UK's product safety regime.[119] In particular, the consultation focused on ensuring that product safety laws properly address new forms of supply and emerging products and technologies, such as artificial intelligence and 3-D printing. In its response to the consultation, the Government concluded that:[120]

> **"while the current framework has strengths, it is facing significant and growing challenges and needs to be radically reformed to be more adaptable and capable of responding to accelerating change".**

Thus, in a similar fashion to the ongoing proposals for reform at EU level, it seems likely that the domestic framework will also undergo potentially significant reform in the not-too-distant future. Of course, following the UK's withdrawal from the EU, the UK is not required to adopt whatever comes of the EU's current scheme of reform: to what extent the two frameworks diverge in their respective approaches remains to be seen.

General Reading

B. Van Leeuwen, P. Verbruggen, "Resuscitating EU Product Liability Law?" (2015) 23 European Review of Private Law 899.

L. Bergkamp, "Is There a Defect in the European Court's Defect Test? Musings about Acceptable Risk" (2015) 6(2) European Journal of Risk Regulation 309.

P. Cartwright, "Total recall? the future of consumer product safety regulation" [2006] L.M.C.L.Q. 390.

J. Eisler, "One step forward and two steps back in product liability: the search for clarity in the identification of defects" (2017) 76(2) C.L.J. 233.

D. Fairgrieve and G. Howells, "General product safety—a revolution through reform?" (2006) 69 M.L.R. 59.

118 The OPSS is the regulator for all consumer products, except for vehicles, medicines and food. It is part of the Department for Business, Energy and Industrial Strategy and was established in January 2018.

119 UK Product Safety Review: Call for Evidence (March 2021).

120 UK Product Safety Review: Call for Evidence Response (November 2021) at p.24.

D. Fairgrieve and G. Howells, "Rethinking Product Liability: A Missing Element in the European Commission's Third Review of the Product Liability Directive" (2007) 70 M.L.R. 962.

D. Fairgrieve, "Product Liability in the United Kingdom" (2019) 8(4) *Journal of European Consumer and Market Law* 170.

R. Freeman, "Strict product liability laws—Consumer Protection Act provisions fail to assist claimants in three recent cases" [2001] J.P.I. Law 26.

R. Goldberg, "Paying for bad blood: strict product liability after the hepatitis C -litigation" [2002] Med. Law Rev. 165.

M. Mildred and G. Howells, "Infected blood: defect and discoverability. A first exposition of the EC Product Liability Directive" (2002) 65 M.L.R. 95.

M. Mildred, "Pitfalls in Product Liability" [2007] J.P.I.L. 141.

C.S. Newell, Product liability after the Consumer Protection Act 1987 (London: Longman, 1989).

D.L. Parry, "Product safety: European style—an appraisal" [1995] J.B.L. 268.

P. Shears, "The EU Product Liability Directive—twenty years on" [2007] J.B.L. 884.

A. Tettenborn, "Components and product liability: damage to 'other property'" [2000] L.M.C.L.Q. 338.

10

Exemption Clauses and Unfair Terms

Introduction

An exemption clause is a term of the contract intended to exclude or restrict the liability of one of the parties, usually the seller. Sometimes a seller is so financially powerful that he can blatantly insist on such a clause being included in the contract; he can adopt a "take it or leave it" attitude. More common is the seller who, having inserted an exclusion clause into his conditions of sale, relies on his buyer not bothering to read (or not understanding) the small print; for example, the exclusion clause may be contained in the small print of a guarantee which he gives to the buyer. 10-001

An exemption clause may, contrary to appearances, have little or no effect. Such clauses are not looked upon with favour either by the courts or by Parliament. They are subject to several common law rules evolved by the courts as well as to certain pieces of legislation. In this respect the Unfair Contract Terms Act 1977 and the Consumer Rights Act 2015 are particularly important. These Acts will be considered later in the chapter. At the moment it is worth noting that s.55(1) of the Sale of Goods Act reads:

> **"Where a right, duty or liability would arise under a contract of sale of goods by implication of law, it may (subject to the Unfair Contract Terms Act 1977) be negatived or varied by express agreement, or by the course of dealing between the parties, or by such usage as binds both parties to the contract."**

Moreover, s.31 of the Consumer Rights Act provides that a term which seeks to exclude or restrict a trader's liability arising under many of the Act's provisions will not be binding on a consumer. Before turning to the legislative framework we shall first examine the common law rules relating to incorporation, misrepresentation, privity of contract and scope of the clause.

Incorporation

10-002 A clause is of no effect unless it is incorporated (included) as a term in the contract. It must be incorporated when the contract is made. Any attempt to incorporate it after the contract is made will be unsuccessful. Thus a document which is first brought to the purchaser's notice after the contract is made will not incorporate into the contract terms printed on the document. It is for this reason that a seller will usually be unable to rely on an exclusion clause printed on a receipt. Receipts are not usually handed over until the purchaser has paid (i.e. after the contract has been made). This rule, that a clause cannot be subsequently be incorporated, was applied in *Olley v Marlborough Court*.[1] There the claimant had booked in at the reception desk of a hotel and only subsequently, on entering her room, did she discover behind the door a notice which claimed to exclude the hotel's liability for guests' property. The Court of Appeal held that the notice was not incorporated in the contract, since it was not displayed at a spot visible to the claimant before she made the contract. The defendant would have been better advised to display his notice in a prominent position near the reception desk.

We can now consider individually the different methods of incorporation.

Oral Agreement Between Buyer and Seller

10-003 This method is not commonly used for two main reasons. First, it involves bringing the exclusion clause directly to the attention of the buyer. Secondly, there may be difficulty in proving that the buyer orally agreed to the exclusion.

Signed Contractual Document

10-004 The buyer will find it difficult to argue that the clause was not agreed upon if it is contained in a document signed by him. It will not help him to plead that he had not read the clause or was unaware of its existence. In *L'Estrange v Graucob*[2] a café proprietor bought a vending machine on the terms of a sales agreement which she signed without having read. Although she had been unaware that the small print contained a wide exclusion clause, the Court of Appeal held that the clause protected the seller from liability in respect of defects in the machine.

A clause will not be incorporated by a document which is not a contractual document. A document will be "contractual" if a reasonable person in the position of the prospective buyer would expect it to contain terms affecting his rights and liabilities. A buyer who has taken the

1 [1949] 1 K.B. 532.
2 [1934] 2 K.B. 394.

formal step of signing a document will therefore find it difficult to show that it was not a contractual document.

Unsigned Contractual Document

There are two significant differences between signed and unsigned documents. First, an exemption clause in an unsigned document is not incorporated unless at the time of making the contract either the buyer was aware of its existence or else reasonable steps had been taken to bring it to his attention. The harsher the clause, the greater the effort needed to bring it to the attention of the buyer.[3] In *A.E.G Ltd v Logic Resources Ltd*[4] the seller's confirmation of order form stated "Orders are subject to our conditions of sale—for extract see reverse". The term which excluded liability for breach of the implied terms in the Sale of Goods Act and left the buyer with no choice but to return defective goods was not included in the extract on the reverse. The Court of Appeal held that insufficient steps had been taken to bring the exclusion clause to the buyer's attention and therefore the clause was not incorporated into the contract. Secondly, in the case of an unsigned document the buyer may find it easier to establish that it was not a contractual document. In *Chapelton v Barry UDC*.[5] Mr Chapelton wanted to hire a deck chair on the beach. He saw a pile of them and a notice nearby, "Hire of chairs 2d. per session of three hours". The notice continued by "respectfully requesting" the hirer to obtain a ticket from the attendant. This he did. He later brought an action claiming damages for injuries he received when his chair collapsed. As a defence, the Council pleaded an exemption clause printed on the back of the ticket. As Mr Chapelton had obtained his ticket from the attendant at the time of making the contract (i.e. when he collected his chair from the pile), the ticket had changed hands in sufficient time. The Court of Appeal rejected the Council's defence on the ground, not that the ticket changed hands too late, but that it was not a contractual document; for no reasonable person would expect to find contractual terms in a document which was no more than a receipt for him to prove that he had paid and which in many instances (i.e. in the absence of the attendant) would not change hands until long after the contract was made.[6] 10-005

Displayed Notices

As with an unsigned contractual document, this method of incorporation will work only if at the time of making the contract the buyer actually knew of the existence of the term or else 10-006

3 See *Interfoto Picture Library v Stiletto Visual Programmes*, para.7-004, above.

4 (1995) unreported.

5 [1940] 1 K.B. 532.

6 For consideration of contractual documents and invoices, see *Transformers & Rectifiers Ltd v Needs Ltd* [2015] EWHC 269 (TCC).

reasonable steps had been taken to bring them to his attention. Thus the notice must be reasonably large and prominently displayed at a spot visible to the buyer when the contact is made. Exactly what amounts to "reasonable steps" is a question of fact in each case. The wider and more drastic the clause, the more care must be taken to bring it to the buyer's attention.

Even if reasonable steps have been taken to bring the exemption clause to the notice of the buyer, it will not be incorporated if it does not clearly cover the particular transaction in question. In *D & M Trailers (Halifax) Ltd v Stirling*[7] an extensive exemption clause was included in the conditions of sale posted up around an auction room. One of these conditions stated, "'Sale' used in these conditions shall include sale by private treaty as well as by auction". Mr Stirling attended the auction and bought some vehicles. On returning a day or two later to pay for them, he saw in the yard a Scania tractor which had been included but not sold at the auction which he had attended. He spoke privately with the auctioneers and agreed to buy the Scania (i.e. he agreed by private treaty and not in an auction). The Scania soon proved to be seriously defective and not of satisfactory quality. The buyer's claim for breach of condition succeeded. The court held that the exemption clause, though it had been incorporated in the auction sales, had not been incorporated in the later sale by private treaty. This was a separate transaction from the auction and the auctioneers had not made it clear that the exemption clause was being incorporated into it.

Previous Course of Dealing

10–007 If, in the past, parties have regularly made contracts with each other upon the same terms (including exemption terms), then that course of dealing can incorporate those terms into a later contract between them. This later contract must be merely the latest in the established course of dealing. Thus three requirements must be satisfied before a course of dealing can incorporate an exemption clause into a later contract:

(i) The transactions between the parties must have been sufficiently numerous to constitute a "course of dealing".

(ii) The established course of dealing must have been consistent.

(iii) The established course of dealing must not have been deviated from on the occasion in question.

7 [1978] R.T.R. 468.

In *Hollier v Rambler Motors*[8] the first of these requirements was not satisfied. The Court of Appeal held that three or four transactions in the course of five years were not sufficient to establish a course of dealing.

In *Kendall v Lillico*[9] all the requirements were fulfilled. Just as he had done on over 100 occasions during the previous three years, the seller sold some animal food to the buyer. As had always previously happened, they made an oral agreement followed by the seller giving to the buyers a "sold note" which had on the back an exclusion clause. Plainly the clause was not on this occasion incorporated by virtue of the sold note, which had been handed over only after the bargain was struck. However, there had been a long and consistent course of dealing which was adhered to on this occasion. It was by virtue of this that the clause was incorporated. The House of Lords held this to be so, even though the buyers were unaware of the precise terms on the sold notes. Lord Pearce said:[10]

> **"The only reasonable inference from the regular course of dealing over so long a period is that the buyers were evincing an acceptance of, and a readiness to be bound by, the printed conditions of whose existence they were well aware of although they had not troubled to read them."**

Trade Usage

Whereas a course of dealing can incorporate a term that has in effect become customary between the two parties in question, trade usage can incorporate a term that has become a custom amongst all the buyers and sellers dealing in the environment in question. In the latter case there is no need for the particular seller and buyer to have dealt previously with each other, or, indeed, previously in the particular environment. It is sufficient that the custom was established in the market in which on this occasion the buyer bought from the seller. By dealing in this market, they are taken, unless they expressly agreed otherwise, to have been dealing in accordance with all the customs of the market. Thus in *Cointat v Myham*[11] where the claimant bought bad meat in the Central London Meat Market, it was held that any warranty as to the 10-008

8 [1972] 2 Q.B. 71.

9 [1969] 2 A.C. 31.

10 [1969] 2 A.C. 31 at 113. Incorporation of contractual terms on the basis of a previous course of dealing is a very fact sensitive matter. Thus each case will turn on its particular facts. See, for example, *Balmoral Group Ltd v Borealis (UK) Ltd* [2006] EWHC 1900 (Comm) and *Capes (Hatherden) Ltd v Western Arable Services* Ltd [2009] EWHC 3065 (QB). Similarly, in *Provimi France SAS v Stour Bay Co Ltd* [2022] EWHC 218 (Comm) at [234] it was said that "whether or not terms are incorporated by a prior course of dealing is ultimately a question of fact and degree, which depends, amongst other things, on the number of previous contracts, how recent they are, the similarity of subject matter, and the manner in which they were concluded".

11 (1914) 110 L.T. 749.

fitness or quality of the meat was excluded, because there was an established custom of the market to that effect.

Overriding oral warranty

10–009 An exclusion clause which would otherwise be incorporated by one of the methods referred to above may nevertheless be overridden by later statements made by the seller to the buyer. The claimant in *Harling v Eddy*[12] bought a heifer at a cattle auction. One of the printed conditions of sale in the auction catalogue was that no warranty was given in respect of any animal sold. However, when there had been some difficulty in getting the bidding started, the seller announced that there was nothing wrong with the heifer and he would absolutely guarantee her. After this the heifer was knocked down to the claimant. The Court of Appeal held that the oral statement overrode the exclusion clause which therefore did not form part of the contract.

Misrepresentation

10–010 The seller cannot rely on any exclusion clause, no matter what liability it claims to exclude, to the extent that he or his agent has misrepresented the effect of the clause. In *Curtis v Chemical Dyeing Co*[13] the claimant took a wedding dress to the defendants for cleaning. The shop assistant asked her to sign a receipt, telling her that this was because the cleaners took no responsibility for damage to beads and sequins on the dress. In fact this was literally true but the clause on the receipt went further. It claimed to exempt the defendants from liability for "any damage howsoever caused". The claimant signed the receipt without reading it. The assistant had not deliberately or knowingly misled the claimant. Nevertheless she had, by revealing part of the clause's effect, concealed its full effect. This amounted to a misrepresentation. The Court of Appeal held the defendants liable in negligence for damage caused to the dress. The misrepresentation, albeit an innocent one, "was a sufficient misrepresentation to disentitle the cleaner from relying on the exemption, except in regard to beads and sequins".

12 [1951] 2 K.B. 739.
13 [1951] 1 K.B. 805.

Privity of Contract

The privity of contract principle is that someone who is not privy to (i.e. not a party to) a contract can neither rely upon the contract nor be bound by it. Generally, a contract can affect the rights and liabilities only as between the parties to it. Thus an exclusion clause in a contract is a defence available, generally, only to a contracted party and only against the other contracted party: *Scruttons v Midland Silicones*.[14] The Contracts (Rights of Third Parties) Act 1999, however, creates a limited exception whereby a third party, who is described or identified in the contract, can rely on an exclusion clause if either (a) the parties expressly provide that he may, or (b) the exclusion clause purports to enable the third party to rely on it.[15] Consider a common situation: a manufacturer sells a number of his products to a wholesaler, the wholesaler sells some of them to a retailer and the retailer sells one of them to a consumer. Here there are three separate contracts of sale. If the product proves to be defective, then this could give rise to three separate claims for damages for breach of contract—one by the consumer against the retailer, one by the retailer against the wholesaler and one by the wholesaler against the manufacturer. There is a chain of contracts and a breach of one may well cause a chain reaction, i.e. a breach of each of the others.[16] The law does not allow the consumer to ignore the intermediate links in the chain. He cannot sue the manufacturer for breach of the latter's contract of sale. However, in certain circumstances, the law of tort gives a consumer a right to sue a manufacturer with whom he has no contract.[17] In our example, if the manufacturer was careless in the manufacture of his product and this had injured the consumer, the latter will have a claim (in the law of tort) in negligence against the manufacturer even though he did not buy the goods from him. Whilst an exclusion clause in the manufacturer's contract of sale could provide the manufacturer with a good defence to a claim by the wholesaler, it would provide him with no defence to a claim in negligence by the consumer. 10-011

Sometimes a manufacturer sells directly to a member of the public, e.g. via mail order or door-to-door salesmen. In such a case an exclusion clause could, if appropriately worded (and, subject to the provisions of the Unfair Contract Terms Act and the Consumer Rights Act), provide the manufacturer with a good defence against a claim by the purchaser in negligence. However, someone other than the purchaser could be injured on account of the article's negligent manufacture and an exclusion clause would provide no defence in an action brought by him against the manufacturer. Furthermore, a manufacturer can now be liable to his immediate purchaser or to anyone else who is caused injury (or private property damage) by a defective product. This liability, under Pt I of the Consumer Protection Act 1987, cannot be limited or excluded at all.[18]

14 [1962] A.C. 446.
15 See para.7-003, above.
16 See para.9-006, above.
17 See Ch.9.
18 See paras 9-007–9-016, above.

Scope of the Clause

10-012 An exclusion clause is construed contra proferentem, i.e. narrowly against the interest of the person relying upon it. An exclusion clause is usually inserted for the sole benefit of one of the parties: in a contract of sale, the seller. The court, in interpreting the clause, leans against the seller. If the clause is ambiguous, the court will adopt the meaning less favourable to the seller and any ground of liability not clearly excluded will remain.[19] In *Andrews v Singer*[20] the claimant made a written contract to buy a "new Singer car". The car delivered to him had in fact done a considerable mileage. It was held that a clause excluding all "implied conditions and warranties" did not exclude the seller's liability for breach of the express condition that he would supply a "new" car. A further illustration is to be found in *Wallis & Wells v Pratt and Haynes*[21] where the House of Lords held that the clause "Sellers give no warranty, express or implied" did not exclude conditions. A clause which does not expressly mention conditions will not normally exclude liability for breach of condition. Similarly in The *Mercini Lady*[22] an exclusion clause which purported to exclude liability for "guarantees, warranties or representations" in respect of "merchantability, fitness or suitability" was not effective in excluding liability under the implied condition as to satisfactory quality under s.14 of the Sale of Goods Act 1979. This decision reinforces the strictness of the approach to construction regarding exclusion clauses and serves as a reminder to make specific reference to conditions and warranties.

Old Approach to Interpretation

10-013 Until the 1970s there was no statutory control upon exemption clauses. So, if an exemption clause was part of the contract and if on its wording it excused one party from a given liability, then the court had to give effect to the clause, i.e. that party (usually the seller) had a valid defence. That is what happened in *L'Estrange v Graucob*.[23] The courts, however, did not very much like this sort of result and, when interpreting an exemption clause, used to adopt a hostile approach. There were two aspects to this. First the court would sometimes place a strained or tortured meaning on the words of the exemption clause in order to deprive it of effect. Secondly, the courts developed the doctrine of fundamental breach of contract. According to this doctrine, a party who had committed a fundamental breach of contract could not (at least, sometimes could not) rely for his defence upon an exemption clause. This doctrine was never, however, approved by the House of Lords.

19 Note that the Consumer Rights Act 2015 s.69(1) provides that where a term in a consumer contract is ambiguous, "the meaning that is most favourable to the consumer is to prevail".

20 [1934] 1 K.B. 17.

21 [1911] A.C. 394.

22 *KG Bominflot Bunkergesellschaft für Mineraloele mbH & Co v Petroplus Marketing AG, The Mercini Lady* [2010] EWCA Civ. 1145.

23 [1934] 2 K.B. 394, see para.10-004, above.

New Approach to Interpretation

As will be explained later in this chapter, Parliament in the 1970s passed legislation which renders certain exemption clauses absolutely ineffective and imposes a test of reasonableness on many others. As we will see shortly, in the context of consumer contracts, the Consumer Rights Act also renders certain clauses ineffective and imposes a test of fairness on others. This means that, even though an exemption clause on its wording apparently provides a defence, it may nevertheless be ineffective. This enabled the courts to adopt a less hostile approach to the interpretation of the wording of exemption clauses. 10-014

In *Photo Production Ltd v Securicor Transport Ltd*[24] the House of Lords swept away the doctrine that a fundamental breach of contract could prevent an exemption clause from providing a defence. Their Lordships overruled earlier decisions saying otherwise. After the Photo Production there were two more decisions of the House of Lords, *Aisla Craig Fishing Co Ltd v Malvern Fishing Co Ltd*[25] and *George Mitchell Ltd v Finney Lock Seeds Ltd*.[26] From this trilogy of cases the modern approach to the interpretation of exemption clauses emerged: an approach which avoids artificial or strained interpretations and that gives effect to context and objective meaning.[27]

Exemption clauses are still construed contra proferentem, i.e. if a clause is ambiguous the court will adopt the meaning which is less favourable to the party (usually the seller) wishing to rely upon the clause. The court will not, however, read an ambiguity into clear words by giving them a strained or tortured meaning. Clear and plain words will be given their clear meaning. Indeed, in *K/S Victoria Street v House of Fraser (Stores Management) Ltd*[28] Lord Neuberger MR observed that:

> **". . . 'rules' of interpretation such as contra proferentem are rarely decisive as to the meaning of any provisions of a commercial contract. The words used, commercial sense, and the documentary and factual context, are, and should be, normally enough to determine the meaning of a contractual provision."**

One aspect of the contra proferentem rule is that, if there is more than one possible head of liability one of which is liability for negligence, then an exemption clause will not be interpreted as excluding liability for negligence unless it does so in clear terms. For example a manufacturer who sells his goods to a wholesaler may in the contract exclude liability in respect of defects in the goods. This clause might well be interpreted as excluding the manufacturer's liability

24 [1980] A.C. 827.

25 [1983] 1 W.L.R. 964.

26 [1983] 3 W.L.R. 163.

27 See the observations of Lord Leggatt in *Triple Point Technology, Inc v PTT Public Co. Ltd* [2021] UKSC 29 at [107].

28 [2011] EWCA Civ 904 at [48].

to the wholesaler under the implied terms as to satisfactory quality and fitness for purpose. In the absence of clear words, however, it will not be interpreted as excluding the manufacturer's liability to the wholesaler for negligence, under the principle of *Donoghue v Stevenson*.[29] On the other hand the Aisla Craig case established that the contra proferentem rule is not applied quite as rigorously in interpreting clauses which merely limit the defendant's (usually the seller's) liability, as it is to clauses which claim to exclude his liability.[30]

In *George Mitchell Ltd v Finney Lock Seeds Ltd*[31] some farmers contracted to buy from some seed merchants 30lb of Finney's "Late Dutch Special" cabbage seed. Unknown to the buyers, the sellers negligently delivered the wrong seed. The buyers planted the seed but only leaves came up and the crop proved worthless, causing the buyers a loss of £61,000. In defence to a claim for that loss, the sellers sought to rely on a contractual clause limiting the sellers' liability to the cost of replacement seeds, i.e. the clause excluded the sellers' liability for any consequential loss arising from "use or failure in performance of or any defect in any seeds or plants supplied or for any other loss or damage whatsoever", except for the cost of replacement of the seed. In interpreting the clause, their Lordships observed that this was a limitation of liability clause and not a complete exclusion clause. They unanimously held that on its wording it limited the sellers' liability to the cost of replacing the seed. That was so even though the breach of contract had been a negligent one. That, however, did not mean that the clause necessarily gave the sellers a valid defence because the clause still had to satisfy the legislation on exemption clauses.[32]

Introduction to the Unfair Contract Terms Act 1977

10–015 The Unfair Contract Terms Act 1977 is a major landmark in the development of the law of contract. It deals with exemption clauses and it replaced and greatly extended certain provisions previously in the Supply of Goods (Implied Terms) Act 1973. The 1973 Act was confined to exemption clauses which claimed to exclude or restrict the statutory implied terms relating to title, description, quality and sample (implied by ss.12–15 of the Sale of Goods Act). The 1977 Act places severe curbs upon the effectiveness of exemption clauses of many sorts. Since the

29 [1932] A.C. 562, see para.10-018, above.

30 In *Mott MacDonald Ltd v Trant Engineering Ltd* [2021] EWHC 754 (TCC) it was said that "a limitation of liability can be regarded as reflecting an agreed allocation of risk and as being a lesser departure from the norm than would be a total exclusion of liability with the consequence that the court is more likely to conclude that a limitation of liability was intended than it would a total exclusion" at [65].

31 [1983] 3 W.L.R. 163.

32 See further, para.10-018, below.

enactment of the Consumer Rights Act 2015, however, the 1977 Act only applies in the context of business-to-business contracts.[33] Neither does the 1977 Act deal with liability under the Consumer Protection Act 1987.[34] The Consumer Protection Act itself provides, in ss.7 and 41(4), that such liability cannot be excluded or limited.

Two preliminary matters must be explained. First, the 1977 Act applies to exemption clauses and these include not only the clauses which claim to exclude liability for breach of contract but also those which claim[35]:

(i) to prevent liability from arising in the first place (e.g. "Seller gives no warranty as to fitness for purpose or satisfactory quality");

(ii) to restrict liability (e.g. to a maximum amount);

(iii) to restrict the buyer's remedies (e.g. to prevent him from rejecting the goods and to confine him to damages for breach of condition);

(iv) to restrict the time within which a remedy may be claimed (e.g. "No claims to be made more than six weeks after purchase"). The general rule is that a claim for damages for breach of contract can be brought at any time up to six years after the breach occurred. If the claim is for personal injuries the period is reduced to three years. A clause claiming to shorten these periods is an exemption clause; and

(v) to make the enforcement of any remedy subject to a restrictive condition (e.g. "Seller accepts no liability unless the goods are first returned to him carriage paid").

The other preliminary matter is that the Unfair Contract Terms Act 1977 does not tell you whether the seller is liable. To put it another way, it does not alter the basis of liability. It simply curbs the effectiveness of exemption clauses. Suppose a contract of sale contains an exemption clause; suppose also that exemption clause is rendered ineffective by the Unfair Contract Terms Act. There still remains the question "What, if any, is the liability of the seller?" That question can be answered only by examining the express and implied terms of the contract, including those implied by the Sale of Goods Act. Now let us turn to exemption clauses and the effect upon them of the provisions of the Unfair Contract Terms Act.

Section 55(1) of the Sale of Goods Act was quoted at para.10-001 above. It allows an exemption clause to take effect subject to the common law rules already outlined and subject also to the provisions of the Unfair Contract Terms Act 1977. We shall examine first the effect of the 1977 Act upon exemption clauses which claim to exempt from liability under the

33 The Act also has (limited) application to private sales (i.e. one where the seller does not sell in the course of business) by virtue of s.6(4). See para.10-023, below.

34 Explained at paras 9-007–9-016 above.

35 By s.13 of the 1977 Act.

statutory implied terms as to title, description, quality and sample and then its effect upon other exemption clauses.

Exemptions from ss.12–15 of the Sale of Goods Act: s.6

10–016 Section 6 of the Unfair Contract Terms Act 1977 applies to any clause claiming to exempt the seller from any of the terms implied by ss.12–15 of the Sale of Goods Act, i.e. the terms as to title, description, satisfactory quality, fitness for purpose and sample.[36] The effect of s.6 is as follows. It is impossible for the seller to exempt himself from liability under s.12 of the Sale of Goods Act. It is, however, possible for the seller to be exempted from liability under ss.13–15 of the Sale of Goods Act, but only in so far as the seller can show that the exemption clause satisfies the requirement of reasonableness, i.e. that it was a "fair and reasonable one to be included having regard to the circumstances which were, or ought reasonably to have been, known to or in the contemplation of the parties when the contract was made".[37]

Schedule 2 provides "guidelines" for the application of the reasonableness test:

> **"(a) the strength of the bargaining positions of the parties relative to each other, taking into account (among other things) alternative means by which the customer's requirements could have been met;**
>
> **(b) whether the customer received an inducement to agree to the term, or in accepting it had an opportunity of entering into a similar contract with other persons, but without having to accept a similar term;**
>
> **(c) whether the customer knew or ought reasonably to have known of the existence and extent of the term (having regard, among other things, to any custom of the trade and any previous course of dealing between the parties);**
>
> **(d) where the term excludes or restricts any relevant liability if some condition is not complied with, whether it was reasonable at the time of the contract to expect that compliance with that condition would by practicable;**

36 It will be recalled that these terms are implied only where the contract is not governed by the statutory rights regime under the Consumer Rights Act, see para.7-007 above.

37 s.11.

(e) whether the goods were manufactured, processed or adapted to the special order of the customer."

It would appear from para.(a) that a seller who has a monopoly over the supply of the kind of goods in question is unlikely to convince the court of the reasonableness of a wide exemption clause, especially if it was a large demand for the product which enabled him to insist on the clause being in the contract. In the light of para.(b) the seller having a monopoly will be more likely to succeed if the buyer had been offered the chance of buying the goods, perhaps at a slightly higher price, on terms not including the exemption clause. Obviously, if the alternative offer had involved a considerably or prohibitively higher price, that would tell against the seller.

Paragraph (c) would appear not to affect decisions in cases such as *Kendall v Lillico*[38] and *Cointat v Myham*.[39] These examples being cases where the purchaser chooses to buy goods for his business from a seller whose terms he has in a consistent course of dealing been apparently quite happy to accept or where the purchaser buys goods in a market in which a trade custom shows that merchants have found exclusion terms to be acceptable. 10-017

In light of para.(d), a clause excluding, for example, all liability "other than that in respect of defects and defaults notified to the seller within three days of purchase" would clearly not be reasonable.[40]

Paragraph (e) would be particularly relevant where the purchaser required the goods to be made or adapted from some use for which the seller did not normally supply goods. It would seem reasonable for the seller to stipulate that he will not guarantee the goods' suitability for that purpose.

Paragraphs (a)–(e) are only guidelines and all the circumstances of the case should be taken into account. So, for example, the scope and harshness (or otherwise) of the clause will also be relevant. 10-018

The leading case on the requirements of reasonableness arose, not under the Unfair Contract Terms Act 1977, but under the earlier provisions of the Supply of Goods (Implied Terms) Act 1973 which were replaced by the 1977 Act. The requirement of reasonableness under the earlier Act was different in two respects. First, the onus of proof was upon the buyer to show that the exemption clause did not pass the test, whereas under the 1977 Act the onus is on the seller to show that the clause passes the test. Secondly, under the 1973 Act the test was whether it was fair and reasonable to allow reliance upon the exemption clause, whereas under the 1977 Act the test is whether the clause is a fair and reasonable one to have been included in the contract. Nevertheless the former test and the current test are very similar and indeed the "guidelines" laid down by the two Acts are the same. The leading case is *George Mitchell v Finney Lock Seeds*.[41] There the exemption clause, according to its wording limited the liability

38 [1969] 2 A.C. 31, see para.10-007, above.

39 (1914) 110 L.T. 749, see para.10-008, above.

40 *Green v Cade* (1978) 1 Lloyd's Rep. 602, see para.10-018, below.

41 [1983] 3 W.L.R. 163, for the facts see para.10-014, above.

of some seed merchants (for supplying defective seed) to the cost of replacing the seed; it excluded liability for consequential loss of the buyers' crop. These limitation terms were incorporated in all contracts between seedsman and farmers and had been for many years. They had not been negotiated by any representative body of farmers, such as the National Farmers' Union. They had been introduced by seed merchants putting them into their catalogues and invoices—and never objected to by farmers. It was held that the exemption clause did not in the circumstances pass the test of reasonableness and that therefore the sellers could not rely on it to limit their liability. The relevant circumstances were that: (i) the limitation terms had not been negotiated by any representative body; (ii) the buyers could not have discovered the error, (i.e. that the wrong seed had been delivered) until the crop was sown, whereas the sellers were in a position to have known; (iii) the buyers could not reasonably have been expected to cover such a risk (i.e. of crop failure) by insurance, whereas it was possible for seedsmen to cover their liability by insurance at a modest premium which would not have put up the cost of the seeds by very much; and (iv) the error could not have occurred without some negligence on the part of the sellers.

George Mitchell v Finney Lock Seeds[42] was different from *Green v Cade*,[43] which had involved the sale of seed potatoes on the standard terms of the National Association of Seed Potato Merchants. In that case one clause which on its wording excluded liability if the buyers had not given notice of any defects within three days of purchase was held to fail the reasonableness test. Another clause, restricting the sellers' liability for a consequential loss and limiting that liability to the amount of the contract price, was held to pass the reasonableness test. The latter clause, however, had had the approval of negotiating bodies representing both potato merchants and farmers; no blame for the infection of the seed potatoes was attributable to either side; and, further, the buyers, if they had so wished, could have bought at a small extra cost, seed potatoes certified by inspectors of the Ministry of Agriculture.[44]

In *St Albans City and District Council v International Computers Ltd*[45] the court had to apply the requirement of reasonableness to a limitation of liability clause in an international computer firm's standard conditions in a contract made with a local council to supply the council with a database for a large community charge register. At that time the community charge was a local tax. The clause limited the computer firm's liability to a maximum of £100,000. The database supplied was defective in that it overstated the local population by 2,966. This in turn had the effect that the rate of tax levied was lower than it would have been if the population had been accurately stated. This in turn caused a loss of tax revenue to the council of over £1.3 million. The relevant factors taken into account by the court were: (a) the parties were of unequal bargaining power; (b) the figure of £100,000 was small in relation to the potential and

42 [1983] 3 W.L.R. 163.

43 (1978) 1 Lloyd's Rep. 602.

44 The Law Commission has recently rejected a suggestion that terms negotiated by trade bodies, etc. should be exempted from the reasonableness test under the draft Unfair Contract Terms Bill, see the discussion of the Law Commission Report at para.10-026, below.

45 [1996] 4 All E.R. 481.

the actual risk; (c) the computer firm was insured for an aggregate sum of £50 million world-wide; and (d) it was in practical terms easier for the computer firm to secure insurance and to pass the cost of that on to its customers and it was not unreasonable that the firm which made the profit by supplying the program should carry the risk. Thus the clause failed to satisfy the requirement of reasonableness and was unenforceable.[46]

Exemptions from Other Terms of the Contract: s.3

We have just considered the extent to which the Unfair Contract Terms Act 1977 allows the seller to exclude his liability under ss.12–15 of the Sale of Goods Act. However, the contract will doubtless contain other terms, some of them expressly agreed between the parties (e.g. the date of delivery) and some of them implied (often by other sections of the Sale of Goods Act, e.g. as to the place of delivery, s.29(2)). The Unfair Contract Terms Act does not totally prohibit the seller from exempting himself from liability for breach of these other terms.[47] Section 3 of that Act, however, does, in certain circumstances, render some exemption clauses subject to the requirements of reasonableness where one of the contracting parties deals on the other's written standard terms of business. 10-019

The Act does not define "written standard terms of business". This expression clearly covers the situation where a seller insists that all (or a considerable proportion of) his buyers buy on the terms of his written contract, there being no variation in the terms from one buyer to another. This would still seem to be so if most, though not all, the terms are standard—if, say, there are minor variations from one buyer to another (e.g. as to the commodity or the quantity bought or the price to be paid). Even where the only "standard" terms of the seller are those in the exemption clause itself, still a buyer whose contract includes that exemption clause could well be regarded as buying on the seller's "written standard terms of business".

Where this requirement is satisfied, s.3 applies and its effect is that the seller cannot:[48]

> **"(a) when himself in breach of contract, exclude or restrict any liability of his in respect of the breach; or**

46 On the question of whether the contract in this case was a sale of goods contract see para.1-012, above.

47 See *Kevin Berwick v Lloyds Bank TSB Bank plc; Michael Haughton v Lloyds TSB Bank Plc* (2007) unreported, where s.3 (and s.4) was not applicable to an action seeking to recover various charges applied to a bank account since there had been neither a breach of contract (or negligence) on the part of the bank. For a discussion of this case, see E. White, "Banker's duties: bank charges" [2007] J.I.B.L.R. 22(10) N100.

48 s.3(2).

> **(b) claim to be entitled—**
> **(i) to render a contractual performance substantially different from that which was reasonably expected of him, or**
> **(ii) in respect of the whole or any part of his contractual obligation, to render no performance at all, except in so far as the contract term [i.e. exemption clause] satisfies the requirement of reasonableness."**

10-020 There is a great deal of room for the courts to interpret these words.[49] Confining ourselves to the obvious, it is clear that for para.(a) to apply the seller must be in breach of contract. Clearly, therefore, a maximum damages clause would be caught by it.

Three important points must be made. First, s.3, where it applies, does not render a clause ineffective if the clause is shown to satisfy the requirement of reasonableness. This requirement has already been explained in relation to s.6 of the Unfair Contract Terms Act.[50] It is exactly the same here except that the Act does not say that the "guidelines" in Sch.2 should be referred to. Nevertheless it seems likely that similar factors will in fact be taken into account by the courts. Secondly, an exemption clause may be partially effective if it is shown to be to some extent reasonable. A clause might for example claim (i) to exclude liability for certain fundamental breaches of contract, and (ii) to limit any damages to a maximum of £5,000. A court might well be persuaded that the clause is reasonable as to (ii) but not as to (i).

The third point is that where an exemption clause is not invalidated (or not completely so) by s.3 of the Unfair Contract Terms Act 1977, the buyer may still be able to defeat the exemption clause by relying on ss.6, 8 or 2 of that Act. Section 6 has already been considered and applies where the buyer's claim is based upon a breach by the seller of the terms implied by ss.12–15 of the Sale of Goods Act. Section 8 applies where the claim is based upon misrepresentation and will be returned to later. Section 2 applies where the claim is based upon negligence.

Exemptions from Liability for Negligence: s.2

10-021 In Ch.9 we saw that a manufacturer can be liable for any loss or damage caused by the negligence of the manufacturer or any of his employees. This is so irrespective of whether the consumer bought the goods from the manufacturer. A distributor or seller who was not the manufacturer (e.g. a retailer) could also be liable under the same principle if he was negligent, e.g. if he negligently failed to pass on to the customer a warning label ("Not to be taken

49 See *AXA Sun Life Services Plc v Campbell Martin Ltd, Brendon Partington, Gary Tibor Hosznyak* [2011] EWCA Civ. 133.

50 See paras 10-016–10-018, above.

internally") which he had received with a bottle of medicine. Section 2 of the Unfair Contract Terms Act applies here. Its effect is twofold. First, it is impossible to exclude liability for death or personal injuries caused by negligence. Secondly, it is possible to exclude or restrict liability for other loss of damage (e.g. to property) caused by negligence, but only to the extent that the exemption clause is shown to satisfy the requirement of reasonableness. The requirement of reasonableness is exactly the same here as it is in relation to s.3.[51]

There are three final points about s.2. First, like ss.3 and 5, it applies only to "business liability". Secondly, where an exemption clause is not invalidated by s.2, the buyer may be able to sue the seller for breach of contract and defeat the exemption clause by virtue of ss.6 or 3 of the Unfair Contract Terms Act. Thirdly, he may be able to establish a claim for product liability under the Consumer Protection Act 1987 (such liability cannot be excluded).[52] Alternatively, he may be able to sue for misrepresentation.

Exemptions from Liability for Misrepresentation: s.8

Section 8 of the Unfair Contract Terms Act 1977 amended s.3 of the Misrepresentation Act 1967.[53] The latter section, as amended, renders any exemption clause ineffective except to the extent that the clause is shown to satisfy the requirement of reasonableness. This requirement is exactly the same here as it is in relation to s.3 of the Unfair Contract Terms Act.[54] 10-022

Business Liability

With very limited exceptions, the core provisions of the Unfair Contract Terms Act (ss.2–7) apply to exemption clauses only where those clauses claim to exempt from "business liability". "Business" includes a profession and the activities of any government department or local or public authority.[55] Thus a private householder selling his old lawn mower or even 10-023

51 See para.10-016, above.
52 See para.9-016, above.
53 See para.6-008, above.
54 See para.10-016, above.
55 s.14.

his second-hand car is free to insist on an exemption clause excluding his liability for, say, negligence. Such a clause will be effective, subject only to the common law rules outlined earlier in this chapter. Two provisions of the Unfair Contract Terms Act apply to both business and to non-business liability—ss.6(4) and 8, i.e. where the seller is not acting the course of a business of profession. Thus, by s.8, the private seller cannot exempt himself from liability for misrepresentation unless he can show that the exemption clause satisfies the requirement of reasonableness. By s.6(4), the position is the same if he tries to exempt himself from ss.13–15 of the Sale of Goods Act. All of this does not, however, mean that if the goods prove defective the private seller can easily be made liable for breach of the terms of ss.13–15 of the Sale of Goods Act. He is unlikely to have sold by sample; that rules out s.15. By definition the private seller did not sell in the course of a business; that rules out the conditions in s.14 (i.e. as to satisfactory quality and fitness for purpose). Finally, provided the goods correspond with the description, there will be no liability under s.13.

Mixed Exemption Clauses

10–024 Suppose one exemption falls within more than one section of the Unfair Contract Terms Act 1977. Suppose, for example, it claims to exclude all the following liabilities of the seller; for misrepresentation, for negligence and also for breach of the terms implied by ss.12–15 of the Sale of Goods Act. Which section of the Unfair Contract Terms Act is relevant? The answer depends upon what claim the buyer makes. Section 8 of the Unfair Contract Terms Act is relevant to a claim for misrepresentation; s.2 to a claim for negligence; s.6 to a claim under ss.12–15 of the Sale of Goods Act; and s.3 to a claim for any other breach of contract.

Contracts Other than for the Sale of Goods

10–025 The Unfair Contract Terms Act applies to hire-purchase contracts in exactly the same way as it does to contracts of sale of goods. This will be explained in Ch.25. There are certain other contracts which are not contracts of sale of goods but which are analogous contracts because the ownership of goods passes under them, e.g. contracts of exchange and barter and contracts for labour and materials supplied.[56] The Unfair Contract Terms Act 1977 applies to these

56 See Ch.8, above.

analogous contracts in the same way as it applies to contracts of sale of goods. The statutory terms (as to title, description, quality and sample) implied by ss.2–5 of the Supply of Goods and Services Act 1982 are dealt with in the same way as the corresponding terms implied in contracts of sale of goods.

Turning to hire contracts, it will be remembered that there are statutory implied terms as to title, description, quality and sample implied by ss.6–10 of the Supply of Goods and Services Act 1982.[57] The Unfair Contract Terms Act 1977 applies, with one small difference, to hire contracts as it does to contracts of sale of goods, hire-purchase, barter and exchange, etc. Thus, its effect is the same in relation to a clause claiming to exempt the supplier from liability under the terms relating to description, quality or sample. It is impossible to exclude such liability in a consumer deal and in any non-consumer deal the clause is subject to the requirement of reasonableness. The one difference is that in a hire contract the terms as to title and quiet possession can be excluded or restricted by an exemption clause provided that exemption clause satisfies the requirement of reasonableness.

Finally, let us turn to the third set of terms implied by the Supply of Goods and Services Act 1982. These are the terms implied in a contract where the supplier has agreed to carry out a service.[58] These are terms that: the supplier acting in the course of a business will carry out the service with reasonable skill and care;[59] within a reasonable time;[60] and that the customer will pay a reasonable charge.[61] An exclusion clause, which purports to exclude or limit liability under these terms, is subject to the rules already outlined in this chapter, including the rules laid down in the Unfair Contract Terms Act 1977. In particular, s.3 of that Act will apply.[62] Thus a clause purporting to exclude or limit the supplier's liability will be subject to the requirement of reasonableness, provided the supplier's customer was either dealing as a consumer or else had contracted on the supplier's written standard terms of business. A further explanation is required in relation to the term as to reasonable care and skill implied by s.13 of the Supply of Goods and Services Act 1982. This is because a claim for breach of that term is treated by the Unfair Contract Terms Act s.1, as a claim for negligence. Thus, liability for death or personal injury arising from such a breach of contract can not be excluded or restricted at all; liability for other loss or injury arising from such a breach can be excluded only in so far as the exclusion clause satisfies the requirement of reasonableness.[63]

57 See para.8-008, above.
58 See para.8-009, above.
59 s.13.
60 s.14.
61 s.15.
62 See para.10-019, above.
63 Unfair Contract Terms Act 1977 s.2, see para.10-021, above.

Unfair Terms in Consumer Contracts

10-026 Prior to the enactment of the Consumer Rights Act 2015 unfair terms in consumer contracts was governed by two pieces of legislation, the Unfair Contract Terms Act as discussed above, and by the Unfair Terms in Consumer Contracts Regulations 1999.[64] Where the regulations applied, the effect was that any unfair term was not binding on the consumer. This arrangement was not entirely satisfactory and in 2002 the Law Commission and the Scottish Law Commission released a Consultation Paper assessing the following three issues:[65]

(1) Replacing the Unfair Contract Terms Act 1977 and the Unfair Terms in Consumer Contracts Regulations 1999 with a unified regime.

(2) Extending the scope of the Unfair Terms in Consumer Contracts Regulations to protect businesses, in particular small enterprises.

(3) Making any replacement legislation clearer and more accessible to the reader, so far as is possible without making the law significantly less certain.

The need for a unified regime is well illustrated by the complications considered above by the dual regime surrounding unfair terms. The Unfair Contract Terms Act 1977 applies to exclusion clauses only, yet has a broader application in that it covered consumer and business contracts. The Unfair Terms in Consumer Contracts Regulations 1999 by contrast had a broader remit in applying to any contractual term and not merely to exclusion clauses, yet had a narrower application in applying to only consumer contracts. The difficulties caused by the dual regime were laid down by the Law Commissions' in the following terms:[66]

(1) the statutory controls over unfair terms are split between two pieces of legislation and must be located in each text;

(2) the UTCCR and UCTA contain inconsistent and overlapping provisions;

(3) the scope of application of each piece of legislation is different;

(4) UCTA and the UTCCR use different language and terminology;

64 SI 1999/2083. The 1999 Regulations replaced the Unfair Terms in Consumer Contracts Regulations 1994 (SI 1994/3159) and implemented the Unfair Contract Terms Directive (Directive 93/13/EC).

65 "Unfair Terms in Contracts", Law Commission Consultation Paper No.166; Scottish Law Commission Paper No.119. See the terms of reference at para.1.1.

66 Law Commission Report No.292, (2005) Cmnd. 6464, para.2.4.

(5) UCTA is drafted in a very dense and highly technical style; and

(6) the UTCCR are a fairly literal version of the text of the Directive whose language and, in some instances, concepts are not always easily understood by UK lawyers.

The consequence of these difficulties was that, as Beale and Goriely state:[67]

> **". . .the law on unfair contract terms, which affects ordinary people in their everyday lives, is unnecessarily complicated and difficult to understand. It leads to widespread confusion among consumers, businesses and their advisers."**

The Law Commissions laid down various recommendations, including the creation of a single regime for consumer contracts which ensured an appropriate level of consumer protection but did so in clearer, more readily understandable language.[68] Whilst these proposals were not taken forward by the government at the time, in 2012 the Law Commissions were once again asked to consider the issue of unfair terms in consumer contracts and their recommendations are largely reflected by Pt 2 of the Consumer Rights Act. The aims of Pt 2 of the Consumer Rights Act are described by the Explanatory Notes as follows. It:

- consolidates the legislation governing unfair contract terms in relation to consumer contracts, which currently is found in two separate pieces of legislation, into one place, removes anomalies and overlapping provisions in relation to consumer contracts;
- makes clearer the circumstances when the price or subject matter of the contract cannot be considered for fairness and in particular makes clear that to avoid being considered for fairness those terms must be transparent and prominent; and
- clarifies the role of and extends the indicative list of terms which may be regarded as unfair (the so-called "grey list").

67 H. Beale and T. Goriely, "An unfairly complex law" (155) N.L.J. 318.

68 The Law Commissions also made various recommendations concerning business-to-business contracts and, more radically, the extension of the protections enjoyed by consumers to micro-businesses. This has not been taken forward.

The Consumer Rights Act 2015

When Does the Act apply?

10-027 The unified unfair contract terms regime laid down by Pt 2 of the Consumer Rights Act applies to terms in a contract between a "trader" and a "consumer" (what the Act labels a "consumer contract")[69] and notices which relate to obligations between a "trader" and a "consumer" or which purport to exclude a trader's liability to a consumer (labelled "consumer notice").[70] We have already considered the terms "trader" and "consumer" in the context of Pt 1 of the Act and the same definitions are used in the unfair terms context of Pt 2.[71] Thus a "trader" means "a person acting for purposes relating to that person's trade, business, craft or profession, whether acting personally or through another person acting in the trader's name or on the trader's behalf".[72] A "consumer" on the other hand means "an individual acting for purposes that are wholly or mainly outside that individual's trade, business, craft or profession".[73] It is therefore clear that the protection offered by the Act cannot extend to businesses since they can never fall under the definition of a "consumer".[74] The scope of Pt 2 is therefore very broad indeed, although it is limited by s.61(2) which excludes contracts of employment and apprenticeship. Neither does Pt 2 of the Act apply to a contractual term or notice to the extent that it reflects either (a) mandatory statutory or regulatory provisions, or (b) the provisions or principles of an international convention to which the UK is a party.[75] Thus for example, any term inserted into a consumer contract in order to comply with the Consumer Credit Act 1974 will not be affected by the application of Pt 2.

Assessment for Fairness

10-028 Section 62 requires contractual terms and notices to be fair. It provides:

69 s.61(3).

70 s.61(7). In this context, "notice" includes an "announcement, whether or not in writing, and any other communication or purported communication". It also extends to notices not expressed to apply to consumers provided that it is reasonable to assume that it is intended to be seen or heard by a consumer (s.61(6)).

71 See para.1-009 above.

72 CRA 2015 s.2(2).

73 CRA 2015 s.2(3).

74 This avoids the difficulties encountered by the courts under UCTA 1977 for example, where it was possible for a business to be protected under the Act. See for example, *R & B Customs Brokers v United Dominions Trust* [1988] 1 W.L.R. 321 and *Feldarol Foundry Plc v Hermes Leasing (London) Ltd* [2004] EWCA Civ. 747. Technically, a sole trader would satisfy the definition of an "individual" and therefore potentially be a "consumer" under the Act. However, they would only be protected where they were acting for purposes wholly or mainly outside their business.

75 s.73(1).

> **"(4) A term is unfair if, contrary to the requirement of good faith, it causes a significant imbalance in the parties' rights and obligations under the contract to the detriment of the consumer.**
>
> **(5) Whether a term is fair is to be determined—**
>
> **(a) taking into account the nature of the subject matter of the contract, and**
>
> **(b) by reference to all the circumstances existing when the term was agreed and to all of the other terms of the contract or of any other contract on which it depends."**

The section makes similar provision for notices.[76] Section 62 resembles the wording of reg.5 in the Unfair Terms in Consumer Contract Regulations and makes it clear that any term which creates an imbalance to the detriment of the seller or supplier is not unfair.

The requirement of good faith is not defined within the Act. Recital 16 of the Directive does, however, offer a definition and was considered by Lord Bingham in *Director General of Fair Trading v First National Bank*:[77]

> **"The requirement of good faith in this context is one of fair and open dealing. Openness requires that the terms should be expressed fully, clearly and legibly, containing no concealed pitfalls or traps. Appropriate prominence should be given to terms which might operate disadvantageously to the customer. Fair dealing requires that a supplier should not, whether deliberately or unconsciously, take advantage of the consumer's necessity, indigence, lack of experience, unfamiliarity with the subject matter of the contract, weak bargaining position or any other factor listed in or analogous to those listed in Schedule 2 to the Regulations".**

Moreover, Lord Bingham stated:[78]

> **"The member states have no common concept of fairness or good faith, and the Directive does not purport to state the law of any single member state. It lays down a test to be applied, whatever their pre-existing law, by all member states. If the meaning of the test were doubtful, or vulnerable to the possibility of differing interpretations in differing member states, it might be desirable or necessary to seek a ruling from the European Court of Justice on its**

76 s.62(6) and (7).

77 [2002] 1 A.C. 481 at [17].

78 [2002] 1 A.C. 481 at [17].

> **interpretation. But the language used in expressing the test, so far as applicable in this case, is in my opinion clear and not reasonably capable of differing interpretations."**

The Act does not state upon whom rests the burden of proof, i.e. to establish fairness or unfairness. The burden therefore falls presumably upon the consumer as the party alleging unfairness.[79] In determining whether the term is unfair the court must take into account the nature of the goods or services and must refer to: all the circumstances attending the making of the contract; and all the other terms of the contract and of any contract upon which it is dependant.[80] It should also be noted that under s.71 the court now has a duty to consider whether a term is fair even where the consumer does not raise unfairness as an issue unless the court does not have sufficient legal and factual information to do so.[81] Thus, in *R v Hunter and Smith*[82] the Court of Appeal considered the Consumer Rights Act's unfair terms framework in the context of an appeal against a conviction for fraudulent trading. The court concluded that terms (such as limits on the number of tickets that could be purchased and the right to prevent entry into an event) were a reasonable and proportionate response to secondary ticket sales and touting—a practice that causes significant detriment to consumers. Such terms were, therefore, fair under the Act.

10-029 In Pt 1 of Sch.2 to the Act there is an indicative list (the grey list) of the sorts of terms which may be regarded as unfair. The list, which is not exhaustive, includes exemption clauses, limitation of liability clauses, penalty clauses, and clauses:

- which the consumer had no real opportunity to become acquainted with before the contract;
- giving the trader the discretion to terminate the contract without conferring the same right upon the consumer;
- giving the trader the power to terminate a contract of indefinite duration without giving reasonable notice (except where there are serious grounds to do so);
- automatically extending a contract of fixed duration unless the consumer indicates to the contrary within an unreasonably early deadline;

79 The Law Commission Report, "Unfair Terms in Contracts" suggests that "where an issue has been raised as to whether a term is fair and reasonable, the burden of proving that it is fair and reasonable should rest on the business" (2005) Cmnd. 6464, at para.3.130.

80 See s.62(5).

81 This reflects jurisprudence from the European Court of Justice, see, for example, *Mostaza Claro v Centro Móvil Milenium SL* (C-168/05) (2006).

82 [2021] EWCA Crim 1785. See, in particular the discussion at [164]–[165].

- enabling the trader to retain a deposit or part payment when the consumer cancels the contract, without also giving the consumer a similar right to compensation where it is the seller/supplier who cancels the contract;
- enabling the trader to retain a deposit or part payment for services not yet supplied when it is the supplier who cancels the contract;
- enabling the trader to vary the agreement unilaterally for an invalid reason or for a reason not specified in the contract;
- providing for the trader to raise the price without at the same time giving the consumer the right in such a case to cancel the contract if the price is then high as compared with the original contract price;
- providing for the price to be determined at the time of delivery but not allowing for the consumer to cancel the agreement if the price is then high as compared to the original contract price;
- giving the trader the exclusive right to interpret any term of the contract;
- giving the trader the right to determine whether goods or services are in conformity with the contract;
- giving the trader the possibility of transferring his obligations under the contract, where this may reduce the guarantees for the consumer, without the consumer's agreement; and
- excluding or hindering the consumer's right to take legal action or take any other legal remedy, particularly by requiring the consumer to take disputes exclusively to arbitration not covered by legal provisions.

The "grey list" closely follows the equivalent laid down in the 1999 Regulations albeit with modified language to ensure consistency with the Act generally and, more substantively, three additional paragraphs:

- A term which has the object or effect of requiring that, where the consumer decides not to conclude or perform the contract, the consumer must pay the trader a disproportionately high sum in compensation or for services which have not been supplied.
- A term which has the object or effect of permitting the trader to determine the characteristics of the subject matter of the contract after the consumer has become bound by it.

- A term which has the object or effect of giving the trader the discretion to decide the price payable under the contract after the consumer has become bound by it, where no price or method of determining the price is agreed when the consumer becomes bound.

Under the 1999 Regulations, two kinds of term were not subject to the requirement to be fair:

(i) a term which is individually negotiated; and

(ii) core terms of the contract (in so far as they are in plain and intelligible language).

The Consumer Rights Act has, however, removed the limitation on individually negotiated clauses, although this will be of (it may be presumed) very little practical effect given that (i) consumers will frequently deal on the seller's standard terms and conditions and will rarely have the opportunity to individually negotiate terms, and (ii) where a consumer is perhaps able to individually negotiate a term, it is likely to be a term which either defines the main subject-matter of the contract or the price to be paid under the contract. These terms remain outside of the scope of the fairness test other than the extent to which they are detailed in Sch.2's list of grey terms. Section 64 provides:

> **"(1) A term of a consumer contract may not be assessed for fairness under section 62 to the extent that—**
> **(a) it specifies the main subject matter of the contract, or**
> **(b) the assessment is of the appropriateness of the price payable under the contract by comparison with the goods,digital content or services supplied under it.**
> **(2) Subsection (1) excludes a term from an assessment under section 62 only if it is transparent and prominent."**

Thus a term which specifies the main subject matter of the contract or the price payable is not subject to the fairness test provided that it is both transparent and prominent. Transparency requires a term to be expressed in plain and intelligible language, and, if a written term, legible.[83] The requirement of prominence is new, having no equivalent under the 1999 Regulations. Section 64(4) defines prominence as a term which "is brought to the consumer's attention in such a way that an average consumer would be aware of the term". The average consumer is one who is "reasonably well-informed, observant and circumspect".[84] The underlying notion at play here is, of course, that an average consumer should not be met with any "nasty

83 s.64(3).
84 s.64(5).

surprises"—provided that they are given ample opportunity to understand the fundamental aspects of the bargain they are entering into, the court will not protect them should they ultimately make a bad bargain. If, however, such terms are buried in small print, the court will be able to assess the term for fairness.

Beyond this requirement however, the terms that are subject to scrutiny under s.62 are those that are ancillary, e.g. those relating to quality; time (of delivery/completion and of payment); arbitration; making complaints; giving (and forfeiting) deposits or down payments; cancellation; powers to vary the agreement, etc. This raises a crucial question: how are we to define "core terms"? 10-030

The issue of core and ancillary terms was considered in *Office of Fair Trading v Abbey National plc*[85] in the context of whether charges for unauthorised overdrafts were subject to the fairness test under the 1999 Regulations, or whether they fell under reg.6 (the predecessor to s.64) and thereby only needed to be drafted in plain and intelligible language. The Court of Appeal took a broad view of the core and ancillary divide and held that payment obligations were exempt from the fairness test only where it formed part of the core bargain between the parties. Since the typical bank customer would view overdraft charges as not being part of the essential bargain it held that the charges were ancillary and therefore open to the general test of fairness. The Supreme Court rejected this approach and found that, viewed objectively, banks offered a package of services and that overdraft charges were part of the consideration provided for that package of services. This was so even though the overdraft fees were contingent, that the majority of bank customers would never pay them and that an average bank customer would not consider such fees to be part of the essential bargain between themselves and the bank. Thus, the OFT was not entitled to assess the fairness of such charges in relation to their adequacy for services provided by the bank. [86]

The Office of Fair Trading v Ashbourne Management Services Ltd[87] involved a number of gym membership contracts. The court held that whilst a term describing the minimum period of membership was part of the core bargain between the parties and therefore not subject to the general fairness test, the consequences of early termination in the light of the minimum membership period was not part of the core bargain and could be assessed for fairness. Notwithstanding the fact that the minimum term clause itself was drafted in plain and intelligible language, the court held that the consequences of early termination were unfair. This was because the average consumer had a tendency to overestimate the extent to which they would use the gym facilities and the defendant's business model was "designed and calculated to take advantage of the naivety and inexperience of the average consumer". This represented a significant imbalance in the parties' obligations and was contrary to the requirement of good faith.[88]

85 [2009] UKSC 6.

86 For a discussion of the bank charges proceedings, see A. Arora, "Unfair contract terms and unauthorised bank charges: a banking lawyer's perspective" [2012] J.B.L. 44 at 60–67.

87 [2011] EWHC 1237 (Ch).

88 [2011] EWHC 1237 (Ch) at [173].

10–031 A useful illustration of the scope of terms which relate to price, and is therefore not to be assessed for fairness is provided by the Supreme Court in *ParkingEye Ltd v Beavis*.[89] The dispute centred on a "parking charge" of £85 payable where a vehicle exceeded the time limit (two-hours). The Supreme Court explained that the clause was subject to the fairness test since whilst the label "parking charge" was used, it was very clear that the sum of £85 was not a charge at all, i.e. it was not remuneration for the service (car parking) provided. Rather, it was a charge payable where a user of the car park breached the terms of the contractual licence. The majority of the Supreme Court (Lord Toulson dissenting) held that the charge was not unfair under the 1999 Regulations. This was the case since it did not arise contrary to the requirements of good faith: ParkingEye had a legitimate interest in efficiently managing the car park for the benefit of other users and the wider community (such as nearby shops for example). The charge of £85 was no higher than was necessary to achieve that purpose and the reasonable motorist would have agreed to such a charge being due in cases where the permitted time limit had been exceeded.

In *CMA v Care UK Health & Social Holdings Ltd*[90] the court had to consider an administration fee payable by elderly residents before being admitted to a care home. The Competition and Markets Authority sought to establish that the term was unfair, since the care home provided no material service in return for the fee. The court rejected the CMA's argument, and found that the term was fair. The charge related to a distinct service being provided in assessing and preparing the consumer ahead of their being admitted. Further, Care UK were able to demonstrate that they took steps to properly explain the agreement. Accordingly, the term did not cause a significant imbalance to the parties' rights and obligations contrary to the requirement of good faith.[91]

Oceano Grupo Editorial S.A. v Rocio Muriciano Quintero[92] involved a number of contracts by a company which had its principal place of business in Barcelona, each such contract being a contract to sell, on instalment credit terms, an encyclopedia to a consumer domiciled in another part of Spain. Each contract contained a clause, not individually negotiated, giving exclusive jurisdiction to the Barcelona courts, which is where the seller commenced proceedings against consumers who had defaulted on their repayments. The European Court clearly considered the clause to be unfair (within the meaning of the Directive). It was held that the Barcelona court should of its own motion (a) determine whether the jurisdiction clause was unfair, and (b) it being unfair, should decline the jurisdiction it conferred.

89 [2015] UKSC 67.

90 [2021] EWHC 2088 (Ch).

91 The CMA also failed to establish any contravention of the Consumer Protection from Unfair Trading Regulations 2008, see Ch.16, below.

92 27 June 2000 (C-240/98) ECJ.

Effect of a Term Being Unfair

An unfair term in a consumer contract, or an unfair consumer notice, is not binding on the consumer.[93] The consumer can, however, continue to rely on the term or notice if they wish to do so.[94] Furthermore, s.67 provides that: 10-032

> **"Where a term of a consumer contract is not binding on the consumer as a result of this Part, the contract continues, so far as practicable, to have effect in every other respect."**

Thus the contract is treated as if the unfair term were not in it. Therefore, provided the contract is capable of subsisting without the unfair term, the rest of the contract survives.

Terms that Cannot be Excluded

Certain terms are always rendered ineffective by the Act.[95] These "blacklisted" terms are therefore never binding upon consumers and are automatically unenforceable irrespective of the fairness test. Of particular importance in our context are certain terms in goods contracts we have discussed previously.[96] Accordingly, s.31 provides that the liability of a trader cannot be excluded or restricted in respect of: 10-033

(a) s.9 (goods to be of satisfactory quality);

(b) s.10 (goods to be fit for particular purpose);

(c) s.11 (goods to be as described);

(d) s.12 (other pre-contract information included in contract);

(e) s.13 (goods to match a sample);

(f) s.14 (goods to match a model seen or examined);

(g) s.15 (installation as part of conformity of the goods with the contract);

(h) s.16 (goods not conforming to contract if digital content does not conform);

93 s.62(1) (terms); s.62(2) (notices).
94 s.62(3).
95 See s.62(8).
96 See, for example, Ch.7 in respect of statutory rights.

(i) s.17 (trader to have right to supply the goods, etc.);

(j) s.28 (delivery of goods); and

(k) s.29 (passing of risk).

Section 31(2) extends this to ensure that a term of the contract will not be binding where it would:

> **"(a) exclude or restrict a right or remedy in respect of a liability under a provision listed in subsection (1),**
> **(b) make such a right or remedy or its enforcement subject to a restrictive or onerous condition,**
> **(c) allow a trader to put a person at a disadvantage as a result of pursuing such a right or remedy, or**
> **(d) exclude or restrict rules of evidence or procedure."**

In respect of contracts to supply digital content s.47 prescribes a similar, though obviously less extensive, list which extends to matters of satisfactory quality, fitness for purpose, description, pre-contract information, and the right to supply. Likewise, in respect of a contract to supply services, any attempt to exclude liability for liability for reasonable skill and care (s.49); information about the trader or service to be binding (s.50); and reasonable price and time (ss.51 and 52), will be ineffective. Finally, s.65 provides that a "trader cannot by a term of a consumer contract or by a consumer notice exclude or restrict liability for death or personal injury resulting from negligence". This reflects the position under s.2 of the Unfair Contract Terms Act discussed above.[97]

Clarity and Interpretation

10–034 Any written term (or notice) must be legible and expressed in plain, intelligible language.[98] There is no express sanction available to a consumer where a written term is not transparent, i.e. is not legible and in plain, intelligible language. However, if there is any doubt about the meaning of a written term or notice, the interpretation most favourable to the consumer prevails.[99] Furthermore, a lack of transparency will be reflected within the assessment of fairness, and, in the context of terms which relate to the subject matter or price, it will render such clauses amenable to an assessment for fairness.

97 Note the limitations laid down in s.66, e.g. for contracts of insurance.

98 s.68.

99 s.69. Note the exception in s.69(2) which ensures that in the context of enforcement activity, the *least* favourable interpretation (to the consumer) can be adopted.

Enforcement

One imagines the Act being of significance in contractual disputes between consumer and trader. However, the Act also gives a power of enforcement to the Competition and Markets Authority (CMA) (formerly the Office of Fair Trading).[100] The CMA, on receiving a complaint that a contract term is unfair, can bring proceedings for an injunction to stop a trader using an unfair term. In addition, the CMA is given the power to accept undertakings from traders and will take these into account in determining whether to start proceedings for an injunction. To facilitate this power, the CMA may require any person to provide copies of any relevant documentation (e.g. copies of their standard contracts) and information regarding their use. The Act affords similar enforcement powers to various other regulatory bodies (e.g. water and gas regulators), to local weights and measures authorities and to a non-statutory body, the Consumers' Association. 10-035

General Reading

J. Adams and R. Brownsword, "The Unfair Contract Terms Act: A Decade of Discretion" (1988) 104 L.Q.R. 94.

A. Arora, "Unfair Contract Terms and Unauthorised Bank Charges: a Banking Lawyer's Perspective" [2012] J.B.L. 44.

I. Brown and A. Chandler, "Unreasonableness and the Unfair Contract Terms Act" (1993) 109 L.Q.R. 41.

S. Hedley, "Defective Software in the Court of Appeal" (1997) 56 C.L.J. 21.

Law Commission Consultation Paper, "Unfair Terms in Contracts", No.166 (2002).

Law Commission Report, "Unfair Terms in Contracts", No.292 (2005) Cmnd. 6464.

E. Macdonald, "Mapping the Unfair Contract Terms Act 1977 and the Directive on Unfair Terms in Consumer Contracts" [1994] J.B.L. 441.

E. Macdonald, "Unifying Unfair Terms Legislation" (2004) 67 M.L.R. 69.

C. Macmillan, "Evolution or Revolution? Unfair Terms in Consumer Contracts" [2002] C.L.J. 22.

N.E. Palmer, "Limiting Liability for Negligence" (1982) 45 M.L.R. 763.

E. Peel, "Reasonable Exemption Clauses" (2001) 117 L.Q.R. 545.

F.M.B. Reynolds, "Unfair Contract Terms" (1994) 110 L.Q.R. 1.

A. Samuels, "The Consumer Rights Act 2015" [2016] J.B.L. 159.

S. Whittaker, "Unfair Contract Terms, Unfair Prices and Bank Charges" (2011) 74 M.L.R. 106.

100 See Sch.3 to the 2015 Act.

11

Delivery and Payment

Introduction

The parties can make what agreement they wish about the time, place and manner of delivery 11-001
and payment. What follows is an explanation of the rights and duties between the seller and buyer when they have not agreed anything different in their contract. As we will see, where the contract is a sales contract under the Consumer Rights Act 2015, the position is governed by both that Act and Sale of Goods Act. Where the contract is not a sales contract under the Consumer Rights Act, for example, non-consumer sales and private sales, the rules applicable are those laid down by the Sale of Goods Act only.

Concurrent Conditions

Section 28 of the Sale of Goods Act provides: 11-002

> **"Unless otherwise agreed, delivery of the goods and payment of the price are concurrent conditions . . ."**

Thus, although s.49 states that the seller can sue for the price in certain circumstances,[1] he will nevertheless not be able to do so unless he is also ready and willing to deliver the goods.[2] Equally, the buyer will not be able to sue for non-delivery unless he was ready and willing to pay or else it had been agreed that he could have credit. The rule that delivery and

1 See Ch.12.

2 *Abraaj Investment Management Ltd v Bregawn Jersey Ltd* [2010] EWHC 630 (Comm) at [19].

payment are concurrent conditions ties in with the unpaid seller's lien[3] which entitles him in the absence of contrary agreement to retain the goods until payment.

Delivery

11-003 Delivery is the voluntary transfer of possession from one person to another.[4] Delivery may be achieved in one of several ways. The seller may physically hand over the goods, i.e. actual delivery. He may hand over the means of control of the goods, e.g. the key to the premises where they are housed which may amount to constructive delivery (where actual delivery does not occur but control of the goods is transferred from seller to buyer). Alternatively, the seller may, where the goods are at the time of the sale in the possession of a third party (e.g. at a warehouse), instruct the third party to hold the goods to the order of the buyer. In that case, delivery occurs when the third party attorns, i.e. acknowledges to the buyer that he holds the goods on his behalf.[5] Delivery can be made in an appropriate case by the transfer of a document, or documents, of title, as in c.i.f. contracts.[6] Sometimes there could be confusion between the last two methods of delivery. For example, X could own a cargo in course of transit which is therefore in the hands of a third party, the carrier. If X sells it by dealing with the documents of title, then delivery occurs when he transfers the bill of lading to the buyer, irrespective of whether the carrier attorns.[7]

Place of Delivery

11-004 Section 29 of the Sale of Goods Act provides:

> **"(1) Whether it is for the buyer to take possession of the goods or for the seller to send them to the buyer is a question depending in each case on the contract, express or implied, between the parties.**
>
> **(2) Apart from any such contract, express or implied, the place of delivery is the seller's place of business, if he has one, and if**

3 See Ch.12.

4 Defined in both SGA 1979 s.61(1) and CRA 2015 s.59.

5 s.29(4). It may be possible to establish a right to immediate possession notwithstanding the absence of an acknowledgement by the third party, see *Pendragon Plc v Walon Ltd* [2005] EWHC 1082 (QB).

6 See para.3-022, above.

7 SGA 1979 s.29(4).

> **not, his residence: except that, if the contract is for the sale of specific goods, which to the knowledge of the parties when the contract is made are in some other place, then that place is the place of delivery."**

Thus, unless otherwise agreed, it is not for the seller to convey the goods to the buyer but for the latter to collect them. If the seller does agree to convey them, he must do so within a reasonable length of time—s.29(3) of the Sale of Goods Act. This position is slightly different where the Consumer Rights Act applies, i.e. where a trader sells goods to a consumer. In this situation, unless agreed otherwise, s.29(3) does not apply and there is a statutory implied term that the trader must deliver the goods to the consumer.[8]

If on arrival the seller hands them over to someone whom he reasonably assumes to be authorised to receive them, then he has carried out his duty of delivery: *Galbraith and Grant v Block*.[9] One possible consequence of this is exemplified in the recent decision of the Court of Appeal in *Computer 2000 Distribution Ltd v ICM Computer Solutions plc*[10] where a rogue convinced the buyer to arrange delivery to an address where they were received by a security guard and subsequently handed over to the rogue. The Court held that the (legitimate) buyer must pay for the goods since they had been delivered.

Time of Delivery

We have already seen[11] that, in a commercial contract, the time of delivery is normally "of the essence". Thus, if a delivery date is stipulated and the seller cannot make delivery by that date, that is a breach of condition and the buyer is entitled to repudiate the contract and sue for non-delivery. 11-005

When no time is stipulated and it is for the buyer to collect, the seller must be ready to hand over the goods (against payment) to the buyer on demand at any time after the making of the contract.[12] If he fails to do so, he is in breach of condition; the buyer can treat the contract as repudiated and sue for non-delivery.

This situation is a little different where the contract is one to which the Consumer Rights Act applies: if the trader is bound to deliver the goods to the consumer (and the parties have not agreed a time for delivery), the trader must deliver the goods without undue delay and in any event, within 30 days from the day after the day the contract was concluded.[13] Irrespective of whether the parties had agreed a time for delivery, where the trader is late in delivering the

8 CRA 2015 s.28(2).
9 [1922] 2 K.B. 155.
10 *The Times*, 17 November 2004.
11 At para.7-006, above.
12 Provided made at a reasonable hour, SGA 1979 s.29(5).
13 CRA 2015 s.28(3).

goods to the consumer, the consumer can, in certain circumstances, treat the contract as at an end. This will be the case where:[14]

(a) The trader has refused to deliver the goods.

(b) Delivery of the goods at the agreed time or within the agreed period is essential, taking into account all the relevant circumstances at the time the contract was entered into.

(c) The consumer told the trader (before the contract was entered into) that delivery in accordance within the standard 30-day period, or at the agreed time, was essential,

In any other circumstances, the consumer has the right to "specify a period that is appropriate in the circumstances and require the trader to deliver the goods before the end of that period".[15] If the trader is unable to deliver the goods within that period, the consumer may treat the contract as at an end.[16] Where a consumer elects to treat the contract as at an end, the trader must reimburse all payments made under the contract without undue delay.[17]

Expenses

11-006 Unless otherwise agreed, the seller must bear the expenses, if any, connected with putting the goods into a deliverable state.[18]

Delivery of Wrong Quantity

11-007 The consequences where the seller delivers the wrong quantity of goods are dealt with by the Consumer Rights Act (for trader to consumer sales contracts) and the Sale of Goods Act (for all other sale of goods contracts). The general approach under both frameworks is the same: a buyer may reject the goods if the wrong quantity is delivered.

Section 30 of the Sale of Goods Act provides:

> **"(1) Where the seller delivers to the buyer a quantity of goods less than he contracted to sell, the buyer may reject them, but if the buyer accepts the goods so delivered he must pay for them at the contract rate.**

14 CRA 2015 s.28(6).
15 CRA 2015 s.28(7).
16 CRA 2015 s.28(8).
17 CRA 2015 s.28(9).
18 SGA 1979 s.29(6).

> **(2) Where the seller delivers to the buyer a quantity of goods larger than he contracted to sell, the buyer may accept the goods included in the contract and reject the rest, or he may reject the whole."**

This is recast for trader to consumer sales contracts by s.25 of the Consumer Rights Act. Under either s.30 or s.25 the buyer is allowed to reject the goods (all of them) if too many or too few are delivered. Where the buyer elects to accept the quantity as delivered, thus accepting either a shortfall or an excess, they must pay for them at the contract rate.

There is one important distinction between these two provisions: where s.30 applies the buyer does not have the right of rejection if the shortfall or excess is so slight as to make rejection unreasonable.[19] Thus whilst the commercial buyer will always have the ability to reject any excess delivered, they will not be able to reject all of the goods unless it is reasonable to do so.

It should also be noted that the law ignores trifling breaches of contract. This is, however, very narrowly defined, as illustrated by the facts of *Shipton, Anderson v Weil Bros*[20] the sellers were entitled to deliver 4,950 tons. They in fact delivered 4,950 tons 55lb. It was held that this did not entitle the buyers to reject the whole consignment. 11-008

Section 30(1) entitles the buyer to reject all the goods if less than the contract quantity is delivered. Section 30(1) does not, however, apply where a contract is severable, i.e. where the parties have agreed that delivery can be made in instalments and, on a true construction of the contract, the parties did not intend that a breach of one consignment was to justify rejection of them all: *Regent v Francesco*.[21] In that case a shortfall in one instalment will normally only justify rejection of that one instalment. It would not entitle the buyer to reject all other instalments unless the seller's breach was so serious as to amount to a repudiation of the contract.[22]

Delivery by Instalments Under the Sale of Goods Act

There are three possible situations: 11-009

(i) The parties did not agree that delivery could be by instalments. In this case the buyer is not bound to accept delivery by instalments.[23] In *Behrend v Produce Brokers*[24] part of the goods were delivered which the buyers accepted. It was held, applying s.30 of the Sale of Goods Act, that the buyers were entitled to refuse to accept later delivery of the rest of the goods and that they should pay pro rata for those they had accepted.

19 SGA 1979 s.30(2A).
20 [1912] 1 K.B. 574.
21 [1981] Com. L.R. 78.
22 See para.11-009, below.
23 SGA 1979 s.31(1).
24 [1920] 3 K.B. 530.

(ii) The parties agreed that delivery could be by instalments but the contract is not severable. A breach of condition (e.g. as to quality) in relation to the first instalment will entitle the buyer to repudiate the whole contract. If, however, he has accepted one or more instalments (or any part thereof), he will not be able to reject later instalments if there is a breach of condition in relation to them—s.11(4).[25] This appears to remain the position even after the introduction in 1995 of the right of partial rejection.[26]

(iii) The parties agreed that delivery could be made by instalments (either on specified dates or "as required") and the contract is severable (divisible). The contract is severable if, on its true construction, the parties did not intend that a breach as to one consignment would justify rejection of all the consignments. If the parties had agreed that each consignment was to be separately paid for, the court will normally construe the contract as severable. That, however, is not an essential requirement of a severable contract. In the case of a severable contract, acceptance of one or more instalments does not preclude rejection of later instalments for breach of condition—s.11(4). In *Jackson v Rotax Motor and Cycle Co*[27] the buyer accepted as satisfactory the first delivery of motor horns but claimed to reject the later deliveries because they were not of merchantable quality. It was held that he was entitled to do this.

A more difficult question in relation to severable contracts is whether a breach of condition in relation to one or more instalments entitles the innocent party to regard the whole contract as repudiated or whether it is a severable breach confined to the instalments in question. It is a question of fact in each case depending upon the circumstances.[28] *Maple Flock Co v Universal Furniture Products (Wembley)*[29] concerned a severable contract for the sale of 100 tons of flock by instalments. The first 15 instalments were satisfactory, the 16th was defective, and there were four more satisfactory deliveries. The buyers claimed to regard the whole contract as repudiated. It was held that they could not. The court said that whether the breach was a repudiatory one depended on two factors:

(a) the ratio the breach bore quantitatively to the whole contract; and

(b) the likelihood of the breach being repeated in later instalments.

On neither factor did the breach appear serious in this case. Sometimes the contract includes a clause such as "each instalment to be considered as a separate contract". This has little effect and the courts will still regard the contract as one contract (albeit a severable one)

25 Unless he can bring himself within s.30 above.
26 See para.13-009, below.
27 [1910] 2 K.B. 937.
28 SGA 1979 s.31(2).
29 [1934] 1 K.B. 148.

and therefore it is possible for a sufficiently serious breach to be a repudiation of the whole contract: *Smyth (Ross) v Bailey*.[30]

The problem of classifying the contract as either non-severable (i.e. (ii) above) or severable (i.e. (iii) above) arose in *Rosenthal v Esmail*.[31] Under a c.i.f. contract which provided "each shipment to be regarded as a separate contract", the sellers had an option whether to send separate shipments or to send all the goods by one shipment. They chose the latter course but they sent to the buyer separate shipping documents in respect of two different lots in the one ship. The buyer claimed that the contract was severable, accepted one lot and rejected the other for breach of condition. The House of Lords held that since the sellers had opted for the one shipment, albeit with separate documents, the contract was not severable. Therefore, the buyers having accepted part of the goods could not reject the rest.[32] This decision must now, however, be read in the light of the right of partial rejection introduced in 1994.[33]

Delivery by Instalments Under the Consumer Rights Act

Section 26 of the Consumer Rights Act deals with delivery by instalments in sales contracts with broadly the same effect as s.31, previously discussed in relation to contracts of sale of goods under the Sale of Goods Act. Thus, unless otherwise agreed, a consumer is not bound to accept delivery of the goods by instalments.[34] Where the contract provides for the goods to be delivered by instalments (which are to be paid for separately) s.26(3) states that: 11-010

> **"If the trader makes defective deliveries in respect of one or more instalments, the consumer, apart from any entitlement to claim damages, may be (but is not necessarily) entitled—**
> **(a) to exercise the short-term right to reject or the right to reject under section 19(6) (as applicable) in respect of the whole contract, or**
> **(b) to reject the goods in an instalment."**

The ability of a consumer to exercise the rights in s.26(3) is dependent upon the terms of the contract and the circumstances of the case.[35] They are not available, however, where the rules relating to delivery laid down in s.28 are not complied with. Section 26(5) makes it clear that in this situation, the rights of a consumer are those laid down by s.28 itself.

30 [1940] 3 All E.R. 60.
31 [1965] 1 W.L.R. 1117.
32 SGA 1979 s.11.
33 See para.13-009, below.
34 CRA 2015 s.26(1).
35 CRA 2015 s.26(4).

Conversely, s.26(6) addresses the position of the trader where the consumer refuses to take delivery of or pay for one or more instalments. In this situation, the trader may be entitled to treat the whole contract as at an end or, where the contract is severable, have a claim for damages but not a right to treat the whole contract as at an end. Again, the ability to exercise these rights depends upon the terms of the contract and the circumstances of the case.

Delivery to a Carrier

11-011 In general, where the seller is authorised or required to send the goods to the buyer, delivery to a carrier for that purpose will normally constitute complete performance of the seller's duty of delivery (s.32). This is modified, however, where the Consumer Rights Act applies. Where there is a trader-to-consumer sales contract, s.32 of the Sale of Goods Act does not apply.[36] As we have already discussed, where there is a sales contract under the Consumer Rights Act, risk will normally remain with the trader until the goods are in the physical possession of the consumer.[37]

In *Scottish & Newcastle International Ltd v Othon Ghalanos Ltd*[38] the House of Lords was required to determine the place of delivery of various consignments of cider shipped from Liverpool to Limassol (Cyprus). The question of where delivery occurred was paramount since if delivery had occurred in Liverpool, the seller's action for the price could be heard in the English courts whereas if delivery took place in Limassol the seller would have to pursue its claim in the Cypriot courts.[39] Their Lordships found that the cider had been delivered to the buyers at Liverpool since (i) the buyers selected the carrier, and (ii) the seller reserved no right of disposal over the goods and had no commercial interest in the goods once the cider was in the possession of the carrier.

Where s.32 applies, the seller must, unless otherwise authorised, make the best reasonably possible contract with the carrier on behalf of the buyer.[40] In *Thomas Young v Hobson*[41] the seller made a contract for the goods to be carried at the "owner's risk". The carrier would have agreed to carry them for the same price at the carrier's risk. The goods were damaged in transit and it was held that the seller was in breach of his duty under s.32(2) and the buyer was entitled to reject the goods.[42]

Where customary, the seller must give sufficient information to the buyer to enable him to insure the goods whilst in transit by sea.[43]

36 See SGA 1979 s.32(4).

37 See the discussion of CRA 2015 s.29, considered at para.3-029, above.

38 [2008] UKHL 11. See generally, C. Hare and P.J. Hinks, "Sale of Goods and the Brussels I Regulation" (2008) L.M.C.L.Q. (3) 353.

39 In accordance with art.5(1)(b) of the Judgments Regulation (EC) No 44/2001 (Brussels I) (now revoked).

40 SGA 1979 s.32(2).

41 (1949) 65 T.L.R. 365.

42 As to risk generally during transit, see para.3-026, above.

43 SGA 1979 s.32(3).

Payment

Normally, in the absence of contrary agreement, the buyer need not make payment until delivery is made.[44] However, where the goods have been destroyed or stolen at a time when they were at the buyer's risk,[45] then of course he is under a duty to pay, even though delivery is impossible. 11-012

Apart from that situation, if the buyer has paid and the goods are not delivered, he is entitled to recover the price because he has received no consideration for it.[46] Two matters are dealt with elsewhere, the amount of the price[47] and when the seller can sue for the price.[48]

44 SGA 1979 s.28.
45 See para.3-028, above.
46 s.54.
47 See paras 2-009–2-010, above.
48 See para.12-003, below.

[illegible] in the absence of contrary agreement [illegible] payment [illegible] delivery is made. However, where the goods have been destroyed [illegible] they were at the buyer's risk [illegible] is under a duty to pay even though delivery is impossible.

[illegible] from that situation [illegible] and the goods are not delivered [illegible] entitled to recover the price because he has received no consideration [illegible] dealt with elsewhere [illegible] and where the seller [illegible] for the price.

12

Seller's Remedies

A seller has two sets of remedies available, personal remedies enforceable by taking action in the courts against the buyer and remedies exercisable against the goods (referred to as "real remedies"). 12–001

Personal Remedies

The seller has two possible actions; for the price or for damages for non-acceptance. 12–002

The Price

Section 49 allows the seller to maintain an action for the price where both the following conditions are fulfilled: 12–003

(i) The buyer has wrongfully refused or neglected to pay according to the terms of the contract.

(ii) Either property has passed to the buyer or "the price is payable on a day certain irrespective of delivery".

The buyer's refusal or failure to pay must have been wrongful. It is not wrongful if he has rightfully rejected the goods for breach of condition (subject to contrary agreement). Similarly, he is entitled (subject to contrary agreement) to refuse to pay except in exchange for taking delivery of the goods—s.28. Therefore the seller will be unable to sue for the price unless, at the time of the neglect or refusal to pay, he was ready and willing to deliver. Again, if the seller has granted the buyer credit, he cannot sue for the price before the end of the agreed credit period; until then the buyer's failure to pay is not wrongful.

In relation to the second requirement, if a particular date has been stipulated for payment then an action can be maintained after that date irrespective of whether property has passed to the buyer. When no "day certain" has been agreed, the seller will succeed only if property has passed to the buyer. A "day certain" may be a fixed date or could be fixed by reference to the seller's performance of his part of the contract. Different days certain may be agreed for the payment of different instalments of the price. In *Workman Clark v Lloyd Brazileno*[1] the seller was building a vessel for the buyer and the price was to be paid by instalments on dates to be determined by reference to the stage of construction. It was held that at the relevant stages the seller could sue for the instalments then due.

In *Readie Construction Ltd v Geo Quarries Ltd*[2] the buyer refused to accept, nor pay for, a delivery of building aggregate having discovered that previous deliveries had turned to slurry following heavy rainfall. The contract stipulated that the buyer was to make "payment in full without any deduction or withholding whatsoever" with payment falling due by the end of the month following the month in which the relevant invoice was dated. It was held that the buyer could not withhold payment for defective goods following the expiration of the credit period extended by the agreement.

In *FG Wilson (Engineering) Ltd v John Holt & Co Ltd*[3] the Court of Appeal held that a seller can only bring an action for price where s.49 applies, i.e. where property has passed or where the price is due on a day certain. This is consistent with previous judicial statements on the matter, however, the Supreme Court has recently suggested, obiter, that s.49 does not provide an exhaustive list of situations where the price may be recoverable. In *PST Energy 7 Shipping LLC v OW Bunker Malta Ltd*[4] the contract was not one of sale of goods, however, the Supreme Court stated that if it had been a sale of goods, they would have overruled the decision in *FG Wilson*. The Supreme Court noted that the "precise limits of such circumstances . . . must be left for determination on some future occasion"[5] though it may be argued that a seller will be able to claim for the price where the contract, expressly or impliedly so provides.

12–004 In addition to an action for the price, the seller may have a claim under s.37 which provides:

> **"(1) When the seller is ready and willing to deliver the goods, and requests the buyer to take delivery, and the buyer does not within a reasonable time after such request take delivery of the goods, he is liable to the seller for any loss occasioned by his**

1 [1908] 1 K.B. 968.
2 [2021] EWHC 3030 (QB).
3 [2013] EWCA Civ 1232.
4 [2016] UKSC 23.
5 [2016] UKSC 23 at [57].

> neglect or refusal to take delivery, and also for a reasonable charge for the care and custody of the goods.
> (2) Nothing in this section affects the rights of the seller where the neglect or refusal of the buyer to take delivery amounts to a repudiation of the contract."

This might apply, if, for example, the goods had perished or contaminated others.

Where a buyer has paid with a cheque which has been dishonoured, he is still liable to pay and can be sued for the price. Where, however, he has paid with a credit or charge card and then the card issuing company fails to pay, the seller is not able to sue the buyer for the price.[6]

Damages for Non-acceptance

If the seller cannot maintain an action under s.49, he may still have a claim for damages which he can bring under s.50 "where the buyer wrongfully neglects or refuses to accept and pay for the goods". The measure of damages is considered in Ch.14. Usually damages will be much less than the price and the seller also has the inconvenience of having to find another buyer. 12-005

Remedies Against the Goods

There are three possible remedies against the goods—lien, stoppage in transit and resale. They are available to an "unpaid seller". By s.38 a seller is an "unpaid seller", 12-006

> "(a) when the whole of the price has not been paid or tendered;
> (b) when a bill of exchange or other negotiable instrument has been received as conditional payment, and the condition on which it was received has not been fulfilled by reason of the dishonour of the instrument or otherwise."

A cheque is a bill of exchange. Thus a seller who in the normal way has accepted a cheque which is later dishonoured, is an unpaid seller.

6 See generally paras 12-006, above and also 17-025, below.

Lien

12-007 The unpaid seller has a right in the circumstances provided by s.41(1) to retain possession of the goods until he is paid or payment is tendered to him. As a matter of strict terminology, this right is called a "lien" if property has passed to the buyer and a "right of retention" if property is still with the seller.[7] This right complements the rule in s.28 that, in the absence of contrary agreement, payment and delivery are concurrent conditions. By s.41(1) the right exists in each of the following circumstances:

> **"(a) where the goods have been sold without any stipulation as to credit;**
>
> **(b) where the goods have been sold on credit, but the term of credit has expired;**
>
> **(c) where the buyer becomes insolvent."**

Obviously, agreement by the seller to allow credit is agreement contrary to the rule in s.28. In such circumstances the seller is not entitled to refuse delivery unless the agreed period of credit has already expired. Usually by that time, delivery will already have been made, thus depriving the seller of his lien. Section 41(1)(c) represents an exception to the rule that the seller has no lien during an agreed period of credit. In spite of having agreed to grant credit, the seller does have a lien if, before the seller relinquishes possession, the buyer becomes insolvent. A person is insolvent (whether or not he is bankrupt) "if he has either ceased to pay his debts in the ordinary course of business or he cannot pay his debts as they become due".[8]

The seller's lien relates only to the price. He is not entitled to withhold the goods until other debts owed to him by the buyer are paid. Thus there is no lien for damages due by the buyer under s.37.[9]

12-008 Where delivery is made in instalments, the extent of the unpaid seller's lien depends upon whether the contract is severable. If it is not severable, the seller can retain any part of the goods to compel payment of any part or all of the price. Section 42 provides:

> **"Where an unpaid seller has made part delivery of the goods, he may exercise his lien or right of retention on the remainder, unless such part delivery has been made under such circumstances as to show an agreement to waive the lien or right of retention."**

A severable contract is generally one where goods are to be delivered in instalments which are to be separately paid for.[10] In this case the seller has no lien over one instalment of goods

7 s.39(2).

8 s.61(4).

9 See para.12-004, above.

10 See para.11-009, above.

to compel payment for a different (earlier) instalment. However, if the buyer's failure to pay amounts to a repudiatory breach of contract,[11] the seller can refuse to make further deliveries, not by virtue of any lien, but because the buyer's repudiatory breach excuses the seller from further performance of his contractual obligations. If the reason for the buyer's failure to pay is his insolvency, then the breach is a repudiatory one, although in this case the seller must deliver those instalments which have actually been paid for.

The seller's lien is lost if any of the following situations arises:

(i) The seller ceases to be unpaid, i.e. if the whole of the price is paid or tendered to him.

(ii) One of the terminating events in s.43 occurs.

(iii) An innocent third party acquires title free from the lien, under one of the exceptions to the *nemo dat* principle.

The last two of these require explanation. Section 43 states: 12–009

> **"(1) The unpaid seller of goods loses his lien or right of retention in respect of them**
> **(a) when he delivers the goods to a carrier or other bailee or custodier for the purpose of transmission to the buyer with-out reserving the right of disposal of the goods;**
> **(b) when the buyer or his agent lawfully obtains possession of the goods;**
> **(c) by waiver of the lien or right of retention."**

Although delivery to a carrier without the reservation of a right of disposal terminates the unpaid seller's lien, he may still be able to recover the goods by exercising his right of stoppage in transit. Lawful acquisition of possession by the buyer will deprive the seller of his rights of lien and stoppage and those rights will not revive even if the buyer later returns the goods to the possession of the seller. Allowing the buyer to have access to the goods, e.g. to paint or repair, will not amount to giving him possession provided the seller retains control over the goods. If the buyer without authority from the seller seizes possession of the goods, that is unlawful and does not destroy the seller's lien.

Waiver of his lien by the seller may take the form of: first an express agreement to forego the lien, secondly an act that clearly indicates an intention to forego it, or thirdly a wrongful act inconsistent with delivery to the buyer. Examples of the last of these are consumption of the goods by the seller or a resale of them by the seller when he has no right to resell. In these cases the buyer can lawfully bring an action for damages against the seller but the damages

11 See para.11-009, above.

will be awarded only after deducting the price still owed by the buyer. An example of the second form of waiver is assent by the seller to a sub-sale by the buyer. To amount to a waiver it must be such an assent as to show that the seller intends to renounce his rights against the goods. In *Mordaunt v British Oil & Cake Mills Ltd*[12] the seller was told of the sub-sale by the buyer only after it had been made. It was held that the seller's acknowledgment of the existence of the sub-sale was not assent such as to defeat his lien. In spite of the sub-sale the seller was entitled to retain possession of the goods until they were paid for.

12–010 If the buyer disposes of the goods within one of the exceptions to the *nemo dat* principle,[13] the innocent sub-purchaser obtains title free from the seller's lien. In this case the seller must surrender the goods to the sub-purchaser and will be reduced to pursuing his personal remedies against the buyer. Most of the exceptions to the *nemo dat* principle apply only if the goods are disposed of by someone in possession of them and if the buyer is lawfully in possession of the goods, the seller's lien is lost anyway.[14] The exceptions may, however, be relevant where the buyer has unlawfully obtained possession. Further, certain exceptions can apply where the buyer has possession only of documents of title. The seller can lose his lien by virtue of one of these. The provisions of s.25 of the Sale of Goods Act and s.9 of the Factors Act have already been considered.[15] However, there is a further provision by virtue of which an innocent sub-purchaser may acquire title free from the seller's lien, s.47. It reads:

> **"(1) Subject to this Act, the unpaid seller's right of lien or retention or stoppage in transit is not affected by any sale, or other disposition of the goods which the buyer may have made, unless the seller has assented to it.**
>
> **(2) Where a document of title to goods has been lawfully transferred to any person as buyer or owner of the goods, and that person transfers the document to a person who takes it in good faith and for valuable consideration, then—**
>
> **(a) if the last-mentioned transfer was by way of sale the unpaid seller's right of lien or retention or stoppage in transit is defeated; and**
>
> **(b) if the last-mentioned transfer was made by way of pledge or other disposition for value, the unpaid seller's right of lien or retention or stoppage in transit can only be exercised subject to the rights of the transferee."**

12 [1910] 2 K.B. 502.

13 See Ch.5.

14 s.43(1)(b).

15 See para.5-024, above.

Subsection (2) was applied in *Ant. Jurgens Margarinefabrieken v Louis Dreyfus & Co.*[16] Some mowra seed was sold. The buyers paid by cheque and the sellers gave the buyers a delivery order which the buyers endorsed and transferred to a sub-purchaser. The cheque was dishonoured and the sellers claimed to have a lien over the mowra seed which was still in their possession. It was held that since all the requirements of subs.(2) were fulfilled, the seller's lien was defeated. Subsection (2) is clearly an exception to the *nemo dat* principle, since the buyers were able to confer upon the sub-purchaser a title better than that which the buyers had themselves, namely, a title free from the sellers' lien and which therefore gave to the sub-purchaser the right to immediate possession.

In the last mentioned case the delivery order transferred by the buyers to the sub-purchaser was the same document as that which has been transferred to the buyers by the sellers. If, instead of transferring the same document, the buyers had transferred a different one, then s.47(2) would not have applied. This was held by Salmon J in *Mount v Jay & Jay Ltd*[17] where the buyers wrote their own delivery order which they sent off to the sub-purchaser. His Lordship thought, however, that s.25 applied to defeat the sellers' lien.[18] Nevertheless, he did not base his decision upon s.25 but held that the sellers' lien was defeated because the sellers, who knew in advance of the sub-sale, had assented to it in a way that indicated their intention to forego the lien.

Stoppage in Transit

Section 44 provides that the seller can resume possession of the goods and retain them until payment or tender of the price to him, if two conditions are both fulfilled: 12-011

(i) The buyer has become insolvent.

(ii) The goods are "in course of transit".

The meaning of "insolvent" has already been considered when dealing with the seller's lien.

Section 45 is a long section dealing with the "course of transit". Broadly, goods are in course of transit from the time that they are delivered to an independent middleman for the purpose of transmission to the buyer, until the time that the buyer actually obtains or is entitled to obtain possession. The carrier will of course be paid for his service by the buyer or seller. Apart from that, however, he must be independent. If, for example, the buyer sends his own lorry driven by one of his own employees to collect the goods, then the goods, once loaded on to the lorry, are not in the course of transit but are in the buyer's possession.

16 [1914] 3 K.B. 40.
17 [1960] 1 Q.B. 159.
18 See para.5-027, above.

12-012 The course of transit ends:

(i) when the buyer obtains delivery,

(ii) when the carrier acknowledges that he holds for and on behalf of the buyer, e.g. by accepting and acting upon the buyer's instructions not to convey the goods as far as their original destination or to convey them to a further destination, or

(iii) when the carrier wrongfully refuses to deliver the goods to the buyer.

Part delivery to the buyer does not prevent the remainder being stopped in transit unless the part delivery is made under such circumstances as to show an agreement to give up possession of the whole of the goods.

Section 46 deals with how stoppage in transit may be effected by the seller either taking actual possession of the goods or giving notice of his claim to the carrier. The carrier is under a duty to comply with the seller's instructions as to redelivery, although the seller must bear the expenses involved. The seller can give his instructions to the person in actual possession of the goods, but it may be difficult for him to discover who that is, if, for example, the goods are on the railways. If, as is more likely, the seller gives his instruction to that person's employer or principal, he must allow reasonable time for the instructions to be communicated to the person in actual possession before delivery is made to the buyer.

With one exception, the right of stoppage in transit is lost in the same circumstances as is the seller's lien. It can therefore be lost by waiver or the operation of s.47(2), etc. The exception is of course that delivery to a carrier without the reservation of a right of disposal will terminate the seller's lien whereas it marks the commencement of the "course of transit".

Resale

12-013 Section 48 governs the right of the unpaid seller to resell the goods. Section 48(1) reads:

> **"(1) Subject to this section, a contract of sale is not rescinded by the mere exercise by an unpaid seller of his right of lien or retention or stoppage in transit."**

Since the contract is not rescinded by the seller exercising his rights of lien or stoppage, the seller's obligations under the contract remain, including his obligation to deliver the goods against payment of the price. Thus he has no right to resell the goods other than that allowed him by later subsections of s.48. In fact ss.48(3) and (4) allow him quite generous rights of resale:

> **"(3) Where the goods are of a perishable nature, or where the unpaid seller gives notice to the buyer of his intention to resell, and the buyer does not within a reasonable time pay or tender the price, the unpaid seller may resell the goods and recover from the original buyer damages for any loss occasioned by his breach of contract.**
>
> **(4) Where the seller expressly reserves the right of resale in case the buyer should make default, and on the buyer making default, resells the goods, the original contract of sale is rescinded, but without prejudice to any claim the seller may have for damages."**

When the seller exercises his right of resale—whether under subs.(3) or under subs.(4)—the contract with the first buyer is thereby rescinded. The effect of rescission is that property (title), if it had passed to the buyer, reverts to the seller. Thus, on exercising his right of resale, the seller resells as owner. Since he resells as owner it follows that he can keep any profit he makes by reselling at a higher price than the original buyer had agreed to pay. That is in addition to keeping any deposit he obtained from the original buyer.[19] In the more likely event that the seller makes a loss on the resale, he can claim that loss from the original buyer as damages together with any other damage caused to him by the buyer's failure to pay.

Ward v Bignall[20] concerned a contract for the sale of two cars for £850. After paying a deposit of £25 the buyer refused to pay the rest. The seller informed the buyer in writing that, if he did not pay the balance by a given date, the seller would try to resell the cars. The buyer still did not pay. The seller sold one car for £350 but failed to find a purchaser for the other. He brought a claim against the original buyer for the balance of the purchase price (£475) and advertising expenses (£22.10s). It was held that the seller could not recover any of the cost since the buyer was no longer the owner of either of the cars, the ownership having reverted to the seller on the resale. The seller was entitled to damages. The remaining car being worth £450, the seller's loss on the resale was £850 minus (£450 plus £350) equals £50. From that figure was deducted the amount (£25) of the deposit paid by the original buyer. The seller was also entitled to his reasonable advertising expenses for the resale, i.e. £22.10s. Therefore, the damages awarded to him totalled £47.10s. 12-014

It is, of course possible for the unpaid seller to resell the goods in circumstances where he has no right to do so. If he does, he will confer good title on the new purchaser provided the resale falls within one of the exceptions to the *nemo dat* principle. One particular exception which may well apply is that contained in s.8 of the Factors Act and s.24 of the Sale of Goods Act. This exception applies where the seller continues or is in possession of the goods

19 See para.2-011, above.

20 [1967] 1 Q.B. 534.

or documents of title and subsequently delivers them to a new innocent purchaser.[21] A further exception is to be found in s.48(2) of the Sale of Goods Act:

> **"(2) Where an unpaid seller who has exercised his right of lien or retention or stoppage in transit resells the goods, the buyer acquires a good title to them as against the original buyer."**

This provision can apply in much the same circumstances as s.24, namely where someone who has sold goods to one person then later resells them to another. However, for the subsequent purchaser to acquire good title under this provision there are different requirements to be fulfilled:

(i) The seller must have been "unpaid" by the first buyer.

(ii) He must also have exercised his right of lien or retention or stoppage in transit.

(iii) He must "sell" the goods. Thus someone taking only a pledge cannot acquire good title by virtue of this provision.

12–015 Unlike s.24, s.48(2) has no requirement that there be a delivery to the second purchaser and no requirement that the latter should be bona fide.

Finally, it should be noted that if the seller does resell the goods and confer good title upon the new purchaser, the original buyer will be able to bring an action against the seller for non-delivery, provided the seller did not have the right to resell.

General Reading

J.N. Adams, "Damages in sale of goods: a critique of the provisions of the Sale of Goods Act and Article 2 of the Uniform Commercial Code" [2002] J.B.L. 553.

L. Gullifer, "'Sales' on retention of title terms: is the English law analysis broken?" (2017) 133 L.Q.R. 244.

21 It was considered in para.5-021, above.

L. Gullifer, "The interpretation of retention of title clauses: some difficulties" [2014] L.M.C.L.Q. 564.

V. Mak, "The Seller's Right to Cure Defective Performance—a Reappraisal" [2007] L.M.C.L.Q. 409.

13

Buyer's Remedies

Introduction

This chapter considers the remedies available to a buyer when faced with a seller in breach of contract. Traditionally this was a relatively straightforward issue with the available remedies being: 13-001

- specific performance of the contract;
- rejection of the goods; and
- damages.

This framework was extended in 2003 by the Sale and Supply of Goods to Consumers Regulations 2002[1] which introduced a new Pt 5A and laid down a two-tier system of additional remedies for consumers. Under the 2002 Regulations a consumer buyer was given the ability to elect for either repair of the goods or a replacement. Where such a remedy was not forthcoming the consumer could then elect to receive a reduction in the purchase price of the goods or rescind the contract. The current law is to be found in the Consumer Rights Act which revoked the 2002 Regulations and introduced a more nuanced set of remedies where a trader supplies goods to a consumer. Whilst the rights to repair and replacement, etc. remain in effect, the operation of the consumer remedies framework under the Consumer Rights Act is, as we will see, considerably more complex than was the case under the 2002 Regulations.

1 SI 2002/3045. For an account of Pt 5A remedies the reader may be directed to the 8th edn of this text. Part 5A remedies remain relevant only for consumer contracts of sale of goods entered into between 31 March 2003 and 30 September 2015.

There is one further point to be made. Prior to the enactment of the Consumer Rights Act the additional remedies available to a consumer buyer were just that—additional, i.e. the traditional remedies available under the Act co-existed with the special remedies available to consumers. This is no longer the case. The Consumer Rights Act (unlike the 2002 Regulations) dis-applies the remedies available under the Sale of Goods Act where a trader supplies goods to a consumer. The remedies available under the Consumer Rights Act will be dealt with later and this chapter will begin by considering the remedies available to a buyer under the Sale of Goods Act.

Remedies Under the Sale of Goods Act

13-002 The Sale of Goods Act offers a number of remedies, however, it should be emphasised that the Act's scheme of remedies now only apply where the Consumer Rights Act does not.[2] Thus as noted above, where a trader sells goods to a consumer, the consumer's remedies are prescribed by the Consumer Rights Act and not by the Sale of Goods Act. Nonetheless, the 1979 Act remains important since it still details remedies available in business sales and private sales.

Specific Performance

13-003 Section 52 allows the court to make an order of specific performance against the seller in the case of a contract to deliver specific or ascertained goods. Thus an order under s.52 cannot be made in the case of a contract for the sale of unascertained goods which have not been appropriated to the contract—*Re Wait*.[3]

An order for specific performance is one which requires the seller actually to deliver the goods and does not give him the option of paying damages instead. Even in the case of specific or ascertained goods the court will not make such an order unless damages for non-delivery would not be an adequate remedy. This is likely to be the case only where similar goods are unobtainable elsewhere, e.g. if the goods are unique or virtually so, as in *Behnke v Bede*

2 See para.1-009 above for an explanation of when the Consumer Rights Act applies.

3 [1927] 1 Ch. 606, see para.3-030, above. Note, however, more recently the courts have entertained the possibility of specific performance of contracts for unascertained goods, though only in exceptional cases where the market is not functioning. In *VTB Commodities Trading DAC v JSC Antipinsky Refinery* [2020] EWHC 72 (Comm) it was said that there was a "strong presumption" that specific performance was limited to specific or ascertained goods.

Shipping Co.[4] A German shipowner had agreed to buy for immediate use a specific ship, the "City", which had engines and boilers which were practically new and satisfied German regulations. There was only one other such ship afloat. An order for specific performance was granted since damages would not have been an adequate remedy. Since the situations where damages would be an inadequate remedy are rare, it should not be surprising that the courts have been reluctant to make an order of specific performance against a seller.[5]

Rejection of the Goods

A breach of condition by the seller gives the buyer, as well as a claim to damages, the right to reject the goods (and therefore not to have to pay for them). The buyer can exercise this right by refusing to take delivery or informing the seller that he rejects the goods. He need not return them to the seller, who if he wants them must come and collect them.[6] If the seller fails to collect goods which the buyer has rightly rejected and as a result the buyer reasonably incurs storage expenses, the buyer is entitled to claim those expenses from the seller as damages for breach of contract: *Kolfor Plant Ltd v Tilbury Plant Ltd*.[7] The buyer has no lien over rejected goods and therefore must hand them over on request even though he has not received the return of his purchase money: *Lyons v May & Baker*.[8] He can bring an action to recover his price on the ground of a total failure of consideration. 13-004

The right of rejection is not given for an ordinary breach of warranty. Unless the seller commits a breach of condition or commits a breach of warranty which is so serious as to deprive the buyer of substantially the whole benefit of the contract, the buyer has no right to reject the goods or recover the price.[9] If he unjustifiably rejects them, the seller may sue him for damages for non-acceptance or, possibly, will have an action for the price.

Trivial breaches of implied condition

The normal rule is that any breach of condition by the seller, however small or trivial, entitles the buyer to reject the goods. Section 15A creates an exception where there is a minor breach of one of the implied conditions as to description, quality and sample contained in ss.13, 14 and 15.[10] Section 15A provides that if the breach "is so slight that it would be unreasonable for him to reject them . . . the breach is not to be treated as a breach of condition but may be treated 13-005

4 [1927] 1 K.B. 640.
5 See further, D. Harris, "Specific Performance—A Regular Remedy for Consumers?" (2003) 119 L.Q.R. 541.
6 s.36.
7 (1977) 121 S.J. 390.
8 [1923] 1 K.B. 695.
9 See para.7-005, above.
10 See Ch.7, below.

as a breach of warranty". This is the position "unless a contrary intention appears in, or is to be implied from, the contract". It would seem extremely likely that if this provision had been in force at the time, the decision in *Re Moore and Landauer*[11] would have been different.[12] In that case the only breach by the seller was that, although he had delivered the correct quantity of tins of pears, he had delivered them packed in cases of 24 tins instead of in cases of 30 tins. In a situation where this breach would cause the buyer no loss or inconvenience, this breach would seem to be so slight that it would be unreasonable for the buyer to reject the goods. Section 15A, which denies the buyer the right to reject for a slight breach of condition, applies only to breaches of the conditions in ss.13–15.[13]

Acceptance

13-006 Faced with a breach of condition, the buyer's choice is either to reject or to accept the goods. Acceptance of any part of the goods will preclude the buyer from later rejecting the goods accepted and may cause him to lose the right to reject other goods under the contract.

Simply taking delivery does not amount to acceptance. Acceptance may take one of three forms:[14]

(i) If the buyer informs the seller that he has accepted the goods.

(ii) If the buyer takes delivery and he does some act inconsistent with the seller being the owner of them (e.g. by selling them).

(iii) If the buyer retains the goods for more than a reasonable length of time without informing the seller that he rejects them.

Neither of the first two of these, however, will amount to acceptance unless either the buyer examined the goods before the contract was made or, alternatively, has had a reasonable opportunity after delivery of the goods to examine the goods for the purpose of ascertaining whether they are in conformity with the contract.[15] Thus, reselling the goods does not constitute acceptance unless the buyer has had a reasonable opportunity of examining them. For example, where a manufacturer sells goods in sealed containers to a distributor who resells them, that distributor does not thereby lose his right of rejection. If the distributor's buyer opens them up and finds them not to comply with a condition in the contract between

11 [1921] 2 K.B. 519.

12 See para.7-013, above.

13 Prior to the enactment of the Consumer Rights Act, this special provision for trivial breaches did not apply to a buyer who dealt as a consumer. Thus there is no equivalent provision within the 2015 Act.

14 s.35.

15 s.35(2).

himself and the distributor, he may reject them. If they also do not comply with a condition in the contract between the manufacturer and distributor, the latter may also reject them.[16]

In *Lee v York Coach and Marine*,[17] the buyer had been supplied in March with a second-hand car which was not of merchantable quality because its brakes were defective. Because the buyer did not claim to reject the car until September, it was held that she had accepted it and that therefore she was entitled only to damages. This is an example of the third form of acceptance, which occurs if the buyer retains the goods for more than a reasonable length of time without intimating to the seller that he is rejecting them. It used to be thought that this meant a reasonable length of time to try the goods out (i.e. a relatively short period) and not a reasonable length of time in which to discover any defects there might be in the goods: *Bernstein v Pamsons Motors (Golders Green) Ltd*.[18] In that case the buyer of a new Nissan car had had it for less than three weeks and had made two or three short journeys in it for the purpose of trying it out, before the engine seized up because of a latent manufacturing fault. Rougier J held that, before the seizure the buyer had already had the car a reasonable length of time for trying it out generally. Therefore the buyer had accepted the car and was entitled only to damages. Since then, however, s.35 has been amended by the Sale and Supply of Goods Act 1994. Thus we now know that in measuring whether a reasonable length of time has elapsed, the court has to take into account whether the buyer has had a reasonable opportunity of examining the goods for the purpose of ascertaining whether they are in conformity with the contract. 13-007

In *Fiat Auto Financial Services v Connelly*[19] the buyer purchased (with a loan provided by a finance company) a new car which quickly manifested a wide range of problems, including a fault with the engine management system which led to poor engine performance generally and also caused the car to break down 10 days after delivery. This fault was investigated by the dealer but never diagnosed and the fault persisted throughout the time the buyer had the car. After nine months (and over 40,000 miles) use the buyer sought to reject the car since the engine management system had not been satisfactorily repaired. The finance company sought to enforce the loan agreement and maintained that the buyer had accepted the car under s.35, thereby losing the right to reject. This claim was made on two alternative bases. First, it was argued that the buyer's use of the car amounted to an act inconsistent with the ownership of the seller. Secondly, that the period of nine months from delivery to rejection was more than a reasonable length of time without intimating rejection.

16 For a good illustration of this, see *Local Boy'z Ltd v Malu NV* [2021] EWHC 2439 (Comm) where a UK re-seller, Local Boy'z, purchased face masks at the start of the Covid-19 pandemic from Malu, an importer based in Belgium. The goods were delivered directly to a sub-buyer who sought to sell them on in turn. At this point, around five months after the initial supply contract, the masks were deemed substandard by prospective purchasers. Local Boy'z were entitled to reject and had not lost that right through either re-sale nor the passage of reasonable time.

17 [1977] R.T.R. 35.

18 [1987] 2 All E.R. 220.

19 [2007] S.L.T. (Sh. Ct.) 111.

The court held that neither argument could succeed since throughout the nine-month period the buyer was in regular contact with the seller regarding the faults with the car and his continued use of the car did not constitute an act inconsistent with the reversionary interest of the seller. Furthermore, the period where the buyer is waiting for information to make an informed decision as to whether to accept or reject does not count towards an unreasonable length of time. This decision does, it seems, leave the seller vulnerable to a buyer rejecting the goods at any point in the future where the goods are subject to a continuous period of failed repairs such as that which occurred in *Connelly*.[20]

13–008 The 1994 amendments to s.35 introduced two further new provisions which clarify what is not acceptance. First, the buyer will not be deemed to have accepted the goods merely because he asks for, or agrees to, their repair by or under an arrangement with the seller. Secondly, he will not be deemed to have accepted the goods merely because they are delivered to another under a sub-sale or other disposition. Suppose, however, that the sub-purchaser retains the goods for more than a reasonable length of time so that, vis-à-vis the buyer, the sub-purchaser has accepted them. In that case the buyer will then be deemed to have accepted the goods vis-à-vis his seller. These provisions were considered in *Truk (UK) Ltd v Tokmakidis GmbH*.[21] It involved a contract between two businesses for the sale and fitting of some lifting equipment to be paid for six months after delivery. The equipment was to be fitted to, and form part of, a towing vehicle which the buyer was then going to re-sell. Approximately six months after delivery the buyer was informed by a potential purchaser of the towing vehicle that the equipment was defective. The buyer immediately informed the seller and refused to pay the price pending investigation (by an appropriate company). About three months later, promptly upon receipt of the result of the investigation which confirmed the allegation, the buyer unequivocally rejected the goods. The judge held as follows. Where goods are sold for resale, a reasonable time in which to give notice of rejection should normally be the time actually taken to resell the goods, together with an additional period in which they can be inspected and tried out (by the sub-purchaser). Where the price is payable at a date after delivery, that reasonable period of time should normally last at least until the date for payment. The reasonable time had not expired when about six months after delivery, the buyer first questioned compliance. The buyer was entitled to a further period in which to investigate that issue. Accordingly the buyer had not accepted the goods when he (validly) rejected them nine months after delivery.

The impact of an agreement to have the contract goods inspected and, if possible repaired, upon acceptance and the right to reject goods under s.35 was considered by the House of Lords in *J & H Ritchie Ltd v Lloyd Ltd*.[22] In that case the buyer carried on a farming business and bought some equipment from the seller, a supplier of agricultural machinery. The

20 Contrast the position where a latent defect in a car did not reveal itself until a year following delivery and the car was not rejected until a further 15 months had passed during which the seller attempted repairs. Rejection was unavailable: *Douglas v Glenvarigill Co Ltd* [2010] CSOH 14.

21 [2000] 1 Lloyd's Rep. 543.

22 [2007] 1 W.L.R. 670.

equipment (which was sold as a single item) consisted of a seed drill and a power harrow and was delivered in early March 1999. The buyer first used the harrow in late April 1999 and discovered that it appeared to have a fault causing it to vibrate. The buyer contacted the seller who sent a member of staff who, with the agreement of the buyer, removed the harrow for inspection and, if possible, for repair. A few weeks later the seller informed the buyer that the harrow had been repaired and was ready for collection. The buyer asked the seller to explain what the problem had been but this request was refused and the seller would only say that the harrow had been repaired to "factory gate specification". The buyer was not satisfied and was concerned, inter alia, that the fault (missing bearings) could have caused other damage to the harrow and that it would not be clear until the next sowing season (i.e. spring the following year) whether the harrow had been satisfactorily repaired. Therefore the buyer sought to reject the goods (both harrow and seed drill) and reclaim the purchase price.

The House of Lords held that the agreement to have the harrow inspected and, if possible, repaired, did not amount to an acceptance of the goods which would take away the buyer's right of rejection under the sale of goods contract. The agreement of inspection and repair was subject to an implied term that, if asked, the seller would tell the buyer the nature of the defect and what repairs had been made in order to rectify that defect. This was necessary in order that the buyer can, where the nature of the defect is not readily apparent, make an informed choice as to whether or not to accept the re-tendered goods. The seller's refusal to provide that information was a breach of the inspection and repair agreement. Thus the buyer was entitled to treat that agreement as repudiated and exercise his right under the sale of goods contract to reject the goods. Accordingly the buyer was entitled to recover the purchase price.[23]

Partial rejection

Until s.35 was amended by the 1994 Act, there was a rule that acceptance by the buyer of all or any part of the goods precluded the buyer from being able to reject any of the goods. There were exceptions to that rule: (a) in the case of a severable contract, where acceptance of goods under one severable part of the contract did not preclude the possibility of rejecting the goods under another part; and (b) where goods more than the contract quantity were delivered, in which case the buyer had the option of accepting the contract quantity and rejecting the rest. These two exceptions remain. However, there is also now a general exception to that rule. Section 35A was inserted into the Sale of Goods Act and it states: 13-009

"(1) If the buyer—

(a) has the right to reject the goods by reason of a breach on the part of the seller that affects some or all of them, but

23 For a critique of this decision, see K.C.F. Loi, "Sale of Goods in Scotland—Repairing Defects in the Law: J&H Ritchie Ltd v Lloyd Ltd" [2007] J.B.L. 807.

> **(b) accepts some of the goods, including, where there are any goods unaffected by the breach, all such goods, he does not by accepting them lose his right to reject the rest.**
>
> **(2) In the case of a buyer having the right to reject an instalment of goods, subsection (1) above applies as if references to the goods were references to the goods comprised in the instalment.**
>
> **(3) For the purposes of subsection (1) above, goods are affected by a breach if by reason of the breach they are not in conformity with the contract.**
>
> **(4) This section applies unless a contrary intention appears in, or is to be implied from, the contract."**

Thus, in order to exercise a right of partial rejection under this provision, the buyer must first have a right to reject the goods, e.g. because of a breach of condition, and must secondly accept all the goods which comply with the contract. Providing he accepts all the goods which comply with the contract, he is not precluded from rejecting some, or all, of those which do not. It should be observed that although s.35A(4) states that this section applies only if a contrary intention does not appear, nevertheless, a clause in a contract which purported to deprive the buyer of his right of partial rejection would be an exclusion clause and therefore could well be rendered ineffective by the Unfair Contract Terms Act 1977.

There is one qualification to the right of partial rejection just mentioned. This lies in the concept of a "commercial unit". A commercial unit is a unit of goods, "division of which would materially impair the value of the goods or the character of the unit". An example might be a two-volume dictionary, the first volume dealing with, say, A to K and the second with L to Z. Suppose that one of the volumes is, and the other is not, of satisfactory quality. By virtue of s.35(7), a buyer accepting any goods in the commercial unit is deemed to have accepted all the goods in that unit. Thus the buyer could not accept one of the volumes and reject the other.

Waiver

13-010 The buyer may lose his right to reject by waiver of that right.[24] This may be particularly relevant where the seller is, to the buyer's knowledge, in breach of condition before the goods are delivered. If the buyer indicates that he will nevertheless accept delivery in spite of the breach of condition, that may well amount to waiver.[25]

24 s.11(2).

25 See *Rickards v Oppenheim* [1950] 1 K.B. 616 discussed at para.7-006, above.

Treatment of the Contract as Repudiated

The buyer's right to treat the contract as repudiated arises in the same circumstances as his right to reject the goods, i.e. if the seller commits a breach of condition or a breach of warranty which deprives the buyer of substantially the whole benefit of the contract.[26] Often the buyer will exercise both remedies at once, i.e. will reject the goods and will also indicate that he is not going on with the contract, e.g. by demanding his money back. He can, however, reject the goods without treating the contract as repudiated. If he does, then the seller is at liberty, if he can do so, to re-tender the goods which comply with the contract. If the seller does so, he will be entitled to the price. It can of course also occur that the buyer treats the contract as repudiated by the seller and yet does not reject any goods. This could occur if the breach by the seller is a failure to deliver the goods by the contractual delivery date, or if the seller commits an anticipatory repudiation, e.g. informs the buyer that he will not be delivering or will not be delivering by the contractual delivery date. In the circumstances where the buyer accepts the seller's breach as a repudiation of the contract, the buyer will be entitled to damages assessed as for non-delivery of the goods.[27] To exercise his right to treat the contract as repudiated by the seller's repudiatory breach, the buyer must inform the seller that he regards the contract as being at an end. 13-011

Suppose the seller commits a wrongful anticipatory repudiation which the buyer does not accept as a repudiation. This latter point would be clear if, for example, the buyer responded to the anticipatory breach by indicating that due delivery was still expected. If then the seller duly makes delivery in accordance with the contract, the buyer must accept it. This is because an anticipatory repudiation terminates a contract only if it is accepted by the innocent party: *Fercometal S.a.r.l. v Mediterranean Shipping Co.*[28] If after having failed to accept the seller's breach as a repudiation, the buyer himself subsequently repudiates the contract, e.g. by rejecting goods which conform to the contract, he will himself be liable to the seller for damages assessed as for non-acceptance (see Ch.14). These principles work exactly the same vice versa. Thus where the buyer commits an anticipatory repudiation which the seller fails to accept as terminating the contract, the seller will be liable if he himself subsequently fails to perform the contract.

Where one of the parties, say the buyer, treats the contract as repudiated giving a bad reason (e.g. simply that he has changed his mind about buying) or even giving no reason at all, that repudiation will not be wrongful if at the time of the repudiation he in fact had a valid reason for it. A party who gives a bad reason for his refusal to perform the contract, does not thereby deprive himself of a justification which in fact existed, whether or not he was aware of it, *Glencore Grain Rotterdam BV v Lebanese Organisation for International Commerce.*[29] The only exceptions to this are: (i) where that party is estopped from relying on the valid reason by

26 See para.7-005 above.

27 See Ch.14.

28 [1988] 3 W.L.R. 200.

29 [1997] 4 All E.R. 514.

virtue of an earlier representation of his, and (ii) where the valid reason later relied upon is one which if given at the time, could have been put right by the other party. In this regard, however, note that in the case of a c.i.f. contract, the fact that goods were not shipped in conformity with the contract does not justify the buyer in rejecting documents which conform to the contract.

Action for Damages

13-012 The buyer can claim damages for non-delivery or for breach of any other condition or warranty. This right is an addition to any right to reject the goods or to recover the purchase price. The measure of damages will be considered in Ch.14.

Recovery of Purchase Price

13-013 Where the consideration has totally failed, the buyer can recover any payments he has already paid. This rule clearly applies in the case of a non-delivery. It also applies where the buyer exercises his right to reject the goods and treat the contract as repudiated because of a breach of condition. We have also seen a surprising application of it in the case of *Rowland v Divall*.[30]

Of course, in the situation where the buyer can and does accept part and reject part of the goods,[31] he is entitled to recover any part of the price that he has paid in respect of the rejected part of the goods and remains liable to pay, if he has not done so already, pro rata for the goods he has accepted.

Remedies Under the Consumer Rights Act

13-014 The Consumer Rights Act replaces the scheme of remedies laid down by the Sale of Goods Act in its entirety and instead provides an intricate framework of remedies covering the range of contracts to which the Act applies. Thus, where a trader supplies goods or digital content to a consumer in breach of one of the numerous statutory rights prescribed by the Act, the remedies available to the consumer are those laid down by the Act.[32] We have already considered the

30 [1923] 2 K.B. 500, discussed at para.7-008, above.

31 See para.13-009, above.

32 The 2015 Act does, however, expressly preserve the right of a consumer to pursue other remedies prescribed by the general law, such as, for example, specific performance (provided this would not lead to recovery for the same loss twice). Thus whilst, as we noted earlier in this chapter s.52 of the SGA 1979 does not apply to consumer sales, the court retains a discretionary power to require specific performance.

definitions of "trader" and "consumer".[33] There are therefore two fundamental questions to be considered. First, what remedies are available under the Consumer Rights Act, and secondly what remedies are available for each statutory right. Before we consider these questions two further points can be made. First, as we will see, the approach of the Act to remedies cannot be said to be straightforward and this is problematic given the consumer protection context. Secondly, broadly speaking, the remedies apply to all contracts for the supply of goods which fall under the broad remit of the Act, and not merely to sales contracts.

The Remedies Which May be Available

Sections 19–24[34] set out the remedies which may apply where a consumer's rights under ss.9–17 are not met, e.g. where goods do not match their description or are of unsatisfactory quality, etc. In most, but not all, cases where the trader does not comply with a statutory right, the consumer will be able to rely on statutory remedies of: 13-015

- A "short-term" right to reject.
- The repair or replacement of the goods.
- A price reduction or a "final" right to reject.

These remedies will be considered shortly, however, certain specific matters can be addressed at this stage. First, the Act makes special provision for the situation where the trader is in breach of s.17. Where the trader does not have the right to supply the goods the consumer always has the right to reject.[35] Section 20(3) distinguishes this right to reject from the restrictions governing the "short-term" right to reject (s.22) and the "final" right to reject (s.24). Where the trader's breach relates to one of the other rights laid down by s.17, such as the right that the goods will remain free from any such charge or encumbrance until the time when property is to pass, the consumer is not empowered to claim for any of the statutory remedies but instead must claim damages.[36]

Secondly, the Act also makes special provision where the trader does not comply with s.12 under which the consumer must be provided with information regarding the main

33 See para.1-009 above.

34 In addition, ss.25 and 26 deal with delivery of the wrong quantity and instalment contracts respectively. These have been noted above, see para.11-007.

35 s.19(6).

36 s.19(9).

characteristics of the goods (as required by the Consumer Contracts (Information, Cancellation and Additional Charges) Regulations 2013). In this situation, the consumer has no right to any of the statutory remedies (i.e. there is no right to reject the goods, nor to repair, replacement or a price reduction) but has instead the right to recover from the trader the amount of any costs he incurs as a result of the breach.[37]

Thirdly, the difficulty of establishing non-conformity at the time of delivery has, however, been removed where the consumer seeks to claim the remedies of repair, replacement, price reduction and the "final" right of rejection. Under s.19(14) there is a rebuttable presumption that where goods develop a fault within six months of delivery, those goods were not in conformity with the contract at the time of delivery. This presumption is removed in two situations:[38]

1. where it is established that the goods did so conform at that date; and
2. where its application is incompatible with the nature of the goods or the nature of the lack of conformity.

An obvious example of the second situation would be where the goods have a life span of less than six months such as cut flowers. Note, however, that this reversal of the burden of proof does not apply where the consumer pursues the "short-term" right of rejection (nor to a claim for damages). In these cases, the consumer must demonstrate that the goods (or digital content) did not conform at the time of the contract.

The "Short-term" Right to Reject

13-016 Where a trader is in breach of the statutory rights as to satisfactory quality, fitness for purpose, description, or compliance with a sample or model examined, the consumer has the right to reject the goods.[39] This right entitles the consumer to reject the goods and treat the contract as being at an end provided they do so within a prescribed time frame of (generally) 30 days. The operation of this time frame is outlined below, but it is worth noting at this stage that one consequence of dis-applying the Sale of Goods Act remedies in consumer sales and providing instead for the "short-term" right of rejection is that difficulties around when the right to rejection under the 1979 Act is lost through "acceptance" of the goods is avoided. Of course, this may or may not be a good thing for consumers since, as discussed earlier in the chapter, on occasion the courts have been prepared to extend the period of time where rejection is

37 s.19(5). The costs recoverable cannot exceed the price paid or the value of any other consideration given for the goods.

38 s.19(15).

39 These rights are also available where the goods do not conform to the contract by virtue of containing defective digital content under s.16.

available to well beyond 30 days. Nonetheless, it does offer both consumers and traders considerably more certainty than the doctrine of acceptance did.[40]

The "short-term" right of rejection can be exercised by any clear indication by the consumer to the trader that he is rejecting the goods and treating the contract as being at an end.[41] Where the goods are rejected, the consumer is entitled to a refund and has a duty to make the goods available for collection by the trader.[42] The refund must be given without undue delay, and in any event within 14 days from the day upon which the trader agrees that the consumer is entitled to a refund.[43]

If the consumer paid money under the contract, the trader must refund the same amount of money and cannot unilaterally insist on refunding the price paid through different means (for example, through store vouchers or shop credit).[44] Where the consumer transferred anything else under the contract, they are entitled to receive back the same amount of what was transferred unless this is impossible, in which case, the consumer is entitled to receive the actual thing transferred.[45] Two examples from the Explanatory Notes are useful in explaining this provision:

> **"A toy 'bought' with vouchers collected from cereal packets. In this case it would be possible to return equivalent vouchers (even though they would not necessarily be the actual vouchers that the consumer cut out) and a 'refund' could therefore take that form.**
>
> **A microwave supplied to the consumer by a trader specialising in refurbishment of white-goods, in exchange for the consumer's old fridge-freezer. In this case, if the fridge-freezer was still available in an unchanged state, then this could be returned to the consumer as a 'refund' under subsection (11), but if it was no longer available, or had been refurbished, then a refund would not be possible."**

40 The doctrine of affirmation applied to analogous contracts, e.g. of hire purchase. The same point regarding certainty in consumer supplies applies.

41 s.20(5) and (6).

42 s.20(7). Where there is an agreement for the consumer to return rejected goods, his duty is instead to return them as agreed. In any case, the costs must be met by the trader other than any costs incurred by the consumer in returning the goods to the place he took physical possession of them (s.20(8)). Note the special rules for contracts of hire, hire purchase and conditional sale in s.20(13) and (14).

43 s.20(15).

44 s.20(16). Neither can the trader impose any fee on the consumer in respect of the refund: s.20(17).

45 s.20(11) and (12).

As the closing words of this example indicate, there is no right to a refund where the thing transferred by the consumer cannot be returned in its original state.[46] In this situation, the consumer can claim damages instead.[47]

Section 22 explains the time limit applicable to the "short-term" right to reject and provides:

> **"(3) The time limit for exercising the short-term right to reject (unless subsection (4) applies) is the end of 30 days beginning with the first day after these have all happened—**
>
> **(a) ownership or (in the case of a contract for the hire of goods, a hire purchase agreement or a conditional sales contract) possession of the goods has been transferred to the consumer,**
>
> **(b) the goods have been delivered, and**
>
> **(c) where the contract requires the trader to install the goods or take other action to enable the consumer to use them, the trader has notified the consumer that the action has been taken."**

To this, four points may be added. First, note that the time limit starts when *all* of the relevant actions laid down in s.22(3) have happened. Thus, for example, the fact that ownership has passed is not, in and of itself, relevant. Invariably, in most consumer sales (leaving aside supply and installation contracts) the time limit will start to run the day after the goods have been delivered. Secondly, the time limit would obviously be inappropriate in the case of perishable goods such as, for example, cut flowers. Here the Act provides that in such cases, the period for exercising the short-term right to reject lasts only as long as it would be reasonable to expect the goods to last.[48] Thirdly, it is possible for the parties to agree that the "short-term" right to reject may be exercised later than the limits prescribed by the Act (but not sooner).[49] Fourthly, as we will see in the next section, the consumer can elect to request that the trader either repairs or replaces non-confirming goods. The effect of this in relation to the "short-term" right to reject is that the time period mentioned above (normally 30 days) stops running for what the Act describes as a "waiting period". The waiting period begins on the day the consumer requests or agrees to the repair or replacement of the goods and ends with the day on which the consumer receives goods supplied by the trader in response to the request or agreement.[50] If the repaired or replaced goods still do not conform to the contract, the consumer can

46 s.20(18).
47 See s.20(19).
48 s.22(4).
49 s.22(1) and (2).
50 s.22(8).

exercise the "short-term" right to reject the goods within (i) seven days following the conclusion of the waiting period, or (ii) the remainder of the original 30-day period if that is longer.[51]

Repair or Replacement

Prior to 31 March 2003 (when the Sale and Supply of Goods to Consumers Regulations 2002 took effect) there was no legal right to demand either a replacement or a repair where goods did not conform to the contract. This was so irrespective of the fact that (i) this is generally the remedy consumers will seek, and (ii) this is generally the remedy retailers will offer. The right of a consumer to require either a repair or a replacement[52] therefore more accurately reflects current business practice in most cases and these rights are repeated under the Consumer Rights Act.[53] 13-017

The right to request either a repair or replacement of the goods is expanded by s.23(2) which states:

> **"If the consumer requires the trader to repair or replace the goods, the trader must—**
>
> **(a) do so within a reasonable time and without significant inconvenience to the consumer, and**
>
> **(b) bear any necessary costs incurred in doing so (including in particular the cost of any labour, materials or postage)."**

Thus it is clear that the initial decision as to whether to elect repair or replacement is down to the consumer and not to the trader. Equally, the cost of such repair or replacement must be borne by the trader, including, for example, the costs of returning the defective goods to the manufacturer for the repair to be carried out.

It is likely that there will be judicial consideration of what exactly is meant by "reasonable time" and "significant inconvenience". As a starting point, s.23(5) is of relevance, stating that: 13-018

> **"Any question as to what is a reasonable time or significant inconvenience is to be determined by reference to:**

51 s.22(7). It is possible, therefore, that a consumer will have both the "short-term" right to reject and the "final" right to reject. The latter will be considered shortly, however, it will generally be advisable for the consumer who finds himself in this position to exercise the "short-term" right to reject due to the different treatment of any use the consumer has enjoyed of the goods.

52 "Repair" is defined by s.23(8) as bringing the goods into conformity with the contract.

53 See s.23. Note that under s.23 the repair or replacement is the right to have the repair or replacement carried out *by the trader*, see *Pendragon v Coom* (Unreported, Cardiff County Court, 22 March 2021) at [63]. In situations where business practice is reluctant to replace goods (such as in the sale of motor vehicles) this clearly represents an important right for the consumer.

> **(a) the nature of the goods, and**
> **(b) the purpose for which the goods were acquired."**

Where, for example, the non-conforming goods are required for a specific purpose, such as a wedding dress, the time reasonably necessary to effect either a repair or a replacement may be taken into account in determining what is a "reasonable time". This may therefore trigger the second set of additional remedies, reduction in purchase price or, more likely in the wedding scenario, the rescission of the contract.[54] The definition of "significant inconvenience" raises similar issues. Would, for example, the seller of a motor vehicle need to offer a courtesy car whilst a faulty car is being repaired in pursuance to a request under s.23? There is a cross-over here between the concepts of "reasonable time" and "significant inconvenience" since a minor fault would presumably be repaired in very little time whereas a more substantial one might reasonably take longer to repair, therefore necessitating the provision of a courtesy car in order to avoid "significant inconvenience". Whilst the exact meaning and scope remains to be determined, it is clear that these provisions give considerable power to the consumer.

It is, however, not entirely bad news for retailers. Under s.23(3) the consumer may not require the trader to repair or replace the goods where that remedy is either:

(a) impossible, or

(b) disproportionate in comparison to the other of those remedies.

Under the 2002 Regulations, the consumer was not able to request repair or replacement where the remedy sought was disproportionate in comparison to an appropriate reduction in the purchase price, or rescission (what is now labelled the "final" right to reject under the 2015 Act). This element has not been retained by the Consumer Rights Act.

The issue of proportionality is expanded within s.23(4) which provides:

> **"Either of those remedies is disproportionate compared to the other if it imposes costs on the trader which, compared to those imposed by the other, are unreasonable, taking into account—**
> **(a) the value which the goods would have if they conformed to the contract,**
> **(b) the significance of the lack of conformity, and**
> **(c) whether the other remedy could be effected without significant inconvenience to the consumer."**

13-019 The impact of these subsections is such that a trader will be entitled to refuse a request for a repair of the goods where, for example, a repair would cost considerably more to effect

54 Considered at para.13-020, below.

than a replacement. Where both repair and replacement options would be considerably more expensive than the value of the goods once repaired or replaced, the seller is entitled to refuse both options and the consumer may then pursue either a reduction in price to reflect the non-conformity of the goods, or exercise the "final" right to refund.

Note that a consumer who requests a repair under s.23 cannot go onto request a replacement or exercise the "short-term" right to reject considered above, without having first given the trader a reasonable time to repair them.[55] The converse situation is also true if the consumer elects to request a replacement.[56]

Finally, where the seller fails to comply with a request for either repair or replacement of the goods, the consumer may either ask the court to compel the seller to comply under s.58(2).

Price Reduction or the "Final" Right to Reject

Under s.24 a consumer may require the trader either to reduce the purchase price in order to appropriately reflect the non-conformity in question or alternatively, to exercise the "final" right to reject and treat the contract as at an end. Section 24(5) makes it clear that these remedies are exclusive (the consumer may select only one or the other but not both) and, furthermore, are only available where: 13–020

(a) after one repair or one replacement, the goods do not conform to the contract;[57]

(b) the repair or replacement of the goods is not possible under s.23(3); or

(c) the trader has not complied with the request for repair or replacement within a reasonable time and/or without causing significant inconvenience. The ability of a consumer to pursue either a price reduction or treat the contract as at an end is therefore secondary to the first set of remedies within s.23.

The ability to elect to receive a reduction in purchase price certainly offers flexibility to the consumer, but will be relevant (presumably) only to certain goods. It will be of little use or interest, for example, to a consumer who discovers that a board game has pieces missing or

55 s.23(6).

56 s.23(7). Note that the Act envisages only one attempt at repair or replacement before the consumer may proceed to request either a reduction in the price paid or exercise the "final" right to reject. Of course, the consumer may prefer to allow the trader repeat attempts to rectify the situation.

57 In *Van Gordon v Volkswagen Financial Services (UK) Ltd (t/a Audi Finance)* (Unreported, Nottingham County Court, 30 April 2019) a consumer entered into a hire-purchase agreement in respect of motor vehicle. The vehicle was found to be of unsatisfactory quality under s.9 CRA due to a persistent rattle. The judge found that requests made to the dealer to repair the rattle were requests made to the trader (i.e. the finance company) as required under s.24(5) since the dealer acted as agent for the trader. The "final" right to reject was, therefore, available.

that a set of nine golf clubs contains only six clubs. In such a case, assuming that s.24 applies, the consumer would seek to exercise the "final" right to reject and reclaim the purchase price. The general principles laid down in s.20 which we discussed above in relation to the "short-term" right to reject are equally applicable here. Thus for example, the right can be exercised by any clear indication of the consumer's intention to treat the contract as being at an end.[58] When exercised, the trader is under an obligation to give a refund without undue delay and the consumer is under an obligation to make the goods available for collection by the trader.[59] One significant distinction between the "short-term" right to reject under s.22 and the "final" right to reject under s.24 is the nature of the refund provided. In particular, the issue of whether the buyer would be entitled to receive a full or partial refund is addressed by s.24(8) which provides:

> **"If the consumer exercises the final right to reject, any refund to the consumer may be reduced by a deduction for use, to take account of the use the consumer has had of the goods in the period since they were delivered, but this is subject to subsections (9) and (10)".**

It follows that there is no automatic right to a full refund within s.24. Where the goods have already been used, a partial refund may be the more appropriate remedy. However, under s.24(10), no deduction for use is permissible where the final right to reject is exercised within six months of the goods being delivered and property passing.[60] This is so unless the goods are a motor vehicle which are excluded from this provision on the grounds that a trader would face significant detriment were they unable to make any reduction to take into account the depreciation in value of the vehicle due to the use of it by the consumer.[61] The trader cannot, however, take into account the general depreciation in value of the motor vehicle: the only deduction permitted under s.24 is that which corresponds to the use of the goods enjoyed by the consumer.

Action for Damages

13-021 The consumer can claim damages if the trader has broken a term of the contract.[62] This applies to conditions, warranties and for unclassified terms such as those introduced by the Consumer Rights Act, e.g. for non-delivery or where goods are not fit for purpose.

The measure of damages will be considered in Ch.14.

58 s.20(5) and (6).
59 s.20(15) and (7).
60 See also s.24(11)(c).
61 s.24(10)(b) enables other goods to be similarly specified through statutory instrument.
62 See s.19(11) for example.

Remedies in Supplies of Digital Content

Where defective digital content is supplied with goods, s.16 provides that the goods supplied will not confirm to the contract. This means that the consumer's remedies are those we considered above, including rights of "short-term" and "final" rejection. This will cover supplies of digital content via a tangible medium (e.g. the software which runs on an internet capable television or where software is supplied on a DVD disk). The position is different, however, where the digital content is supplied otherwise than on tangible media, e.g. by download. In this situation the Consumer Rights Act prescribes an alternative framework of remedies under s.42. Accordingly, where the trader is in breach of the right to supply under s.41, the consumer will have the right to a refund under s.45. This is broadly comparable to the equivalent remedy in a contract to supply goods under s.17, and the consumer is entitled to receive a refund of the money paid under the contract. There is one fundamental distinction however: under s.45, the consumer is not required to return (or even delete) the digital content supplied. This is sensible given the context—how, for example, would a consumer "return" software which has been downloaded? 13-022

Where the digital content does not confirm to the contract due to a breach of the rights laid down by ss.34–36 (satisfactory quality; fitness for purpose; and description) the consumer is entitled to the remedies of repair or replacement and the right to a price reduction. Thus, unlike contracts for the supply of goods, there is no right of "short"-term or "final" rejection in contracts to supply digital content. The remedies available to a consumer under a supply of digital content follow the same pattern as for other supply contracts noted above.[63] One substantive additional right is that prescribed by s.46 which deals with the situation where defective digital content damages a device owned by the consumer (e.g. where a consumer downloads software which contains a virus which damages the consumer's computer). In this situation, provided that the "damage is of a kind that would not have occurred if the trader had exercised reasonable care and skill" the consumer can require the trader to either repair the damage or compensate the consumer for the damage.

Repeat Performance and Price Reduction in Service Contracts

In Ch.8 we considered the impact of the Consumer Rights Act on contracts where a trader supplies a service to a consumer. Thus we saw that s.49 requires a trader to carry out the service with reasonable skill and care and within a reasonable time frame, etc. In a substantial departure from the previous position (i.e. that laid down by the Supply of Goods and Services Act 13-023

63 See ss.43 (repair and replacement) and 44 (reduction in price). See also s.42(4) where the trader fails to provide the required pre-contract information. As with the corresponding right in contracts for the supply of goods, the consumer is limited to recovering the amount of any costs incurred as a result of the breach, up to the amount of the price paid for the digital content.

1982) the Consumer Rights Act provides for two new statutory remedies: Where a trader fails to perform the service with reasonable skill and care[64] the consumer now has a right to repeat performance (s.55), and where that is not possible, the right to a price reduction (s.56). Repeat performance is defined as the "right to require the trader to perform the service again, to the extent necessary to complete its performance in conformity with the contract".[65] When requested, the trader must carry out the repeat performance within a reasonable time and without significant inconvenience to the consumer. Moreover, the trader must bear any costs associated with the repeat performance. This is significant, since in many cases, the costs of repeat performance (including labour and materials) will be significant. Where repeat performance is not possible or has not been carried out within a reasonable time (or without significant inconvenience to the consumer), the consumer may pursue a price reduction.[66] This operates in a very similar way to the equivalent position in respect of supply contracts considered above.

Private Redress Under the Consumer Protection from Unfair Trading Regulations 2008

13-024 The Consumer Protection from Unfair Trading Regulations 2008 provide for remedies where a consumer enters into a contract (or makes a payment) due to a trader's misleading action or aggressive commercial practice. This scheme of remedies, which is separate from that under the Consumer Rights Act, will be considered in Ch.16.[67]

Additional or Alternative Defendant

13-025 Of course, the seller will be liable for his own breach of contract. However, as an exception to the general rule, s.75 of the Consumer Credit Act 1974 allows the buyer in certain circumstances to bring against someone else (the creditor) a claim for the seller's breach of contract or

64 Or in line with information provided under s.50 and which is deemed a term of the contract.
65 s.55(1).
66 See s.56.
67 See para.16-013, below.

misrepresentation. Section 75 has already been noted in connection with misrepresentation.[68] It applies in exactly the same way in the case of a breach of contract by the seller. The claim that the buyer can bring against the creditor (e.g. the credit card company when the buyer has used his credit card to buy an item for more than £100) is the same as that which he can bring against the seller. The section only enhances the buyer's rights and therefore does not in any way reduce his right to sue the seller. The circumstances in which s.75 applies are set out in Ch.25.

General Reading

J.N. Adams, "Damages in sale of goods: a critique of the provisions of the Sale of Goods Act and Article 2 of the Uniform Commercial Code" [2002] J.B.L. 553.

W.C.H. Ervine, "The Sale and Supply of Goods to Consumers Regulations 2002" 2003 SLT 8 at 67–71.

B. Hacker, "Rescission of contract and revesting of title: a reply to Mr Swadling" (2006) 14 R.L.R. 106.

D. Harris, "Specific performance—a regular remedy for consumers?" (2003) 119 L.Q.R. 541.

K.F.K. Low, "Repair, rejection & rescission: an uneasy resolution" (2007) 123 L.Q.R. 536.

J. O'Sullivan, "Rescission as a self-help remedy: a critical analysis" [2000] C.L.J. 509.

A. Samuels, "The Consumer Rights Act 2015" [2016] J.B.L. 159.

W. Swadling, "Rescission, property, and the common law" (2005) 121 L.Q.R. 123.

C. Willett, M. Morgan-Taylor and A. Naidoo, "The Sale and Supply of Goods to Consumers Regulations" [2004] J.B.L. 94.

68 See para.6-009, above.

14

The Measure of Damages

General Contractual Principles

According to the rules in *Hadley v Baxendale*[1] damages for breach of contract can be obtained for two kinds of loss: 14–001

(i) any loss naturally arising from the breach; and

(ii) any loss which at the time of making the contract the defendant could have predicted as likely (or not unlikely) to result from the breach of it.

These principles were applied in *Victoria Laundry v Newman Industries*[2] where the laundry had agreed to buy a new (larger) boiler. In breach of contract the boiler was delivered five months late. For that period the buyers were therefore without its larger capacity and therefore unable to cater for a larger volume of business. They were awarded damages for this loss of ordinary business which arose naturally from the late delivery. They received no damages for the loss of some exceptionally lucrative government dyeing contracts which they would have secured if the boiler had been delivered on time. This loss did not arise naturally—in the usual course of business. Neither was it within the second type of loss above, because the sellers were unaware of the buyers' chance of obtaining those lucrative contracts.

1 (1854) 9 Exch. 341.
2 [1949] 2 K.B. 529.

Prima Facie Rules Applicable to Non-Consumer Rights Act Sale of Goods Contracts

14-002 The general principles outlined above apply in sale of goods, for although there are sections of the Sale of Goods Act 1979 governing the assessment of damages, those sections do little more than embody the general principles. The position in sales contracts under the Consumer Rights Act 2015 is a little different, as we will highlight later.

Non-acceptance

14-003 Section 50 provides:

> **"(1) Where the buyer wrongfully neglects or refuses to accept and pay for the goods, the seller may maintain an action against him for damages for non-acceptance.**
>
> **(2) The measure of damages is the estimated loss directly and naturally resulting, in the ordinary course of events, from the buyer's breach of contract.**
>
> **(3) Where there is an available market for the goods in question the measure of damages is prima facie to be ascertained by the difference between the contract price and market or current price at the time or times when the goods ought to have been accepted, or (if no time was fixed for acceptance) at the time of the refusal to accept."**

Subsection 3 lays down the prima facie measure of damages. The idea is that if the seller can sell the goods elsewhere at the same or a higher price than the buyer had agreed to pay, the seller has lost nothing, in which case he will receive only nominal damages.[3] However, if the market price is less than the contract price, the difference between the two represents the seller's loss. The market price for these purposes is the price which in normal business dealings those goods would have fetched on the date when the buyer should have accepted the goods. If the market price subsequently rose or fell, that is irrelevant, even if the seller actually sold at that subsequent greater or lower price. This is clear from some words of Salmon LJ in *Pagnan v Corbisa*[4] which are quoted below.

3 On the issue of there being no available market under s.50(3), see *Aercap Partners 1 Ltd v Avia Asset Management AB* [2010] EWHC 2431 (Comm) where displacing the prima facie rule was deemed preferable to artificially extending the concept of "reasonable time" under s.50(3) at [107]–[117].

4 [1970] 1 W.L.R. 1306.

The measure of damages in subs.3, being prima facie, does not apply where it does not represent the seller's loss. In *Thompson v Robinson*[5] the purchaser ordered from a motor trader a Vanguard car and later refused to accept it. The price of Vanguard cars did not fluctuate and the contract price and market price at the date of the buyer's breach were the same. However, the trader's loss was not merely nominal because he had lost a sale. It was held that the prima facie rule was displaced and the seller received as damages his loss of profit on one transaction. This was his loss "directly and naturally resulting".

That case was distinguished in *Charter v Sullivan*[6] where the buyer refused to accept a Hillman Minx which he had ordered from a trader. The difference was that in *Charter v Sullivan* there was a shortage of Hillman Minx cars. The number of sales the trader could make was limited to the number of cars he could get. Demand exceeded supply. Thus when one purchaser backed out, the trader did not lose a sale. He received only nominal damages. 14-004

Thompson v Robinson was distinguished also in *Lazenby Garages v Wright*[7] where Mr Wright refused to accept a second-hand car which he had previously agreed to buy for £1,670 from a car dealer. The dealer sold it a little later to another buyer for £1,770. The dealer claimed from Mr Wright the loss of profit on one sale. However, it could not be said with any certainty that because Mr Wright had backed out, the dealer had sold one car less. This was because second-hand cars are all unique. It was held that since the dealer had sold the car for more than the price Mr Wright had agreed to pay, he had suffered no damages at all.

Even when it is not displaced, the prima facie rule does not exclude any further loss which was reasonably foreseeable as a result of the buyer's breach. So, for example, the seller will also be able to recover any reasonable extra storage expenses he has had to incur.[8]

Non-delivery

Section 51 provides: 14-005

> **"(1) Where the seller wrongfully neglects or refuses to deliver the goods to the buyer, the buyer may maintain an action against the seller for damages for non-delivery.**
>
> **(2) The measure of damages is the estimated loss directly and naturally resulting, in the ordinary course of events, from the seller's breach of contract.**
>
> **(3) Where there is an available market for the goods in question the measure of damages is prima facie to be ascertained by the difference between the contract price and market or current**

5 [1955] Ch. 177.
6 [1957] 2 Q.B. 117.
7 [1976] 2 All E.R. 770.
8 s.37.

> **price of the goods at the time or times when they ought to have been delivered, or (if no time was fixed) at the time of the refusal to deliver."**

This section is converse of s.50. If on the date the seller fails or refuses to deliver, the buyer can buy similar goods from elsewhere at the same or a cheaper price, then prima facie the buyer's damages are only nominal. If the market price is higher, then the prima facie measure of damages is the extra, i.e. the difference between the contract price and the market price on the date of the seller's breach. Again, it is the market price on the date of the breach which is important. In *Pagnan v Corbisa*[9] Salmon LJ explained the prima facie rule:

> **". . . the innocent party is not bound to go on the market and buy or sell at the date of the breach. Nor is he bound to gamble on the market changing in his favour. He may wait if he chooses; and if the market turns against him this cannot increase the liability of the party in default; similarly, if the market turns in his favour, the liability of the party in default is not diminished."**

Thus, if the buyer does not immediately buy replacement goods but does so subsequently and at a different price from the market price at the date of the breach, that is normally irrelevant. His subsequent purchase is an "independent and disconnected" transaction.

The prima facie rule would be displaced by a subsequent transaction which was not "independent and disconnected", as illustrated by the facts in *Pagnan v Corbisa*. The sellers delivered goods which did not comply with the conditions of the contract. The buyers rejected them but, before doing so, obtained from an Italian court a sequestration order which gave them the right to detain the goods against payment of damages. They then negotiated a new contract with the sellers whereby they bought the goods at a price considerably less than the market price—the price being depressed because of the sequestration order. The buyers nevertheless claimed under the first contract damages based on the difference between the contract price and market price on the date of the breach. The claim failed. The second contract could not be ignored since it was not an "independent and disconnected" transaction; the same buyer bought the same goods from the same seller. On the facts, the benefit of the second contract price being depressed was greater than the loss caused by the breach of the first contract. Therefore the buyers obtained no damages.

9 [1970] 1 W.L.R. 1306.

Anticipatory Breach

Often a contract is to be performed in the future, i.e. delivery of the goods is to be in the future, either at a fixed date or within a reasonable length of time. In such a case it is possible for either the seller or the buyer to commit an anticipatory breach of contract, i.e. to repudiate the contract before the time for performance. This can be done by the seller informing the buyer that he will not deliver the goods or the buyer informing the seller that he will not accept them. When one side commits an anticipatory breach, the other party (the innocent party) is given an option. Either he can at once accept the anticipatory breach as a repudiation and immediately claim damages or else he can refuse to accept it as a repudiation and wait until there has been actual failure to perform the contract (as opposed to an anticipatory one). 14-006

If the innocent party adopts the latter alternative then he can claim damages if and when the actual breach (non-delivery or non-acceptance) occurs. In that case his damages are assessed on the principles already given (ss.50 and 51 above).[10] Thus the measure of damages is the difference between the contract price and the market price on the date for actual performance. *Tai Hing Cotton Mill Ltd v Kamsing Knitting Factory*[11] established that the same principle applies where the innocent party immediately accepts the anticipatory breach as a repudiation of the contract. The measure of damages is still the difference between the contract and the market price. The relevant market price is still that prevailing on the date for actual performance and not that prevailing on the earlier date of the anticipatory breach. This is so irrespective of whether the contract had a fixed future date for delivery or whether delivery was to be within a reasonable length of time.

Consider an example. On 1 May B agrees to buy from S 50 tonnes of cob nuts at £100 per tonne, delivery to be on 1 December. On 1 June, when the market price of cob nuts is £101 per tonne S informs B that S will not supply the nuts. B may refuse to accept that as a repudiation by S. In that case B will be able to sue for damages for non-delivery if on 1 December S does not deliver. The market price of cob nuts on 1 December is £110 per tonne. Thus B is entitled to the market price (£110 x 50) less the contract price (£100 x 50) = £500. Suppose that B had in June accepted S's repudiation of the contract. Then the assessment of B's damages would be on the same basis and B would similarly be entitled to £500.

There are just two qualifications to this last point, i.e. which apply where the innocent party immediately accepts the repudiation. First, if B's claim for damages comes to trial before 1 December (i.e. before the actual date of delivery), the court must determine the market price on that future date as best it can: *Melachrino v Nickoll and Knight*.[12] This will often be little more than guesswork. The second qualification is that an innocent party who accepts an anticipatory breach becomes under a duty to mitigate (minimise) his loss. Thus if B accepts S's repudiation in June and he sees the market price begin to rise, he has a reasonable opportunity to minimise his loss by buying replacement nuts immediately at less than £100 per tonne. In that case the 14-007

10 See paras 14-003 and 14-005 above.

11 [1978] 2 W.L.R. 62.

12 [1920] 1 K.B. 693.

court may well reduce his damages from the £500. It will do so irrespective of whether the buyer actually used the opportunity to buy replacement nuts.

Suppose now, however, that B, having accepted S's repudiation in June, sees the market beginning to rise rapidly in July and, in an attempt to minimise his loss before the market rises further, buys replacement goods on 15 July at £115 per tonne—only to discover that by the delivery date under the original contract (1 December) the market price has fallen back to £110 per tonne. In that case the court has a discretion (in order to avoid injustice) to award damages at the higher level of £750 (i.e. by reference to the market price at 15 July instead of the later contract delivery date of 1 December): *Johnson v Agnew*.[13]

The duty to mitigate does not apply where the innocent party refuses to accept the anticipatory breach as a repudiation. Because he is waiting to see if the anticipatory breach turns into non-performance in fact, he is not expected to buy any replacement goods until the date of actual non-performance.

14-008 Now suppose that the buyer commits a wrongful anticipatory repudiation of the contract and the seller immediately accepts that repudiation as terminating the contract and sues for damages. Clearly the seller does not have to remain ready and willing to deliver. The buyer is the only party to have broken the contract and the seller will be entitled to damages from him according to the principles just outlined. What, however, is the position if, at the time of the buyer's wrongful anticipatory repudiation, the seller had already been disabled from completing the essential terms of the contract (e.g. the seller's factory making the goods was already so far behind in production that the seller could not possibly have delivered the goods by the contractual delivery date)? In that case the seller's damages would be reduced from the prima facie level in s.50: *British & Benningtons v North West Cachar Tea Co*.[14] To achieve a reduction, however, the burden of proof rests upon the buyer to show that the seller would have been unable to comply with the essential terms of the contract if it had not been terminated: *Gill & Duffus v Berger & Co*.[15] Even if the buyer were able to do that, the greatest reduction the buyer could achieve would still leave the seller entitled to nominal damages.

Late Delivery

14-009 In commercial contracts, late delivery by the seller will normally be a breach of condition.[16] If the buyer rejects the goods for breach of condition, his damages are assessed as in the case of non-delivery. If it is only a breach of warranty or if the buyer accepts the goods, the damages are prima facie assessed according to the difference between the value of the goods on the date they should have been delivered and their value (if lower) when actually delivered.

13 [1970] A.C. 367.
14 [1923] A.C. 48.
15 [1984] 2 W.L.R. 95.
16 See para.7-006, above.

As always, the prima facie method of assessment may be displaced and damages awarded for any loss which falls within the rules in *Hadley v Baxendale*.[17] *Victoria Laundry v Newman Industries*[18] (above) is an example of this.

Breach of Condition

If the buyer rejects the goods, damages are assessed as in the case of non-delivery. If he accepts the goods, the damages are assessed as if it were a breach of warranty under s.53. 14-010

Breach of Warranty

Section 53(2) and (3) provide: 14-011

> **"(2) The measure of damages for breach of warranty is the estimated loss directly and naturally resulting, in the ordinary course of events, from the breach of warranty.**
>
> **(3) In the case of breach of warranty of quality such loss is prima facie the difference between the value of the goods at the time of delivery to the buyer and the value they would have had if they had fulfilled the warranty."**

The prima facie rule in subs.(3) can be termed a "capital value" assessment. In fact the buyer has a choice. He can claim either his capital loss or his loss of profit. He cannot claim both: *Cullinane v British Rema*.[19] In that case the sellers had warranted that a clay pulverising machine would process clay at six tons per hour. In fact it could not do so. The purchaser claimed under two heads, first for the capital loss and secondly for his loss of profits—the latter head being based on the difference over three years between the profits made at the machine's actual rate of output and the higher profits which would have been made at the warranted rate of output. The Court of Appeal held that both claims could not succeed and disallowed the first (that being the smaller claim). It was also pointed out that the buyers could have claimed loss of profits for the whole of the estimated useful life of the machine (10 years in this particular case).

In addition to a claim for capital loss or loss of profits, a claim can be made for any consequential loss which falls within the rules in *Hadley v Baxendale*, i.e. loss of a type which at the time of the contract could reasonably have been predicted by both parties as liable (i.e. not unlikely) to occur in the event of the breach. Indeed this is sometimes the only claim

17 (1854) 9 Exch. 341.
18 [1949] 2 K.B. 529.
19 [1954] 1 Q.B. 292.

made, as in *Frost v Aylesbury Dairy Co.*[20] It does not matter that the extent of the damage could not have been foreseen. Damage is recoverable provided the type of damage and the way it occurred were predictable. In *Vacwell Engineering v B.D.H. Chemicals*[21] the sellers supplied (in glass ampoules) a chemical for use in the buyer's factory. The chemical was liable to explode on contact with water. No warning was given of this. Indeed, the sellers were unaware of it. The sellers were in breach of the implied condition that the goods should be reasonably fit for their purpose. Had the sellers known, they could have predicted that perhaps water would come into contact with the contents of an ampoule and cause an explosion. This is what occurred in the buyer's factory but, because a number of ampoules were being washed together, the explosion was much greater than might have been predicted and the damage much more extensive. Rees J held that nevertheless the sellers were liable for all the damage.

14-012 It should be apparent from this case that in assessing what damages are recoverable (i.e. within the rules in *Hadley v Baxendale*) for breach of a term as to quality, one does not ask simply "What type of damage could the seller at the time of the contract have predicted?" Rather one asks, "Had he known of the defect, what type of damage could the seller at the time of the contract reasonably have predicted?" A similar point arose in *Parsons v Uttley Ingham*.[22] The buyers, who were pig farmers, bought a 28 ft-high hopper which, as the sellers knew, the buyers intended to use for the storage of pig nuts. On delivery the ventilator on top of the hopper was shut and nobody noticed. As a result nuts stored in the hopper became mouldy. A large number of the buyers' pigs died from an infection, E. Coli, triggered by eating the mouldy pig nuts. The sellers were in breach of the implied condition that the hopper would be reasonably fit for the purpose for which the buyers required it. Was the resulting loss of the pigs recoverable under the rules in *Hadley v Baxendale*? E. Coli was a hitherto unknown disease and also, apparently, it could not reasonably have been expected that pigs would become ill from eating mouldy pig nuts. However, the breach of contract by the sellers consisted not of feeding mouldy pig nuts to the buyers' pigs, but of supplying an unventilated hopper. If the sellers had known they were supplying an unventilated hopper, could they reasonably have regarded illness in pigs as a not unlikely consequence of that breach? It was held that they could and were therefore liable for the loss of the pigs. It was immaterial that the seller could not have predicted either the particular illness that resulted nor the severity of it.

Section 53(1) allows the buyer to set off damages due to him for breach of warranty against the price he owes the seller. He can of course sue for any excess under s.53(4).

20 [1905] 1 K.B. 608, see para.7-023, above.

21 [1971] 1 Q.B. 88.

22 [1978] Q.B. 791.

Sub-sales

Non-delivery

Suppose that on 1 December X agreed to buy from Y for £100 one tonne of corn to be delivered on 1 January. Y does not deliver the corn and market price on 1 January is £105. Prima facie X is entitled to £5 damages. Suppose further that on 15 December X had agreed to sell a tonne of corn to Q, delivery to be on 1 January. That sub-sale can affect X's loss. His loss could be less than £5 if, for example, in his contract with Q the price was £104. Alternatively, it might be greater if for example the price in Q's contract was £106 or if he himself is liable to Q for breach of contract. Does the law take sub-sales into account? 14-013

Generally, the effect of a sub-sale is ignored and the prima facie rule prevails. In *Williams v Agius*,[23] Williams agreed to buy from Agius a cargo of coal at 16s. 3d. per ton. Later he agreed with a sub-purchaser to sell him a similar cargo at 19s. per ton. Agius failed to deliver. Williams' damages were assessed at the difference between the contract price (16s. 3d.) and the market price on the date when delivery should have been made (23s. 6d.).

In *Re Hall & Pim's Arbitration*[24] the House of Lords established an exception. The prima facie rule will be displaced and a sub-sale taken into account when the following circumstances all exist:

(i) The first contract contemplated the creation of sub-sales—so that the seller could predict from the outset that in the event of non-delivery the buyer might suffer loss in connection with sub-sales.

(ii) The sub-contract was for the sale, not merely of similar goods, but of the very same goods as were to be supplied under the first contract.

(iii) The sub-contract was not an extravagant or unusual bargain.

(iv) The sub-contract was created before the delivery date under the first contract.

If these circumstances all exist then the loss connected with the sub-sale(s) falls within the second rule in *Hadley v Baxendale*.[25] This was the position in *Re Hall & Pim's Arbitration*. On 3 November the buyers agreed to buy a cargo of wheat at 51s. 9d. per quarter. The contract clearly referred to the possibility of sub-sales. On 21 November the buyers made a sub-sale of the same cargo at 56s. 9d. per quarter. On 22 March, when the seller refused to deliver, the

23 [1914] A.C. 510.
24 (1928) 139 L.T. 50.
25 (1854) 9 Exch. 341.

market price was 53s. 9d. per quarter. The buyers were awarded damages assessed at 5s. per quarter and also damages which the buyers had to pay to their sub-buyer.

Late Delivery

14-014 From *Wertheim v Chicoutimi Pulp Co*[26] it appears that sub-sales are taken into account more readily in the case of a late delivery. The contract price was 25s. per ton. Before the delivery date, the buyer made a sub-contract to sell similar goods at 65s. per ton. On the date when delivery should have been made under the first contract, the market price was 70s. When delivery was actually made, the market price had dropped to 42s. 6d. The buyer used the goods to fulfil his sub-contract. The Privy Council took the buyer's sub-sale into account and awarded damages assessed at only 5s. per ton.

Breach of Term as to Quality

14-015 Here also sub-sales are taken into account more readily than in the case of non-delivery. The buyer can include in his claim for damages the amount of the damages he has had to pay out to his sub-purchaser for breach of contract, see *Godley v Perry*[27] For this, it is sufficient that the seller knew or ought to have known that the buyer bought the goods for resale.

Sub-sales which are within the reasonable contemplation of the parties, can result in the seller's damages being either more or less than the prima facie measure laid down in s.53(3). *Bence Graphics v Fasson UK*[28] involved the sale of vinyl film. The sellers knew that the buyer was going to make it into decals (identification labels for bulk containers) and sell them to companies involved in the international container business. Over a period of years the sellers supplied the buyer with vinyl film which, in breach of an express contract term, was not such that it would survive in good legible condition for at least five years. This was discovered only much later. The value of the film supplied with this latent defect was in fact zero and thus the prima facie measure of damages laid down in s.53(3) (i.e. difference between the value the goods should have had on delivery and the lower value of the goods actually supplied) was the whole of the contract price. The breach meant, however, that the buyer was exposed to the risk of claims by their sub-buyers, which would have greatly exceeded that prima facie amount. Nevertheless, no such claims were made. The Court of Appeal held that the prima facie measure of damages was displaced. Just as the buyer could have claimed a greater figure if he had had to meet claims in excess of the prima facie amount, equally the sellers did not have to pay the prima facie amount where it exceeded the buyer's actual loss.

26 [1911] A.C. 301.

27 [1960] 1 W.L.R. 9, see para.9-006, above.

28 [1997] 3 W.L.R. 205.

The Consumer Rights Act 2015

Whilst much of what has been said is of relevance to both commercial and consumer sales contracts, the Consumer Rights Act has had an impact in this area, with some rules embodied in the Sale of Goods Act no longer applying to sales contracts under the 2015 Act. In particular, it dis-applies various provisions which are inconsistent with the framework of consumer remedies laid down by the Act. Thus, whilst s.50, discussed above, remains applicable in the event of a consumer buyer wrongfully refusing to accept the goods, ss.51 and 53 are dis-applied where there is a sales contract under the CRA 2015. Instead, non-delivery is dealt with under CRA s.28. As we have already noted, this provides that a consumer buyer can treat the contract as at an end in various situations.[29] Under s.28(9) the trader must reimburse all payments made under the contract without undue delay and the consumer may seek other remedies, such as damages, however they must establish actual loss. Thus, for example, if a trader is unable to deliver a wedding dress, purchased by a consumer, the consumer buyer will be able to treat the contract as at an end, recover any money already paid and claim for damages in respect of additional costs incurred by having to buy a replacement wedding dress. 14-016

Mitigation

The innocent party is under a duty to take reasonable steps to mitigate (minimise) his loss. Any loss which he could reasonably have avoided will be deducted from his damages. 14-017

His duty is to act reasonably. So, in the case of non-delivery, the buyer is not expected to hunt the globe to find similar goods: *Lesters Leather & Skin Co v Home & Oversees Brokers*.[30] Similarly, a purchaser need not force defective goods upon his sub-purchaser (even if contractually entitled to do so) if that would involve damaging his own commercial reputation: *Finlay v Kwik Hoo Tong*.[31]

Sometimes the party in default makes an offer to put things right, e.g. the seller offers to buy back defective goods. If the offer is a reasonable one then it is likely to be reasonable to accept it. An unreasonable refusal will be a breach of the duty to mitigate: *Payzu v Saunders*.[32]

Occasionally, albeit rarely, steps taken by the claimant in an attempt to minimise his loss result in fact in increasing it. In that case the extra loss is recoverable in a claim for damages. 14-018

29 See para.11-005.
30 [1848] W.N. 437.
31 [1929] 1 K.B. 400.
32 [1919] 2 K.B. 581.

The defendants in *Hoffberger v Ascot International Bloodstock Bureau*[33] had contracted to buy a mare from Mr Hoffberger for £6,000 in October 1973 provided that on that date the mare was in foal. When the time came the mare was in foal but they failed to buy her and finally refused to do so in December 1973. Mr Hoffberger was unable to sell the mare at the December 1973 sales because she was ill. In an attempt to obtain a good price, he paid a stud fee of over £1,400 to have her covered again so that he would be able to sell her in foal at the December 1974 sales. In fact the market fell and the mare in foal fetched only £1,085 at those sales. Mr Hoffberger was awarded damages of over £7,000. This sum included all the loss and expenses he had incurred in attempting to mitigate his damages. This was because those steps had been reasonable ones to take even though they had in the event aggravated the losses.

Penalties

14-019 Sometimes the contract stipulates how much is to be paid by the party in breach, e.g. "£100 per day for each day delivery is delayed". Such a clause is a liquidated damages clause and is binding upon the parties provided it is not a penalty. If it binds the parties, the stipulated amount is the amount payable and that is the case, whether the loss actually caused is greater or smaller. Therein lies the advantage of liquidated damages clauses. As Lady Arden has said:[34]

> **"Parties agree a liquidated damages clause so as to provide a remedy that is predictable and certain for a particular event . . . . . . The employer does not then have to quantify its loss, which may be difficult and time-consuming for it to do."**

However, such a clause is a penalty if it was not a genuine attempt by the parties to pre-estimate the likely damages but was intended to hang in terror over one party to ensure that he carried out the contract. Some sentences of Lord Dunedin's in *Dunlop Pneumatic Tyre Co v New Garage Motor Co* are particularly instructive:[35]

> **"Though the parties to a contract who use the words 'penalty' or 'liquidated damages' may prima facie be supposed to mean what they say, yet the expression used is not conclusive. The**

33 (1976) 120 S.J. 130.

34 *Triple Point Technology Inc v PTT Public Co Ltd* [2021] UKSC 29 at [35].

35 [1915] A.C. 79.

court must find out whether the payment stipulated is in truth a penalty or liquidated damages. . .It will be held to be a penalty if the sum stipulated for is extravagant and unconscionable in amount in comparison with the greatest loss that could conceivably be proved to have followed from the breach. . .

There is a presumption (but no more) that it is a penalty when 'a single lump is made payable by way of compensation, on the occurrence of one or more or all of several events, some of which may occasion serious and others but trifling damage. . .'

On the other hand: it is no obstacle to the sum stipulated being a genuine pre-estimate of damage, that the consequences of the breach are such as to make precise pre-estimation almost an impossibility. On the contrary, that is just the situation when it is probable that pre-estimated damage was the true bargain between parties."

In *Cavendish Square Holding BV v Talal El Makdessi; ParkingEye v Beavis*[36] the Supreme Court took the opportunity to revisit this issue. The court observed that whilst Lord Dunedin's presumptions had proven to be "perfectly adequate" in the context of "simple damages clauses in standard contracts" they were less satisfactory in more complex cases.[37] Thus, rather than focusing upon whether the clause in question is a liquidated damages clause or an unenforceable penalty, the question is:[38]

". . . whether the impugned provision is a secondary obligation which imposes a detriment on the contract-breaker out of all proportion to any legitimate interest of the innocent party in the enforcement of the primary obligation."

This approach would seemingly give the parties considerably more flexibility when making provision for damages within the contract itself. This is particularly likely to be the case where the parties are of equal bargaining power and have access to legal advice. If the clause serves a legitimate interest and is not grossly out of proportion to the protection of that interest, it will not be regarded as penal and will be enforceable. The facts of Beavis demonstrate the application of this revised test. It will be recalled that the case concerned a charge of £85 imposed on a motorist who had parked his car in the car park for nearly an hour longer than

36 [2015] UKSC 67.

37 [2015] UKSC 67 at [25].

38 [2015] UKSC 67 at [32].

the maximum permitted time.[39] The Supreme Court concluded that the charge was not a penalty clause. Whilst it did not represent a pre-estimate of the damage sustained by the failure to comply with the conditions of parking (i.e. using a parking bay for nearly an hour longer than was permitted), the amount was not unreasonable, and was necessary to protect the legitimate interests of the management company in ensuring that the parking facilities were not abused.

The Supreme Court took a similarly favourable approach to liquidated damages clauses in *Triple Point Technology Inc v PTT Public Co Ltd*.[40] The dispute concerned a scheme of works to replace and upgrade an IT system to be used in commodity trading. The scheme consisted of various phases, with the completion of various phases serving to trigger payments under the contract. At the time when PTT terminated the contract due to the lack of progress, the first phase of the work was only partially complete. The contract contained a clause which provided that Triple Point were liable to pay a penalty at an agreed rate each day whilst the work remained unfinished "up until PTT accepts such work". The Court of Appeal interpreted the clause as meaning that liquidated damages would only be available where in fact the supplier eventually completes the work since otherwise PTT could not 'accept' work that had not been completed. The Supreme Court said that this interpretation "would be to render the liquidated damages clause of little value in a commercial contract". Instead, the true construction "provided for liquidated damages if Triple Point did not discharge its obligations within the time fixed by the contract irrespective of whether PTT accepted any works which were completed late". [41] Thus, liquidated damages will accrue during a period of relevant delay until termination (unless the parties agree otherwise).

14–020 Whether a clause is properly regarded as a penalty or a liquidated damages clause is a matter of construction.[42] Thus in *Azimut-Benetti SpA v Healey*[43] a clause which provided for termination and 20 per cent of the purchase price was not an unenforceable penalty clause since its purpose was not to act as a deterrent to default and was commercially justifiable not least since the clause also imposed obligations on the supplier.

If it is a penalty, the clause is void and the innocent party can sue in the usual way for whatever is his actual loss. That loss will be calculated according to the principles outlined in the earlier parts of this chapter. Finally, a penalty within a consumer contract might well be rendered ineffective by the Consumer Rights Act 2015 even if it were not struck down by the doctrine of penalties.[44]

39 See para.10.031, above.

40 [2021] UKSC 29.

41 [2021] UKSC 29 at [48].

42 *Lordsvale Finance Plc v Bank of Zambia* [1996] Q.B. 752 at 762–3.

43 [2010] EWHC 2234 (Comm) at [29].

44 See paras 10-027–10-033.

General Reading

N. Bridge, "Mitigation of damages in contract and the meaning of avoidable loss" (1989) L.Q.R. 398.

B. Coote, "Contract damages, Ruxley, and the performance interest" (56) 1997 C.L.J. 537.

R. Lawson, "Contract law: incorporation of terms—rejection of goods and the measure of damages" (1995) Tr. Law 14(5) at 418.

M. McInnes, "Breach of contract and compound interest as damages" (2002) 118 L.Q.R. 516.

G. McMeel, "Contract damages: the interplay of remoteness and loss of a chance" [2004] L.M.C.L.Q. 1(Feb) 10–14.

B.R. Opeskin, "Damages for breach of contract terminated under express terms" (1990) 106 L.Q.R. 293.

S. Watterson, "The law of damages in the 21st century" [2004] L.M.C.L.Q. 4(Nov) 513–534;

C. Webb, "Performance and compensation: an analysis of contract damages and contractual obligation" [2006] 26(1) O.J.L.S. 41–71.

15

Auction Sales

In most respects a purchase made at an auction constitutes an ordinary contract for the sale of goods. 15-001 Thus, in general, the provisions of the Sale of Goods Act and the Consumer Rights Act apply in the same way as they do in relation to non-auction sales. As we will see, the Sale of Goods Act also makes special provision in relation to auction sales. It should be noted that the Consumer Rights Act excludes, to a large extent, individuals who buy second-hand goods at an auction where they have the opportunity to attend the auction in person from the definition of "consumer" for the purposes of Ch.II Pt I of the Act.[1] Thus an individual who buys new goods at an auction or second-hand goods where there is no opportunity to attend the auction in person will remain within the definition of "consumer" under the Consumer Rights Act. Where this exclusion applies, the buyer may still be protected by the general provisions of the Sale of Goods Act (e.g. if the goods breach an implied term within the Act) but will not be able to avail themselves of the extended range of remedies available to consumers under the Consumer Rights Act.

Advertisements Before the Auction Sale

An advertisement that an auction is to be held is not an offer or a promise that the auction will 15-002 be held. There is no liability if the auction is not in fact held. In *Harris v Nickerson*[2] the claimant

1 See s.2(5) and s.2(6). In some respects however, such a person would remain a consumer for the purposes of Ch.II, e.g. the rules relating to delivery and risk in ss.28 and 29 as well as any information to be provided under the Consumer Contracts (Information, Cancellation and Additional Charges) Regulations 2013.

2 (1873) L.R.8 Q.B. 286.

travelled to the advertised place for the auction sale which he then found to be cancelled. It was held that he was not entitled to claim his travelling expenses from the advertiser.

It seems, however, that if the auction is in fact held, then anything advertised to be "without reserve" must be sold to the highest bidder. If it is withdrawn, then the advertiser is in breach of contract with any bidder who had come in response to the advertisement: *Warlow v Harrison*.[3]

Section 57 of the Sale of Goods Act

15-003 Section 57 states:

> **"In the case of a sale by auction –**
>
> **(1) Where goods are put up for sale by auction in lots, each lot is prima facie deemed to be the subject of a separate contract of sale.**
>
> **(2) A sale by auction is complete when the auctioneer announces its completion by the fall of the hammer, or in other customary manner; and until such announcement is made any bidder may retract his bid.**
>
> **(3) A sale by auction may be notified to be subject to a reserve or upset price, and a right to bid may also be reserved expressly by or on behalf of the seller.**
>
> **(4) Where a sale by auction is not notified to be subject to a right to bid on behalf of the seller, it is not lawful for the seller to bid himself or to employ any person to bid at such a sale, or for the auctioneer knowingly to take any bid from the seller or any such person.**
>
> **(5) A sale contravening subsection (4) above may be treated as fraudulent by the buyer.**
>
> **(6) Where, in respect of a sale by auction, a right to bid is expressly reserved (but not otherwise) the seller or any one person on his behalf may bid at the auction."**

3 (1859) 1 E. & E. 309, confirmed in *Barry v Heathcote Ball & Co* [2000] 1 W.L.R. 1962 CA.

Reserve Price

A problem arises if the seller (i.e. the person who puts the goods into the sale) imposes a reserve price and the auctioneer nevertheless accepts a bid for less than the reserve price. If the reserve price had been notified as allowed by s.57(3), then the bidder has no claim against the seller or auctioneer who will not be liable for refusing to deliver the goods: *McManus v Fortescue*.[4] If the reserve price had not been notified and the bidder had no reason to know of it, then the bidder will have an action against the auctioneer for breach of the auctioneer's warranty of authority. That is the implied warranty given by any agent (whether auctioneer or not) that he is acting within his principal's (in this case the seller's) authority.[5] 15-004

Position of the Auctioneer

In selling goods, an auctioneer is an agent of the owner. In *Chelmsford Auctions v Poole*[6] Lord Denning MR explained that on a sale by auction there are three contracts. They are: 15-005

(i) Between the owner (vendor) and the highest bidder (purchaser).

(ii) Between the owner (vendor) and the auctioneer.

(iii) Between the auctioneer and the highest bidder (purchaser).

The first of these is a simple contract of sale to which the auctioneer is no party. The auctioneer's rights and obligations arise under the other two contracts.

Contract Between Auctioneer and Owner (Vendor)

Of this contract Lord Denning said:[7] 15-006

> **"The understanding is that the auctioneer should not part with possession of them [the goods] to the purchaser except against**

4 [1907] 2 K.B. 1.
5 On breach of warrant of authority, see Ch.30, below.
6 [1973] Q.B. 542.
7 [1973] Q.B. 542 at 548.

payment of the price; or if the auctioneer should part with them without receiving payment, he is responsible to the vendor for the price . . . The auctioneer is given as against the vendor, a lien on the proceeds for his commission and charges."

The above comment means that the auctioneer when he receives payment from the purchaser can deduct his commission charges before passing on the money to the vendor. *Chelmsford Auctions v Poole* involved the sale of a car which the auctioneers knocked down to the purchaser for £57. The purchaser paid an immediate deposit of £7. The auctioneers retained possession of the car. The auctioneers, without waiting for further payment from the purchaser, paid to the vendor the full amount of the price less their commission charges (£3.50). This deduction was quite proper. Subsequently the auctioneers, as they were entitled to, sued the purchaser for the outstanding balance of the price.

The terms of the contract between the auctioneer and the vendor can of course be varied by contrary agreement (i.e. usually by the printed auction conditions).

Contract Between Auctioneer and Highest Bidder (Purchaser)

15–007 In the absence of contrary agreement, the common law implies the following terms into the contract:

(i) a warranty by the auctioneer that he has authority to sell;

(ii) a warranty by the auctioneer that he will give the purchaser possession of the goods against the price paid into his hands;

(iii) a warranty by the auctioneer that the possession given to the purchaser will be undisturbed by the vendor or by himself; and

(iv) a warranty that he knows of no defect in the vendor's title.

The auctioneer, however, does not warrant the vendor's title in the case of a sale of specific goods (or unascertained goods out of a specific bulk) which the purchaser knows do not belong to the auctioneer. In *Benton v Campbell, Parker Co*[8] the auctioneer knocked down the car to the highest bidder. It turned out that the person who put the car into the auction (the vendor) was not the owner. It was held that the auctioneer was not liable to the purchaser. (The purchaser could, of course, have brought an action against the vendor under the Sale of Goods Act s.12.)

8 [1925] 2 K.B. 410.

As well as giving the implied warranties listed above, the auctioneer has certain rights at common law. He has a special property in the goods, which gives him a lien over the goods until the whole of the price is paid or tendered. In *Chelmsford Auctions v Poole*[9] it was held that he also had the right personally to sue the purchaser for the price. Lord Denning further pointed out:

> **"... the purchaser cannot avoid his liability to the auctioneer by paying the vendor direct without telling the auctioneer. If he does so, the auctioneer can make the purchaser pay the full price again, even though it means that the purchaser pays twice over."**

These rights and obligations can be varied by the auction conditions.

Auctions (Bidding Agreements) Acts 1927–69

These Acts are aimed at preventing auction rings. A ring is an arrangement whereby several dealers all of whom are interested in a given item agree not to compete in outbidding each other at the public auction but instead allow one of their number to buy it as cheaply as possible.[10] The idea is that they subsequently hold their own private auction amongst themselves. Under the Acts it is a criminal offence for a dealer to offer or agree to give an inducement or reward to another for abstaining or having abstained from bidding. If goods are sold at an auction to someone who has been a party to such an agreement to abstain from bidding, then the seller can rescind the contract.[11] 15–008

It should be noted that these rules relate only to agreements where at least one dealer is involved and also that they do not apply in the case of an agreement to purchase the goods bona fide on a joint account, e.g. where two dealers in partnership together wish to purchase goods for their business and agree that only one of them will bid. For the purpose of the Acts a dealer is "a person who in the normal course of his business attends sales by auction for the purpose of purchasing goods with a view to reselling them".

Apart from cases where the Auctions (Bidding Agreements) Acts apply, there is nothing illegal in two potential bidders agreeing that one of them will not bid with the result that the

9 [1973] Q.B. 542 at 549.
10 See, for example, s.1(1) of the 1969 Act.
11 See s.3 of the 1969 Act.

one who does bid obtains the property more cheaply than he otherwise would. The auction sale to the one who does bid remains perfectly valid: *Harrop v Thompson*.[12]

Mock Auctions

15–009 Mock auctions are sham auctions designed to entice unsuspecting members of the public to buy shoddy goods at over-inflated prices by creating the appearance that the auctioneer is offering goods at a fraction of their normal retail price. The Mock Auctions Act 1961, now repealed (see below), defined a mock auction as an auction where persons were invited to buy goods by way of competitive bidding and:

- (i) any goods of a type listed in the Act were sold to a bidder for less than his highest bid or part of the price is repaid or credited to him (or stated to be so);
- (ii) the right to bid for any such goods was (or was stated to be) restricted to persons who had bought or agreed to buy one or more articles; or
- (iii) any articles were given away or offered as gifts.

One form of mock auction was exemplified by the facts of *Allen v Simmons*[13] where the defendant offered just one set of glasses and asked his audience who would pay him 30 pence for the set. A number of hands went up. The defendant then selected one of them and then sold the set to the person for one penny. It was held that the defendant was guilty, since in raising their hands the members of the audience were engaging in competitive bidding—namely in competing against one another for the chance of getting in first by raising a hand before anyone else or for the chance of attracting the defendant's favour in selecting the lucky buyer.

The Mock Auctions Act 1961 has now been repealed by the Consumer Protection from Unfair Trading Regulations 2008[14] which easily apply to mock auctions which are therefore prohibited as an unfair commercial practice. The operation of a mock auction may well fall under the activities automatically deemed unfair through the "Black List" in Sch.1. The majority of mock auctions will no doubt fall foul of one or more of the following activities:

12 [1975] 1 W.L.R. 545.

13 [1978] 1 W.L.R. 879.

14 SI 2008/1277. The Regulations came into effect on 26 May 2008.

- Making an invitation to purchase products at a specified price and then refusing to show the advertised item to consumers (bait and switch).[15]
- Falsely stating that a product will only be available for a very limited time, or that it will only be available on particular terms for a very limited time, in order to elicit an immediate decision.[16]
- Claiming that the trader is about to cease trading or move premises when he is not.[17]
- Creating the impression that the consumer cannot leave the premises until a contract is formed.[18]

Where the auction does not fall under the practices detailed in Sch.1, it is likely, nevertheless, that the auction will be deemed unfair either as a "misleading commercial practice"[19] or alternatively, as an "aggressive practice".[20] The Regulations are explained in more detail in Ch.16 below.

General Reading

A. Breward and D. Miller, "Online Auctions—when the virtual hammer falls, who does it hit?" (2000) E.B.L. 2(3), 11–12.

B.W.M. Downey, "Mock Auctions" (1962) 25 M.L.R. 224.

B. de Groote and K. de Vulder, "European framework for unfair commercial practices: analysis of Directive 2005/29" [2007] J.B.L. 16.

J. Hörnle, "Is an online auction an 'auction' in law?" (2007) E.B.L. 8(12) at 7–9.

C. Reifa, "Consumer protection on online auction sites: just an illusion?" (2005) Computers & Law 16(3) 34.

H.P. Wiesemann and E. Falletti, "Internet Auctions and Harmonisation. A Comparison between Italy and Germany" (2006) European Review of Private Law 14(1) 3.

15 Sch.1 para.6.
16 Sch.1 para.7.
17 Sch.1 para.15.
18 Sch.1 para.24.
19 Under reg.3(3).
20 Under reg.7.

16

Unfair Trading Practices

Introduction

This chapter deals with the law relating to unfair trading practices and in so doing introduces an area of law which has recently undergone significant (and substantial) reform. In particular the chapter considers the Unfair Commercial Practices Directive 2005 and its implementation into domestic law through the Consumer Protection from Unfair Trading Regulations 2008. These regulations have, as shall be discussed shortly, radically affected much of the previous legislation designed to protect the consumer in ways other than conferring rights upon individual consumers, including, for example the Trade Descriptions Act 1968 and Pt III of the Consumer Protection Act 1987. This chapter will now only offer a brief account of these pieces of legislation since the regulation of such activities has now been subsumed within the Consumer Protection from Unfair Trading Regulations 2008. Where the reader requires a detailed account of previous legislation such as the criminal offences under ss.1 and 14 of the Trade Descriptions Act 1968 the 6th edn of this text will prove useful. The chapter will also introduce the Enterprise Act 2002 which confers powers on enforcement authorities to secure court orders against traders guilty of malpractices. Such enforcement action is vital to the consumer protection movement and has also undergone considerable reform in recent years. 16-001

The Unfair Commercial Practices Directive 2005

16-002 The Unfair Commercial Practices Directive 2005[1] was incorporated into domestic law on 26 May 2008 by the Consumer Protection from Unfair Trading Regulations 2008.[2] This section will briefly outline the purpose of the Directive before focusing upon its implementation into domestic law through the regulations. The purpose of the Directive is deceptively simple and is stated in art.1 in the following terms:

> **"...to contribute to the proper functioning of the internal market and achieve a high level of consumer protection by approximating the laws, regulations and administrative provisions of the Member States on unfair commercial practices harming consumers' economic interests."**

The Directive therefore imposes a legal framework designed to govern unfair commercial practices in business-to-consumer dealings. Moreover, it does so uniformly in that the Directive is one of full (or maximum) harmonisation, i.e. it lays down the standard which must be transposed into domestic law by the Member States, which cannot provide a lesser or greater level of protection to consumers than that required by the Directive.[3]

Scope of the Consumer Protection from Unfair Trading Regulations 2008

16-003 The regulations create a broad system of prohibitions upon unfair commercial practices. As originally enacted, the regulations did not alter or enhance the consumer's contractual rights, i.e. an agreement would not be unenforceable where a trader had breached the regulations. This position has been modified following recommendations of the Law Commissions and consumers now have rights of redress under the (amended) regulations.[4] These additional rights, however, do not apply to every instance of an unfair commercial practice however, and we will consider their effect later in the chapter. Before analysing the approach of the regulations in prohibiting

1 Directive 2005/29 EC. Note that the Enforcement and Modernisation Directive (EU) 2019/2161/EU makes some significant amendments to the 2005 Directive, especially with regard to enforcement. Since the date for implementation falls after IP completion day, the UK is not obligated to implement the new Directive.

2 SI 2008/1277. The regulations came into effect on 26 May 2008.

3 The significance of maximum harmonisation is clearly demonstrated through Sch.2, which lists 115 amendments to previous legislation required in order to comply with the Directive.

4 See reg.29. See also, Law Commission and the Scottish Law Commission Report "Consumer Redress for Misleading and Aggressive Practices" (Law Com. No.332; Scot. Law Com. No.226) (March 2012).

unfair practices it is necessary to define certain key concepts which run throughout the regulations. Fundamental is the definition of "commercial practice" laid down in reg.2(1) as meaning:

> **"any act, omission, course of conduct, representation or commercial communication (including advertising and marketing) by a trader, which is directly connected with the promotion, sale or supply of a product to or from consumers, whether occurring before, during or after a commercial transaction (if any) in relation to a product".**

When understood in conjunction with the definition of "product"[5] which includes both goods[6] and services and also "immovable property, rights and obligations", this is clearly extensive in scope. The definition extends well beyond simply the supply of goods (or offer thereof) by a trader to a consumer.[7] Indeed, as the definition above makes clear, there need not actually be any commercial transaction, thus the advertising of a product to consumers will constitute a commercial practice under the regulations. Moreover, it is clear that the definition of "commercial practice" does not require repeated patterns of behaviour. In *R v X Ltd* the Court of Appeal observed that the definition was capable of covering both single incidents and repeated patterns of behaviour.[8] Similarly, the Court of Justice of the EU has recently held that an incorrect communication, caused by administrative error, to a single consumer was an unfair commercial practice: *Nemzeti Fogyasztóvédelmi Hatóság v UPC Magyarország Kft.*[9]

The reference to trader and consumer within the definition of "commercial practice" is instructive and ensures that the regulations comply with the Unfair Commercial Practices Directive which employs the term "business-to-consumer commercial practices".[10] The definition of "consumer" under the regulations adopts the standard European meaning, focusing upon the idea of a natural person (i.e. not a company or other corporate body) acting for purposes outside his trade, business or profession.[11] The definition of "trader" also has the meaning expected and includes any person (whether natural or legal) "acting for purposes relating to his trade, business, craft or profession".[12] The regulations do not apply to consumer-to-consumer

5 reg.2(1).

6 Defined in reg.2(1) as including "ships, aircraft, animals, things attached to land and growing crops".

7 Something recently noted by the Court of Appeal in *R. v Scottish and Southern Energy Plc* [2012] EWCA Crim 539 at [34]. Note the modified definition of "product" under the civil redress system under Pt4A. See reg.27C and 27D.

8 [2013] EWCA Crim 818 at [23].

9 [2015] (C-388/13).

10 See art.2(d). In *Warwickshire CC v Halfords Autocentres Ltd* [2018] EWHC 3007 (Admin) the court held that the definition of commercial practice under art.2(d) encompassed 'test-purchases' i.e. where the actual purchaser was not a consumer but instead a trading standards officer.

11 reg.2(1).

12 reg.2(1). In adopting this definition, the difficulties evident through *Havering London Borough v Stevenson* [1970] 3 All E.R. 609 and *Davies v Sumner* [1984] 1 W.L.R. 1301 should be avoided, with the broader definition under *Havering* being preferred under the regulations.

dealings (in the same way, for example, that the old Trade Descriptions Act 1968 did not) nor do the regulations apply to business-to-business dealings.[13] This particular issue will be returned to below in relation to the Business Protection from Misleading Marketing Regulations 2008.[14]

Now that the concepts of "commercial practice", "consumer" and "trader" have been considered, the key issue is that of defining what is meant by unfair.

Unfair Commercial Practices

16–004 Under the Consumer Protection from Unfair Trading Regulations there are five categories of "unfair commercial practice".[15] Accordingly, a commercial practice is unfair if:

- it is contrary to the general prohibition against unfair commercial practices under reg.3(3);
- it is a misleading action under reg.5;
- it is a misleading omission under reg.6;
- it is aggressive under reg.7; or
- it is listed in Sch.1 (in which case it is considered unfair in all circumstances).[16]

Where a business commits an offence under the regulations, any officer (such as a director or manager) of the business can be liable where the offence is either committed due to their consent or connivance or attributable to neglect on their part.[17]

Practices deemed unfair as being contrary to the general prohibition of unfair commercial practices

16–005 The general prohibition under reg.3(3) has two requirements. First, the practice must be contrary to the requirements of professional diligence and secondly it must materially distort (or be likely to materially distort) the economic behaviour of the average consumer with regard the product. Furthermore, where the practice is directed to a specific group of consumers, the test

13 At least not directly, there may well be some advantages flowing from the Directive to legitimate businesses, see further, M. Griffiths, "Unfair commercial practices—a new regime" [2007] *Communications Law* 196 at 196.
14 SI 2008/1276.
15 reg.3(2) referring to regs 3(3) and 3(4).
16 See Annex.1 of the 2005 Directive.
17 reg.15.

is that of whether the practice materially distorts (or is likely to materially distort) the economic behaviour of the average member of that group, rather than consumers generally.[18]

The meaning of "professional diligence" here is crucial, and is defined in Sch.2 in the following terms:[19]

> **"the standard of special skill and care which a trader may reasonably be expected to exercise towards consumers, commensurate with either:**
> **(a) honest market practice in the trader's field of activity; or**
> **(b) the general principle of good faith in the trader's field of activity".**

Compliance with industry standards and market practice may not satisfy this requirement, where for example, the industry standard is not what may be reasonably expected.[20] The material distortion test is defined with reference to the ability of a consumer to make an informed decision. Therefore, where the commercial practice "appreciably" impairs the ability of the average consumer to make an informed decision, and consequently, consumers make or are likely to make transactional decisions that they would not have taken otherwise, this element of the test will be satisfied.

OFT v Ashbourne Management Services Ltd[21] was concerned with various business practices of a gym management company where consumers were required to make membership payments notwithstanding the fact that they had been misled in pre-contract negotiations, for example, by being informed that they could resign their gym membership at any time when in fact there were minimum membership periods, or being informed that certain exercise classes were free when in fact they were not. The court held that demanding payment where liability was disputed was contrary to reg.3(3), reg.5 (misleading actions) and reg.7 (aggressive practices). Furthermore, reporting or threatening to report gym users to credit reference agencies where no debt was owed was similarly contrary to the regulations.

Where a trader knowingly or recklessly engages in a commercial practice which contravenes the requirements of professional diligence and materially distorts (or is likely to do so) the economic behaviour of an average consumer, he is guilty of an offence under reg.8. Regulation 8(2) explains that a trader cannot avoid committing this offence by not considering whether the commercial practice contravenes the requirements of due diligence. This is so even where the failure is an innocent one. Such a trader is deemed to have recklessly engaged

18 See also, art.5(3) which creates a similar provision in respect of vulnerable consumers (those with mental or physical infirmity and age, etc.).

19 See also, *Tiscali UK Ltd v British Telecommunications Plc* [2008] EWHC 3129 (QB).

20 For parallels with the similar attitude towards industry standards in product liability under the Consumer Protection Act 1987, see Ch.9.

21 [2011] EWHC 1237 (Ch).

in the commercial practice and therefore satisfies the test laid down in reg.8(1)(a).[22] Where guilty of an offence under reg.8 the trader is liable, on conviction on indictment, to either a fine or imprisonment for up to two years, or both.[23]

Misleading actions

16–006 Under reg.5 of the Consumer Protection from Unfair Trading Regulations 2008 there are two ways in which a commercial practice may be deemed misleading. First, under reg.5(2) a commercial practice is misleading if it contains false information and is therefore untruthful in relation to one or more of the specified matters (see below) or if the practice (or its overall presentation) deceives, or is likely to deceive, an average consumer in relation to any of the specified matters. In addition, the practice must also cause (or be likely to cause) an average consumer to take a transactional decision he would not have otherwise taken. The second category of misleading commercial practices is laid down in reg.5(3) and relates to marketing practices which either: (i) create confusion with any products of a competitor,[24] or (ii) relate to a breach of any code of conduct which the trader has signed up to, and cause (or be likely to cause) an average consumer to take a transactional decision he would not have otherwise taken.

The matters to be considered in determining whether the practice is misleading under the first subcategory of misleading actions are detailed in reg.3(4) and include:

- the existence or nature of the product;
- the main characteristics of the product;[25]
- the extent of the trader's commitments;[26]
- the price or the manner in which the price is calculated;[27]
- the need for a service, part, replacement or repair;

22 For judicial consideration of recklessness under the old Trade Descriptions Act 1968 s.14 see *MFI Warehouses v Nattrass* [1973] Crim. L.R. 196.
23 reg.13(b). See, *R v Garfoot* [2011] EWCA Crim 2043. See also, reg.13(a) (summary conviction).
24 Including, though obviously not limited to, comparative advertising.
25 e.g. fitness for purpose; availability; quantity, etc. see the list laid down by reg.5(5).
26 Including any statement as to approval of either the trader or product (whether direct or indirect), reg.5(4)(c).
27 Including the existence of any price advantage, reg.5(4)(g).

- the nature, attributes and rights of the trader or his agent;[28] and
- the consumer's rights.[29]

The fundamental test to be applied here is therefore twofold. First, the practice must contain false information or be such that it deceives (or is likely to deceive) the average consumer. Secondly, that falsity or deception must be such that it "causes or is likely to cause him to take a transactional decision that he would not have taken otherwise". The definition of "transactional decision" is laid down in reg.2(1) in the following terms:

> **"any decision taken by a consumer, whether it is to act or to refrain from acting, concerning:**
> **(a) whether, how and on what terms to purchase, make a payment in whole or in part for, retain or dispose of a product; or**
> **(b) whether, how and on what terms to exercise a contractual right in relation to a product".**

The concept of a "transactional decision" is a recurring feature within the regulations and is arguably "not dissimilar to a test considering whether the trader's actions would cause a reasonable person to act in reliance on these to his detriment".[30]

This does represent a departure from the traditional approach of, for example, the Trade Descriptions Act 1968. Under the 1968 Act there was no need to establish any transactional impact whatsoever once it had been found that the trade description was false (or literally true, yet still misleading). It remains to be seen whether this additional requirement under the Directive causes any loss to domestic consumer protection. 16–007

Where a trader engages in a commercial practice which is a misleading omission under reg.5,[31] he is guilty of an offence under reg.9 and is thereby liable, on conviction on indictment, to either a fine or imprisonment for up to two years, or both.[32]

28 Including his identity; qualifications or status, reg.5(4)(j).

29 e.g. as to a repair or replacement, etc. under s.23 of the Consumer Rights Act.

30 C. Twigg-Flesner, "Deep impact? The EC Directive on unfair commercial practices and domestic consumer law" (2005) 121 L.Q.R. 386 at 387. Note the discussion of a transactional decision in *CMA v Care UK Health & Social Holdings Ltd* [2021] EWHC 2088 (Ch) at [142]-[152].

31 Other than the offence under reg.5(3)(b) (failure by the trader to comply with the code to which he has agreed to comply with).

32 reg.13(b). See also, reg.13(a) (summary conviction).

Misleading omissions

16–008 There is a similar provision to that of misleading actions in respect of misleading omissions which cause the consumer to make a transactional decision that he would not have taken otherwise.[33] Under reg.6(1) a commercial practice will constitute a misleading omission where it: (i) causes, or is likely to cause, the consumer to make a transactional decision as considered above, and (ii) the practice either:

- omits material information;
- hides material information;
- provides material information in an unclear, unintelligible, ambiguous or untimely manner; or
- fails to identify its commercial intent (unless this is clear from the context of the practice).

In making this assessment reg.6 provides that the following matters must be taken into account. First, all of the features and circumstances of the commercial practice and secondly, the limitations, if any, of the medium used to communicate the commercial practice (e.g. advertising through text messaging services). Thirdly, where there are limitations imposed by the nature of the communication medium, any measures taken by the trader to make the information available through other means (such as, for example, using the trader's internet site to provide all material information where the text message advertisement does not allow for this information to be included).[34] In *CMA v Care UK Health & Social Holdings Ltd*[35] the court had to consider the regulations in the context of residential care homes. The Competition and Markets Authority sought to establish that Care UK's practice of not mentioning an administration fee on its website or in response to initial telephone enquires instead highlighting indicative weekly fees for accommodation was both a misleading action and a misleading omission under the regulations. The court rejected the CMA's arguments. The practice was not misleading since no "reasonably well-informed, reasonably observant and circumspect average family member . . . could have believed that the indicative fee given represented the weekly price that would be charged to that particular resident, still less that the figure included all elements of the fees charged by Care UK".[36] Further, it was "logical and reasonable" that fees would be discussed only once the consumer had visited the home

33 art.7.

34 Similarly, contrast, for example, a sales brochure with an advertising poster.

35 [2021] EWHC 2088 (Ch).

36 [2021] EWHC 2088 (Ch) at [121].

and expressed a serious interest in becoming a resident.[37] Thus the practice of revealing the administration fee only after the consumer had visited and made an emotional commitment to it, did not constitute an aggressive practice under reg.7. The fee was disclosed sufficiently early particularly given the nature of any transactional decision in the context of choosing a long-term residential care home.

Unsurprisingly, the definition of "material information" has been drafted in broad terms and is heavily context sensitive.[38] The definition has two elements (which will no doubt overlap). The first is any information which the average consumer needs to make an informed transactional decision. In *OFT v Purely Creative Limited* Briggs J stated that the key word was "need". Thus where the omitted information would be merely useful or relevant, it would not be material for the purposes of reg.6.[39] The second element of the definition is any information which must be included within commercial communications as a result of an EU obligation, e.g. the information requirements under the Electronic Commerce Directive 2000[40] as implemented by the Electronic Commerce (EC Directive) Regulations 2002.[41]

Where the commercial practice is an invitation to purchase, reg.6(4) expands the definition of "material information" to include the following:[42]

(a) the main characteristics of the product, to the extent appropriate to the medium by which the invitation to purchase is communicated and the product;

(b) the identity of the trader, such as his trading name, and the identity of any other trader on whose behalf the trader is acting;

(c) the geographical address of the trader and the geographical address of any other trader on whose behalf the trader is acting;

(d) either—

  (i) the price, including any taxes; or

  (ii) where the nature of the product is such that the price cannot reasonably be calculated in advance, the manner in which the price is calculated;

(e) where appropriate, either—

  (i) all additional freight, delivery or postal charges; or

37 [2021] EWHC 2088 (Ch) at [132]–[133].

38 *Secretary of State for Business, Innovation and Skills v PLT Anti-Marketing Ltd* [2015] EWCA Civ 76.

39 [2011] EWHC 106 (Ch) at [74].

40 Directive 2000/31/EC.

41 SI 2002/2013, e.g. reg.6 (general information relating to the service provider).

42 Unless, of course, context of the practice is such that the information would be required in any event for the average consumer to make an informed transactional decision under reg.6(3).

(ii) where such charges cannot reasonably be calculated in advance, the fact that such charges may be payable;

(f) the following matters where they depart from the requirements of professional diligence—

(i) arrangements for payment;

(ii) arrangements for delivery;

(iii) arrangements for performance;

(iv) complaint handling policy; and

(g) for products and transactions involving a right of withdrawal or cancellation, the existence of such a right.

Where a trader engages in a commercial practice which is a misleading omission under reg.6, he is guilty of an offence under reg.10 and is thereby liable, on conviction on indictment, to either a fine or imprisonment for up to two years, or both.[43]

Aggressive practices

16–009 An aggressive commercial practice is defined by reg.7(1) as any commercial practice that:

(i) significantly impairs or is likely to significantly impairs the average consumer's freedom of choice or conduct in relation to a product through either harassment, coercion[44] or undue influence[45]; and

(ii) causes, or is likely to cause, the consumer to make a transactional decision he would not have taken otherwise.

Under reg.7(2), harassment, coercion and undue influence is to be assessed in light of various factors including:

- its timing, location or persistence;
- threatening or abusive language or behaviour;

43 reg.13(b). See also, reg.13(a) (summary conviction).

44 Including the use of physical force, reg.7(3)(a).

45 See reg.7(3)(b).

- exploitation by the trader of any specific misfortune thereby impairing the consumer's judgment and influencing the consumer's decision regarding the product;
- onerous or disproportionate non-contractual barrier in relation to the consumer's rights under the contract; and
- the threat of legal action where none can legally be taken.

Where a trader engages in an aggressive commercial practice under reg.7, he is guilty of an offence under reg.11 and is thereby liable, on conviction on indictment, to either a fine or imprisonment for up to two years, or both.[46]

Unfair in all circumstances

Schedule 1 of the Consumer Protection from Unfair Trading Regulations 2008 implements the "blacklist" prescribed by art.5(5) and Annex 1 of the Directive. Where a practice is included on the list (which can only be amended through revision of the Directive itself) it will be regarded as unfair in all circumstances. The blacklist is as follows:[47] 16-010

> **"1. Claiming to be a signatory to a code of conduct when the trader is not.**
> **2. Displaying a trust mark, quality mark or equivalent without having obtained the necessary authorisation.**
> **3. Claiming that a code of conduct has an endorsement from a public or other body which it does not have.**
> **4. Claiming that a trader (including his commercial practices) or a product has been approved, endorsed or authorised by a public or private body when he/it has not or making such a claim without complying with the terms of the approval, endorsement or authorisation.**

46 reg.13(b). See also, reg.13(a) (summary conviction).

47 The Department of Business, Energy & Industrial Strategy has recently consulted on wide-ranging reforms to consumer protection (and competition) law and intends to amend the "blacklist" so as to capture the recent phenomenon of "fake reviews". See, *Reforming Competition and Consumer Policy: Government Response to Consultation* (April 2022, CP 656) at para.2.27. Similarly, at the EU level, the Enforcement and Modernisation Directive (Directive 2019/2161/EU) has revised the Unfair Commercial Practices Directive with Member States required to apply the new provisions from 28 May 2022. In particular, the revised Directive extends the definition of "product" to capture digital services and adds four new entries to the blacklist of prohibited practices including fake reviews and failing to disclose "paid-for" search results. It may well be that the outcomes of the UK consultation, above, serves to make similar amendments to the 2008 Regulations notwithstanding the fact that it is not required to implement the updated Directive following the UK's withdrawal from the EU.

5. Making an invitation to purchase products at a specified price without disclosing the existence of any reasonable grounds the trader may have for believing that he will not be able to offer for supply or to procure another trader to supply, those products or equivalent products at that price for a period that is, and in quantities that are, reasonable having regard to the product, the scale of advertising of the product and the price offered (bait advertising).
6. Making an invitation to purchase products at a specified price and then:
   (a) refusing to show the advertised item to consumers; or
   (b) refusing to take orders for it or deliver it within a reasonable time; or
   (c) demonstrating a defective sample of it, with the intention of promoting a different product (bait and switch)
7. Falsely stating that a product will only be available for a very limited time, or that it will only be available on particular terms for a very limited time, in order to elicit an immediate decision and deprive consumers of sufficient opportunity or time to make an informed choice.
8. Undertaking to provide after-sales service to consumers with whom the trader has communicated prior to a transaction in a language which is not English (in the case of a trader located in the United Kingdom) or not an official language of the EEA State where the trader is located and then making such service available only in another language without clearly disclosing this to the consumer before the consumer is committed to the transaction.
9. Stating or otherwise creating the impression that a product can legally be sold when it cannot.
10. Presenting rights given to consumers in law as a distinctive feature of the trader's offer.
11. Using editorial content in the media to promote a product where a trader has paid for the promotion without making that clear in the content or by images or sounds clearly identifiable by the consumer (advertorial).
12. Making a materially inaccurate claim concerning the nature and extent of the risk to the personal security of the consumer or his family if the consumer does not purchase the product.
13. Promoting a product similar to a product made by a particular manufacturer in such a manner as deliberately to mislead the consumer into believing that the product is made by that same manufacturer when it is not.

14. Establishing, operating or promoting a pyramid promotional scheme where a consumer gives consideration for the opportunity to receive compensation that is derived primarily from the introduction of other consumers into the scheme rather than from the sale or consumption of products.
15. Claiming that the trader is about to cease trading or move premises when he is not.
16. Claiming that products are able to facilitate winning in games of chance.
17. Falsely claiming that a product is able to cure illnesses, dysfunction or malformations.
18. Passing on materially inaccurate information on market conditions or on the possibility of finding the product with the intention of inducing the consumer to acquire the product at conditions less favourable than normal market conditions.
19. Claiming in a commercial practice to offer a competition or prize promotion without awarding the prizes described or a reasonable equivalent.
20. Describing a product as 'gratis', 'free', 'without charge' or similar if the consumer has to pay anything other than the unavoidable cost of responding to the commercial practice and collecting or paying for delivery of the item.
21. Including in marketing material an invoice or similar document seeking payment which gives the consumer the impression that he has already ordered the marketed product when he has not.
22. Falsely claiming or creating the impression that the trader is not acting for purposes relating to his trade, business, craft or profession, or falsely representing oneself as a consumer.
23. Creating the false impression that after-sales service in relation to a product is available in the UK or in an EEA State other than the one in which the product is sold.
24. Creating the impression that the consumer cannot leave the premises until a contract is formed.
25. Conducting personal visits to the consumer's home ignoring the consumer's request to leave or not to return except in circumstances and to the extent justified, under national law, to enforce a contractual obligation.
26. Making persistent and unwanted solicitations by telephone, fax, e-mail or other remote media except in circumstances and to the extent justified under national law to enforce a contractual obligation.

27. **Requiring a consumer who wishes to claim on an insurance policy to produce documents which could not reasonably be considered relevant as to whether the claim was valid, or failing systematically to respond to pertinent correspondence, in order to dissuade a consumer from exercising his contractual rights.**
28. **Including in an advertisement a direct exhortation to children to buy advertised products or persuade their parents or other adults to buy advertised products for them.**
29. **Demanding immediate or deferred payment for or the return or safekeeping of products supplied by the trader, but not solicited by the consumer.**
30. **Explicitly informing a consumer that if he does not buy the product or service, the trader's job or livelihood will be in jeopardy.**
31. **Creating the false impression that the consumer has already won, will win, or will on doing a particular act win, a prize or other equivalent benefit, when in fact either:—there is no prize or other equivalent benefit, or—taking any action in relation to claiming the prize or other equivalent benefit is subject to the consumer paying money or incurring a cost."**

The operation of para.31 has been considered by the courts in some detail. In *OFT v Purely Creative Ltd*[48] Briggs J had to consider various promotional schemes whereby consumers were invited, through scratch-cards, individually addressed letters and other similar means, to claim one of a number of various "prizes", the value of which varied greatly, however, in 99 per cent of cases, the lowest value prize was awarded. The value of this prize was generally equal to or indeed less than, the costs incurred by the consumer in claiming the prize. The court held that the promotions were in breach of the regulations and stated that the crucial requirement under para.31 was that a false impression was created. This was a matter to be determined in light of the whole communication, including the words used and the layout of the promotion. If, as the court held in Purely Creative, the substance of the transaction was one of the consumer purchasing the goods rather than winning them, there will be a breach of para.31 of the blacklist. The decision was appealed to the Court of Appeal which stayed both the appeal and the OFT's cross-appeal in order to refer the matter to the European Court of Justice.[49]

The European Court of Justice stated that "the concept of a true 'prize' should be preserved, by interpreting paragraph 31. . .as meaning that a prize in respect of which the consumer is obliged to make a payment of whatever kind cannot be regarded as a 'prize'." Thus

48 [2011] EWHC 106 (Ch).

49 [2011] EWCA Civ 920.

even where the costs associated with claiming the prize are minimal, or indeed trivial, such as the cost of a postage stamp to return a claim form, there will be a breach of para.31. The Court also rejected the argument that there should be no breach where the trader provided a range of options to claim the prize, one of which did not incur any charges whatsoever.

Where a trader engages in an activity listed within Sch.1[50] he is guilty of an offence under reg.12 and is thereby liable, on conviction on indictment, to either a fine or imprisonment for up to two years, or both.[51]

Defences

If the defendant can establish any of the defences under regs 17 and 18 he has a good defence to the offences laid down in regs 9–12. Under reg.17 the trader must prove that: 16-011

1. the commission of the offence was due to:
   - a mistake;
   - reliance on information supplied to him by another person;
   - the act or default of another person;[52]
   - an accident;
   - another cause beyond his control; and
2. that he took all reasonable precautions and exercised all due diligence to avoid the commission of the offence.

This is a recasting of the old defences laid down in s.24(1) of the Trade Descriptions Act 1968.[53] The old case law under s.24 is therefore instructive in considering the nature of the defences laid down by reg.17 and what follows is an overview of such case law.

In *Simmons v Potter*[54] the defendants, second-hand car dealers, succeeded in proving that the commission of the offence was due to "reliance upon information supplied to him" but failed to prove that they themselves had taken "all reasonable precautions", etc. They had sold a car with the wrong mileage recorded on the odometer. Before doing this they had first made enquiries about the car's history from its previous owner and learnt nothing suggesting that the odometer reading was false. It was held that the defendants had no defence under s.24 because they had, in failing to display a disclaimer, failed to take all reasonable precautions.

50 With the exception of Sch.1 paras 11 and 28.
51 reg.13(b). See also, reg.13(a) (summary conviction).
52 See also, reg.16.
53 See also the Consumer Protection Act 1987 s.39.
54 [1975] R.T.R. 347.

They had failed to adopt an obvious and easy method of avoiding commission of the offence. If they had displayed a disclaimer (sufficiently bold, precise and compelling) they would have avoided commission of the offence even without having to rely upon s.24.[55] There is, however, no absolute rule that a failure to display an effective disclaimer will rule out the defences in s.24. There can be exceptional cases where, despite a failure to display an effective disclaimer, the defendant might be held to have taken all reasonable precautions. Thus in *Ealing LBC v Taylor*[56] the Divisional Court declined to overturn the magistrates' finding that the defendant car dealer had taken all reasonable precautions (in relation to the mileage reading) in checking the consistency of the condition of the car with the recorded mileage and in obtaining from the person who sold him the car a signed warranty guaranteeing the accuracy of the mileage reading.

In *Hurley v Martinez*[57] the defendant had supplied bottles of German wine on which the labels indicated the alcoholic strength as 8 per cent instead of 7.2 per cent, the bottles having come to him from Germany thus labelled. It was held that the defendant could rely upon the defence in s.24, it not being necessary for him to have indulged in sample testing the accuracy of the statement on the labels.[58]

16–012 When the defence relied upon is "act of default of another person" or "reliance on information supplied by another person" the defendant will have a good defence only if he has also made available to the prosecution such information as he has identifying that other person.[59] This is to enable the prosecution to find and charge the other person. The other person will often be the employee of the defendant, as he was in *Tesco Supermarkets Ltd v Nattrass*.[60] There, the defendant company, which operated a large number of supermarkets, had instituted in their stores an effective system to prevent the commission of an offence. One of their employees, a store manager, failed to properly carry out the system with the result that Radiant washing powder was advertised in the window at 2s. 11d. when in fact the only packets available in the shop were 3s. 11d. The House of Lords held that the defendant company was not guilty; the commission of the offence was due to the default of "another person" (the store manager) and the defendant company had, by instituting an effective system, taken all reasonable precautions, etc. in the circumstances.

Thus where, for example, the defendant owns a chain of stores he can rely upon the acts of a store manager provided that the defendant can show that he (the defendant) took all reasonable precautions to avoid the commission of the offence. These precautions will usually consist of instructions sent out to managers. The defendant must show that he sent out

55 See *Norman v Bennett* [1974] 1 W.L.R. 1229.

56 [1995] Crim. L.R. 166.

57 [1991] C.C.L.R. 1.

58 For a comparison with the defence of due diligence when used by someone charged with a consumer safety offence, see para.9-023, above.

59 See reg.17(2).

60 [1973] Crim. L.R. 196.

adequate instructions. He will have no defence if the instructions were such that even if they were followed the offence was still likely to be committed.[61]

Regulation 18 allows a defence where an offence under regs 9–12 has been committed by the (innocent) publication of an advertisement. The defendant will have a good defence where he can prove that:

(a) he is a person whose business it is to publish (or to arrange for the publication of advertisements);

(b) he received the advertisement for publication in the ordinary course of business; and

(c) he did not know, and had no reason to suspect, that its publication would amount to an offence.

Like that in reg.17, this is a recasting of the "innocent publication" defence found in previous consumer protection measures, including s.25 of the Trade Descriptions Act 1968 and s.24 of the Consumer Protection Act 1987. So, for example, a newspaper which innocently publishes an advertisement which contravenes one or more of the offences in regs 9–12 will have a good defence provided the advertisement was received in the ordinary course of business and they did not know and had no reason to, suspect that its publication constituted an offence.

Private Redress

As noted above, as originally enacted, the Consumer Protection from Unfair Trading Regulations 2008 did not affect the validity of any agreement made between a consumer and a trader in breach of the regulations. Thus, in such a position, in order to seek redress, the consumer was forced to raise an action for a different claim, such as misrepresentation.[62] Accordingly, the Law Commissions recommended that a limited private right to redress should be introduced and the 2008 Regulations have been amended to include private rights of redress for consumers who have suffered a loss or detriment through unfair commercial practices. This was achieved through the insertion of Pt 4A into the 2008 Regulations. Accordingly, a right to private redress will be available if the following conditions are met:[63] 16-013

61 See *Haringey London Borough v Piro Shoes Ltd* [1976] Crim. L.R. 462 (instruction that goods were not to leave the shop without the label having first been removed was insufficient).

62 See Ch.6, above. Note that following the introduction of Pt 4A, where a consumer has a right to redress under the 2008 Regulations they are precluded from claiming damages under the Misrepresentation Act 1967, see. s.2(4).

63 Note, however, the limitations regarding immoveable property and financial services, see reg.27C and reg.27D.

The first condition relates to the type of agreement entered into by the consumer. It must be one of the following:[64]

- A "business to consumer contract"—the consumer enters into a contract with a trader for the sale or supply of a product by the trader.

- A "consumer to business contract"—the consumer enters into a contract with a trader for the sale of goods to the trader.

- A "consumer payment"—the consumer makes a payment to a trader for the supply of a product.

This is obviously a much more restrictive approach then under the regulations generally where as we have seen, in broad terms, the focus is placed on practices which materially distort, or are likely to materially distort, the economic behaviour of a consumer. In contrast, in order for a consumer to have a private right to redress under Pt 4A, a contract or payment must have been made. The second condition is that either the trader has engaged in a "prohibited practice" or a producer has engaged in a "prohibited practice" and the trader could reasonably be expected to be aware of the practice at the time the contract was made.[65] This serves to limit the scope of the rights of private redress, since not all breaches of the regulations or unfair commercial practices are deemed to constitute a "prohibited practice". Under reg.27B a "prohibited practice" is defined as either a misleading action (under reg.5) or an aggressive practice (under reg.7).[66] Thus, for example, a breach of the general prohibition under reg.3 will not afford the consumer a right of redress nor will a misleading omission under reg.6. Where a trader engages in a practice which is prohibited as being in all circumstances unfair, the consumer will have a private right to redress only where the practice also constitutes a misleading action or aggressive practice under reg.5 or reg.7. This means that, for example, the practice must practice cause, or be likely to cause, the average consumer to take a transactional decision he would not have otherwise taken.

The third condition is that the prohibited practice is a significant factor in the consumer's decision to enter into the contract or make the payment.[67] Thus in order to claim private redress, the consumer must:[68]

> **"...provide some evidence that they saw or heard the misleading statement, or experienced the aggressive practice before making the**

64 reg.27A(2).

65 reg.27A(4).

66 Note the modified definition of "transactional decision" under Pt 4A of the regulations, see reg.27B(2).

67 reg.27A(6).

68 Law Commission and the Scottish Law Commission Report "Consumer Redress for Misleading and Aggressive Practices" (Law Com. No.332; Scot. Law Com. No.226) (March 2012), para.7.115.

decision to buy or pay and that they were influenced by it. Thereafter, it will normally be enough if the misleading or aggressive practice is sufficiently serious to cause a reasonably well informed, observant and circumspect consumer to enter into the contract or make a payment."

Under the regulations there are three potential forms of redress open to consumers. First, there is what is labelled the "right to unwind" which restores the consumer to the position he was in before he entered into the contract (or made the payment). Under reg.27E, the consumer has the right to bring the contract to an end within a 90-day period.[69] Where the consumer sold goods to the trader or where the consumer made a payment to the trader, this time limit does not apply and the consumer can unwind the contract at any time. However, in order to exercise the right to unwind it must be possible to return the parties to their original position. Thus the product must be capable of being rejected which means that the goods or digital product has not been fully consumed, or that the service has not been fully performed.[70] Where a consumer has sold goods to a trader as a result of a prohibited practice, the trader must return the goods in exchange for the price paid or, if that is not possible, a monetary equivalent based on the market value of the goods.[71] 16-014

Where the consumer has not claimed the right to unwind the contract, for example, where the 90-day period has expired or the goods have been fully consumed, the consumer can instead look to claim the right to a discount on any sums paid (or which are payable).[72] Where the goods or services cost less than £5000, the regulations create four fixed percentage discounts based on the seriousness of the prohibited practice:[73]

(a) if the prohibited practice is more than minor, it is 25 per cent,

(b) if the prohibited practice is significant, it is 50 per cent,

(c) if the prohibited practice is serious, it is 75 per cent, and

(d) if the prohibited practice is very serious, it is 100 per cent.

69 This period commences on the day the contract is made, or, if later, the happening of another specific event such as delivery of the goods. See reg.27E(4). Note that in general, there is no allowance made for any use of the goods within the 90-day period. However, this is modified where the contract is one of continuous supply, e.g. utility contracts for the supply of gas or electricity. See reg.27F.

70 reg.27E(8).

71 reg.27G(5).

72 reg.27I.

73 reg.27I(4). Where the goods or services cost more than £5000 and there is evidence as to the market value of the goods or service at the time of contract, the reduction is instead calculated by reference to that market value as against the price paid. See reg.27I(6) and (7).

Under reg.27I(5) the seriousness of the prohibited practice, i.e. the misleading action or aggressive practice, is determined by consideration of the behaviour of the person who engaged in the practice, the impact of the practice on the consumer and the time that has elapsed since the prohibited practice took place.

The final private right to redress under the 2008 Regulations is the right to damages. The consumer has the right to damages where he:[74]

(a) has incurred financial loss which the consumer would not have incurred if the prohibited practice in question had not taken place, or

(b) has suffered alarm, distress or physical inconvenience or discomfort which the consumer would not have suffered if the prohibited practice in question had not taken place.

There is no right to damages where the losses incurred are not reasonably foreseeable, nor where the trader was not at fault for the prohibited practice. In order to avoid liability for damages under the regulations, the trader must prove that he took all reasonable precautions and exercised all due diligence to avoid the occurrence of the prohibited practice and that the occurrence of the prohibited practice was due to a mistake, an accident or some other cause beyond the trader's control.[75]

Enforcement

16-015 The duty to enforce the Consumer Protection from Unfair Trading Regulations 2008 falls on every local weights and measures authority (the CMA also has the power to enforce in appropriate cases).[76] Enforcers are aided by various powers prescribed in the (now unified) scheme of investigatory powers created by the Consumer Rights Act 2015. Thus an enforcer has powers to, amongst other things, make test purchases, inspect products and entry premises without a warrant.[77] In addition, the Regulations have been added to the list of "Schedule 13 infringements"[78] under the Enterprise Act 2002 and therefore the framework of Pt 8 powers (in that Act) now extends to breaches of the Directive. This framework is explained at para.16-024, below.

74 reg.27J(1).

75 reg.27J(5).

76 reg.19.

77 See Sch.5 to the 2015 Act.

78 Formerly "Community infringements", the change in terminology being necessitated by the UK's withdrawal from the EU: Consumer Protection (Enforcement) (Amendment etc.) (EU Exit) Regulations 2019 (SI 2019/203).

Impact on Previous Consumer Protection Measures

The implementation of the Unfair Commercial Practices Directive 2005 into domestic law through the regulations considered above has necessitated considerable amendments to a wide range of legislation previously in force. This section will outline some of these changes and summarise the law replaced by the Consumer Protection from Unfair Trading Regulations 2008.[79] It will also introduce a second set of regulations, the Business Protection from Misleading Marketing Regulations 2008 which have come into force in parallel with the Consumer Protection from Unfair Trading Regulations 2008. 16-016

Trade Descriptions Act 1968

This Act created criminal offences to protect the consumer, although, similarly to the Consumer Protection from Unfair Trading Regulations 2008 as originally enacted, it in no way enhanced his contractual rights.[80] The Act had three main sets of provisions. First, the Department of Trade and Industry was empowered to make certain orders. These could specify and require information to be included in advertisements or descriptions of goods and they could specify and require instructions to be supplied with the goods. Secondly, the Act laid down offences intended to prevent anyone wrongly claiming to have supplied goods to the Queen (or to anyone else) or wrongly claiming royal approval, e.g. by displaying an emblem resembling that of the Queen's Award to Industry. Thirdly, and most significantly, the Act created two offences relating to misdescriptions of goods and misleading statements about services. The majority of the Trade Descriptions Act 1968, including the various criminal offences dealing with misdescriptions of goods and services, has been repealed by the Consumer Protection from Unfair Trading Regulations 2008.[81] 16-017

Part III of the Consumer Protection Act 1987

Part III of the Consumer Protection Act 1987 replaced earlier provisions dealing with misleading price indications. These were the Trade Descriptions Act 1968 s.11 and the Price Marking (Bargain Offers) Order 1979. These provisions had loopholes and proved technical and obscure with the result that enforcement was difficult. Part III of the 1987 Act adopted a different approach to the problem of defining the mischief which it sought to stamp out, i.e. the giving of misleading price information. It contained a statement of the offence[82] and a generally worded definition of "misleading"[83] and provided for a code of practice to be approved by 16-018

79 For a more detailed account of these historical laws, the reader may be directed to the 6th edn of this book.
80 As the Act made clear through s.35.
81 Sch.2 para.8.
82 s.20.
83 s.21.

the Secretary of State which gives practical guidance.[84] Part III has been repealed by the Consumer Protection from Unfair Trading Regulations 2008.[85]

Control of Misleading Advertisements Regulations 1988

16–019 These regulations implemented the Misleading Advertisements Directive.[86] They required the Office of Fair Trading (or OFCOM where the advertisement was broadcast) to consider complaints (other than vexatious or frivolous ones) about misleading advertisements.[87] The OFT could bring proceedings for a High Court injunction to stop the publication of a misleading advertisement.[88] The OFT, before considering a complaint, could require the complainant to satisfy him that alternative methods of dealing with the matter have been tried and found inadequate. Thus where the advertisement constituted a criminal offence, it was pointless to complain to the OFT. It was more sensible to complain to the local trading standards department. Even where the advertisement did not amount to an offence, the OFT could consider that an approach to the Advertising Standards Authority (a non-statutory body with no legal powers) would be an adequate way of dealing with the complaint. The regulations were clearly useful as a last resort, where the advertisement was not caught by any other legal provision and there was no other effective way of dealing with it, e.g. an advertisement falsely stating "closing down sale".[89] Before the OFT could take action under the regulations, the advertisement had to be such that it both deceived or was likely to deceive and was likely to affect the economic behaviour of those whom it reached or to injure a competitor of the trader (usually the advertiser) whose interests the advertisement was promoting.

The Control of Misleading Advertisements Regulations 1988 have been revoked and replaced by the Consumer Protection from Unfair Trading Regulations 2008.[90]

Business Protection from Misleading Marketing Regulations 2008

16–020 The Unfair Commercial Practices Directive was directed solely at protecting consumers from unfair business practices. In implementing the Directive the approach adopted was, as set out above, to repeal, either in whole or in part, various pieces of legislation which had performed

84 s.25.
85 Sch.2 para.34.
86 84/450/EEC replaced by Directive 2006/114/EC.
87 See reg.4. Regulation 4A details various conditions which must be satisfied in respect of comparative advertisements.
88 See regs 5 and 6. Where the court grants an injunction (other than an interlocutory injunction) it must be satisfied that the advertisement is either misleading or a type of prohibited comparative advertising under reg.4A.
89 See para.16-010, above.
90 Sch.2 para.81.

similar roles in domestic law. The difficulty was that many of those pieces of legislation were not aimed specifically at consumers. For example, the offences within the Trade Descriptions Act 1968 were general provisions of the criminal law. In repealing the offences in ss.1 and 14 of the 1968 Act the Consumer Protection from Unfair Trading Regulations 2008 risked creating a distinct gap. Where there had traditionally been protection in a business context there would, if the problem was left unaddressed, be no protection following the implementation of the Directive. Moreover, the repeal of the Control of Misleading Advertising Regulations 1988 by the Consumer Protection from Unfair Trading Regulations 2008 also required action in order to implement the EU Directive on misleading and comparative advertising.[91] These issues led to the introduction of a second set of regulations, the Business Protection from Misleading Marketing Regulations 2008.[92]

The key feature of these regulations is the prohibition on advertising which misleads traders.[93] The concept of advertising which is misleading is set out in reg.3(2) and is explained as requiring one of the following two elements. It is misleading if it:

> **"(a) in any way, including its presentation, deceives or is likely to deceive the traders to whom it is addressed or whom it reaches; and by reason of its deceptive nature, is likely to affect their economic behaviour; or**
>
> **(b) for those reasons, injures or is likely to injure a competitor."**

In assessing whether an advertisement is misleading, reg.3 requires account to be taken of all its features, although the following are of particular relevance:

(i) the characteristics of the product;

(ii) the price or manner in which the price is calculated;

(iii) the conditions on which the product is supplied or provided; and

(iv) the nature, attributes and rights of the advertiser.

The first feature, that of the characteristics of the product, includes availability; composition; method, place and date of manufacture; fitness for purpose; and quantity.[94] *Croydon LBC v Hogarth*[95] involved an advertising campaign which sent "invoices" marked as "paid" to

91 Directive 2006/114/EC which replaced Directive 84/450/EEC. See the discussion of the Control of Misleading Advertising Regulations 1988 at para.16-019, above.

92 SI 2008/1276. The Regulations came into effect on 26 May 2008.

93 reg.3(1).

94 See reg.3(4). These characteristics are broadly similar to the list previously to be found in s.2 of the Trade Descriptions Act 1968.

95 [2011] EWHC 1126 (QB).

businesses when in fact the "invoice" was actually a contract. The advertising campaign was held to be misleading under reg.3 since it led traders to believe that they already had a contract with the defendant business.

Where a trader engages in advertising which is contrary to reg.3, he is guilty of an offence as he is liable to either a fine on summary conviction or to a fine and/or imprisonment for up to two years on indictment.[96]

16-021 The regulations also contain a framework for the use of comparative advertising under reg.4. Broadly speaking, comparative advertising will be permitted under the new regulations only where certain conditions are satisfied. Those conditions are that:

(i) it is not misleading under reg.3;

(ii) it is not a misleading action under reg.5 of the Consumer Protection from Unfair Trading Regulations 2008 or a misleading omission under reg.6 of those regulations[97];

(iii) it compares products meeting the same needs or intended for the same purpose;

(iv) it objectively compares one or more material, relevant, verifiable and representative features of those products, which may include price;

(v) it does not create confusion among traders;

(vi) it does not discredit or denigrate the trade marks, trade names, other distinguishing marks, products, activities, or circumstances of a competitor;

(vii) for products with designation of origin, it relates in each case to products with the same designation;

(viii) it does not take unfair advantage of the reputation of a trade mark, trade name or other distinguishing marks of a competitor or of the designation of origin of competing products; and

(ix) it does not present products as imitations or replicas of products bearing a protected trade mark or trade name.

As in the equivalent pieces of legislation which preceded the regulations the two core defences are replicated, namely: due diligence and innocent publication. These have already been considered.[98]

96 See regs 6 and 7.
97 See the discussion at paras 16-006–16-008, above.
98 See para.16-011, above.

Like the Consumer Protection from Unfair Trading Regulations 2008, the Business Protection from Misleading Marketing Regulations 2008 are to be enforced by all local weights and measures authorities and, in appropriate cases, by the CMA.[99] Moreover, enforcers benefit from the powers of investigation laid down by the Consumer Rights Act 2015. Thus, for example, an enforcer has the power to make test purchases, etc. in order to ascertain whether the regulations are being breached.[100]

Fair Trading Act 1973 and the Enterprise Act 2002

The Fair Trading Act created the office of Director General of Fair Trading, giving that official certain functions in relation to consumer affairs. This was amended by the Enterprise Act which abolished the office of Director General and transferred his powers to the Office of Fair Trading.[101] The principal functions of the OFT were laid down by the Enterprise Act 2002 and included: 16-022

- The duty to produce an annual plan and report (s.4).[102]
- The acquisition of information regarding commercial activity impacting upon consumers (ss.5 and 6).[103]
- The duty to provide information and advice to Ministers (s.7).[104]
- The duty to promote good practice (s.8).[105]

---

99 reg.13.

100 See the Consumer Rights Act 2015 Sch.5 Pt.4 para.21.

101 See ss.2 and 273.

102 The obligation under s.4 of the Enterprise Act 2002 replaces the previous duty to produce annual reports under legislation where so required under s.125 Fair Trading Act 1973.

103 The OFT is also required to provide "information or advice in respect of matters relating to any of its functions to the public" under s.6(1)(b).

104 This replaces the old duty under the Fair Trading Act 1973 to provide recommendations for action under s.2 to the Secretary of State.

105 s.8 is a considerable extension of role in this regard from the previous general obligation to encourage trade associations to develop codes of practice safeguarding and promoting the interests of consumers under s.124(3) of the Fair Trading Act 1973.

The OFT has itself been abolished by the Enterprise and Regulatory Reform Act 2013 which transferred various functions of the OFT to the (newly created) Competition and Markets Authority with effect from 1 April 2014.[106] The consumer advice and representation functions of the OFT have been transferred to the Citizens Advice service and Trading Standards.[107] The aim of these reforms is to create a more efficient and cost-effective competition regime and consumer protection framework with Trading Standards acting as lead enforcer for much of the consumer law landscape. However, concerns have been raised as to the ability of, for example, Citizens Advice, to adequately take on the functions hitherto undertaken by the OFT.[108] Whether the functions of the OFT can be transferred without any loss in the level of consumer protection remains to be seen and much will depend on how the acquired knowledge of the OFT in what can be very complex investigations is retained by any new organisations.[109]

Neither the Fair Trading Act nor the Enterprise Act were designed to enhance consumers' individual rights: Pt II of the Fair Trading Act 1973 established a mechanism for creating new criminal offences to combat, as they arise, trading malpractices adverse to consumers. Part III gives the Director General powers of enforcement against traders guilty of malpractices. In addition the opportunity was taken to deal with pyramid selling, a particular malpractice which had become a nuisance at the time the Act was being passed. This will now be considered first, before we turn to Pts II and III.

In their heyday, before 1973, pyramid selling schemes worked something like this. The typical scheme was ostensibly concerned with marketing goods or services through a chain of private distributors. An individual was persuaded to join the scheme as a "distributor" (or "agent", "representative" or whatever). He may have been persuaded to pay a large sum of money (perhaps hundreds or thousands of pounds) for the privilege of joining. Whether he could recover this sum would depend upon whether he could introduce further people into the scheme, for he would receive a payment for each new participant whom he introduced. Sometimes the fee he paid for joining was expressed to be payment for a consignment of the goods which the scheme was supposed to be marketing. However, he could still find it difficult to recoup his joining fee if he could not find new members for the scheme, because he would find it difficult to sell the goods. It was not always easy for a private householder to find buyers for a large number of packets of soap!

Sections 118–123 deal with pyramid selling.[110] Section 120(3) makes it an offence for a promoter or participant to receive any payment (or the benefit of any payments) which some other participant is induced to make by reason that the prospect is held out to him of receiving

---

106 See the Enterprise and Regulatory Reform Act 2013 s.26.

107 For example, the Consumer Direct advice service is now maintained by Citizens Advice as the Citizens Advice consumer helpline. See the Enterprise Act 2002 s.8A (the CMA is not able to support such a scheme).

108 See, for example, the OFT's response to the consultation available from *https://webarchive.nationalarchives.gov.uk/ukgwa/20140402142426/http://www.oft.gov.uk/shared_oft/consultations/consumer-landscape/Consumer_Landscape.pdf* [Accessed 2 April 2022].

109 Together with the extent of the resources these organisations are awarded in order to fulfil their new responsibilities.

110 Pt VI of the Act which deals with pyramid selling survived the repeals made by the Enterprise Act 2002.

payments or other benefits for introducing other persons into the scheme. Further, s.119 empowers the Secretary of State to make regulations for the purpose of preventing participants being unfairly treated. These powers have been used thereby effectively banning pyramid selling as it was previously practised.[111]

Creation of Criminal Offences—an Outdated Mechanism

The aim of Pt II of the Fair Trading Act was to discover, and by ministerial order prevent, consumer trade practices which adversely affected the economic interests of consumers. It established a legislative mechanism for the creation of criminal offences to combat malpractices. The intention was to have a fast legislative response to malpractices as and when they arose in the market place, in the event the legislative mechanism proved cumbersome and slow. This included a requirement for a committee report before any regulations could be made. In fact only three Orders were ever made under this mechanism, which soon fell into disuse until it was eventually repealed by s.10 of the Enterprise Act 2002. None of these Orders are of any effect any longer. The only legal consequence of infringing one of the Orders was that a criminal offence was committed contrary to s.23 of the Fair Trading Act 1973—and that section was repealed by the Consumer Protection from Unfair Trading Regulations 2008. The fact is that the mechanism in Pt II of the Fair Trading Act had become outmoded in the modern legislative climate. Now we have the Consumer Protection from Unfair Trading Practices Regulations 2008 which are a widely drafted set of Regulations controlling unfair trading practices. There is no longer any need for additional legislation targeted at specific narrowly defined malpractices, since such practices will be banned by the 2008 Regulations anyway. This is surely true, for example, of the following malpractices which were previously banned under Orders made under Pt II of the Fair Trading Act 1973: 16-023

(i) The misleading use of void or unenforceable exemption clauses (e.g. signs displayed in shops stating that goods will in no circumstances be returnable), leading to the impression that defective goods can not be rejected.[112]

(ii) The advertising of goods for sale by a trader in circumstances where the reader would not realise that the advertisement was placed by a trader and not by a private seller.[113]

111 See the Trading Schemes Regulations 1997 (SI 1997/30).

112 Previously banned by the Consumer Transactions (Restrictions on Statements) Order 1976.

113 Previously banned by the Business Advertisements (Disclosure) Order 1977 (SI 1977/1918).

Power to Enforce the General Law on Protection of Consumers

16-024 Part III of the old Act (ss.34–43) gave the Director power to act against someone who in the course of business persistently breaks the law (civil or criminal) in a way detrimental to the interests of consumers.[114] These provisions, unlike those just outlined, are concerned not only with the economic interests of consumers but also their "interests in respect of health, safety or other matters".[115] Sections 34 to 43 were repealed by the Enterprise Act and a new system introduced which operates not through "consumer detriment" but through listed infringements. These infringements are listed in two parts: First, domestic infringements under s.211 and secondly, Schedule 13 infringements under s.212.[116] Whether the infringement is classified as "domestic" or "Schedule 13" the requirements of s.210 must be satisfied. Namely:

1. goods or services are (or are sought to be) supplied to the individual (whether by way of sale or otherwise) in the course of a business; and
2. the individual receives or seeks to receive the goods or services otherwise than in the course of a business.

The ambit of Pt 8 is therefore very broadly defined. In principle there must be an infringement which harms the collective interests of consumers. Under the Enterprise Act (Pt 8 Domestic Infringements) Order 2003[117] the following Acts, amongst a very long list, were all specified as "domestic infringements":

- Administration of Justice Act 1970.
- Consumer Credit Act 1974.
- Misrepresentation Act 1967.
- Sale of Goods Act 1979.

Unsurprisingly Pts 1 and 2 of the Consumer Rights Act 2015 are also specified as "domestic infringements".[118] A similar list is laid down in Sch.13 for the purposes of detailing a "Schedule

114 Collective harm to consumer interests could be inferred from the accumulation of individual infringements. See *OFT v Miller* [2009] EWCA Civ. 34 at [44]–[46] per Arden LJ.

115 s.34.

116 Formerly "Community infringements", the change in terminology being necessitated by the UK's withdrawal from the EU: Consumer Protection (Enforcement) (Amendment etc.) (EU Exit) Regulations 2019 (SI 2019/203).

117 SI 2003/1593.

118 Enterprise Act 2002 (Part 8 Domestic Infringements) Order 2015 (SI 2015/1727).

13 infringement". It includes Consumer Contracts (Information, Cancellation and Additional Charges) Regulations 2013;[119] The Consumer Credit Act 1974 and associated secondary legislation (other than to the extent they apply to consumer hire agreements; Consumer Protection from Unfair Trading Regulations 2008;[120] and substantial parts of the Consumer Rights Act 2015.[121]

Where a trader is committing a listed infringement (under either ss.211 or 212) the CMA is a general enforcer of Pt 8 (along with every local weights and measures authority)[122] and must engage in "appropriate consultation" with the trader before applying for an enforcement order. "Appropriate consultation" is defined in s.214(2) as being consultation for the purpose of: 16–025

> **"(a) achieving the cessation of the infringement in a case where an infringement is occurring;**
> **(b) ensuring that there will be no repetition of the infringement in a case where the infringement has occurred;**
> **(c) ensuring that there will be no repetition of the infringement in a case where the cessation of the infringement is achieved under paragraph (a);**
> **(d) ensuring that the infringement does not take place in the case of a Schedule 13 infringement which the enforcer believes is likely to take place."**

There is no need for such a consultation where the CMA thinks that enforcement should be made without delay.[123]

During this consultation, the enforcer may accept from the trader in question an undertaking that he:[124]

---

119 SI 2013/3134.

120 SI 2008/1277.

121 Including those dealing with statutory rights (and remedies) and unfair terms. See Sch.13, para.27.

122 See s.213 which also enables any person or body to be designated as an enforcer under Pt 8, e.g. the Information Commissioner. See also, s.216 on the co-ordination role of the CMA.

123 s.214(3).

124 s.219(4). These undertakings may also be sought in respect of an "online interface order" where there is, or is likely to be, a Sch.13 infringement. See ss.218ZA-218ZD, inserted by Consumer Protection (Enforcement) (Amendment etc.) Regulations 2020 (SI 2020/484) with the aim of improving enforcement of consumer protection law in the digital sphere. See also, the action taken by FaceBook and Instagram in light of CMA action against fake reviews online: *https://www.gov.uk/cma-cases/fake-and-misleading-online-reviews* [Accessed 2 April 2022]. Nevertheless, it seems likely that legislative intervention to address "fake reviews" will soon be forthcoming: The Department of Business, Energy & Industrial Strategy has recently stated its intention to amend the "blacklist" so as to capture the recent phenomenon of "fake reviews". See, *Reforming Competition and Consumer Policy: Government Response to Consultation* (April 2022, CP 656) at para.2.27.

> **"(a) does not continue or repeat the conduct;**
> **(b) does not engage in such conduct in the course of his business or another business;**
> **(c) does not consent to or connive in the carrying out of such conduct by a body corporate with which he has a special relationship."**

Following the enactment of the Consumer Rights Act the scope of undertakings open to an enforcer has been expanded considerably. With effect from 1 October 2015, an enforcer may also seek an undertaking from the trader that he will take what the Act calls "enhanced consumer measures". Under s.219A there are three forms of enhanced consumer measures: "redress", "compliance" and "choice". The redress category is explained in s.219A(2):

> **"The measures in the redress category are—**
> **(a) measures offering compensation or other redress to consumers who have suffered loss as a result of the conduct which has given rise to the enforcement order or undertaking,**
> **(b) where the conduct referred to in paragraph (a) relates to a contract, measures offering such consumers the option to terminate (but not vary) that contract,**
> **(c) where such consumers cannot be identified, or cannot be identified without disproportionate cost to the subject of the enforcement order or undertaking, measures intended to be in the collective interests of consumers."**

Thus, the undertaking can, for example, require the trader to offer compensation to consumers who have suffered a loss stemming from an infringement, or to enable the consumer to terminate the contract. The "compliance" category enables the undertaking to specify measures intended to reduce the risk of the infringement continuing, or to enhance compliance with consumer law more generally. Undertakings which would readily fall under this category include those committing to improve training for staff or, in larger businesses, the appointment of a specific individual with consumer law compliance responsibilities. The "choice" category extends to measures which enable the consumer to choose more effectively between traders. Thus an undertaking here could require the trader to declare their breach of the law, perhaps on their website or instore, along with the measures adopted to prevent the breach from recurring. The rationale for the introduction of this category of measures is succinctly put by the Department for Business Innovation and Skills (BIS) its Guidance: "If consumers are not aware of a business' past performance, there is no incentive for that business to change their practices and put consumers first".[125]

125 BIS, "Enhanced Consumer Measures: Guidance for enforcers of consumer law" (2015), para.71.

There are, however, limitations on the exercise of these powers in addition to requirement of an infringement which has harmed the collective interests of consumers. First, the enhanced consumer measures can only be included within an undertaking to the extent that the enforcer considers them to be "just and reasonable". Thus the measures must be proportionate, taking into account the likely benefit of the measures to consumers, the costs likely to be incurred by the subject of the enforcement order or undertaking, and the likely cost to consumers of obtaining the benefit of the measures.[126] 16-026

Where such an undertaking is not forthcoming (or breached), the CMA[127] can apply for an enforcement order under s.215.[128] This order must detail both the trader and the conduct which constitutes an infringement and will be drafted in the same terms as the s.219 undertaking considered above.[129]

In April 2022 the Government announced its intention to reform consumer law enforcement.[130] Though it recognised that the current "system of enforcement of consumer law generally works and delivers significant benefits" it identified various weaknesses around procedural barriers, weak sanctions for breaching the law, and low engagement with alternative dispute resolution services.[131] Consequently, the Government announced its intention to legislate so as to enable the Competition and Markets Authority to enforce "core" consumer law, such as unfair commercial practices and unfair contract terms directly, i.e. without the need to apply to the courts for an enforcement order as outlined above. Under the proposals, the CMA would be able to determine when a company breaches the rules and impose fines of up to 10% of a company's annual global turnover. Whilst the current scheme of court-based enforcement would remain, the reforms proposed constitute a fundamental shift of enforcement strategy and the detail of any forthcoming legislation is eagerly anticipated.[132] 16-027

126 s.219B(2).

127 As for the CMA and others, see s.217.

128 Also see s.218ZB regarding online interface orders where, for example, the order may require infringing content to be removed or warnings issued to the consumer ahead of accessing such content.

129 Note that in this case, it is for the court to determine whether the inclusion of enhanced consumer measures is just and reasonable, rather than the enforcer.

130 *Reforming Competition and Consumer Policy: Government Response to Consultation* (April 2022, CP 656).

131 *Reforming Competition and Consumer Policy: Government Response to Consultation* at para.3.1. See also, J. Penrose, *Power To The People: Stronger Consumer Choice and Competition So Markets Work For People, Not The Other Way Around* (February 2021) available here: *https://www.gov.uk/government/publications/power-to-the-people-independent-report-on-competition-policy* [Accessed 28 April 2022].

132 In particular to see how closely, or not, UK reform resembles those effected in the EU through the Enforcement and Modernisation Directive (Directive 2019/2161/EU). The Directive, for example, provides for fines of up to 4% of a business's annual turnover.

General Reading

P. Cartwright, "Trade descriptions, corporations and mens rea" [1997] J.B.L. 465–471.

P. Cartwright, "Servicing and supplying: a judicial muddle" [2000] Crim. L.R. 356.

P. Cartwright, "Unfair Commercial Practices and the Future of the Criminal Law" [2010] J.B.L. 618.

P. Cartwright, "Redress Compliance and Choice: enhanced consumer measures and the retreat from punishment in the Consumer Rights Act 2015" [2016] C.L.J. 271.

H. Collins, "Harmonisation by Example: European Laws Against Unfair Commercial Practices" (2010) 73 M.L.R. 89–118.

P. Dobson, "Does the Ban on Pyramid Promotional Schemes Challenge the Business Model of a Typical Direct Selling Company?" [2011] J.B.L. 194.

M. Griffiths, "Unfair commercial practices—a new regime" [2007] Comms. L. 196.

B. De Groote and K. De Vulder, "European framework for unfair commercial practices: analysis of Directive 2005/29" [2007] J.B.L. 16.

G. Howells, "The End of an Era—Implementing the Unfair Commercial Practices Directive in the United Kingdom" [2009] J.B.L. 183–194.

P. Milne, "The Trade Descriptions Act and breach of contract" (1997) 113 L.Q.R. 382–385.

P. Shears, "Overviewing the EU Unfair Commercial Practices Directive: concentric – circles" (2007) E.B.L.Rev. 18(4) 781–796.

J. Stuyck, E. Terryn and T. Van Dyck, "Confidence through fairness? The new Directive on unfair business to consumer commercial practices in the internal market" (2006) C.M.L.Rev. 43(1) 107–152.

C. Twigg-Flesner, "Deep impact? The EC Directive on unfair commercial practices and domestic consumer law" (2005) 121 L.Q.R. 386.

C. Twigg-Flesner, D. Parry, G. Howells and A. Nordhausen, "An Analysis of the Application and Scope of the Unfair Commercial Practices Directive", DTI Report 2005.

Part II

Consumer Credit

17

Introduction and Definition of Hire Purchase and Other Forms of Never-Never

A contract of hire-purchase, as its name suggests, contains two elements. It is a contract of hire which also gives the hirer an option to purchase the goods. Hire is a form of bailment which is a word used to describe the situation where one person is put in possession of goods belonging to another. The hirer is a bailee. Thus a hire-purchase agreement is an agreement for the bailment of goods whereby the bailee has an option to purchase them. 17-001

Two particular contracts relating to goods have long been recognised by the law, one of bailment and one of sale. Of which type, then, is a hire-purchase agreement? Is it bailment or is it sale? To put it another way, is it hire or is it purchase? The emphatic answer is that it is not a contract of sale. Thus the parties to a hire-purchase agreement are termed not "seller" and "buyer" but "owner" and "hirer". Under the Consumer Credit Act 1974 they are termed "creditor" and "debtor".

Distinction Between Hire Purchase and Sale

It is the hallmark of a contract of sale of goods that the parties enter into a mutual commitment that the buyer thereby acquires or will acquire ownership of the goods. A "buyer" is described in s.61 of the Sale of Goods Act as "a person who buys or agrees to buy goods". If the buyer does not commit himself to acquire ownership of the goods there is no contract of sale and indeed it is inaccurate to describe him as "buyer". This was made clear by the House of Lords in the leading case of *Helby v Matthews*.[1] The agreement in that case was between the owner 17-002

1 [1895] A.C. 471.

of a piano (a dealer) and his customer. The latter agreed to hire the piano for 36 months at a rent of 10s. 6d. per month. The agreement provided that the piano would become the property of the customer on payment of all the instalments of rent but that he could at any time before then terminate the hiring by returning the piano to the dealer. In the event of the hiring being terminated, the hirer would be liable only for arrears of rent in respect of the period prior to the termination. The House of Lords held that this agreement was not a contract of sale and that the customer was not a "buyer". The fact that he could terminate the hiring meant that he was under no commitment to acquire ownership of the goods. He had in effect an option to purchase, which he could exercise by not terminating the agreement and by paying all 36 monthly instalments. An option is not a commitment. Their Lordships said that the option was an irrevocable offer by the owner to sell. That offer could be accepted only when the option was exercised. Until then there was no purchase and no contract of sale. Therefore, the hire-purchase agreement was not a contract of sale within the meaning of the Sale of Goods Act. Thus a hire-purchase contract is a contract of bailment, albeit one with a difference—namely an option to purchase.

In deciding *Helby v Matthews* their Lordships distinguished the case of *Lee v Butler*.[2] In that case the agreement provided that the customer should have immediate possession of the goods (furniture) and should pay £1 on 6 May and £96 on 1 August. These sums were termed "rent". The agreement further provided that the furniture would become the customer's property when the instalments had both been paid and not before. There was no clause in the agreement giving the customer the right to terminate it, although there were provisions entitling the dealer to do so (and to repossess the goods) if the customer defaulted. The Court of Appeal held that this agreement was a contract of sale. The difference between this and *Helby v Matthews* is that here the customer was committed to making all the payments and therefore to acquiring ownership of the goods.

It will be observed that in *Lee v Butler* the goods were not to become the buyer's property until he had paid all the money. This, however, did not prevent the agreement from being a contract of sale. Indeed, as we saw in Ch.3, ss.17 and 18 of the Sale of Goods Act expressly recognise that property passes to the buyer at the time the parties intend it to.

17–003 In each of the cases mentioned above, the customer disposed of the goods (in return for money) to an innocent third person and he did so before completing his payments. The importance of the distinction between hire-purchase and sale becomes apparent when it is realised that different legal results followed. In neither case was the customer owner of the goods at the time he disposed of them. In *Helby v Matthews* he was merely hiring them and in *Lee v Butler* it had been expressly agreed that the furniture was not to become his property until the payments had been completed. However, in *Lee v Butler* he was a "buyer" in possession of the goods and thus, although he was not the owner, he could pass good title to an innocent purchaser.[3] So in *Lee v Butler* the dealer could not recover the goods from the innocent purchaser to whom his customer has sold them. In *Helby v Matthews*, on the other hand, the dealer was

2 [1893] 2 Q.B. 318.

3 Factors Act s.9, see Ch.12, above.

held entitled to recover the goods. Someone hiring goods under a hire-purchase agreement is not a "buyer" and therefore cannot pass good title under either the Factors Act s.9 or the Sale of Goods Act s.25. Therefore, from the dealer's point of view, the hire-purchase transaction has the advantage that he will not be prevented by either of those sections from recovering the goods after they have been passed on by the hirer to an innocent third party. It should be remembered that there are other provisions which could in certain circumstances prevent him from doing so.[4] In particular the Hire Purchase Act 1964, Pt. III can have this effect in the case of a motor vehicle. Also note that, since *Lee v Butler*, ss.9 of the Factors Act and 25 of the Sale of Goods Act have been amended. The result is that the rule in *Lee v Butler* (that under those sections a buyer under a conditional sale agreement can pass good title to an innocent purchaser) applies only if the conditional sale agreement is not regulated by the Consumer Credit Act 1974.[5]

Since the House of Lords decision in *Helby v Matthews*,[6] the hire-purchase agreement has become very common indeed. The usual form it has come to take is an agreement whereby the customer (a) agrees to hire the goods for an agreed fixed period (e.g. 48 months) in return for a monthly payment, and (b) is given an option to purchase the goods for a nominal amount (e.g. £1) which option is exercisable only after the customer has first completed payment of all the monthly instalments. In economic terms the customer has paid for the goods by means of the monthly instalments. Having paid all the monthly instalments, he would be mad not to exercise his option to buy for the nominal amount. Nevertheless he is not legally bound to do so and thus the agreement is still only a hire-purchase agreement and is not a contract of sale unless and until the customer exercises his option to buy: *Close Asset Finance v Care Graphics Machinery Ltd*.[7] Suppose, on the other hand, that the customer is contractually bound to pay all the monthly instalments, is not required to pay anything at all for exercising his "option to buy" and is deemed to have exercised that option simply by completing his instalment payments without informing the owner that he wishes not to exercise it. In that unusual case, the agreement is a sale of goods contract (a conditional sale agreement) and not a hire-purchase agreement: *Forthright Finance Ltd v Carlyle Finance Ltd*.[8] Following the decision of the Court of Appeal in *Forthright Finance Ltd* it is clear that the distinction between contracts of conditional sale and hire-purchase is one of substance, and the language used by the parties is not conclusive. Phillips LJ observed that "this contract has all the ingredients of a conditional sale agreement" and that the option not to take title did "not affect the true nature of the agreement". Consequently the fact that the contract referred to the agreement as one of hire-purchase was irrelevant.

Consider the emergence in modern times of a new species of hire purchase agreement: the "Lease Purchase" or "Personal Contract Purchase" commonly used within the motor industry

4 See Ch.12, above.
5 See para.5-025, above.
6 [1895] A.C. 471.
7 [2000] C.C.L.R. 43.
8 [1997] 4 All E.R. 90.

to finance sales of new motor vehicles. Rent is payable throughout the agreement period and is calculated on the amount of depreciation likely on the vehicle. At the end of that period, the lessee has the option to purchase the vehicle for a sum calculated to be the capital/residual value of the vehicle. What is the economic objective of such a contract? Clearly it is distinct from that of a hire-purchase agreement, which is in effect a secured sale.[9] That much is self-evident from the nature of the instalment payments being calculated on the estimated depreciation of the vehicle (or goods) over the contract period. This however, may be contrasted with the payment structure of a typical modern hire-purchase agreement, where the option to buy the goods at the end of the contract period is frequently only a nominal fee, and certainly not representative of the estimated value of the goods at the end of the contract period. The courts have not yet had the opportunity to determine whether this new form of instalment contract should be regarded as a simple hiring or as a hire-purchase agreement.

Conditional Sale and Credit Sale Agreements

17–004 Each of these is a type of contract of sale of goods and each has the characteristic that the buyer is committed to acquiring ownership of the goods. "Conditional" and "Credit" are commonly used to describe contracts of sale of goods where the price is payable in instalments. In that respect they therefore have some similarity with hire-purchase agreements.

At common law there is only one difference between a credit and a conditional sale agreement. It is that in a conditional sale agreement the passing of property to the buyer is expressly postponed until some condition (usually all the instalments being paid) is fulfilled. So, the agreement in *Lee v Butler*[10] can be described as a conditional sale agreement. In a credit sale agreement there is no such condition to the passing of property and the goods therefore normally become the buyer's immediately after the contract is made.[11] Thus under a credit sale agreement, the buyer will, as soon as he takes delivery, be in possession of goods of which he is the owner. Under a conditional sale agreement the buyer will be in possession of goods which will continue to belong to the seller until all the instalments have been paid. Apart from this, there is at common law no difference between credit sale and conditional sale agreements.

Although this is the position at common law, we shall see that the Consumer Credit Act 1974 radically alters the position with respect to conditional sale agreements regulated by its provisions, thus making them significantly different in effect from credit sale agreements.

9 Indeed, this fact is responsible for the number of cases examining the sale of goods by a non-owner. In many instances, a hirer under a hire-purchase agreement sells the goods on due to the (mistaken) belief that he or she is entitled to do so.

10 [1893] 2 Q.B. 318.

11 SGA 1979 s.18 r.1.

The Finance Company

In both *Helby v Matthews*[12] and *Lee v Butler*,[13] the customer took the goods under an agreement between himself and the dealer. There was no intermediate party. No doubt some dealers still do business in that way. Today, however, it is common for the dealer to sell goods for cash to a finance company which then parts with them on instalment terms to the customer. Thus today's customer often finds that he is hiring or buying the goods, not from the dealer, but from a remote and powerful finance company. This is a classic example of a weak party (the customer) contracting with a strong one (the finance company). Finance companies, by adopting a "take it or leave it" attitude, used to insist on inserting terms that were very onerous for the customer—terms to the effect that all implied conditions and warranties were excluded; that in the event of the customer's payments falling into arrears the finance company could repossess the goods; that in order to repossess the goods the company's agents could trespass upon the customer's premises; and in the event of the customer terminating the agreement he should pay a large sum of money to the finance company, etc. The Consumer Credit Act 1974, the Consumer Rights Act 2015, and the Unfair Contract Terms Act 1977 largely prevent these abuses, but it is true that, in so far as those Acts allow them to, finance companies still insist on the terms being as beneficial to them as possible. 17-005

The usual process by which the contract is made is as follows. The customer selects the goods from the dealer's stock. He asks for instalment terms. At the dealer's request (and sometimes with his assistance) he fills in a form. This form will have been supplied to the dealer by a finance company with whom the dealer maintains regular contact. When completed and signed by the customer, it will constitute an offer to the finance company by the customer to take the goods either on hire-purchase or on credit sale or conditional sale terms. The customer will leave that form with the dealer. The dealer will himself complete another form which will constitute an offer by him to the finance company to sell it the goods. The dealer will send both forms to the finance company which will either accept or reject both offers. It will accept offers only if made on its own forms and thus incorporating the terms that it wishes to include. If it accepts the offers, the finance company will have agreed with the dealer to buy the goods from him and with the customer to supply the goods to him on hire-purchase (or credit sale or conditional sale) terms.

12 [1895] A.C. 471.

13 [1893] 2 Q.B. 318.

The Dealer

17-006 Much of the following chapters is devoted to the contractual relationship between the customer and the person (often a finance company) from whom he hires or buys the goods. However, a little time should be spent considering the position of the dealer who sells his goods to the finance company.

Dealer and Customer

17-007 The relationship between these two is not that of seller and buyer, because the dealer has sold the goods, not to the customer, but to the finance company. It follows that, if the goods prove defective, the customer has no action against the dealer under the Sale of Goods Act s.14 or the Consumer Rights Act s.9.[14] Nevertheless he may well still have a remedy against the dealer. In *Andrews v Hopkinson*[15] the dealer told the customer "It's a good little bus. I would stake my life on it". After this the customer made a hire-purchase contract, in the usual way, with a finance company. Soon after taking delivery of the car, he had a crash in it, due to its defective steering mechanism. McNair J held that the dealer was liable in damages to the customer for two reasons.

(i) There was a contract, albeit not one of sale, between the dealer and the customer. The contract consisted of the dealer promising that the car was a "good little bus" in return of the customer applying to the finance company to acquire it on hire-purchase terms. The dealer was therefore liable for breach of his warranty (i.e. his promise).

(ii) The defect in the steering mechanism was due to negligent lack of inspection and servicing by the dealer who was therefore liable—irrespective of whether there was a contract—to anyone foreseeably injured by his negligence. This was an application of the general principle in *Donoghue v Stevenson*.[16]

Dealer and Finance Company

17-008 The relationship of dealer and finance company is primarily that of seller and buyer. Their contract will therefore, in the absence of contrary agreement, be subject to the provisions of the Sale of Goods Act. However, the finance company will often require the dealer to take on further obligations and to enter into a recourse agreement. The extent of the dealer's liability under one of these will depend upon the terms of his particular agreement. Often it will be

14 *Drury v Victor Buckland* [1941] 1 All E.R. 269.

15 [1957] 1 Q.B. 229.

16 [1932] A.C. 562. See para.9-005, above.

worded so as to constitute a contract of indemnity under which the dealer must make good any loss suffered by the finance company in the event of the customer defaulting on his payments or terminating his agreement.

The question of to what extent the dealer in dealing with the customer is the agent of the finance company will be discussed in Ch.21.

Guarantors and Indemnifiers

There are risks involved in credit trading. Apart from the chance that the customer may default on his payments (perhaps even go bankrupt), there is the risk that he may also sell, damage or even destroy the goods. In the typical transaction, it is the finance company which runs these risks. The finance company can to some extent safeguard itself by including certain terms in the contract it makes with the customer. For example, in the case of a motor vehicle the contract may require the hirer/buyer to have comprehensive insurance. However, this does not provide any safeguard against the irresponsible customer who does not comply with such terms of the agreement or against the out and out rogue who, having paid his initial deposit, disappears with the goods without trace. 17-009

Thus it is quite possible for a finance company to insist that some third person acts as a safeguard against the finance company making a loss on the transaction. The contract made between the third person and the finance company will, depending upon its terms, be a contract either of guarantee or of indemnity. The difference between these two types of contract has already been considered.[17] From the finance company's point of view a contract of guarantee is the less satisfactory, for two reasons. First, it is enforceable only if there is sufficient written evidence of its existence,[18] though this is perhaps not very important since the agreement will usually be in writing anyway. Secondly, a contract of guarantee is enforceable only if the principal contract is valid (i.e. the one between the finance company and the customer). Put another way, if the customer has a defence to a claim against him under the hire-purchase agreement, then any guarantor will also be able to use the same defence. An indemnifier, however, can be liable when the customer has a valid defence and can sometimes be liable to a greater extent than the customer.[19]

It is useful at this stage to indicate that guarantors and indemnifiers are of two types, those who act as such at the request of the customer and those who were not requested by the customer to do so. An example of the latter is the dealer who has a recourse agreement with the finance company.

17 See Ch.9.

18 See the Statute of Frauds 1677.

19 See *Goulston Discount Co Ltd v Clark*, para.24-024.

Other Forms of Never-Never

17-010 With the coming of the affluent society the consumer credit business has boomed. Indeed, in December 2016 the extent of outstanding consumer lending stood at the staggering figure of £198 billion.[20] In earlier days, having goods on hire-purchase or similar terms came to be known colloquially as having them on the "never-never"—because the repayment periods were so long it sometimes seemed as though they would never be paid for. Hire-purchase is today only one of the ways in which the consumer can obtain credit. The rest of this chapter is a "whistle-stop tour" of the rest of the "never-never land", a quick passing look at a number of different ways in which credit is provided and security taken. It is concerned not so much with the law as with the way business is carried on.

Hire-purchase, conditional sale and credit sale have in common that the goods and the credit are provided in the same agreement. The same agreement regulates both the supply of the goods and also the indebtedness of the hirer or buyer. However, there is no legal or practical reason why this should be the case with every credit agreement. Take the typical situation where a finance company lets goods on hire-purchase terms to a customer. From a practical view (though not a legal one) the finance company is not really the supplier of the goods. The dealer is the real supplier of the goods. Indeed, when the agreement has been made, it is from the dealer that the customer will collect the goods which he is hiring on hire-purchase terms from the finance company. Practically speaking, the finance company is in business, not really to sell or hire out goods, but to give loans. It supplies goods (i.e. purchases them from the dealer and lets them to the borrower on hire-purchase terms) in order to make the loan and at the same time to retain some collateral for the loan. The collateral is the finance company's right to recover possession of the goods in the event of the hirer defaulting on his payments or disposing of the goods.

Why does the finance company not achieve the same result (i.e. the giving of a loan on the collateral of the goods) by granting a loan to the purchaser and taking a mortgage of the goods? This is how house purchases are financed and it would have the advantage that the borrower buys the goods directly from the person who is actually the supplier of them, i.e. the dealer. The finance company would not then be cast in the role of a seller or owner (i.e. supplier) of the goods. The reason that finance companies do not commonly take mortgages of goods lies in the Bills of Sale Acts 1878–1882.[21]

However, there are various methods in use today by which credit is quite commonly granted under an agreement which is separate from that which regulates the selling or hiring of the goods, e.g. the customer borrows the money from X and uses it to buy the goods from Y. We are about to examine some of these methods but two preliminary points need to be made.

20 *http://www.themoneycharity.org.uk/money-statistics/* [Accessed 18 April 2021]. This figure has fallen from a peak of £238 billion in September 2008, however, it represents an increase of over £19 billion from December 2015.

21 See "Mortgages of Goods", below.

First, the credit (i.e. the loan) does not necessarily have to be for the supply of goods. It could be for the purchase of services (e.g. a holiday or the erection of a garage) or for the purchase of a plot of land or for any other use to which the borrower wants to put it. Secondly, the two agreements (i.e. loan and purchase) could be with the same person, e.g. the borrower borrows money from X and uses it to buy goods also from X. Now let us examine first some general categories and then some more particular examples.

Unsecured Loan

The notion of an unsecured loan is very simple. It consists of the lender giving money to the borrower in return for a promise by the borrower to repay it. The only means for the creditor to enforce the agreement is for him to sue the borrower in the courts. If the borrower becomes insolvent or bankrupt, the creditor has no other remedy open to him and therefore runs a considerable risk of losing part or all of his money. Since the lender runs high risks, the cost of the loan (i.e. the interest) will usually be high. Unsecured loans can be obtained from various sources, mainly banks and finance companies. 17-011

It is worthwhile comparing an unsecured loan with a credit sale agreement. The effect of both is that the creditor provides unsecured credit. Under a credit sale agreement the credit is, by the nature of the transaction, directly related to the purchase of the goods in the credit sale agreement, i.e. the credit is for the purchase of particular goods. (Incidentally, this last statement is true also of hire-purchase and conditional sale agreements.) A direct loan, on the other hand, need not be associated with the purchase of a specific item or items. The vast majority of hire-purchase, conditional sale and credit sale agreements involve the giving of credit by a finance company which has business connections with the dealer. These agreements often arise out of a regular relationship between a dealer and a finance company to whom the dealer regularly introduces potential purchasers who require credit terms. A direct loan may also be given by such a connected lender but, equally, may be given by a lender completely unconnected with the dealer (i.e. a lender contacted by the borrower for himself, whether it be a bank, a finance company or even a friend).

Unsecured Credit

An unsecured loan is only one type of unsecured credit and is in reality no different from any other form. The word "loan" conjures up a picture of money passing physically from the lender to the borrower who then uses it as desired and makes repayments later. A loan is but one way of creating a debt and a credit. (It must of course create both, since one person's debt is another person's credit.) However, a debt can be created in other ways. Whenever there is an agreement that a debt may be paid later there is something which can be called a credit agreement. A credit sale agreement provides an excellent example. Others (e.g. credit card and trading check agreements) will be given shortly. 17-012

Secured Credit

17-013 The purpose of security for the creditor is to reduce the risk for him that he will not recoup the debt that is owing to him—the main risks being either that the debtor does not have the means to pay (i.e. becomes insolvent) or that he disappears without trace. The main advantage to the debtor of giving security is that the creditor may offer better terms (i.e. charge less interest) because the risks are reduced.

Generally, the fact that a credit agreement is secured does not in any other way alter its nature. Generally, even if for some reason the security fails, the creditor will still be able to sue the debtor on his promise to repay.

Guarantee or Indemnity

17-014 The notion of someone acting as guarantor or indemnifier has already been considered in relation to hire-purchase agreements. His position and function are exactly the same in relation to any other credit agreement. He does in a very real sense provide security. He is someone to whom the creditor can look if the debtor defaults. He may be the only security that the creditor has or, equally, may be additional to security in one of the following forms.

Mortgage of Goods (Chattel Mortgage)

17-015 A mortgage of goods is created when the owner of goods (the borrower) transfers ownership to the lender (e.g. a finance company) on condition that the lender will retransfer the ownership when the loan is duly repaid. The borrower retains possession throughout. The borrower could create a mortgage over goods he has owned for some time or could do it at the time he purchases them. Mortgages of goods are seldom used, because any document creating one must comply with the very technical and obscure requirements of the Bills of Sale Acts 1878–1882 and must be registered. Failure to comply with these requirements is likely to render the security void.

In 2013 there were around 50,600 registered bills of sale and lending using bills of sale was estimated at £38–40 million in 2010. Notwithstanding the relatively small scale of this form of lending, deepening concerns surrounding the use of bills of sale as security in consumer lending coupled with the an increase in the use[22] of bills of sale (largely in respect of motor vehicles, i.e. "log-book" loans) led to the Government introducing proposals in 2009 to reform the sector.[23] In its response to the consultation the Government noted that there was

22 In 2001, for example, there were only 2840 registered bills of sale.

23 BIS, "Consultation on Proposals to Ban the Use of Bills of Sale for Consumer Lending" December 2009.

some support for a prohibition on the use of bills of sale for consumer lending. This focused on various features of bills of sale, all of which are detrimental to the consumer:[24]

- bills of sale use archaic language and are difficult for consumers to understand;
- consumers have fewer rights under bills of sale than they do under other secured lending agreements (e.g. pawn-broking and hire purchase);
- bills of sale loans are generally very expensive and involve punitive fees and charges that can quickly add up; and
- better alternatives, in particular credit unions, are available.

The Government, however, declined the opportunity to impose a ban on consumer lending through bills of sale and instead introduced, inter alia, a code of practice with increased protections for consumers and improved consumer information provided in plain English. The Law Commission has recommended the repeal of the Bills of Sale Acts in order to provide appropriate protection to both borrowers and subsequent purchasers (where they unknowingly buy goods that are subject to a bill of sale). It has been announced, however, that the Law Commission's Goods Mortgages Bill has not been taken forward following the Government's most recent consultation.[25]

Pledge

A pledge is created when the owner of goods transfers possession of them (or of the documents of title) to a lender as security for a loan. A pledge differs from a mortgage in that with a pledge the borrower retains his ownership throughout and parts with possession, whereas with a mortgage of goods the borrower parts with ownership and retains possession throughout. 17-016

Mortgage of Land

This is a particularly sound form of security—more so than any security over goods, which can be lost, stolen or destroyed or can simply depreciate in value. Land on the other hand tends to increase in value and cannot be moved. It is this last fact which has made land mortgages increasingly widely used in the consumer credit field. It is well known that someone who buys a house is able to mortgage the house as security for the loan of the money to buy it. After he has 17-017

24 BIS, "Government Response to the Consultation on Proposals to Ban the Use of Bills of Sale for Consumer Lending", January 2011, p.35.

25 See further, Law Commission, *Bills of Sale* (Law Com. No.369, 2016) and HM Treasury "Goods Mortgages Bill: response to the consultation" (April 2018).

occupied it for a while it may have increased in value and would be good security for a further loan. Thus there exists what might be termed second mortgage companies which will give the house owner a loan and take a second mortgage as security for the loan. The agreement will usually allow the borrower to use the loan for whatever he likes.

Assignment of Life Assurance Policy

17–018 A policy of this type presents for the assured person a means of saving combined with seeing that in the event of his premature death his dependents are not left without money. The policy is an agreement whereby he agrees to pay for, say, 20 years a regular premium to the insurance company. In return, the company agrees to pay him a fixed sum (perhaps plus bonuses) at the end of the period; it further agrees that if he dies earlier it will immediately pay the fixed sum (perhaps plus any bonuses already accumulated). That is a typical agreement. Now, suppose the agreement has been running for 10 years. It has by then got some value and could, for example be sold (i.e. surrendered) back to the insurance company for an immediate cash payment.

Instead of doing that, the insured could obtain a loan and assign (i.e. transfer the benefit of) the policy to the lender until the loan is repaid. A bank will sometimes accept an assignment of such an insurance policy as security for a loan and may then charge a lower rate of interest.

Methods of Providing Credit

17–019 Arrangements vary. There are three different roles which may or may not be combined in one person:

(i) That of creditor, i.e. the lender, the person who provides the credit for the debtor.

(ii) That of seller/supplier, i.e. the person who makes a contract with the debtor to supply him with goods or services.

(iii) That of dealer, i.e. the retailer of the goods (or services).

There are three common combinations:

(a) All three roles are combined in the same person, e.g. when a dealer makes a credit sale or hire-purchase agreement directly with the customer, as occurred in *Helby v Matthews*.[26]

26 [1895] A.C. 471.

(b) The first two roles are combined in one person but the dealer is someone else, e.g. in the typical hire-purchase or credit sale agreement where a finance company is involved.

(c) The last two roles are combined in one person, the creditor being someone else, e.g. when a bank makes a personal loan to a customer who uses it to buy goods directly from the dealer.

It is useful to bear this analysis in mind when considering the following methods that are used to provide credit.

Bank Loan

This term is usually used to describe an arrangement whereby the customer borrows a fixed sum at a fixed rate of interest and agrees to pay it off by fixed regular (usually monthly) instalments. The repayments will often be made by automatic deductions from the customer's current account at the bank. The loan will usually be unsecured but may be secured, e.g. by the assignment of a life policy. A bank loan will invariably be an example of the third possibility (c) above. 17-020

Bank Overdraft

This is an arrangement whereby the customer is allowed to overdraw (i.e. borrow) on his current account. Like a bank loan, it will fall within the third possibility (c) above. Unlike a bank loan, it will be flexible in a number of ways. First, the interest rate is liable to fluctuate over the period of the loan. Secondly, the debtor may not be required to pay it off at any particular rate but may be trusted to pay it off as and when he can. Thirdly, it may not be for a fixed sum but may simply allow the customer to overdraw up to a maximum amount. Lastly, it may not be restricted to one occasion. The customer is usually allowed, as he pays it off, to overdraw again and again—always subject to a maximum amount. 17-021

Bank's Revolving Credit

This is simply a version of a bank loan but has one feature of an overdraft—namely that the debtor, as his debt becomes reduced by his regular repayments, is automatically allowed to borrow again up to the original or an agreed figure. He can do this again and again. 17-022

Shop's Revolving Credit

17–023 Some large shops and chain stores, e.g. men's tailors, operate a system whereby the customer agrees to pay a certain amount of money a month (say, £30) and at the same time the customer can buy goods on credit up to a certain value (e.g. 12 times his monthly payments). Thus, in this example the customer could immediately buy £360 worth of clothes and will take about 12 months to pay for them. If that was all that the arrangement was, it would be no more than an ordinary credit sale agreement. However the customer is normally allowed to "top up" his debt, i.e. as his repayments reduce his outstanding debt, he can then purchase more clothes so as to bring his debt back up to £360. This sort of arrangement is often termed by the shop a "budget account". It is an example of the first possibility (a) above. The credit is usually unsecured.

Check Trading

17–024 A trading check is a piece of paper or token or voucher. It is a device for providing a fixed amount of credit which is (usually) unsecured. Check trading traditionally involved quite small sums (i.e. up to about £100) with weekly repayments and were often acquired from a door-to-door representative of the check trading company (who would also collect the repayments). Check trading has been overtaken by more common methods of providing credit, but it operated as follows: The customer will acquire the check first and then use it to buy goods or services. Suppose the check has a face value of £90. Then the customer can buy goods up to that value at any shop prepared to accept the check. The value of the goods he has bought, say £45, will be marked on the back of the check thus leaving the customer free to spend the rest of the check elsewhere. The shops will actually get payment from the check trading company from which the customer acquired the check. The customer will pay off the check trading company in instalments over a period of weeks, e.g. 36 weekly instalments of £3. The total of his instalments will of course be more than the face value of the check, the extra representing the interest. Check trading is an example of the third possibility (c) above. The creditor is one person (i.e. the check trading company). The seller and supplier of the goods is another person (i.e. the shop which accepts the trading check in payment). The contract between the customer and the shop which accepts the trading check in payment is a contract of sale of goods: *Davies v Customs and Excise*.[27] A trading check can be used only at those shops which are prepared to accept them. There will be an arrangement between the check trading company and a large number of stores whereby the latter agree to accept the checks.

A trading check or voucher is not a revolving credit. Once the debtor has spent the value of his check he cannot, as his repayments are made, automatically have more credit. He must apply again to the check trading company (or, rather, to its representative) for another check.

27 [1975] 1 All E.R. 309. See para.8-006, above.

Credit Cards[28]

The credit card system has much in common with that of trading checks. It is a further example of the third possibility (c) above. Again three parties are involved, the customer, the creditor (in this case the credit card company) and the seller/supplier. A credit card is used in much the same way as a trading check. The buyer (i.e. the credit card holder), having decided what to purchase, buys it but does not pay either cash or by cheque; instead he uses his credit card. The seller is then paid by the credit card company and the latter within about two to seven weeks sends an account to the customer for payment. The normal arrangement between a credit card company and a retailer is that the retailer gives the card company a discount. Thus if a card holder uses his card to pay for an item costing £100, the card company will pay only about £95 or £96 to the retailer. This discount is part of the card company's profit. The card holder will of course still be required to pay the card company the full amount. Now, those card companies which require the customer to pay the whole amount at once are providing no more than a sophisticated form of general trade debt—debt deferred for a short time to be repaid in one instalment (e.g. Diner's Club and traditional American Express cards). Such cards are often termed charge cards to differentiate them from credit cards properly so-called. Some companies, e.g. American Express, offer charge card agreements and credit card agreements. With the latter the card holder is allowed to pay the account off in monthly instalments. The best known of these are "Visa" and "Mastercard". 17-025

The legal nature of a typical credit card or charge card arrangement was considered in *Re Charge Card Services Ltd*.[29] There were two underlying agreements. One was between the card company and card holder and regulated the basis on which credit could be obtained and was to be paid off. The other was between the card company and retailer; under it the retailer agreed to accept payment by means of the card and was to receive payment, less a discount, from the card company. In the case a number of card holders had used their cards to pay for petrol at various garages before the card company became insolvent. This left a number of the garages owed money by the card company. Being unable to get it from the insolvent company, the garages claimed it from the individual card holders. The garages claimed that payment by credit or charge card was like payment by cheque. If a customer's cheque had been dishonoured by the bank, the garage would be entitled to claim the price direct from the customer. This is because payment by cheque is conditional upon the cheque being honoured. A number of the card holders had, however, already paid the card company for the petrol in question. So if they now had to pay the garage, they would end up having to pay twice for the same petrol. The Court of Appeal held that payment by means of a credit or charge card is not conditional, but absolute. It is a complete payment by the card holder who is not liable to pay the garage if the card is not honoured. Thus it is the retailer who runs the risk that the card company may become insolvent. It was also held, interpreting the agreement between the card company and the card holder, that the company had the right to claim payment from the card holder

28 See generally, S.A. Jones, "Credit Cards, Card Users and Account Holders" [1988] J.B.L. 457.

29 [1989] Ch. 497.

irrespective of whether the card company had paid the garages. Thus the neat result was that those card holders who had not yet paid the card company in respect of petrol purchased using their card remained liable to do so, but no card holder was liable to pay the garage for such petrol. It should be added that a card might be dishonoured for a reason other than the card company becoming insolvent, i.e. because the person using the card was doing so in excess of his credit limit or had stolen the card. It might be, under the terms of the agreement between the card company and the retailer, that in those circumstances the card company is not liable to pay the retailer. If so, there is no doubt that the retailer in those circumstances would be entitled to claim payment from the person who had used the card, though probably not the full cash price but only the lesser amount that the retailer had expected to be paid by the card company. This is the only amount the retailer has lost because of the customer's representation (implied by his action of using the card) that he was authorised by the card company to use the card on that transaction.

There are two significant differences between the credit card system and the trading check system. First, the credit card holder does not actually draw upon any credit (i.e. owe any money) until he uses his credit card to purchase something. Thus when the credit card holder obtains his credit card he does not agree to any fixed amount of credit. The amount of the credit he obtains will depend upon the value of what he chooses to buy with the card. However, there will be a credit limit which he must not exceed at any one time. Secondly, a credit card provides a type of revolving credit. Thus the card holder can use the card again and again to obtain more credit, subject to the promise that his total credit does not at any one time exceed the credit limit stipulated in his credit card agreement. The credit card will normally be valid for two years but on expiry a replacement card will usually be sent automatically to the card holder.

17–026 A credit card provides an extremely useful and flexible form of credit. Even if the card is not used, the card holder has the knowledge that he can obtain instant credit. He can use it (or not) as and when he chooses. Although he can use it only at shops and other establishments which have an arrangement with the credit card company, it is true to say that a great many places at home and abroad have made such arrangements to accept both Visa and Mastercard. Further, the debtor can make repayments more or less as he pleases. He can pay it all off when the first account is sent to him or he can pay off some (not necessarily the same amount) each month. The only restriction is that there is normally a minimum amount which he must repay each month. Naturally, the longer he takes to make repayment, the more he will have to pay in interest.

A further point needs to be made. A credit card can usually be used not only to buy goods or services but also to obtain a cash loan from a bank. The bank will then obtain immediate repayment from the credit card company. The latter can be repaid by the card holder in the flexible way described above.

Visa and Mastercard can both be used by the card holder at any shop which has an agreement with the relevant credit card company enabling the shop to accept that company's cards. However, some large stores or chains of stores have their own credit card schemes under which the card holder is limited to being able to use the card in that company's own stores. Some of these "in-house" credit cards are operated by the company which owns the store.

These are therefore sometimes termed in the trade "two party" credit cards. There are only two persons involved in the transaction, the card holder and the company owning the store. This arrangement is an example of the first possibility (a) mentioned at para.17-019, above. The roles of creditor, seller and dealer are all combined in one person. Sometimes one of these "in-house" credit card schemes (e.g. the John Lewis Partnership Card) will be operated, not by the store itself, but by a subsidiary company or by a bank or finance company in arrangement with the store. The main difference between this "three party" type of "in-house" credit card and the more common Visa and Mastercard cards is that the in-house card can be used only in the store (or chain of stores) with which it is connected. Many stores operating in-house schemes also have arrangements with the major operators (e.g. Visa and Mastercard) enabling them to accept payment via the major credit cards. Some stores are more exclusive and recognise only their own in-house cards. Besides stores, other large-scale retail operators, e.g. hotel chains and petrol companies, also operate in-house credit card schemes.

Rental Agreements

Where goods are hired but the hirer is given no option to purchase the agreement is not a hire-purchase agreement but is simply an ordinary bailment. There is in a sense no element of credit, since the hirer pays each week for what he gets each week (i.e. one week's use of the goods). There is no element of "have now, pay later". However, it is becoming quite common with certain types of goods (e.g. televisions) for the goods to be hired by the same person for virtually the whole of the useful life of the goods. It is true that the hirer never becomes owner of the goods but he does have them (to keep indefinitely) and pay later. This is in a very real sense never-never, even though it is not a "credit" agreement. 17-027

Credit-hire Agreements

The "credit-hire" agreement, a modern phenomenon, is a hire agreement which does involve the provision of credit.[30] The hirer is typically a motorist whose car has been put off the road in an accident caused entirely by the other's driver's fault. The agreement provides for the motorist to hire a replacement car for so long as her own is off the road, and also provides that the hire charges will become payable, not at the end of the hire period but only when the motorist's damages are recovered from the other motorist whose negligence caused the accident. Commonly the credit-hire company (or its chosen solicitor) will pursue that claim on his behalf, recover his damages and deduct the credit-hire charges before handing those damages over to him. A credit-hire agreement undoubtedly involves an element of "have now" (i.e. the hire of the car) and "pay later". Unsurprisingly, hire charges under credit-hire agreements are much 17-028

30 J.K. Macleod, "Credit hire in the House of Lords" [2001] J.B.L. 14.

higher than under conventional hire agreements (known as "spot hire"). The higher charges reflect the fact that, under a typical credit-hire agreement, the hirer receives the following benefits not provided under a spot hire agreement:

(i) he is relieved of having to lay out money for the car hire;

(ii) he is relieved of having to pursue a claim against the other motorist, i.e. because normally the credit-hire company does that for her; and

(iii) he is thus also relieved of having to bear the costs of pursuing litigation against the other motorist.

The majority of the House of Lords in *Dimond v Lovell*[31] considered, obiter, that the cost of these extra benefits was not compensatable in damages obtainable from the other motorist. This, if correct, means that the hirer can recover, in damages from the other motorist, hire charges only at the equivalent spot hire rate. Thus the difference between the credit-hire charges and the lower spot hire rate will have to be borne either by the hirer or by the credit-hire company (i.e. if it chooses not to, or cannot, enforce the credit-hire agreement fully against the hirer).

The extent to which credit-hire agreements are regulated by the Consumer Credit Act is explained later in Ch.18.[32]

General Reading

N. Curwen, "Hire-Purchase Agreements: the unfortunate triumph of form over function" (2007) 11 Mountbatten Journal of Legal Studies 21.

L. Gullifer and S. Hurst, "Bills of Sale Acts: ripe for reform?" (2013) 11 J.I.B.F.L. 685.

H. Johnson, "Problems with Hire-Purchase" [1993] I.B.F.L. 39.

S.A. Jones, "Credit Cards, Card Users and Account Holders" [1988] J.B.L. 457.

J.K. Macleod, "Credit hire in the House of Lords" [2001] J.B.L. 14.

G. McBain, "Repealing the Bills of Sale Acts" [2011] J.B.L. 475.

G. McCormack, "Hire-Purchase, Reservation of Title and Fixtures" [1990] Conv. 275.

M.E. Raczynska, "Replacing the Bills of Sale Acts" [2017] L.M.C.L.Q. 196.

D. Sheehan, "The Abolition of Bills of Sale in Consumer Lending" (2010) 126 L.Q.R. 356.

31 [2000] 2 All E.R. 897.

32 For a detailed and comprehensive account see A. Dobson, "Recovery of Credit Hire Charges" [1988] C.I.C.C. 25.

18

The Consumer Credit Act 1974

Introduction

This chapter introduces the Consumer Credit Act 1974 and outlines the recent developments 18-001
in this area of law introduced by the Consumer Credit Act 2006 and the implementation of the Consumer Credit Directive.[1] The 1974 Act followed the Crowther Committee's Report on Consumer Credit[2] and in large part implemented its recommendations. The basis of the Report was that consumer credit, although it might take many different forms, was always basically the same thing. Thus the Act, which is concerned with providing reasonable protection for those consumers who obtain credit, brings under one umbrella consumer credit agreements generally—whatever form they take. The Act repealed previous Acts which applied only to particular forms of consumer credit, i.e. the Pawnbrokers Acts 1872 and 1960, the Moneylenders Acts 1900–1927, the Hire Purchase Act 1965, and the Advertisements (Hire Purchase) Act 1967. Two sets of provisions, however, remain in force—the Bills of Sale Acts and the Hire Purchase Act 1964 Pt III. The former means that chattel mortgages are likely to remain relatively uncommon.[3] The latter was dealt with at para.5-030 above.

The repeal of the Hire Purchase Act 1965 did not mean that the whole of the law relating to hire-purchase was recast—rather the reverse. Before 1974 the law of hire-purchase was generally thought to be satisfactory. Thus, in the Consumer Credit Act 1974, it was largely re-enacted with little alteration except that much of it applies to other consumer credit agreements as well. In the 1974 Act the terms "creditor" and "debtor" are used. The creditor means the person who provides the credit, i.e. in the case of a hire-purchase agreement, the owner; in the case of a direct loan, the lender; and in the case of a credit sale agreement, the seller. The

1 Directive 2008/48/EC.
2 (1971) Cmnd. 4596.
3 See para.17-015.

debtor means the person who receives the credit, i.e. in the above examples, the hirer, borrower or buyer.[4]

The regulation of consumer credit has been changed significantly by the implementation of the Consumer Credit Directive 2008.[5] The Directive repealed the first Consumer Credit Directive[6] and is designed to further the harmonisation of consumer credit regulation across Europe and increase the level of consumer protection. The Directive takes a mixed approach in implementing these aims. On the one hand, a number of the requirements of the Directive are of maximum harmonisation, i.e. a Member State cannot maintain or introduce lesser or greater provisions than those prescribed in the Directive. On the other hand, certain requirements are merely minimum harmonisation measures and consequently a Member State may elect to retain or implement more stringent legal measures.

18-002 In the UK the Directive has been implemented through amendments to the Consumer Credit Act itself and by various sets of regulations focused on specific issues including the form and content of agreements, disclosure of information and advertising. The Directive has introduced a number of new obligations such as the duty of a creditor to investigate the creditworthiness of a debtor before offering or providing credit,[7] the obligation to provide an "adequate explanation" of the credit agreement to the debtor,[8] and the debtor's right to withdraw from a regulated consumer credit agreement without giving any reason.[9] The impact of the Directive will be discussed where relevant throughout the following chapters. It is important to note, however, that the ambit of the Directive does not completely mirror that of the Act. There are a number of matters, such as hire purchase and business lending, which are regulated by the Consumer Credit Act but which are outside of the scope of the Directive. These are referred to as "out of scope" agreements. As we will see, the Government adopted a case-by-case approach to these agreements. Thus some "out of scope" agreements remain unaffected by the Directive whereas others will be integrated into the new Consumer Credit Directive compliant framework.

The Consumer Credit Directive 2008 is not the sole driver of recent reforms to consumer credit law. In 2010 HM Treasury and the Department for Business, Innovation and Skills issued a joint consultation under which it was proposed to transfer consumer credit regulation from the Office of Fair Trading to the Financial Conduct Authority.[10] In 2013 a further joint consultation was launched to set out the way in which consumer credit was to be integrated into the same regulatory regime as other financial services (i.e. that under the Financial Services and

---

4 Note that the Financial Conduct Authority's Consumer Credit Sourcebook (CONC) and the Financial Services and Markets Act 2000 (Regulated Activities) Order 2001 (SI 2001/544) instead use the terminology "borrower" and "lender".

5 Directive 2008/48/EC.

6 Directive 87/102/EEC (as amended).

7 See para.21-027, below.

8 See para.21-028, below.

9 See para.21-040, below.

10 A New Approach to Financial Regulation: Consultation on Reforming the Consumer Credit Regime (December 2010).

Markets Act 2000) whilst retaining existing consumer rights and protections in the Consumer Credit Act 1974. Thus, with effect from 1 April 2014 the Financial Conduct Authority replaced the Office of Fair Trading as the consumer credit regulator with a number of changes to, for example, licensing (replaced by authorisation under the FSMA 2000) and advertising (replaced by the financial promotion regime under the FSMA 2000). The impact of these changes will be considered where relevant throughout the following chapters.[11]

Despite these wide-ranging changes the Consumer Credit Act remains central to the regulation of consumer credit. In particular, it continues to regulate virtually the whole range of consumer credit agreements. That is to say, it controls the contractual position, the rights and duties existing between the creditor and debtor and continues to do to notwithstanding the Financial Conduct Authority's recent review of the Consumer Credit Act.[12] The FCA was required to complete the review with a particular focus on considering whether the remaining provisions of the Act could be replaced by rules or guidance made under the FSMA and it published its findings in March 2019.[13] It concluded that whilst some of the statutory protections offered by the Act could be maintained through FCA rules,[14] a significant proportion could not be repealed and replaced without reducing the level of consumer protection currently in place, for example, those relating to antecedent negotiations, connected lender liability and unfair relationships.[15] Thus it appears that, for the time being, the Consumer Credit Act will continue to occupy a central position in the regulation of consumer credit although it may well be that reforms are not too far around the corner. In particular, the Woolard Review[16] (commissioned by the FCA) has made 26 wide-ranging recommendations to the FCA and the Government aimed at making the unsecured credit market fit for purpose, particularly given the changes to the sector in the years following the transfer of responsibility from the OFT to the FCA. In particular, the Review highlighted the emergence of unregulated Buy Now Pay Later schemes which have the potential for consumer harm. The Report identified the potential of such products to create high levels of indebtedness and also raised concerns over late payment fees and consumer understanding. The Review recommended urgent legislative intervention to bring current forms of unregulated Buy Now Pay Later credit into FCA regulation and the

11 Further reform to consumer credit law has been necessitated by the Mortgage Credit Directive (Directive 2014/17/EU). It is beyond the scope of this text to consider the Directive in detail. However, its primary effect has been to amalgamate the law relating to first and second charge mortgages. Historically the CCA 1974 regulated second charge mortgages, however, with effect from 21 March 2016 both first and second mortgages are being dealt with by the FCA under the Mortgages and Home Finance Conduct of Business sourcebook (MCOB) in the FCA Handbook.

12 See art.20 of the Financial Services and Markets Act 2000 (Regulated Activities) (Amendment) Order 2014 (SI 2014/366).

13 FCA, *Review of retained provisions of the Consumer Credit Act: Final report* (March 2019).

14 Such as the right under s.155 to the reimbursement of credit brokerage fees where an introduction effected by the broker is unsuccessful.

15 See, for example, the rights and protections analysed in Ch.5 of the Final Report. The inability of FCA rules to replicate the sanctions framework was also a concern highlighted in the Report, see Ch.7.

16 *The Woolard Review—A review of change and innovation in the unsecured credit market* (February 2021).

Government has recently consulted on how best to achieve this.[17] The Woolard Review also made a number of broader recommendations as to the regulation of consumer credit in the UK. In particular, it recommended that the FCA engage with the Government "to prioritise work the work on CCA reform" stating that much of the "groundwork" had been completed as part of the FCA's 2019 Report.[18] It is worth noting that the FCA's Report took the position that "substantive changes to provisions implementing the [Consumer Credit Directive] will not be possible at this time".[19] Indeed, fundamentally, consumer credit regulation was largely unaffected by the UK's withdrawal from the EU: the same broad framework continues to apply, with rather complex results since, as we will see over this, and following chapters, a consumer credit agreement could engage any one, or more, of frameworks laid down by the Consumer Credit Act 1974, various associated regulations, the FCA's Consumer Credit Sourcebook, and the FCA's Mortgage Conduct of Business Sourcebook.

This, however, may not be the case for much longer. Recommendation 25 of the Woolard Review commented on the "additional flexibility" in the regulation of consumer credit afforded by the UK's withdrawal from the EU. It recommended that the FCA conduct a further review in order to explore this flexibility, particularly as to facilitate consumer awareness. Indeed, it is hard to think of a more opportune time for such a review: In June 2021, the European Commission adopted a proposal to replace the Consumer Credit Directive.[20] The proposed Directive would retain much of the content of the 2008 Directive, but would make some significant changes, including reforms to:

- capture emerging credit products such as Buy Now, Pay Later loans and Peer-to-Peer lending;
- revise the financial thresholds, in particular to capture short-term, high-cost credit which may fall under the current €200 limit;
- prohibit certain practices that exploit consumer behaviour, such as pre-ticked boxes and unsolicited sales;
- revise rules around the assessment of credit-worthiness and pre-contract information.

It will be interesting to observe what approach the UK takes to the new Directive. It may now, of course, simply choose to ignore it! However, that would lead to the rather absurd position that

17 HM Treasury, *Regulation of Buy-Now Pay-Later Consultation* (October 2021). In the meantime, the FCA has worked with Buy Now Pay Later companies to secure changes to terms and conditions around late penalties and cancellation rights. See, for example, *https://www.fca.org.uk/news/press-releases/fca-secures-contract-changes-buy-now-pay-later-customers* [Accessed April 4 2022].

18 The Woolard Review, Recommendation 24.

19 FCA, *Review of retained provisions of the Consumer Credit Act: Final report* (March 2019) at para.1.13.

20 COM (2021) 347 final.

much of the UK's consumer credit law, as a former Member State, would be based on an out-of-date Directive whilst all current Member States would have implemented the new Directive. It has been argued that this "is a huge opportunity for the UK to get away from the previous EU legislation".[21] Given that it is not anticipated that any of the changes proposed by the new Directive will apply (in Member States) before 2024, it may be hoped that this will be sufficient time for the FCA to complete a further review of consumer credit regulation and take the opportunity to consider the rationalisation (and simplification) of consumer credit law so as to improve consumer outcomes and the coherence of statutory and regulatory intervention in this area.

The following two chapters will deal with the Financial Conduct Authority's authorisation regime and with its rules relating to financial promotion as they relate to credit activities. After that the remaining chapters will be primarily concerned with the way in which the Consumer Credit Act deals with the rights and liabilities between the creditor and debtor, i.e. which deal with the formation, validity and enforcement of a consumer credit agreement. These provisions of the Act cannot be circumvented. Two sections see to that. First, s.173 prevents the parties from contracting out of the effect of the Act's provisions. A term of an agreement regulated by the Act is void to the extent that it is inconsistent with any provision in the Act (or any regulations made under the Act) for the protection of the debtor.[22] Where the Act imposes upon the debtor a duty or liability, that duty or liability cannot be increased by any term of the agreement.[23] 18-003

The second section referred to is s.113, which prevents the Act being evaded by the use of security. Thus where an agreement is regulated by the Act, the creditor cannot enforce any security so as to benefit himself to an extent greater than if the debtor carried out his obligations to the full extent that they would be enforced under the Act. The effect of this is that the creditor can take security as an added safeguard to ensure that the debtor carries out all his obligations to the full extent that they would be enforced against him under the Act. However, where an obligation would not be enforced under the Act, the creditor cannot use the security to enforce that obligation.

The rest of this chapter will deal with the definitions (mainly of different types of agreement which fall within the Act) in ss.8–20.

Definitions

Those agreements that are regulated agreements under the Act are of two types—consumer credit agreements and consumer hire agreements. 18-004

21 F. Philpott, "Consumer credit—which way forward?" [2021] 171 New L.J. 7949, p.11 at p.12.
22 s.173(1).
23 s.173(2).

Consumer Credit Agreements

18–005 The definition of a consumer credit agreement is to be found in s.8(1) which reads:[24]

> **"A consumer credit agreement is an agreement between an individual ('the debtor') and any other person ('the creditor') by which the creditor provides the debtor with credit of any amount."**

This was supported by s.8(2) which restricted the definition of a personal credit agreement to those agreements providing credit not exceeding £25,000.[25] This credit ceiling was abolished by s.1 of the Consumer Credit Act 2006[26] which repealed s.8(2) and thus for agreements made on or after 6 April 2008 the amount of credit provided under the agreement is no longer relevant to whether or not the Act applies.[27] The role and operation of s.8(2) will be considered shortly since it still plays an important role in relation to agreements entered into before its repeal came into effect.

Section 8 has recently been amended in light of the Mortgage Credit Directive.[28] It is beyond the scope of this text to consider the Directive in detail. However, its primary effect has been to amalgamate the law relating to first and second charge mortgages. Historically the CCA 1974 regulated second charge mortgages, however, with effect from 21 March 2016 both first and second mortgages are being dealt with by the FCA under the Mortgages and Home Finance Conduct of Business sourcebook (MCOB) in the FCA Handbook.[29]

Section 9(1) completes the picture:

> **"(1) In this Act 'credit' includes a cash loan, and any other form of financial accommodation."**

24 Note the special position of "green deal plans", defined in the Energy Act 2011 s.1, whereby s.8(1) does not apply. A green deal plan will be treated as a consumer credit agreement under the Act where the requirements of s.189B are met. The Green Deal is a government initiative to support energy saving installations (such as insulation) and the financing thereof.

25 For agreements made before 20 May 1985 the figure of £25,000 was £5,000. For agreements made on or after that date and before 1 May 1998, the figure was £15,000.

26 For an account of the policy considerations behind the 2006 Act, see J. Patient, "The Consumer Credit Act 2006" [2006] J.I.B.L.R. 309. See also, E. Lomnicka, "The reform of consumer credit in the UK" [2004] J.B.L. 129.

27 Where the business purposes exception does not apply, see para.18-019, below.

28 Directive 2014/17/EU.

29 s.8(3). Following the UK's withdrawal from the EU, the wording of s.8(3) has been modified by the Financial Services and Markets Act 2000 (Amendment) (EU Exit) Regulations (SI 2019/632) with the reference to the Directive removed and replaced so that s.8 does not capture agreements "the purpose of which is the acquisition or retention, by an individual acting for purposes outside those of any trade, business or profession carried on by the individual, of property rights in land or in an existing or projected building".

Because of the word "individual" in s.8(1), any agreement where the debtor is a company (or any other corporate body) is outside the definition of a consumer credit agreement.[30] On the other hand small partnerships and other unincorporated associations are treated as individuals.[31]

The definition of a consumer credit agreement does not include rental agreements which are dealt with under the definition of consumer hire agreement but it does include the other types of agreement considered in the last two chapters. Thus it includes credit sale and conditional sale agreements, bank loans, check trading and credit card agreements. Section 9(3) specifically states that it includes hire-purchase agreements.[32] 18-006

No agreement falls within the definition unless it provides "credit". The explanation of "credit" in s.9(1) is less than complete. An element of "have now, pay later" is a fairly good indication of credit. Sometimes it is said that credit involves the "deferment of a debt" or the "deferment of an obligation to pay". Professor Goode, in his Consumer Credit Legislation, suggested that credit is provided "whenever the contract provides for the debtor to pay, or gives him the option to pay, later than the time at which payment would otherwise have been earned". *Dimond v Lovell*[33] involved a "credit-hire" agreement.[34] As explained above, this did not require the hirer to pay the car hire charges at the end of the hire period, but allowed her to postpone paying them until the conclusion of her claim against another motorist whose negligence had damaged the hirer's own car. In holding that the agreement thus provided credit to the hirer, the House of Lords applied Professor Goode's test, although Lord Hobhouse thought that it would not always be a satisfactory one to apply. The result is that a credit-hire agreement can be regulated under the Act as being both a consumer credit agreement and, if the hire period is capable of lasting over three months, also a consumer hire agreement.[35]

It can be difficult to ascertain whether there has been an element of "have now, pay later" in the case of a contract which provides for access to facilities over a set period of time. In *OFT v Ashbourne Management Services Ltd*[36] the OFT unsuccessfully argued that certain gym membership agreements provided credit. Kitchen J stated that:[37]

> **"a distinction must be drawn between the following two classes of case: the first comprises cases in which a liability or obligation to pay is incurred or, but for the payment terms, would have been**

30 See, for example, *Bank of Ireland (UK) plc v McLaughlin* [2014] NIQB 104 at [39] and [41].

31 s.189(1) as amended by the CCA 2006 s.1, which limits the application of the 1974 Act to partnerships consisting of two or three partners only (one of those partners must not be a body corporate).

32 Necessary since a hire purchase agreement would not otherwise be regarding as extend credit to the hirer during the period of hire.

33 [2000] 2 W.L.R. 1121.

34 See, J.K. Macleod, "Credit hire in the House of Lords" [2001] J.B.L. 14.

35 For the definition of consumer hire agreement, see para.18-011, below.

36 [2011] EWHC 1237 (Ch).

37 [2011] EWHC 1237 (Ch) at [95].

incurred at the outset, and is discharged in instalments; the second comprises cases in which payment falls due in stages as the contract is performed."

Within the meaning of the Act, credit is only provided in the first case. Where, as in Ashbourne, the agreement is one under which the consumer makes monthly payments in return for access to and use of the gym facilities for that month no credit is provided.[38]

In *CFL Finance Ltd v Laser Trust*[39] the Court of Appeal considered the definition of credit in the context of settlement or compromise agreements. It is clear that the concept of credit extends to an agreement to refinance existing debt obligations[40] but can the same be said for an agreement to settle a legal dispute where the terms of the settlement enable the payment of the debt at a later date? The Court of Appeal determined that settlement agreements are capable of providing financial accommodation and therefore can, in certain circumstances, fall within the ambit of the Act. The court emphasised that the concept of credit was grounded in a contractual deferment of an obligation to pay: thus, a contractual settlement in respect of an undisputed debt that is to be repaid through instalments is capable of falling within the definition of credit since it defers an individual's debt obligations. The words "contractual" and "undisputed" here are crucial. The Act does not apply where a creditor, without receiving consideration, merely allows a debtor more time to pay. Only where there is consideration for the financial accommodation will there be credit under s.9. Similarly, where the existence of a debt is not certain and the compromise agreement was merely to settle that disputed claim, then it cannot be said to provide financial accommodation since the debtor may, in fact, owe nothing![41]

Former financial ceiling

18–007 No agreement made prior to the repeal of s.8(2) (i.e. before 6 April 2008) is a consumer credit agreement unless it is within the financial limit of £25,000. For the purpose of applying the

38 Contrast this position with the monthly payment of an annual insurance premium, which almost certainly does involve the provision of "credit", since the full amount of the premium will customarily be due at the start of the insurance period.

39 [2021] EWCA Civ 228.

40 See, for example, s.11(1)(c). See *Holyoake v Candy* [2017] EWHC 3397 (Ch) where the court held that a settlement agreement that compromised liability under a number of pre-existing credit agreements did extend credit since it deferred the debt obligations under those pre-existing agreements.

41 The court noted the fine line to be drawn between a debt which is genuinely disputed and one which is not, see for example the observations of Lord Justice Newey at [51]. This is particularly problematic when one considers the consequences of a settlement agreement falling unexpectedly within the CCA. Where, for example, the various formalities of the Act (e.g. pre-contract information) are not followed, an agreement will generally be unenforceable without a court order. See Ch.21 below. There could well also be consequences under the FCA's authorisation regime, which will be considered in the next Chapter.

financial limit, a distinction is made between fixed-sum credit and running-account credit. The idea of fixed-sum credit is easy. It is a once-only credit, e.g. a single loan. It is still fixed-sum credit even if later the creditor agrees to make a further loan to the debtor and even if he does so before the first loan is repaid. There will then be two fixed-sum credit agreements. Hire-purchase agreements, credit sale agreements, conditional sale agreements, ordinary bank loans and trading checks are all examples of fixed-sum credit. Running-account credit is what is often termed in the credit trade as revolving credit. This is where the debtor does not have to re-apply for a further credit but automatically as part of his original credit agreement has the right to further credit (usually subject to a credit limit). Examples of running-account credit are bank overdrafts, revolving credit from a bank or a shop and credit card agreements.

If a credit agreement provides fixed-sum credit of £25,000 or less then it is within the definition. The relevant figure is not the total amount which the debtor is to pay but the amount of the credit. That is, roughly speaking, the capital amount which the debtor is borrowing and it therefore does not include the interest payable by the debtor. To be precise, the amount of the credit does not include any item in the "total charge for credit". What is meant by the "total charge for credit" is considered a little further on.[42] All that can be said now is that the total charge for credit will reflect the cost to the debtor of having the credit. Thus the biggest item in the total charge for credit will be the interest charged to the debtor, which will therefore not be part of the "credit". Thus an agreement would fall within the definition of a consumer credit agreement if it gave the debtor a cash loan of £25,000 to be repaid by him in 50 monthly instalments of £560. The amount of the credit would be £25,000 even though the repayments would total £28,000. The extra £3,000 is interest, falls within the "total charge for credit" and therefore is not part of the "credit". For the definition of a consumer credit agreement, the relevant figure is the credit (the amount borrowed), not what it costs the debtor to borrow it.

With a hire-purchase agreement the calculation is not quite so easy but the principle is the same. Suppose Sam wishes to buy a yacht for which the retail cash price is £33,000. Sam has only £8,000 saved up. So he acquires the yacht under a hire-purchase agreement under which he makes an immediate deposit of £8,000 and agrees to pay 50 monthly instalments of £560 each. The agreement gives him an option to buy the yacht for £2 provided he has first paid the deposit and all the instalments. This hire-purchase agreement would fall within the definition of a consumer credit agreement because the amount of the credit is £25,000.

Suppose, however, that the retailer had offered to insure (or buy insurance for) the yacht 18-008
for two years at an additional price of £100. To buy the yacht thus insured would cost £33,100 in cash. However, since Sam still only has £8,000 saved up, he takes it on hire-purchase terms whereby he pays an immediate deposit of £8,000 and agrees to pay 50 monthly instalments of £562 each (the option money still being £2). Now, in this case the agreement would seem to fall outside the definition since the amount of the credit is £25,100. Thus where the credit would otherwise be at or just under £25,000 it is possible to get the agreement outside the definition by persuading the prospective debtor to borrow just a little bit more. This could be

42 At para.18-024.

done by offering some optional extra item which is sufficiently tempting to persuade the debtor to have it. In the case of a yacht a particularly tempting extra might be the provision of a mooring for a certain number of years. A similar service is sometimes provided in the "mobile home" (i.e. caravan) business where one can buy a caravan and sometimes with it also the right to have it on a given site for a given number of years.

A warning must be given. A point made earlier must be repeated. It is that a distinction must be made in every case between (a) the amount of the credit, and (b) the total charge for credit. These terms are mutually exclusive. The amount of credit does not include any sum which is within the total charge for credit. In the example just given about Sam and his yacht the £100 for the insurance was not within the total charge for credit. In *Humberclyde Finance Ltd v Thompson*[43] the Court of Appeal considered the status of a payment waiver insurance premium. Thompson acquired a car on finance supplied by Humberclyde Finance Ltd. The amount of credit was £14,497 but the agreement also included a payment of £796 as an insurance premium in the event of the debtor being unable to make the necessary repayments. At first instance the Court held that the insurance payment was part of the credit supplied under the agreement and that the agreement was therefore not regulated since the credit ceiling at the time was £15,000. The Court of Appeal held that the insurance premium was properly regarded as part of the total charge for credit and was not part of the credit. Consequently the agreement was regulated under the Act since the amount of credit fell under the s.8(2) limit. It would seem therefore that the courts are prepared to extend the natural meaning of what is part of the total charge for credit so as to ensure that where a debtor has been tempted to take an "extra" which would take the agreement over the credit ceiling he is still protected by the provisions of the Act. This approach does leave the question of what extras will be regarded as part of the credit and which will not rather unpredictable.[44]

This distinction has in recent years been given attention by the courts not least because of the consequences for an agreement falling within the old definition of a regulated agreement but also because of the consequences if a regulated agreement wrongly identified a fee which was part of the total charge for credit, as being within the credit itself. In *Wilson v Robertsons (London) Ltd*[45] a pawnbroking agreement for a six-month loan of £400 was struck. From that loan an £8 documentation fee was deducted, although the agreement referred to the amount of credit as £400. At trial on preliminary issues Laddie J held that the documentation fee was properly to be regarded as part of the total charge for credit and therefore not, as part of the credit itself. Thus the loan was in fact for £392 since the £8 fee was to be ignored under s.9(4). Consequently the agreement was not properly documented and was unenforceable.[46]

43 [1997] C.C.L.R. 23.

44 See, for example, *London North Securities Ltd v Meadows* [2005] EWCA Civ. 956 where the Court of Appeal held that the insurance premium was part of the total charge for credit whereas payments against the arrears of previous mortgages were part of the credit. See also, *Black Horse Ltd v Hanson* [2009] EWCA Civ. 73.

45 [2005] 3 All E.R. 873.

46 On the issue of unenforceable agreements see Ch.24.

The same principle was applied in *Southern Pacific Personal Loans Ltd v Walker*[47] where the Supreme Court held that a broker administration fee of £875 was part of the charge for credit under s.9(4) even where interest was charged on that fee. Thus the amount of credit provided had been properly documented as £17,500 and the agreement was enforceable.

The £25,000 financial limit applies also in relation to running-account credit agreements. Here the governing figure is the credit limit, i.e. the maximum debt which the debtor is allowed to run up. If the debtor's credit limit is £25,000 or less, the agreement is within the financial limit and, providing the debtor is an individual (not a company), it is a consumer credit agreement. The agreement will still be a consumer credit agreement even if the debtor is allowed temporarily to exceed this credit limit. However, even where the agreement has no credit limit or has one in excess of £25,000, there are three situations when it will still be within the financial limit. These three situations are where: 18-009

(i) The debtor is unable on any one occasion to draw credit in excess of £25,000.

(ii) The terms of the agreement are such that if the debt (the debit balance) exceeds a certain figure (of £25,000 or less) the terms (e.g. the rate of interest) become more onerous for the debtor.

(iii) It is probable, at the time the agreement is made, that the debt will not at any time rise above £25,000.

Thus most running-account credit agreements will be within the definition. A clear example of one which would not, would be one restricted to large credits of over £25,000 and which could not be used (even on one occasion) to acquire a credit of £25,000 or less.

Abolition of financial ceiling

The removal of the financial limit for agreements made on or after 6 April 2008 has for the most part removed such difficulties and it is now clear that the amended Consumer Credit Act regulates all consumer credit agreements and all consumer hire agreements, unless exempt, with no distinction based on the amount of credit provided. It is, however, still very important to understand the approach of the courts to the old s.8(2) issue of calculating the amount of credit provided. First, as mentioned above, agreements entered into before April 2008 will only be regulated agreements where the financial limit is satisfied. Secondly, the issue of distinguishing between "credit" and the "total cost for credit" is still vitally important for other sections of the Act. Thirdly, the business purpose exemption retains a 18-010

47 [2010] UKSC 32.

financial limit of £25,000 and for the purposes of that exemption the same calculations must be made.[48]

Consumer Hire Agreements

18–011 A consumer hire agreement is any agreement for the bailment (hiring) of goods which fulfils three conditions:[49]

(a) It is not a hire-purchase agreement.

(b) It is capable of lasting more than three months.

(c) The hirer is not a body corporate.

The first condition does not, of course, mean that a hire-purchase agreement is not regulated. We have just seen that hire-purchase agreements fall within the definition of a consumer credit agreement. The second condition means that, for example, an agreement to hire a car for two months would fall outside the Act. Like s.8 previously discussed, s.15 in its original form also included a financial limit. The agreement was not regulated if it required the hirer to make payments exceeding a specified figure. For agreements made before 20 May 1985 the specified figure was £5,000. For agreements made on or after that date and before 1 May 1998, the figure was £15,000. For agreements made on or after 1 May 1998 and before 6 April 2008, the figure was £25,000. This financial limit has also been removed following the implementation of the Consumer Credit Act 2006. Thus for agreements made on or after 6 April 2008, a consumer hire agreement, unless exempt, will be regulated irrespective of the amount of the hire payments. The former financial limit coupled with the requirement that the agreement is "capable of subsisting for longer than three months" is best understood through an example. Consider a hire agreement made in March 2008 which is not a hire-purchase agreement and which provides:

(i) That the hirer (an individual) shall pay a deposit of £15,000.

(ii) That the hirer shall pay a monthly rental of £10,000.

(iii) That the hiring shall continue for a maximum of one year but that the hirer shall be able to terminate it at or at any time after the end of the first month.

48 Formerly to be found in s.16B, though now replicated in the Financial Services and Markets Act 2000 (Regulated Activities) Order 2001 art. 60C(3). See para.18-019, below.

49 s.15.

This agreement falls within the definition since it might last longer than three months and the payments might not exceed £25,000. If the same agreement had been made in May 2008 (i.e. after the removal of the financial limit) the outcome would be exactly the same (i.e. it would be regulated under s.15) but the amount of the deposit and monthly rental would be irrelevant in arriving at this conclusion. Consider another example—a hire agreement which is not a hire-purchase agreement and which provides:

(i) That the hirer (an individual) shall not pay any deposit but shall pay a rental of £100 per month.

(ii) That the hiring shall last three months.

(iii) That the hirer shall have the right to renew the agreement for a further three months.

This agreement is capable of lasting more than three months and is also within the definition.

In *TRM Copy Centres (UK) Ltd v Lanwall Services Ltd*[50] the House of Lords was required to consider whether a "location" agreement fell within the definition of a consumer hire agreement under s.15. The location agreement concerned a photocopier which was placed in a shop. The shopkeeper earned a commission whenever the machine was used and was under an obligation to account for the proceeds of the photocopier (minus his commission) to the supplier. The House of Lords held that the agreement was not a consumer hire agreement since the shopkeeper was under no obligation to pay anything for the photocopier and that this payment, whether in cash or in kind, was the "most obvious badge of an agreement for hire".[51] 18–012

It was necessary for the Act to have a separate definition of a consumer hire agreement since, as explained in the last chapter a hire agreement does not normally involve any -element of credit and thus does not fall within the definition of consumer credit agreement. A "credit-hire" agreement is an unusual type of agreement which involves both hire and credit and thus can fall within both definitions, consumer credit agreement and consumer hire agreement.

It will be found that a great many sections of the Act refer to the "creditor or owner" and the "debtor or hirer". The words "owner" and "hirer" refer to the parties to a consumer hire agreement and not to the parties to a hire-purchase agreement. The words "creditor" and "debtor" include (and refer to) the owner and hirer respectively under a hire-purchase agreement. This is because, as we have just seen, a hire-purchase agreement falls within the definition of a consumer credit agreement under s.8.

50 [2009] UKHL 35.

51 [2009] UKHL 35 at [12] per Lord Hope.

Regulated Agreements

18–013 Most of the provisions of the Act apply, not to all consumer credit agreements, but only to regulated agreements. This is true in particular of those sections which relate to the formation, validity and enforcement of agreements.[52] Following the transfer of consumer credit regulation to the Financial Conduct Authority, the definition of "regulated agreement" is now to be found in the Financial Services and Markets Act 2000 (Regulated Activities) Order 2001.[53] Thus a "regulated credit agreement" is defined as "any credit agreement which is not an exempt agreement" and a "regulated consumer hire agreement" is defined as "a consumer hire agreement which is not an exempt agreement".[54]

The question of which agreements are exempt agreements will be examined a little later. First, it is necessary to consider certain sub-categories of consumer credit agreement.

Restricted Use and Unrestricted-Use Agreements

18–014 Credit will be either restricted-use credit or unrestricted-use credit as explained by s.11. It is unrestricted-use credit if it is in fact provided in such a way as to leave the debtor free to use it as he chooses. Thus hire-purchase agreements, credit sale and conditional sale agreements, check trading agreements, credit-hire agreements and a shop's revolving credit are all examples of restricted-use credit agreements. A bank loan or overdraft will almost always be unrestricted-use credit, since the money is usually paid directly to the borrower who is therefore free to use it as he chooses. In this case it is still unrestricted-use credit even if the borrower had agreed to use it only for one particular purpose, e.g. to repay a debt to X. It would of course be a restricted-use credit agreement if the bank stipulates that the money is to be paid directly by the bank to X.

A credit card agreement is an example of a multiple agreement, i.e. it can be used to buy goods or services at a restricted number (albeit a large number) of shops, etc. and it can be used to obtain a cash loan. This is an unrestricted-use credit agreement with respect to the provision of cash, and a restricted-use credit agreement with respect to the provision of goods or services.

52 Note that the mere labelling of a consumer credit agreement as being "regulated" does not result in an otherwise unregulated agreement being regulated under the Act. The borrower was therefore not entitled to the protections afforded by the Consumer Credit Act: *NRAM Plc v McAdam* [2015] EWCA Civ 751.

53 SI 2001/544 as amended by the Financial Services and Markets Act 2000 (Regulated Activities) (Amendment) (No.2) Order 2013 (SI 2013/1881).

54 art.60B(3) (regulated credit agreements) and art.60N(3) (regulated consumer hire agreements).

Debtor-Creditor and Debtor-Creditor-Supplier Agreements

Every regulated consumer credit agreement must be either a debtor-creditor-supplier agreement or a debtor-creditor agreement under ss.12 and 13 respectively.[55] The former describes the type of agreement where either there is a business connection between the creditor and the supplier of the goods (as occurs in check trading) or the creditor is also the supplier of the goods (as in every credit sale, conditional sale, hire-purchase and credit-hire agreement). In order to determine whether there is a business connection between the creditor and supplier (i.e. whether the credit agreement is a debtor-creditor-supplier agreement) it must first be decided whether the credit agreement is for restricted-use or for unrestricted-use credit. 18-015

The rule can be formulated as follows. The following agreements are debtor-creditor-supplier agreements:

(a) An agreement for restricted-use credit where the creditor and supplier are one and the same person.

(b) A restricted-use credit agreement "made by the creditor under pre-existing arrangements, or in contemplation of future arrangements, between himself and the supplier".

(c) An unrestricted-use credit agreement made by the creditor under pre-existing arrangements between himself and the supplier, in the knowledge that the credit is to be used to finance a transaction between the debtor and the supplier.

Any agreement not in one of these three categories is merely a debtor-creditor agreement.

In many cases a restricted-use credit agreement will be a debtor-creditor-supplier agreement and an unrestricted-use credit agreement will be a debtor-creditor agreement. These are the common combinations. Thus hire-purchase, conditional sale, credit sale, trading check agreements and credit-hire are all restricted-use debtor-creditor-supplier agreements. Further illustrations are provided by a typical credit card agreement which is, as has been seen, a multiple agreement. In so far as it relates to a cash loan, it is an unrestricted-use credit agreement and is a debtor-creditor agreement. In so far as it relates to goods or services it is a restricted-use credit agreement and is also a debtor-credit-supplier agreement. It is the latter because the supplier of goods or services who accepts payment by means of a credit card does so under an arrangement between himself and the credit card company—an arrangement which either pre-existed, or was contemplated by, the credit agreement.

It is, however, possible for the combination to be different. For example a bank loan may be granted to the debtor to pay off a pre-existing debt of his and it may be payable directly 18-016

55 The terms "borrower-lender" and "borrower-lender-supplier" are utilised in the Financial Services and Markets Act 2000 (Regulated Activities) Order 2001 (SI 2001/544) art.60L(1) as amended by the Financial Services and Markets Act 2000 (Regulated Activities) (Amendment) (No.2) Order 2013 (SI 2013/1881).

by the bank to the person to be paid off. This would be an agreement for restricted-use credit but would merely be a debtor-creditor agreement. Exactly the same result occurs where a bank agrees to enable its customer to buy a new car by making him a loan, but at the same time stipulates that the money is to be payable directly by the bank to the supplier (i.e. the car dealer). The agreement between the bank (creditor) and its customer (debtor) is clearly for restricted-use credit but it is still merely a debtor-creditor agreement because it is not made under pre-existing arrangements or in contemplation of future arrangements between the bank and the car dealer.

Take one further example, this time of an agreement in the third category (above) of debtor-creditor-supplier agreements—namely, an agreement where the creditor furnishes the credit in such a way as to leave the debtor free to use the credit as he likes but where the creditor makes the agreement under pre-existing arrangements between himself and the supplier in the knowledge that the credit is to be used to finance a transaction between the debtor and the supplier. This situation could arise on facts like these: Shiver wants central heating installed in his house. He approaches Warmitup Ltd who indicate that they will deal only on a cash payment basis and suggest that Shiver gets in touch with Hotmoney Ltd who have an arrangement with Warmitup Ltd whereby Hotmoney Ltd will make loans to potential customers of Warmitup Ltd. After some negotiations, Hotmoney Ltd make a loan to Shiver which is paid directly into Shiver's hands. This is a debtor-creditor-supplier agreement even though it is an unrestricted-use credit agreement.

The Act nowhere uses the words "business connection". Nevertheless the policy behind the classification into debtor-creditor-supplier agreements and debtor-creditor agreements is to identify the former as credit agreements where there is some business connection between the creditor and supplier. The policy is that where there is that business connection between the creditor and the supplier, both of them (and not just the supplier) should be answerable to the customer if the goods or services supplied do not correspond with representations made to him before he bought them or if the supplier is in breach of contract with the customer. This point will be returned to later.[56]

Electronic Funds Transfer and debit cards

18–017 In the light of the foregoing, consider one particular development in banking services, namely Electronic Funds Transfer (EFT). This is a modern means of payment in supermarkets, department stores and other places. In the shop at the point of sale there will be a terminal which will have a direct electronic link with the major clearing banks. A bank customer who holds a "debit" card is able to hand his debit card to the shop's checkout assistant who will run it through the terminal. That terminal via its electronic link automatically transfers the money (more or less immediately) from the customer's own bank account to the shop's bank account.

56 See paras 21-017 and 22-004 below.

The Consumer Credit Act does not apply at all to a "debit" card unless the customer has an agreed overdraft authority with his bank. In the absence of an overdraft (or an agreement of the bank authorising one), there will be no credit agreement.

One piece of plastic may serve several purposes. It may be a "debit" card, a cash withdrawal token and a credit card. In that case, how can the agreement be classified for the purposes of the Consumer Credit Act? The answer is to regard each aspect of the card as a separate agreement and to classify that. Thus when used as a debit card by a holder who has an agreed overdraft authority it is a debtor-creditor agreement. When used as a regulated credit card to purchase goods or services, it is a debtor-creditor-supplier agreement. When used as a regulated credit card to draw cash it is a debtor-creditor agreement. In short, the agreement is a multiple one and some aspects of it may be regulated and others not; some aspects of it may be within one category of regulated agreement and others within another.[57]

Exempt Agreements

Subject to one important exception, exempt agreements are not regulated by the Act. The exception is that the court has power to reopen an exempt consumer credit agreement if it gives rise to an unfair relationship between creditor and debtor.[58] We have already noted that a regulated agreement is any credit or consumer hire agreement other than an exempt agreement. Following the transfer of consumer credit regulation to the Financial Conduct Authority on 1 April 2014, various types of agreement have been defined as being exempt under the Financial Services and Markets Act 2000 (Regulated Activities) Order 2001. In general, however, the categories of exempt agreements remain largely the same as those previously laid down under the Consumer Credit Act.[59] Some of the principal exempt agreements under the Order are: 18-018

(i) Credit agreements secured on land (i.e. a mortgage) and made by a local authority.[60]

(ii) A "fixed-sum" "borrower-lender-supplier" agreement under which the borrower is to repay the credit in no more than twelve instalments and within a period of 12 months and where the credit is either provided without interest and without any other charges (such as an administrative fee) or is secured on land.[61] The 12-month

57 On credit cards and multiple agreements see paras 18-014 and 18-015, below. On cash withdrawal tokens, see para.23-021, below.

58 Under ss.140A–140C, see para.23.006, below.

59 Through, for example, the now repealed s.16 and the Consumer Credit (Exempt Agreements) Order 1989 (SI 1989/869) (as amended). Needless to say, this remains an exceedingly complex area of consumer law.

60 art.60E(2). Note the impact of art.60HA for agreements entered into on or after 21 March 2016.

61 art.60F(2). Prior to 18 March 2015 the maximum number of instalments permissible under this exemption was four. This was amended by the Financial Services and Markets Act 2000 (Miscellaneous Provisions) (No.2) Order 2015 art.2(a) to ensure that, for example, insurance contracts where annual premiums are paid through

period begins with, and includes, the date the agreement is made. Thus an agreement requiring the repayments to be made within 12 months after the date of the agreement will not qualify for this exemption.[62] Some credit-hire agreements stipulate that the hire charges must be paid before the first of the following events: (i) conclusion, settlement or abandonment of the hirer's claim against the other motorist; or (ii) expiry of a period of 365 days beginning with the date the agreement is made. Such an agreement appears to satisfy the requirements for this exemption and the House of Lords, obiter, said as much in *Dimond v Lovell*.[63]

(iii) A "borrower-lender-supplier" agreement financing the purchase of land where the number of payments to be made by the borrower does not exceed four and the credit is either secured on land or provided without interest and any other charges.[64]

(iv) A "running-account" "borrower-lender-supplier" agreement where the borrower is required to pay the whole of each periodical account (which must be three months or less) by a single payment and impose no significant charge for the credit (or is secured on land).[65] This exemption means that the milk, newspaper and grocery accounts of many households will be exempt. So also are those charge card agreements (e.g. Diners Club and American Express) which require the card holder to settle each account by a single repayment and where no significant charge is imposed for the credit. In determining whether an agreement falls within this exemption, some caution is needed because some card issuers (e.g. American Express) operate two different kinds of agreement; one which allows extended credit and is a regulated agreement; and another which is exempt because it requires each periodical account to be settled with a single payment.

(v) A "borrower-lender" agreement which is of a type offered only to a certain class or classes of individuals and not offered to the public generally, where there is no charge for credit other than interest and where the rate of that interest, though possibly variable, is low, i.e. cannot at any time exceed a rate of 1 per cent higher than the highest of the base rates operated by the main English and Scottish banks 28 days earlier.[66]

---

monthly instalments are treated in the same way as premiums which are paid in quarterly instalments, i.e. in both cases, the agreement will be exempt.

62 *Zoan v Rouamba* [2000] 2 All E.R. 620; cf. *Ketley v Gilbert* [2001] 1 W.L.R. 986; *Clark v Tull (t/a Ardington Electrical Services)* [2003] Q.B. 36; *Thew v Cole, King v Daltry* [2003] C.C.L.R. 2.

63 [2000] 2 All E.R. 897. On credit-hire agreements generally, see paras 17-028 and 18-006, below.

64 art.60F(4).

65 art.60F(3).

66 art.60G(3). Note the impact of art.60G(8) for agreements entered into on or after 21 March 2016.

(vi) A credit agreement providing credit to be used by the borrower in connection with overseas trade.[67]

(vii) Consumer hire agreements for the hire of metering equipment (for metering gas, water or electricity) hired from a corporate body (e.g. British Gas plc) authorised to supply gas, water or electricity.[68]

(viii) A credit agreement providing credit of £25,000 or less entered into by the borrower in connection with his or her business under the Bounce Back Loan Scheme.[69]

The Consumer Credit Act 2006 introduced two further important categories of exempt agreement under the (now repealed) ss.16A and 16B both of which have been replicated under the Financial Services and Markets Act 2000 (Regulated Activities) Order 2001.[70] The first of the new exceptions relates to high net worth borrowers (and hirers)[71] and allows a borrower or hirer to exempt themselves from all provisions of the Act, barring those provisions relating to unfair agreements. In order for this exemption to apply, four requirements must be satisfied:[72]

(a) the borrower or hirer is a natural person;

(b) the agreement includes a declaration made by him to the effect that he agrees to forgo the protection and remedies that would be available to him if the agreement were a regulated agreement;

(c) a statement of high net worth has been made in relation to him; and

(d) that statement is current in relation to the agreement and a copy of it was provided to the creditor or owner before the agreement was made.

Thus, for an agreement to be exempted under art.60H or art.60Q, the borrower or hirer must be a natural person and the agreement must include a declaration, in the specified form, that the borrower or hirer agrees to forgo the protection which would be available under the 1974 Act if the agreement were a regulated agreement. In addition a statement of high net

67 art.60C(8).

68 art.60P.

69 art.60C(4A). The Bounce Back Loan Scheme was designed to enable businesses to access credit quickly (and on favourable terms) during the coronavirus pandemic. The scheme offered loans from 4 May 2020 until it closed on 31 March 2021.

70 SI 2001/544 as amended by the Financial Services and Markets Act 2000 (Regulated Activities) (Amendment) (No.2) Order 2013 (SI 2013/1881).

71 Introduced by s.3 of the CCA 2006 (now repealed).

72 Laid down in art.60H (credit agreements) and art.60Q (consumer hire agreements).

worth must be made in relation to the debtor or hirer. The form and content of such a statement is laid down by the FCA's Consumer Credit Sourcebook (CONC).[73] CONC App 1.4.3 R provides that the statement must be made by either the creditor or owner[74] or an accountant.[75] In order to be deemed a "high net worth" individual the debtor or hirer must satisfy at least one of the two threshold tests. The first threshold is that the debtor received a net income of at least £150,000 during the previous financial year. Alternatively, the debtor may nevertheless obtain the required statement where, throughout the previous financial year, he held net assets with a total value of £500,000 or more.

18-019 The scope of this exception as it applies to credit agreements (as opposed to consumer hire agreements) has been restricted following the implementation of the Consumer Credit Directive 2008 and will not apply to any credit agreement which provides credit of less than £60,260 unless it is an agreement secured on land.[76] Thus, for art.60H will not exempt a hire purchase agreement for £60,000 entered into by a high-net worth debtor. Since consumer hire agreements are not within the scope of the Directive, this additional restriction does not apply to those agreements. Where the exemption does apply, its effect is to allow greater freedom of contract between high net worth individuals and the credit industry. Moreover, it is a natural consequence of the financial limits being removed coupled with the general prohibition on contracting out.

The second new category of exempt agreement originally introduced by the 2006 Act is where the agreement is entered into for business purposes. It has already been seen that the definition of "individual" under the Act extends protection to agreements entered into for business purposes. This may occur in a number of situations. First, for example, an unincorporated business (e.g. a sole trader) may enter into a regulated agreement. Secondly, a partnership (of up to three partners) may similarly enter into a regulated agreement. Thus, agreements are exempt where the amount of credit provided is greater than £25,000 and where "the agreement is entered into by the debtor or hirer wholly or predominantly for the purposes of a business carried on, or intended to be carried on, by him".[77] The test for whether an agreement has been entered into solely or predominantly for business purposes is one of fact for the court to decide on a case-by-case basis. This represents a significant change in approach since in -relation to agreements made prior to the introduction of the business purpose exemption

73 CONC App 1.4.

74 Though only where the creditor or owner is authorised to accept deposits under Pt IV of the Financial Services and Market Act 2000.

75 Who is a member of one of the professional organisations listed in CONC App 1.4.3 R, for example, the Institute of Chartered Accountants in England and Wales.

76 Where the agreement was entered into on or after 21 March 2016 there is a further requirement in order for the agreement to be exempt. Not only must the credit exceed the financial threshold, the credit provided must be for a purpose other than the renovation of residential property or the acquisition or retention of property rights in either land or a building. See further, art.60H(b).

77 Financial Services and Markets Act 2000 (Regulated Activities) Order 2001 art.60C (credit agreements) and art.60O (consumer hire agreements). This essentially replicates the exemption (now repealed) in s.16B of the Consumer Credit Act.

under the Consumer Credit Act 2006, the purpose behind the agreement was irrelevant to the question of whether it was regulated. Now, under art.60C and art.60O of the Financial Services and Markets Act 2000 (Regulated Activities) Order 2001, the courts must enquire as to the purpose of the agreement and, where that purpose is exclusively or predominantly business it is once again the amount of credit provided that will determine whether or not the agreement is regulated.

For example, if a solicitor leases a new car on hire purchase terms for £30,000 the agreement will be regulated where the car is intended primarily for private use (notwithstanding the fact that the agreement is on the books of the partnership). Where the car is predominantly intended for business use, the agreement will be unregulated. In *Bassano v Toft*[78] a professional musician had secured a number of loans against her expensive viola. The fact that the borrower was a professional viola player was insufficient, however, to infer that the agreement was exempt under the business purpose exemption. The crucial matter is the purpose of the credit being advanced, not the status of the borrower.

Perhaps the greatest challenge for the courts here will be to ascertain where the division lies between predominantly business use and predominantly private use. To alleviate this difficulty the prospective borrower or hirer can, under art.60C(5) make a declaration.[79] If he makes a declaration to the effect that the agreement is entered into by him wholly or predominantly for the purposes of a business carried on (or intended to be carried on) by him, the agreement shall be presumed to have been entered into by him wholly or predominantly for such purposes. 18-020

In order to prevent abuse of this exemption, art.60C(6) provides that any such presumption does not apply if, when the agreement is entered into the lender, or any person acting on their behalf in forming the agreement, knows, or has reasonable cause to suspect, that the declaration is not true. In *Wood v Capital Bridging Finance Ltd*[80] a borrower signed a business purpose declaration notwithstanding that the loan was in fact for her son-in-law's business (and thus not a business of the borrower). Since the lender knew that the purpose of the loan was to support the son-in-law's business, they were not able to rely on the declaration.

There is one further category of exempt agreement to be mentioned: art.60D is concerned with buy-to-let (or investment) properties. Thus, where the credit agreement is secured by a mortgage and less than 40 per cent of the property is to be occupied by the debtor (or a close family member), the agreement will be exempt.

Small Agreements

A regulated agreement which does not exceed a specified financial limit (presently £50) is a small agreement—s.17. A fixed-sum credit agreement is a small agreement provided the 18-021

78 [2014] EWHC 377 at [27].

79 For the equivalent provision for consumer hire agreements, see art.60O(2) and art.60O(3).

80 [2015] EWCA Civ 451.

"credit" does not exceed £50 (the credit is the capital amount, i.e. excluding the total charge for credit). A running-account credit agreement is a small agreement if it has a credit limit of £50 or less.

There are exceptions to all of this. First, no hire-purchase or conditional sale agreement falls within the definition of a small agreement.[81] Secondly, neither does any agreement which is secured by anything other than a guarantee or indemnity. Thirdly, it is not possible artificially to contrive to make several small agreements in place of one larger one.[82] If, where one agreement would exceed the £50 limit, two or more agreements are made so as to bring each agreement below the limit, the agreements will be regarded together as one agreement which exceeds the limit.

The object of defining small agreements is so that it is easy for later sections to exclude such agreements (i.e. where small sums are involved) from some of the technical requirements of the Act (e.g. from the formality and cancellation provisions).

Non-commercial Agreements

18–022 Section 189(1) defines a non-commercial agreement as "a consumer credit agreement or a consumer hire agreement not made by the creditor or owner in the course of a business carried on by him". Thus an agreement for a loan between friends or from a father to his son would be a non-commercial agreement. It will be seen that non-commercial agreements are excluded from many provisions of the Act (e.g. the formality and cancellation provisions).[83]

In *Hare v Schurek*[84] the claimant carried on business as a car dealer and did not normally extend credit to his customers. On one occasion, however, he agreed to supply a car to a friend of his on hire-purchase terms. The Court of Appeal held that the word "business" in the definition of non-commercial agreement meant a consumer credit or consumer hire business. It was held that, since the claimant did not carry on a consumer credit business or consumer hire business, this agreement was not made in the course of a business and was therefore a non-commercial agreement; thus the creditor did not need a consumer credit licence. This reasoning was probably wrong, since there is, in the definition of non-commercial agreement, no qualification to the word "business" and the claimant did not need a licence in any event.[85]

In *Khodari v Tamimi*[86] the claimant, a bank manager, lent money (in a personal capacity) to a customer of the bank. The Court of Appeal held that in order to ascertain whether or not the loans were made in the course of a business the features of the transactions must be taken

81 s.17(1)(a).
82 s.17(3).
83 For an explanation of "carrying on a business" see para.19-002, below.
84 [1993] C.C.L.R. 47.
85 See para.19-002, below.
86 [2009] EWCA Civ. 1109.

as a whole. Thus, the Court held that the agreement between the parties was, on balance, not a commercial one since the loans were made ad hoc, at the request of the borrower and not recorded in writing. In arriving at this decision, the Court was also persuaded by the following facts: that the claimant's loans were almost all to the defendant; that there was no indication that the claimant would lend to someone he did not know; and also that the creditor had not asked for any security in respect of the loans.

Linked Transactions

The object of the definition in s.19 is to enable later sections to provide for what will be the effect on linked transactions in the event of the debtor or hirer withdrawing an offer to enter a regulated agreement or exercising his right of cancellation of a regulated agreement. The effect will be that any linked transaction is similarly (and automatically) withdrawn from or cancelled—ss.19(3) and 69. It is therefore not possible for a creditor or owner to get around the cancellation provisions of the Act by persuading the debtor or hirer to enter a linked transaction. 18–023

The following are linked transactions:

(a) A transaction which the debtor or hirer has to enter as a condition of the principal agreement, e.g. if his credit agreement requires him to take out an insurance policy to ensure that the debt will be repaid if he dies.

(b) A transaction financed or to be financed by the credit agreement where the credit agreement is a debtor-creditor-supplier agreement. Thus an agreement to buy goods by using one's credit card is a linked transaction in relation to the credit card agreement.

(c) A transaction which includes all three of the following characteristics:

   (i) It was suggested to the debtor by someone who knew that the principal agreement had been or might well be made, e.g. the creditor or owner himself, the credit broker, or, depending upon the circumstances, the dealer.

   (ii) It was a transaction between the debtor or hirer and a person who knew that the principal agreement had been (or might well be) made or for whom the dealer acted as credit broker in negotiating the transaction.

   (iii) The debtor entered the transaction to induce the creditor or owner to enter the principal agreement or for another purpose related to the principal agreement or for a purpose related to the transaction to be financed by the principal agreement (provided in the last case that the principal agreement was a restricted-use credit agreement).[87]

There are three further points in the definition. First, no agreement will be a linked one except in relation to a regulated agreement. Secondly, no security agreement (e.g. one of guarantee or indemnity) can be a linked agreement. Thirdly, a transaction which would be a linked agreement if the debtor were a party to it will still be a linked agreement even though it is a relative who instead of the debtor or hirer is a party to it.

It will be appreciated that the definition is indeed a complex one. It may become easier if it is remembered that the definition is intended to embrace those transactions which, if the debtor or hirer is allowed to cancel his regulated agreement, ought also to be automatically cancelled. Assistance may also be gained from a few examples:

(i) X agrees to buy on credit sale terms a deep freezer from Y, a dealer. X also enters a separate agreement with Y whereby Y agrees to install the freezer. X enters a further agreement with Y that Y shall restock the freezer six months after delivery. The credit sale agreement is the principal agreement and the other two agreements are linked transactions.

(ii) The situation is exactly the same as in (i) except that the principal agreement is made by X not with the dealer Y but with a finance company. The other two agreements with Y, the dealer, are still linked agreements.

(iii) The situation is the same as in (i) or (ii) except that X's wife is the person who makes the installation or stocking agreement with Y, the dealer. The installation and stocking agreements are still linked transactions.

(iv) An agreement by a supplier, Z, to sell goods to X for which X pays by using a trading check is a linked transaction.

(v) In the example at para.18-016 (above) the agreement between Shiver and Warmitup Ltd is a linked transaction—the principal agreement being that between Shiver and Hotmoney Ltd.

There are three provisions of the Act which apply directly to linked transactions. Their effect is as follows. First, a linked transaction made before the regulated agreement is made

87 In *Holyoake v Candy* [2017] EWHC 3397 (Ch) the court held that a settlement agreement was a linked transaction under s.19. The settlement was initiated by the creditor and entered into by the debtor for a purpose related to the principal credit agreement (specifically, to gain the creditor's agreement to an extension to the principal agreement).

is of no effect unless and until the regulated agreement is made.[88] Secondly, if the regulated agreement is cancelled, then any linked transaction is similarly withdrawn from or cancelled under s.69(1). Thirdly, if for any reason the debtor's indebtedness is discharged early, the debtor is discharged from any further liability under any linked transaction under s.96(1). To see what all of this means, suppose that the credit sale agreement in example (i) above is one which X has the right to cancel.[89] Then if X were to cancel the agreement before the freezer was installed, he would not be obliged to have it installed and thus would not be obliged to pay for the installation. That is all very sensible since if X has cancelled the credit sale agreement then he is not going to have the freezer. If X did not cancel the credit sale agreement but paid off the whole of his credit within six months of delivery he would not be obliged to have Y restock the freezer. As we shall see later, a debtor has a right to pay off the credit early at any time he wishes.[90]

The Total Charge for Credit

The Act makes a basic distinction between the credit and the cost to the debtor of having it. The idea behind having a definition of the "total charge for credit" is that the definition should produce a figure which, if stated to the debtor, will accurately tell him the cost of having the credit. The "credit" and the "total charge for credit" are mutually exclusive. Any sum which is part of the total charge for credit cannot be part of the credit. A simple agreement to borrow £25,000 and to repay it at the end of a year with £25,000 + £3,000 interest involves credit of £25,000 and a total charge for credit of £3,000. A creditor may, however, try to conceal his charges. He may require a repayment of only £25,000 whilst at the same time requiring the debtor, as a precondition to getting the loan, to buy a peanut for £3,000. More subtly, he may, as condition of the loan, require the debtor to take out an insurance policy with a particular insurance company—a company which, perhaps, has agreed to pay the creditor a handsome commission on such new business. There are numerous ways in which a debtor may find that he has to pay for having credit. The definition of the total charge for credit is designed to include such costs so that when the total charge for credit is stated, it represents the true cost of the credit.[91] 18-024

The amount of the total charge for credit may have to be calculated for any one of a number of reasons, including the following:

88 s.19(3).

89 See para.21-039, below.

90 For exceptions to the general rule see the Consumer Credit (Linked Transactions) (Exemptions) Regulations 1983 (SI 1983/1560).

91 See generally, J. Devenney and N. Ryder, "The cartography of the concept of 'total charge for credit' under the Consumer Credit Act 1974" [2006] Conv. 475.

(i) It is a necessary first step towards the calculation of the annual percentage rate of charge.[92]

(ii) It may in some cases have to be included in the agreement in accordance with the formality requirements.[93]

(iii) It will be relevant in determining the debtor's liability under a debtor-creditor agreement after cancellation.[94]

(iv) In conjunction with the annual percentage rate of charge, it will be relevant in determining whether an agreement creates an unfair creditor/debtor relationship.[95]

Prior to the transfer of consumer credit regulation to the Financial Conduct Authority on 1 April 2014, there were two sets of regulations concerning the total charge for credit: the Consumer Credit (Total Charge for Credit) Regulations 2010 and the Consumer Credit (Total Charge for Credit) Regulations 1980.[96] The 2010 regulations were introduced in order to ensure compliance with the Consumer Credit Directive[97] and had the effect of replacing the 1980 regulations in respect of all credit agreements except certain credit agreements secured on land.[98] Both sets of regulations have, with effect from 1 April 2014 been repealed, however, the substance of each has been incorporated into the Financial Conduct Authority's Consumer Credit Sourcebook (CONC).

18–025 The CONC offers a broad definition of what it terms the "total cost of credit to the -borrower". It includes "all costs, including interest, commissions, taxes and any other kind of fees which are required to be paid by or on behalf of the debtor or a relative of the debtor in connection with the consumer credit agreement." It is irrelevant whether the charges are to be paid to the creditor or another person. Compulsory ancillary service costs, such as brokerage fees or payment protection insurance premiums (PPI)[99] are expressly included within the meaning of the total charge. The total charge for credit includes the following:[100]

(a) any fee or charge payable by the borrower to a credit broker in connection with the agreement (if the fee or charge is known to the lender);

92 See the Consumer Credit Directive art.19.
93 See para.21-039, below.
94 See para.21-029, below.
95 See para.23-006, below.
96 SI 2010/1011 and SI 1980/51 respectively.
97 Directive 2008/48/EC.
98 For an account of the 1980 Regulations, see the 7th edn of this book.
99 This is a policy to ensure that the creditor is repaid (fully or partially) in the event of the death, invalidity, illness or unemployment of the debtor.
100 CONC App 1.2.3(2) R.

(b) the costs of maintaining an account recording both payment transactions and drawdowns;

(c) the costs of using a means of payment for both payment transactions and drawdowns; and

(d) other costs relating to payment transactions.

This is subject to two exceptions. First, where the opening of the account is optional and the costs of the account have been clearly and separately shown in the consumer credit agreement (or other agreement with the debtor). Secondly, in the case of an overdraft facility, where the costs to the debtor do not relate to that facility.[101]

More generally, default or non-compliance charges are excluded by these exceptions from the total charge for credit as are any charges which would be payable by a customer buying the same goods or services for cash instead of on credit terms.[102] Default charges are excluded because they are not payable if the debtor honours his agreement. Charges which would be payable by a cash customer (e.g. delivery charges payable on a new car) are excluded because, as a matter of common sense, they are not part of the cost of the credit. This rule also means that if a discount is given to cash customers, and not to credit customers, then the discount is part of the total charge for credit.[103]

General Reading

N. Bamforth, "Human rights and consumer credit" (2002) 118 L.Q.R. 203.
J. Devenney and N. Ryder, "The cartography of the concept of 'total charge for credit' under the Consumer Credit Act 1974" [2006] Conv. 475.
E. Lomnicka, "The reform of consumer credit in the UK" [2004] J.B.L. 129.
J.K. Macleod, "Credit hire in the House of Lords" [2001] J.B.L. 14.
J.K. Macleod, "Credit Hire" [1999] J.B.L. 452.
J. Patient, "The Consumer Credit Act 2006" [2006] J.I.B.L.R. 309.
F. Philpott, "E-Commerce and Consumer Credit" [2001] J.I.F.M. 131.

101 CONC App 1.2.3(3) R.
102 CONC App 1.2.3(5) R
103 *R. v Baldwin's Garage* [1988] Crim. L.R. 438.

19

Authorisation

From Licensing to Authorisation

In March 2013 the government announced that responsibility for consumer credit regulation was to be subsumed into the regulatory framework for financial services generally, spearheaded by the Financial Conduct Authority. Its consultation stated that consumer credit regulation was an area "ripe for reform" and that:[1] 19-001

> **"Consumers are not sufficiently protected from harm in this market. The National Audit Office (NAO) recently highlighted that the current regulatory regime lacks the capacity and powers to tackle the bulk of detriment in the consumer credit market: the NAO estimated unaddressed detriment cost consumers £450 million in 2011–12."**

One key consequence of this reform was the demise of the licensing framework created by the Consumer Credit Act 1974 and operated by the Office of Fair Trading. Thus following the transfer of consumer credit regulation to the Financial Conduct Authority on 1 April 2014 the licensing system created by the 1974 Act was replaced by the authorisation system applicable to activities regulated under the Financial Services and Markets Act 2000. To put it another way, the control over entry to the consumer credit market moved from a licensing regime under the control of the Office of Fair Trading to the authorisation framework for financial services generally, under the remit of the Financial Conduct Authority. Thus Pt 3 of the Consumer

1 HM Government, "A New Approach to Financial Regulation: Transferring Consumer Credit Regulation to the Financial Conduct Authority" March 2013, at para.1.3.

Credit Act 1974 was repealed in its entirety with effect from 1 April 2014.[2] This represents a fundamental shift in the approach toward consumer credit regulation, with the government suggesting that "greater scrutiny at the gateway to the market, especially for higher risk firms, will improve standards and root out rogue firms before they enter the market".[3] As we will see, it is clear that the authorisation framework under the FCA is considerably more demanding on consumer credit businesses than the licensing regime which preceded it.[4]

Business Needing Authorisation

19–002 Broadly, if a business intends to engage in regulated activity it must apply for authorisation from the Financial Conduct Authority. In the context of consumer credit and hire a wide range of activities are classified as "regulated activity" including:[5]

- Entering into a regulated credit or regulated consumer hire agreement (as lender or owner respectively).
- Exercising, or having the right to exercise, the lender's (or owner's) rights and duties under a regulated credit agreement (or regulated consumer hire agreement).
- Credit broking.
- Debt adjusting.
- Debt counselling.
- Debt-collecting.
- Debt administration.

2 Financial Services and Markets Act 2000 (Regulated Activities) (Amendment) (No.2) Order 2013 (SI 2013/1881) art.20(10).

3 HM Government, "A New Approach to Financial Regulation: Transferring Consumer Credit Regulation to the Financial Conduct Authority" March 2013, at para.1.18.

4 For an account of the old law, the reader may be directed to the 8th edn of this text. Since all existing consumer credit licenses lapsed on the transfer of regulation to the FCA, it is generally of historical interest only, although it may be that various pre-1 April 2014 agreements remain unenforceable under CCA 1974 s.40.

5 Thus authorisation is not required for a business which only offers credit (or hire) to companies or partnerships of over three persons, or which provides credit only under exempt agreements.

- Providing credit information services.
- Providing credit references.
- Operating an electronic system in relation to lending.

With one key exception, these activities broadly replicate the previous position under the Consumer Credit Act's licensing framework. The exception is the final category noted above: the operation of an electronic system in relation to lending. This is a new category of activity requiring authorisation and is intended to address electronic peer-to-peer lending which has grown in popularity (and prominence) in recent years.

The definition of regulated activity makes it clear that authorisation is only required where the activity is carried on by way of business.[6] In the context of consumer credit and hire activities, this term is left undefined in the Financial Services and Markets Act 2000. FCA guidance highlights that this is a matter of judgement which will take into account of a variety of factors, including the degree of continuity, the existence of a commercial element, the scale of the activity and the proportion which the activity bears to other activities carried on by the same person but which are not regulated.[7] Thus if someone on one occasion lends money to a friend—even if the friend is to pay interest—the lender would not be regarded as thereby carrying on a business. Similarly, a car dealer who never normally provides credit but who on one occasion agrees to supply a car to a friend on hire-purchase terms will not necessarily be carrying on a regulated activity by way of business.[8] A garage proprietor who (more than occasionally) hired out cars under regulated consumer hire agreements would be engaging in regulated activity even if the main part of his business consisted of selling cars and petrol for cash.

Authorisation and the Financial Conduct Authority

In order to qualify for authorisation, a firm must satisfy the threshold conditions as laid down 19-003
in s.55B and Sch.6 to the Financial Services and Markets Act 2000.[9] These are the minimum conditions which the FCA must ensure the firm will satisfy (and continue to satisfy) and they

6 FSMA 2000 s.22.

7 PERG 2.3.3.G. See *Helden v Strathmore Ltd* [2011] EWCA Civ 542.

8 See *Hare v Schurek*, para.28-022, above (no licence required under the old CCA system). Note that technically the equivalent definitions in CCA s.189 are not relevant to the FCA regime.

9 As supplemented by the Threshold Condition Code.

vary according to the nature of the credit activity to be offered, i.e. the level of risk associated with the product or service to be provided. There are a number of threshold conditions relevant to consumer credit firms:[10]

1. Location of Offices (where the firm is incorporated in the UK, both its head office and registered office must be in the UK).

2. Effective Supervision (the business must be capable of effective supervision by the FCA).

3. Appropriate Resources (both financial and non-financial, e.g. skills and expertise).

4. Suitability (is the applicant a "fit and proper person"?).

Under the FCA's scheme of authorisation there are two types of permission: "full" permission and "limited" permission. These labels distinguish the level of risk involved and, in general, firms that require full authorisation will face additional authorisation conditions, together with heightened scrutiny and monitoring. The following activities require full permission:

- most consumer credit lending;[11]
- credit broking;[12]
- debt adjusting and debt counselling (unless not-for-profit);
- debt collection;
- debt administration;
- providing credit information services (unless not-for-profit);
- providing credit reference agency services; and
- peer-to-peer lending.

10 See paras 2B–2E of Sch.6 Pt 1B of FSMA 2000.

11 Full permission is required for consumer credit lending (e.g. credit cards, hire purchase, personal loans, etc.) unless the trader's main business is selling goods and non-financial services other than by hire-purchase or conditional sale and there is no interest or charge for the finance. Thus a retailer offering goods such as home furnishings on credit sale terms, with no interest or charges being applied, would require only limited permission.

12 Unless the main business is selling goods or non-financial services and broking is a secondary activity or where it relates to the Green Deal.

Whereas the following activities require limited permission:

- consumer credit lending where the trader's main business is selling goods and non-financial services other than by hire-purchase or conditional sale and there is no interest or charge for the finance;
- consumer hire;
- credit broking by non-financial business (e.g. a car dealership who introduces customers to lenders);
- not-for-profit debt counselling and debt adjusting;
- not-for-profit credit information services; and
- lending by local authorities within the scope of the Consumer Credit Directive.

This is an important change to the old consumer credit licensing regime under the 1974 Act which made no such risk-based distinction and ought to enable a more focused and proportionate regulatory approach to consumer credit. Another likely change can be noted. Under the licensing framework of the 1974 Act consumer credit providers would have been well advised to apply for a license covering all consumer credit activity, not merely that which they intended to engage with. This would ensure that they would not inadvertently enter into agreements which were not covered by their license and thereby face criminal and civil sanctions. The increased scrutiny of applications for authorisation (when compared to the grant of a license), coupled with the possibility of heightened ongoing supervision by the FCA, mean that it is now advisable for consumer credit providers to consider carefully the nature of the authorisation applied for.

A more significant consequence of consumer credit regulation being subsumed into the general framework of financial services supervision under the FCA is the application of the "Approved Person" regime to consumer credit firms. Under the 1974 Act, the OFT was primarily concerned with the suitability (or fitness) of the licensee, whether that was an individual or a company. The FCA framework, however, extends not only to the business, but also to formal approval of key individuals within that business such as senior management or with specific roles of particular importance (such as the individual responsible for anti-money laundering reporting). This is achieved through s.59 of the Financial Services and Markets Act which requires an authorised person to take reasonable care to ensure that no person performs a "controlled function" in relation to regulated activity. The controlled functions which are relevant to consumer credit firms vary by firm, but include matters such as governing functions, compliance oversight and money laundering reporting. In general every consumer credit firm must have at least one approved person (there are exceptions such as that for most not-for profit debt advice organisations) and comes with a number of responsibilities, 19–004 including understanding how the regulatory requirements apply to their controlled function (or functions).

The aim of these various levels of supervision is to ensure that consumer credit businesses and key individuals within those firms are fit and proper to enter the consumer credit market, and that relevant standards are maintained post-authorisation. One crucial element of being authorised as a consumer credit business is the FCA Handbook which contains various rules (which are legally binding) and guidance (which is not binding). It is only possible to outline the broad impact of the FCA Handbook here. However interested readers may locate it on the FCA webpages.[13] In brief, the Handbook specifies various "High Level Standards" that apply to consumer credit firms. These standards include:

- Principles for Businesses (PRIN)[14]
- Threshold Conditions (COND)[15]
- General Provisions (GEN)[16]
- Senior Management Arrangements, Systems and Controls (SYSC)[17]
- Statements of Principle and Code of Practice for Approved Persons (APER)[18]
- The Fit and Proper Test for Approved Persons (FIT)[19]

The Principles for Business offer a useful insight into the broad approach of FCA regulation since it lays down the fundamental principles with which authorised firms must comply. Of particular relevance to the consumer credit industry are the following:[20]

13 Available here: *https://www.handbook.fca.org.uk/handbook* [Accessed 11 April 2022].
14 These are the fundamental principles with which authorised firms must comply.
15 As noted above at para.19.003, these are the minimum conditions which firms must meet in order to be authorised.
16 This sets out standards for all firms with regard to, for example, how the firm interacts with the FCA.
17 This details the expectations operative on senior management regarding their responsibilities for the running and oversight of their firm.
18 This describes the standards that the FCA require of individuals who hold, or will hold, a "controlled function" in a firm.
19 This addresses the criteria that will be considered when assessing the fitness and propriety of an application by an individual for a controlled function, as discussed above. The most important considerations are the person's honesty, integrity and reputation, competence, capability, and financial soundness.
20 CONC.1.1.4.G.

- Principle 1 (a firm must conduct its business with integrity).
- Principle 2 (a firm must conduct its business with due skill, care and diligence).
- Principle 3 (a firm must take reasonable care to organise and control its affairs responsibly and effectively, with adequate risk management systems).
- Principle 6 (a firm must pay due regard to the interests of its customers and treat them fairly).
- Principle 7 (a firm must pay due regard to the information needs of its clients, and communicate information to them in a way which is clear, fair and not misleading).[21]
- Principle 9 (a firm must take reasonable care to ensure the suitability of its advice and discretionary decisions for any customer who is entitled to rely upon its judgement).
- Principle 10 (a firm must arrange adequate protection for clients' assets when it is responsible for them).
- Principle 11 (a firm must deal with its regulators in an open and co-operative way).

Another important element of the Handbook is the specialist Consumer Credit Sourcebook (CONC). The purpose of the Consumer Credit Sourcebook is to set out the detailed obligations that are specific to the consumer credit industry. Many of the rules laid down in CONC derive from provisions within the Consumer Credit Act, related statutory instruments or OFT Guidance and we will discuss a number of these in the next chapter. It is interesting to note, however, that the FCA wasted little time in using CONC to extend the ambit of consumer credit regulation where it deemed it necessary such as in the "pay-day loan" (or High-Cost Short-Term Loan) market. This form of consumer credit now has various, highly targeted, rules designed to combat various undesirable elements of this market, including a cap on the maximum interest permitted (0.8 per cent per day); a cap on the total of the interest and fees chargeable (which must not exceed 100 per cent of the loan) and limiting the number of "roll-overs" permitted (to two).[22] It would appear that the FCA's intervention has been successful with Citizens Advice

21 The FCA has recently concluded a second consultation on a new "consumer duty" whereby a new Principle 12 ("A firm must act to deliver good outcomes for retail customers") is to impose a higher standard in replacing Principles 6 and 7 where it applies. See further: *https://www.fca.org.uk/publication/consultation/cp21-36.pdf* [Accessed 11 April 2022]. It is expected that new rules will be introduced by 31 July 2022 and implementation is expected no later than 30 April 2023.

22 See further, CONC.5A.

reporting that there has been an 86 per cent reduction in the number of clients seeking their guidance regarding payday loans between 2013 and 2016.[23]

The Consequences of Being Unauthorised

19–005 Section 19 of the Financial Services and Markets Act 2000 imposes what is termed "the general prohibition". This means that it is prohibited for any person to undertake regulated activity unless they are either an authorised person or an exempt person.[24] It is a criminal offence to breach the general prohibition.[25] Under s.23 the authorisation offence is one of strict liability, though there is a due diligence offence available. Further, the Act also makes it a criminal offence for an authorised person to carry on a "credit related regulated activity" without the necessary permission.[26] This is significant since it maintains the criminal sanction available under the old CCA licensing regime where a licensed business entered into agreements outside of the scope of their licence. Broadly, under the FCA authorisation framework, it is not a criminal offence for an authorised person to engage in regulated activities which are outside of the scope of their authorisation however s.23(1A) of FSMA 2000 ensures that this level of consumer protection is maintained under the new FCA-led system.[27] This is achieved by designating certain activities as credit-related regulated activity, though their powers are limited (for example, no regulated credit activity secured on land can be designated). Indeed, not all regulated credit activities have been designated as "credit-related regulated activity" though the Treasury have designated lending under regulated agreements and debt collection as such.[28]

There are further consequences stemming from unauthorised activity. Under s.26(1) of FSMA 2000 a person who contravenes the general prohibition is unable to enforce the agreement. This mirrors the position previously laid down by s.40 of the 1974 Act whilst the agreement is enforceable as against the lender or voidable at the election of the consumer. Similarly, s.26A renders a credit-related regulated activity agreement unenforceable against the consumer where the business exceeds the terms of their authorisation under s.20. As with s.26, agreement is voidable at the election of the consumer who is also entitled to claim for compensation. These agreements are not, however, permanently unenforceable. Under s.28A, the business who breached the general prohibition or exceeded the terms of their authorisation can

23 Citizens Advice, "Payday loans: An Improved Market?" March 2016.

24 For the definition of "exempt persons" see s.417(1). Note that under s.24 it is a criminal offence to falsely claim to be authorised or exempt.

25 See for example, *R v Gopee* [2019] EWCA Crim 601 where the Court of Appeal held that a sentence of three and half years' imprisonment for unlawful money lending was not manifestly excessive.

26 s.23(1A).

27 Though it would contravene s.20 of FSMA 2000.

28 See the FSMA 2000 (Consumer Credit) (Designated Activities) Order 2014 (SI 2014/334).

apply to the FCA who have the discretion, where it is just and equitable to enforce the credit-related regulated activity agreement. Where the agreement does not concern credit-related regulated activity, the equivalent discretion lies with the court. In either case, the FCA or the court must consider whether the firm "reasonably believed that by making the agreement the relevant firm was neither contravening the general prohibition nor contravening section 20".[29]

29 See s.28 and s.28A of FSMA 2000.

20

Advertising and Seeking Business

Introduction

Following the transfer of consumer credit regulation to the Financial Conduct Authority on 1 April 2014 the regulation of consumer credit advertising, including matters such as the content of advertisements and quotations, is dealt with through the FCA's Consumer Credit Sourcebook (CONC). In consequence, various provisions of the Consumer Credit Act have been repealed. Nonetheless, the Consumer Credit Act places controls and restrictions upon canvassing off trade premises and totally prohibits certain kinds of promotion of credit facilities.[1] 20-001

Canvassing Off Trade Premises

The Act has a two-pronged method of protecting the consumer from what can loosely be termed "doorstep selling" of credit. By one prong, it gives consumers a right of withdrawal from most regulated consumer credit agreements by entitling the consumer to cancel the agreement after he has made it without giving the creditor any explanation. This prong does not, however, place any restriction or control upon the way in which a customer may be persuaded to make an agreement. The second prong places restrictions and controls upon canvassing off 20-002

1 The FCA was required to review the remaining CCA 1974 provisions to consider whether they could effectively be moved into the FCA Handbook. The Final Report was published in March 2019, see further: *https://www.fca.org.uk/publication/corporate/review-of-retained-provisions-of-the-consumer-credit-act-final-report.pdf* [Accessed 11 April 2022].

trade premises. The first prong, which deals with withdrawal (and cancellation) will be considered in Ch.24 and will not figure any more in the present chapter.

There are two different kinds of canvassing off trade premises. One is concerned with persuading a member of the public (a consumer) to make a regulated agreement and the other with persuading someone to agree to engage the services of an ancillary credit trader. We shall consider them separately.

Canvassing a Consumer to Make a Regulated Agreement

20–003 The definition in s.48 of "canvassing off trade premises" is technical. It deals with oral persuasion aimed at getting a customer to make a regulated agreement. Making oral representations in an attempt to induce a consumer to enter into a regulated agreement amounts to canvassing off trade premises if:

(a) the oral representations are made during a visit by the canvasser carried out for the purpose of making them,

(b) the visit is to somewhere other than where a business is carried on by any of the following—namely the canvasser, the creditor or owner, the supplier or the consumer, and

(c) the visit is not made in response to a request made on a previous occasion.[2]

It is only if the canvassing falls within this definition that it is controlled in the ways shortly to be explained. Thus, there is no control upon visits made to the consumer at the consumer's business premises. A visit made, for example to a shop in order to persuade the shopkeeper to take a loan is not canvassing off trade premises. Nor would it be canvassing off trade premises if the canvasser, having visited some premises (e.g. his golf club) for just one purpose (e.g. to play golf), fell, whilst there, into conversation (e.g. with another member) during which he found himself suggesting that the other should consider taking credit (perhaps to buy a new set of golf clubs). It is only if the canvasser made the visit for the purpose of making such a suggestion that he will be canvassing off trade premises.

There are two controls upon activity which does fall within the definition. First, there is a total ban on the canvassing off trade premises of debtor-creditor agreements (e.g. ordinary cash loans). It is a criminal offence under s.49. Even if the visit is made in response to an earlier request, it will still be an offence unless that request was in writing and signed.[3] The second control relates to other regulated agreements. These are not totally prohibited. However, for

2 The request must be to invite discussions in respect of a regulated agreement, see *PF (International) Ltd v The Financial Conduct Authority* [2018] UKUT 400 (TCC).

3 s.49(2).

it to be lawful to canvass off trade premises these other regulated agreements, the canvasser must be operating under a licence which specifically authorises canvassing off trade premises.[4] Thus, whilst doorstep attempts to persuade the consumer to take an ordinary loan are totally banned, the doorstep sale of trading checks and the doorstep promotion of goods or services (e.g. double glazing) on credit terms is allowed.

There is one very limited exception to what has been said so far. It arises from a determination by the Financial Conduct Authority under s.49(3). It applies only in the case of an ordinary current account (a cheque book account), only where the canvasser is trying to persuade an account holder to take an overdraft on a current account, and only where the canvasser is the creditor or an employee of the creditor. In this case, there is no ban on canvassing off trade premises. Thus, a bank manager can visit an existing customer in the customer's home to try to persuade that customer to take an overdraft on a current account.

Canvassing the Services of an Ancillary Credit Trader

An ancillary credit trader is anyone who carries on a business as a credit broker, debt collector, debt counsellor, debt adjuster, debt administrator, credit information service, or credit reference agency.[5] The definition here (in s.153) is the same as the definition of the first kind of canvassing off trade premises, except that here the object of the canvassing is to persuade the person who is the target of it to enter into an agreement to engage the services of an ancillary credit trader. 20-004

Thus, making oral representations for that purpose amounts to canvassing off trade premises if:

(a) the oral representations are made during a visit by the canvasser carried out for the purpose of making them,

(b) the visit is to somewhere other than where a business is carried on by any of the – following—namely, the canvasser, the canvasser's employer or principal or the person to whom the representations are made, and

(c) the visit is not made in response to a request made on an earlier occasion.

4 s.23(3).

5 s.145(1). The new categories of debt administration and credit information services were added to the list of ancillary credit traders by the Consumer Credit Act 2006.

There is just one very strict control upon this second kind of canvassing off trade premises. It is a criminal offence to canvass off trade premises the services of a credit broker, debt adjuster, debt counsellor or a provider of credit information services.[6]

Criminal Offences

Circulars to Minors

20–005 It is an offence, with a view to financial gain, to send to a minor (someone under the age of 18) a circular inviting him to obtain credit (or goods on hire) or to seek further information about it.[7] If, however, a circular is sent to a minor which includes a statement that loans are not available to anyone under 18, then the offence is not committed because the circular does not amount to an invitation to the minor to obtain credit.[8] The same case decided that if the advertiser had a policy and system to ensure that applications from minors were refused, then also the offence would not be committed, since the advertiser would then clearly not have sent the circular to the minor "with a view to financial gain".

Unsolicited Credit Tokens

20–006 Prior to 1 April 2014, it was an offence to issue a credit token[9] to someone who has not asked for it in writing signed by himself.[10] This was intended to prevent the unsolicited sending out of credit cards.[11] When consumer credit regulation was transferred from the Office of Fair Trading to the Financial Conduct Authority, the offence was repealed and replaced by rules under the FCA's Consumer Credit Sourcebook (CONC). Thus, an FCA-authorised person is prohibited from issuing a credit token to someone who has not requested it in writing.[12] As with the former CCA offence, there is an exception where the credit token is issued as a renewal or replacement for a previous one.[13]

---

6 s.154.

7 s.50.

8 *Alliance & Leicester Building Society v Babbs* [1993] C.C.L.R. 77.

9 Defined in s.14. See para.23-022, below.

10 s.51.

11 As occurred, for example, when, before the Consumer Credit Act was passed, the Access credit card scheme was launched.

12 CONC 2.9.2 R.

13 For an example of a conviction under s.51, *see Elliott v Director-General of Fair Trading*, para.23-023, below.

Advertising

Prior to the transfer of consumer credit regulation to the Financial Conduct Authority, the Consumer Credit Act together with the Consumer Credit (Advertising) Regulations 2010 served to control the form and content of various types of consumer credit and related advertisements.[14] In general, the advertisements which were controlled were those which indicated that the advertiser was willing to provide credit or goods on hire. By way of illustration, *Jenkins v Lombard North Central*[15] concerned an advertisement for a car which bore not only the price of the car but also the words "Lombard North Central Limited" together with that company's logo. This was held not to be a controlled advertisement because, although it suggested that the company might provide credit, it did not state as a fact that the company was willing to provide credit. 20-007

With effect from 1 April 2014 however, the form and content of consumer credit advertisements is no longer dealt with by the Consumer Credit Act (and the regulations) and is instead controlled through the Financial Services and Markets Act 2000 and the FCA's Consumer Credit Sourcebook.

Financial Promotion Under the FSMA 2000

The fundamental approach of the FMSA 2000 to financial promotion is to ensure that such activity is only undertaken by, or with the approval of, authorised persons. As such, s.21 of the Act prohibits an unauthorised person from making a "communication" which "invites or induces" another to engage in "investment activity" where that communication is made in the course of business.[16] The term "communication" is not defined, but is clearly very wide and will cover conveying or making information known to another irrespective of the form. It is, therefore, capable of extending far beyond only advertisements. Similarly, the concept of invitation or inducement is not defined, though it is clear that the words connote a promotional element, thus, a communication which seeks to inform or educate and does not have an element of persuasion or incitement to engage in investment activity will not fall under s.21.[17] In order to fall under the s.21 prohibition, the communication must relate to engaging in an investment activity. The phrase "engage in investment activity" has a specific meaning and refers to, inter alia, entering into (or offering to enter into) a "controlled activity".[18] The activities which are "controlled" are specified in the Financial Services and Markets Act 2000 (Financial Promotion) 20-008

14 For an account of the approach of the Act to advertisements, see s.43 and s.151 (now repealed), and the 8th edn of this book.

15 [1984] 1 All E.R. 828.

16 s.21 was amended by the Financial Guidance and Claims Act 2018 to extend its ambit to claims management activity.

17 See the FCA's Perimeter Guidance Manual (PERG), 8.4.

18 See FSMA 2000 s.21(8).

Order 2005.[19] In the context of consumer credit, controlled activities extend to the various activities considered earlier in relation to the authorisation framework. Thus the provision of credit agreements, consumer hire agreements, credit broking, and various ancillary activities such as debt counselling are all forms of "controlled activity".[20]

A breach of the prohibition on financial promotion is deemed to be an "unlawful communication".[21] Agreements made as a consequence of an unlawful communication are unenforceable and the customer is entitled to recover any money or property transferred by him under the agreement and compensation for losses incurred as a result of that transfer.[22] The court has discretion to allow enforcement of the agreement, money or property transferred under the agreement to be retained where it is just and equitable to do so. In considering whether to exercise this discretion, the court must have regard to two specific matters laid down in s.30(6) and s.30(7). First, if the lender or owner was responsible for the unlawful communication, the court must consider whether the lender or owner reasonably believed that he was not making an unlawful communication. Secondly, if the lender or owner did not make the unlawful communication, the court must consider whether the lender or owner knew that the agreement was entered into in consequence of an unlawful communication. In either case, these considerations are not conclusive and the court will consider any matters relevant to whether or not it would be fair and equitable to enforce the agreement. Thus, for example, the general question of whether the communication was fair and not misleading will be of importance.

It is a criminal offence to breach the restriction on financial promotion laid down in s.21.[23] The offence is one of strict liability, although there is a due diligence offence laid down in s.25(2). The offence cannot be committed by an authorised person (or where the content of a communication has been approved by an authorised person).[24] Instead an authorised person must comply with the Financial Conduct Authority's rules relating to financial promotion.

The Financial Conduct Authority and Advertisements

20-009 Chapter 3 of the FCA's Consumer Credit Sourcebook (CONC) deals with financial promotions and communications with customers. In so doing, it employs the same terminology of financial promotion as previously considered in relation to the s.21 offence. In general, the rules laid down in CONC replicate the provisions of the (now revoked) Consumer Credit (Advertisement)

19 SI 2005/1529, as amended in the context of credit related activities by the Financial Services and Markets Act 2000 (Regulated Activities) (Amendment) (No.2) Order 2013.

20 See Sch.1 to the Financial Services and Markets Act 2000 (Financial Promotion) Order 2005. The Order also exempts certain, narrowly defined, communications from the restriction on financial promotion in s.21. See, for example, art.48 (certain communications to high net worth individuals).

21 FSMA 2000 s.30(1).

22 FSMA 2000 s.30(2).

23 FSMA 2000 s.25.

24 FSMA 2000 s.21(2).

Regulations, however, the consequences of non-compliance are significantly different.[25] The Consumer Credit Act made it a criminal offence for consumer credit and hire advertisements not to comply with the relevant set of advertisement regulations. Where an authorised person breaches the financial promotion rules laid down in CONC 3, however, no criminal offence will be committed. Instead, such breach could give rise to civil remedies under s.138D whereby a private person can bring a civil claim in respect of loss suffered as a result of the breach. The authorised person could, additionally, face disciplinary action for the failure to comply with the rules in the Consumer Credit Sourcebook.

The detail of the rules in CONC 3 is too great to be given here. Their broad thrust can be outlined. Their aim is to see that the consumer is given sufficient information[26] in such a way that he gains a fair impression of what is being advertised and also can make a meaningful comparison between different sources of credit. Thus it is a fundamental requirement that financial promotions are fair, clear, and not misleading.[27] This requirement is a corollary of the high-level Principles for Businesses which operate as fundamental obligations under the FCA regulatory regime. In particular Principle 6 states that a "firm must pay due regard to the interests of its customers and treat them fairly". Similarly, Principle 7 requires a firm to "pay due regard to the information needs of its clients, and communicate information to them in a way which is clear, fair and not misleading".[28] Further to this general requirement, CONC 3.3.2 R dictates that every communication or financial promotion must:

(a) use plain and intelligible language;

(b) be easily legible (or, in the case of any information given orally, clearly audible); and

(c) specify the name of the person making the communication or financial promotion.

The FCA's Guidance on the fair, clear and not misleading requirement explains that a firm should ensure that communications and financial promotions are accurate and avoid emphasising potential benefits of a product or service without also giving a fair and prominent

25 The Rules laid down in CONC also replicate the old offence (now repealed) in s.45 of the CCA 1974 (a firm must not indicate a willingness to supply goods or services on credit terms at a time when the firm (or supplier) is not also prepared to supply the goods or services for cash), see CONC 3.5.2. R.

26 See, for example, CONC 3.5 which lays down rules as to the content of financial promotions about credit agreements not secured on land and CONC 3.7 which lays down rules in relation to financial promotions in relation to credit broking activities.

27 CONC 3.3.1. R.

28 Note that the FCA has recently concluded a (second) consultation on a new "consumer duty" whereby a new Principle 12 ("A firm must act to deliver good outcomes for retail customers") is to impose a higher standard in replacing Principles 6 and 7 where it applies. See further: *https://www.fca.org.uk/publication/consultation/cp21-36.pdf* [Accessed 11 April 2022]. It is expected that new rules will be introduced by 31 July 2022 and implementation is expected no later than 30 April 2023.

indication of any relevant risks. Where a firm takes reasonable steps to ensure that this broad requirement is satisfied, any breach will not give rise to a right of action under s.138D.

In order to ensure that a consumer is not misled by the terminology of a financial promotion CONC 3 also imposes certain restrictions. These include banning (i) the use of the term "overdraft" for a general running account credit arrangement (i.e. where the facility is not drawing on a current account), and (ii) the use of the term "gift" or similar unless there are no conditions requiring the debtor to return either the credit or the free item.[29]

General Reading

R. Azim-Khan, "Those Winter Sales Offers—Festive Cheer or New Year Gloom?" (2004) 66 Commercial Law 54.

F. Besemer, "New Rules on Misleading and Comparative Advertising" [2008] Entertainment Law Review 115.

H.A. Johnson and H. Johnson, "Advertisers Beware! The Impact of the Unfair Commercial Practices Directive" [2005] Communications Law 164–169.

29 See CONC 3.5.12 for a complete list. Similar restrictions were previously effected through the Advertising Regulations.

21

Formation of a Consumer Credit Agreement

Because different types of consumer credit agreements are made in different ways, it will be necessary to deal with the different types separately. Many of the problems arising in connection with hire-purchase, conditional sale and credit sale agreements are due to the fact that the agreement between debtor and creditor (finance company) is often negotiated through the dealer. Thus these agreements will be considered first. Before embarking upon that, we should note that the formality and cancellation provisions of the Consumer Credit Act apply to regulated agreements of all types. These provisions and also provisions relating to credit brokers' fees and credit reference agencies will be considered later in this chapter. 21-001

Hire Purchase, Conditional Sale and Credit Sale Agreements

Offer, Acceptance and Revocation

As we have seen, the customer usually makes an offer to the finance company by filling in a form and leaving it with the dealer. That offer will usually be accepted by the finance company posting their acceptance to the customer. In that case the contract will be made when the acceptance is put in the post. It usually takes several days and sometimes much more. At any time before the letter of acceptance is posted (or the offeror is in some other way informed of the finance company's acceptance) the offeror can revoke his offer. Normally, in order for revocation to be effective, it must actually be notified to the other party before the contract is made. So, if the customer 21-002 (i.e. the offeror) posts the finance company a revocation of his offer, that revocation will be effective only if it actually arrives before the finance company posts its letter of acceptance. However, there is no need for the revocation to be in writing. Furthermore, the dealer is agent of the finance company for the purpose of receiving revocations. Thus, when the customer tells the dealer that he revokes his offer to the finance company, that has the same effect as if he had told the finance company. Provided he does so before the finance company posts its letter of acceptance, there will be no contract between the customer and the finance company.

In *Financings v Stimson*[1] the customer filled in at the dealer's premises a hire-purchase proposal form and he was allowed to drive the car away. The dealer sent the form off in the usual way to the finance company. After four days the customer returned the car to the dealer declaring that he did not want it. Shortly after that the car was stolen from the dealer's premises. It was recovered fairly quickly but in a badly damaged state. The following day the finance company purported to accept the customer's offer and sent him a copy of the "agreement". The Court of Appeal held that there was no agreement and therefore no contract for two reasons: (i) by returning the car to the dealer and declaring that he did not want it, the customer revoked his offer to the finance company. Communication of that revocation to the dealer was sufficient, as the latter was the finance company's agent for the purpose of receiving a revocation; and (ii) the customer's offer to the finance company must be taken to have been conditional upon the goods being in substantially the same state at the time of acceptance as they were at the time the offer was first made. Thus for two reasons the customer's offer was, at the time in question, incapable for being accepted. There being no contract, the customer was under no liability to the finance company.

The position as so far stated is that at common law. The customer's position at common law is strengthened where s.57 of the Consumer Credit Act applies. That section applies to all regulated hire-purchase and conditional sale agreements other than non-commercial ones and it applies to all regulated credit sale agreements other than non-commercial agreements and small agreements. It has two important provisions. First, the dealer is agent of the creditor for the purpose of receiving notice (oral or written) that the debtor's offer is withdrawn.[2] This reinforces the rule in *Financings v Stimson*. Secondly, the withdrawal of either party from a prospective agreement takes effect as if the agreement:[3]

(i) had been actually made,

(ii) had been a cancellable one, and

(iii) had been cancelled by the debtor under s.69.

1 [1962] 3 All E.R. 386 (followed by the Court of Appeal in *CF Asset Finance v Okonji* [2014] EWCA Civ 870).
2 s.57(2) and 57(3).
3 s.57(1) and s.57(4).

Thus the debtor will be in the same position as he would be in after cancelling a cancellable agreement. As we shall see shortly the debtor is in a strong position after cancellation. Thus s.57 has the effect of strengthening his position after withdrawal from a prospective agreement. 21-003

A withdrawal from a prospective agreement means that there is no agreement and therefore no obligation under the agreement. If the debtor has taken delivery of any goods he will have to return them and if he has made any payments he will be entitled to recover them. However, where s.57 applies, the effect of treating it as a cancelled agreement is that the debtor has, in addition, a lien over the goods to compel the repayment. This entitles him to retain possession of the goods until he is repaid. This could be very useful where for example the dealer has allowed the customer to drive away the car as soon as the customer had signed the proposal form and paid the deposit. If the debtor then withdrew his offer to the finance company, he could retain possession of the car until his deposit was repaid.

Uncertainty

It is true of any agreement that it is not a contract unless the parties have agreed on the basic terms. We saw in Ch.2 that an agreement for the sale of goods will not normally constitute a contract if the parties have not agreed on something as basic as the price. 21-004

Similarly, a hire-purchase agreement may be void for uncertainty. In *Scammell v Ouston*,[4] Ouston had been negotiating to acquire a van from Scammell on hire-purchase terms. They reached an agreement "that the balance of purchase price can be had on hire-purchase terms over two years". Ouston sued Scammell for non-delivery. The House of Lords found Scammell not liable because there was no contract, the agreement being too vague. The parties had not reached any agreement as to what the hire-purchase terms were to be.

Mistake

It may happen that the parties, though believing themselves to have agreed the terms, have not in fact done so. In *Campbell Discount v Gall*[5] the customer selected a car from the dealer's stock. They agreed that the customer would apply to a finance company to acquire it on hire-purchase terms—the cash price being £265. The customer signed the finance company's proposal form in the usual way and left it with the dealer for the latter to fill in the details and send it off to the finance company. The dealer filled in the cash price as £325. The finance company accepted this proposal. The Court of Appeal held that there was no contract between the finance company and the customer, because they were not agreed on the price. In law one is 21-005

4 [1941] A.C. 251.

5 [1961] 1 Q.B. 431.

bound by an agreement made by one's agent.[6] However, the Court rejected any idea that the dealer was, for the purpose of completing the form, agent for either party. Thus, although the dealer is agent of the finance company for the purpose of receiving revocations, it was held that he is not, unless expressly authorised, their agent for the purpose of making a hire-purchase contract. This is the position at common law.

The rule that the dealer is not normally the agent of the finance company was confirmed in *Branwhite v Worcester Works*.[7] The facts were the same as in *Campbell Discount v Gall*.[8] The customer signed the proposal form leaving the cash price still to be filled in. He paid to the dealer the initial deposit (£130) which would be due to the finance company if the proposal was accepted. The dealer filled in the wrong cash price on the proposal form, which he sent off, together with his own offer to sell the vehicle, to the finance company. The finance company accepted both these proposals and sent to the dealer the cash price less the deposit (£130) which the dealer had already received from the customer. It was assumed and accepted that following *Gall's* case there was no valid contract between the finance company and the customer because they were not agreed on the price. The customer therefore claimed the return from the finance company of his deposit of £130, arguing that the dealer who had received it was agent of the finance company in doing so and that therefore the dealer receiving it was equivalent to the finance company itself receiving it. This argument was rejected. The dealer is not, unless expressly authorised, agent of the finance company for the purpose of receiving deposits. However, the customer was held entitled to the return of his money on a different ground—namely that the finance company had itself received the deposit. Although the dealer had not actually sent the £130 to the finance company, the latter had nevertheless obtained it by deducting it from the purchase money which it had sent to the dealer. There being no contract between the customer and the finance company, the customer was entitled to the return of his initial deposit on the ground of a total failure of consideration.

Branwhite's case (like *Gall's* case) was decided upon the assumption that there was no contract between the customer and the finance company. This assumption was wrong. It does not follow that there is no contract just because the dealer is nobody's agent and sends the finance company a form with figures different from those intended by the customer. This is because of the rule that normally someone who signs a document intended to have legal effect is bound by the terms of that document if the other party (here the finance company) relies upon that signature and is unaware that the document does not accord with the signer's intentions. In *United Dominions Trust Ltd v Western*[9] the customer and dealer agreed a price for a car and the dealer produced a finance company's proposal form for the customer to sign. This he did, leaving the dealer subsequently to fill in the agreed figures. He believed it to be a hire-purchase proposal form but it was in fact a proposal for a loan agreement. The dealer did not disillusion him and, unknown to the customer, filled in, not the agreed figures, but inflated figures. He then sent the

---

6 See generally, Pt.3, below.

7 [1969] 1 A.C. 552.

8 [1961] 1 Q.B. 431.

9 [1976] Q.B. 513.

form off to the finance company, which duly accepted the proposal as it then appeared. The Court of Appeal held that the customer was bound by the terms of the document he had signed, including the figures subsequently inserted by the dealer. Thus the position at common law can be summarised as follows. The dealer (unless expressly authorised by the finance company) is not the finance company's agent. The customer is bound by the terms of the document he signs unless the finance company knows that it does not accord with the customer's intentions. That is so, irrespective of whether he signs a completed document or he signs an uncompleted one leaving it to be completed by someone else. The position would be very different if the dealer were the agent of the finance company. In that case there would be no binding agreement because the finance company would be regarded as knowing what its agent knows, namely that the proposal form does not represent the customer's intended offer.

The common law rule, settled in *Branwhite's* case, is that the dealer, who typically has possession of the finance company's proposal forms, has knowledge of the finance company's charges and who may help the customer complete the form, is not normally agent of the finance company. It is possible, however, that exceptional facts could exist which in a particular case could establish the dealer as agent. That occurred in *Purnell Secretarial Services v Lease Management Services Ltd*.[10] The dealer was Canon (South West) Limited, from whom the customer had bought several photocopiers over a period of years. During a visit by the dealer's sales representative, the customer made it plain that it was essential that any new machine should be capable of making "paper plates" as indeed the demonstration model was. On this basis the customer signed an agreement to hire a new machine, only to discover after delivery that the machine was incapable of making "paper plates". It transpired that the customer had made the hire agreement not, as the customer had thought, with the dealer, but with a finance company, Lease Management Services Limited. This was a surprise to the customer since the agreement was headed "Canon (South West) Finance" and below that in a large box beside the word "supplier" appeared "Canon (South West) Limited", the word "Canon" being printed in that company's distinctive logo. Much further down, in more tightly typed print, there appeared the words "Lessor/Owner: Leaser Management Services Limited trading as Canon (South West) Finance". It was held that the finance company, Lease Management Services, by customising its form, had chosen to identify itself with Canon (South West) Limited and had thereby misled the customer into thinking the contract was with Canon (South West) Limited. Therefore the finance company was estopped from denying the authority of Canon (South West) Limited's staff to speak for the finance company. The dealer was agent (by estoppel) of the finance company which was thus liable for misrepresentations and breaches of promises made by the dealer. This case involved a hire agreement and not a hire-purchase agreement but the common law principles are the same in relation to each. 21-006

The common law rule that for most purposes the dealer is not the finance company's agent has in the case of regulated agreement, been overturned. Section 56(2) of the Consumer Credit Act provides that antecedent negotiations in relation to the goods shall be deemed to

10 [1994] C.C.L.R. 127.

be conducted by the dealer "in the capacity of agent of the creditor as well as in his actual capacity".

The dealer is by virtue of s.56 agent of the finance company in any antecedent negotiations with the customer—and negotiations include any dealings between customer and dealer. That means that any deposit received by the dealer from the customer is received by him as agent for the finance company. Thus if there is no binding agreement between the finance company and the debtor, the latter can reclaim the deposit from the finance company; and that is so even if the finance company never received it from the dealer.

Non Est Factum

21-007 Someone who signs a document in the mistaken belief that it is of a totally different type can evade liability on his signature provided he was not careless in signing. He can plead *non est factum*—that it was not his deed. If the plea succeeds, his signature is null and void. There are two requirements for the plea to succeed:

(a) The document must be radically different from what the signer believed.

(b) The signer must not have been careless in signing.

A mistake merely as to the details, e.g. as to the number of instalments or the dates when due, will not be sufficient. Believing a personal loan agreement to be a hire-purchase agreement is not a sufficient mistake either.[11] However, if the signer believes himself to be witnessing a will or to be guaranteeing a friend's debt when he is in fact signing a hire-purchase agreement, that is a sufficient difference.[12]

Even if the signer can establish a sufficient mistake, he will usually fail because it will usually have been careless of him not first to have read what he signed. He will therefore find it easier for the plea to succeed if he is illiterate or blind or if, like the old lady in *Gallie v Lee*,[13] he had just lost his glasses.

Misrepresentation

21-008 If before the contract is made, one party makes an untrue statement of fact which induces the other party to make the contract, the latter may have a remedy for misrepresentation. The principles applicable and remedies available were set out in Ch.6.

11 See *United Dominions Trust v Western* above.

12 *Muskham Finance v Howard* [1963] 1 Q.B. 904.

13 [1971] A.C. 1004.

A particular problem arises where goods are selected from a dealer's stock and subsequently acquired on instalment terms from a finance company. The problem is that most of the statements made to the customer to persuade him to have the goods are made not by the other party to the instalment contract (the finance company) but by the dealer.

We have already seen that if such a statement proves to be untrue, the customer may have a claim for damages from the dealer for breach of collateral warranty.[14] Does the customer have a remedy also against the finance company for misrepresentation? This is an important question because if he does, not only may he be entitled to damages from the finance company, but he may also be able to rescind the contract in accordance with the principles set out in Ch.6. However, the answer at common law is "no". There is a remedy for misrepresentation only in respect of statements made by one party or his agent to the other party. For most purposes (other than receiving revocation of an offer) the dealer is not agent of the finance company. Thus when a dealer makes statements about the goods, he is not, unless expressly authorised, doing so as agent of the finance company.

Although that is the common law position, it has in the case of regulated agreements been reversed by the Consumer Credit Act. By s.56 the dealer is a negotiator in antecedent negotiations and in conducting these negotiations the dealer is deemed to be an agent of the finance company. Antecedent negotiations begin when the dealer and the customer first get into communication and that includes communication by advertisement. The antecedent negotiations include any representations made by the dealer. Section 56 is important in that, in respect of misrepresentations about the goods by the dealer, it confers upon the customer the armoury of the law of misrepresentation with which to attack the finance company. In particular he will be entitled to rescind the regulated agreement. It is sufficient that he gives notice of rescission to the dealer, for by s.102 of the Consumer Credit Act the dealer is agent of the finance company for receiving notice of rescission. 21-009

By the terms of s.56(1)(b), the antecedent negotiations in which the dealer is deemed to be agent of the creditor are those conducted by him "in relation to goods sold or proposed to be sold" by the dealer to the creditor. Consider the following situation. A customer has a car on hire-purchase terms and is still paying off the instalments under her hire-purchase agreement with finance company X. She approaches a car dealer asking to trade in her existing car and to acquire a new one on hire-purchase. Enquiries made of finance company X reveal that the settlement figure needed to pay off the customer's existing debt is £1,000. The car dealer suggests that the customer acquires the new car under a hire-purchase agreement with finance company Z. The customer agrees and they come to an arrangement. It is that: the cash price of the new car is £6,000; the trade-in allowance for the existing one is £3,000; the customer completes a hire-purchase proposal form of finance company Z proposing to take the new car on hire-purchase terms, make a down payment of £2,000 and pay the balance of £4,000 (plus credit charges) in monthly instalments over three years. The car dealer undertakes to receive the trade-in car, to pay off the £1,000 owing to finance company X and to use the

14 See *Andrews v Hopkinson*, para.17-007, above.

balance of the trade-in allowance as the customer's £2,000 down payment under the new hire-purchase agreement. Finance company Z accepts the customer's proposal and pays the car dealer £4,000 (i.e. the cash price of £6,000 less the £2,000 down payment received, as part of the value of the traded-in car, by the car dealer direct from the customer). The customer takes delivery of the new car and subsequently discovers that the car dealer has gone out of business, disappeared and has never kept his promise to pay the £1,000 to finance company X. Can the customer claim that finance company Z is liable for breach of the dealer's (its agent's?) promise to pay the settlement figure to finance company X? Yes. For the customer her buying of the new car and the trade-in arrangement and settlement of her debt on her traded-in car was all one transaction. Thus the dealer's promise to pay off the customer's existing debt was something done "in relation to" the car she was buying.[15]

Legality

21–010 A party who makes a contract knowing it to be illegal will be unable to sue the other party. In *Snell v Unity Finance*[16] the customer made a hire-purchase contract in the usual way with a finance company. He had not enough money to pay the minimum deposit required by regulations then in force. The cash price of the car was £185. The minimum deposit required by the regulations was 20 per cent, but the customer had only £25. The dealer and the customer filled in the forms to show (wrongly) that the customer had paid a deposit of £50 and that the cash price was £210. The finance company accepted the proposals. Later the customer sued the finance company on the ground that the car was defective and not reasonably fit for its purpose. He lost because the court would not allow him to enforce an illegal contract. Incidentally, there have been no regulations requiring a minimum deposit, since the last regulations were revoked in 1982.

Suppose that in *Snell v Unity Finance*[17] the customer had defaulted in his payments. In that case the finance company could have enforced the agreement against him and sued him for the arrears, because the finance company was not *in pari delicto*, i.e. as much to blame as the customer. The finance company could also have exercised its right to recover possession of the goods on default by the customer, for the same reason. However, there is also an alternative reason. Under a hire-purchase agreement ownership does not pass until all the instalments have been paid and the option exercised. Until then, the finance company is the owner and that ownership gives it the right to recover the goods (or their value) unless the customer can

15 *Forthright Finance Ltd v Ingate* [1997] 4 All E.R. 99. The same reasoning applies to s.56(1)(c) discussed below, at para.21-013. In *Scotland v British Credit Trust Ltd* [2014] EWCA Civ 790 the customer wanted to take out a loan to finance the supply of new doors and windows. Salesmen wrongly told the customer that in order to take out the loan, it would be necessary also to take out a Payment Protection Insurance policy (PPI). The negotiations about the PPI were made "in relation to" to new doors and windows, i.e. the customer had no interest in taking out PPI other than as a means of securing the loan for the goods.

16 [1964] 2 Q.B. 203.

17 [1964] 2 Q.B. 203.

establish a right to retain them.[18] If, on the other hand, the customer pays off all the instalments and exercises his option, then ownership passes to him and this happens even under an illegal contract.[19] The right (if any) of the creditor (i.e. the owner) to recover possession of the goods on default by the debtor (i.e. the customer) will be considered further at paras 24-012 and 24-013, below.

Other Regulated Agreements

The contracts we have considered so far in this chapter (i.e. hire-purchase, conditional sale and credit sale agreements) have one thing in common—namely that the credit agreement and the contract by which the customer agrees to have the goods are one and the same thing. That being so they are (i.e. it is) made at the same time. However, we come to consider a number of other kinds of credit agreement where often the seller and the creditor are two different people, where the customer therefore makes two agreements and where he will usually make one before the other. This fact can be crucial. Usually the credit agreement will be made first so that the debtor then has the funds or the credit facilities to make the purchase. Thus someone who has a credit card will have made his credit agreement (i.e. the credit card agreement) when he accepted his card by signing it or first using it.[20] When some time later he uses his card to purchase some goods he will not be making a new credit agreement but simply using the credit facilities available under the credit agreement made earlier. Thus although the dealer who sells him the goods is made by the Act agent of the creditor, he is not the agent of the creditor in the making of the credit agreement. This is because the debtor will not have made contact with the dealer until after the credit agreement was made. 21-011

There are two people who are to a greater or lesser extent deemed to be the agent of the creditor or owner—namely the debtor's or hirer's representative in negotiations and the negotiator in antecedent negotiations.

Customer's Representative

The Act uses the formula "any person who, in the course of a business carried on by him, acts (or acted) on behalf of the debtor or hirer in any negotiations for the agreement".[21] This formula clearly includes those persons who run businesses whereby they arrange loans or other 21-012

18 *Bowmakers v Barnet Instruments* [1945] K.B. 65.
19 *Belvoir Finance v Stapelton* [1971] 1 Q.B. 210.
20 s.66.
21 s.57(3)(b).

forms of credit for the customer. They do not grant the credit themselves but will negotiate on behalf of the customer with a prospective creditor. They sometimes describe themselves as finance brokers. It is also possible for a customer's own solicitor or accountant to fall within the formula—if for example the customer got him to negotiate a loan for the customer. Anyone falling within the formula is deemed for three limited purposes to be agent of the creditor or owner. Someone falling within the formula will in this book be described as the customer's representative. The customer's representative is of course primarily an agent of the customer and is not agent of the creditor or owner except where the Consumer Credit Act states that he is.

The three purposes for which he is made the agent of the creditor or owner are:

(i) For receiving notice from the customer that the customer withdraws his offer to enter a regulated agreement.[22]

(ii) For receiving notice of cancellation.[23]

(iii) For receiving notice from the customer that the customer rescinds his regulated agreement.[24]

Section 102 should not be misunderstood. The customer's representative is not the agent of the creditor or owner for the purpose of making representations. Therefore s.102 does not mean that misrepresentations by the customer's representative will entitle the customer subsequently to rescind his agreement with the creditor. It means simply that if for some other reason (e.g. a misrepresentation made by the creditor himself) the customer is entitled to rescind a regulated agreement, it is sufficient that he gives notice of that rescission to the customer's representative. Whenever the Act makes someone the agent of the creditor or owner for the purpose of receiving a notice or payment, he is under a duty to the creditor or owner to transmit it to him forthwith.[25]

Negotiator in Antecedent Negotiations

21-013 A negotiator in antecedent negotiations is a deemed agent of the creditor or owner. The purpose for which he is deemed the creditor's or owner's agent include and are wider than those for which the customer's representative is a deemed agent. Thus if a customer's representative falls also within the definition of a negotiator in antecedent negotiations, he can be regarded simply in the latter capacity.

22 s.57.

23 s.69, see para.21-039, below.

24 s.102.

25 s.175.

There are just three types of person who fall within the definition of a negotiator in antecedent negotiations:[26]

(a) The creditor or owner. Plainly no question of agency arises here.

(b) The dealer in the case of a hire-purchase, conditional sale or credit sale agreement. This was considered in the earlier part of this chapter.

(c) The dealer (termed by the Act, the supplier) in the case of any other debtor-creditor-supplier agreement.

Our concern here then is with who falls within category (c). Debtor-creditor-supplier agreements other than those mentioned in (b) include credit card agreements and trading check agreements.[27] Thus the trader who supplies goods under a credit card agreement (i.e. because the buyer uses his credit card instead of paying cash) is a negotiator within s.56.

Any person (except the creditor) falling within the definition of a negotiator in s.56 is deemed in conducting negotiations with the debtor (the customer) to be an agent of the creditor.[28] This does not however alter any other capacity he may have. Thus the supplier of goods under a credit card agreement is a seller of goods to the customer as well as being an agent of the creditor in negotiations with the customer. Section 56 gives a wide meaning to the "negotiations" during which the negotiator is agent of the creditor. These negotiations begin when the negotiator and the customer first get into communication (including communication by advertisement). The negotiations include any representations made by the negotiator to the customer and any other dealings between them. Thus statements (e.g. about the quality of the goods)[29] made by the negotiator during the negotiations are made by him in two capacities. They are regarded as made not only by the dealer but also by the creditor (because they are made by his agent). The exact effect of them being so regarded will be considered a little later. 21–014

"Antecedent" needs to be explained. Section 56 talks of a negotiator in antecedent negotiations. Antecedent means previous or earlier—but previous to what, earlier than what? It is clear from category (c) above that it is possible for a supplier to be a negotiator in antecedent negotiations which occur after the relevant credit agreement has been made, e.g. the supplier of goods under a credit card agreement. Thus antecedent sometimes means previous to the making of a credit agreement (e.g. in categories (a) or (b) above) and sometimes means previous to the making of an agreement to be financed by an already existing credit agreement.

26 s.56.

27 See Ch.18.

28 s.56(2).

29 See, for example, *Hodgson v Creation Consumer Finance Ltd* [2021] EWHC 2167 (Comm) where the finance company was liable for the misrepresentation of the supplier who misrepresented the ability of solar panels to "pay for itself" within 10 years.

Put it another way, in the case of a hire-purchase agreement antecedent negotiations will occur before the credit agreement (i.e. the hire-purchase agreement) is made. In the case of a purchase of goods by use of a credit card, the antecedent negotiations will occur before the purchase but after the credit agreement was made. Although representations made by the dealer to the customer will in both cases be treated as if made also by the creditor, the effect of that will be much more significant when those statements were made before the credit agreement was made (i.e. in the hire-purchase case). In that case a misrepresentation by the creditor will entitle the debtor to rescind the whole credit agreement in accordance with the principles outlined in Ch.6. However, a misrepresentation by the creditor after the credit agreement was made (e.g. in the credit card situation) will not entitle the debtor to rescind the whole credit agreement. It will, however, entitle him (as we shall shortly see) to rescind that aspect of the credit agreement relating to the purchase in question.

Offer and Acceptance

21–015 It is true of any contract that it is made at the time when both sides agree to be bound by the same terms, i.e. when one side makes an offer which the other accepts.

To discover whether or when an acceptance occurred, the communications between the parties must be examined. We have seen that in the case of a hire-purchase agreement the finance company will require the customer to make an offer by filling in its proposal form containing the terms of the prospective agreement. The agreement (i.e. the contract) will be made if and when the finance company communicate to the customer their acceptance of his offer. Other credit agreements are not always made in the same way. Thus a customer who wishes to have a credit card—i.e. to enter into a credit card agreement—will no doubt be asked to fill in an application form. He may find, however that the credit card company, although it is satisfied with the application, regards the application not as an offer but as only a request for the company to make an offer. Thus the customer is likely to receive an offer (together with the credit card) from the company.

The offer will state that the customer will accept the offer when he signs or uses the credit card. The agreement will be made therefore when the customer first signs or first uses the card. Arrangements vary from one creditor to another. Some will insist on the customer making the offer and others will insist on making the offer themselves and leaving the customer to accept it. Yet other creditors will not invariably be insistent one way or the other. Thus a bank manager may make an offer of an overdraft to one customer and from another customer receive an offer to take an overdraft. Whichever party makes an offer, the agreement will be made when the acceptance of it by the other party takes effect. In the case of regulated agreements the exact point of time when the agreement is made has added significance. Not only is it important because a withdrawal of an offer cannot be effective after acceptance of the offer but it also marks the beginning of the seven-day period within which a second copy of the agreement may have to be served upon the customer. This will be dealt with later under the formalities provision.

Withdrawal of Offer

An offer can be withdrawn at any time before the offer has been effectively accepted. The time when acceptance takes effect was explained in Ch.2—in particular, if the post was expected to be used, the acceptance takes effect upon posting. This is a general rule of the law of contract and applies therefore to regulated agreements. There is also a general rule that a withdrawal of an offer does not take effect upon posting but only upon its receipt or communication to the other party. Thus a withdrawal will have no effect unless it actually arrives before the acceptance is posted. If it does not, both sides are bound and neither can back out.[30] 21-016

Section 57 applies to prospective regulated agreements which are subject to the formalities requirements—and that includes most regulated agreements. Its effects are twofold as they are in relation to hire-purchase agreement. First, the customer's representative and the negotiator in antecedent negotiations are deemed to be agents of the creditor or owner for receiving notice of withdrawal by the customer. Secondly, where either party withdraws from a prospective agreement, the debtor or hirer will be in the same position as he would be if the agreement had been made and had been cancellable and had subsequently been cancelled under s.69. That position will be explained later.

We will now consider some particular types of regulated agreement in the light of what has so far been said in this chapter.

Credit Cards

By s.57 a negotiator in antecedent negotiations—i.e. the supplier of goods under the credit card agreement—is agent of the creditor for the purpose of receiving from the debtor notice withdrawing an offer to enter the credit agreement. However, this will be of little importance in practice because an offer cannot be withdrawn once it has been accepted and the debtor is unlikely to attempt to get credit by means of his credit card agreement until after the offer has been accepted (and after the credit card agreement has therefore been made). In any case a great many credit card agreements are made, not by an offer from the debtor which the creditor accepts, but by an offer by the creditor to the debtor (the card holder), which the latter accepts by signing or using his credit card. 21-017

It has already been seen that by virtue of s.56 representations by the supplier to the debtor are made by him also as agent of the creditor. It was also seen that this would not enable the debtor to rescind the whole credit card agreement. It would, however, entitle him to rescind that part of the credit card agreement relating to the transaction in relation to which the

30 i.e. unless it is a cancellable agreement, see para.21-039, below.

misrepresentation was made. This requires explanation. There is no doubt that a credit card agreement (unless it is exempt like certain American Express and Diners Club agreements) is itself a regulated running-account credit agreement.[31] As a matter of ordinary contract law, that agreement is a standing offer under which the credit card company is offering credit to the card holder. The card holder is not committed to take any particular amount of credit or indeed any credit at all. He may keep the card and never use it. When he uses it to pay, say, £40 for a pair of shoes he accepts the standing offer to provide him with credit and the accepts it to the extent of £40 worth of credit. In thus accepting the standing offer he creates a contract with the credit card company for the provision to him of £40 worth of credit. Each time he uses the card he make a new contract with the credit card company. Suppose the supplier makes a misrepresentation (e.g. the shoe seller falsely states the shoes to be 100 per cent leather). If the credit card agreement is a regulated one, that is a misrepresentation by the credit card company, i.e. through their agent, a negotiator in antecedent negotiations. It has presumably induced not just the sale of the shoes but also the accompanying use of the credit card. The card holder therefore has the right to rescind the contract for the £40 worth of credit. This is because a misrepresentation by the other party to that contract (the credit card company) induced him to make it. He could exercise this right by informing the credit card company that he is rescinding the transaction. He would then be entitled to refuse to make any payments relating to that particular transaction. Of course, if he had made some repayment of the £40 to the credit card company, he might be regarded as having affirmed the contract and thereby having lost the right of rescission. In an appropriate case the card holder may even wish to claim damages from the credit company for the misrepresentation.[32]

As already observed, at common law a credit card agreement amounts to a standing offer and thus each new use of the card creates a new contract between the card holder and the credit card company. It is therefore tempting to regard each such new contract as a new regulated agreement. Such an approach would be wrong, contrary to the scheme of the Act.[33] Every time a new regulated agreement is made, the formality and documentation provisions have to be complied with. The Act clearly contemplated that with a running-account credit agreement those formalities could be satisfied when the agreement was first made and would not apply each time the agreed credit facility was used.[34]

In practice it will be in only very rare cases that a card holder will need to rely upon s.56 to make a claim against the credit card company. He has considerable rights against the supplier and will usually get satisfaction direct from him for any misrepresentation or breach of contract by the supplier.[35] Where the supplier agrees to take back the goods and give a refund, he will not usually hand money over to the card holder but will instead credit the card holder's credit card account with the credit card company. Even where he cannot obtain satisfaction from the

31 See para.18-005, above.

32 For an explanation of the remedies available for misrepresentation see Ch.6.

33 See P. Dobson, "Connected Lender Commencement Controversy" [1978] New L.J. 448.

34 For a fuller analysis, see P. Dobson, "Credit Cards" [1979] J.B.L. 331.

35 See Ch.6 and Ch.7.

supplier (perhaps because the latter has disappeared or become insolvent), the card holder will very often be able to make a claim under s.75 against the credit card company for the supplier's misrepresentation or breach of contract. It is only where s.75 does not apply (e.g. where the cash price of the item in question did not exceed £100) that the card holder will be forced to rely upon s.56.[36] So far it has been assumed that there is just one card holder. Sometimes, however someone with a credit card agreement has a second person (often the husband or wife) who also has a card which can be used on the same account. Where it is the latter who has used his card on the purchase in question, can he rely on s.56 in the same way as if he were the principal card holder? The answer depends upon the same arguments as apply to whether he may claim under s.75. A similar point is that s.56 probably cannot be relied upon by any card holder who made his credit card agreement before 1 April 1977—though there probably are not too many such credit card agreements which are still operating. Here again there is a similar issue in relation to s.75.[37] The debtor might not use his credit card as a means of paying the dealer, but might instead use his credit card to obtain a cash loan and then use the cash to make a purchase from the dealer. In this case the credit card agreement will, in relation to the loan and subsequent purchase, be for unrestricted-use credit and will be a debtor-creditor agreement.[38] If in this case the debtor were able to show a misrepresentation or breach of contract by the dealer, that would not give him any claim against the creditor. The dealer would not be an agent of the creditor because he would not in this case fall within the definition of a negotiator in antecedent negotiations. Also s.75 would not apply to give a remedy against the creditor. The debtor would thus be left to his remedies against the dealer.

Check Trading

The supplier will always be a negotiator within the meaning of s.56 and will therefore be agent of the creditor. Also the credit agreement will usually already have been made before the debtor approaches the supplier of the goods or services. 21-018

With check trading it can happen that the customer first sees the item in the supplier's showroom, indulges in antecedent negotiations with the salesman and then goes to the creditor to make the necessary credit agreement. This situation is likely to occur with more expensive items in which case the document he obtains from the creditor is likely to be termed a trading voucher and be specifically restricted to the purchase of the specified item. If this sequence of events has occurred, any misrepresentation made by the supplier to the customer before the latter made his trading voucher agreement will entitle the customer to rescind both

36 s.75 is explained at para.22-004, below.

37 See generally the treatment of s.75 at para.22-004, below.

38 See Ch.21, above.

his agreements, i.e. not only the agreement with the supplier but also the trading voucher agreement. Furthermore, in order to rescind the latter (as well as the former) it is sufficient that the customer gives notice of rescission to the supplier since by s.102 the supplier is agent of the creditor for the purpose of receiving notice of rescission.

Section 75 may enable the debtor to bring a claim against the creditor for a breach of contract or a misrepresentation by the supplier.

Cash Loan

21-019 It is with a cash loan that there is more likely to be a customer's representative involved, who is agent of the creditor for certain purposes including the receiving of a withdrawal of the customer's offer to enter the regulated agreement. Also, even though the debtor borrows the cash from the creditor and uses it to buy goods or services from the dealer, it is nevertheless possible for the latter to be a negotiator in antecedent negotiations, i.e. agent of the creditor. It would happen where, for example, the dealer has a regular arrangement with the creditor whereby the latter is prepared to make loans to potential customers of the dealer, i.e. to put a potential customer in a financial position to make a purchase from the dealer. Such arrangements between dealers and lenders tend to occur where the dealer does not wish (or cannot afford) himself to give credit terms to this customer.

If in pursuance of such an arrangement between creditor and dealer, the creditor agrees to make a cash loan to the customer, the resulting regulated credit agreement will be a debtor-creditor-supplier agreement and the dealer will be a negotiator in antecedent negotiations. This is exactly the situation in the example given at para.21-019 above, where Warmitup Ltd is therefore agent of Hotmoney Ltd in conducting negotiations with Shiver.

However, most cash loans are not made in such circumstances but are mere debtor–creditor agreements. This is certainly the case with the vast majority of bank loans and overdrafts. In these cases the position is as with a cash loan obtained under a credit card agreement. Thus the dealer is not the bank's agent for the purpose of any representations about the goods or services he supplies, i.e. s.56 does not apply. That being so, the bank is free of any liability for any misrepresentation or breach of contract by the dealer.

Consumer Hire Agreements

21-020 There is with this type of contract no question of the prospective hirer obtaining the goods from one person (the owner) and credit from another. There is after all no element of credit. Thus in the case of a consumer hire agreement there is only one person who falls within the definition of a negotiator in antecedent negotiations—namely the owner himself. There is therefore no negotiator in antecedent negotiations who is deemed to be the agent of the owner. However, if there is "any person who, in the course of a business carried on by him, acts on behalf of the hirer in any negotiations for the agreement" then that person (the customer's representative) is deemed to be agent of the owner for the purposes indicated earlier.[39]

Just as with hire-purchase agreements, so with consumer hire agreements, there is sometimes a triangular arrangement whereby the dealer sells the goods to a finance company which contracts with the customer to supply them to him. This process was explained at para.17-005 in relation to hire-purchase. The difference is that here the finance company supplies the goods to the customer on hire instead of hire-purchase terms. We saw that at common law the normal rule is that the dealer is not the agent of the finance company.[40] This is the position at common law in relation to hire-purchase and it is exactly the same where the agreement is a hire agreement.[41] This is so unless, as in Purnell Secretarial Services v Lease Management Services Ltd,[42] there is some very exceptional factual material which establishes an agency.

Although the common law position is the same as it is in the case of hire-purchase, the application of the Consumer Credit Act is not the same. This is because where it is a consumer hire agreement instead of a consumer credit agreement, the dealer is not made agent of the finance company.[43] As just stated, the owner is the only negotiator in antecedent negotiations, (i.e. the finance company).

Credit Broker's Fees and Credit Reference Agencies

There are two types of ancillary credit trader[44] who may have a role to play in connection with the making of a regulated agreement, a credit broker and a credit reference agency. 21-021

39 See para.21-012, below.

40 At para.21-005, below.

41 *Woodchester Equipment (Leasing) Ltd v BACFID* [1995] C.C.L.R. 51.

42 [1994] C.C.L.R. 127.

43 *Moorgate Mercantile Leasing Ltd v Gell and Ugolini* [1988] C.C.L.R. 1.

44 See generally, s.145.

Credit Broking

21–022 An individual consumer will sometimes go to a credit broker[45] for an introduction to a source of credit. The definition of credit broking now includes activities previously separately categorised as "credit brokerage" and "credit intermediaries" prior to the transfer of consumer credit regulation to the Financial Conduct Authority. The FCA's Consumer Credit Sourcebook imposes a number of pre-contractual obligations on a firm that engages in credit broking activities with the aim that the relationship between a credit broker and the lender is clearly communicated to the borrower before he enters into any credit agreement. In particular, the broker must disclose to the prospective customer the extent to which he is independent and whether he works exclusively with one or more lenders.[46] Furthermore, prior to any regulated consumer credit or consumer hire agreement being concluded the broker must disclose the extent of any monetary consideration payable to him by the customer for his services.[47]

Section 155 establishes a rule designed to prevent the credit broker from charging the consumer more than £5 for any introduction which does not result in the consumer obtaining credit. The rule applies where, for example, the consumer wants to enter into a regulated credit or consumer hire agreement.[48] The rule is that if the credit-broker's introduction of the consumer does not result in an agreement within six months of the introduction, the consumer cannot be liable to pay the credit broker any fee or commission in excess of £5. If he has already paid such a fee or commission, he is entitled to recover it all (except the £5). He is of course not entitled to recover it until the six months have elapsed.

Credit Reference Agencies

21–023 The general function and definition of a credit reference agency has already been explained in para.20-003. The bank of knowledge that an agency has about any one person can be formidable and, if it indicates that the person is not creditworthy, can mean that it is very difficult for that person to obtain credit—except perhaps from the most speculative of creditors who lend without reference to the borrower's creditworthiness and who also charge correspondingly high interest rates.

Concern has been felt at the secrecy with which credit reference agencies have in the past operated. Very often their information has been available only to the trade (i.e. finance companies, etc.) so that an individual has been unable to discover the accuracy of reports about his

45 Credit broking is defined in art.36A of the Financial Services and Markets Act 2000 (Regulated Activities) Order 2001 (SI 2001/544).

46 CONC 3.7.3. R (previously required under s.160A(3) of the CCA 1974).

47 CONC 4.4.2. R (previously required under s.160A(4) of the CCA 1974). As to the disclosure of commission or fees payable to the credit broker by the lender, see CONC 4.5.3 R and CONC 4.5.4. R.

48 See further, s.155(2) and s.155(2A).

creditworthiness, or indeed whether any such reports have in fact been obtained. The aim of ss.157–159 is to rectify the situation.

Where a creditor under a prospective regulated agreement, other than a consumer hire agreement or an agreement secured on land, does not continue with the agreement as a consequence of information proffered by a credit reference agency, s.157(A1) applies. Under this provision, the creditor must inform the consumer that the decision not to proceed was the consequence of information provided by a credit reference agency and give the details of the agency concerned, including its name, address and telephone number. Moreover, s.157(1) entitles the debtor or hirer to discover from the creditor, owner or negotiator in any antecedent negotiations, the name and address of any credit reference agency which has been consulted as to the creditworthiness of the debtor or hirer. The obligations laid down by s.157(A1) and s.157(1) do not apply where the creditor's disclosure would:[49]

(a) contravene the UK General Data Protection Regulation;

(b) be prohibited by any retained EU obligation;

(c) create (or be likely to create) a serious risk that any person would be subject to violence or intimidation; or

(d) prejudice (or be likely to prejudice) the prevention or detection of crime, the apprehension or prosecution of offenders, or the administration of justice.

Where the obligations under s.157(1A) or s.157(1) are not complied with the creditor, owner or negotiator (as appropriate) commits an offence.[50] 21-024

Once that information has been obtained, the debtor or hirer is then in a position to take advantage of s.45 of the Data Protection Act 2018 or, in the case of a partnership or other unincorporated body, s.158 of the Consumer Credit Act. This entitles an individual (or unincorporated body) to make a request for details of information relating to the individual (or body) which is kept at the agency.[51] Such a request can be made, irrespective of whether the person making it has obtained credit or has merely tried to obtain it or has not even tried to do so.

By s.159, an individual (labelled the 'objector') who considers an entry in the file relating to him to be incorrect and likely to prejudice him if not corrected, can require the agency either to remove the entry or to amend it. Then the agency must within 28 days either do that and notify the objector that it has done so or else notify him that it has not.[52] If the latter course is taken the objector can require the agency to add to his file an accompanying notice of correction of

49 s.157(2A).

50 s.157(3).

51 Under the 2018 Act, such requests are generally free (see s.12). Under the CCA 1974, a fee is payable (currently £2, s.158(1)(c)). Note that the failure to comply with s.158 is an offence (s.158(4)).

52 s.159(2).

not more than 200 words drawn up by the objector.[53] If the agency refuses to do so, either the objector or the agency can refer the matter to the relevant authority, who may make such order as he or she thinks fit.[54] Failure to obey the order is a criminal offence. The relevant authority is the Information Commissioner unless the objector is an unincorporated body, in which case it is the Financial Conduct Authority.

Formalities

21–025 Sections 60–65 deal with formalities which must be complied with in the making of a regulated agreement. The aim is to ensure:

(i) That the debtor is fully aware of the nature and cost of the transaction he is about to enter (including the cost of the credit).

(ii) That his written agreement gives him a clear account of his rights and obligations.

Agreements Subject to the Formalities Requirements

21–026 These provisions apply only to regulated agreements. However, certain agreements are not required to comply with some of the formalities requirements laid down in Pt V of the Act. The extent of the exemption varies according to the type of agreement. Thus non-commercial agreements are exempted from all formalities with the exception of the rules relating to antecedent negotiations under s.56,[55] whereas some other agreements, as we shall shortly see, are exempted from fewer formalities. The reason that non-commercial agreements are not subject to the formalities requirements is that those requirements are intended to protect the consumer against the financially powerful creditor (whether that be the dealer or, say, a finance company). It is however quite possible for two private individuals to enter into what is in fact a regulated consumer credit agreement. For example, the man who sells his car privately (perhaps following a small advertisement in the local paper) may agree to his buyer paying him later—perhaps in instalments.[56]

53 s.159(3).

54 s.159(4).

55 s.74(1A).

56 A similar example would be where a private individual lends money to a friend to be repaid over a period of time. In these cases the law would be unreasonable and unrealistic to insist that the agreement be put into writing and copies of it served on the debtor, etc.

A small debtor-creditor-supplier agreement for restricted use credit is exempt from all formalities other than those relating to pre-contract disclosure under s.55, antecedent negotiations under s.56 and the right of withdrawal under s.66A.[57] Additionally, where the agreement is in writing, the provisions as to form and content under s.60(1).[58] An example of an agreement which fulfils these conditions is a trading check agreement for £50 or less. Another example is a credit sale agreement under which the credit does not exceed £50.[59] A regulated hire-purchase or conditional sale agreement will always be subject to the formalities requirements unless it is a non-commercial agreement. This is because hire-purchase and conditional sale agreements are excluded from the definition of "small agreements" in s.17.

Under s.74 a number of other agreements are excluded from having to comply with some of the formality requirements. They are certain agreements to overdraw on a current account and certain agreements to finance payments arising out of a death. The latter might be an agreement to finance the paying of inheritance tax or court fees payable in order to get probate of a will.[60] As to the former, imagine the situation where the bank manager is presented with a cheque which if he pays it, will put the customer's account into the red. If the manager pays out on the cheque—as often happens in practice—he is in effect agreeing to the customer having an overdraft. It would be plainly unrealistic to require every such agreement to be in writing, etc. The overdraft exception applies to all debtor-creditor agreements for overdrafts on current accounts but is limited in application; thus, for example, the formalities under, inter alia, ss.55B, 60 and 61B are still applicable.[61]

Pre-contract Assessment of Creditworthiness

Following the implementation of the Consumer Credit Directive 2008, lenders are required to assess a borrower's creditworthiness before concluding a regulated consumer credit agreement.[62] This inquiry must also occur before the amount of credit provided under an existing agreement is increased and in the case of running-account credit, such as a credit card, before the credit limit is increased.[63] The assessment must consider (i) the potential for the commitments under the credit agreement to adversely impact the customer's financial situation, 21-027

57 s.74(1)(d).

58 s.74(2).

59 Unless the agreement is one to which Pts 2 or 3 of the Consumer Contracts (Information, Cancellation and Additional Charges) Regulations 2013 applies, in which case the relevant financial threshold is £42.

60 See s.74(1F) as to what formalities must be complied with in such cases.

61 See s.74(1C) as to formalities for an authorised non-business overdraft and s.74(1D) for an authorised business overdraft.

62 This requirement was initially introduced by the Consumer Credit (EU Directive) Regulations 2010 which inserted s.55B(1) (now repealed) into the Act. It is now incorporated as a rule in the FCA's Consumer Credit Sourcebook, CONC 5.2A.1. R. This obligation does not extend to any pawn agreement or an agreement secured on land.

63 CONC 5.2A.4. R.

taking into account information which the lender is aware of at the time the agreement is to be entered into, and (ii) the ability of the borrower to repay the credit. The assessment must be based on "sufficient information" obtained from the debtor where appropriate and a credit reference agency, where necessary.[64]

Pre-contract Disclosure

21-028 In order that a debtor can understand the nature and effect of a credit agreement the creditor must disclose "in good time" before the contract is made, key information relating to the agreement. The majority of regulated consumer credit agreements will fall under the Consumer Credit (Disclosure of Information) Regulations 2010[65] which lay down requirements as to both the information which must be provided and also the manner in which it must be provided. In both cases the Regulations are highly prescriptive, which has the advantage of allowing for the clear and accessible presentation of the information to the debtor. Uniformity of presentation is also important in order that a debtor can more easily compare different agreements.[66] As to the contents of the pre-contract disclosure the Regulations require the inclusion of such things as:[67]

(i) the type of credit;

(ii) the name and address of the creditor;

(iii) the APR and the total amount payable under the agreement; and

(iv) the amount of the credit (or the credit limit).

The Consumer Credit (Disclosure of Information) Regulations 2010 do not apply to all regulated consumer credit agreements. In particular, they do not apply at all to non-business overdrafts which are either secured on land or which provide credit in excess of £60,260. Furthermore, the Regulations will, prima facie, not apply to any of the following agreements unless the creditor "opts in" and elects to provide the required information under the 2010 Regulations:

(a) an agreement under which the creditor provides the debtor with credit exceeding £60,260;

64 CONC 5.2A.7. R.

65 SI 2010/1013.

66 See reg.8 and Sch.1.

67 reg.3(4). The Regulations also lay down special rules for agreements made by telephone, certain distance contracts, pawn agreements and overdraft agreements.

(b) an agreement secured on land;

(c) an agreement entered into by the debtor wholly or predominantly for the purposes of a business; or

(d) an agreement made before 1 February 2011.

Where the Consumer Credit (Disclosure of Information) Regulations 2010 are inapplicable, pre-contract disclosure will continue to be prescribed by the Consumer Credit (Disclosure of Information) Regulations 2004[68] or the Financial Services (Distance Marketing) Regulations 2004.[69]

The pre-contract disclosure provisions have recently been reinforced by a further obligation. Before a regulated consumer credit agreement is made the creditor (or credit intermediary) must give the debtor an "adequate explanation" of various matters regarding the credit agreement in order that the debtor is able to assess whether the agreement is suitable to his needs and specific financial situation.[70] The matters which must be explained include: whether the credit provided under the agreement is such that it is unsuitable for particular types of use;[71] features of the agreement which may have a significant adverse effect on the customer in a way which he is unlikely to foresee;[72] any consequences of failing to make payments under the agreement;[73] and information surrounding any right to withdraw from the agreement.[74]

The obligation to offer this explanation to the customer does not apply to an agreement where the credit provided exceeds £60,260 or to an agreement which is secured on land.[75]

Form and Content

The form and content of regulated agreements was significantly altered by the Consumer Credit Directive 2008 which established a sharp distinction between those agreements which fall under the Directive and those which do not. Accordingly, every regulated agreement must comply with either the Consumer Credit (Agreements) Regulations 1983 (regulated agreements 21-029

68 SI 2004/1481.

69 SI 2004/2095.

70 This requirement was originally introduced by the Consumer Credit (EU Directive) Regulations 2010 which inserted s.55A(1) (now repealed) into the Act with effect from 1 February 2011. It is now incorporated as a rule in the FCA's Consumer Credit Handbook, CONC 4.2.5. R.

71 e.g. the use of a credit card for long-term borrowing.

72 e.g. differing introductory rates of interest on credit card borrowing.

73 e.g. additional charges for late payments.

74 In addition to this general requirement the lender must also give the customer the opportunity to ask any questions he may have regarding the agreement and advise the customer how he can get further information should he require it at a later stage.

75 See CONC 4.2.1. R.

which are outside of the Directive)[76] or the Consumer Credit (Agreements) Regulations 2010 (where the agreement is inside of the ambit of the Directive). Both sets of regulations were made under ss.60 and 61.[77] The majority of regulated agreements will fall under the scope of the 2010 Regulations with notable exceptions including:

- regulated consumer hire agreements;
- regulated consumer credit agreements made prior to 1 February 2011;
- regulated consumer credit agreements secured on land;
- regulated consumer credit agreements extending credit over £60,260; and
- regulated consumer credit agreements which extend business credit.

These Regulations lay down detailed requirements as to the form, legibility and contents of agreements. In particular an agreement must have whichever is the appropriate one of the following headings: Hire-Purchase Agreement regulated by the Consumer Credit Act 1974; Conditional Sale Agreement regulated by the Consumer Credit Act 1974; Fixed Sum Loan Agreement regulated by the Consumer Credit Act 1974; Credit Card Agreement regulated by the Consumer Credit Act 1974; or the Agreement modifying a Credit Agreement regulated by the Consumer Credit Act 1974. Where none of these headings is relevant, the agreement must be headed "Credit Agreement regulated by the Consumer Credit Act 1974" and include a description of the type of credit. As to the contents of an agreement the Regulations require the inclusion of such things as:

(ii) names and addresses of the parties;[78]

(ii) the duration of the agreement, or in the case of and open-ended agreement, a statement indicating that the agreement has no fixed duration;

(iii) A statement indicating how and when the credit to be advanced under the agreement is to be drawn down;

(iv) the amount of the credit (or the credit limit);

(v) the APR;

76 SI 1983/1553 as amended by the Consumer Credit (Agreements) (Amendment) Regulations (SI 2004/1482).

77 See generally, *HSBC Bank Plc v Brophy* [2011] EWCA Civ 67 and *Watchtower Investments Ltd v Payne* [2001] EWCA Civ 1159.

78 Including any credit intermediary.

(vi) the total amount payable;

(vii) the amount of each payment;

(viii) details of default charges; and

(ix) details of any security provided by the debtor or hirer.

In addition the agreement will have to contain notices, in a precise form laid down in the Regulations, informing the debtor or hirer of certain of his statutory rights and protections. These include his right of withdrawal or cancellation (where applicable) and his rights of early termination and early repayment. These rights and protections are explained in later chapters of this book.

Apart from complying with the Regulations, the agreement must embody all the terms of the agreement (other than implied terms).[79]

Signatures

By s.61 the agreement must be contained in a document which is signed:[80] 21-030

(i) by the debtor or hirer, and

(ii) by or on behalf of the creditor.

Thus the debtor must sign it in person, unless the debtor or hirer is a partnership or other unincorporated body in which case it can be signed by one person on behalf of the debtor or hirer. It is not sufficient that the debtor or hirer signs it when it is still blank. When it is presented or sent to him for signature, it must include all the terms of the agreement (other than implied terms) and it must be readily legible. This means that deals ought not to follow the practice whereby the dealer persuades the customer to sign the form (say a hire-purchase proposal form) in blank and then the dealer fills in the spaces later—see, for example, *Campbell Discount Co v Gall*.[81]

The Consumer Credit (Agreements) Regulations 1983 require the agreement to include a signature box in a particular form. The debtor or hirer must sign within that box. Other signatures, e.g. of the creditor or of a witness, must be made outside the box. Normally the date of each signature must be inserted, although this is not necessary if the agreement is not a cancellable one and the date when the agreement becomes an executed agreement is inserted.

79 s.61(1)(b).

80 An electronic signature will suffice, see *Bassano v Toft* [2014] EWHC 377.

81 At para.21-005, above.

The agreement becomes executed when the completed document is signed by (or on behalf of) both sides. The Consumer Credit (Agreements) Regulations 2010 apply similar rules although there is no requirement for the debtor to sign in a signature box.

Copies

21–031 The rules relating to copies have been significantly altered by the implementation of the Consumer Credit Directive 2008 with new rules for draft and executed agreements consumer credit agreements. Under s.55C(1), before a regulated consumer credit agreement is made, the creditor must give the debtor a copy of the prospective agreement. This obligation is not automatic and only applies where the debtor specifically requests a copy, thus raising concerns over the protection afforded to those prospective debtors who are ignorant of this right.

Section 61A places a creditor under a duty to supply a copy of the executed consumer credit agreement to the debtor unless the agreement is in identical terms to an unexecuted copy.[82] Where this is the case, the debtor must instead inform the debtor: that the agreement has been executed; that the executed copy is in identical terms to the unexecuted copy previously provided; and that the debtor has the right to request a copy of the executed agreement in accordance with s.66A.

These rules apply only where the agreement is not an excluded agreement under s.61A(6). Accordingly, there is no obligation to provide a copy of the executed agreement under s.61A where the agreement is cancellable; secured on land; provides credit in excess of £60,260; or which provides credit for business purposes. Where s.61A does not apply, the old rules under ss.62 and 63 will apply.

21–032 Sections 62 and 63 provide for the debtor or hirer to receive a copy or copies of the agreement. Depending upon the circumstances, the debtor or hirer must be given either one or two copies of the agreement. Whatever the circumstances, he should always receive one copy when he signs the agreement. If the agreement is sent to him for his signature then the copy should be sent at the same time. If the agreement is presented personally to him for his signature, then the copy should be given to him there and then. A further (i.e. second) copy must be given to the debtor or hirer if the agreement was not actually made on the occasion when he signed it.[83] This situation commonly arises. An agreement is not made until both sides accept it—or to be more accurate until one side makes an offer which the other side accepts. Now, often, when a customer signs a finance company's form (e.g. for hire-purchase) that is no more than a proposal (i.e. an offer) by the customer. There is no agreement and therefore no contract until the finance company accepts the proposal. The finance company will seldom agree immediately. It (or rather one of its officials) will probably sign the form a few days later and post it or a copy of it back to the customer. That will constitute acceptance of the customer's offer and that will therefore be when the agreement is made (i.e. when the fully signed, executed, agreement is

82 When an agreement is signed by or on behalf of both parties it is an "executed" agreement, s.189(1).
83 s.63.

posted or given back to the debtor). That being so, the agreement will not have been made when the debtor signed the agreement. This will normally be the situation where the customer signs a finance company's hire-purchase proposal form at the dealer's place of business.[84]

In addition to those copies which must be given to the customer at or about the time of making the agreement, the customer is entitled at any time during the currency of the agreement to request, inter alia, a further copy of the executed agreement under ss.77–79. Section 77 is reinforced by the new s.77A[85] which requires creditors in the case of regulated fixed sum agreements to provide debtors with annual statements. Where an annual statement is not provided there are three consequences, none of which are favourable to the creditor:[86]

(i) the creditor is unable to enforce the agreement during the period of non-compliance;

(ii) the debtor is not liable to pay any interest during the period of non-compliance; and

(iii) the debtor will not be liable to pay any default sum which is incurred during the period of non-compliance.

One further point must be made in relation to all copies. Whenever the Consumer Credit Act requires a copy of a regulated agreement to be given or posted, it is part of that requirement that the copy is given or posted together with a copy of any document referred to in the agreement.

Each copy must, in its form and contents, comply with the Consumer Credit (Cancellation Notices and Copies of Documents) Regulations 1983.[87] Those Regulations also contain certain stated exemptions from the requirement that each copy must be accompanied by a copy of any document referred to in the agreement. Otherwise, every copy would have to be accompanied by a copy of the Consumer Credit Act!

Special Formalities for Second Mortgages

Sections 58 and 61(2) are intended to protect the debtor against high pressure sales methods of what are loosely termed second mortgage companies, i.e. finance companies who will lend money usually for unrestricted-use to any houseowner provided he gives to the finance company security in the form of a mortgage on his land (i.e. his house). This need not in fact be a "second" mortgage but in practice usually will be, because the houseowner will probably have created a first mortgage in order to raise the money to purchase the house. Sections 58 21-033

84 For a more detailed account of ss.62 and 63, see the 7th edn of this book.

85 Inserted by the Consumer Credit Act 2006 s.6, with effect from 1 October 2008.

86 s.77A(6).

87 SI 1983/1557, as amended.

and 61(2) do not apply to any mortgage created specifically to finance the purchase of the land which is in fact mortgaged or to any bridging loan connected with the purchase of land.

The effect of s.58 is that the customer must receive a copy of the prospective agreement in advance of receiving the actual agreement to sign. The copy is for his information for him to think about and is not for him to sign. By s.61(2) the agreement (i.e. for his signature) must be sent to him by post but must not be sent until a lapse of at least seven days after the earlier copy was given to him. During that lapse of time the prospective creditor or owner must leave the customer alone to make up his own mind. The creditor must not in any way approach the customer during the interval between delivery of the copy and of the agreement for signature. He must continue to stay away until either a further seven days have elapsed after delivery of the agreement for signature or the customer has signed and returned the agreement.

The aim and effect of these arrangements is that there may be a reasonable period during which the prospective customer is relieved of the "sales" pressure of the prospective creditor or owner. The length of this consideration period will depend upon whether and when the customer signs and returns the agreement. He will have in any case a minimum of seven days and, if he does not sign and return the agreement, he will have at least a further seven days. During the consideration period, the only circumstance in which the prospective creditor or owner will be entitled to approach the customer will be if the customer has during the consideration period specifically requested him to do so. Furthermore, the advance copy must clearly indicate to the customer his right to withdraw from the prospective agreement. It must contain a notice to this effect in the form laid down in the Consumer Credit (Cancellation Notices and Copies of Documents) Regulations 1983.[88]

The advance copy required to be given by s.58 is in addition to those required by ss.62 and 63.[89]

Effect of Non-compliance with the Requirements

21-034 Any agreement which does not comply with all the formality requirements is "improperly executed". The debtor or hirer will not in any way be penalised for this. Thus he can if he wishes enforce the agreement even if it was never signed or never even put into writing. For example he may wish to claim damages under a hire-purchase agreement for breach of an implied condition that the goods will be of satisfactory quality.[90]

It is the creditor or owner who may find it either impossible or difficult to enforce an improperly executed agreement. Where the agreement was made before 6 April 2007 the creditor is entirely unable to enforce it (or any security) if the formality requirements were infringed in any of the following three respects:[91]

88 SI 1983/1557.

89 See para.21-031, above.

90 See para.22-002, above.

91 s.127.

(i) If the debtor or hirer did not sign the agreement or a document containing certain minimum basic terms of the agreement (then set out in Sch.6 to the Consumer Credit (Agreements) Regulations 1983).

(ii) If, in the case of a cancellable agreement, the requirements of s.64 were not complied with, i.e. if any copy given to the debtor did not contain the required details of the right of cancellation or if a notice of those rights should have been served separately and was not.

(iii) If, in the case of a cancellable agreement, the creditor has failed to serve the copy (or copies) required by ss.62 and 63 and has also not served, at some time before commencing proceedings, a copy of the fully-signed agreement.

Only in these very restricted situations will it be entirely impossible for the creditor or owner to enforce the agreement.

These three situations could cause hardship to the creditor. In *Wilson v First County Trust Ltd (No.2)*[92] the agreement was properly documented except that a documentation fee of £250 was included as part of the credit provided under the agreement rather than as part of the total charge for credit. The Court of Appeal held that this misstatement rendered the agreement permanently unenforceable under s.127(3) and that therefore the loan was unrecoverable. This view was confirmed by the House of Lords and resulted in the £5000 loan being unrecoverable due to the inclusion of a £250 documentation fee being incorrectly assigned as part of the credit. This was certainly a windfall for the debtor under such an agreement! To rectify this injustice the Consumer Credit Act 2006 repealed ss.127(3)–127(5) which results in the enforceability of such improperly documented agreements being subject to judicial discretion as considered below.

Where an agreement is not subject to the (now repealed) provisions of s.127(3)–(5), the creditor can enforce it—but subject to five restrictions: 21-035

(i) He can enforce it only by action in court.[93]
(ii) He cannot, without an order of the court, retake possession of the goods or land associated with the agreement (even if otherwise he would be entitled to) because that would constitute enforcement of the agreement.[94]
(iii) He cannot enforce any security except to the extent that the court allows him to enforce the regulated agreement[95] This is

92 [2001] 3 All E.R. 229, affirmed [2004] 1 A.C. 816 (HL). See, A. Seager, "Wilson v First County Trust: first declaration of incompatibility under the Human Rights Act 1998" [2001] J.I.B.L. 163.

93 s.65(1). Reporting to a credit reference agency does not amount to "enforcement", see *McGuffick v Royal Bank of Scotland Plc* [2009] EWHC 2386 (Comm); [2010] C.C.L.R. 2.

94 s.65(2).

95 s.113.

important where the security is provided otherwise than in the regulated agreement itself, e.g. in the case of a guarantor or indemnifier.

(iv) The court has power in granting any order enforcing the agreement:

(a) To reduce or extinguish any sum payable by the debtor or hirer (i.e. so as to compensate him for any prejudice caused to him by reason of the default).[96]

(b) To impose any conditions (e.g. the delivery of a further copy to the hirer).[97]

(c) To suspend the operation of an enforcement order or any part of it (e.g. until certain conditions have been fulfilled).[98]

(d) To amend the agreement as the court considers just.[99]

These powers, especially those given by ss.135 and 136 are very wide and will enable the court in many cases to wipe out or minimise any prejudice caused to the debtor by the non-compliance with the formalities requirements. For example, in *Rank Xerox Finance v Hepple and Fennymore*[100] the county court granted an enforcement order but in doing so significantly reduced the amount of money payable by the customer because the agreement had not fully indicated the charges payable upon default.

(v) Before the court will make any order enforcing the agreement, the creditor or owner will have to convince the court that in view of the non-compliance it is nevertheless just and fair that the order be made. The court must consider to what extent the debtor or hirer has been prejudiced by the non-compliance and to what extent the creditor or owner is to be blamed for it.[101]

Plainly the court has power to waive purely technical infringements of the requirements. Moreover, in view of the wide powers given to the court to minimise the prejudice caused to the debtor or hirer, it would seem unlikely that the court will often refuse to grant an enforcement order. It must of course refuse in the three situations mentioned earlier where the agreement was entered into before 6 April 2007. One rare situation where the court would be also likely

96 s.127(2) and 127(1)(i).
97 s.135(1)(a).
98 s.135(1)(b).
99 s.136.
100 [1994] C.C.L.R. 1.
101 s.127.

to refuse would be where the creditor or owner has knowingly not complied with the requirements with the deliberate intention of prejudicing the debtor or hirer. In the unlikely event that the court cannot minimise or remove the prejudice caused to the debtor by the creditor's non-compliance, no order will be granted and thus, the agreement will remain unenforceable by the creditor.

Security

Often the security (if any) will be given by the debtor or hirer. In that case the security should be described in the regulated agreement or in a document referred to in the regulated agreement—Consumer Credit (Agreements) Regulations 2010.[102] 21-036

However, the position is not so simple where the security is given by another person—in the case of a contract of guarantee or indemnity. As we have seen finance companies quite often demand that someone acts as guarantor or indemnifier of a credit agreement—particularly when the prospective debtor is a young person under the age of 25.[103] Such a guarantor or indemnifier is often a parent or friend and will normally agree to the arrangement at the request of the debtor or hirer—because otherwise the finance company will not agree to the credit transaction.

On the other hand someone may act as guarantor or indemnifier without any request to do so from the debtor or hirer. Recourse agreements made between finance companies and dealers are examples. The Consumer Credit Act applies to security only if given at the request (express or implied) of the debtor or hirer.[104] Thus a recourse agreement does not have to comply with formalities laid down in the Act and will still be enforceable even though the principal agreement between creditor and debtor did not comply with the formalities requirements.

A guarantor or indemnifier who acted as such at the request (express or implied) of the debtor or hirer is given a considerable measure of protection by the Act. First, where the court refuses or would, if asked, refuse to enforce a regulated credit agreement because it was improperly executed, any security (i.e. the guarantee or indemnity) will also be unenforceable.[105] 21-037

Secondly, certain formalities must be observed in relation to the security (guarantee or indemnity) itself.[106] The person providing the security (the guarantor or indemnifier) is termed the surety. Section 105 requires the security agreement to be in writing and signed by or on behalf of the surety. It authorises regulations to be made as to the form and contents of the

102 Or, where relevant, the Consumer Credit (Agreements) Regulations 1983, see para.21.029, above.

103 See para.17-009, above.

104 s.189.

105 s.113, see para.18-003, above.

106 See s.105.

written document and it requires copies of that document and of the principal agreement (the credit agreement) to be given to the surety.[107]

If any of the above formalities are not complied with, the security is "improperly executed" and is not enforceable against the surety except on an order of the court. In deciding whether to make an order to enforce the security, the court has to weigh similar considerations to those it must take into account in deciding whether to enforce an improperly executed regulated agreement. To put it another way, ss.127, 135 and 136 apply in both cases. Thus the court has wide powers to put right any prejudice suffered by the surety (e.g. by reduction of any sum payable by the surety or by amending the security document). There is one significant difference. Whereas a regulated agreement which, contrary to the formalities requirements is not in writing or not signed by the debtor is never enforceable, there is no such rigid rule in the case of an unsigned or unwritten security agreement. There is simply the rule that the court must have regard to the prejudice caused to the surety and the degree of culpability of the creditor or owner.

21-038 At this stage three notes of warning must be sounded. First, the fact that a security document is improperly executed does not affect the validity or enforceability of the credit agreement to which it relates. The credit agreement is still valid even though the security may be unenforceable.[108]

Secondly, the formalities requirements in s.105 of the Consumer Credit Act apply only to security given in relation to a regulated agreement. The third warning is that those formalities (which apply to security whatever form it takes) are in addition to formalities laid down by other Acts of Parliament in relation to particular form of security, e.g. the Bills of Sale Acts 1878–1882 (mortgages of goods), the Policies of Assurance Act 1867, the Law of Property Act 1925 s.136 (assignment of life assurance policies), and the Statute of Frauds 1677 (guarantees).

Withdrawal and Cancellation

21-039 The cancellation provisions and the new right of withdrawal (ss.67–73 and s.66A) represent an attempt to combat a particularly undesirable selling technique. Door-to-door salesmen used to persuade people to commit themselves to acquire on credit terms goods or services for which the payments might be crippling and the need for which would seem to recede in the cool light of reason after the salesman had left. At one time, certain encyclopaedia salesmen were guilty of this. Thus the cancellation provisions are aimed at what might be termed doorstep credit agreements. Where an agreement is cancellable, the debtor has a short period of a few days in which he may cancel the agreement, even after it has been made. These provisions, therefore,

107 See the Consumer Credit (Guarantees and Indemnities) Regulations 1983 (SI 1983/1556).

108 The same is not true vice versa, s.113, see para.18-003, above.

create an important exception to the principle that after a contract is made, neither party can back out of it. A contract not cancellable under these provisions (of the Consumer Credit Act) about to be discussed may be cancellable under the Consumer Contracts (Information, Cancellation and Additional Charges) Regulations 2013.[109] These regulations extended the principle of a cooling-off period to doorstep and distance selling contracts with effect from 13 June 2014.[110]

Right of Withdrawal

The protection offered by the Consumer Credit Act in respect of cancellable agreements has been extended by the right of withdrawal laid down by s.66A inserted into the Act by the Consumer Credit (EU Directive) Regulations 2010.[111] Section 66A affords a debtor under a regulated consumer credit agreement the automatic right of withdrawal without offering any explanation. This right is exercisable only where the agreement is not excluded. Excluded agreements are defined as: 21-040

(a) an agreement for credit exceeding £60,260;[112]

(b) an agreement secured on land;

(c) a restricted-use credit agreement to finance the purchase of land; or

(d) an agreement for a bridging loan in connection with the purchase of land.

The right to withdraw applies only to the credit agreement. Thus it does not allow the debtor to return any goods or services purchased using the credit supplied under the agreement. The right to withdraw lasts for 14 days from what the Act refers to as the "relevant day". This is defined variously depending on the nature of the regulated agreement as being the later of either:

(a) the day on which the agreement is made;

(b) the day on which the creditor first informs the debtor of the credit limit (where the creditor is required to inform the debtor of the credit limit);

109 SI 2013/3134.
110 See above, Ch.2.
111 SI 2010/1010.
112 Other than a "residential renovation agreement" as defined in s.189(1).

(c) the day on which the debtor receives a copy of the executed agreement where s.61A applies (i.e. the creditor is under a duty to supply copy of executed consumer credit agreement); and

(d) the day on which the debtor receives a copy of the executed agreement where s.63 applies (i.e. the creditor is under a duty to supply a copy of the executed agreement).

The debtor can, at any stage before the expiry of the 14-day period, give notice of withdrawal either in writing or orally. In either case it must be given using the contact details provided in the agreement.[113]

Where the debtor exercises his right under s.66A it has two effects on the agreement. First, that agreement is treated as if it had never been entered into. The debtor must repay the amount of credit provided, together with any accrued interest (at the rate indicated in the agreement) within 30 days.[114] However, the debtor is not liable for any other fees with the exception of non-returnable charges paid by the creditor to a public administrative body.[115] Secondly, where any ancillary contract relating to the credit agreement has been made, that too will be regarded as if it had never been made. This will cover, for example, any payment protection policy the debtor signed on entering the credit agreement.[116]

Cancellable Agreements

21-041 Section 67 offers a considerably more limited mechanism for a debtor to cancel a regulated agreement and now applies only where the broader right of withdrawal under s.66A does not apply.[117] Thus the main application of s.67 is now reduced to agreements over the £60,260 threshold for s.66A and to consumer hire agreements. A regulated agreement is cancellable under s.67(1) if two conditions are fulfilled:

(i) The antecedent negotiations included oral representation made when in the presence of the customer by or on behalf of the negotiator. It will be recalled that either the creditor or owner or the dealer may be a negotiator in antecedent negotiations—though in the case of a consumer hire agreement, the dealer will not be a negotiator in antecedent negotiations.[118]

113 s.66A(4) and s.66A(5).

114 This period commences on the day after the debtor notifies the creditor of their withdrawal, s.66A(10).

115 s.66A(9).

116 Note that the ancillary contract must relate to the credit and not any goods supplied under the credit agreement. Thus, notification of withdrawal under s.66A will not have any effect on, for example, a warranty purchased in respect of a motor vehicle.

117 s.67(2).

118 *See Lloyds Bowmaker Leasing Ltd v MacDonald* [1993] C.C.L.R. 65 (Sh. Ct.) and para.21-020, above.

(ii) The customer signed the agreement elsewhere than at certain business premises—namely those of the creditor or owner, of the dealer and of any party to a linked transaction (other than the customer or his relative).

The first requirement will be fulfilled in almost any case where the agreement is made after the prospective customer has spoken face to face either with the dealer or with the creditor or owner. It would not of course be fulfilled where the agreement was negotiated by the customer entirely through the post. Suppose the only oral representations made to the customer by the dealer or the creditor or owner were made over the telephone. Here again the first requirement would not be fulfilled. Not every statement made during antecedent negotiations will amount to a "representation" for the purposes of s.67. For example a simple greeting, "Good day" or an inconsequential bit of small talk, "Nice day isn't it?" would not suffice. A statement will amount to a representation for the purposes of s.67 only if it is a statement of fact, an opinion, or an undertaking as to the future, which is capable of inducing the proposed customer to enter into the regulated agreement: *Moorgate Services Ltd v Kabir*.[119] It is sufficient if there is at least one such statement made in the presence of the customer during the antecedent negotiations.

The second requirement is fulfilled if the customer signed the agreement away from the business premises mentioned, e.g. at his own business premises or at his home. Thus an agreement which the debtor signs at the dealer's premises is not cancellable. On the other hand if, after listening to the dealer's sales talk, the customer takes the agreement away and signs it at home, then the agreement will be cancellable. Thus although the cancellation provisions were aimed at what might loosely be termed "doorstep" credit agreements, their net was cast rather more widely than that.

To exercise his right of cancellation the debtor or hirer must serve a written notice indicating his intention of withdrawing from the transaction. The notice of cancellation must be served upon one of the following persons[120]—the creditor or owner (or his agent), the person specified in the agreement as being a person to whom such notice may be sent, the dealer, and any person who in the course of a business acted on behalf of the customer in negotiations for the agreement. The notice can be sent by post and must be sent or served within the time limit stated in s.68.[121]

119 [1995] C.C.L.R. 74.

120 s.69.

121 For analysis of cancellation under the Consumer Credit Act, including the duration of the cancellation period and the effect of cancellation, see the 7th edn of this book.

22

Creditor's Liability in Respect of Goods or Services Supplied

Introduction

A distinction can be drawn between two types of contractual terms—those relating to the credit and its repayment and those relating to the goods or services supplied. It is the latter with which this chapter is concerned. These include terms relating to the quality of the goods supplied, the time of delivery, the title of the seller, etc. Sometimes both types of terms (i.e. as to the credit and as to the goods or services supplied) are contained within the same agreement—i.e. in the case of hire-purchase, conditional sale and credit sale agreements. Most of this chapter will be devoted to dealing with these agreements. However, first we shall consider those situations where there are two agreements—one relating to the credit and a separate one relating to the supply of goods or services. This occurs for example in the case of a bank loan, a credit card purchase or a trade check purchase. The credit agreement is with one person (the bank or finance company) and the agreement to buy goods or services is with another (the supplier). In relation to the latter agreement two questions arise: 22-001

(i) What are the terms of the agreement to buy goods or services?

(ii) To what extent is the creditor (as well as the supplier) liable for breaches of those terms by the supplier?

Terms of the Goods or Services Agreement

22-002 The debtor may use his credit (be it a bank loan, credit card or whatever) to buy either goods or services. If he buys goods, then it will be a contract of sale of goods that he makes with the supplier. The terms of that contract will include those which were discussed in Ch.7. If he buys services then the terms of the agreement will be those that are expressly agreed between him and the supplier plus any terms that are implied. The terms of a contract for services will therefore vary a great deal according to the type of agreement made. He may buy a package holiday or a cruise, have central heating installed or an extension built, have his garden landscaped or his yacht repaired, etc. All these are contracts for services and the terms expressly agreed or implied will be different in each case. There is no room here to consider them all, but only to make some general observations.

In contracts for services the implied terms will include those implied by the Consumer Rights Act 2015 (where the service is supplied by a trader to a consumer) or the Supply of Goods and Services Act 1982 (where the service is supplied in the course of a business to a non-consumer). These were explained in Ch.8 and the circumstances in which they could be excluded were explained in Ch.10. Without repeating the detail it might be useful to recall that the following terms are implied by both the Consumer Rights Act 2015 and the Supply of Goods and Services Act 1982:

(i) There is an implied term that the work will be done with reasonable care and skill.[1]

(ii) If no time is mentioned in the contract, then there will usually be an implied condition that the services will be provided and completed within a reasonable length of time.[2]

(iii) Where the contract involves the supply of some goods, there are implied terms as to title, description, quality and sample.[3]

Creditor's Liability for the Supplier's Breach

22-003 The concern here focuses on the situation where the debtor has two contracts—a credit agreement with the creditor and a contract with the supplier to buy goods or services. It is a basic

1 CRA 2015 s.49; SGSA 1982 s.13.

2 CRA 2015 s.52; SGSA 1982 s.14.

3 See, for example, CRA 2015 ss.9–11 and SGSA 1982 ss.1–5. These are similar to those in Sale of Goods Act ss.12–15.

common law rule that only a party to a contract can be liable for breach of that contract. Therefore, at common law even if the seller who sells the goods or services is in breach of contract, the buyer will have no remedy against the creditor because the latter was not a party to the contract to sell the goods or services. The buyer will have a remedy only against the seller.

Section 75

Section 75 of the Consumer Credit Act 1974 has made a considerable inroad into the rule just stated. This section, which applies to debtor-creditor-supplier agreements, has already been quoted in connection with misrepresentation.[4] Section 75 provides that if the debtor has: 22-004

> **"any claim against the supplier in respect of a misrepresentation or breach of contract, he shall have a like claim against the creditor".**

Thus the debtor can bring the claim against the seller or the creditor or both.[5] Take an example: X uses his credit card[6] to buy an armchair (cash price £145) from a shop. The armchair is not of satisfactory quality and collapses, causing X some injury. By virtue of s.75, X can sue the credit card company (as well as the shop) for damages for injury and damage caused. This right to sue the creditor could be very valuable in the situation where the shop has become insolvent. If X exercises his right to claim against the creditor, the creditor (the credit card company) can claim against the supplier under a right of indemnity.[7] The effect of s.75 is therefore that it is the creditor who stands the risk of the supplier becoming insolvent.

Turning briefly to debit cards used in conjunction with Electronic Funds Transfer, these debit card agreements, unlike credit card agreements, are debtor-creditor agreements. Thus s.75 does not apply to them because it applies only to debtor-creditor-supplier agreements.

As just observed, s.75 applies only in the case of a debtor-creditor-supplier agreement, i.e. broadly, where there is some business connection between the creditor and supplier, as in the example of Shiver, Warmitup Ltd and Hotmoney Ltd given at para.22-004, above. However, there are two further restrictions upon the operation of the section. First, it does not apply to a non-commercial agreement.[8] Secondly, it does not apply to a claim in respect of "any single item to which the supplier has attached a cash price not exceeding £100 or more than £30,000".[9] So, if X, as well as buying an armchair, had used his credit card to buy a hot water

4 See paras 21-017 and 21-018, below. For a recent discussion of s.75 in the context of a misrepresentation claim, see *Hodgson v Creation Consumer Finance Ltd* [2021] EWHC 2167 (Comm) (creditor liable for misrepresentations by the supplier as to the financial benefits of domestic solar panels).

5 For the general criticism of the policy behind s.75, see A. Dobson, "Connected Lender Substantive Controversy" [1978] N.L.J. 703.

6 Though not a charge card, see s.75(3)(c).

7 s.75(2).

8 s.75(3)(a).

9 s.75(3)(b).

bottle which had burst and ruined his bed, he could not make a claim for that damage against the credit card company because the hot water bottle will not have had a cash price in excess of £100. That is so even if the damage caused was in excess of £100. X would of course still have his remedies against the seller. Section 75 applies to items having a cash price of over £100 but not over £30,000.

22-005 Section 75 probably cannot be relied upon by any credit card holder who made his credit card agreement before 1 July 1977.[10] It seems unlikely, however, that many credit card agreements made so long ago are still active.[11]

Whenever a regulated credit card agreement was made, a complication arises where there is a second authorised user. This occurs where someone with a credit card agreement has as part of that agreement an arrangement whereby a second person (often husband or wife) has a card which can be used on the same account. The latter person, the authorised user, is not, however, made liable to pay the debts incurred. Thus there is one account and one person liable to make repayments on that account, although there are two card holders each able to draw on the account. Where it is the authorised user who has used his card on the purchase in question, can that authorised user rely on s.75 in the same way as if he were the principal card holder? Exactly the same question could be asked in relation to s.56 and the answer is exactly the same. At first sight the answer appears to be no, since the wording of both sections makes it clear that they operate only in favour of the debtor. Imagine a wife, Joan, who is an authorised user of a card on her husband Darby's account. Suppose she uses the card to pay £200 for a coat from Bill's shop. She is clearly the person who makes a contract with Bill's shop.[12] She is not acting as her husband's agent in making that contract but is clearly buying the coat herself. If the coat is not fit to wear, it is she who has a claim against Bill for the coat not being of satisfactory quality. Is she perhaps Darby's agent in using the credit card to debit his credit card account? If she is, then could he (instead of her) rely on the sections? The answer still appears to be no. In relation to s.75, the debtor is given a right to bring against the creditor any claim which he could have brought against the supplier, but Darby has no claim against Bill. Joan's problem is that ss.56 and 75 confer rights only on the debtor and the debtor is Darby. In order to succeed under either section, Joan needs to show that she too is a debtor. Perhaps she can. The word "debtor" in the Act does not have the simple meaning of someone who owes a debt. It means the "individual receiving credit under a consumer credit agreement"—s.189(1). Presumably Joan got her card (of which she is the authorised user) by agreement of the credit card company. In that case the card company in making the agreement with her provided her with a financial accommodation, credit upon which she can draw. If that is so, the credit card company has a credit agreement with Darby and also has one with Joan. The difficulty with that is that if the card company has provided a financial accommodation to Joan, then one would

10 Similarly, s.56 probably cannot be relied upon by a card holder who made his credit card agreement before 1 April 1977.

11 Thus for a full explanation readers are referred to the 5th edn of this book and to A. Dobson, "Connected Lender Commencement Controversy" [1978] N.L.J. 448.

12 It is a sale of goods contract, see para.8-006, above.

have expected Joan to have to be responsible for repaying any credit she draws. It is surely much more accurate to say that in letting Joan have a card on Darby's account, the card company has granted a further financial accommodation to Darby and that Joan when she uses her card is actually acting as Darby's agent to pledge his credit. The plain fact is that the legal position of the second authorised card holder needs clarifying, preferably by an amendment to s.75. Clearly, as matter of policy, the law should be that the second authorised card holder has exactly the same rights against the credit card company as if she had been the principal card holder.[13]

Leaving the problem of the second authorised card holder, we can turn to another situation in which the card companies have sought to avoid liability under s.75. This is where the card holder has used his card to make a purchase abroad. The contract of purchase abroad may be governed by the law of the country (e.g. Japan) in which that purchase occurs. Nevertheless the credit card agreement, if made in England between a card issuer in England and a card holder resident in England, will be governed by English law, including s.75. It should still be possible first to discover whether the card holder has a claim against the supplier (i.e. according to whatever law governs the supply contract) and secondly to hold the card issuing company jointly and severally liable for that claim. The credit card companies' attempts to avoid s.75 liability in respect of transactions when the card is used abroad were in each case a "try on". In *Office of Fair Trading v Lloyds TSB Bank Plc*[14] the Court of Appeal held that s.75 applies where the transaction is conducted abroad. The decision was confirmed by the House of Lords and thus it is now settled that s.75 is capable of supporting an action by a card holder in respect of a transaction conducted abroad. Whilst this could be unfair on the card issuer, (who may well struggle to impose liability on the foreign supplier in question) it reflects the consumer protection orientation of s.75.[15]

In *Porter v General Guarantee Corporation*[16] Brown J said in relation to a hire-purchase agreement that s.75 was relevant. He was plainly wrong. In fact s.75 does not apply to hire- 22-006
purchase, conditional sale and credit sale agreements. This is, after all, only common sense, since in these cases there are in the credit agreement itself terms relating to the delivery, description and quality of the goods and if one of those terms is broken the creditor will in any case be liable for what is his own breach of contract. Where a finance company makes a hire-purchase, conditional sale or credit sale agreement with the debtor, the finance company buys the goods from the dealer and contracts with the debtor to supply the goods to the debtor. Thus the finance company supplies the goods on credit terms to the debtor.

13 For a fuller discussion of the position of the second authorised card holder see A. Dobson, "Connected Lender Liability" [1994] S.J. 1212.

14 [2006] EWCA Civ. 268, [2007] Q.B. 1 affirmed [2007] UKHL 48, [2007] 3 W.L.R. 733. See also *Jarrett v Barclays and Royal Bank of Scotland* [1999] Q.B. 1 (purchaser of timeshare in Portugal held entitled to succeed under s.75 against British banks which had financed the purchase).

15 See further, C. Hare, "Your Flexible Friend?" (2005) 64 C.L.J. 287.

16 [1982] R.T.R. 384.

The situation is different, however, where the finance company does not itself buy the goods and then supply them to the debtor but instead lends the debtor the money to enable the debtor himself to buy the goods direct from the dealer. In this situation the agreement between the finance company and the debtor is not a hire-purchase, conditional sale or credit sale agreement. It is simply a loan contract. If the loan contract is a regulated debtor-creditor-supplier agreement (i.e. made as a result of business arrangements between the dealer and the finance company), s.75 will apply. That was the situation in the Scottish case, *United Dominions Trust v Taylor*[17] where a finance company lent money to Mr Taylor to enable him to buy a car from Parkaway Cars. The finance company brought proceedings against him to enforce the loan agreement. He based his defence on s.75. He said he had a claim against Parkaway Cars for breach of contract and for misrepresentation because the car had been misrepresented to be in a good condition when in fact it was unroadworthy. It was held that this, if proved, gave him a good defence under the loan agreement. Where the debtor had a right to rescind the supply contract (i.e. his contract of sale of goods with Parkaway Cars), he had under s.75 a "like claim" against the finance company; a "like claim" meant a claim to rescind the loan agreement.[18]

However, in a recent Scottish case, *Durkin v DSG Retail Ltd*,[19] the Supreme Court confirmed that the words "a like claim" should be given their ordinary meaning and that the broader interpretation in *United Dominions Trust v Taylor* was not correct. Lord Hodge, in explaining this conclusion, suggested that the words "a like claim" meant that "a debtor, who has a right of action against the supplier for misrepresentation or breach of the contract of supply, can sue the creditor for that misrepresentation or breach of the supply contract". Thus the claim against the creditor must be in relation to the supply not the credit agreement. A right to rescind the credit agreement with the creditor was not a "like claim" since it was not a claim which the debtor could have pursued against the supplier.

22-007 Whilst s.75 could not be invoked to rescind the credit agreement, however, that was not the end of the matter. The Supreme Court considered that the debtor was entitled to rescind the credit agreement by an alternative method. Since the credit provided was tied into a specific supply transaction, where that supply transaction was brought to an end by the supplier's breach of contract the debtor is obligated to repay the funds borrowed. Thus Lord Hodge stated that:[20]

> **"in order to reflect that reality, the law implies a term into such a credit agreement that it is conditional upon the survival of the**

17 [1980] C.C.L.R. 29.

18 For an analysis of this case, see A. Dobson, "Consumer Credit—A Connected Lender Conundrum" [1981] J.B.L. 179. Despite a certain amount of academic criticism (see for example, F.P. Davidson, "The Missing Link Transaction" (1980) 96 L.Q.R. 343 and N.V. Lowe, "Missing Link Transactions—Further Observations" (1981) 97 L.Q.R. 532) the decision in *U.D.T. v Taylor* was followed in *Forward Trust Ltd v Hornsby* [1996] C.C.L.R. 18.

19 [2014] UKSC 21.

20 [2014] UKSC 21 at [26].

> **supply agreement. The debtor on rejecting the goods and thereby rescinding the supply agreement for breach of contract may also rescind the credit agreement by invoking this condition."**

Thus Mr Durkin was entitled to rescind the credit agreement, albeit not through s.75. Perhaps a more straightforward approach would be for the debtor in such a position to rely upon s.56 and argue that the supplier's misrepresentation which gave rise to his right to rescind the supply contract was also made by the supplier as agent for the creditor and thus amounted to a misrepresentation by the creditor entitling him to rescind his credit agreement with the creditor. Alternatively, the debtor could have sought damages from the supplier, including as damages his liabilities from having to make payments under the now pointless credit agreement. That claim for damages would have constituted a "like claim" under s.75, even though such a remedy was perhaps less "obvious" than rescission of the finance contract itself.

Section 75A

Following the implementation of the Consumer Credit Directive into UK domestic law there is now one further mechanism for imposing liability on the creditor for the supplier's breach—s.75A. This section allows a debtor to claim against the creditor for a breach of contract[21] by the supplier where there is a "linked credit agreement". This is defined as: 22-008

> **"a regulated consumer credit agreement which serves exclusively to finance an agreement for the supply of specific goods or the provision of a specific service and where—**
> **(a) the creditor uses the services of the supplier in connection with the preparation or making of the credit agreement, or**
> **(b) the specific goods or provision of a specific service are explicitly specified in the credit agreement."**

Thus where only general credit is provided, such as through a credit card, s.75A will not apply. Furthermore, s.75A will not apply where the cash price (as opposed to the amount of credit supplied) of the goods or services is less than £30,000[22] nor where the amount of credit supplied under the linked credit agreement is greater than £60,260.[23]

Where s.75A does apply its effect is different from that under s.75. Under s.75 a debtor can pursue either the creditor or the supplier at the debtor's sole determination, whereas under s.75A the debtor must pursue the supplier first, and only where the debtor is unable to obtain

21 Unlike s.75, however, misrepresentation is insufficient, s.75A(1).

22 s.75A(6)(a).

23 s.75A(6)(b).

satisfaction from the supplier is the debtor empowered to bring an action against the creditor. Section 75A is therefore available only when either:[24]

(a) the supplier cannot be traced;

(b) the debtor has contacted the supplier but the supplier has not responded;

(c) the supplier is insolvent; or

(d) the debtor has taken reasonable steps to pursue his claim against the supplier but has not obtained satisfaction for his claim.

Hire Purchase

22–009 We now come to discuss the terms title, description, quality, sample and delivery which are implied in hire-purchase agreements. First, a few words must be said about terminology. Traditionally the parties to a hire-purchase agreement have been called "hirer" and "owner". These are the words that have usually appeared in the agreement itself and they therefore have also tended to be used in the judgments of decided cases. However, the Consumer Credit Act has brought about a change. That Act and other Acts of Parliament now use the words "debtor" and "creditor" to describe the parties.[25] This change of terminology has not changed the essential nature of a hire-purchase contract. The debtor under a hire-purchase agreement will still be the hirer of goods with an option to purchase them. Many finance companies continue to use the old terminology in their hire-purchase agreements. There is nothing wrong with that and it is not inaccurate. Indeed it serves to make it clear that the agreement is a hire-purchase agreement and not a credit sale agreement or some other kind of credit agreement. In this chapter, however, the terms "debtor" and "creditor" will be used. The written hire-purchase agreement seldom contains many terms securing the debtor's interest. Indeed, in the past, such agreements have often included exemption clauses designed to prevent the debtor being able to make a claim for the creditor's breach of the agreement. Parliament has stepped in to protect the interests of debtors.

Following to the consolidation of consumer rights under supply contracts through the Consumer Rights Act 2015, the position is regulated according to the status of the parties involved. Where a trader supplies goods to a consumer on hire purchase terms, the position is

24 s.75A(2).

25 We have already noted that in some situations, the equivalent terminology employed by the Financial Conduct Authority is "borrower" and "lender".

regulated by the Consumer Rights Act 2015 which addresses both the ability of the creditor to exclude his liability and the content of hire-purchase contracts. Where the 2015 Act does not apply, for example, where the debtor is not a consumer, the position is regulated by the Supply Goods (Implied Terms) Act 1973 and the Unfair Contract Terms Act 1977.

The Supply of Goods (Implied Terms) Act and the Consumer Rights Act 2015 imply terms into hire-purchase agreements which are virtually identical to the corresponding terms implied into sale contracts whether under the Sale of Goods Act or the Consumer Rights Act. The result is that, whether a customer buys goods or whether he takes them on hire purchase terms, his rights as to title, description, quality and sample are the same. For example, where a trader supplies goods to another business on hire purchase terms, apart from necessary changes of wording, ss.8, 9, 10 and 11 of the 1973 Act are identical to ss.12, 13, 14 and 15 of the Sale of Goods Act. Similarly, where a trader supplies goods to a consumer on hire purchase terms, the consumer can rely on the implied terms under ss.9, 10, 11, 14 and 17 of the CRA 2015, Since the implied terms under both the 1979 Act and the 2015 Act have been considered in detail in Ch.7, ss.8–11 of the 1973 Act and the corresponding sections in the 2015 Act will be considered here only to the extent that there are matters specially relevant to hire-purchase contracts.

Terms implied in a hire-purchase contract at common law have in large measure been rendered redundant and superseded by the terms implied by the 1973 Act. Nevertheless in one or two instances they may be significant and this will be seen as the chapter proceeds—particularly in relation to delivery and acceptance.[26]

Title

Section 8 of the Supply of Goods (Implied Terms) Act 1973 is virtually identical to s.12 of the Sale of Goods Act. It corresponds to the equivalent term laid down in s.17(1) of the Consumer Rights Act where a trader supplies goods to a consumer on hire purchase terms. Section 8(1) reads: 22-010

> **"In every relevant hire-purchase agreement, other than one to which subsection (2) below applies, there is—**
> **(a) an implied term on the part of the creditor that he will have a right to sell the goods at the time when the property is to pass."**

In hire-purchase contracts, it is usually some time before property passes to the debtor. Property will not pass until the debtor exercises his option to buy and that option will not be exercisable until he has paid all his instalments. Provided the creditor has the right to sell the goods at the time the debtor exercises his option, the creditor is not in breach of the condition in s.8(1)(a) nor of the term implied into consumer contracts by s.17(1) of the Consumer Rights Act.

26 Note that s.28 of the CRA 2015 (the trader must deliver the goods to the consumer unless otherwise agree) only applies to sales contracts under the Act, i.e. it does not apply to hire purchase agreements.

However, there are three other grounds upon which the creditor may be liable unless he has the right to sell much earlier than the time at which the debtor exercises his option. The first ground is breach of the condition implied by the common law as to title—namely that the creditor will have good title to the goods at the time when the debtor takes delivery. In the situation where goods are handed over as soon as the agreement is made, the creditor must have good title right from the start. On the other hand, where the goods are not to be delivered until some time after the making of the agreement, the creditor will not be in breach of the condition provided he acquires good title to the goods before the debtor takes delivery of them. *Mercantile Guarantee v Wheatley*[27] concerned an agreement made by a finance company on 7 February to let out a lorry on hire purchase terms. On that date the finance company did not own the lorry but subsequently purchased it on 11 February. Thus the finance company had good title when, on 8 March the debtor took delivery of the lorry. Goddard J held that the common law condition as to title was not broken since the relevant time was when the goods were delivered.

22-011 The second ground of possible liability of the creditor who does not have the right to sell the goods is for breach of an express term of the agreement. *Barber v NWS Bank*[28] involved an agreement which included an express term that until full payment the property in the goods would remain vested in the creditor. It was conceded that this amounted to an express term that at the time of the contract the creditor had good title and it was held that this amounted to a condition of the contract. The case involved a conditional sale agreement but the law is the same in the case of hire purchase.

The other ground of possible liability of the creditor who does not have the right to sell the goods is breach of the warranty implied by s.8(1)(b) of the Supply of Goods (Implied Terms) Act—the warranty of quiet possession and freedom from undisclosed charges or encumbrances.[29] This warranty relates to the period of hire, i.e. the period before the debtor exercises his option to buy. The warranty of quiet possession (as in sale of goods) also relates to the future, i.e. after the debtor has exercised his option and acquired ownership in the goods.[30]

Breach of a condition as title—whether the one implied by s.8(1)(a),[31] the one implied by the common law or an express one—gives the debtor the right to treat the contract as repudiated and to reclaim all the payments he has made. The reason he can recover all his payments is that he can be said to have suffered a total failure of consideration. This is just a way of saying that the law regards him as having received no benefit from the contract. Because he has received no benefit, he can recover the whole amount that he has paid. We saw in Ch.7 that this was the position in sale of goods when the seller is in breach of the condition as to

27 [1938] 1 K.B. 490.

28 [1996] 1 All E.R. 906.

29 Again, the same is true in respect of hire purchase agreements which fall under the equivalent provision in the Consumer Rights Act s.17(2).

30 See *Microbeads v Vinhurst Road Markings*, para.7-010, above.

31 In respect of hire purchase agreements falling under the Consumer Rights Act the question is not answered by reference to the status of the term but by s.19 of that Act.

title in s.12 of the Sale of Goods Act, i.e. the buyer can recover the whole price he has paid as was held in *Rowland v Divall*.[32] *Rowland v Divall* has been followed in a hire purchase case, *Warman v Southern Counties Finance*.[33] The facts in the latter case were that the debtor had paid all instalments and had enjoyed the use of the goods for some months before having to surrender them to their true owner. Finnemore J said that the true basis of a hire-purchase agreement was that the debtor should be able to acquire ownership of the goods. The debtor was unable to acquire ownership and his Lordship held that therefore the debtor had suffered a total failure of consideration and was entitled to the return of all his payments. The result, as in *Rowland v Divall*, was that the plaintiff enjoyed the use of the goods for some months at no cost to himself. The basis of these decisions—that the plaintiff derived no benefit from the contract—would appear questionable! Nevertheless these cases, both decisions at first instance, were approved and followed by the Court of Appeal in *Barber v NWS Bank*.[34]

The situation could come about that a creditor is in breach of a condition as to title but subsequently manages to cure his defect in title. He could do this, for example, by buying the goods from their true owner. If this occurs whilst the debtor is still enjoying the use of the goods, then the debtor will not subsequently be able to treat the contract as repudiated: *Butterworth v Kingsway Motors*.[35] Also he will not suffer a total failure of consideration, since the creditor will now be able to give him good title—even if a little belatedly. He will therefore not be able to reclaim all his payments. His claim will be simply for damages for the fact that he did not obtain good title as soon as he should have done. If the creditor cures his defect in title before property is to pass to the debtor, i.e. before payment of the final instalment—then the debtor will suffer no delay in obtaining good title. He will acquire it at exactly the time that he should do so, i.e. on exercising his option. In this case he will be entitled only to nominal damages. Thus the debtor who discovers that his creditor is in breach of a condition as to title would be well advised to treat the contract as repudiated immediately, i.e. before the creditor cures his defect in title. If the debtor does this, he will be able to recover all his payments. If, instead, he waits until after the defect is cured, he may be reduced to a claim for nominal damages. His method of treating the contract as repudiated is to inform the creditor that he rejects the goods and regards the contract as repudiated.

Description

Section 9 of the Supply of Goods (Implied Terms) Act is virtually identical to s.13 of the Sale of Goods Act. Section 9 reads: 22-012

32 [1923] 2 K.B. 500.

33 [1949] 2 K.B. 576.

34 [1996] 1 All E.R. 906.

35 [1954] 2 All E.R. 694, see para.7-009, above.

> **"(1) Where under a relevant hire-purchase agreement goods are bailed or (in Scotland) hired by description, there is an implied term that the goods will correspond with the description, and if under the agreement the goods are bailed or hired by reference to a sample as well as a description, it is not sufficient that the bulk of the goods corresponds with the sample if the goods do not also correspond with the description.**
>
> **(1A) As regards England and Wales and Northern Ireland, the term implied by subsection (1) above is a condition.**
>
> **(2) Goods shall not be prevented from being bailed by description by reason only that, being exposed for sale, bailment or hire, they are selected by the person to whom they are bailed or hired."**

Where a trader supplies goods on hire purchase terms to a consumer, s.11 of the Consumer Rights Act imposes the same obligation on the trader to supply goods which correspond to the description given. As previously noted, the Consumer Rights Act, unlike the Supply of Goods (Implied Terms) Act equivalent, does not classify the term as being a condition and we must look to s.19 as discussed above to determine the remedy where the term is not complied with.[36]

Where the debtor has agreed to take the goods as a result of a previous inspection, the creditor's obligation may be greater than merely to see that the goods match the description in the written agreement. As Denning LJ said in *Karsales v Wallis*:[37]

> **"When the hirer has himself previously seen and examined the [item] and made application for hire-purchase on the basis of his inspection, there is an obligation on the lender to deliver the [item] in substantially the same condition as when it was seen. It makes no difference that the lender is a finance company which bought the [item] in the interval without seeing it."**

The facts in that case were that the debtor had inspected at the dealer's premises a roadworthy Buick car which, after he had made the usual hire-purchase agreement with the finance company, was delivered to him in such a deplorable condition that it was incapable of self-propulsion without a major overhaul. The Court of Appeal held the creditor liable for what was in fact a fundamental breach of its obligation—so radically different was the car from that which the debtor had contracted to take.

36 See Ch.13, above.

37 [1956] 2 All E.R. 866.

Quality

There are no fundamental differences between the terms implied into hire purchase contracts regarding the quality of the goods supplied. Section 10 of the Supply of Goods (Implied Terms) Act is, apart from changes of working necessary to make it apply to hire-purchase agreements, identical to s.14 of the Sale of Goods Act for non-consumer contracts and ss.9 and 10 of the Consumer Rights Act applies to both sales contracts and hire-purchase contracts. 22-013

It may be remembered that the condition that the goods be reasonably fit for a particular purpose is not implied unless that particular purpose, for which the goods are required, is made known before the contract is made. It is sufficient that the debtor makes it known either to the creditor or to the negotiator in antecedent negotiations. Thus it is sufficient that he tells the dealer for what purpose he requires the goods.[38]

Sample

The same can be said of the conditions relating to the hire purchase of goods by reference to a sample. There is no significant difference between s.11 of the Supply of Goods (Implied Terms) Act and s.15 of the Sale of Goods Act. Where the supply is by a trader to a consumer, the Consumer Rights Act similarly requires the goods to match the sample previously seen or examined.[39] Note that s.14 of the Consumer Rights Act also applies where the trader supplies goods on hire purchase terms to a consumer. This term has no corresponding equivalent in the Supply of Goods (Implied Terms) Act. 22-014

Delivery and Payment

There are no statutory implied terms relating to delivery and acceptance.[40] That leaves us to consider what terms are implied at common law. There is a lack of authority but there seems no reason to suppose that the terms are any different from those in sale of goods. 22-015

Thus, in the absence of any contrary agreement by the parties, it is the creditor's duty to hand over the goods upon demand, i.e. it is up to the debtor to collect them and it is not the creditor's obligation to arrange transport for the goods. If the goods are known to be at the premises of a third party, then those premises will be the place of delivery, i.e. it is from the dealer's premises that the debtor must collect them.

38 See SOGIT 1973 s.10(3) and CRA 2015 s.10(2).

39 CRA 2015 s.13.

40 Note that s.28 of the CRA 2015 (the trader must deliver the goods to the consumer unless otherwise agree) only applies to sales contracts under the Act, i.e. it does not apply to hire purchase agreements.

If the creditor refuses to deliver (i.e. to hand over) the goods, that is a breach of condition and the debtor can treat the contract as repudiated and reclaim any money paid and also claim damages (if he has suffered any).

22-016 Where the subject matter of the hire-purchase agreement is a second-hand motor vehicle, the creditor is under an obligation also to hand over the registration document. In *Bentworth Finance v Lubert*[41] Lord Denning MR said of the debtor:[42]

> **"She was entitled to say 'Produce the log book. Until you do, there is no contract'. There may, of course, be circumstances in which the condition may be waived by taking delivery of the car and using it."**

The debtor is under a duty to accept the goods, provided that those supplied fulfil the contract. When he fails to do so, the proper remedy for the creditor is not to claim arrears of instalments but to claim damages for the debtor's failure to take delivery: *N.C.R. v Stanley*.[43] The measure of damages is the same as that in sale of goods—*Inter-Office Telephones v Freeman*,[44] i.e. the loss arising naturally from the breach of contract. Thus the creditor will be able to recover his loss of profit on the transaction. That loss will normally include:

(a) the difference between the creditor's purchasing price and the retail cash price of the goods, and

(b) the creditor's lost finance charges, i.e. the extra profit he would have made by disposing of the goods on instalment terms instead of by a cash sale.

However, if the debtor had gone through with the hire-purchase agreement, the creditor would have received his profit over a period of time. Thus, when awarding damages to the creditor for loss of profit, the court will make a deduction to take account of the fact that the creditor is then receiving his profit immediately in one lump sum, i.e. earlier than he otherwise would have received it.

Remedies

22-017 Where the Consumer Rights Act applies, the framework of remedies laid down by the Act is the same for hire-purchase agreements and sales contracts.[45] Where the Consumer Rights

41 [1968] 1 Q.B. 680.
42 [1968] 1 Q.B. 680 at 687.
43 [1921] 3 K.B. 292.
44 [1958] 1 Q.B. 190.
45 See above, Ch.13.

Act does not apply, broadly speaking, the remedies are similar to those in sale of goods. Thus where the creditor is in breach of a warranty the only remedy normally available to the debtor is to sue for damages. Where the creditor is in breach of condition, the debtor has, in addition to a claim for damages, a right to treat the contract as repudiated and reclaim money that he has paid. As in sale of goods, the method of treating the contract as repudiated is either to refuse to take delivery of the goods or, if delivery has already been taken, to reject them. He can reject them simply by informing the creditor that he does so. Just as in sale of goods, a debtor who is not dealing as a consumer will not have a right to reject for a breach of an implied condition as to description, satisfactory quality, fitness for purpose or as to sample, if the breach is so slight that it would be unreasonable to reject the goods. For this purpose someone buying in the course of a business is not dealing as a consumer.[46]

We saw in Ch.13 that under the Sale of Goods Act the right to treat a breach of condition as having repudiated the contract is lost when the buyer "accepts" the goods.[47] When that occurs, the buyer can treat the breach of condition only as if it were a breach of warranty and it follows that his only remedy is a claim for damages. In hire purchase law there is no exact equivalent to s.11(4) of the Sale of Goods Act. However, there is a somewhat similar rule that, if after the breach of condition, the debtor affirms the contract, he will then be able to treat it only as a breach of warranty. In sale of goods, we saw that the buyer may be taken to have accepted goods if after a fairly short time he has not indicated that he is rejecting them. It may be that in hire purchase rather more time has to elapse before he will be taken to have affirmed the contract. In any case, if he returns the goods requiring them to be repaired that is quite likely to be interpreted as not being an affirmation. In *Farnworth Finance Facilities v Attryde*[48] the subject matter of the hire-purchase agreement was a new motorcycle. After taking delivery, Mr Attryde found that the motorcycle had a lot of defects and he repeatedly returned it to be put right. The repairs were never satisfactory and eventually, when the rear chain broke, he rejected the cycle. Up to this time he had had the cycle for four months and had driven it some 4,000 miles. Nevertheless the Court of Appeal held that he had not in fact affirmed the contract. His conduct indicated rather the reverse—namely that he was prepared to affirm the contract only if the defects were remedied. It followed that he was within his rights when he rejected the cycle, thereby treating the contract as repudiated. It was further held that he was entitled to recover all of the payments that he had made. No deduction was made for the use he had had of the cycle because that was offset by the inconvenience caused by the defects.

It used to be thought that in hire purchase, if the debtor affirmed the contract and the goods remained unfit for their purpose (or otherwise in breach of condition) after the affirmation, the debtor's right to reject the goods revived. This, however, is not so: *U.C.B. Leasing Ltd v Holtom*.[49] Once the debtor has affirmed the contract, he has lost for good his right to reject. If he subsequently rejects the goods or otherwise repudiates the contract, he will himself be in

46 See para.7-005, above.

47 Sale of Goods Act s.11(4).

48 [1970] 1 W.L.R. 1053.

49 [1987] C.C.L.R. 101.

breach and liable to pay damages to the creditor. This may not be as disastrous for the debtor as at first appears. It is true that if the goods are not of satisfactory quality (or the creditor is in breach of some other condition) affirmation by the debtor removes the debtor's right to reject the goods. Nevertheless the debtor will still be able to claim damages for that breach of contract. So when the debtor is sued by the creditor for damages for wrongful rejection, the debtor has a counterclaim. The amount of that counterclaim will be assessed on the basis that the debtor is entitled to recover as damages all of his payments already made and all his outstanding liabilities to the creditor. The only deduction that will be made will be in respect of such use as the debtor has had of the goods before they were rejected. In *Charterhouse Credit Co Ltd v Tolly*[50] he was awarded the total of his initial deposit, the damages awarded to the hire purchase company on its claim and the cost of new tyres he had had fitted to the car, less a small deduction for the slight use he had had of the car. The same principles were applied in *U.C.B. Leasing Ltd v Holtom*, where the sum awarded to the debtor also included an amount for inconvenience and distress. These were caused by the fact that, during the time the debtor had it, the car had persistent electrical problems, sometimes suffering a complete electrical failure, which on a couple of frightening occasions could have led the debtor to have an extremely serious accident.

Exclusion

22–018 The law relating to exemption clauses in hire-purchase contracts is the same as that relating to those in contracts of sale of goods. The common law rules are equally applicable. The Unfair Contract Terms Act 1977 and the Consumer Rights Act 2015 applies to hire-purchase agreements in precisely the same way as it does to contracts of sale of goods.

Credit Sale and Conditional Sale

22–019 A credit sale agreement is a contract of sale of goods under the Sale of Goods Act, and where a trader sells to a consumer on credit sale terms, that agreement will be a sales contract under the Consumer Rights Act. Thus the implied terms and statutory rights previously discussed in Ch.7 apply in the same way to credit sale agreements. So also do the provisions of the Unfair Contract Terms Act 1977 and the Consumer Rights Act in respect of unfair terms. The same is true of conditional sale agreements.

50 [1963] 2 Q.B. 683.

One thing explained in relation to hire purchase was that, in connection with the statutory term as to fitness for purpose, it is sufficient that the debtor has told the dealer (i.e. the negotiator in antecedent negotiations) the particular purpose for which the goods were required. The same is true in relation to contracts of sale of goods.

General Reading

C. Bisping, "The case against s.75 of the Consumer Credit Act 1974 in Credit Card Transactions" [2011] J.B.L. 457.

A. Campbell, "Credit cards and section 75: time for a change in the law?" [1996] J.I.B.L. 527.

D.M. Collins, "Connected lender liability: clarification from the Supreme Court" [2014] J.I.B.L.R. 522.

C.V.M. Hare, "Your Flexible Friend?" (2005) 64 C.L.J. 287.

I. Griffiths and M. Griffiths, "Joint Liability under the Consumer Credit Act 1974" [1995] I.B.F.L. 103.

23

Enforcement by the Creditor or Owner

Introduction

This chapter outlines the broad principles relating to the enforceability of the credit agreement. In particular, it will focus upon the recent developments whereby the old extortionate credit provisions have been replaced by the new law of unfair credit relationships and it will explain default notices and time orders. 23-001

Broad Principles of Enforcement

This is the most important part of the chapter and deals with certain provisions of the Act which apply to all regulated agreements. Running through them all is Parliament's intention to protect the debtor from harsh terms in the agreement and generally to ensure that he receives fair treatment. 23-002

County Court

Any court action by the creditor or owner to enforce the agreement or any security for it must be brought in the county court.[1] Not only must the debtor or hirer be made a party to the proceedings but so also must any surety. While the action is still undecided the court can, on 23-003

1 s.141.

application by the creditor, make any order it thinks just for protecting any property of the creditor or owner, or any property which is subject to any security, from damage or depreciation.

Payment Ahead of Time

23–004 The debtor under a regulated consumer credit agreement is entitled to discharge his debt ahead of time whenever he wishes by giving notice to the creditor and making full payment of all his payments due under the agreement.[2] Early payment by the debtor of all sums payable under the agreement will mean that if the agreement is a hire-purchase or conditional sale agreement, the debtor will become the owner of the goods at an earlier date than he otherwise would.

The Consumer Credit (Early Settlement) Regulations 2004[3] provide for a rebate to a debtor who pays off his debt ahead of time. The rebate is calculated according to the Regulations or according to the terms of the agreement, whichever give the higher rebate.[4] The amount required to discharge the debt under s.94 is reduced by the amount of the rebate.

The debtor under a regulated consumer credit agreement is also entitled to discharge part of his debt ahead of time whenever he wishes by giving written notice to the creditor and making partial payment. This right was introduced by the Consumer Credit (EU Directive) Regulations 2010[5] in order to comply with the Consumer Credit Directive. Under s.94(4)(c) a partial payment must be made either within 28 days from the day following that on which the creditor received the notice or on or before any later date specified in the notice itself.[6]

Where a debtor makes a full or partial repayment the creditor is entitled to compensation under the rules laid down by s.95A. There are, however, a number of restrictions on the ability of a creditor to claim compensation. First, the right only exists where the agreement is not secured on land and provides for the rate of interest on the credit to be fixed for a period of time and the debtor makes full or partial repayment during that period. Secondly, the right does not exist unless the repayment exceeds £8,000 or, if multiple partial repayments are made, the sum of those repayments exceeds £8,000 in a 12-month period. Thirdly, there is no right to compensation for early repayment of an overdraft. Fourthly, there is no right to compensation where the early repayment is made from the proceeds of a payment protection

2 s.94. The notice need not be in writing unless it is a regulated consumer credit agreement secured on land, s.94(6)(a).

3 SI 2004/1483. The Regulations came into force on 31 May 2005 and revoked the Consumer Credit (Rebate on Early Settlement) Regulations 1983 (SI 1983/1562).

4 See, inter alia, regs 3 and 4.

5 SI 2010/1010.

6 See also, s.97A which imposes a duty on the creditor to provide information when requested to do so by the debtor following a partial repayment. This information includes matter such as whether the debtor is entitled to any rebate and the amount of indebtedness remaining following a partial repayment.

insurance policy. Where the creditor is able to claim compensation, the amount must be fair and objectively justifiable.[7]

Payment Behind Time

It is not uncommon for a debtor to be late in paying off his debt or some instalments of it. In these circumstances the creditor does not receive his money as soon as he ought to. It is quite possible for the agreement to state that in that event the creditor shall be entitled to an additional payment as interest for the period of the delay. However, that interest must not be at a rate higher than that which the debtor was already paying under the agreement. If the agreement stipulates for a higher rate to be payable on default, the creditor will be able to recover only interest calculated at the rate payable under the contract as a whole.[8] 23-005

Unfair Agreements

The Consumer Credit Act 2006 introduced a new concept of unfair relationships (between debtor and creditor). This was designed to remedy some of the difficulties evident with the previous provisions (ss.137–140) which permitted the court to "re-open" a credit agreement where that agreement was extortionate.[9] In particular the requirement that the agreement must be grossly exorbitant, under the old s.138(1), placed a high threshold which had to be reached before the court could intervene. This threshold led to reluctance on the part of the courts to intervene with any frequency.[10] This was accepted by the government in the White Paper, "Fair Clear and Competitive: The Consumer Credit Market in the 21st Century"[11] where it was noted that only 30 extortionate credit cases had reached the courts![12] Accordingly, ss.137–140 were replaced by the new ss.140A–140D which allow the court to re-open agreements where there is an unfair credit relationship. 23-006

7 s.95A(3).

8 s.93.

9 The new provisions came into effect, for the most part, on 6 April 2007. For a discussion of the previous law, see the 6th edn of this book.

10 See, for example, the comments of Dyson LJ in *Broadwick Financial Services Ltd v Spencer* [2002] 1 All E.R. (Comm) 446. See also, *Paragon Finance Plc (formerly National Home Loans Corp) v Pender* [2005] 1 W.L.R. 3412.

11 Cmnd. 6040 (2003).

12 Furthermore, few of those cases were actually proven.

Under s.140A the court may make an order (under s.140B) where it determines that the relationship between debtor and creditor arising out of the agreement[13] is unfair due to one or more of the following:[14]

(i) Any of the terms of the agreement or of any related agreement.[15]

Thus, for example, the court will consider whether the term is commonplace and supported by sound commercial reasons. The relative strength of the debtor's bargaining position will also be relevant as will the question of whether terms have been individually negotiated, and if not, whether they have been presented on a "take it or leave it" basis.[16]

(ii) The way in which the creditor has exercised or enforced any of his rights under the agreement or any related agreement.[17]

Thus any demand from the creditor that is prompted by an "improper motive" or is the consequence of an "arbitrary decision" is indicative of an unfair relationship.[18] In *Re London Scottish Finance (In Administration)*[19] the creditor sent letters to debtors in arrears demanding repayment and warning that they might lose their homes if they did not comply. This was untrue since the loan agreements did not properly document the amount of credit provided and were therefore irredeemably unenforceable under the now repealed s.127(3). This conduct was held to give rise to an unfair relationship where the threat led to debtors making repayments.[20]

(iii) Any other thing done (or not done) by, or on behalf of, the creditor (either before or after the making of the agreement or any related agreement).[21]

---

13 Thus a loan agreement between a bank and a company will not fall under the ambit of s.140A since the debtor is not an individual: *Bank of Ireland (UK) Plc v McLaughlin* [2016] NICA 33.

14 For a helpful summary of various factors likely to be of relevance, see the comments of Hamblen J in *Deutsche Bank (Suisse) SA v Khan* [2013] EWHC 482 at [346]. See also, *Commercial First Business Ltd v Pickup* [2017] C.T.L.C. 1.

15 s.140A(1)(a). For an example of an unfair relationship arising through a related agreement, see *Link Financial Ltd v Wilson* [2014] EWHC 252.

16 See, for example, *Rahman v HSBC Bank Plc* [2012] EWHC 11.

17 s.140A(1)(b).

18 See, for example, *Paragon Mortgages Ltd v McEwan-Peters* [2011] EWHC 2491.

19 [2013] EWHC 4047.

20 See also, for example, *Pilgrim Rock Ltd v Iwaniuk* [2019] EWHC 203 (Ch) where the creditor's failure to enforce any rights over a credit agreement for four years was found to be unfair.

21 s.140A(1)(c).

The scope of s.140A, though broad, is not without limit. The Supreme Court has recently considered the meaning of the words "on behalf of" in the context of s.140A in *Plevin v Paragon Personal Finance Ltd*.[22] It was held that the phrase should be given its ordinary meaning and therefore required an agency relationship. Thus, under s.140A, unfairness can only derive from things done (or not done) by someone for whom the creditor had legal responsibility. This is a much narrower interpretation than that favoured by the Court of Appeal in *Plevin* whereby it was said that unfairness could derive from the conduct of all persons that play a role in bringing about the agreement.[23] Further, the court cannot consider the potential unfairness of the relationship created by a related agreement, such as a guarantee, in isolation. The court can consider the guarantee only in so far as it speaks to the fairness of the credit relationship: *Clydesdale Bank Plc v Gough*.[24]

Section 140A(2) requires the court to take into account "all matters it thinks relevant". Furthermore, the court must, where appropriate, consider acts done (or not done) by, or on behalf of, an associate (or former associate) of the creditor.[25] In *Pilgrim Rock Ltd v Iwaniuk*[26] it was argued that, following Plevin, it was only the acts of an agent or associate of the creditor that are relevant under s.140A, i.e. that the actions of someone who was neither an agent nor an associate of the creditor were not relevant under s.140A(2). The court had little difficulty in rejecting this argument since such limit to the scope of s.140A(2) would result in a court being "forced to take a credit agreement at face value . . . unable to investigate the evolution and true nature of the creditor-debtor relationship".

The Court of Appeal has recently settled a number of important points regarding the application of s.140A in *Smith and another v Royal Bank of Scotland plc*.[27] First, the assessment of fairness under s.140A may extend to any matters it considers relevant regardless of when in time they took place. Thus, in Smith, the fact that a relevant related agreement (one for PPI in connection to a credit card facility) has come to an end does not prevent the court from including that agreement in its assessment of fairness at a later point in time under s.140A. Second, the fact that a credit relationship was at one point in time unfair did not mean that the unfairness "necessarily has to persist for all time as long as the credit agreement persists, as a matter of law and irrespective of the facts". Accordingly, the fact that a relationship was unfair by virtue of undisclosed PPI payments does not mean that the relationship necessarily remains unfair after the related agreement has ended. What matters is ascertaining the relevant point in time when the assessment of fairness is to be made. This was crucial in Smith since if the unfairness persisted whilst the underlying credit agreement existed, i.e. after the conclusion of the PPI agreement, then the claim against the creditor was not time barred under

22 [2014] UKSC 61.

23 See also, *Scotland v British Credit Trust Ltd* [2014] EWCA Civ 790 where it was held that the misrepresentations of a supplier who was an agent of the creditor by virtue of s.56(2) were relevant to unfairness under s.140A as being things done on behalf of the creditor.

24 [2017] EWHC 2230 (Ch).

25 s.140A(3).

26 [2019] EWHC 203 (Ch).

27 [2021] EWCA Civ 1832.

the Limitation Act 1980. If, on the other hand, the conclusion of the PPI agreement served to end the unfairness in the ongoing credit relationship, then the claim would be time barred. The Court of Appeal held that the limitation period ran from the last date at which the relationship was unfair. On the facts of Smith, this was at the conclusion of the PPI contract since that was the sole source of the unfairness and no economic effect from the PPI contract lingered after its conclusion.[28]

It is important to note that where the debtor alleges that there is an unfair relationship, it is for the creditor to prove that the relationship was not unfair, thus reversing the normal burden of proof.[29]

23–007 Where the court is satisfied that an unfair relationship has arisen under s.140A, s.140B(1) allows the court to make an order for one, or more, of the following:[30]

(a) require the creditor or any associate or former associate of his to repay (in whole or in part) any sum paid by the debtor or by a surety by virtue of the agreement or any related agreement (whether paid to the creditor, the associate or the former associate or to any other person);

(b) require the creditor or any associate or former associate of his to do or not to do (or to cease doing) anything specified in the order in connection with the agreement or any related agreement;

(c) reduce or discharge any sum payable by the debtor or by a surety by virtue of the agreement or any related agreement;

(d) direct the return to a surety of any property provided by him for the purposes of a security;

(e) otherwise set aside (in whole or in part) any duty imposed on the debtor or on a surety by virtue of the agreement or any related agreement;

(f) alter the terms of the agreement or of any related agreement; or

(g) direct accounts to be taken, or (in Scotland) an accounting to be made, between any persons.

28 On the application of the Limitation Act 1980, see also *Canada Square Operations Ltd v Potter* [2021] EWCA Civ 339.

29 s.140A(9). Noted in *Bevin v Datum Finance Ltd* [2011] EWHC 3542 (Ch), [2012] C.C.L.R. 3. For an example where the creditor was able to discharge this burden, see *Consolidated Finance Ltd v Hunter* [2010] B.P.I.R. 1322.

30 Note that the aim of the relief is to "approximate, as closely as possible, to the overall position which would have applied had the matters giving rise to the perceived unfairness not taken place" *Kerrigan v Elevate Credit International Ltd* [2020] EWHC 2169 (Comm) at [214] per HHJ Worster.

It is interesting to note that nowhere in the amended Consumer Credit Act 1974 is the term "unfair" defined. It might have been expected that the approach of, for example, the Unfair Commercial Practices Directive could have been adopted in drafting a list of factors for the court to consider when assessing whether there was an unfair relationship between the parties. No doubt similar considerations will be adopted by the courts but it seems clear that this absence is a response to the strict interpretation of "extortionate" and "grossly exorbitant" under the old provisions. The absence of any such list means that the courts now have considerable flexibility in assessing the relationship between debtor and creditor and will, it may be expected, be more proactive in their approach to unfair relationships.

Patel v Patel[31] involved a series of oral loan agreements made between two friends in the 1980s. In 1992 all of the ongoing agreements were consolidated into one new agreement totaling around £200,000 under which interest would accrue at a rate of 20 per cent per annum compounded monthly. The debt was repayable on demand by the creditor. The debtor made only partial repayments totaling £30,500 after 1992 and by the time the creditor commenced legal action the amount outstanding was around £4.5 million due to the relatively high rate of compound interest.

The court held that following the consolidation in 1992 the relationship became progressively unfair. This was so for a number of reasons. First, due to the extent of the debtor's indebtedness in 1992 "fairness to the defendant would have involved attempting to formulate a realistic schedule of payments which would have enabled him to reduce and ultimately to pay off the debt, with a reasonable rate of interest charged in the meantime".[32] Secondly, the claimant had adduced no evidence to establish that an interest rate of 20 per cent per annum, compounded monthly, was a reasonable commercial rate to charge a borrower in the defendant's position in 1992.[33] This rate was therefore "exorbitant" since it was 13 per cent above the base rate. Indeed, the fall in the base rate in the years following 1992 made this rate seem "more and more exorbitant". The court was also influenced by the conduct of the creditor in the years following the consolidation agreement, in particular, his failure to keep proper records of the amount outstanding or to send any reminders to the debtor. These factors, when taken in combination were such that the agreement was unfair. Accordingly the court made an order under s.140B and reduced the amount -outstanding to £207,465, that being the amount outstanding at the time of the 1992 agreement. 23-008

31 [2009] EWHC 3264 (QB), [2010] C.C.L.R. 6.

32 [2009] EWHC 3264 (QB) at [73].

33 Compare this with the reasoning in *Khodari v Tamimi* [2009] EWCA Civ. 1109, [2010] C.C.L.R. 3, where the court held that a fee of 10% was "fairly normal" for the circumstances of that case. Similarly, in *Shaw v Nine Regions Ltd* [2009] EWHC 3514, an agreement with an interest rate of 119% per annum did not give rise to an unfair relationship. Thus, whilst interest rates and other charges will often be relevant factors under s.140A, they are not necessarily conclusive. Further, interest rates and fees will be assessed as against the market rate for that type of lending.

In *Harrison v Black Horse Ltd*[34] the Court of Appeal considered the implications of non-disclosure of payment protection insurance on s.140A. Tomlinson LJ stated that although the commission payments received by financial institutions in respect of payment protection insurance was "on any view quite startling" and could be viewed as "unacceptable conduct" the mere size of the undisclosed commission did not equate to an unfair relationship.[35] The Court was also persuaded by the fact that there was no legal duty under the relevant regulatory framework on the creditor to disclose the existence of a commission payment. Accordingly, the Court suggested that it would be an anomalous result were the creditor required to disclose a commission payment in order to avoid s.140A whilst being under no legal duty to disclose it under the regulatory framework. This decision has, however, been overruled by the Supreme Court in *Plevin v Paragon Personal Finance Ltd*.[36] Lord Sumption stated that the "view which a court takes of the fairness or unfairness of a debtor-creditor relationship may legitimately be influenced by the standard of commercial conduct reasonably to be expected of the creditor" and that the relevant regulatory framework was evidence of that standard. It was not, however, determinative of whether there was an unfair relationship since compliance with the regulatory rules and s.140A were separate matters. Accordingly:[37]

> **"An altogether wider range of considerations may be relevant to the fairness of the relationship, most of which would not be relevant to the application of the rules. They include the characteristics of the borrower, her sophistication or vulnerability, the facts which she could reasonably be expected to know or assume, the range of choices available to her, and the degree to which the creditor was or should have been aware of these matters."**

On the facts, the non-disclosure of commission payments for PPI (which constituted 71.8 per cent of the PPI premium paid) gave rise to an unfair relationship. Had the creditor disclosed the size of the commission paid, there would have been no unfair relationship since the debtor would have been able to make a properly informed decision about whether to take out PPI in the first place.

23-009 It is important to note that decisions under s.140A will always be heavily fact-dependent—factors which suggest an unfair relationship between one debtor and a creditor may be not be sufficient to establish unfairness in another relationship. This is exemplified by the decision

34 [2011] EWCA Civ. 1128, [2012] C.C.L.R. 2. The failure to disclose payment protection insurance has given rise to a number of County Court judgments on the question of unfair relationships under s.140A, see *Yates v Nemo Personal Finance* (2010) (unreported) and *MBNA Europe Bank Ltd v Thorius* [2010] E.C.C. 8.

35 In *Harrison* the commission was 87% of the total premium.

36 [2014] UKSC 61.

37 [2014] UKSC 61 at [17].

in *Rahman v HSBC Bank plc*[38] where the claimant unsuccessfully argued that there was an unfair relationship. The case involved large scale lending of a commercial nature and, unlike in the majority of cases, the debtor and creditor were of essentially equal bargaining power. In this context the court had little difficulty in finding that neither a cross default clause (which allowed the debtor to demand repayment on all sums outstanding on various loan agreements if the debtor defaulted on one of the agreements) nor a provision for the repayment of overdraft facilities on demand created an unfair relationship.

It remains to be seen how far the courts will push their powers under s.140A but it is, in any event, clear that the new law is considerably more generous to debtors than under the former "extortionate credit bargain" provisions as to both the threshold to be satisfied and the breadth of the court's powers under s.140B(1) once the threshold is satisfied.

Alternative Legislative Provisions

Where a debtor is unable to persuade a court to re-open an agreement under the unfair relationship provisions, he may nevertheless be able to challenge the agreement, or part of it, under other provisions. First, where the court makes any order under the Act, it has a supplementary power under s.136 to amend the agreement "in consequence of a term of the order". This can, for example, involve reducing the rate of interest when a time order is granted.[39] Secondly, a contract term can be challenged as being an unfair term under the Consumer Rights Act 2015 as previously noted.[40] 23-010

Default Notice

Section 87 operates where the debtor is in breach of the agreement. Its effect is to prevent the creditor from pursuing certain remedies unless and until a default notice has first been served upon the debtor giving him a chance to put right his default. In *Doyle v PRA Group (UK) Ltd*[41] the Court of Appeal held that s.87 had the effect of qualifying the substantive legal rights of the creditor. In the absence of a default notice the debtor would have a complete defence to the creditor's action. The remedies which the creditor is thereby prevented from pursuing are, broadly, those which would involve the debtor in more than just being compelled to honour the agreement and put right his default, i.e. those remedies of the creditor which operate as a sort of threat to induce the debtor to honour the agreement. 23-011

38 [2012] EWHC 11 (Ch), [2012] C.C.L.R. 4.

39 s.136 is discussed at para.23-018, below.

40 See Ch.10.

41 [2019] EWCA Civ 12.

Thus by s.87(1) a notice of default must be served before the creditor or owner is entitled:

> **"(a) to terminate the agreement, or**
> **(b) to demand earlier payment of any sum, or**
> **(c) to recover possession of any goods or land, or**
> **(d) to treat any right conferred on the debtor or hirer by the agreement as terminated, restricted or deferred, or**
> **(e) to enforce any security."**

By way of exception to s.87(1) no default notice need be served before the creditor can become entitled to treat the debtor's right to draw upon any credit as restricted or deferred. Thus, for example, a credit card company which discovers that a card holder has exceeded his credit limit can take immediate steps to prevent him using the card to obtain still further credit. No default notice is required where the creditor seeks a remedy which would do no more than compel the debtor to honour the agreement in the normal way. Thus where the debtor is in arrears, no default notice is required before the creditor can sue for the arrears.

When the default notice is required, it must make certain things clear to the debtor:[42]

(i) The nature of the alleged breach.

(ii) What action is required to remedy it or, if it is not remediable, how much (if anything) is required to be paid in compensation.

(iii) The exact date by which the breach must be remedied or the compensation paid.

(iv) The consequences if the debtor does not comply with the notice.

(v) A copy of the default information sheet under s.86A

23-012 The time allowed must be at least 14 days[43] from the date the notice is served upon the debtor. If the default notice overstates the amount owing, it will be invalid, unless (possibly) the error was so small as to be insignificant: *Woodchester Lease Management Services Ltd v Swain.*[44] The default notice must also be in the form prescribed by the Consumer Credit (Enforcement, Default and Termination Notices) Regulations 1983.[45] If the debtor complies

42 s.88.

43 Increased from seven days by the CCA 2006 s.14(1).

44 [1999] C.C.L.R. 8.

45 SI 1983/1561 (as amended). See, for example, the Consumer Credit (Information Requirements and Duration of Licences and Charges) Regulations (SI 2007/1167) with effect from 1 October 2008 and in particular, the Consumer Credit (Enforcement, Default and Termination Notices) (Coronavirus) (Amendment) Regulations

with the notice within the specified time by rectifying the breach or paying the stipulated compensation, the breach must be treated as if it had never occurred.[46]

If at the end of the specified time the breach has not been remedied or the compensation has not been paid, then the creditor is free to pursue any of the remedies in s.87(1), provided that under the terms of the agreement he is entitled to do so. If the default notice included no requirement for the breach to be remedied or for any compensation to be paid, then after 14 days the creditor is free to pursue any of the remedies in s.87(1), again, provided that he is entitled to do so under the terms of the agreement. Two points of explanation are required. First, s.87 does not confer any remedies or rights upon the creditor. It simply restrains him from pursuing certain remedies. Thus, when the restraint is lifted, he can pursue any given remedy only if, quite apart from s.87 (i.e. under the terms of the agreement), he is entitled to do so. Secondly, the creditor cannot avoid giving the debtor a chance to put things right by the simple expedient of failing to include in the default notice any requirement for the breach to be remedied or compensation paid. If the breach can be remedied then a requirement for that must be included. If it cannot, and compensation is required, then a requirement for payment of compensation must be included.

Consider an example. Flotsam buys a boat under a credit sale agreement in which there is a condition that Flotsam will not sell the boat until he has paid all the instalments. The agreement states that if Flotsam breaks the agreement by selling the boat, all the remaining instalments shall fall due immediately. Flotsam does sell the boat. Now, the breach cannot be put right, since the boat now belongs to someone else and the creditor will not require compensation. In this situation the creditor can serve a default notice without any requirement for the breach to be remedied or for any compensation. After 14 days he can commence an action against Flotsam for the whole of the remaining instalments.[47]

The default notice requirement is exactly the same where a hirer is in breach of a regulated consumer hire agreement as it is where the debtor is in breach of a regulated consumer credit agreement.

Death of the Debtor

Consumer credit agreements quite often include a clause which provides for what is to be the position if the debtor dies. The agreement may, for example, provide that on the death of the debtor, all remaining instalments shall immediately become payable in one lump sum. Hire-purchase agreements sometimes provide that the hiring and the agreement shall terminate upon the debtor's death. 23-013

2020 (SI 2020/1248). The 2020 Regulations came into force on 2 December 2020 and are intended to make the prescribed wording less intimidating (e.g. using bold or underlined text rather than capital letters) and signpost sources of free debt advice.

46 s.89.

47 Less any rebate for early payment under s.95, see para.23-004, above.

Section 86 applies to any regulated agreement where the debtor dies. Its effect depends upon whether the agreement was "fully secured" or not. Where the regulated agreement is fully secured and the debtor or hirer dies, then by s.86(1) the creditor or owner cannot do any of the acts specified in paras (a)–(e) of s.87(1).[48] There is a complete embargo. In short, this means that, in spite of anything written in the agreement, the death of the debtor or hirer will not affect the operation of the agreement. The debtor's or hirer's personal representatives will simply take over his rights and duties under the agreement.

Where the agreement is not fully secured, s.86 does not place an absolute embargo upon the operation of clauses in the agreement which would, upon the death of the debtor or hirer either (for example) terminate the agreement or cause the remaining payments to fall due immediately. Nevertheless it does severely restrict the operation of such clauses. The creditor or owner can do one of the acts specified in paras (a)–(e) of s.87(1) only if two requirements are both fulfilled:

(i) the creditor or owner applies to the court, and

(ii) the creditor or owner proves to the court that he has been unable to satisfy himself that the present and future obligations of the debtor or hirer under the agreement are likely to be carried out.

23-014 In practice this will involve showing that none of the personal representatives or relations of the debtor or hirer are willing to take over the agreement.

There are three qualifications to s.86. First, the credit agreement may provide that on the death of the debtor or hirer, the outstanding debt (or part of it) shall be paid out of the proceeds of a policy of life assurance taken out on the debtor's or hirer's life for that purpose. Such a provision in the agreement is enforceable and not affected by s.86. Secondly, s.86 does not prevent the creditor from treating the right to draw on any credit as terminated by the debtor's death. Thus, for example, the debtor's personal representatives would not be able to use his credit card or to draw money under his overdraft agreement. Section 86 is concerned only with debts which the debtor had before he died. Thirdly, s.86 does not apply in relation to the termination of an agreement which is of an unspecified duration or where the specified period of duration has expired.

Let us examine the effect of s.86 in some particular examples:

(i) The debtor dies owing money under an ordinary unguaranteed credit sale agreement. Unguaranteed is used here to mean that the debtor had no guarantor. In this case the agreement will be unsecured. The debtor's personal representatives will be entitled to continue the agreement (i.e. to pay the instalments as and when due from the debtor under the agreement). However, if they refuse to do so and the creditor is unable to

48 See para.23-011, above.

make satisfactory arrangements with anyone else (e.g. the debtor's relatives) for the carrying out of the agreement, then the creditor could ask the court to enforce a term of the credit sale agreement (if it contained such a term) which stipulates that the whole outstanding balance becomes due on the death of the debtor.

(ii) The debtor died owing money borrowed on an unsecured bank loan. If the loan was for a specified period then the result would be exactly the same as with the credit sale agreement. If the loan was not for a specified period and included a term that the creditor (the bank) could terminate it and demand immediate repayment at any time, then there would be no restriction upon the bank doing just that.

(iii) The debtor died owing money under this credit card agreement, which is of unspecified duration and includes a term that on the death of the debtor the agreement shall terminate and the outstanding debt become repayable immediately. Because the agreement is of unspecified duration, s.86 will not apply and the effect of the debtor's death will be as stated in the agreement.

(iv) The debtor died owing money under an unexpired regulated agreement of specified duration (e.g. a credit sale agreement) under which the liability of the debtor and of his personal representatives was fully guaranteed by someone who acted as guarantor at the express or implied request of the debtor. Now, such a guarantee is within the definition of "security"[49] and therefore such an agreement would be "fully secured". That being so, the creditor (even if satisfactory arrangements could not be made for the carrying out of the debtor's obligations) could not do any act within paras (a)–(e) of s.87(1). Thus the creditor could not regard the agreement as terminated by the debtor's death, nor could he sue for any instalment earlier than it would have been due from the debtor had he lived.

(v) The hirer under an unguaranteed consumer hire agreement of specified duration dies while the agreement is still running. Under such agreements there is usually no security given for the payments due under the agreement. Nevertheless the owner will be able to regard the agreement as terminated and recover the goods only if he applies to the court and can show that he was unable to satisfy himself that the hirer's obligations under the agreement would be carried out.

(vi) The debtor dies leaving outstanding instalments to be paid under an unguaranteed hire-purchase agreement. A hire-purchase agreement will in practice always be of a specified duration. The debtor's personal representatives will have the right to continue the agreement just as if he had not died. The problem arises if such satisfactory

49 s.189.

arrangements cannot be made for the carrying out of the debtor's obligations. Is the agreement "fully secured"? If it is, the position is the same as in the case of a credit sale agreement with a guarantor of the liability of the debtor and of his personal representatives. If it is not "fully secured", then the creditor (in the absence of satisfactory arrangements) could ask the court to enforce any provisions in the agreement allowing the creditor to terminate it, to take possession of the goods, etc.

Nowhere does the Act define "fully secured" which presumably describes an agreement where the creditor or owner has taken security which, if realised at the time of the debtor's or hirer's death, would cover the whole of the outstanding payments under the agreement. Section 189 defines "security" as:

> **". . . a demanding earlier payment debenture, indemnity, guarantee, bill note or other right provided by the debtor or hirer, or at his request (express or implied) to secure the carrying out of the obligations of the debtor or hirer under the agreement."**

Has the creditor under a hire-purchase agreement got any "security"? In any ordinary sense of the word he has, because he has the right to the return of his goods (subject to the provisions of the Consumer Credit Act) if the debtor defaults in circumstances entitling the creditor to terminate the agreement.[50] However, is this right "provided by the debtor"? The answer would appear to be that the agreement is "fully secured" if in the agreement itself the debtor gives the creditor the right to take possession of the goods upon termination of the agreement. If, however, the agreement does not give the creditor such a right then there is no "security" and it follows that the agreement cannot be "fully secured". This is so even though the creditor may still be entitled to recovery of the goods on termination of the agreement, because in this case the right to recovery of the goods is not "provided by the debtor" but derives from the basic property rights which belong to the owner of goods (the creditor under the hire-purchase agreement). Since most hire-purchase agreements do not today expressly provide for what is to happen to the goods upon termination of the agreement, it follows that in relation to the vast majority of hire-purchase agreements there is no "security" and that they are therefore not "fully secured".

Non-default Notice

23–015 In the event of the debtor or hirer being in a breach of a regulated agreement, there is a list of things (in s.87(1)) which the creditor or owner by reason of the breach become entitled to do without first serving a default notice. Sections 76 and 98 contain similar provisions which

50 See paras 24-012 and 24-013, below.

apply where the creditor or owner is entitled to do one of those things otherwise than by reason of a breach of the agreement by the debtor or hirer. For example, an agreement may provide that the creditor can terminate it at any time or that he can terminate it if the debtor is convicted of an offence of dishonesty, is sent to prison or changes his address, or becomes unemployed, etc.

Section 98 prevents the creditor or owner terminating a regulated agreement without first serving on the debtor or hirer a notice of his intention to do so. Section 76 requires the creditor or owner to serve a similar notice before enforcing a term of regulated agreement by:

> **"(a) demanding earlier payment of any sum, or**
> **(b) recovering possession of any goods or land, or**
> **(c) treating any right conferred on the debtor or hirer by the agreement as terminated restricted or deferred."**

The notice must give the debtor or hirer at least seven days' warning of the creditor's or owner's intention and must be in the form prescribed by the Consumer Credit (Enforcement, Default and Termination Notices) Regulations 1983. Like a default notice, the notice in this case does not prevent the creditor from treating the right to draw on any credit as restricted or deferred.

Unlike s.87 (default notice), ss.76 and 98 apply only to agreements which have a specified period of duration. Thus they apply to hire purchase, conditional sale and credit sale agreements. They do not, however, apply to open-ended consumer credit agreements which are instead subject to s.98A with the effect that the creditor must give notice. Note, however, that certain agreements are excluded from s.98A, including bank overdrafts. If such an agreement gives the bank the right at any time to demand immediate repayment of the whole debt then no notice need be served before the bank can do just that. 23-016

The Act does not give any name to the notice which ss.98 and 76 require to be served. In this book it is termed a non-default notice to distinguish it from a default notice. It will be appreciated that these two types of notice are very close cousins. In the case of an agreement of specified duration, before the creditor or owner can take certain kinds of action (e.g. terminating the agreement) he will have to serve one of these types of notice. Which one he must serve will depend upon whether the creditor's right to take that action derives from the debtor's breach of the agreement (default notice) or some other event (non-default notice). Whichever one it is, service of the notice will entitle the debtor to apply for a time order. With a default notice the debtor normally has an opportunity to put right his default, whereas plainly there is no question of that with a non-default notice.

Time Order

The debtor or hirer can ask the court for a time order in any court action brought by the creditor 23-017
or owner to enforce a regulated agreement. Alternatively when the debtor or hirer has been served either with a default notice (under ss.87 and 88) or with a non-default notice (under

ss.76 or 98), then he can apply for a time order without waiting for the creditor or owner to sue him.[51]

The power given by s.129 to the court to make a time order is twofold. It can allow time (a specified period) for the debtor or hirer to remedy any breach of the agreement other than non-payment. It can also give time for the payment of any sums owed by the debtor or hirer under the agreement. Where the court does make a time order, it can make the payment(s) "payable at such times, as the court having regard to the means of the debtor or hirer and any surety, considers reasonable." The court's power is confined to sums which at the time the order is made have already fallen due. It does not extend to future instalments. Thus the debtor under a credit sale agreement cannot ask the court to alter the amount or dates of future instalments but can ask it to give him time to pay instalments which have already fallen due. There are three exceptions to the rule that the power to make a time order does not extend to future instalments. First, if there has come into operation a term (an accelerated payments clause) of the agreement which stipulates that all remaining instalments are due immediately, the debtor can ask the court to give him time to pay those because they have (owing to that term of the agreement) fallen due already. The second exception arises where a mortgage of land has been granted as security for a loan and, after the debtor's default, the creditor (no doubt after having served a default notice) commences repossession proceedings. It has been held that commencing repossession proceedings amounts to a "calling-in" of the loan, i.e. causes the creditor to be entitled to the whole of the outstanding balance: *Southern District Finance plc v Barnes*.[52] Thus it has the same effect as the operation of an accelerated payments clause and thus the court is empowered to make a time order in respect of the whole debt including future instalments. The third exception arises where the agreement in question is a hire-purchase or conditional sale agreement. In that case the court has special powers when asked for a time order.[53] In particular it can, even in the absence of an accelerated payments clause, make a time order in respect of future instalments which have not yet fallen due and thus is able (if it considers it just and reasonable to do so) to rewrite the whole instalment pattern.

The court has power to vary or revoke any time order it makes. So, for example, the debtor could come back to the court later and ask that he be given a further extension of time in which to make the payments subject to the time order. Alternatively the creditor could ask that the time order be revoked (e.g. if the debtor was not in fact making payments as required under the time order). In that case the creditor might ask for immediate judgment in his favour for the total amount then due or for any other remedy (e.g. enforcement of any security).

---

51 s.16 of the CCA 2006 allows the debtor or hirer to make an application under the new s.129(1)(ba) and s.129A where he has been given a notice under s.86B (notice of sums in arrears under fixed-sum credit agreements) or s.86C (notice of sums in arrears under running-account credit agreements) and 14 days have passed.

52 [1995] C.C.L.R. 62. See H. Johnson, "Time Orders" [1995] I.B.F.L. 6; A. Dunn, "'Footprints on the sands of time': sections 129 and 136 Consumer Credit Act 1974" [1996] *Conveyancer and Property Lawyer* 209.

53 s.130(2).

Court's Supplementary Powers

Suspended and conditional court orders

Section 135 gives the court certain extra powers in making any order in relation to a regulated agreement. It can make any order (or any term of the order) conditional upon the doing of specified acts. It can also suspend the operation of any order or term of an order. 23–018

The court's powers under s.135 can be particularly useful where the creditor or owner brings an action to recover possession of goods to which the agreement relates (e.g. in the case of a hire purchase, conditional sale or consumer hire agreement). He will probably be bringing the action because the debtor or hirer is in arrears. In that case the court could make a time order (giving the debtor or hirer time to make up his arrears) and could also order the debtor to return the goods. The court could then suspend the operation of the return order so that it will not take effect unless the debtor or hirer fails to comply with the time order. Alternatively it could suspend the order indefinitely, requiring the creditor to return to the court again before being able to enforce it.

This is only an example and the court's power to impose conditions or to suspend the operation of an order apply in relation to any order relating to a regulated agreement.

Amendment of agreement

Section 136 provides: "The court may in an order made by it under this Act include such provision as it considers just for amending any agreement or security in consequence of a term of the order." Can the court vary the rate of interest when granting a time order? The court clearly has power to vary the rate of interest where it finds that an agreement gives rise to an unfair debtor/creditor relationship. Apart from that, however, the court when granting a time order can vary the interest rate (under s.136) only where that variation in the interest rate is "in consequence of a term of the time order": *Southern and District Finance plc v Barnes*.[54] This could come about as follows. It could very well be, for example, that the effect of making a time order is to delay the receipt of payments by the creditor, e.g. by the court in the time order providing for a greater number of smaller payments over an extended repayment period. If no reduction were made in the contractual rate of interest, that rate would continue to apply to the monthly deficiency arising between the contractual monthly instalment and the monthly instalment directed by the court. This would result in the creditor on the one hand receiving overall a higher total amount of interest whilst on the other receiving a slower rate of repayment. In the case of an agreement with a high, albeit not extortionate, rate of interest, it would then be appropriate for the court to reduce the rate of interest "in consequence of" the time order. The fact is that if the court is able to reduce the interest rate, that may well be a way of achieving 23–019

54 [1995] C.C.L.R. 62.

justice. Suppose the court is dealing with a loan secured by a mortgage at a rate of interest which, though not extortionate, is nevertheless very high. The debtor has got into arrears. These are piling up at an alarming rate because interest is accumulating on the arrears. The creditor commences repossession proceedings. The court is then facing a choice of either granting an immediate repossession order or else giving the debtor a chance to catch up by making a time order: a time order being normally made for a stipulated period on account of temporary financial difficulty. The court cannot make a time order unless the debtor has some reasonable chance of keeping up with the payments required under the time order. If the court is able to find a reason to reduce the interest rate, i.e. "in consequence of a term of the time order", then that may make all the difference, thereby enabling the court to make a time order for payments which the debtor has some chance of maintaining.

Subsidiary Matters

Appropriation of Payments

23-020 It may happen that the debtor or hirer has more than one credit agreement with the same person. Alternatively he may have separate agreements with two different persons but have to make payments under them to the same person (e.g. if he has to make payments to X who is the agent for both creditors). Suppose the debtor makes a payment. To which agreement does the payment relate? It may not seem an important question because, regardless of which agreement is the relevant one, the total amount still remaining outstanding will be the same. However, the question will be important if one of the agreements is unenforceable for any reason. Where the customer has two or more regulated agreements and has to make payments in respect of them to the same person, the customer has the right to appropriate any payment as between the different agreements as he sees fit. If he does not indicate any appropriation then the payment is automatically appropriated towards the different agreements proportionately according to the sums then due under the different agreements (i.e. ignoring any future instalments which have not yet fallen due). Thus, if he wishes, the customer can indicate that all his payments are to go to pay off sums due under an enforceable agreement—thereby leaving the creditor to "whistle for" payments under any unenforceable agreements.[55] Even if the customer makes no such appropriation, the creditor or owner cannot appropriate all the payments to an unenforceable agreement. The payments must be appropriated proportionately.[56]

There is one qualification to what has just been said. Where none of the agreements in question is a hire purchase, conditional sale agreement or a consumer hire agreement and where there is no security in respect of any of them, there is no automatic appropriation. The

55 CONC 6.4.2. R (replicating the now repealed s.81(1)).

56 CONC 6.4.2. R (replicating the now repealed s.81(2)).

result in that case is that if the debtor does not indicate to which agreement a payment relates, the recipient of the payment can appropriate the payment as he wishes.

In *Julian Hodge Bank Ltd v Hall*[57] the debtor had just one agreement, a regulated hire purchase agreement. He was in arrears. Ignoring future payments which had not yet fallen due, he owed two sets of money: (i) arrears of payments which he should have made; and (ii) default interest which, at the contract rate, had accumulated on the arrears. When he made a further payment which was less than the total of (i) and (ii), the debtor could have made his own appropriation of it as between (i) and (ii). Since he did not, the creditor was free to make such an appropriation. It was held that the creditor's appropriation is not effective until communicated to the debtor and once it is communicated it is irrevocable. It might, for example, be communicated by a letter or invoice, showing the revised amounts of (i) and (ii) owing. Whichever way it is appropriated, it will still have the same effect on the overall amount outstanding. In a hire purchase case, however, appropriation of the payment to (i) may, as it did in Julian Hodge, increase the chances of the goods being "protected goods".[58]

Misuse of Credit Facilities

With certain kinds of credit facilities, there is a particularly high risk that someone other than the debtor will manage to gain access to the facilities and thereby obtain credit. This is so, for example, where the credit is obtained by the production by the debtor of a trading check or credit card. If the check or card falls into the wrong hands then it may be used by someone who is never afterwards found. 23-021

The question arises as to whether the original debtor has to pay for that. There are special rules in s.84 relating to credit tokens and they will be dealt with a little later.[59] However, apart from those special rules, there is a general all-embracing rule in s.83 that the debtor under a regulated agreement shall not be liable for any use of credit facilities by another person who is not the debtor's agent and not authorised by the debtor to use them. This section is not confined to trading checks and covers any kind of credit facilities which are provided under a regulated agreement.

We must now consider the position where a bank provides a current account customer with a withdrawal token, i.e. an ATM card. An ATM card (usually indistinguishable from a credit card in appearance) enables the customer to obtain cash from this current account outside the bank's opening hours by using the card to operate a machine situated, usually, outside the bank. Normally this facility is not used to obtain credit; it is provided under a current account agreement. In fact, assuming that the customer has got some money in his current account, he is not a debtor but a creditor (i.e. the bank owes him money, not vice versa). When he uses his ATM card that will have the effect of reducing the amount in his current account and he will

57 [1998] C.C.L.R. 14.

58 See para.25-014, below.

59 See para.23-002, below.

therefore not be obtaining credit. Rather he will be obtaining money which the bank owes him. However, if the customer uses his ATM card so as to cause his bank to pay out more than the funds in the customer's current account, then he has obtained credit from his bank. When the bank provided him with those facilities whereby it obliged itself to give him this credit it made with him a regulated consumer credit agreement. If it is a regulated agreement then it is still a regulated agreement even if in fact the customer never afterwards actually obtained credit under it.

The result of all this would appear to be that s.83 applies to ATM cards. However, there are two things which affect the simplicity of that. The first complication arises as a consequence of the fact that a withdrawal token falls within the definition of a credit token and is therefore subject to the special rules relating to credit tokens—the effect of which is basically that the customer can be liable for the first £50 of any loss. The second complication is that s.83 and the special rules (in s.84) relating to credit tokens applies only to misuse of credit facilities. Thus they apply to an ATM card only when it is used to draw on credit. Nothing in these sections prevent the debtor from being made fully liable for a misuse of the ATM card which merely reduces the amount of money in his account, i.e. which occurs when his account is not overdrawn. However, the Payment Services Regulations 2017[60] includes provisions similar to those in ss.83 and 84 and will apply in such a situation. Under reg.77 the customer is only liable up to a maximum of £35 unless he has acted fraudulently or has with either intent or gross negligence failed to comply with his obligations under reg.72. These obligations include using the payment instrument in accordance with the terms of the agreement and taking all reasonable steps to ensure the security features of the card are maintained, e.g. not writing the PIN number for a debit card on its reverse. Under reg.77(4) the customer will not be liable for any losses occurring after he has notified the card issuer that the card has been lost or is liable to be misused unless he has acted fraudulently.

Credit Token Agreements

23-022 A credit token is, broadly, a card, check, voucher, coupon, stamp, form, booklet or other document or thing, which is given to the debtor by the creditor and which can be used by the debtor to obtain cash or services or goods on credit.[61] Thus a credit card is a good example of a credit token.

Prior to 1 April 2014, it was a criminal offence to supply a credit token to someone who has not asked for it.[62] That offence has now been replaced by equivalent rules in the Financial Conduct Authority's Consumer Credit Sourcebook (CONC) which prohibit the supply of unsolicited credit tokens by FCA-authorised persons. Except in the case of a small

60 SI 2017/752. See regs 76 and 77. The 2017 Regulations (for the most part) came into effect on 13 January 2018 and replaced the Payment Services Regulations 2009 (SI 2009/209).

61 s.14(1).

62 s.51.

borrower-lender-supplier agreement the customer's request must be in a document signed by himself. There is further exception whereby no prior request is needed before a credit card is sent out in renewal or replacement of an earlier one (for credit cards normally expire after a couple of years or so).[63]

One particular risk with a credit card is that before it reaches the person for whom it was intended, it falls into the wrong hands, i.e. someone else might acquire it and use it to obtain credit. By s.66 the debtor (i.e. the person who was intended to receive it) will not be liable for any use made of a credit token unless he has himself accepted it. This is so whether the credit token was sent to him unsolicited or after he had requested it or agreed to its being sent. Even if it has actually reached him, it does not follow that he has accepted it. He does not accept it until he either signs it, signs a receipt for it or uses it.[64]

Someone (e.g. a thief) may make unauthorised use of the credit token after the debtor has accepted it. It is quite likely that in these circumstances the credit agreement will make the debtor liable to the creditor for any loss caused by this unauthorised use. Section 84 permits this but restricts the liability of the debtor in four respects. First, if he has lost possession of the credit token at the time of the authorised use, his liability cannot exceed £35 (or the credit limit if lower) in respect of the whole period that he is out of possession. This restriction does not, however, apply to the debtor's liability in respect of any misuse by someone who obtained possession with the debtor's consent.[65] Secondly, the debtor is not liable for any unauthorised use that is made of the credit token after he has given notice that it is lost, stolen or for any other reason likely to be misused.[66] Notice may be given orally (e.g. by telephone) but in that case the notice will be ineffective if the agreement requires it to be confirmed in writing and it is not confirmed in writing with the period stipulated in the agreement (the period allowed must be at least seven days).[67] Thirdly, the debtor will be under no liability at all for unauthorised use unless the name, address and telephone number of the person to whom notice can be given that the credit token is lost or stolen or is for any other reason liable to misuse, was shown clearly and legibly in the agreement.[68] Fourthly, the debtor is not liable for any unauthorised use that is made of the credit token in connection with a distance contract (other than an excepted contract).[69] Nothing in s.84 prevents the debtor being made liable by the terms of his contract for any loss which does not arise from misuse of a credit facility, e.g. if a cash withdrawal token is used by a thief to withdraw £200 from the debtor's current account at a time when the debtor had £300 in the account.[70] 23-023

63 See CONC 2.9.2 R.
64 s.61(2).
65 s.84(2).
66 s.84(3).
67 s.84(5).
68 s.84(4).
69 s.84(3A).
70 See, however, the equivalent provisions of the Payment Services Regulations 2017. See, for example, reg.76 and reg.77.

Section 171 completes the protection for the debtor by putting the onus of proof of certain matters firmly upon the creditor. In proceedings brought by the creditor under the agreement it is for the creditor to prove that the credit token was lawfully supplied and was accepted by the debtor.[71] Where the debtor alleges that any use of the credit token was not authorised by him, it is for the creditor to prove either that it was or that the unauthorised use occurred before the creditor had been given notice that the credit token was lost, stolen or likely to be misused.[72]

Finally, observe an oddity. It is possible to have a credit token without there being either a credit token agreement or an offer to make such an agreement. In *Elliott v Director-General of Fair Trading*[73] a footwear retailing company instituted a promotional scheme whereby the company sent to members of the public unsolicited plasticised cards which looked very much like credit cards. The idea was that a holder of such a card could use it at an Elliott shop to obtain goods on credit. The company was charged, under s.51 (now repealed), with sending out an unsolicited credit token. Clearly, when a card was received by a member of the public, there was no credit agreement. The sending of the card was either an offer or it was merely an invitation to treat. It was not clear which. The wording on the card was ambiguous. On the one hand it said "This card is available for immediate use" and "credit is immediately available". On the other, it also said ". . . it can only be used when a signature has been accepted at an Elliott shop" and other literature which was sent out with the cards made it clear that the customer would have to complete further forms and formalities before being able to use the card. The court held that the company was guilty. The card was a credit token irrespective of whether it amounted to an offer. A card is a credit token within the statutory definition (in s.14) if on its face or its reverse side there is an undertaking that on its production credit will be given.

71 s.171(4)(a).
72 s.171(4)(b).
73 [1980] 1 W.L.R. 977.

24

Termination of Hire Purchase Contracts

At the outset the parties will no doubt expect that the contract will run its full course—that the debtor will pay all his instalments and at the end will exercise his option to purchase the goods. Nevertheless, the hiring may be terminated before the debtor has paid all his instalments. This chapter is concerned with the causes and consequences of such premature termination. It is not, however, concerned with the right of cancellation which is given for the first few days to some debtors who sign the agreement elsewhere than at certain trade premises. That was considered in Ch.21. 24-001

Unlike withdrawal or cancellation, termination is seldom in the debtor's best interest. The normal consequences of termination are that the debtor has no right to retain the goods and that he is unable to recover any payments he has already paid; he may even have to make a further payment. Thus it is rarely a positive decision on the debtor's part to terminate the agreement. The most common cause is in fact the debtor's inability or failure to keep up his payments. We shall see, however, that the debtor whose agreement is a regulated agreement has much less to fear from termination. The Consumer Credit Act gives him considerable protection. One set of provisions of the Consumer Credit Act will not, however, be mentioned further in this chapter; those relating to unfair creditor/debtor relationships.[1] It should nevertheless be borne in mind throughout that these provisions can be used if the court finds that the agreement creates an unfair debtor/creditor relationship and that they are not confined to regulated agreements but can be used in relation to any consumer credit agreement even if it is an exempt agreement.

We shall be dealing with the position at common law, i.e. where the agreement is not regulated by the Consumer Credit Act, as well as the position in relation to regulated agreements. Although this chapter will be concerned only with hire purchase agreements, the practice will be continued, in line with the Consumer Credit Act, of referring to the parties as creditor and

1 Consumer Credit Act 1974 ss.140A–140C.

debtor rather than owner and hirer, although it is true that many of the creditor's rights derive from the fact that he is the owner of the goods. This is especially so in relation to his rights against third parties.

This chapter will be devoted to answering four questions, in the following order:

(1) What events cause termination?

(2) After termination, is the creditor entitled to recover the goods from the debtor?

(3) After termination, is the creditor entitled to any further payment from the debtor?

(4) After termination, is the creditor entitled to recover the goods if they have passed to a third person?

Events Causing Termination

24-002 Broadly, termination may come about as a result of one of four things: subsequent agreement between the parties; exercise by the debtor of a right of termination; breach of the agreement by the debtor; or, lastly, the occurrence of an event stipulated in the agreement as liable to cause termination. When termination occurs it is not always easy to identify which of these things was the cause. It can, however, be important, for the consequences of termination vary according to the cause.

Mutual Agreement

24-003 It is quite possible for the creditor and debtor to come to a subsequent agreement whereby they terminate the hire-purchase contract. In practice, this will seldom be done except where a new hire-purchase agreement is substituted for the old one. The debtor will hardly wish to return the goods and also to sacrifice the payments which he has already made. On the other hand, the creditor will not usually be too willing to forgo a substantial part of the payments and also have the problem of disposing of the goods. The creditor is more likely to try to persuade the debtor to replace his existing contract with another hire-purchase agreement, spreading the remaining payments over a longer period of time.

The parties may of course decide that it is not necessary to terminate the agreement and substitute a new one and decide instead simply to agree to vary the first one. However, if they do this then the provisions of the Consumer Credit Act will operate as if they had terminated the first agreement and made a new one producing the combined effect of the first agreement and the later variation.[2]

Termination by mutual agreement seldom gives rise to any legal difficulty. The problems with which this chapter is concerned are associated rather with termination which comes about in some other way.

Exercise by the Debtor of a Right of Termination

Often a hire-purchase agreement will contain a term expressly allowing the debtor to terminate the contract, although there will usually also be a provision to the effect that the debtor must, as the price of doing so, make a further stipulated payment (i.e. in addition to payments falling due before termination). Notice in writing to the creditor will normally be required. Since the contract expressly allows him to terminate it, the debtor does not commit a breach of contract by exercising the contractual right. This can be an important point in relation to whether the creditor is entitled to recover the further payment stipulated to be due on the debtor exercising his right of termination.[3] It will be important where the agreement is not a regulated one but not where the agreement is a regulated agreement because in the latter case the amount of money recoverable by the creditor is governed by s.100. 24-004

In the case of a regulated agreement, s.99 gives the debtor a right to terminate the contract by giving notice in writing to the creditor or any person entitled or authorised to receive payments under the agreement. The debtor may have both the above rights of termination, i.e. if the agreement both gives to the debtor an express right of termination and is also a regulated agreement. If in that situation the debtor exercises his right of termination, the consequences will be those that are the more lenient and beneficial for the debtor, i.e. those in s.100 or those stipulated in the agreement. The reason for this is that by s.173 the agreement cannot increase but can only reduce the debtor's liability as stated in the Act.

Where the agreement is not a regulated one, the debtor will not have a right to terminate under s.99 but may still have a contractual right of termination. In this case a stipulation for a further payment may be enforceable even though it is excessive. Thus it might exceed the actual loss caused to the creditor by the termination. It might mean that he receives in all more than he would have received if the agreement had never been terminated and had been fully carried out. To put it another way, it could result in the creditor receiving in all (i.e. including the sums already paid by the debtor before the termination and the value of the goods returned to the creditor at the time of the termination) more than the whole of the total price.[4] This means that where the agreement is not a regulated one, the consequences of the debtor exercising a contractual right of termination could be very harsh for the debtor. They certainly could be worse than if he broke his contract (i.e. simply allowed his payments to get into arrears). For

2 See s.82.

3 See *Associated Distributors v Hall* [1938] 1 All E.R. 511, at para.24-026, below.

4 See *Associated Distributors v Hall* [1938] 1 All E.R. 511, para.24-026, below.

this reason the court will not hold that the debtor has exercised a contractual right of termination unless it is sure that he was fully aware of the consequences. In *United Dominions Trust v Ennis*[5] the subject-matter of the agreement was a Jaguar car and the debtor was a London docker who found he could not keep up his payments when the dockers went on strike. He wrote to the creditor saying, "I wish to terminate my agreement with you as I find I cannot fulfil the terms". The Court of Appeal held that the debtor was not exercising his contractual right of termination but was, in effect, giving the creditor notice of his breach of contract. Referring to the debtor's contractual right (option) of termination, Lord Denning MR said, "A hirer (i.e. debtor) is not to be taken as exercising such an option unless he does so consciously, knowing of the consequences and avowedly in exercise of his option". Since the debtor had not exercised his right of termination, it was the creditor who had terminated, as he was entitled to do, for the debtor's breach of contract. This meant that the creditor had no right to the stipulated further payment which was excessive and therefore void as a penalty.

Breach of the Agreement by the Debtor

24-005 Not every breach by the debtor will terminate the agreement. Those breaches which may result in termination are:

(i) An act by the debtor wholly repugnant to the agreement, e.g. if he sells the goods or otherwise indicates by acts or words that he repudiates the contract. If the debtor does such an act, the creditor is not bound to regard the agreement as terminated but is entitled to do so. If he does so, the law will regard the termination as having been caused by the debtor's repudiation. This fact will tell against the debtor if the creditor claims damages.[6]

(ii) A breach by the debtor which does not amount to repudiation but which is specified in the agreement as giving to the creditor the right to terminate the hiring. The usual breaches specified in this way are first, failure by the debtor to take reasonable care of the goods and, secondly, the debtor falling into arrears with his payments. Sometimes the contract states that it is automatically terminated on the occurrence of one of the specified breaches. Sometimes it gives the creditor the right of termination after giving notice. When the creditor exercises his right of termination for the debtor's breach then, unless the debtor repudiated the agreement, the law regards the termination as having been caused by the creditor. This fact will be in the debtor's favour if the creditor claims damages.[7]

---

5 [1968] 1 Q.B. 54.

6 See para.24-021, below.

7 See *Financings v Baldock* [1963] 2 Q.B. 104, para.24-022, below.

(iii) A breach of a term which is a condition of the contract. If the contract clearly indicates that a term is a condition (as opposed to a warranty) then any breach of it by the debtor has the same effect as an act by the debtor which is wholly repugnant to the contract. A statement in the contract that a given term is "of the essence" clearly labels it as a condition. Thus where the contract states that punctual payment of all moneys due by the debtor is "of the essence", then, if the debtor is late (even if only by one day) in making one of the payments, he can be treated by the creditor as having repudiated the contract.[8] The damages to be paid by the debtor will be assessed accordingly. Thus there is a fine, but important, line between a contract provision that if the debtor is 10 days late in making any payment the creditor has the right to terminate the hiring (*Financings v Baldock*)[9] and one which states that punctual payment of all moneys due under the contract is "of the essence" (*Lombard North Central v Butterworth*).[10] Both give the creditor the right to terminate the contract for late payment, however the latter can result in the debtor having to pay greater damages.[11]

If the agreement so specifies, it appears to be possible for the contract to be terminated if the debtor is late with one instalment. However, in the case of an agreement which is a regulated agreement, this cannot happen without the debtor first being given a chance to bring his payments up to date. Section 87 applies where the debtor is in breach of the agreement. It provides that the creditor cannot (amongst other things) either terminate the agreement or treat any right of the debtor's as terminated without first serving a default notice on the debtor. The section applies to regulated agreements and it applies irrespective of whether the debtor's breach was a repudiatory one or not. Default notices were considered in the last chapter.[12] By way of reminder it may be said here that where the debtor's only breach is non-payment of instalments the default notice must make a number of things clear to the debtor, including:

(i) The exact amount required to bring his payments up to date. If the amount is overstated, the notice is invalid.[13]

(ii) Exactly how long (a minimum of 14 days) he has got in which to pay it (i.e. the date of expiry of the default notice).

(iii) The consequences of failure to comply with the notice.

8 *Lombard North Central v Butterworth* [1987] Q.B. 527.
9 [1963] 2 Q.B. 104.
10 [1987] Q.B. 527.
11 See para.24-023, below.
12 See para.23-011, below.
13 *Woodchester Lease Management v Swain* [1999] 1 W.L.R. 263.

(iv) The provision of the agreement (if any) under which the agreement can be terminated.

(v) That if the breach is duly remedied the agreement will not terminate.

Some of these requirements were not made clear in *Eshun v Moorgate Mercantile Co.*[14] The debtor had paid £115 out of a total hire purchase price of £405 17s. 3d. The default notice served on him stated correctly that he was £23 3s. 6d. in arrears. It then said:

> **"Unless we do hear from you with payment within the course of the next nine days after the date on which you would normally be expected to receive this letter, we shall have no alternative but to assume that you do not wish to continue the hiring under the Agreement and are, in effect terminating by repudiation."**

24–006 The court held that this notice was invalid on three grounds. First, the creditor had no right to assume from the mere non-payment of two instalments that the debtor was in effect terminating by repudiation. The creditor cannot put upon the debtor a repudiation when he has never repudiated. Secondly, the notice did not refer to the provision of the hire-purchase agreement under which it was given and under which the amounts in default were due. Thirdly, it did not clearly state exactly how long the debtor had before the period for payment expired. Since the notice was invalid, the agreement was never terminated and therefore the creditor had no right to recover possession of the goods. The creditor therefore had to pay compensation to the debtor for having done so.

A further interesting point to emerge from the case was that even if the agreement had not been regulated by an Act of Parliament, it still could not have been terminated without a notice of default being served. Lord Denning MR said:[15]

> **"I think that even at common law a notice of default may be necessary . . . the agreement being a one-sided one with stringent terms, the plaintiff was entitled to a reminder that his instalments were in arrear before it could be terminated".**

14 [1971] 1 W.L.R. 722.

15 [1971] 1 W.L.R. 722 at 725, citing with approval the words of Sellers LJ in *Reynolds v General & Finance Facilities Ltd* (1963) 107 S.J. 889.

Other Stipulated Events

Hire purchase agreements commonly provide for termination on the occurrence of any one of certain stipulated events (other than breach of the agreement), e.g. on the death of the debtor, on his becoming insolvent or on his being sentenced to a term of imprisonment. Either the contract will provide that it is terminated automatically by a given event or it will give the creditor the right (option) to terminate it on the occurrence of the event. At common law the effect of such an event occurring is as stated in the contract, i.e. either that the contract terminates automatically or that it becomes terminable at the creditor's option. 24-007

Where the agreement is a regulated agreement the common law position is modified in two respects. One of these modifications applies where the stipulated event is the death of the debtor. The other modification (the requirement for a non-default notice) applies whatever the stipulated event.

Section 86 applies to any regulated agreement where the debtor dies. This section has already been fully considered in the last chapter.[16] It is sufficient to say here that usually the death of the debtor will not cause the agreement to terminate, notwithstanding anything said in the agreement. The result will be that on the debtor's death, his rights and obligations under the agreement will transfer to his personal representatives, i.e. those responsible for administering his estate.

Sections 76 and 98 apply to regulated agreements where the stipulated event is anything other than a breach of the agreement by the debtor. Their effect is that the creditor cannot (amongst other things) either terminate the agreement or treat any right of the debtor as terminated without first serving on him a notice (a non-default notice) giving him at least seven days' warning. These sections also have already been considered once.[17] However, there are two remaining questions that need answering in relation both to default and also to non-default notices.

Default Notice and Non-default Notice

It will be apparent that where termination occurs other than by mutual agreement or by the debtor exercising his right of termination, one of these notices has to be served. Two questions arise in relation to such notices: 24-008

Exactly when will termination occur?

When the creditor has a right (i.e. option) to terminate the agreement on a breach or other stipulated event, then termination cannot occur before expiry of the notice served on the 24-009

16 See para.23-013, above.

17 See para.23-015, above.

debtor. That (i.e. expiry of the notice) will in practice be when termination will occur—because the notice will state so. However, sometimes a hire purchase agreement states that the agreement is to terminate automatically upon a certain type of breach by the debtor or upon some other event. At common law, of course, this would mean that termination occurred as soon as (and at the same time as) the stipulated event. Section 87 (default notice) or s.76 (non-default notice) prevents the creditor, until the expiry of the notice, from being entitled to "treat" any right to the debtor as terminated. So we have the position that it is not until the expiry of the notice that the creditor can treat the contract as terminated. At the expiry of the notice he can treat the contract as terminated—but, as terminated when? The answer is that he can then treat the contract as having terminated upon the happening of the event which was stipulated as causing the automatic termination. This is because the sections requiring the notice to be given to the debtor do not (with one exception) prevent automatic termination occurring but only prevent (i.e. delay) the creditor treating the termination as having occurred. The exception brings us on to the next question.

24–010 In one situation they can. That is where, after a default notice is served and before it expires, the debtor complies with the notice by remedying his breach or paying compensation as required in the notice. If he does this, then the debtor's breach is treated as not having occurred.[18] In this case it follows that the breach cannot give rise to termination (either automatically or otherwise).

Apart from that one situation, service of a notice will not prevent termination. It does, however, give the debtor the opportunity to apply for a "time order" and the court then has power to give the debtor another chance, to allow the debtor to keep the goods, to spread his repayments over a longer period, etc. However, if the court exercises these powers, that will not prevent the agreement being technically terminated. It may seem odd that on the one hand the debtor will in these circumstances be in possession of the goods, paying instalments and having the ability to exercise his option to buy them, while on the other hand the agreement has terminated. The explanation is that the debtor is then in possession of the goods under the time order made by the court. It is true that he will be "treated" as in possession under the terms of the agreement, but this will not alter the fact that the agreement has technically terminated. It may in these circumstances seem irrelevant that the agreement had, technically speaking, been terminated, and so it is, as between the creditor and debtor. However, as we shall see, it may be an important point in the creditor's favour if the debtor's landlord later seizes the goods from the debtor's possession in order to pay for the debtor's rent. More will be said on this later.

One more thing needs to be said at this stage about time orders. The court's power to make a time order includes the power to allow time (a specified period) during which the debtor can remedy a breach (other than one consisting of non-payment). This will cause a postponement of the time when the creditor will be able to terminate the agreement or to treat it as terminated.

18 s.89.

Recovery of the Goods by the Creditor from the Debtor

Whether the creditor is entitled to recover the goods after termination may depend upon whether the hire-purchase agreement is a regulated agreement within the Consumer Credit Act or not. The common law position, i.e. where it is not a regulated agreement, will be examined first. 24-011

Common Law

At common law the rule is that once the hiring has been terminated, the debtor has no right to retain possession of the goods. The creditor is entitled to recover possession. This is so even if the contract does not expressly say so: *Bowmakers v Barnet Instruments*.[19] If on request the debtor refuses or fails to hand over the goods, he commits conversion of the goods. There are two ways in which the creditor can enforce his right to possession. He can either seize physical possession of them or he can commence court proceedings against the debtor for conversion. There may be difficulty in the first method because, if the goods are on the debtor's premises, the creditor may be unable to seize them without trespassing and thus laying himself open to an action by the debtor. For this reason sometimes the hire-purchase agreement will contain a clause expressly authorising the creditor to enter the debtor's premises to recover possession of the goods after termination. If the creditor brings an action for conversion, he is most unlikely to obtain a court order compelling the debtor to return the goods. He will obtain damages instead. The damages will not be the full value of the goods, only the outstanding balance of the hire-purchase price, i.e. the remaining payments which the debtor would have been liable to pay if the agreement had not been terminated.[20] If the result of an award of damages to the creditor is that he gets payment of the balance of the hire purchase price earlier than he would have got it if the agreement had not been terminated, then a reduction will be made to take account of this accelerated payment. 24-012

The Torts (Interference with Goods) Act 1977 allows the creditor, if he wishes, to choose a different judgment in place of a simple award of damages—namely a judgment giving the debtor an option either to pay damages (assessed as just explained) or to return the goods. If the debtor opts to return the goods then the debtor is entitled to receive from the creditor a financial allowance, i.e. a sum equal to the amount by which the value of the goods exceeds the alternative damages awarded.

19 [1945] K.B. 65.

20 *Wickham Holdings v Brooke House Motors* [1967] 1 All E.R. 117.

Regulated Agreements

24-013 The position is different in three ways where the agreement is a regulated agreement:

(i) Section 92 provides that the creditor is not entitled to enter any premises to take possession of the goods except under an order of the court. This means that in practice, unless the creditor can persuade the debtor voluntarily to hand over the goods, the creditor will have to bring a court action to recover them. If he does that then the court has power to make a time order.

(ii) Where the debtor wrongfully retains possession of the goods after termination, the court will normally order the debtor to return the goods to the creditor. The debtor will not be given the option of paying their value instead.[21] The court may, however, refuse to make an order for the return of the goods if a refusal would be "just". Of course, there would be such a refusal or else the operation of the return order would be suspended where the court makes a time order.

(iii) Where the goods are "protected goods", the creditor is not entitled to recover possession of them without bringing a court action.

It is still the position that where the agreement is terminated otherwise than by the debtor's breach, the creditor is entitled to seize physical possession of the goods without trespassing. The creditor is similarly entitled, even where the agreement has been terminated by reason of the debtor's breach unless the goods are "protected goods". However, no doubt when the court gives the debtor another chance and therefore makes a time order, it will simultaneously deprive the creditor of the right to seize possession while the time order is in force.

Protected Goods

24-014 For the debtor the consequences of termination can be unfortunate in that he may have the goods repossessed by the creditor in spite of the fact that he has paid a considerable amount towards them. He may then find that the creditor claims also a further money payment for termination of the agreement. We shall shortly be seeing that the court, by making a time order, can give the debtor another chance of maintaining payments under the agreement. The effect of the protected goods provision is to see that the creditor has not seized possession

21 s.100(5).

of the goods before the court has considered whether to give the debtor that second chance. However, these protected goods provisions apply only where the goods fall within the definition of "protected goods".

The Definition

Goods which are let under a regulated hire purchase agreement fall within the definition of protected goods in s.90 if three conditions are fulfilled: 24-015

(a) The debtor is in breach of the agreement.

(b) The debtor has paid or tendered to the creditor one-third or more of the total price of the goods.

(c) The property in the goods remains in the creditor.

The last of these will cause no difficulty since property (i.e. ownership) will remain with the creditor until the debtor exercises his option to buy (i.e. until he has paid all the money due under the agreement).

The first condition is satisfied only if the debtor is in breach of the agreement. If the agreement has been terminated for some other reason the creditor will be entitled to seize the goods, providing he does not trespass to do so, or he can sue for their return under s.100(5). Where the debtor falls into arrears, the goods will be protected goods provided one-third of the total price has been paid or tendered.

The total price is the total sum payable by the debtor under the agreement, i.e. the deposit plus all the instalments plus the option money. The calculation will normally be easy. However, it will be complicated if either the total price includes charges in respect of the installation of the goods or the debtor has more than one regulated agreement with the same creditor. 24-016

For the purposes of the calculation, any installation charges have to be separated from the rest of the total price. By s.90(2) the debtor will not be regarded as having paid or tendered one-third of the total price unless he has paid or tendered both:

(i) the whole of the installation charges, and

(ii) one-third of the remainder of the total price.

This calculation may be made more complicated where the debtor has, in addition to the agreement in question, a further regulated agreement under which he has to make payments to the same person as he does under the agreement in question. In such a situation, CONC 6.4.2R provides that any payment made by the debtor can be appropriated by him as between the different agreements.[22] If the debtor does not indicate to which agreement any given payment is appropriated, then that payment is appropriated between the agreements proportionately according to the amount of the sums due under each agreement. If on the other hand the debtor has just one agreement under which he owes, both (i) arrears of payments which have already fallen due, and (ii) default interest which has accrued on those arrears, then in the absence of an appropriation by the debtor, there is no automatic appropriation and the creditor can appropriate any payment received to either (i) or (ii).[23] If it is appropriated to (ii) then it will not go towards payment of the one third of the total price, since default interest is not part of the "total price".

Goods will not be (or will cease to be) protected goods if the debtor exercises his right of termination (i.e. under s.99). Thus where the debtor falls into arrears, it may be much to his advantage not to exercise his right of termination but simply to do nothing and let the creditor, if he wishes, serve a default notice and terminate the agreement. Since in these circumstances it would not be in the debtor's interest for him to exercise a right of termination, the court would be reluctant to find that he had done so, unless he had done it consciously and was fully aware of the consequences.[24]

The Protection

24–017 The creditor is not entitled, otherwise than by court action, to recover possession of protected goods from the debtor (s.90). Thus he must not seize physical possession of them. It is not a criminal offence for him to do so. However, if, contrary to s.90, he does so, then the agreement is terminated and all payments made under the agreement are returnable to the debtor who is relieved of further liability under the agreement.[25] There are three significant exceptions to the protection given by s.90, i.e. three situations where the creditor can recover physical possession of the goods without contravening s.90:

(i) If the debtor has disposed of the goods to a third party, the creditor can seize them from the third party without contravening s.90. This is because s.90 prevents him seizing them "from the debtor". If the debtor has not disposed of the goods but has simply, for example, lent them to a friend or left them to be mended by a repairer, the creditor would be contravening s.90 if he seized them. Lord Denning MR in *Bentinck v Cromwell Engineering Ltd*[26] was referring to the section of the Hire Purchase Act 1965

22 Prior to the transfer of consumer credit regulation from the OFT to the FCA in April 2014, this was dealt with under s.81 with identical effect.

23 *Julian Hodge Bank Ltd v Hall* [1998] C.C.L.R. 14 CA.

24 See *United Dominions Trust v Ennis*, para.24-004, above.

25 s.91.

26 [1971] 1 Q.B. 324.

which was replaced by s.90 (and which used the word "hirer" instead of "debtor") when he said:

> "In the ordinary way, once goods are 'protected goods', i.e. more than one-third has been paid, the finance company cannot recover possession—except by action—from the hirer, nor from any garage or repairer with whom the hirer may have left it. The words 'from the hirer' include all those to whom the hirer has bailed it."

(ii) If the debtor has abandoned the goods, the creditor can seize them without contravening s.90, for he is not then seizing them "from the debtor". In Bentinck's case, the debtor paid the deposit and first few instalments before falling into arrears. The car was badly damaged in an accident and he left it at a garage but did not give orders to repair it. Three months later the finance company, the creditor, traced him. He paid none of the arrears, gave a false telephone number and disappeared without trace. After a further six months the finance company took the car from the garage where it had been left by the debtor some nine months earlier. The court held on these facts that the debtor had abandoned the car and the finance company had not contravened s.90.

(iii) The creditor does not contravene s.90 if the debtor consents to the creditor repossessing the goods.[27] To be effective, the consent has to be given at the time of the repossession. Even then the consent will not be effective unless the debtor knows, or has been informed, what his rights would be if he refuses consent.[28] Those rights would (if the creditor brought legal proceedings to recover possession of the goods) be the right to ask the court to reorganise his repayments and let him retain possession under a time order.

Court Action

If the creditor wishes to recover possession of protected goods he must bring an action in the county court. Even if he can show that the agreement has terminated he will not automatically be granted a "return order", i.e. an order for the goods to be returned. The court may decide that such an order would not be just and may instead grant a time order. The court's powers will be further considered after we have looked at what money claim the creditor can make. 24-018

27 *Mercantile Credit Co v Cross* [1965] 2 Q.B. 205 and s.173(3).

28 *Chartered Trust v Pitcher* [1988] R.T.R. 72.

Money Claim by Creditor from Debtor

24-019 When termination occurs, the situation is different according to whether the agreement is or is not a regulated agreement. Regulated agreements will be considered second. Turning first to the position at common law, i.e. where the agreement is not a regulated one, the creditor may have two alternative claims against the debtor. He may be able to claim damages for the debtor's breach of contract or he may be able to claim the amount stipulated in the agreement as being payable upon termination (i.e. the minimum payment).

Damages

24-020 Damages can be obtained for the debtor's breach of contract. Since termination is usually preceded by the debtor falling into arrears, there is usually a reason for claiming damages. The amount, however, will depend upon whether the debtor repudiated the contract or whether he simply got into arrears. If he has simply got into arrears, the amount of damages will depend upon whether punctual payment was of the essence of the contract.

Damages for repudiation

24-021 These are assessed according to the rule in *Yeoman Credit v Waragowski*[29] where at the time of termination the debtor had paid only the initial deposit, £72. After termination the creditor recovered possession of the goods, a car, which was then worth £205. The creditor was awarded the following damages:

1. Arrears of instalment due before termination			£60
and			
2. A sum arrived at by taking the total hire purchase price and then deducting certain items:		£434	
payments already made	£72		
the amount awarded under (a)	£60		
the option money in the agreement	£1		
the value of the goods recovered	£205		
	£338	£338	
		£96	£96
Total:			£156

29 [1961] 3 All E.R. 145.

When the creditor is awarded damages assessed on the *Waragowski* basis, he is in effect put in the same position as if the whole transaction had gone through as originally contemplated. Adding up the amounts he receives before termination, the value of the goods he has recovered and the damages awarded, it can be seen that he receives virtually the whole hire-purchase price.

Sometimes when termination occurs early on, the creditor gets this sum earlier than he would have done if the agreement had never been terminated. If it had not been terminated, he would have had to await payment of the instalments as the months went by. If it does occur that the creditor receives payment earlier than he would have, the court will make a deduction from the award of damages to take account of that earlier payment.[30]

Damages where the debtor does not repudiate

Where the debtor simply gets into arrears but does not repudiate the contract, the agreement may give the creditor the right of termination. If the creditor exercises that right then the termination is caused not by the debtor's breach but by the creditor exercising his right. That being so, the creditor cannot claim for loss of future payments as damages. He is limited to a claim for arrears of instalments due before termination. This was decided in *Financings v Baldock*.[31] The debtor had been in arrears; he had told the finance company (the creditor) that he hoped to pay off the arrears. The finance company later terminated the agreement. It was held that since at the time of termination the debtor could not be said to have repudiated the contract, he was liable only for arrears of instalments up to the date of termination. It is clear then that a debtor who finds he cannot maintain his payment is best advised not to repudiate the agreement but to indicate that he hopes and intends to make up the instalments. The court's sympathy in these cases tends to be with the debtor rather than the creditor who is normally a finance company. The court will tend, if possible, to find that the debtor's conduct has not amounted to a repudiation and it will not allow the finance company to put upon the debtor a repudiation when the debtor has not in fact repudiated.[32] One clear case of repudiation, however, is where the debtor sells or otherwise wrongfully disposes of the goods, in which case the damages will be assessed on the *Waragowski* basis. 24-022

Where damages are assessed on the *Financings v Baldock* basis and the creditor therefore receives only arrears up to the date of termination, there will be added to that amount a sum equal to the creditor's loss caused by the debtor's failure, if any, to take reasonable care of the goods. The hire purchase agreement will have included a term requiring the debtor to take reasonable care of the goods. If he does not do so then the goods when recovered by the creditor may be worth a certain amount less than if reasonable care had been taken of them. It is

30 *Overstone v Shipway* [1962] 1 All E.R. 52.

31 [1963] 2 Q.B. 104.

32 *Eshun v Moorgate Mercantile Co*, see para.24-005, above.

that amount which will in the award of damages be added to the arrears due up to the date of termination.

The law as established in *Financings v Baldock*[33] does not apply where the debtor has broken a condition of the contract.

Damages where debtor's breach is a breach of condition

24–023 In *Lombard North Central v Butterworth*[34] the contract provided that punctual payment of instalments under the contract was of the essence of the agreement. This clearly meant that punctual payment was a condition (as opposed to a warranty). In accordance with the general law of contract, the Court of Appeal held that therefore any lateness in payment, even if it did not amount to a repudiation by the debtor, could nevertheless be treated by the creditor as if it were such a repudiation. This meant that the creditor's damages after termination were to be assessed not on a *Financings v Baldock* basis but on a *Waragowski* basis. This decision may well have resulted in the law in *Financings v Baldock* becoming a dead letter, since many hire purchase companies have, after *Lombard North Central v Butterworth*, drafted their contracts to state that prompt payment by the debtor is of the essence of the contract. Thus, as Nicholls LJ said in the Lombard case, the conclusion in that case "emasculates the decision in *Financings v Baldock*".

Claim against a guarantor or indemnifier

24–024 As already explained, if, when the debtor has neither repudiated the contract nor broken a condition, the creditor exercises a right of termination, the creditor cannot claim loss of future payments from the debtor. He is entitled only to the return of the goods and arrears which were due before termination. That is what happened in *Goulston Discount Co v Clark*[35] where the creditor recovered from the debtor £157 less than he would have recovered if the debtor had repudiated the contract. The question in *Goulston* was whether the creditor, a finance company, could recover that £157 from the car dealer. Under a recourse agreement between the finance company and the dealer, the dealer had, in consideration of the finance company entering into a hire purchase agreement with W (the debtor), agreed as follows. He had agreed that he would "indemnify" the finance company against any loss that the finance company might suffer by reason of the fact that W did not, for any cause whatsoever, pay all the amounts which he would pay if he completed his hire purchase agreement. It was held that since this was an indemnity, the finance company was entitled to recover the £157. If it had been a guarantee, the finance company would have failed in this claim because a guarantor is under no

33 [1963] 2 Q.B. 104.

34 [1987] Q.B. 527.

35 [1967] 2 Q.B. 493.

greater liability than the debtor. The decision in *Goulston* would be exactly the same if the facts occurred again today. The claim under the indemnity (the recourse agreement) would not be reduced or affected at all by s.113 of the Consumer Credit Act, since the recourse agreement would not be "security" within the definition in the Act.

Minimum Payments

Hire-purchase agreements commonly contain a provision that on termination the debtor must pay a stipulated amount. From the creditor's point of view, one advantage of claiming this minimum payment instead of damages is that no damages can normally be claimed where the termination has occurred not as a result of the debtor's breach of contract but as a result of some event, e.g. the debtor terminating under a right to do so. Another advantage is that the minimum payment clause will usually provide for a fixed sum, whereas in a claim for damages there may be a dispute about the creditor's actual loss. However, the principal advantage is that the minimum payment clause may provide for a larger sum than the creditor could claim as damages. This last fact has caused neither the courts nor Parliament to look with favour upon minimum payment clauses. Thus a minimum payment clause may either (i) be void because of the common law doctrine of penalties, (ii) be ineffective because of the provisions of the Consumer Credit Act relating to unfair creditor/debtor relationships (if they apply), or (iii) be ineffective by virtue of the unfair terms framework laid down in the Consumer Rights Act 2015. 24-025

Penalties

The common law doctrine of penalties is concerned with a certain type of contractual clause—namely, the sort of clause which stipulates how much will be payable in the event of a breach of contract. Such a clause is a liquidated damages clause and is void if it amounts to a penalty. It will not be a penalty if it was a genuine attempt by the parties to pre-estimate the likely damages in the event of the breach. It will be a penalty if the stipulated minimum payment is large, out of all proportion to the likely damages.[36] In the words of Lord Dunedin in *Dunlop Pneumatic Tyre Co v New Garage Motor Co*:[37] 24-026

> **"It will be held to be a penalty if the sum stipulated for is extravagant and unconscionable in amount in comparison with the greatest loss that could conceivably be proved to have followed from the breach."**

36 See, generally, Ch.14 above.

37 [1915] A.C. 79.

In *Bridge v Campbell Discount Co*[38] the clause in question required the debtor to pay on termination:

(a) arrears of payments due before termination, plus

(b) an amount which together with payments made and due before termination amounted to two-thirds of the hire-purchase price.

This was in addition to the fact that the creditor was entitled to the return of the goods. The clause was held to be a penalty because, including the value of the returned goods, it would in nearly all cases give the creditor more than 100 per cent of the hire-purchase price, i.e. more than damages assessed on the *Waragowski* basis.

Even a clause where the amount stipulated is the same as would be awarded as damages assessed on the *Waragowski* basis can be a penalty. It will be a penalty if it provides for that amount to be payable where the damages, if awarded, would be assessed on the *Financings v Baldock* basis. In *Anglo Auto Finance Co v James*[39] the clause required the debtor to pay:

1. arrears of payments due before termination, plus
2. the amount by which the hire-purchase price exceeded the sum of:
   (i) payments made and due before termination, and
   (ii) the value of the goods when recovered and resold.

The Court of Appeal held that this was a penalty and awarded damages instead. Since the debtor had not repudiated the agreement the damages were assessed on the *Financings v Baldock* basis.

The doctrine of penalties applies where an excessive sum is stipulated to be payable on a breach of contract. However, termination can and does sometimes occur where there is no breach of contract, e.g. where the debtor exercises a contractual right of termination or where the contract terminates automatically on some specified event such as the debtor's bankruptcy. The Court of Appeal in *Associated Distributors v Hall*[40] held that the doctrine of penalties does not apply where a sum is stipulated payable on a termination which occurs without the debtor being in breach of the agreement. The creditor can sue for the stipulated amount, however great. This decision has proved a controversial one, although it still stands as part of the law. In *Bridge v Campbell Discount Co*[41] the House of Lords was evenly split on the question

38 [1962] A.C. 600.
39 [1963] 3 All E.R. 566.
40 [1938] 2 K.B. 83.
41 [1962] A.C. 600.

of whether it was correct. The decision leads to the situation where, if the debtor exercises his contractual right of termination, he may have to pay a larger sum than if he breaks his contract, thus causing termination. It is for this reason that the court will not hold that the debtor has exercised his right of termination unless he did so fully aware of the -consequences.[42] Of course it is now possible that a clause providing for a very high sum to be payable on a termination occurring in the absence of a breach by the hirer would be rendered ineffective by the Consumer Rights Act 2015.[43]

Regulated Agreements

Where the creditor brings a money claim against the debtor, it is an action to enforce the regulated agreement. That being so, the court will have the power to make a time order which is to be considered in the next section of this chapter. However, what money award could the creditor expect if the court were to make an immediate "return order"? The Consumer Credit Act does not state what size of award should be made. Thus the answer is that the award would equal whatever sum would be obtainable by the creditor as damages at common law—unless the agreement stipulated a different amount. However, it should be added that if the agreement stipulated an excessive amount, the court could reduce that amount. Even if the doctrine of penalties did not apply, the court could reopen the agreement under the unfair creditor/debtor relationships provisions. 24-027

By way of exception to what has just been said, the Act does state in s.100 how much money award should be made where the termination has occurred by the debtor exercising his right of termination under s.99. In that case the debtor's liability is to pay any loss caused by his failure to take reasonable care of the goods, plus all the arrears due before termination, plus whichever is the smallest of the following three amounts:

(i) The amount of the minimum payment stipulated in the agreement. If none is stipulated then the amount under this head is zero.

(ii) The amount, if any, by which one-half of the total hire-purchase price exceeds the total of the sums paid by the debtor and the arrears due before termination.

(iii) The amount of the creditor's actual loss arising from the termination by the debtor (i.e. the amount of damages assessed on the *Waragowski* basis).

Thus where the debtor exercises his right of termination the most that he will have to pay (assuming he took reasonable care of the goods) is the amount required to clear off his arrears due before termination, plus enough to bring up his payments to one-half of the total price. In

42 See *United Dominions Trust v Ennis*, para.24-004, above.

43 See Ch.10, above.

calculating one-half of the total price, difficulties will arise if the total price includes installation charges or if the debtor has a further regulated agreement with the same creditor. For the purposes of the calculation, the installation charges have to be separated from the rest of the total price. By s.100(2) one-half of the total price is to be regarded as equal to the whole of the installation charge plus one-half of the remainder of the total price. CONC 6.4.2R applies where the debtor has, in addition to the agreement in question, a further regulated agreement with the same creditor.[44]

Powers of the Court in the Case of Regulated Agreements

24-028 Hire purchase has been picturesquely described as the fertile mother of litigation. The vast majority of this litigation takes the form of an action by the creditor against the debtor in circumstances where the latter has defaulted on paying his instalments. There can be no doubt that the vast majority of hire-purchase agreements fall within the category of regulated agreements. Thus the court's powers, which we are about to examine, are designed to enable the court to deal with the situation where the debtor has defaulted.

A hire-purchase agreement will usually give the creditor the right to terminate it if the debtor becomes a certain amount in arrears. Thus when the debtor gets into arrears the action brought against him by the creditor will be one of two sorts:

(i) The creditor chooses to regard the agreement as terminated and (after serving the necessary default notice) brings an action claiming repossession of the goods and damages or the stipulated payment.

(ii) The creditor chooses not to regard the agreement as terminated and sues simply for arrears.

In the latter case the court will either give immediate judgment to the creditor for the arrears due or it will make a time order under s.129 allowing the debtor extra time to pay.

If the creditor adopts the first alternative and claims repossession, then the court can make a time order or it can exercise its powers under s.133. A time order will have the effect of allowing the debtor another chance of making his payments—perhaps over a longer period. The court's powers under s.133(1) are to make either a return order or a transfer order. A return

44 See para.24-016, above.

order is an order for the return of the goods to the creditor. The court must make a return order unless it would not be just to do so. Such an order would therefore be made if there were clearly no chance of the debtor paying off the debt. In that case the creditor will be likely to ask for damages also. The amount of such an award has already been considered.[45]

A transfer order is an alternative to making a return order but one which will in practice be available only occasionally. It is an order that the debtor return part of the goods but which allows him to keep the other part as his own without making further payment. This order can be made only where the court can divide the goods and where the payments already made by the debtor under the agreement are at least equal to a minimum amount. The minimum amount which he must have paid is a combination of (i) that part of the total price which is attributable to the goods he is being allowed to keep, and (ii) one-quarter of the rest of the total price. The total price includes the deposit, all the instalments and the option money which were scheduled under the agreement. The reason a transfer order will seldom be available is that the goods cannot very often be divided. It is not common, except perhaps in the case of some items of furniture (e.g. a three-piece suite), for one hire-purchase agreement to embrace more than one item. 24-029

Even after a return order or transfer order is made, there may be some delay before the creditor enforces the order. In this situation, if the debtor can find the financial resources to do so, he is still entitled to pay the whole outstanding balance of the total hire-purchase price and thereby become the owner of all the goods. He has this right until the creditor actually recovers possession.[46]

Recovery of the Goods by the Creditor in the Hands of a Third Party

The main concern here focuses on the position where someone other than the creditor or debtor also claims to have an interest in the goods. We have seen that on termination the creditor has a right as against the debtor to possession (subject to the provisions of the Consumer Credit Act). When some third party claims an interest, whose claim takes priority—the creditor's or the third party's? 24-030

45 See para.24-027, above.
46 s.133(4).

Sale of the Goods by the Debtor

24-031 When the debtor sells the goods before completing his payments, the goods will be in the hands of the purchaser. The general rule is that the creditor is entitled to recover the goods from the purchaser: *Helby v Matthews*.[47] This is the reason that hire purchase has proved so popular with finance companies. It gives the creditor this high degree of protection even when the debtor wrongfully sells the goods. The reason for the general rule is that the creditor under a hire-purchase agreement remains the owner of the goods until the debtor has paid off all the instalments and exercised his option to buy. He remains the owner even though the debtor sells the goods. It is his ownership that entitles him to recover the goods from the purchaser and he has that right regardless of whether the hire-purchase agreement has been terminated. Of course, if one of the exceptions to the nemo dat principle applies (see Ch.5 above), then the creditor will lose his rights over the goods and the innocent purchaser will acquire good title. From the creditor's point of view the important thing about hire purchase is that one exception in particular does not apply, i.e. the exception in s.9 of the Factors Act and s.25 of the Sale of Goods Act—because the debtor is not a "buyer" in possession.

The general rule then is in favour of the creditor rather than the innocent purchaser. The rule is the same if, instead of selling the goods, the debtor pledges them with a pawnbroker. The pawnbroker is in the same position as the innocent purchaser.

The general rule is very hard on the innocent third party and has been reversed where the subject-matter of the hire-purchase agreement is a motor vehicle which the debtor sells to an innocent private purchaser. In this case the innocent private purchaser acquires good title to the vehicle by virtue of the Hire Purchase Act 1964 Pt III.[48]

24-032 In a case where none of the exceptions to the nemo dat principle applies, the creditor may nevertheless not discover that the debtor has disposed of the goods and may therefore do nothing to recover them. If the debtor continues to pay his instalments, eventually completes his payments and exercises his option to purchase, that will operate to feed the title down to the person who acquired the goods from the debtor.[49] If this happens, it follows that, since the creditor under the hire-purchase agreement is no longer the owner, he has no right to the goods.

Even where the creditor under the hire-purchase agreement is still the owner, as in *Helby v Matthews*,[50] it does not follow that he will actually recover possession of the goods. If the third party refuses to hand them over, the creditor can bring a court action, i.e. a claim for conversion. The refusal of the creditor's demand to hand them over is a conversion. However, the court will not order the goods to be returned but will award damages to the creditor. Now, the damages will not necessarily be the full value of the goods at the date of conversion. The debtor has already paid some sums to the creditor (i.e. the initial deposit and perhaps some

47 [1895] A.C. 471, see Ch.12, above.

48 See Ch.5, above.

49 *Butterworth v Kingsway Motors*, see para.7-009, above.

50 [1895] A.C. 471.

instalments). If the debtor had not disposed of the goods but had kept them he could have bought them by paying the outstanding balance of the hire-purchase price. Thus, all that the creditor has lost is that outstanding balance. It is that amount which will be awarded to him as damages against the third party.[51] To look at it another way, the debtor, by selling the goods to the third party (albeit wrongfully), has transferred to the third party his (the debtor's) rights—in particular his option to buy the goods for the outstanding balance of the hire-purchase price. The Torts (Interference with Goods) Act 1977 allows the creditor, if he wishes, to choose a different judgment in place of an award of damages—namely a judgment giving the third party (the innocent purchaser) an option either to pay damages (assessed as just explained) or to return the goods. If the third party opts to return the goods then the debtor is entitled to receive from the creditor a financial allowance, i.e. a sum equal to the amount by which the value of the goods exceeds the alternative damages awarded.

There is an important qualification to the rule in *Wickham Holdings v Brooke House Motors*.[52] It is that the creditor cannot recover from the third party any more than the value of the goods at the date of conversion: *Chubb Cash Ltd v John Crilley & Son*.[53] It can happen, for example, that at the date when the third party refuses the creditor's demand to hand over the goods, their value is less than the outstanding balance of the hire-purchase price. The amount recoverable by the creditor from the third party is the smaller of the two following amounts: (i) the outstanding balance owing under the hire-purchase agreement; or (ii) the value of the goods at the date of conversion, i.e. the date the third party refused the creditor's demand to hand them over.

It should be added that an innocent purchaser who is liable in conversion to the creditor will have an action against the debtor, from whom he bought the goods, for breach of the condition as to title in s.12 of the Sale of Goods Act.[54] 24-033

Suppose that the innocent purchaser to whom the debtor sold the goods has himself resold them to a sub-purchaser. In that case the creditor may be able to bring a claim against the sub-purchaser. He will be able to do so provided, again, that none of the exceptions to the nemo dat principle applies. The creditor's claim against the sub-purchaser will be on exactly the same basis as that (just explained) against the innocent purchaser who has not disposed of the goods. It is a claim in conversion. Now suppose that such a claim is impossible because one of the exceptions to the nemo dat principle does apply. This might occur where a motor vehicle is involved. Thus, a debtor who has a car on hire-purchase terms might sell the car to a car dealer who in turn sells it to an innocent sub-purchaser. Here the innocent sub-purchaser obtains good title by virtue of the Hire Purchase Act 1964 Pt III.[55] The Act does not however, protect the car dealer. Thus the creditor has the possibility of a claim against the debtor or against the car dealer, the latter claim being a claim for damages for conversion. If the sale by

51 See *Wickham Holdings v Brooke House Motors* [1967] 1 All E.R. 117.

52 [1967] 1 All E.R. 117.

53 [1983] 1 W.L.R. 599.

54 See para.7-008, above.

55 See para.5-030, above.

the car dealer was a sale at a car auction, the creditor also has a claim against the auctioneers for conversion. All of this is because selling someone else's goods without authority amounts to conversion. The owner (the creditor) can succeed in a claim for conversion provided that he was either in possession of the goods at the time of conversion (unlikely) or else had a right, at the time of conversion, to immediate possession (more likely).

Union Transport Finance v British Car Auctions[56] arose out of facts which occurred before the Consumer Credit Act 1974 was passed. A hire-purchase agreement required the debtor not to remove or alter the identification marks on the car and not, without the creditor's permission, to sell it or offer it for sale. The agreement also provided that, if the debtor made any default in his monthly rentals or committed any other breach, the creditor had the right to terminate the agreement by serving a default notice on the debtor. Before completing his payments under the agreement, the debtor altered the car's registration number and without authority took it to a car auction where it was sold. Subsequently the creditor learnt what had happened and brought a claim for conversion against the auctioneers. The auctioneers, in defending the action, asserted that at the time of the conversion (the auction sale) the creditor did not have a right to immediate possession because the creditor had not at that time served a default notice upon the debtor. The defence failed. It was held that the terms of the agreement allowing the creditor to terminate the agreement by serving a default notice on the debtor, conferred rights on the creditor additional to his rights at common law. The latter included the right to terminate the hire-purchase agreement without notice if the debtor did any act wholly repugnant to the agreement. When the debtor put the car into the auction the creditor therefore had the right to immediate possession, i.e. the right to terminate the agreement without notice. If the facts of this case were to occur again after the coming into force of s.87 of the Consumer Credit Act, the result might well be different. Section 87[57] applies to any breach by the debtor and requires the creditor to serve a default notice giving at least 14 days' notice before he can be entitled to terminate the agreement or recover possession of the goods. It thus prevents the creditor having a right to immediate possession unless and until a default notice has been served and has expired.

Debtor Creates a Lien

24–034 At common law a repairer to whom goods are entrusted for repair has a lien over them for his charges. The lien is the right to retain possession of the goods until his charges are paid. A lien does not arise where maintenance alone is involved but only where the work is to improve the goods. Now, it is not uncommon for a debtor to have the goods repaired. This may happen if it is a car that has been in an accident. If the debtor has it repaired and later the hire-purchase contract is terminated, the repairer's lien takes priority over the creditor's right to recover possession. This means that the creditor is not entitled to possession without first paying the

56 [1978] 2 All E.R. 385.

57 See para.23-011, above.

repair bill. This is because the essence of hire purchase is that the debtor shall have the use and enjoyment of the goods and therefore is authorised to have them repaired if need be. It therefore makes no difference that the repairer knows that his customer is hiring the goods on hire purchase, for the repairer is entitled to assume that the debtor is authorised to have them repaired. This is still so, even if the hire-purchase agreement expressly states that the debtor is not authorised to create a lien. In *Albemarle Supply Co v Hind*[58] the subject-matter of the hire-purchase agreement was a taxi cab. In the agreement the debtor agreed not to create a lien for repairs. The garage where he took the cab for repair knew that he was hiring it on hire-purchase terms but was unaware of the restriction on the debtor creating liens. The Court of Appeal held that the lien was good even against the creditor. The decision would of course have been different if the garage had known of the restriction in the agreement. In that case the creditor would have been entitled to the taxi free of the lien, i.e. without having to pay off the repair charges.

Another situation where the creditor is entitled to recover the car free of lien is where the debtor deposits it for repair after the hire-purchase agreement has been terminated. This was the position in *Bowmakers v Wycombe Motors*[59] where, since the hire-purchase agreement had been terminated, the debtor had no more authority to use the car or to have it repaired. The garage therefore could not establish a lien against the creditor and this was so even though the garage was unaware that the car was or had been the subject of a hire-purchase agreement. In this case the garage had to surrender the goods to their owner (the creditor) but could of course still sue its customer (the debtor) for the repair charges.

Suppose that at the time the debtor deposits goods for repair, he is in possession of those goods under a time order. Section 130 expressly provides that in such circumstances the debtor "shall be treated as a bailee of the goods under the terms of the agreement, notwithstanding that the agreement has terminated". The position where the debtor deposits the goods for repair after a time order has been made is exactly the same as where he does so during the currency of the agreement before a time order is made.

Debtor Goes Bankrupt

As a general rule when someone goes bankrupt all his property passes to his trustee in bankruptcy whose task it is to collect in all the bankrupt's assets and use them to pay off the creditors. This does not, however, affect goods which do not belong to the bankrupt, such as goods he is hiring on hire-purchase terms. 24-035

58 [1928] 1 K.B. 307.
59 [1946] K.B. 505.

Sheriff Levies Execution on the Debtor

24-036 When a defendant has a judgment entered against him by a court, the claimant can enforce that judgment by having the enforcement officer execute it for him. The enforcement officer is entitled to enter the defendant's premises and seize his goods so that he can sell them and use the proceeds to pay the amount of the judgment. The risk is that he seizes goods which the defendant is hiring on hire-purchase terms. If he does so unknowingly and sells them, the owner (i.e. the creditor) thereupon loses all rights in the goods and the purchaser acquires good title. However, if the creditor becomes aware of the fact that his goods have been seized, then he can recover possession of them at any time before the enforcement officer disposes of them. If it is too late and they have been sold, he is entitled to the proceeds of sale.

25

Termination of Credit Sale, Conditional Sale and Consumer Hire Agreements

Credit Sale Agreements

Under a credit sale agreement property passes to the buyer before he has paid the instalments of the price. If he sells the goods, the person buying them from him will acquire good title. The buyer is free to sell the goods at any time. Some credit sale agreements provide that if he does so, the full outstanding balance of the purchase price shall immediately become payable. This means that the seller can commence proceedings against him immediately for the whole outstanding balance. However, if the agreement is a regulated agreement within the Consumer Credit Act, the creditor (i.e. the seller) will first have to serve a default or non-default notice and the court will also have power to make a time order under s.129, i.e. to allow the debtor (i.e. the buyer) to pay the sum off in instalments. 25-001

A credit sale agreement may provide that the whole outstanding balance of the price shall become payable on certain specified breaches by the buyer (e.g. if his payments get more than a certain time in arrears). Here again if the agreement is a regulated agreement within the Consumer Credit Act, then the creditor could not sue for that sum until he had first served on the debtor a default notice. Again, the court would have the power to make a time order.

A credit sale agreement does not give the seller the right to recover possession of the goods on default by the buyer. It will not give the buyer a right to terminate it prematurely and s.100 of the Consumer Credit Act does not apply; so the buyer has no statutory right of termination (other than, in the case of a regulated agreement, to pay off his debt early—s.94). Thus the question of "protected goods" does not arise and the protected goods provisions do not apply to credit sale agreements. From a finance company's point of view, a credit sale agreement is a device for the company to give what in effect is an unsecured loan for the purchase of particular goods.

Conditional Sale Agreements

25–002 A distinction must be drawn between conditional sale agreements which are regulated agreements within the Consumer Credit Act and those which are not. Where the debtor is a company, the agreement will, for example, not be regulated.

Agreements that are not Regulated Agreements

25–003 Under these agreements property does not pass to the buyer until the stipulated conditions are fulfilled (i.e. usually not until he has paid all the instalments). However, the essence of a contract of sale is that the buyer either buys or commits himself to buying, i.e. to acquiring property in the goods. Therefore, as with a credit sale agreement, a conditional sale agreement will not give the buyer a right of premature termination of the agreement. It may, however, give the seller a right to recover possession of the goods and to retain ownership in the event of the buyer's default, death, bankruptcy, etc. If it does, then the common law rules relating to penalties and damages will apply.

If the buyer disposes of the goods before property has passed to him, he may nevertheless confer good title upon the person who buys them from him. Any of the exceptions to the nemo dat principle might apply.[1] In particular, the exception in ss.9 of the Factors Act and 25 of the Sale of Goods Act might apply.[2]

Regulated Agreements

25–004 The scheme of the Consumer Credit Act is to make regulated conditional sale agreements the same in effect as regulated hire-purchase agreements. Thus the provisions of the Act apply to regulated conditional sale agreements as they do to regulated hire-purchase agreements. That includes not only the provisions of the Act that apply to regulated agreements generally but also certain provisions which apply only to hire-purchase and conditional sale agreements. It follows that the following provisions are amongst those that apply to regulated conditional sale agreements:

(a) The "protected goods" provisions—ss.90 and 91.

(b) The provisions requiring service of default notice or non-default notice—ss.87, 76 and 98.

1 See Ch.5, above.

2 *Lee v Butler* [1893] 2 Q.B. 318.

(c) The provision preventing termination upon death of the debtor—s.86.

(d) The provision empowering the court to make a time order—s.129.

(e) The provision empowering the court to modify the agreement or to make a return order or a transfer order—s.133.

(f) The provisions giving a statutory right of termination to the debtor and stating the amount payable by the debtor in that event—ss.99 and 100.

The last of these is important because it makes the agreement different in kind from what it is in theory. The agreement involves a commitment by the debtor (the buyer) that he will pay all the instalments and thereby become the owner of the goods. Otherwise it would not be a contract of "sale" at all.[3] The reality is that s.99 gives him (as it does to a debtor under a regulated hire-purchase agreement) a statutory right to terminate the agreement prematurely. As we have seen, this is a right to get out of the agreement without buying the goods which will have to be returned to the creditor.

We come now to the situation where the debtor (the buyer) has disposed of the goods to an innocent third party. The problem arises as to who has the better right—is it the third party or is it the creditor (the seller) under the conditional sale agreement? Remember, the creditor is, until property passes to the debtor, the owner of the goods. Here again, statute makes a conditional sale agreement which is a consumer credit agreement the same, in effect, as a hire-purchase agreement. Thus, for example, s.25(2) of the Sale of Goods Act provide that, for the purpose of s.25 of the Sale of Goods Act, a buyer under a conditional sale agreement which is a consumer credit agreement shall be deemed not to be a person who has bought or agreed to buy goods. Thus someone to whom the buyer sells the goods will not acquire good title under s.25. It should be noted that in the case of a motor vehicle, a "private purchaser" could acquire good title under Pt III of the Hire Purchase Act 1964 which applies to a purchase from the debtor under a conditional sale agreement as it does to one from the debtor under a hire-purchase agreement.[4]

Consumer Hire Agreements

A consumer hire agreement is in one essential respect different from a hire-purchase, conditional sale or credit sale agreement. The difference is that it is not contemplated that the customer (the hirer) will ever buy the goods. 25-005

3 See Ch.1, above.

4 See Ch.5, above.

As in the case of a hire-purchase agreement, termination of a consumer hire agreement can occur in a number of ways—mutual agreement, on breach of the agreement by the hirer, on some other stipulated event, or on the hirer exercising a right of termination. Nothing more needs to be said on termination by mutual agreement. After considering the other terminating events in the order just given, consideration will be given to the owner's right to recover possession of the goods and to other rights arising on termination.

Breach by the Hirer

25-006 As with a hire-purchase agreement here there are three types of breach by the hirer, any of which may entitle the owner to terminate the agreement:

(i) A repudiatory breach, e.g. a failure (not mere delay) to make payments over such a period that it seems clear that he is not going to keep the agreement.

(ii) A breach stipulated in the agreement as giving the owner a right of termination, e.g. the hirer becoming more than 10 days late in making any payment.

(iii) A breach of a condition (as opposed to a warranty) of the contract, e.g. late payment when the contract states punctual payment to be the essence of the contract.

Section 87 applies whenever the owner is entitled to terminate the agreement by reason of the hirer's breach, i.e. it applies to regulated consumer hire agreements just as it does to other regulated agreements. Thus the owner cannot terminate the agreement, cannot recover possession of the goods and cannot enforce any security without first serving a default notice. As with other regulated agreements the serving of the default notice enables the customer to rectify his default within the period of notice and it also enables him to apply for a time order. The court's power to make a time order is restricted to payments that have already fallen due. Thus it cannot alter the future payment pattern and can give the hirer extra time only in respect of payments already due. The court has no power to extend the period during which the hirer is entitled under the terms of the agreement to remain in possession of the goods.[5] It has that power in respect of hire-purchase and conditional sale agreements; for it can make a return order and suspend the operation of the return order for so long as the time order is complied with. Section 135(3), however, prevents the court from doing this in order to extend the period during which the hirer is entitled to possession of the goods under the terms of a consumer hire agreement.

5 s.135(3).

Other Stipulated Events

The agreement may state that, upon the occurrence of any one of certain stipulated events, the owner can terminate the agreement (or, alternatively that the agreement will terminate automatically). Where the stipulated event is a breach of the agreement by the hirer then s.87, which has just been mentioned, applies. We are now dealing with the situation where the stipulated event is something other than a breach by the hirer, e.g. his death, his being sentenced to prison or committing an act of bankruptcy, etc. 25-007

Section 86 applies to regulated consumer hire agreements as it does to other regulated agreements, with the result that the death of the hirer under an agreement of specified duration will seldom entitle the owner to terminate the agreement against the wishes of the debtor's personal representatives.

Also, ss.76 and 98 apply in the same way as they do in relation to other regulated agreements. Thus the owner will not be able to treat an agreement of specified duration as terminated upon any stipulated event without first serving a non-default notice upon the hirer. The hirer will then be entitled to ask the court for a time order.

Exercise by the Hirer of a Right of Termination

Section 101 gives the hirer under certain regulated consumer hire agreements a right of termination, provided he gives due written notice. Section 101 does not entitle him to terminate the agreement before it has run for 18 months and the hirer must give a minimum period of notice. That minimum period is the lesser of: 25-008

(i) three months, and

(ii) the shortest interval between the due dates of the hirer's payments under the agreement.

Thus if the agreement provides for the hirer to pay rent monthly, then one month's notice is sufficient. The notice can be given to any person entitled or authorised to receive payments under the agreement. Therefore all the hirer need do is to hand the notice to the person to whom he pays his rent.

The agreement can improve the hirer's rights given to him by s.101 but it cannot diminish them.[6] It might improve them, by, for example, allowing him to give a shorter period of notice or allowing him to terminate the agreement before 18 months has expired.

6 s.173.

Certain agreements are excluded from the application of s.101. They are:[7]

(i) Any agreement under which the hirer's payments are to exceed £1,500 per year.

(ii) Certain agreements involving specialised goods required by the hirer for business purposes.

(iii) Any agreement where the hirer requires the goods so that he in turn can in the course of his business let them out to someone else.

(iv) Agreements, if any, excluded by the FCA from the application of s.101.

Recovery of the Goods by Owner from Hirer

25–009 The owner under a regulated agreement will not be entitled to enter any premises to take possession of the goods unless at the time he obtains the permission of the occupier to do so. This is because s.92 applies to regulated consumer hire agreements as it does to hire-purchase and conditional sale agreements. Apart from that, however, the owner does have the right, after termination of the agreement, to recover possession of the goods. He has this right as soon as he is entitled to treat the agreement as terminated, i.e. when the default notice expires. This right is enforceable in the courts or the owner can alternatively enforce it by seizing physical possession. The latter alternative will seldom be very practicable without the hirer's consent, because of the restriction on entering premises imposed by s.92.

Financial Relief for the Hirer

25–010 Where the owner recovers possession of the goods (whether by court action or otherwise) the court can grant the hirer financial relief if it appears just to do so—s.132. The financial relief can take either or both of two forms:

(i) An order that any payment still due from the hirer shall be reduced by an amount stated by the court (even, if the court so decides, reduced to nothing).

(ii) An order that the whole or any part of any sum already paid by the hirer shall be repaid.

7 See s.101(7), s.101(8) and s.101(8A).

The purpose of s.132 is no doubt to enable the court to ensure that when the agreement is terminated the hirer does not end up having to pay or having paid an amount which is equivalent to rent for a much longer period than the agreement actually lasted. Thus when deciding if and how to exercise its powers under s.132, the court must have regard to "the extent of the enjoyment of the goods by the hirer".

Hirer Wrongfully Disposes of the Goods

If the hirer sells the goods then the owner will have a right to recover possession from the purchaser unless the latter acquired them under an exception to the nemo dat principle. It will not be very likely, however, that the hirer will sell under any such exception. In particular the hirer is not a buyer in possession and (even if the goods are a motor vehicle) the Hire-Purchase Act 1964 will not apply.[8] 25-011

8 For other possible exceptions to the *nemo dat* principle, see Ch.5, above.

Part III

Agency

26

The Law of Agency

Introduction

The role and importance of agency in commercial law has already been considered in Ch.1. What follows in this chapter is an introduction to the law of agency and an analysis of the two models of understanding the creation and operation of agency law: consent and authority. This chapter also introduces the various types of authority which will be explored in the following chapters and are fundamental to the law of agency. Those types of authority are: express actual authority; implied actual authority; usual authority; and apparent authority. 26–001

Definition

Agency is a relationship between one person, the principal, and another, the agent, under which the agent will fulfil the intentions of the principal and act on his behalf generally through the creation, modification or termination of contracts with a third party. This relationship is, as a general rule, created through the consent of both agent and principal whereby the agent is granted the authority (power) to fulfil his principal's instructions. In *UBS AG (London Branch) v Kommunale Wasserwerke Leipzig GmbH*[1] the Court of Appeal observed that the usual characteristics of a common law agency agreement were that the agent: i) has authority to affect the principal's legal relationship with third parties; ii) owes a fiduciary duty to the principal; and iii) 26–002

1 [2017] EWCA Civ 1567.

is subject to a degree of control by the principal. Whilst the Court recognised the possibility of exceptional cases, the absence of these characteristics would be "a significant pointer away from the characterisation of a particular relationship as one of agency".[2] The relationship may, however, be created through express or implied agreement.[3] Moreover, the courts may find that the parties have entered into an agency relationship without even realising it.[4]

Clearly therefore, the law of agency involves three possible relationships. First, there is the internal relationship between the principal and the agent. Secondly, there is the external relationship between the agent and the third party. Thirdly, there is the (possible) relationship between the principal and the third party. The law treats these relationships separately and so each has its own legal rules, traditionally imposed by the common law.[5] These relationships are important in defining the authority of the agent to act on behalf of his principal.

Authority

26-003 Clearly crucial to the law of agency is the concept of authority. Authority in this sense refers to the scope of the agent's ability to affect the legal position of the principal. In many situations the agent's authority may be defined in very narrow terms and specific instructions given, e.g. "sell my Vauxhall car for no less than £10,000". This instruction is the express actual authority granted by the principal (the car's owner) to the agent. This type of actual authority is reinforced by a second type of actual authority, that of implied actual authority. Implied actual authority gives the agent the ability to do whatever associated tasks are necessary to ensure that the instructions of his principal are met. So, in the example given above, it would be reasonable for the agent to show the car to prospective buyers. Equally, it may well be necessary to demonstrate the car to them, i.e. take them on a test drive. These activities are not expressly permitted under the principal's instructions and so would not fall within the express actual authority of the agent. They would, however, fall under the remit of implied actual authority since both are tasks reasonably connected to, and necessary for, the fulfilment of the principal's instructions.

There are two further categories of authority which should be mentioned at this point. First, there is the concept of usual authority. This means that an agent will be deemed to have the authority that an agent in his position would normally have. So, for example, a store manager will have the usual authority, amongst other things, to hire staff to work in the store

2 [2017] EWCA Civ 1567 at [91].

3 See, for example, *Dinglis Management Ltd v Dinglis Properties Ltd* [2019] EWCA Civ 127.

4 In so far as the parties may not recognise that their relationship is recognised as one of agency. The parties must still, of course, have established that relationship: *London Borough of Haringey v Ahmed* [2017] EWCA Civ 1861.

5 See also, however, the Commercial Agents Regulations considered in Ch.31.

and to purchase stock to sell in the store. Even if the agreement between the principal and the agent does not expressly authorise such actions, the principal will be bound where the court is satisfied that they fell within the usual (or customary) authority of the agent concerned. There is, of course, a clear overlap between usual authority and implied actual authority which will be explored in the next chapter.

Secondly, there is the concept of apparent authority. Apparent authority may at first glance seem very similar to usual authority. It is, however, very different. By virtue of this concept, an agent who acts outside his actual authority will still be able to bind his principal where the principal has made a representation to the third party that the agent is acting within his authority. In such a situation the court is able to use estoppel to bind the principal to the actions of the agent even where the agent knew that he was acting outside his authority.

Consent

The consent model of agency law dictates that the crucial element in the relationship is the voluntary grant of authority from the principal to agent and the voluntary acceptance of such authority by the agent.[6] This fits fairly neatly into a contractual analysis of agency law and as such describes the majority of agency relationships and the concept of authority which underlines them. The difficulty here, however, as will be seen in detail in the following chapter, is that it does not adequately describe every situation where the courts may find an agency relationship to exist. Broadly speaking there are two methods of creating an agency relationship which in turn give rise to two broad categories of authority: those with consent and those without. The consent model describes those agency relationships created by agreement and explains the nature of actual authority (both express and implied). The consent model fails, however, when it comes to the non-consensual methods of creating an agency relationship and the nature of the agent's authority in such relationships. As will be seen, the courts can find that an agency relationship has been created through necessity. Consider the following example: a courier of valuable goods encounters difficulty en route to his destination. Here, the agency relationship between the courier and his employer will be created by agreement and the authority of the agent defined by that agreement. What if however, the goods are in danger of being destroyed by virtue of the courier having encountered difficulties? There will be no agreement between the courier and the owner of the goods as to what actions the agent may take in that scenario. Therefore, a consensual agency relationship will not have been created. Despite this, the courts have been able to find that the courier is an agent of necessity for the owner of the goods and 26-004

6 *Garnac Grain Co Inc v HMF Faure & Fairclough* [1968] AC 1130 at 1137 per Lord Pearson.

that consequently the owner would be liable to reimburse the agent's costs associated with the necessary emergency action.

A second illustration of the shortcomings of the consent model of agency is found in what is referred to as "apparent authority". It has been noted above that where a principal makes a representation to the third party that the agent has authority to do a particular act, the principal will be bound by that act. This does not fit with the consensual model of agency law at all, since here the authority (and even the existence of an agency relationship in the first place) is determined by the relationship between the principal and the third party rather than the relationship between principal and agent.

Certainly neither the concept of consent nor that of authority provides an entire description of the agency relationship suitable for every situation. However, both concepts play an important role in the agency relationship and both add to an understanding of such relationships and the rights and duties of all parties involved.

General Reading

I. Brown, "Authority and Necessity in the Law of Agency" (1992) 55 M.L.R. 414

I. Brown, "The significance of general and special authority in the development of the agent's external authority in English law" [2004] J.B.L. 391.

F.E. Dowrick, "The Relationship of Principal and Agent" (1954) 17 M.L.R. 24.

F.M.B. Reynolds, "Agency: Theory and Practice" (1978) 94 L.Q.R. 224.

27

The Creation of Agency

Introduction

This chapter examines the different ways in which the relationship of agent principal can be created. This is closely related to the issue of the authority of an agent since the manner in which the relationship is created will clearly impact upon the ability of the agent to act on behalf of his principal. As has already been mentioned there are various methods through which this relationship can be established but the central difference is that between creation with consent and creation where there is no consent. This distinction is important as it will affect the nature of agent's authority, i.e. the extent to which his acts will bind the principal. 27-001

Creation With Consent

Actual Authority

Certainly the most straightforward situation is that where the agency relationship is created by express agreement. In such a case, the agreement will, to some extent at least, dictate the scope of the agent's authority. This is called "actual authority": the agent can properly do anything detailed within the agreement. Whilst this agreement will commonly be a formal contract, there is no requirement under the common law for it necessarily to be so. Thus, a parent sending a child on an errand to the shops is forming an agency relationship even though there is obviously no contract. In that example, the extent of the child's authority as agent would 27-002 most likely be defined by the instructions given by the parent, e.g. "take this money and buy a loaf of bread".

The extent of an agent's actual authority depends on the proper construction of the terms of the agreement. Historically much argument turned on ambiguous instructions of the principal. The courts were generally prepared to find that the principal was bound by the acts of his agent where the agent had honestly interpreted those instructions in a manner not intended by the principal. In *Ireland v Livingston*[1] for example, the principal's instructions were ambiguous and capable of more than one interpretation. Since the agent acted reasonably and in good faith on one of the possible interpretations of the instructions, the principal was bound. This argument is now much less likely to find favour and it may well be that even in the case of ambiguous instructions, the principal will not be bound if the agent has the opportunity to confirm the meaning of the instructions with the principal before acting on his behalf. This is obviously much more likely in modern times given the ability of speedy, worldwide communications.[2] The nature of "actual authority" is neatly summed up by Diplock LJ in *Freeman & Lockyer (A Firm) v Buckhurst Park Properties (Mangal) Ltd* in the following terms:[3]

> **"An 'actual' authority is a legal relationship between principal and agent created by a consensual agreement to which they alone are parties. Its scope is to be ascertained by applying ordinary principles of construction of contracts, including any proper implications from the express words used, the usages of the trade, or the course of business between the parties."**

The words "including any proper implications" is a reference to the second category of authority, implied actual authority, and it is to this issue we shall now turn.

Implied Authority

27–003 In the same way that a contract can be created through implication, so too can an agency relationship. In such a situation the normal rules of contract law will apply. A clear (and important) illustration of both implied actual authority and also the creation of the agency relationship through implication is that of *Hely-Hutchinson v Brayhead Ltd*.[4] The chairman of a company, a Mr Richards, acted as managing director for the company and entered into various contracts on behalf of the company. The board of directors of the company were aware of Mr Richards acting as de facto managing director. One contract Mr Richards entered into on behalf of

1 (1872) L.R. 5 H.L. 395.
2 See, for example, the observations in *European Asian Bank A.G. v Punjab & Sind Bank (No. 2)* [1983] 1 W.L.R. 642 at 655 per Goff LJ.
3 [1964] 2 Q.B. 480 at 502.
4 [1968] 1 Q.B. 549.

the company was for the company to act as guarantor for various debts of a third party. The company sought to avoid honouring the guarantee arguing that Mr Richards had no authority to enter into the contract. The Court of Appeal held that the company was liable since Mr Richards had actual authority to enter into the guarantee implied from the conduct of the parties and the circumstances of the case. Lord Denning MR explains the matter thus:

"It is implied when it is inferred from the conduct of the parties and the circumstances of the case, such as when the board of directors appoint one of their number to be managing director. They thereby impliedly authorise him to do all such things as fall within the usual scope of that office."

This goes to the root of implied actual authority. Even where there is a formal contractual document detailing the scope and extent of the agent's authority, this will generally not be so detailed as to cover every possible situation the agent may face. The nature of implied actual authority is to confer upon the agent such authority as is necessary to comply with the instructions given by the principal.[5] One important point follows from this understanding. Implied actual authority cannot be employed contrary to the express actual authority granted by the principal. Thus even if the agent's actions are reasonably required by the principal's instructions, if the act is expressly prohibited within the express agreement between agent and principal, the notion of implied actual authority will not be applicable.

A second feature of implied actual authority also stems from the nature of this type of authority and that is that it cannot exist in isolation. Implied actual authority is an aid to allow the agent to fulfil the express instructions of his principal. It therefore requires there to be an express actual authority in the first place which is then supported by the secondary notion of implied actual authority. This feature was considered by the Court of Appeal in *The Choko Star*[6] where the issue arose as to whether a ship's master was able to make salvage contracts acting as agent for the cargo-owner. It was clear that the ship's master was, at all times, acting as agent for the ship owner and it was equally clear that he could also be the agent for the cargo-owner where the concept of agency of necessity applied. What was not clear, however, was whether the master had implied actual authority to act on behalf of the cargo-owner in salvaging the cargo in the absence of some compelling and immediate situation which invoked the rules of necessity.[7]

At first instance Sheen J held that the ship's master was bestowed with an authority to arrange for salvage of the cargo by implication by virtue of such an authority being implied into the contract of carriage, i.e. that the cargo-owners should reasonably expect that it may become necessary for the cargo to be salved at some point on the voyage, and that thus the ship's master should reasonably have the authority to enter into the necessary contracts in order to secure the salvage of the cargo. The Court of Appeal, however, disagreed and reversed the decision since there was no basis to establish a relationship of agent-principal between the ship's master and the cargo-owners. That being so, it was not possible to consider any implied

5 Traditionally known as "medium powers", see for example, *Howard v Baillie* (1876) 2 Hy Bl 618.

6 *Industrie Chimiche Italia Centrale and Cerealfin S.A. v Alexander G. Tsavliris & Sons Maritime Co, Panchristo Shipping Co S.A. and Bula Shipping Corporation* [1990] 1 Lloyd's Rep. 516.

7 Agency of necessity is deal with at paras 27-011, below.

actual authority of the ship's master since there was no agency relationship or authority by implication or otherwise. This decision would of course have been very different had the Court of Appeal been able to find that this was a situation where the ship's master was an involuntary agent of the cargo-owner as an agent of necessity.

Creation Without Consent

Apparent Authority

27-004 The first situation (termed apparent or ostensible authority) where an agency relationship can be formed despite there being no express agreement to that effect is that where estoppel is established. In short, this means that where an individual (the principal) leads a third party to believe that another person is acting as his agent, the courts can find that there is an agent-principal-third party relationship in effect and enforce the contract between the principal and third party accordingly.[8] It will be recognised immediately that the creation of agency through estoppel has certain distinct features which set it apart from agency created through agreement. First, it applies through the conduct of the principal towards the third party and is not defined by the conduct between the principal and his agent. This is unusual since it appears to run contrary to the general rationale behind agency relationships where the principal will generally have no interaction with the third party, since the agent will have been appointed to fulfil such duties. Secondly, estoppel in this context has two distinct abilities. It can be employed by the courts to discover the existence of an agency relationship. It can also be used, however, in order to expand on the nature of the agent's authority where, for example, the agent's actual authority does not extend to encompass the particular agreement with the third party.

In order for a third party to argue successfully that the principal is bound by the actions of his agent the following requirements must be satisfied:

1. There must be a representation by the principal to the third party that the agent has authority.
2. The third party must rely on the representation.
3. The third party must not be aware that the agent is acting without authority.

All of these requirements must be satisfied and each will now be considered in turn.

8 *ING Re (UK) Limited v R&V Versicherung AG* [2006] EWHC 1544 (Comm) at [99], per Toulson J.

Representation from the principal to the third party that the agent has authority

Since the nature of apparent authority is defined by the representation from principal to third party, the requirement for there to be a representation is obviously fundamental. The representation must be such that it indicates to the third party that the agent has authority to act on behalf of the principal. This will be satisfied in the simple case where the principal makes a specific representation to the third party. It will also be satisfied, however, where the principal places his agent in such a position that would usually carry certain powers and responsibilities.[9] Certainly the most straightforward situation is where the principal makes an express representation to the third party. It is clear, however, that a representation can be implied through, for example, the conduct of the principal or through the course of prior dealing between the principal and the third party. An example of the former situation is the case of *Freeman & Lockyer (A Firm) v Buckhurst Park Properties (Mangal) Ltd*[10] where Diplock LJ stated that:[11] 27-005

> **"The representation which creates 'apparent' authority may take a variety of forms of which the commonest is representation by conduct, that is, by permitting the agent to act in some way in the conduct of the principal's business with other persons. By so doing the principal represents to anyone who becomes aware that the agent is so acting that the agent has authority to enter on behalf of the principal into contracts with other persons of the kind which an agent so acting in the conduct of his principal's business has usually 'actual' authority to enter into".**

An example of the latter case is that of *Summers v Solomon*[12] where an agent had managed his principal's shop for a number of years. In the course of managing the shop, the agent did, on many occasions, buy goods on behalf of his principal from the third party for which the principal paid. The agent absconded, however, but still purchased goods purporting to do so on behalf of his (old) principal. After absconding, the agent was clearly not acting with any actual authority but the principal was liable on the contract since the previous course of dealing constituted a representation sufficient to clothe the agent with the necessary authority.[13]

9 As to the relationship between apparent authority and usual authority, see para.27-008, below.

10 [1964] 2 Q.B. 480.

11 [1964] 2 Q.B. 480 at 503–04.

12 (1857) 7 E & B 879.

13 For a more recent illustration of a course of conduct establishing apparent authority, see *Lovett v Carson Country Homes Ltd* [2009] EWHC 1143. For a modern example of apparent authority remaining effective beyond the termination of actual authority, see *Benourad v Compass Group Plc* [2010] EWHC 1882 at [113].

Reliance upon the representation

27–006 This requirement means that where the third party is unaware of the representation made by the principal the third party cannot seek to bind the principal into the contract through apparent authority. Similarly, the third party will not be able to demonstrate reliance where it can be shown that he knew the representation to be untrue. The position was clearly stated by Lord Scott in Criterion Properties Plc v Stratford UK Properties LLC.[14]

> **"Apparent authority can only be relied on by someone who does not know that the agent has no actual authority. And if a person dealing with an agent knows or has reason to believe that the contract or transaction is contrary to the commercial interests of the agent's principal, it is likely to be very difficult for the person to assert with any credibility that he believed the agent did have actual authority."**

It seems reasonably clear that the third party need not act upon the representation to his detriment. This is important since it allows for a claim by the third party against the principal where, for example, the third party did enter into a transaction but suffered no detriment. In *Arctic Shipping Co Ltd v Mobilia A.B., The Tatra*[15] Gatehouse J stated unequivocally "the only 'detriment' that has to be shown in such a case is the entering into the contract by the party relying on that authority".

Third party must be unaware of the agent's lack of authority

27–007 It is self-explanatory that where the third party is aware that the agent does not have the necessary authority to act on behalf of his principal, the third party cannot raise apparent authority to bind the principal. In many cases this is a natural consequence of the requirement of reliance previously discussed since, if a third party is aware of the lack of the agent's authority, he cannot rely on a representation to the contrary from the principal. This position can, however, be a little complicated. Thus, whilst it may not be possible to establish that a third party had actual knowledge of the agent's lack of authority to act, the third party may, nevertheless, be "put on notice" by the circumstances of the agent's act. In *Lloyds Bank Ltd v The Chartered Bank of India, Australia and China*[16] an employee of a bank was fraudulently drawing cheques on his principal's account and paying them into an account in his own name with the defendant bank. It was held that the defendant bank, the third party, was put on notice by the fraudulent cheques since, having regard to the position of the agent, the sums involved were large and

14 [2004] UKHL 28 at [31]. However, on the issue of inferring knowledge, see *Lexi Holdings (In Administration) v Pannone and Partners* [2009] EWHC 2590 (Ch).

15 [1990] 2 Lloyd's Rep. 51 at 59.

16 [1929] 1 K.B. 40.

also each of the fraudulent cheques was purported to have been signed by the same officer of the principal. This of course, will not protect the principal where the agent is sufficiently deceptive so as to make sure that every fraudulent transaction appears perfectly normal. The issue is not the fraud of the agent, but rather how the transaction appears to the third party. Thus, in *Quinn v CC Automotive Group Ltd t/a Carcraft*[17] where the third party was held to have an honest belief in the agent's authority and had not turned a blind eye to any suspicion of wrong-doing, Gross LJ suggested that the fact that the exercise of reasonable care would likely have resulted in the fraud being discovered was "neither here nor there".[18] In *Acute Property Developments Ltd v Apostolou* the position was summarised as follows:[19]

"in commercial dealings a person is normally entitled to rely on what he is told and should be protected if he does so honestly; not so if he in fact disbelieves it, or if he turns a blind eye notwithstanding suspicion, or if he acts recklessly. In such cases he will not have relied on the apparent authority."

The basis of the subjective honesty approach adopted in *Quinn* has been subject to doubt in *East Asia Co Ltd v PT Satria Tirtatama Energindo*[20] where the Privy Council suggested, obiter, that a third party would not be able to rely on apparent authority where he has failed to make the enquiries a reasonable person would have made in the circumstances notwithstanding their honest belief in the authority of the agent.[21] The dispute in *Satria* concerned a transfer of shares in a separate company, which represented the principal's sole asset, to a third party buyer. The Privy Council found that the agent did not have any apparent authority to make the transfer but nonetheless suggested that in the event the agent did, the third party would not have been able to rely on the agent's apparent authority. This was so since the third party had not made reasonable inquiries to ascertain the actual authority possessed by the agent in circumstances where the transaction appeared suspicious. In particular, it was clear that the agents purportedly authorising the sale stood to gain significantly from the transaction and the third party was aware (by virtue of earlier due diligence) that only the board of the company had authority to make the transfer. It remains to be seen whether future courts approach the question of reliance as one of subjective honesty or whether the reasonable reliance test will prevail, however, *Quinn* was followed recently in *Harbour Fund III LP v Kazakhstan Kagazy Plc*.[22]

17 [2010] EWCA Civ. 1412.

18 [2010] EWCA Civ. 1412 at [27].

19 [2013] EWHC 200 at [39]. In *Apostolou* there was no reliance on the representation due to the close personal relationship between third party and agent.

20 [2019] UKPC 30.

21 The Privy Council was critical of the earlier decision in *Thanakarn Kasikorn Thai Chamkat (Mahachno) v Akai Holdings Ltd (No 2)* [2010] HKCFA 63 where Lord Neuberger (sitting as a non-permanent judge of Hong Kong's Final Court of Appeal) suggested that a third party was, in the absence of irrationality or dishonesty, entitled to rely on an agent's representation.

22 [2021] EWHC 1228 (Comm).

Usual Authority

27–008 The nature of usual authority has been the subject of much debate in agency law. The debate focuses upon whether usual authority emanates from the other types of authority an agent may possess, particularly actual implied authority and apparent authority, or whether usual authority can exist in its own right as an independent category of authority.

What can be said with confidence is that usual authority is primarily a sub-division of actual, implied authority and it thus emanates from and enlarges the scope of the actual authority which exists between the agent and principal. In *Hely-Hutchinson v Brayhead Ltd*[23] Lord Denning MR said that when the Board of Directors appoints X as a Managing Director "they thereby impliedly authorise him to do all such things that fall within the usual scope of the Office".[24] It is clear therefore that where an agent belongs to a particular trade or profession he will have the usual authority to do whatever is necessary to fulfil his express authority as agent. This obviously depends upon the interpretation of what is "usual" for an agent belonging to the same business or profession as the agent in question. It is also possible for trade usage to give rise to usual authority whereby the agent will have the usual authority to act in accordance with the lawful usages of that place or trade. This is so even where the principal is unaware of the particular trade usage in question provided that the usage is reasonable. A trade usage will be regarded as reasonable where it is not inconsistent with the principal's express instructions (i.e. the agent's actual, express, authority). This is exemplified by *Robinson v Mollett*[25] where an agent was appointed to buy tallow (processed animal fat) on behalf his principal, a tallow merchant in Liverpool. The agent bought the tallow in his own name and allocated the agreed quantities amongst his multiple principals. Upon discovering that the agent had purchased the tallow in his own name, the tallow merchant refused to take delivery of the goods. The agent sought to rely on the customary trade usage in the London tallow markets whereby agents would buy tallow in their own name. The House of Lords accepted that such a trade custom existed but their Lordships were not prepared to allow it to bind the principal since the nature of the custom was such as fundamentally to affect the relationship between the parties. By buying, and therefore selling in his own name, the agent was in a position of conflict between his position as agent (duty bound to achieve the best price possible for his principal) and as owner and seller of the tallow (whereby he would seek to obtain the highest price possible). This conflict resulted in the conclusion that the trade usage was not reasonable and therefore in order for it to be effective, the principal must be aware of it. Since he was not, the agent's action for damages failed.

Usual authority is also utilised in apparent authority when the principal's representation involves appointing the agent to a position which carries a usual authority. Thus, in *First Energy*

23 [1968] 1 Q.B. 549.

24 [1968] 1 Q.B. 549 at 583. In *Lexi Holdings (In Administration) v Pannone & Partners* [2009] EWHC 2590 (Ch), for example, it was held that it was within the usual authority of a managing director to give instructions to the company's solicitors as to the payment of money held on trust in its client account.

25 [1875] L.R. 7 H.L. 802.

(UK) Ltd v Hungarian International Bank Ltd[26] the Court of Appeal found that, a company, by appointing a man to the role of senior manager within the business as a bank, had given him a position which carried usual authority and consequently the company had clothed him with apparent authority. Steyn LJ suggested that:[27]

> **"It seems to me that the law recognises that in modern commerce an agent who has no apparent authority to conclude a particular transaction may sometimes be clothed with apparent authority to make representations of fact".**

This is an example of the situation Lord Keith referred to in *Armagas Ltd v Mundogas S.A. (The Ocean Frost)*[28] as where "the ostensible authority is general in character, arising when the principal has placed the agent in a position which in the outside world is generally regarded as carrying authority to enter into transactions of the kind in question".[29] Whilst the principal has made no representation to the third party that the agent has the authority to perform the specific act carried out, appointing the agent to a role which would usually carry the authority to conduct the transaction in question will be sufficient to bind the principal through recourse to apparent authority.

A further illustration of this aspect of usual authority in the context of apparent authority is to be found in *Panorama Developments (Guildford) Ltd v Fidelis Furnishing Fabrics Ltd*[30] where a company secretary hired cars purporting to do so on behalf of the company. In fact, however, the secretary was hiring the cars for his own purposes. When the car hire charges were not paid, the third party (i.e. the car hire company) sued the company, which denied liability. The Court of Appeal held that a company secretary had the usual authority to enter into contracts in respect of the administrative operation of the company and that by appointing a person to such a position, the company had clothed the agent with apparent authority to enter into such contracts. Consequently, the company was bound by the contracts made by the secretary.

The final issue to consider in relation to usual authority is also the most controversial: is there an independent category of usual authority? Put another way, can an agent 27–009
bind his principal to a contract where the act is outside both express and implied actual authority (for example, where the act is specifically prohibited by the agency agreement) and the principal has not held out the agent to have the authority to act and so apparent authority

26 [1993] 2 Lloyd's Rep. 194.

27 [1993] 2 Lloyd's Rep. 194 at 204.

28 [1986] A.C. 717 at 777.

29 For a similar example, see *Kelly v Fraser* [2012] UKPC 25 where the Privy Council determined that an agent appointed to the role of Vice President of the Employee Benefits Division had, by virtue of his position, apparent authority to communicate that a transfer of sums into a pension fund had been approved.

30 [1971] 2 Q.B. 711.

is not applicable? The decision of the court in *Watteau v Fenwick*[31] answers these questions in the affirmative.

The facts of the case are deceptively straightforward. The owner of a beerhouse sold it to a firm of brewers who retained the former owner as the manager of the business. The licence was always taken out in the manager's name, and it was his name that was painted over the door. Under the agreement made between the manager and the brewers, the manager had no authority to buy any goods for the business except bottled ales and mineral waters. All other goods required by the business were to be supplied by the brewers themselves. Despite the terms of the agreement, the manager entered into contracts with a third party to supply the beerhouse with, amongst other things, cigars and Bovril. Upon discovering that the manager was not the owner of the business, the third party sued the brewers for payment under the supply contracts in respect of the cigars and Bovril.

The court held that the principal was liable under the contracts made by their agent even though (i) they were of a type expressly prohibited in the agreement between the parties, and (ii) since the principal was undisclosed there was no apparent authority extended to the agent. Wills J stated that:[32]

> **". . .the principal is liable for all the acts of the agent which are within the authority usually confided to an agent of that character, notwithstanding limitations, as between the principal and the agent, put upon that authority. It is said that it is only so where there has been a holding out of authority—which cannot be said of a case where the person supplying the goods knew nothing of the existence of a principal. But I do not think so".**

27–010 Wills J was very much influenced by the fact that in Watteau the principal was undisclosed. Had the principal have been disclosed, the standard ambit of usual authority previously considered would have applied, and the principal would have been liable on the contracts made by his agent. In order to prevent a "secret limitation" on the liability of all undisclosed principals Wills J was happy to extend the application of usual authority. This is justifiable on the grounds of public policy but has been strongly criticised in subsequent cases and has been followed only once.[33] In *Rhodian River Shipping Co S.A. and Rhodian Sailor Shipping Co S.A. v Halla Maritime Corporation*[34] Bingham J described Watteau as "a somewhat puzzling case" and went on to state that "I would myself be extremely wary of applying this doctrine, if it exists".[35]

31 [1893] 1 Q.B. 346.
32 [1893] 1 Q.B. 346 at 348–49.
33 In *Kinahan & Co Ltd v Parry* [1910] 2 K.B. 389.
34 [1984] 1 Lloyd's Rep. 373.
35 [1984] 1 Lloyd's Rep. 373 at 379.

It seems likely, therefore, that Watteau will not be followed in the future and that its application will be narrowly construed. Nevertheless, at present, it remains a possibility that an agent could bind his principal despite there being no authority whether actual or apparent.

Necessity

In certain strictly controlled circumstances the law will impose an agency relationship or, where such a relationship already exists, extend an agent's authority to act by virtue of an emergency. Thus, for example, where perishable goods are decomposing en route to their intended destination, it is accepted that a courier can, in certain circumstances, sell the goods on behalf of the principal even though he is not an agent of sale.[36] In *Springer v Great Western Railway Co*[37] a consignment of tomatoes was delayed in transit due, in part, to a strike by dock workers which meant that the tomatoes could not be unloaded upon their arrival at the port. This delay meant that the tomatoes were starting to deteriorate and an "agent" sold the entire cargo and sought to rely on his position of agent of necessity in order to effect a sale before the goods became unmerchantable. The Court of Appeal held that whilst the doctrine of necessity could potentially apply to these facts, it did not in fact do so, since the "agent" had the opportunity to contact the owners of the various consignments of tomatoes and take instructions on how to proceed. Scrutton LJ said:[38] 27-011

> **"The defendants have sold somebody else's goods, and they have no right to do so unless they establish certain conditions. They are agents to carry, not to sell. To give them the right to sell, -circumstances must exist which put them in the position of agents of necessity for the owners to take that action which is necessary in the interests of the owners".**

Since the "agent" could have contacted the owners but failed to do so, he was not an agent of necessity. This will clearly be an important restriction on agency of necessity in modern times since the nature of speedy and effective communications in the 21st century will allow for only a handful of situations where the agent cannot contact the owner of the goods to take instructions on how to proceed.[39] Nevertheless, this case illustrates the sort of situation where a court may be prepared to find agency of necessity.

36 For example, a cargo of grain which was fermenting in *Couturier v Hastie* (1856) 8 Exch. 40.

37 [1921] 1 K.B. 257.

38 [1921] 1 K.B. 257 at 267.

39 It seems that even where the owner can be contacted, but is not in fact giving any instructions to the agent, this will be sufficient to satisfy this requirement of agency of necessity. See *China-Pacific S.A. v Food Corporation of India, The Winson* [1982] A.C. 939.

Lord Diplock in *China-Pacific S.A. v Food Corporation of India, The Winson*[40] considered a two-fold division of agency of necessity:

(i) where an agent enters into a contract with a third party on behalf on the principal, consequently binding the principal contractually to the third party; and

(ii) where a person acts for another and subsequently seeks reimbursement or an indemnity from him.

Lord Diplock suggested that only in the first scenario would agency of necessity properly arise. The issue of reimbursement could be dealt with by reference to the terms of the nature of the agreement between the parties, e.g. bailor/bailee. Regardless, it seems clear that agency of necessity will be deemed to apply in both cases outlined above.

One further point must be made in respect of agency of necessity. The agent must act bona fide in the best interests of the principal. This requirement is exemplified by the case of *Prager v Blatspiel, Stamp and Heacock, Ltd*[41] where hostilities prevented the sellers from delivering a consignment of furs to their buyer. The sellers resold the furs and argued that the condition of the goods was deteriorating and therefore they were agents of necessity in effecting a resale of the goods. McCardie J held that (i) there was no commercial necessity to sell the furs since the deterioration was only slight and the increase in the value of the furs more than compensated for this slight deterioration, and (ii) the sellers had been dishonest in selling the furs and since they were motivated by the increase in their value, they were not acting bona fide in the best interests of their buyer in effecting a resale. Consequently, whilst agency of necessity could have arisen, on the facts it did not.

Ratification

27–012 Normally, an agent's authority is given to him before he acts for the principal. With ratification the position is reversed and the principal agrees to ratify the agent's conduct subsequently. It is, therefore, equivalent to antecedent authority.[42] It follows that the decision whether or not to ratify the agent's conduct is one taken by the principal unilaterally and there is no requirement

40 [1982] A.C. 939.
41 [1924] 1 K.B. 566.
42 See, for example, the analysis of Lord Sterndale MR in *Koenigsblatt v Sweet* [1923] 2 Ch 314 at 325.

to communicate ratification to either the agent or the third party.[43] The concept was explained in the following terms by Lord Macnaghten in Keighley, *Maxsted & Co v Durant*:[44]

> **"And so by a wholesome and convenient fiction, a person ratifying the act of another, who, without authority, has made a contract openly and avowedly on his behalf, is deemed to be, though in fact he was not, a party to the contract."**

In order to ratify, the principal must have full knowledge of the material circumstances in which the unauthorised act was done.[45] In *De Bussche v Alt* Thesiger LJ said that:[46]

> **"before the principal can properly be said to have ratified or adopted the act of his agent or waived his right of complaint in respect of such [unauthorised] acts, it should be shown that he has had full knowledge of its nature and circumstances, in other words, that he has had presented to his mind proper materials on which to exercise his power of election".**

The question of what constitutes "full knowledge" is a highly fact sensitive matter, although in *ING Re (UK) Limited v R&V Versicherung AG*[47] Toulson J suggested that the principal must have knowledge of the "essentials of what happened as between the agent and the third party".

Given the inroad the concept of ratification (what Lord Macnaghten rightly regards as a convenient fiction) could have on the doctrine of privity of contract, it is not surprising that the courts have imposed fairly restrictive requirements which must all be satisfied in order for ratification to be effective. These requirements are as follows:

- The principal must be in existence at the time of the agent's act.
- The agent must profess to act as an agent for the principal.
- The principal must have the capacity to act as a principal at the time of the agent's act.
- The principal must have the capacity to act as a principal at the time of the ratification.

Each requirement will now be considered in turn.

---

43 *Harrisons & Crossfield Ltd v London & North Western Railway Co* [1917] 2 K.B. 755.
44 [1901] A.C. 240 at 247.
45 Or intended to ratify whatever the material facts, *Marsh v Joseph* [1897] 1 Ch 213.
46 (1878) 8 Ch D. 286 at 312.
47 [2006] EWHC 1544 (Comm) at [153].

The Principal Must be in Existence at the Time of the Agent's Act

27-013 This means that the principal must be a live human being or a juristic person at the date of the agent's act. Thus an agent cannot act for a non-existent principal even if he knows that the principal will subsequently come into existence and then will wish to ratify his conduct. The rule has caused difficulties where company promoters enter into contracts on behalf of companies which are in the process of formation but have not yet acquired legal status. Both the requirement and the problem it causes in the context of company promoters are evident in the case of *Kelner v Baxter*[48] where there was a contract of sale of some wine. The contract purported to be made on behalf of the Gravesend Royal Alexandra Hotel Company. The problem was that at the time of contracting the company did not exist. When the company had been incorporated, it attempted to ratify the contract of sale. The court held that the newly formed company could not ratify since it had not been in existence at the time the contract was made. The question of liability on the contract was considered by Erle CJ who stated that "as there was no company in existence at the time, the agreement would be wholly inoperative unless it were held to be binding on the defendants personally".[49]

The Agent Must Profess to Act as an Agent for the Principal

27-014 This requirement prevents, for example, a principal from ratifying a contract which his agent entered into in the agent's own name. This was precisely what happened in the leading case of *Keighley, Maxsted & Co v Durant*:[50] An agent was appointed to buy wheat at a specified price. When he could not find any wheat to buy at the specified price he entered into a contract to buy wheat at a higher price. The contract was made between the seller and the agent in his own name and did not refer to the principal whatsoever. The agent contacted his principal who confirmed that he was happy that the wheat was worth the higher price. When the agent failed to pay for the wheat and take delivery, the sellers claimed that the principal had ratified the contract and was therefore liable under it. The House of Lords, in reversing the decision of the Court of Appeal, unanimously held that ratification was impossible since the contract of sale made no mention of the fact that the agent was acting on behalf of another party. The contract was in the agent's name and thus no other party could be liable under it. Lord Macnaghten, on the question of whether ratification ought to be extended so as to cover such a situation, stated:

48 [1866] L.R. 2 C.P. 174.

49 See also Ch.30 on breach of warrant of authority.

50 [1901] A.C. 240 at 247.

> **"On principle I should say certainly not. It is, I think, a well-established principle in English law that civil obligations are not to be created by, or founded upon, undisclosed intentions."[51]**

The position is the same where the agent forges his principal's signature. In such a case the agent is holding himself out to be the principal and the act is incapable of being ratified by the principal. In *Brook v Hook*[52] an agent forged his principal's signature on a promissory note. The principal did not wish to see his agent prosecuted (since he was his brother-in-law) and agreed to honour the note. The court held that his attempt to ratify the act of his agent forging his signature was not effective since the act of forgery was illegal and the note void. Therefore, ratification was not possible and the principal was not liable to honour the promissory note. This decision can also be explained by the fact that the agent, in forging his principal's signature is not acting as agent but is purporting to act on his own behalf. This would therefore be incapable of ratification under the principle enunciated in *Keighley*.[53]

The case of *Watson v Swann*[54] makes it clear that whilst the principal need not be named by the agent during his business with the third party, it must be possible for the third party to ascertain the identity of the principal on whose behalf the agent is acting. Thus a general reference to the third party that the agent is acting as an agent will not suffice since it does not allow the third party to ascertain the identity of the person who is to be bound by the contract made by the agent. The ascertainment must be sufficient to identify the individual who can ratify the acts of the agent. If this is not possible, ratification is not possible. Therefore, in the case of an undisclosed principal, ratification is not possible.

The Principal Must Have the Capacity to Act at the Time of the Agent's Act

This requirement is well explained by the nature of ratification already considered. The fiction of ratification is that it artificially deems that the principal himself made the contract. In reality of course the position is that the principal is adopting the transaction. Nevertheless, it follows that if ratification is possible, the principal must have had the capacity actually to make the transaction at the time the agent entered into the transaction. A clear example of this requirement in operation is the decision of the court in *Boston Deep Sea Fishing and Ice Co Ltd v Farnham*[55] where it was held that ratification of acts by the French principal was not pos- 27-015

51 [1901] A.C. 240 at 247.
52 (1870–71) 6 Ex. 89.
53 [1901] A.C. 240 at 247.
54 (1862) 11 C.B. (N.S.) 756.
55 [1957] 1 W.L.R. 1051.

sible, since at the time of the acts, the principal was an alien enemy and therefore was "not a competent principal because it could not have done the act itself".[56]

The Principal Must Have the Capacity to Act at the Time of the Ratification

27–016 This requirement is best understood by reference to the reality of the situation where a principal seeks to ratify an unauthorised act made by his agent, i.e. that he adopts the transaction. Consequently, it follows that the principal must have the capacity to enter into the transaction at the time he wishes to ratify it. This rule was effective in *Grover & Grover Ltd v Mathews*[57] where an agent arranged for a factory to be insured without any authority to do so. Unfortunately the factory was destroyed by fire and the principal subsequently sought to ratify the transaction. The court held that ratification was not possible after the subject matter of the insurance policy had been destroyed. The principal would not have been able to make the contract of insurance after the factory had been destroyed and therefore he could not ratify the agent's unauthorised act.

This decision was based on the earlier case of *Bird v Brown*[58] where Rolfe B suggested that in order to ratify, the principal must lawfully be able to enter into the transaction which he seeks to ratify. This has been subject to criticism in recent times, particularly in *Presentaciones Musicales S.A. v Secunda*[59] where solicitors acting without authority issued a writ in April 1988 on behalf of a company in Panama. In May 1991 the company liquidators purported to ratify the solicitor's act (i.e. issuing the writ) but faced the problem that this "ratification" occurred after the expiry of the limitation period under the Limitation Act 1980. Roch LJ considered the principle of ratification and suggested that "the dictum cited from Bird v Brown is not a correct statement of the exceptions to the principles of ratification".[60] Roch LJ then went on to state that the correct view was that laid down by Cotton LJ in *Bolton Partners v Lambert*:[61]

> **"The rule as to ratification by a principal of acts done by an assumed agent is that the ratification is thrown back to the date of the act done, and that the agent is put in the same position as if he had had authority to do the act at the same time the act was done by him".**

Therefore, the Court of Appeal applied *Bolton Partners v Lambert* and held that the ratification was effective since the writ was in existence, i.e. it was not a nullity, and allowing

56 [1957] 1 W.L.R. 1051 at 1058.
57 [1910] 2 K.B. 401.
58 (1850) 4 Exch. 786.
59 [1994] Ch. 271.
60 [1994] Ch. 271 at 284.
61 (1889) 41 Ch D. 295 at 306–307.

ratification in such circumstances did not adversely affect any property rights accrued by the third party as a result of the unauthorised agent's acts. If this position is the law, then it is no longer a general requirement of ratification that the principal must have capacity at the time of ratification.

General Reading

I. Brown, "Authority and Necessity in the Law of Agency" (1992) 55 M.L.R. 414.

I. Brown, "Ratification, Retroactivity and Reasonableness" (1994) 110 L.Q.R. 531.

I. Brown, "The Agent's Apparent Authority: Paradigm or Paradox?" [1995] J.B.L. 360.

R. Munday, "Salvaging the Law of Agency" [1990] L.M.C.L.Q. 1.

J. Payne and D. Prentice, "Company Contracts and Vitiating Factors: Developments in the Law on Directors' Authority" [2005] L.M.C.L.Q 447.

F.M.B. Reynolds, "Authority, Ratification, Warrant of Authority" [2006] J.B.L. 537.

F.M.B. Reynolds, "The Ultimate Apparent Authority" (1994) 110 L.Q.R. 21.

A. Tettenborn, "Agents, Business Owners and Estoppel" (1988) 47 C.L.J. 274.

P. Watts, "Some Wear and Tear on Armagas v Mundogas: The Tension Between Having and Wanting in the Law of Agency" [2015] L.M.C.L.Q. 36.

28

The Duties of an Agent

Introduction

In this chapter we will look at the duties owed by an agent to his principal. This may appear, at first instance to be rather a straightforward investigation. Certainly, where there is an express contract between the parties, the duties of the agent will be defined, in no small measure, by that agreement and any terms which may be implied into it under the normal rules of contract law. Defining the duties of an agent is, however, in fact, somewhat more complicated than might have been expected since, the fact that the agency relationship can be created in numerous different ways, coupled with the consequence that the nature and extent of the authority vested in the agent will vary accordingly, dictates that the duties owed by one agent will not necessarily be the same as those owed by another. This is probably made most evident by a comparison of the duties owed by a contractual agent and those of a gratuitous agent. In both cases there is, as we have seen previously, a consensual undertaking of authority by the agent to act in accordance with the instructions of his principal. What if, for one reason or another, the agent refuses to perform his undertaking as dictated by the agency agreement? If the agent is a contractual agent, the position is straightforward and the principal will be able to pursue an action for breach of contract. In the case of the gratuitous agent, however, the agent would not be liable for failing to perform his agreed undertakings; since there is no consideration to bind the agent's promise, enforcement here is impossible. That is not to say, however, that a gratuitous agent owes no duties to his principal. As we shall see in addition to a non-contractual duty of care, a gratuitous agent can owe fiduciary duties towards his principal. These are obligations arising out of the voluntary undertaking of authority and power in respect of another person and will apply to both contractual and gratuitous agents. It must also be appreciated, however, that in addition to the nature of the agency created (and therefore the nature of authority granted to the agent) affecting the type of obligations the law will impose upon the agent, the specific requirements of such duties will require will vary from agent to agent. Thus, 28–001 for example, the contractual duty of reasonable care and the fiduciary duties owed by an agent to his principal are inherently variable.

Performance of Contractual Undertaking

28–002 As noted above, where there is an express contract the obligations between the agent and principal will be governed by that agreement. The duty of the agent in this regard is strict. So where the principal's instructions are clear and unequivocal, the agent is duty bound to comply with them precisely. Where an agent fails to comply with such instructions, he will be liable in damages. This rule is exemplified by the case of *Turpin v Bilton*[1] where an agent was instructed to insure a ship. The agent, however, failed to do so and as a result, when the ship was lost, the principal was unable to claim on the insurance. The agent was liable in damages for the value of the lost ship since he had not performed his contractual undertaking. A similar scenario arose in *Bertrom, Armstrong & Co v Godfray*[2] where an agent was instructed to sell certain shares when their value reached a precise amount. The agent was required to sell those shares as soon as the specified price was reached and had no discretion to wait in order that the share price might increase beyond the figure specified by the principal.

The obligation to comply with clear and unequivocal instructions is strict. Thus, an agent who disobeys such instructions will be liable even where not following instructions is a reasonable course of action.[3] Furthermore, it follows that where an agent complies with his principal's imprudent or commercially unwise instructions, he will not be liable for losses incurred as a result.[4] Similarly, an agent will not be liable for breach of duty where the principal's instructions would lead to an illegal or void act. In *Cohen v Kittell* the agent was instructed to place bets on various horses at Sandown Park and Newmarket races. When the agent failed to place the wagers as instructed, the principal sued for breach of duty, however, since those wagers were illegal the agent was not liable.

It is clear from the authorities, including *Turpin* and *Bertrom Armstrong*, that the agent's duty of performance extends both to cases of non-performance and also to those of mis-performance. It was seen in the introduction that a gratuitous agent will not be liable for non-performance since to hold otherwise would in effect find there to be a contract where there was none. The situation is different, however, where a gratuitous agent mis-performs under

1 [1843] 5 Man. & G. 455.
2 [1838] 1 Knapp 381.
3 *Fray v Voules* (1859) 1 E&E 839.
4 *Overend & Gurney Co v Gibb* (1871–72) L.R. 5 H.L. 480. The duty of reasonable skill and care may require, in particular, professional agents to advise their principal of the imprudence of the instructions. See further, para.28-005.

the agency agreement. This is exemplified by the facts and outcome of *Wilkinson v Coverdale*.[5] An agent agreed to arrange, without payment, for insurance on behalf of his principal. Due to the agent's negligence in effecting the insurance contract, the principal was unable to claim on the policy when his house was destroyed by fire. The court held that the agent was in breach of his tortious duty in performing on behalf of the principal. This decision raises a clear difficulty since we have already discussed the fact that a gratuitous agent cannot be liable for failing to perform his agreed function. The distinction, albeit a fine one, is said to be that where a gratuitous agent performs (to whatever degree) his functions under the agency agreement, he must carry them out without negligence in order to comply with his tortious duty. Where however, the same agent fails to act whatsoever under the agency agreement, he will not be in breach of his tortious duty. The distinction, therefore, is between misfeasance (performing poorly) and nonfeasance (doing nothing).

The issue of misfeasance by a gratuitous agent will also by definition raise questions over whether such an agent will face liability for breach of a tortious duty of care. This may be contrasted with the contractual (statutory) duty of skill and care which is discussed below. In *Chaudhry v Prabhakar*[6] the plaintiff asked a friend to find a car for her since she knew little about cars. The friend was neither a car trader nor a mechanic but did have some experience in buying and selling cars and had much more knowledge than the plaintiff. The principal stipulated that the car was not to have been in an accident. The friend found a car which he thought was suitable and although he noticed that the bonnet had been either repaired or replaced he did not ask the seller (a car dealer) whether it had been in an accident. After having the car recommended to her by her friend, the principal purchased the car only to discover a couple of months later that it had been in a major accident and had been sold to the car dealer as salvage. The plaintiff argued that (i) the car dealer was in breach of the implied term that the car was of merchantable quality under s.14 of the Sale of Goods Act 1979, and (ii) the agent had breached his duty of care by not taking steps to ensure that he found her a car which met her stipulation that it should not have been in an accident. At first instance, the court easily accepted the first argument. The court also held that agent did owe his principal a duty of care to inquire as to whether the car had been in an accident. The Court of Appeal upheld this decision. Stuart-Smith LJ stated that:[7] 28-003

> **"When considering the question of whether a duty of care arises, the relationship between the parties is material. If they are friends, the true view may be that the advice or representation is made upon a purely social occasion and the circumstances show that there has not been a voluntary assumption of responsibility."**

5 (1793) 1 Esp. 74.
6 [1989] 1 W.L.R. 29.
7 [1989] 1 W.L.R. 29 at 34.

The issue therefore, is how to determine whether or not the relationship in question was a "purely social occasion" or whether there was something more, i.e. a "voluntary assumption of responsibility". On this point Stuart-Smith LJ suggested that the relationship of agent and principal "is powerful evidence that the occasion is not a purely social one". This was further supported by the nature of the relationship between the parties, in particular, the fact that the principal clearly relied upon the agent's skill and judgment which was considerably greater than her own. Moreover, the agent knew that the principal was relying upon his recommendation and even told her that she did not need to have an inspection made of the car prior to buying it.

A related issue is the duty of the agent to perform his obligations personally, i.e. not to delegate. This duty is easily explained by an understanding of the nature of the agency relationship. Where a principal appoints an agent to act on his behalf, he grants that agent authority to stand in his place. It follows, therefore, that the identity of the agent will be very important to the principal and that the agent may not, without consent, hand over the authority vested in him to another person, a sub-agent, in order to fulfil his obligations under the agency agreement. This is referred to by the maxim "delegatus non potest delegare" which was explained by Thesiger LJ in *De Bussche v Alt*[8] as preventing two distinct situations:[9]

(i) the ability of an agent to appoint his own agent as principal; and

(ii) the ability of an agent to devolve his responsibilities to another.

This rule, however, has numerous exceptions. Thesiger LJ in *De Bussche* suggested that the ability of an agent to delegate may well be required due to the "exigencies of business". The Court of Appeal stated that this ability[10]:

> **". . .should be implied where, from the conduct of the parties to the original contract of agency, the usage of trade, or the nature of the particular business which is the subject of the agency, it may reasonably be presumed that the parties to the contract of agency originally intended that such authority should exist".**

28–004 More recently, the Court of Appeal in John McCann & *Co v Pow*[11] has repeated the general rule that an agent may not, without express or implied authority from his principal, delegate his performance under the agency agreement. Mr Pow wished to sell a flat he owned and appointed John McCann & Co as agents to effect such a sale. The agents sent the details of the flat on to a second firm of estate agents in order that both firms might both advertise the property. The second firm found a willing purchaser, Mr Rudd, and after private negotiations

8 (1878) 8 Ch D. 286.
9 (1878) 8 Ch D. 286 at 310.
10 (1878) 8 Ch D. 286 at 310.
11 [1974] 1 W.L.R. 1643.

between Rudd and Pow, the flat was sold. After the sale had been effected, John McCann & Co discovered that Mr Rudd had been introduced to the property through the second firm of estate agents. John McCann & Co claimed commission as agreed under the agency agreement on the basis that the second firm of agents were their sub-agents. The court rejected this claim and held that Mr Pow was not liable to pay commission since there was no express authority to delegate and no implied authority could be found to allow the agent to delegate performance. This latter point was explained thus:[12]

> **"The reason is because an estate agent holds a position of discretion and trust. Discretion in his conduct of negotiations. Trust in his handling of affairs. It is his duty, certainly in the case of a sole agent, to use his best endeavours to sell the property at an acceptable price to a purchaser who is satisfactory and who is ready and willing and able to purchase the property."**

Since these functions required "personal skill and competence" they could not be delegated without express agreement between agent and principal.

Where the functions entrusted to the sub-agent are merely 'ministerial', i.e. acts which could be done by any reasonably competent person, there are two possible views. First, they are sub-agents and are authorised since their role is, for example, purely administrative or clerical. The second view is that such activities are not examples of delegation at all. For example, in *Lord v Hall*[13] an agent gave her daughter the responsibility of endorsing a bill of exchange with the name of her principal. It was held that this was not properly regarded as an example of delegation, since the daughter acted not as a sub-agent, but as her mother's instrument in effecting her function under the agency agreement. In *John McCann & Co v Pow* the agents argued that the functions delegated to the second firm of estate agents were ministerial. This argument was rejected by the Court of Appeal, particularly since the "sub-agents" were able to draft particulars in respect of the property.

Reasonable Skill and Care

An agent owes his principal a duty to fulfil his contractual obligations with due skill and care. In *Keppel v Wheeler*,[14] for example, the Court of Appeal held that an estate agent was generally employed to effect the sale of the principal's property at the highest price achievable. 28–005

12 [1974] 1 W.L.R. 1643 at 1647, per Lord Denning MR.

13 (1848) 2 Car. & Kir. 698.

14 [1927] 1 K.B. 577.

Consequently, when a higher offer was received by the agents they were under a duty to inform the principal of the new offer even though they had already arranged a sale subject to contract on behalf of the principal. The Court of Appeal awarded damages equal to the amount of the difference between the offer accepted and the higher offer which was not brought to the attention of the vendor as principal. The decision of the Court of Appeal is useful in two other respects. First, the Court of Appeal was minded to accept the proposition that the agents had not wilfully breached their duties in respect of their principal, but rather had "misunderstood their position" in believing that they had fulfilled their responsibilities when an offer had been accepted subject to contract.[15] Secondly, the decision of the court also illustrates that an agent is not prevented from claiming his commission simply by virtue of a bona fide mistake which caused him to be liable in damages for a breach of duty.

The common law duty of an agent to perform his undertakings with reasonable skill and care has been reinforced by the Supply of Goods and Services Act 1982 s.13, which provides that:

> **"In a contract for the supply of a service where the supplier is acting in the course of a business, there is an implied term that the supplier will carry out the service with reasonable care and skill".**

Thus where an agent is acting in the course of a business,[16] he must fulfil his undertakings with reasonable skill and care. Obviously what standard must be satisfied in order to comply with this statutory requirement will vary from case to case and will be judged in the context of the particular type of undertaking carried out. An equivalent provision applies where Ch.4 of Pt 1 of the Consumer Rights Act 2015 applies.[17]

Fiduciary Duties

Definition and Application

28–006 The concept of "fiduciary" is notoriously difficult to define in precise terms.[18] Nevertheless, it is clear that the notion of a fiduciary relationship is an expansion of the law of trusts. Fiduciary

15 See, for example, the comments of Bankes LJ at 587.

16 Defined by s.18 of the Act.

17 CRA 2015 s.49(1) requires that: "Every contract to supply a service is to be treated as including a term that the trader must perform the service with reasonable care and skill." See further, para.8-009.

18 See, for example, the observations of A. Mason in "The Place of Equity and Equitable Remedies in the Contemporary Common Law World" (1994) 110 L.Q.R. 238 at 246. Thus, in general terms, the question of

obligations are imposed on the agent and principal relationship because the principal reposes confidence in the agent and trusts him to perform his undertaking with honesty and integrity. The position of an agent as a fiduciary is well understood through the Law Commission's attempt to define the relationship:[19]

> **"Broadly speaking, a fiduciary relationship is one in which a person undertakes to act on behalf or for the benefit of another, often as an intermediary with a discretion or power which affects the interests of the other who depends on the fiduciary for information and advice".**

Clearly, an agent is by definition a person who undertakes to act on behalf of another, his principal, and has been vested with authority or power to so act. This position is the same regardless of whether the agent is being paid. Fiduciary relations are thus "founded on the highest and truest principles of morality"[20] and require the agent to work altruistically, i.e. to do what is best for the principal and not what is in the agent's own best interests.

It is important to realise that the labelling of the agency relationship as one which is fiduciary in nature is of little assistance in defining the scope and application of any fiduciary duties which will be placed upon the agent. It merely acknowledges that such an inquiry must be undertaken.[21] This has received support from the judiciary. In particular, Lord Mustill, sitting on the Privy Council in *Re Goldcorp Exchange Ltd*[22] suggested that merely labelling a person as a fiduciary was meaningless. He continued to quote with approval the comments of Frankfurter J in *SEC v Chenery Corp*:[23]

> **"To say that a man is a fiduciary only begins analysis; it gives direction to further inquiry. To whom is he a fiduciary? What obligations does he owe as a fiduciary? In what respect has he failed to discharge these obligations? And what are the consequences of his deviation from duty?"**

---

whether a fiduciary relationship exists is highly fact sensitive. See, for example, the approach of Newey J in *Miller v Stonier* [2015] EWHC 2796 where fiduciary duties did not arise between partners in a joint venture. See also, *UBS AG (London Branch), UBS Global Asset Management (UK) Ltd v Kommunale Wasserwerke Leipzig GMBH* [2017] EWCA Civ 1567 at [91]–[92].

19 Law Commission Report, *Fiduciary Duties and Regulatory Rules* (Rep. No. 236 November 1995).

20 *Parker v McKenna* (1874) 10 Ch App 96 at 118.

21 See, for example, L.S. Sealy, "Fiduciary Relationships" [1962] C.L.J. 69 at 73. See the analysis of the Court of Appeal as to the dangers of over-defining the scope of fiduciary relationships in *Wood v Commercial First Business Ltd* [2021] EWCA Civ 471 at [45]–[50]. As to whether all agents are fiduciaries, see R. Flannigan, "Fiduciary Agency Denied" [2021] J.B.L. 50.

22 [1995] 1 A.C. 74.

23 (1943) 318 US 80 at 85–6.

Such an inquiry, moving away from a purely definitional investigation is certainly a more purposeful charge, and heeds the warning of Fletcher Moulton LJ against trusting to "verbal formulae".[24] Indeed Fletcher Moulton LJ summarises the situation well in suggesting that:[25]

> **"Thereupon in some minds there arises the idea that if there is any fiduciary relation whatever any of these types of interference is warranted by it. They conclude that every kind of fiduciary relation justifies every kind of interference. Of course that is absurd. The nature of fiduciary relation must be such that it justifies the interference".**

Such sentiments have received recent judicial approval, notably through Lord Browne-Wilkinson in *Henderson v Merrett Syndicates Ltd*,[26] who sought to emphasise the fluid nature of fiduciary duties, in observing that such a term was "dangerous", as it leads to the (mistaken) assumption that "all fiduciaries owe the same duties in all circumstances". His Lordship concluded by stating that "this is not the case".[27]

What follows in this chapter therefore is a loose categorisation of the fiduciary duties which may be owed by an agent to his principal.

Conflict of Interests

28–007 The general position was stated by Lord Cairns in *Parker v McKenna* that "No man can in this Court, acting as an agent, be allowed to put himself into a position in which his interest and his duty will be in conflict."[28] This is exemplified by the facts of *Armstrong v Jackson*[29] where an agent was instructed to purchase some shares on behalf of his principal. The agent already owned some shares of the company in question and instead of purchasing shares in the normal manner, he elected to sell the principal his own shares. The court held that the agent had placed himself in a position where his duty conflicted with his own interest. The conflict is self-evident since the best interests of the principal require the lowest purchase price possible. The best interests of the agent in selling his own shares, however, are to achieve the highest possible sale price. McCardie J suggested that:[30]

24 *Re Coomber, Coomber v Coomber* [1911] 1 Ch. 723 at 728.
25 [1911] 1 Ch. 723 at 729.
26 [1995] 2 A.C. 145.
27 [1995] 2 A.C. 145 at 206. See also, the observations of Ramsey J in *John Youngs Insurance Services Ltd v Aviva Insurance Service UK Ltd* [2011] EWHC 1515 (TCC) at [94].
28 (1874) L.R. 10 Ch. 96 at 118.
29 [1917] 2 K.B. 822.
30 [1917] 2 K.B. 822 at 824.

> **"The prohibition of the law is absolute. It will not allow an agent to place himself in a situation which, under ordinary circumstances, would tempt a man to do that which is not the best for his principal".**

It is irrelevant, therefore, whether the agent sells his shares at the proper market value. Furthermore, it is not necessary to consider whether the principal has suffered a loss through the agent's conflict of interest. The court set aside the transaction and required the agent to repay the payments made under the sale of the shares to his principal. A similar conflict of interest is evident on the facts of *Northampton Regional Livestock Centre Co Ltd v Cowling*[31] where an agent was instructed to assist with the sale of a plot of land. Under the agreement, commission was payable based on the purchase price of the plot. The agent, however, entered into a separate agreement with the purchaser of the land whereby he would act for the purchaser in return for a share of the profit made on any subsequent resale. This arrangement gave rise to a conflict of interest since the agent stood to personally gain from a reduction in the price paid to his principal for the land, as that lower price would bolster the profit margin on any subsequent sale and thereby increase the agent's profit under the separate agreement.

Where there is a conflict of duty the agent is obliged to make full disclosure of all material circumstances so that the principal with full knowledge can elect whether to consent to the agent's act. In *Fullwood v Hurley*[32] Scrutton LJ stated that:[33]

> **"No agent who has accepted an employment from one principal can in law accept an engagement inconsistent with his duty to the first principal from a second principal unless he makes the fullest disclosure to each principal of his interest, and obtains the consent of each principal to the double employment".**

Where an agent discovers that he has a conflict of interest he must take steps to inform his principal of the conflict so that either (i) the principal will appoint another agent, or (ii) will give his consent to the agent acting on his behalf despite the conflict. In *Clark Boyce v Mouat*[34] the plaintiff agreed to mortgage her house in order to secure a loan to her son. The difficulty was that the solicitor had agreed to act for both the son and the plaintiff. The Privy Council had to determine the situation of the solicitor in such a position where there was a clear conflict of interest. Lord Jauncey stated:[35]

31 [2015] EWCA Civ 651.
32 [1928] 1 K.B. 498.
33 [1928] 1 K.B. 498 at 502.
34 [1994] 1 A.C. 428.
35 [1994] 1 A.C. 428 at 435.

> **"There is no general rule of law to the effect that a solicitor should never act for both parties in a transaction where their interests may conflict. Rather it is the position that he may act provided that he has obtained the informed consent of both to his acting."**

Informed consent requires more than simply putting the other party on notice that there is a conflict of interest. According to Lord Jauncey it requires the agent to explain that the conflict may result in him being unable to disclose "to each party the full knowledge which he possesses as to the transaction or may be disabled from giving advice to one party which conflicts with the interests of the other".[36]

Secret Profits

28–008 A secret profit is any financial advantage the agent receives in the execution of the agency relationship which is over and above the amount to which the agent is lawfully entitled. The agent cannot obtain any such profit unless he makes full disclosure to the principal of all relevant facts and the principal consents to the agent retaining the profit.[37] It is well established that it is irrelevant whether the principal suffers any damage as a result of the agent's secret commission or indeed, whether the principal is in fact advantaged by the secret commission. In *Rhodes v Macalister* Bankes LJ said that:[38]

> **"There seems to be an idea prevalent that a person who is acting as agent or servant of another is committing no wrong to his employer in taking a secret commission or bribe from the other side, provided that in his opinion his employer or principal does not have to pay more than if the bribe were not given. There cannot be a greater misconception of what the law is or what the duty of a servant or agent towards his master in reference to such matters is. . ."**

Similarly, in *Murad v Al-Saraj*[39] Clarke LJ explained the position clearly in stating that liability accrued merely by the agent having made a profit without the informed consent of the principal. The fact that the principal makes a profit or avoids a loss that he would otherwise have sustained by the agent's activity is irrelevant. Thus, in *Imageview Management Ltd v Jack*[40] the

36 [1994] 1 A.C. 428 at 435.

37 The burden of proving that the principal has given informed consent falls on the agent, see, for example, *Keown v Nahoor* [2015] EWHC 3418 (Ch) which serves to highlight the importance of record-keeping as an agent.

38 (1923) 29 Comm. Cas. 19 at 20.

39 [2005] EWCA Civ. 959 at [129].

40 [2009] EWCA Civ. 63. See generally, L. Macgregor, "An Agent's Fiduciary duties: Modern Law Placed in Historical Context" [2010] *Edinburgh Law Review* 121.

Court of Appeal had little difficulty in finding the agent liable to account for both the secret profit and the commission already paid under the agency agreement where he, a football agent, had received a secret payment of £3000. Similarly, in *FHR European Ventures LLP v Mankarious*[41] an agent failed to disclose a conflict of interest when he acted on behalf of the principal to secure the purchase of a hotel. Unknown to the buyer the agent was also retained as an agent of the seller. Accordingly, the agent had to account for the secret profit, i.e. the commission he received from the seller, some €10 million. The requirement to account for the secret profit is a well established personal remedy of the principal. The greater significance of the *FHR European Ventures LLP* litigation lies in the clarity it has brought to the long-standing question of whether a proprietary remedy is available to the principal where the agent has received a benefit in breach of his fiduciary duty. In *FHR European Ventures LLP v Cedar Capital Partners LLC*[42] the Supreme Court held that all money and property constituting a bribe, secret commission, or derived from the bribe, will be held on constructive trust for the principal. Thus, the Supreme Court overruled the long-standing decision of the Court of Appeal in *Lister & Co v Stubbs*[43] and confirmed that in such cases, the principal had both a proprietary remedy and a personal remedy against the agent and could elect which of the two to pursue. Importantly, it settled the debate by overruling the Court of Appeal decision in *Sinclair Investments (UK) Ltd v Versailles Trade Finance Ltd (in Administration)*.[44] This case had suggested that only a personal remedy was available for bribes and that a constructive trust would arise only where the fiduciary was acting as an agent of the principal, expressly appointed (or perhaps impliedly appointed) for the purpose of acquiring the property concerned, or where the property acquired by the fiduciary is the proceeds of property (or an opportunity) already beneficially owned by the principal.

In *FHR European Ventures* Lord Neuberger expressly commented upon the public policy arguments underpinning the decision:[45]

> **"Secret commissions are. . .objectionable as they inevitably tend to undermine trust in the commercial world. . .[and] concern about bribery and corruption generally has never been greater than it is now. . .one would expect the law to be particularly stringent in relation to a claim against an agent who has received a bribe or secret commission".**

There are two conceivable situations where a secret profit may arise. First, a secret profit may arise without any active intervention or connivance by the third party. Secondly, a secret

41 [2011] EWHC 2308 (Ch).
42 [2014] UKSC 45.
43 (1890) 45 Ch D. 1.
44 [2011] EWCA Civ 347.
45 [2014] UKSC 45 at [42].

profit may arise with the connivance of the third party, e.g. where the third party bribes the agent.[46]

28–009 The constituents of a bribe were examined in *Industries and General Mortgage Co Ltd v Lewis*[47] as follows:[48]

- the person giving the bribe (third party) makes the payment to the agent;
- the third party makes the payment knowing that the agent acts in that capacity on behalf of a principal;
- the third party does not disclose to the principal that he has made payment to the agent; and
- it is not a prerequisite of the bribe that the principal should sustain any loss and the law will assume that the principal has suffered a loss.

This final point was reinforced in *Hovenden & Sons v Millhoff*[49] where Romer LJ said:[50]

> **"The Court will not enquire into the donor's motive in giving the bribe, nor allow evidence to be gone into as to a motive. . .the Court will presume in favour of the principal and against the [third party] and the agent bribed, . . . that the agent was influenced by the bribe; and this presumption is irrebuttable."**

In *Anangel Atlas Compania Naviera S.A. v Ishikawajima-Harima Heavy Industries Co Ltd*[51] Leggatt J accepted the proposition that the key factor in determining whether or not a payment made to the agent is a bribe was whether the making of such a payment gives rise to a conflict of interest. Leggatt J accepted the following formulation of Anglin J in *Barry v The Stoney Point Canning Co*:[52]

46 In addition to civil liability in respect of bribes, the criminal law on this matter has now been strengthened by the introduction of the Bribery Act 2010. The Act, which came into effect on 1 July 2011, criminalises, inter alia, the giving of a bribe (s.1) and the receiving of a bribe (s.2). See generally, G. Sullivan, "The Bribery Act 2010: Part 1: An Overview" [2011] Crim L.R. 87.

47 [1949] 2 All E.R. 573.

48 [1949] 2 All E.R. 573 at 575.

49 (1900) 83 LT 41.

50 (1900) 83 LT 41at 43.

51 [1990] 1 Lloyd's Rep. 167.

52 (1917) 55 S.C.R. 51 at 73.

> **"The fundamental principle in all these cases is that one contracting party shall not be allowed to put the agent of the other in a position which gives him an interest against his duty. The result to the agent's principal is the same whatever the motive which induced the other principal to promise the commission. The former is deprived of the services of an agent free from the bias of an influence conflicting with his duty, for which he had contracted and to which he was entitled."**

There is, therefore, a clear overlap between the agent's duty to avoid conflicts of interest and the duty not to make secret profits. This relationship was considered by the Court of Appeal in *Hurstanger Ltd v Wilson*[53] in the context of a commissioned credit broker. The defendants applied, through a broker, for a loan of £8000. The lender's standard form pre-contract documents informed the borrowers that a fee would be payable to the credit broker in certain circumstances. The question before the court was whether (i) this declaration negated the secrecy of the commission paid to the broker, and (ii) whether the declaration had resulted in the borrowers giving their informed consent to the conflict of interest. The conflict of interest here is straightforward. In acting on in the best interests of his principals, the broker must recommend the most suitable loan for his principals with no regard to whether the provider of that loan offers the most profitable rate of commission. The Court of Appeal held that whilst the declaration did negate secrecy, it did constitute a breach of the conflicts of interest rule since informed consent had not been obtained.[54] *Hurstanger* was recently applied in *McWilliam v Norton Finance (UK) Ltd*[55] where a credit broker had to account for commission received without the informed consent of the borrower. The Court of Appeal held that informed consent had not been obtained despite the fact that the contract stated that (i) the broker was providing information only (and not advice), and (ii) the credit broker was likely to receive commission for the sale. It would seem that in certain cases, particularly where the borrower has a history of financial difficulty, the need to gain informed consent could extend as far as requiring a statement of the amount which the broker may receive so as to make the potential conflict of interest clear.[56]

53 [2007] 1 W.L.R. 2351. For comment, see A.O. Makinwa,"Wilson v Hurstanger Ltd: secret commissions—extent of duty to disclose" (2007) 18 I.C.C.L.R. 365.

54 This outcome was no doubt influenced by the fact OFT guidance recommends a clear warning stating that the broker may not be in a position to give unbiased advice, see the comments of Tuckey LJ at 2365.

55 [2015] EWCA Civ 186.

56 It should be emphasised, however, that the Court of Appeal made it clear that the appeal was a "very unsuitable vehicle" for the resolution of broader issues applicable generally. See the comments of Tomlinson LJ at [9]. For an example of a situation where the broker need not disclose the precise amount of commission received from the third party, see *Medsted Associates Ltd v Canaccord Genuity Wealth (International) Ltd* [2019] EWCA Civ 83. In *Medsted* the court was influenced by the fact that the clients were wealthy, experienced investors who paid no fees to the broker. They would, therefore, be aware therefore that the broker would receive commission from the third party. In such circumstances, the failure to disclose the amount of commission received did not represent a breach of fiduciary duty.

In *Wood v Commercial First Business Ltd*[57] the Court of Appeal considered the distinction between fully secret commissions and those, such as in *Hurstanger* and *McWilliam*, which are half-secret. In *Wood* the borrowers applied, through a broker, for a mortgage. The borrowers paid a fee to the broker and were also informed that the broker might receive further fees from the lender: the broker's standard form documents said that where the broker received payments from the lender of less than £250 it would inform the borrower that a fee had been paid. On the other hand, where the payments exceeded £250 the documents said that the borrower would be informed of the precise amount paid. When significant fees were subsequently paid to the broker by the lender, those additional fees were fully secret, not half-secret, commissions. This was so since the borrower was entitled to assume that they would be informed of any subsequent payments in line with the terms in the standard form documents. It was argued by the lender that the disclosure of the possibility of commission was inconsistent with a fiduciary duty of loyalty. The Court of Appeal rejected this argument: the nature of the role played by the broker involved the exercise of judgement in selecting the most appropriate loan for the borrower. That required "an impartial and disinterested view" and the duty of loyalty applied.[58] Accordingly, the borrowers were entitled to rescind the loan agreements due to the secret profit made by the broker (subject to counter rescission).

Duty to Account

28-010 Where an agent receives payments intended for his principal he will be under various duties in respect of those payments. First, he is under a duty to keep such moneys separate from his own, unless the agency agreement provides that he may mix such funds with his own.

Secondly, the agent is under a duty to maintain accurate accounts of his transactions. He must also produce these accounts for his principal when he is requested to do so by the principal. It is now clear that the duty of an agent in this regard does not cease to exist by virtue of the termination of the agency agreement. In *Yasuda Fire & Marine Insurance Co of Europe Ltd v Orion Marine Insurance Underwriting Agency Ltd*[59] the agents refused to comply with requests to provide records held in respect of transactions entered into on behalf of the principal by the agents. Colman J was unimpressed by the arguments of counsel acting for the agents that since the agency relationship had been terminated, the duty to provide accounts had ceased to operate. He said:[60]

> **"Because the agent's duty to provide records of transactions to the principal is founded on the entitlement of the principal to the records**

57 [2021] EWCA Civ 471.

58 [2021] EWCA Civ 471 at [125]. In reaching this conclusion, the Court of Appeal held that *CFBL v Pickup and Vernon* [2017] CTLC 1 (no fiduciary relationship between borrower and broker) had been wrongly decided.

59 [1995] Q.B 174.

60 [1995] Q.B 174 at 185–186.

> **of what has been done in his name, termination of the agent's authority to enter into further transactions should have no bearing on the continuance of the duty to provide pre-existing records pertaining to the period when transactions were authorized".**

Colman J stated that a continuing right to inspect the agent's records could be excluded by the terms of the contract between the parties, but that on the facts of the case, this had not occurred. The agents were therefore under a continuing duty to allow the principal access to their records in respect of transactions conducted on behalf of the principal.

The need for such an obligation is easily understood by the nature of the relationship between agent and principal. For example, where the agent is instructed to enter into commercial contracts on behalf of his principal, the principal must be able to discover what contracts have been made in his name. In Yasuda the rationale was explained thus:[61]

> **"That obligation to provide an accurate account in the fullest sense arises by reason of the fact that the agent has been entrusted with the authority to bind the principal to transactions with third parties and the principal is entitled to know what his personal contractual rights and duties are in relation to those third parties as well as what he is entitled to receive by way of payment from the agent."**

If the agent fails to maintain proper accounts there is a presumption that any funds which the agent cannot prove are his own, will be deemed to belong to his principal.[62] This is an example of what Romilly MR *in Gray v Haig*[63] referred to as the court presuming everything unfavourable to the agent. This emphasises both the legal and practical significance of this obligation.

General Reading

A. Bowen, "Principals, Agents and Fiduciary Relationships" (2006) 83 Business Law Bulletin 6.
K. Brinkworth, "Gratuitous Agency: Liable or Not?" (1990) Bus. L.R. 111.
F.E. Dowrick, "The Relationship of Principal and Agent" (1954) 17 M.L.R. 24.
R. Flannigan, "The (Fiduciary) Duty of Fidelity" (2008) 124 L.Q.R. 274.

61 [1995] Q.B 174 at 185.
62 *Lupton v White* (1808) 15 Ves. 432.
63 (1854) 20 Beav. 219 at 226.

R. Flannigan, "Fiduciary Agency Denied" [2021] J.B.L. 50.

J. Getzler, "Inconsistent Fiduciary Duties and Implied Consent" (2006) 122 L.Q.R. 1.

J. Lowry and L. Sloszar, "Judicial Pragmatism: Directors' Duties and Post-Resignation Conflicts of Duty" [2008] J.B.L. 83.

G. Virgo, "Profits Obtained in Breach of Fiduciary Duty: Personal or Proprietary Claim?" [2011] C.L.J. 502.

D. Whayman, "Proprietary Remedy Confirmed for Bribes and Secret Commissions" (2014) 6 Conveyancer and Property Lawyer 518.

29

The Rights of an Agent Against His Principal

Introduction

This chapter explores the position of the agent as against his principal. The common law has traditionally taken the view that it is the principal who requires protection from his agent rather than the other way round. This had led to a situation where the rights of the agent as against his principal are somewhat sparse. Nevertheless, there are a handful of areas where the common law has imposed obligations upon a principal. In particular, this chapter will consider the agent's rights of remuneration and indemnification. Moreover, as has already been seen, statute law has recently been active in this area and there is now a general obligation on a principal to "act dutifully and in good faith" towards his commercial agent. The impact of the Commercial Agents (Council Directive) Regulations 1993 on this matter will be considered in Ch.31. What follows in this chapter is an assessment of the rights on an agent at common law rather than those of a commercial agent under the Commercial Agents (Council Directive) Regulations. 29-001

Right to Remuneration

At common law an agent has no automatic right to remuneration. This is so irrespective of whether the agency is contractual or non-contractual in nature. It is entirely possible for the parties to enter into a gratuitous agency relationship. At common law, therefore, the agent will have the right to remuneration only where there is an express or implied term to that effect in the agency contract.[1] The relationship between express and implied terms of contract in this 29-002

1 An agent may have a restitutionary right to reasonable remuneration on a quantum meruit basis. This could apply where, for example, both agent and principal anticipate that a contract would come into being but it

context is evident on examination of two leading cases: *Way v Latilla*[2] and *Kofi Sunkersette Obu Appellant v A. Strauss & Co.*[3] In *Latilla* the House of Lords held that although there was no express term as to the right to remuneration, since the agreement between the parties was one of employment with a clear understanding that the work was not to be gratuitous, their Lordships were able to imply a contractual right to a reasonable level of remuneration for the agent's services. The court will not imply any right to remuneration unless it is clear that this is what the parties intended, as it was in *Latilla*. Where the agreement is silent on remuneration, the "most usual inference in such a case is that nothing is to happen".[4]

In the *Kofi Sunkersette* case, however, there was an express term in the agency contract detailing the level of remuneration payable to the agent. There was also another term which stated that additional remuneration was available in the form of commission at the discretion of the principal. The Privy Council held that the agent was not entitled to any commission since this was clearly available at the discretion of the principal. It was therefore not open to them to impose a reasonable sum of commission payable to the agent since that would be taking a contractual discretion of the principal and placing it in the hands of the court.

The right or otherwise of an agent to commission has been a topic upon which there has been considerable judicial consideration. In this context a distinction must be drawn between a salary and a commission. Both are obviously forms of remuneration to which the agent might be entitled, however the distinction is that whereas the right to a salary stems from the contract of employment between agent and principal, the right to commission is not automatic. It is a payment due upon fulfillment of certain conditions. Consequently, it is necessary to interpret the agreement between the parties so as to ascertain what event triggers the right to the commission.

29–003 This rule is exemplified by the facts of *Toulmin v Millar*[5] where an agent was employed to find a tenant for a property owned by the principal. The agent found a tenant who went on to purchase the house. The agent claimed that he was entitled to commission as provided for in the agency agreement. The claim failed since he was employed to find his principal a tenant for the house. Since he had found a purchaser for the house, he was not entitled to any commission under the agency agreement.

More recently, in *Fairvale v Sabharwal*[6] an estate agency was instructed to enter a property for sale at public auction. The contract provided that commission would be payable if the

in fact does not do so, as was the case in *William Lacey (Hounslow) Ltd v Davis* [1957] 1 W.L.R. 932, and more recently, in *AMP Advisory and Management Partners A.G. v Force India Formula One Team Ltd (In Liquidation)* [2019] EWHC 2426 (Comm). It can also occur in situations where the contract is not binding, see *Craven-Ellis v Canons Ltd* [1936] 2 K.B. 403. In *Barton v Gwyn-Jones* [2019] EWCA Civ 1999 the Court of Appeal also permitted a quantum meruit claim by a contractual agent. The Supreme Court has recently clarified the process through which a quantum meruit claim is to be calculated, see *Benedetti v Sawiris* [2013] UKSC 50.

2 [1937] 3 All E.R. 759.

3 [1951] A.C. 243.

4 *Att-Gen of Belize v Belize Telecom Ltd* [2009] UKPC 10 at [17], per Lord Hoffman.

5 (1887) 12 App. Cas. 746.

6 [1992] 32 E.G. 51.

sale was effected within 28 days of the auction. Although the auction was unsuccessful since the reserve price was not reached, the agents introduced the seller to one of the unsuccessful bidders who then went on to purchase the property. The sale was effected more than 28 days after the conclusion of the auction. The Court of Appeal held that since the sale of the house fell outside of the terms of the agreement in respect of the payment of commission, the agents were not entitled to any commission.

In *Luxor (Eastbourne) Ltd v Cooper*[7] an agent was appointed to find a purchaser for a number of cinemas. Under the agreement a minimum sale price was agreed as was a commission of £10,000 due to the agent upon completion of the sale. Although the agent found suitable buyers at an acceptable price under the terms of the agency agreement, the principal company decided not to proceed with the sale. The agent, deprived of the substantial commission payment sued the company for the same amount as damages for breach of an implied term that the principal would not, without just cause, act as to prevent the respondent from earning his commission. Although this argument was accepted by the Court of Appeal it was unanimously rejected by the House of Lords who held that the agent's right to commission must be construed in accordance with the express terms of the contract of agency. On that basis, since the sale of cinemas had not been completed, no commission was due. Moreover, it was not possible to introduce the implied term not to deprive an agent of his commission "unless it is necessary to do so for the purpose of giving to the contract the business effect which both parties to it intended it should have".[8] On the facts of Luxor the House of Lords found that it was unnecessary to imply such a term to give commercial efficacy.

The payment of commission to estate agents is still a regular visitor to the courts today. 29-004
Two recent cases (amongst many) reinforce the point developed above that the entitlement or otherwise to commission is a matter of contractual interpretation. In *Your Move v Moore*[9] Moore wished to sell her house and entered into a sole agency agreement with Your Move estate agents. The agreement provided that the agent would be entitled to commission "if at any time unconditional contracts for the sale of the property are exchanged with a Person introduced". Your Move successfully found a buyer for the house and contracts of sale were exchanged between the prospective purchaser and Moore. Despite the exchange of contracts the parties never completed the sale. Your Move sued Moore for the commission due on exchange of contracts as dictated in the agency agreement. Moore, however, argued that since the agreement provided for payment in the event of completion, the agents were not entitled to any commission. The court found in favour of the agents and followed the principle of the House of Lords in Luxor. The agreement between the parties was clear that commission was due on successful exchange of contracts and the clause in the contract providing for payment in the event of completion was designed merely to give the principal more time to pay the commission fee.[10]

7 [1941] A.C. 108.
8 [1941] A.C. 108 at 120, per Viscount Simon LC.
9 [2002] C.L.Y. 68 (County Court).
10 In *Foxtons Ltd v O'Reardon* [2011] EWHC 2946 (QB) it was unsuccessfully argued that such a clause, without a term allowing for deferred payment in the event of completion not occurring, was not unfair under the Unfair

The issue of construction was also fundamental to the outcome in *Dashwood (formerly Kaye) v Fleurets Ltd*.[11] The owner of licensed premises entered into an agency agreement with an estate agent under which the agent had sole selling rights and was thereby entitled to commission where the property was purchased by anyone introduced during the agency agreement. This was so irrespective of whether the agents were the effective cause of the transaction. Since the agreement clearly entitled Fleurets to commission where they had introduced the prospective purchaser, it was not necessary to show that they had done anything else to effect the ultimate transaction and the agents were entitled to their commission. It is unclear, however, whether this reasoning is capable of surviving the recent decision of the Court of Appeal in *Foxtons Ltd v Bicknell*.[12] *Bicknell* involved a sole agency agreement under which commission would be payable on the exchange of contracts with a purchaser introduced by the agents during the period of their sole agency. The agents introduced a prospective purchaser who was looking for a property for his ex-wife. However, when the lady viewed the property she was not keen on it and dismissed it from her mind. She was subsequently re-introduced to the property by a different agent (the claimant's sole agency period had expired by this point) and proceeded to purchase it. At first instance, the court held that the claimants were entitled to their commission under the terms of the sole agency agreement since it was not necessary to show that their introduction had caused the sale. However, this was reversed by the Court of Appeal where Lord Neuberger gave the only judgment. Lord Neuberger stated that the word "purchaser" in the sole agency agreement could be interpreted in one of two ways. On the one hand, it could refer to a person who at some point in the future becomes a purchaser. Alternatively, it could mean a person who becomes a purchaser as a result of an introduction.[13] Lord Neuberger preferred the latter construction which required the agents to have introduced the person to the purchase rather than merely to the property. Since the agents could not prove that they had introduced the buyer to the purchase, their claim for remuneration failed.

Ultimately, the entitlement to commission will turn on the application of general principles to each specific situation and the words of Upjohn LJ in *Ackroyd & Sons v Hasan* are useful in this context:[14]

> **"When an agent claims commission from a principal, there are certain principles of law applicable which cannot be doubted. First, when an agent claims that he has earned the right to commission,**

Terms in Consumer Contracts Regulations 1999. The agent was therefore entitled to commission at the agreed rate.

11 [2007] EWHC 1610 (QB).

12 [2008] EWCA Civ. 419. See P.Watts, "Agents' Entitlements to Commission" [2009] J.B.L. 268 at 270.

13 [2008] EWCA Civ. 419 at [22].

14 [1960] 2 Q.B. 144 at 154. For recent examples of the difficulties which can arise in the context of the interpretation of contractual provisions regarding commission payments, see *Unite The Union v Liverpool Victoria Banking Services Ltd* [2015] EWCA Civ 285; *Winlink Marketing Ltd v Liverpool Football Club and Athletic Grounds Ltd* [2020] EWHC 2271 (Comm); and *EMFC Loan Syndications LLP v The Resort Group Plc* [2021] EWCA Civ 844.

> **the test is whether upon the proper interpretation of the contract between the principal and the agent the event has happened upon which commission is to be paid. Secondly, there are no special principles of construction applicable to commission contracts with estate agents. Thirdly, contracts under which a principal is bound to pay commission for an introduction which does not result in a sale must be expressed in clear language."**

Right to Indemnity

Under the common law a principal must indemnify his agent for losses and liabilities reasonably incurred through the execution of his obligations as agent. Where the agency is contractual, the contract itself will frequently provide for the reimbursement of expenses and indemnity against liabilities incurred by the agent. Where the contract is silent on the issue, an indemnity will be an implied term of the contract.[15] The general rule was stated by Lindley J in *Thacker v Hardy*[16] in the following terms:[17] 29–005

> **"Upon general principles an agent is entitled to indemnity from his principal against liabilities incurred by the agent in executing the orders of his principal, unless those orders are illegal, or unless the liabilities are incurred in respect of some illegal conduct of the agent himself, or by reason of his default."**

The duty to indemnify also exists in situations where the agent is liable in tort. Thus, in *Adamson v Jarvis*[18] where the principal instructed his agent, an auctioneer, to sell goods which he did not own, the principal was under a duty to indemnify the agent for the tortious damages incurred.

Lien

In order to ensure the principal's performance, of for example his obligation to pay commission or indemnity, the agent can, of course, commence an action against his principal for breach of contract. It may well be much more effective (and certainly less time consuming) for the 29–006

15 Where the agency is gratuitous, the indemnity will be restitutionary.
16 (1878–9) 4 Q.B.D. 685.
17 (1878–9) 4 Q.B.D. 685 at 687.
18 (1827) 4 Bing. 66.

agent to exercise his lien over his principal's property. This lien only exists in certain circumstances. First, it is only available where goods belonging to the principal are in the possession of the agent[19] and where those goods are those in relation to which money is owed: *Bock v Gorrissen*.[20] Secondly, the agent's right to lien does not apply where the existence of the lien would be inconsistent with the terms of the agency agreement. This explains the decision on this point in *Rolls Razor Ltd v Cox*[21] where the agent sought to exercise his lien over some of the principal's goods still in his possession after the agency agreement had been terminated. The court held that since there was a term of the agreement requiring the agent to return all property belonging to the principal upon termination of the agency relationship no lien could exist after the termination of the agreement since to find otherwise would run contrary to the terms of the agreement.

General Reading

J.W. Carter, "The Life of an Agent in Commerce is a Precarious One" (1982) 45 M.L.R. 220.
P. Jaffey, "Unjust Enrichment and Contract" (2014) 77 M.L.R. 983.
A. McGee, "Termination of a Commercial Agency—The Agent's Rights" [2011] J.B.L. 782.
P. Watts, "Agents' Entitlements to Commission" [2009] J.B.L. 268.
W. Day and G. Virgo, "Risks on the contract/unjust enrichment borderline" (2020) 136 L.Q.R. 349.

19 Actual or constructive possession will suffice, see *Bryans v Nix* (1839) 4 M & W 775.
20 (1861) 30 L.J. Ch. 39.
21 [1967] 1 Q.B. 552.

30

Contracts Made by Agents

Introduction

This chapter examines the respective relationships between the principal and the third party and between the agent and the third party. We have already looked at the nature of an agent's authority and this will generally explain both the relationship between agent and third party and also that between principal and third party. Thus, generally, where an agent acts within his authority, the principal will be bound to the contract made on his behalf by his agent. Whilst this does explain the normal position between principal and third party, it is not however the full story. There are occasions where, for example, the agent will be liable on the contract made with the third party. Similarly, there are occasions where both the principal and the agent are liable on the contract made with the third party. This chapter explores such issues and begins with the relationship between the principal and the third party. This will depend primarily on the manner in which the agent conducts his dealings with the third party: the agent may name his principal; he may disclose his status as agent (but not name his principal); or alternatively he may not disclose his status as an agent at all. 30-001

The Relationship Between Principal and Third Party

Disclosed principal

The law will generally treat the position of a named principal and that of an unnamed but disclosed principal in the same way.[1] They are both subject, therefore, to the general position 30-002

1 See, however, the comments of Lord Denning MR in *Teheran-Europe Co Ltd v S.T. Bolton (Tractors) Ltd* [1968] All E.R. 886 at 889 which appear to blur unnamed and undisclosed principals.

of disclosed principal, which is that the principal may sue (or be sued) on the contract made with the third party. This is so provided that either the contract is within the actual (express or implied) authority of the agent or, alternatively, where the contract is unauthorised, the principal elects to ratify it. This is a relatively straightforward rule whereby the agent effectively drops out of the arrangement, since his function is to effect legal relations between his principal and a third party. It has, however, an interesting consequence in relation to apparent authority. We have already seen that where apparent authority is created, the principal is bound by the acts of his agent and is estopped from denying the contract with the third party, i.e. the third party can enforce the contract against the principal. However, in order for the principal to enforce the contract against the third party, he must first ratify. If this is not possible for whatever reason, the principal will be unable to enforce the contract despite the fact that the third party may well be able to enforce the contract against him.

Where the agent discloses his agency there will be no privity of contract between himself and the third party. It follows, therefore, that the agent cannot be held liable on any contracts he makes on behalf of his principal, i.e. the third party cannot enforce the contract against the agent. This is so even where the agent in fact has no authority.[2] Where the agent is acting without authority he will, however, face liability for breach of warrant of authority.[3] Although this is the normal position, it has been qualified so that in certain circumstances the agent will face personal liability on the contract.[4]

Undisclosed principal

30–003 Where the agent does not disclose his status as agent, and the third party is thus unaware that he is dealing with an agent, it might be expected that the principal will not be liable on any contract made by his agent, nor be able to enforce such contracts. This would be a natural consequence of the doctrine of privity of contract. In fact, this is not so. An undisclosed principal can both enforce and be made liable on contracts made by his agent. It follows that the doctrine of the undisclosed principal is restricted to situations where there is actual authority. Plainly, an undisclosed principal cannot make any representation to the third party as to the authority of the agent since in so doing he would no longer be an undisclosed principal. The key facets of the doctrine of the undisclosed principal were summarised by Lord Lloyd in *Siu Yin Kwan v Eastern Insurance Co Ltd*:[5]

(i) An undisclosed principal may sue and be sued on a contract made by an agent on his behalf, acting within the scope of his actual authority.

2 *Lewis v Nicholson* (1852) Q.B. 503.

3 See para.30-011, below.

4 See para.30-008, below.

5 [1994] 2 A.C. 199 at 207.

(ii) In entering into the contract, the agent must intend to act to act on the principal's behalf.

(iii) The agent of the undisclosed principal may also sue and be sued on the contract.

(iv) Any defence which the third party may have against the agent is available against his principal.

(v) The terms of the contract may, expressly or by implication, exclude the principal's right to sue and his liability to be sued.

The fact that the doctrine of the undisclosed principal sits uneasily with the traditional rules of contractual privity was noted by Lord Lindley in *Keighley, Maxsted & Co v Durant*[6] where he said that:[7]

> **"as a contract is constituted by the concurrence of two or more persons and by their agreement to the same terms, there is an anomaly in holding one person bound to another of whom he knows nothing and with whom he did not, in fact, intend to contract."**

Whilst this anomaly (and the potential inroad into the doctrine of privity of contract) is clear, two points must be made. First, the doctrine of the undisclosed principal was well established at common law long before that of privity of contract. Secondly, there is strong justification for the doctrine on the basis of commercial efficacy since (i) it allows for the collection of payments due under contracts made between agent and third party where the agent was unable to collect and pass such payments on to his principal (e.g. due to insolvency),[8] and (ii) the identity of the principal (or even the fact that the agent is, in fact, acting on behalf of an undisclosed principal) will rarely be of importance to the third party in a commercial contract. This is recognised in contract law generally and has already been considered in Ch.21 where the issue of mistake as to the identity of the contracting parties was considered. However, there may well be cases where the identity of the agent is crucial to the third party in making the contract. This is most likely to be the case where the contract is one where a service is to be provided and that service depends upon the skills and personal attributes of the agent. Nevertheless, the courts have been faced with the difficult question of establishing when the identity of the agent is so

6 [1901] A.C. 240.

7 [1901] A.C. 240 at 261. In *Playboy Club London Ltd v Banca Nazionale del Lavoro SpA* [2018] UKSC 43 at Lord Sumption observed that the rule "that an undisclosed principal may declare himself and enter upon a contract is an anomalous legacy of eighteenth and nineteenth century jurisprudence, which survives in the modern law on account of its antiquity rather than its coherence" at [12].

8 This is the historical context from which the doctrine originated, see for example, *Burdett v Willett* (1708) 2 Vern. 638.

important that the third party would not have otherwise entered into the contract and where consequently the principal cannot enforce the contract.

In *Said v Butt*[9] an agent was instructed to obtain a ticket for an opening night performance at a theatre. The principal required the services of the agent since he knew that, due to his poor relationship with the third party who managed the theatre, he would be denied a ticket if he attempted to purchase one in his own name. The theatre, not realising that the agent was acting for an undisclosed principal sold the ticket which the principal then attempted to use on the opening night. On being recognised, however, he was refused admission. The principal sought to rely on the doctrine of undisclosed principal, i.e. that he could enforce the contract made between his agent and the third party. The court held that there was no contract between principal and third party since there had been an operative mistake, i.e. that the third party would never have sold a ticket to the principal had he been disclosed and identified. In arriving at this conclusion the court was persuaded by the fact that the ticket was for the opening night and that it was therefore a special occasion where the theatre would be more selective over admittance to the theatre.

30–004 This decision has attracted considerable criticism not least for the fact that it seems to misapply the fundamental doctrine of the undisclosed principal. In such a case the accepted view is that the contract is made between the agent and the third party (and that the undisclosed principal can intervene on that contract which is made on his behalf).[10] It is not correct to say that the principal must establish a contract between himself and the third party. The decision could well have been the same on the facts but it would have required the theatre to establish that the identity of the agent was such that they intended to sell him and only him the ticket in question. It is most unlikely that the theatre manager could have proved this, since the identity of the agent seems to have been irrelevant to his being sold a ticket. A true reflection of the facts seems to be that the theatre would have sold a ticket to anyone, except the undisclosed principal.

The question of whether identity of the agent was sufficiently crucial to the third party so as to prevent an undisclosed principal from enforcing a contract was more satisfactorily dealt with in the subsequent case of *Dyster v Randall & Sons*[11] where a principal instructed his agent to purchase some land on his behalf as undisclosed principal. As in *Said*, the principal knew that the third party would refuse to sell the land to him (or to his agent where his identity was disclosed). The agent did contract to purchase the land but before completion the third party discovered that the purchaser was in fact acting as agent for the undisclosed principal. Consequently, the third party cancelled the agreement at which point the principal sued for specific performance. The court held that the principal could enforce the contract and awarded specific performance since the contract between agent and third party was an ordinary commercial contract for the sale of land in which the identity of the buyer was unimportant. This is so where the agent does not misrepresent his position, for example, by telling the third party

9 [1920] 3 K.B. 497.

10 See, for example, *Welsh Development Agency v Export Finance Co Ltd* [1992] B.C.L.C. 148.

11 [1926] Ch. 932.

that he is not acting as agent for a principal whom the third party will not deal with. Thus in *Dyster* the court distinguished the earlier case of *Archer v Stone*[12] where such a representation was made. In that case, the court refused to grant specific performance since the third party had made it clear that they would not deal with the principal and the agent had lied about not acting for that principal during the course of the negotiations.

It is possible for the third party to protect himself in the situations above by introducing a term of the contract that precludes an undisclosed principal from intervening on the contract made between agent and third party.[13] Thus, if there is an express term to that effect, the doctrine of the undisclosed principal will not apply and the difficulties of establishing that the identity of the agent was sufficiently important so as to preclude the undisclosed principal from intervening on the contract will not arise. There is difficulty however, where there is no express term but only a term which suggests that the agent is in fact acting as principal. In *Fred Drughorn Ltd v Rederiaktiebolaget Transatlantic*[14] an agent hired a ship and signed the contract as "charterer". The third party argued that this meant that the agent was the charterer and that the contract could not therefore be enforced by the undisclosed principal. The House of Lords held that the term "charterer" did not preclude the doctrine of the undisclosed principal and that whether an agent could enter into a contract on behalf of an undisclosed principal was a matter of ordinary business sense. Viscount Haldane sought to emphasise the true nature of a charterparty agreement, i.e. a hiring of a vessel, and the meaning of the term "charterer", i.e. the individual seeking to hire the vessel. The term did not imply that the agent was in fact dealing as principal and was the only person with whom the contract could be made. Neither did the nature of a charterparty agreement result in any assertion being made as to title or ownership of the property. This was important since it allowed the House of Lords to distinguish the previous decision in *Humble v Hunter*[15] where an agent signed a charterparty agreement on behalf of his (undisclosed) principal but signed as "owner". In that case the court held that by signing as owner the agent was contracting as principal and for that reason the undisclosed principal could not enforce the contract against the third party.[16]

The approach of Viscount Haldane has been supported in recent decisions and it seems clear that the courts will make an assessment of the contractual intention in the light of pragmatic "business common-sense".[17] Thus, in *Siu Yin Kwan v Eastern Insurance Co Ltd*[18] the Privy

---

12 (1898) 78 L.T. 34.

13 See, for example, *Aspen Underwriting Ltd v. Credit Europe Bank NV* [2018] EWCA Civ 2590 at [47]. The Court of Appeal has recently considered the (unusual) issue of whether a contract precludes the intervention of a disclosed, but unnamed, principal. See, *Filatona Trading Ltd v Navigator Equities Ltd* [2020] EWCA Civ 109. The court held that the principal was, in the absence of clear and unambiguous words to the contrary, not precluded from enforcing the contract.

14 [1919] A.C. 203.

15 (1848) 12 Q.B. 310.

16 The same logic was applied in *Formby Bros v Formby* (1910) 102 L.T. 116 where the agent described himself as "proprietor" and thus asserted ownership.

17 [1919] A.C. 203 at 207.

18 [1994] 2 A.C. 199.

Council held that the insurance contract, properly constructed, did not prevent the doctrine of undisclosed principal from applying where the agent signed in his own name as the "insured". In giving effect to a pragmatic approach, the decision was in no small part based on the fact that the third party was indifferent as to the identity of the "insured" and that since there was no express term of the contract preventing the principal from intervening to enforce the contract, the doctrine of the undisclosed principal applied.[19]

Merger and election

30–005 As noted previously, where a third party contracts with an agent acting on behalf of an undisclosed principal the agent will be personally liable on the contract. Similarly, where an agent acts on behalf of a disclosed principal but does so in such a way so as to incur personal liability, it is clear that the third party will have two possibilities. First, he may seek to enforce the contract against the principal.[20] Secondly, he may elect to enforce the contract against the agent. Thus liability here is not joint and several but is alternative, i.e. the third party cannot pursue both agent and principal but must instead elect which party to sue.[21]

Third party's right to set-off[22]

30–006 There is a general rule that where an agent, acting on behalf of an undisclosed principal, concludes a contract with a third party and the principal subsequently intervenes on that contract, he does so subject to any defences and equities which would be available to the third party had the agent himself brought the action.[23]

Therefore, where the third party is sued by the principal he may avail himself of all defences, including set-offs, which he would have possessed against the agent. This is so provided that the third party's right of set-off against the agent existed prior to the third party having notice of the principal's existence.[24]

19 Similarly, see *Kaefer Aislamientos de CV v. AMS Drilling Mexico SA de CV* [2019] EWCA Civ 10 at [55].

20 See, for example, *Boyter v Thomson* [1995] 2 A.C. 628.

21 For criticism of this alternative liability in the case of agent and principal, see *Fowler (LC) & Sons v St Stephen's College Board of Governors* [1991] 3 N.Z.L.R. 304.

22 See generally, S.R. Derham, "Set-off and Agency" (1985) 44 C.L.J. 384.

23 *Browning v Provincial Insurance Co of Canada* (1873) L.R. 5 P.C. 263.

24 As to whether the principal's conduct must give rise to an estoppel, see the (much criticised) decision in *Cooke & Sons v Eshelby* (1887) 12 App. Cas. 271.

Settlement

On ordinary principles it would be expected that in the case of disclosed agencies, neither the principal nor the third party would be able to discharge their liabilities by settling with the agent. This is so since where the agency has been disclosed, the standard position is that the agent drops out of the relationship between the parties. Thus, where an agent has purchased goods on behalf of a disclosed principal, payments made by the principal to the agent will not normally discharge the obligation to pay for the goods. This rule is subject to a number of exceptions, for example, where the third party has led the principal to believe that his liability to the third party has been discharged by the agent. In such cases the third party will be estopped from denying that the principal's liability has been discharged.[25] Similarly, where an agent is authorised to receive payment on the principal's behalf the third party's liability to the disclosed principal will be discharged where he provides payment to the agent. Caution is required here, however, since it is not every agent that has the authority to accept payment on behalf of his principal even though, for example, that agent may have authority to sell goods.[26] Where the agent has no authority to accept payment on behalf of the principal, the third party will remain liable to the principal unless the principal ratifies the unauthorised act by, for example, accepting receipt of the payment made by the third party from the agent. 30-007

The position is different where the principal is undisclosed. Where a third party enters into a settlement with an agent acting for an undisclosed principal, that settlement will constitute a complete defence if the principal subsequently attempts to enforce the contract. This is justified on the basis that the undisclosed principal has allowed the agent to appear to the third party as the true principal. Therefore, provided the settlement is made before the third party becomes aware of the existence of the principal, that settlement is binding upon the principal.[27] It may be expected that in undisclosed agencies a principal will not be able to discharge his obligations through settlement with the agent since the third party will know nothing of the principal. In *Armstrong v Stokes*, however, the court held that the settlement made between agent and undisclosed principal discharged the principal's liability to the third party on the grounds that making the principal, in effect, pay twice for the same goods would lead to "intolerable hardship".[28] Hardship or not, it is, however, difficult to see the justification for imposing the burden in such cases on the third party and *Armstrong* was subsequently described as "a very remarkable case".[29] Indeed, Munday has stated that it is "improbable that *Armstrong v Stokes* would be followed today.[30]

25 *Wyatt v Marquis of Hertford* (1802) 3 Est 147.
26 *Butwick v Grant* [1924] 2 KB 483.
27 *Coates v Lewes* (1808) 1 Camp 444.
28 (1872) LR 7 QB 598 at 610.
29 *Irvine & Co v Watson & Sons* (1880) 5 QBD 414 at 417.
30 R. Munday, *Agency: Law and Principles* (Oxford: OUP, 2010), p.267.

The Relationship Between Agent and Third Party

Contractual liability

30–008 It has already been seen that where an agent, having disclosed his authority, effects a contract between a third party and his principal, the standard position is that the agent drops out of the relationship between the parties. Consequently such an agent will face no liability on that contract since it is one between the principal and the third party. This is exemplified by *Wakefield v Duckworth*.[31] A solicitor, acting on behalf of a client, ordered some photographs. The photographer sued the solicitor for the price of the photographs supplied. It was held that he could not succeed since the solicitor was acting as agent on behalf of his client (the principal) and that, since the photographer was aware of this, the action for price should be brought against the principal. This position is not affected by the fact that the agent was acting outside his authority in making the contract with the third party. In *Lewis v Nicholson*[32] Lord Campbell CJ said that "in no case where it appears that a man did not intend to bind himself, but only to make a contract for a principal, can he be sued as principal, merely because there was no authority".[33] The logic here is straightforward. The fact that an agent acts without authority does not alter the privity of contract between his principal and the third party. However, where an agent acts without authority, he could face liability for breach of warranty of authority (considered below).

Although an agent will not normally face liability under a contract made with a third party there are exceptions to this rule. Where an agent acts on behalf of a non-existent principal, for example, the agent may face personal liability on the contract. This is a particular problem for promoters of a company in the process of formation. This issue has already been considered in respect of ratification and it is the same problem here: where the company is never in fact incorporated, who is liable on any pre-incorporation contracts? It is clear that at common law[34] and under statute[35] the promoter (agent) is liable. *Kelner* can be contrasted with the decision in *Newborne v Sensolid (Great Britain) Ltd*[36] where there was a contract for the sale of some goods. The contract was signed "Leopold Newborne (London) Ld" and underneath was the name Leopold Newborne. The Court of Appeal suggested that since the signatory to the contract was "Leopold Newborne (London) Ld" and not "Leopold Newborne, by authority of and as agent for the company" it was clear that Mr Leopold was not undertaking personal liability under the contract. If the contract had been signed "Leopold Newborne, by authority of and as agent for the company" the agent would have signed in his own name and would therefore face liability under the contract under the principle in *Kelner v Baxter*. This issue was resolved by the s.36C(1)

---

31 [1915] 1 K.B. 218.

32 (1852) Q.B. 503.

33 (1852) Q.B. 503 at 511.

34 *Kelner v Baxter* (1866 2 C.P. 174.

35 Companies Act 1985 s.36C(1).

36 [1954] 1 Q.B. 45.

of the Companies Act 1985 and is repeated in s.51(1) of the Companies Act 2006[37] which provides for personal liability of the promoter on pre-incorporation contracts. However, it seems that the issue in respect of the non-existent principal in other contexts depends upon the form of the signature and whether the agent signs in his own name "on behalf" of the principal or signs in the name of his principal.

An agent will also face personal liability under the contract if, on proper construction of the contract, he has undertaken personal liability under the contract. As May LJ put it in *Foxtons Ltd v Thesleff*:[38]

> **"As to the point that the first defendant should not be liable because he was agent to the disclosed principal, this would, of course, normally be the position in law. But there is no principle of law which says that parties may not contract on the explicit basis that the agent also is liable, and this is what the parties here did."**

One example of an agent undertaking personal liability is the decision of *Kelner v Baxter* which we have already encountered. In the case of a written contract the matter will be one of construction. Did both the agent and the third party intend that the agent should be personally liable under the contract? The courts have sought to distinguish between words of description and those of representation. Only in the former will an agent be deemed to have undertaken personal liability on the contract. This raises difficulties of interpretation. In *Universal Steam Navigation Company Ltd v McKelvie*[39] the House of Lords held that the signing of a charter-party "as agents" was to be constructed as representative and therefore the agents were not liable to the third party. By way of contrast, the wording "as agent" was held to be descriptive in *Parker v Winlow*[40] since the phrase was used in a commercial rather than a legal sense. This demonstrates two things very well. First, it serves as an example against trusting to "verbal formulae"[41] and secondly, reinforces the importance of ascertaining the intention of both agent and third party in making the contract. The difficulties of contractual construction as to whether personal liability was intended are illustrated in the case of *Bridges & Salmon, Ltd v The Swan (Owner)*[42] where the plaintiffs sought to claim for work done to a boat owned by J.D.R. Ltd. The company was formed by the owner of the boat, Mr Rodger, with the purpose of maintaining and repairing the boat. To that purpose, the newly-formed company hired the boat from Mr Rodger and entered into contracts with the plaintiffs to effect repairs. The company, before paying for the work completed, became insolvent and ceased trading. The plaintiffs sought payment from Mr Rodger personally and argued that he was personally liable 30-009

37 This provision replaced s.36C of the 1985 Act with effect from 1 October 2009.

38 [2005] EWCA Civ. 514 at [28].

39 [1923] A.C. 492.

40 (1857) 7 E & B 942.

41 *Re Coomber, Coomber v Coomber* [1911] 1 Ch. 723 at 728, per Fletcher Moulton LJ.

42 [1968] 1 Lloyd's Rep. 5.

under the contracts made between J.D.R. Ltd and themselves. Brandon J sought to ascertain the contractual intention (something made more difficult by the contracts having been concluded partly in writing and partly by words) and said:

> **"It seems to me that the defendant did not ever contract expressly as agent in the sense of saying either orally or in writing that he was acting 'as agent for', or 'on account of', or 'on behalf of', or 'for' the company. What he did was to describe himself to both plaintiffs at an earlier stage as 'Mr. Rodger, of J.D. Rodger, Ltd.', and later to write the written orders on the company's notepaper and add the word 'Director' to his signature. On the other hand, the plaintiffs' subsequent conduct shows that they understood clearly that the bills for their work were to be sent to the company".**

The former point would indicate that in making the contract of repair, Mr Rodger was undertaking personal liability. On the other hand, the latter point, would lead to the opposite conclusion. Brandon J even suggested that "the present case appears to be somewhat near the borderline, with strong arguments available either way". It was held that, on proper construction of the facts, Mr Rodger had undertaken personal liability since he had not made it clear to the third parties that, although he, as owner, would benefit from the repairs to the boat, he was disowning any personal liability to pay for the repairs carried out.

In *Gregor Fisken Ltd v Carl*[43] the Court of Appeal considered the position where a buyer was described in the contract heading as "an agent for an undisclosed principal" but signed the contract simply as "Gregor Fisken Ltd", i.e. there was ambiguity between one part of the contract and another. In fact, there was no undisclosed principal. The court held that Gregor Fisken Ltd was the principal not an agent, and was entitled to sue on the contract. Lord Justice Males said that:[44]

> **"Ultimately it is necessary to have some principle of construction to resolve the inconsistency where a person signs a contract as a contracting party without qualification but is described in the body of the contract as an agent. If the contract contains no other means of resolving the inconsistency, English law has decided that the signature is the predominating consideration and has maintained that position over the last 150 years or so".**

43 [2021] EWCA Civ 792.

44 [2021] EWCA Civ 792 at [62].

Lord Justice Males was further persuaded as to the identity of the parties by the wording of the draft bill of sale which confirmed the sale to Gregor Fisken Ltd and transferred title to the company as a result.

Contractual rights

Just as an agent will not normally incur contractual liabilities under any agreements he makes with a third party on behalf of his principal, since he will "drop out" of the picture once he has fulfilled his role, similarly, an agent will generally not incur any contractual rights under such contracts. Thus, normally an agent will not be able to enforce a contract. Where, however, it can be established that the parties intend the agent to be a party to the contract, the agent will be able to enforce the contract against the third party. This is so even though the principal repudiates the contract, again, provided that the third party intends to contract with the agent.[45] 30–010

In *Braymist Ltd v The Wise Finance Co Ltd*[46] a solicitor (the agent) signed an agreement to buy some land as agent for an unformed company. The third party seller did not realise at the time of making the contract that the company did not in fact exist and upon realising this he refused to complete the transaction. The solicitor rescinded the contract and brought an action for breach of contract. We have already seen that s.36C(1) of the Companies Act 1985 imposed personal liability on agents who made contracts on behalf of a company which is not yet in existence. The Court of Appeal held that s.36C(1) also entitled the agent to enforce the contract himself unless ordinary common law principles prevented him from doing so.

Liability for breach of warrant of authority

The situation we are concerned with here is that where an agent represents to the third party that he has the necessary authority but in fact does not. Where the representation of authority induces the third party to take steps that he would not otherwise have done (such as entering into a contract or taking action prior to entering into a contract) then the agent will be deemed to have warranted that he had the authority represented and be made liable for any loss incurred by the third party. The rationale behind this rule is fairly simple: we have already seen that where an agent acts outside his authority the principal will not be bound by the acts of his agent. In order to protect the third party it is necessary to find the agent liable. The liability of the agent in such circumstances stems from a unilateral collateral contract between the agent and the third party under which the agent offers to warrant his authority. This offer will generally be accepted by the third party entering into the contract with the principal, but may also 30–011

45 *Short v Spackman* (1831) 2 B & Ad. 962.

46 [2002] Ch. 273.

be accepted through the third party taking other action, such as entering into a contract with another party (e.g. to purchase stock, etc.).

The existence of an action for breach of warrant of authority was first recognised by the courts in *Collen v Wright*[47] where Willes J stated:

> **"The obligation arising in such a case is well expressed by saying that a person, professing to contract as agent for another, impliedly, if not expressly, undertakes to or promises the person who enters into such contract, upon the faith of the professed agent being duly authorised, that the authority which he professes to have does in point of fact exist. The fact of entering into the transaction with the professed agent, as such, is good consideration for the promise".**

The importance of the decision in *Collen* stems from the fact that it firmly established the strict liability of the agent for breach of warrant of authority. Thus, it does not matter whether the misrepresentation of authority was unintentional, reckless or entirely innocent—the agent is liable to the third party in any event. This is exemplified by the case of *Yonge v Toynbee*[48] where a solicitor continued to act for his principal in defending a legal action after his principal had been diagnosed as suffering from insanity. This ended the agency relationship but the solicitor was unaware of his principal's illness and continued to act on his behalf. He was held liable to the third party for the costs of the legal action since he had (entirely innocently) warranted his authority when in fact he had none since he was no longer an agent at all!

General Reading

A.L. Goodhart and C.J. Hamson, "Undisclosed Principals in Contract" (1931) 4 C.L.J. 320.

R.R. Pennington, "The Validation of Pre-Incorporation Contracts" [2002] Comp. Law. 284.

F.M.B. Reynolds, "Election Distributed" (1970) 86 L.Q.R. 317.

F.M.B. Reynolds, "Personal Liability of an Agent" (1969) 85 L.Q.R. 92.

J. Savirimuthu, "Pre-incorporation Contracts and the Problem of Corporate Fundamentalism: Are Promoters Proverbially Profuse?" [2003] Comp. Law 196.

47 (1857) 8 E & B 647.

48 [1910] 1 K.B. 215.

R. Stevens, "Why do Agents 'Drop Out'?" (2005) 1 L.M.C.L.Q. 101.
Tan Cheng-Han, "Undisclosed Principals and Contract" (2004) 120 L.Q.R. 480.
Tan Cheng-Han, "Implied Terms in Undisclosed Agency" (2021) 84 M.L.R. 532.
C. Twigg-Flesner, "Full Circle: Purported Agent's Right of Enforcement Under Section 36C of the Companies Act 1985" [2001] Comp. Law 274.

31

Commercial Agents

Introduction

Traditionally, the relationship between principal and agent has been left as a matter to be dealt with by common law. The approach adopted by the common law has already been considered. What follows in this chapter is a consideration of the statutory framework which governs the relationship between principal and agent. The Commercial Agents (Council Directive) Regulations 1993[1] implement the European Directive relating to Self-Employed Commercial Agents.[2] Broadly speaking, the aim of the Directive is to harmonise the relationship between principal and agent and to provide protection on certain key issues for the agent. They do not offer any assistance in detailing the rights or obligations of either party as against a third party. Such matters being determined solely by reference to the common law. 31-001

1 SI 1993/3053 as amended by SI 1993/3173 and SI 1998/2868.

2 86/653/EEC.

Commercial Agents (Council Directive) Regulations 1993

Application and Scope

31–002 The regulations deal with the following issues in the relationship between commercial agents and principals:

- rights and obligations of both agent and principal;
- remuneration of agents;
- conclusion and termination of agency contracts; and
- restraint of trade clauses.

Clearly of importance is the definition of "commercial agent" since the regulations only impact upon the relationship between a commercial agent and his principal. The term is defined in reg.2 as:

> **"a self-employed intermediary who has continuing authority to negotiate the sale or purchase of goods on behalf of another person (the 'principal'), or to negotiate and conclude the sale or purchase of goods on behalf of and in the name of that principal".**

This definition serves immediately to restrict the application of the regulations to two types of agency relationship, in each of which the agent has continuing authority: first where the agent has authority to negotiate the sale or purchase of goods, and secondly, where the agent could negotiate and conclude the sale and purchase of goods in the name of the principal. The regulations do not, therefore, apply to employees acting as agents since a commercial agent here refers to "self-employed". Similarly, the reference to "continuing authority" will generally rule out an agent who acts as agent on a one-off basis.[3] The word "negotiate" has not been defined in the regulations.[4] In *Parks v Esso Petroleum Company Ltd*[5] the court afforded the

3 The number of transactions is not, however, the sole determining indicator of continuing authority: *Poseidon Chartering BV v Marianne Zeeschip VOF* [2006] 2 Lloyd's Rep. 105.

4 See the comments of Patten J in *Nigel Fryer Joinery Services Ltd v Ian Firth Hardware Ltd* [2008] 2 Lloyd's Rep. 108 at [17].

5 [2000] E.C.C. 45 at [32].

term a broad meaning of to "deal with, manage or conduct [a sale]". The definition does not require the agent to, for example, conclude agreements or bargain over the price to be paid. It has been held that an individual can fall within the definition of a commercial agent even where their role is not to solicit orders at all, but rather to promote the principal's capabilities to contractors more generally.[6]

In previous editions of this text, it was noted that the difficulties surrounding supplies of computer software, (discussed earlier in Ch.1)[7] in respect of the Sale of Goods Act 1979 were of relevance to the definition of "goods" under the Regulations. To some degree, this difficulty has now been removed by the Software Incubator Ltd litigation. At first instance[8] the court held that software constitutes "goods" for the purposes of the Regulations even when supplied in an intangible format. The Court of Appeal, however, reversed that decision and determined that goods within the Regulations was limited to tangible items.[9] The court was heavily persuaded by the approach of the Consumer Rights Act 2015 (and the Consumer Rights Directive) whereby the definition of goods was not extended to cover intangible supplies of software, but instead a novel category of "digital content" was created instead.[10] The Supreme Court referred the matter to the European Court of Justice for a preliminary ruling on two questions. First, does software supplied only in an intangible medium constitute goods under the Directive, and secondly, where software is supplied via a perpetual licence to use it, is that supply a sale of goods under the Directive? In its ruling, the ECJ answered both questions in the affirmative.[11] However, the Supreme Court has not had the opportunity to determine the appeal since the parties agreed to it being withdrawn. As such, the interpretation of the Regulations is uncertain following the end of the Brexit transition period, though it seems likely that the courts will interpret the Regulations in light of the ECJ's ruling.

The reference to the sale of goods removes agents selling services from the scope of the regulations. In *Mercantile International Group plc v Chuan Soon Huat Industrial Group Ltd*[12] the Court of Appeal had to determine whether the agreement between CSH (manufacturer of timber products) and MIG (the retailer of such products) was one of commercial agency or resale. The agreement between CSH and MIG was headed "agency agreement" and appointed MIG as "sales and forwarding agents on behalf of. . .CSH". Despite this agreement, however, there were certain features of the commercial relationship which appeared to indicate that the proper construction of the relationship was one of sale and resale. These features included the fact that MIG did not account to CSH for any of the sale proceeds obtained from the purchasers,

6 *PJ Pipe & Valve Co Ltd v Audco India Limited* [2005] EWHC 1904 (QB) at [154] and [155]. More recently, in *Green Deal Marketing Southern Ltd v Economy Energy Trading Ltd* [2019] EWHC 507 (Ch) the court held that an agent whose function was to persuade customers to switch energy supplier but who played no role in negotiating terms was a commercial agent.

7 See para.1-012.

8 *Software Incubator Ltd v Computer Associates Ltd* [2016] EWHC 1587 (QB).

9 *Computer Associates UK Limited v The Software Incubator Ltd* [2018] EWCA Civ 518.

10 This is, of course, now no longer possible following the UK's withdrawal from the EU.

11 *Software Incubator Ltd v Computer Associates (UK) Ltd* C410-19.

12 [2002] C.L.C. 913.

having always paid CSH before receiving payment for the goods from the customer. In addition, MIG made and retained a substantial mark-up, the amount of which was unknown and uncontrolled by CSH. CSG argued that the agreement was not one of commercial agency.

There is longstanding support for such a position. In *Re Nevill, Ex p. White*[13] Mellish LJ suggested that:

> **"if the consignee is at liberty, according to the contract between him and his consignor, to sell at any price he likes, and receive payment at any time he likes, but is to be bound, if he sells the goods, to pay the consignor for them at a fixed price and a fixed time—in my opinion, whatever the parties may think, their relation is not that of principal and agent."**

Moreover, in *AMB Imballaggi Plastici SRL v Pacflex Ltd*[14] the Court of Appeal was persuaded that the relationship was not one of commercial agent and principal, not least because of the mark-up of over 5 per cent made and retained by Pacflex. Gibson LJ stated that:

> **"In these circumstances it seems to me plain that Pacflex was never acting as the commercial agent of AMB, on whose behalf it never purported to negotiate, nor did it have a contract or other authority to negotiate a sale on AMB's behalf, still less did it have authority to do so which could be called continuing."**

Nevertheless, the Court of Appeal in *Mercantile International Group* decided that the agreement in that case was one of commercial agent and principal, and that therefore, the Commercial Agents Regulations 1993 did apply to the agreement between the parties. The key distinction between this case and, for example, that of *Pacflex*, was that in the present case there was a written agreement between the parties which was clearly drafted in agent and principal terms.[15] Rix LJ held that MIG had continuing authority to act on behalf of CSH, its principal, and that it was therefore within the meaning of "commercial agent".[16]

31–003 These two recent cases demonstrate that there are still considerable difficulties in distinguishing an agency relationship from other analogous relationships and that, most importantly in our present context, the regulations are of application only where there is a genuine relationship of commercial agent and principal.

---

13 (1871) LR 6 Ch App 397 at 403.

14 [1999] C.L.C. 1391.

15 In *Sagal (t/a Bunz UK) v Atelier Bunz GmbH* [2009] EWCA Civ. 700, the Court of Appeal held that since the claimant contracted in his own name and not in that of the principal, he was not a commercial agent. The Court suggested that as a matter of policy (in limiting the time and expense of factual inquiries as to the existence of an agency relationship between the parties) the contractual documents were crucial.

16 Rix LJ did raise the possibility that the mark-up may well constitute a breach of the fiduciary obligations owed by an agent to his principal.

Regulation 2 continues further to restrict the definition of "commercial agent" by stating that it does not include any of the following:

(i) a person who, in his capacity as an officer of a company or association is empowered to enter into commitments binding on that company or association;

(ii) a partner who is lawfully authorised to enter into commitments binding on his partners; and

(iii) a person who acts as an insolvency practitioner.

The first category would obviously rule out the managing director of a company from the scope of the regulations since a managing director has the authority to enter into commitments binding on the company. The second category imposes the same restriction in relation to members of a partnership. Regulation 2(2) also specifically removes certain other types of commercial agents from the remit of the regulations, including: unpaid commercial agents and commercial agents working in commodity exchanges or markets.

The regulations are of no application to commercial agents whose activities as a commercial agent are considered to be "secondary".[17] The Schedule to the regulations defines "secondary activities" as meaning where the primary purpose of the agency agreement does not meet both of the following requirements:[18]

"(a) the business of the principal is the sale, or as the case may be purchase, of goods of a particular kind; and
(b) the goods concerned are such that—
(i) transactions are normally individually negotiated and concluded on a commercial basis, and
(ii) procuring a transaction on one occasion is likely to lead to further transactions in those goods with that customer on future occasions, or to transactions in those goods with other customers in the same geographical area or among the same group of customers, and that accordingly it is in the commercial interests of the principal in developing the market in those goods to appoint a representative to such customers with a view to the representative devoting effort, skill and expenditure from his own resources to that end."

17 reg.2(4). For a comparative analysis of "secondary" activities, see S. Saintier, "The Interpretation of Directives to Suit Commercial Needs: A Further Threat to Coherence" [2012] J.B.L. 128 at 130–137.

18 para.2. For a recent discussion of the Schedule, see *Green Deal Marketing Southern Ltd v Economy Energy Trading Ltd* [2019] EWHC 507 (Ch).

The Schedule offers the following indications that an agreement falls under the requirements above:[19]

(a) the principal is the manufacturer, importer or distributor of the goods;

(b) the goods are specifically identified with the principal in the market in question rather than, or to a greater extent than, with any other person;

(c) the agent devotes substantially the whole of his time to representative activities (whether for one principal or for a number of principals whose interests are not conflicting);

(d) the goods are not normally available in the market in question other than by means of the agent; and

(e) the arrangement is described as one of commercial agency.

Where these indications are not met by the agreement in question, it is an indication that the agreement is secondary, and not therefore covered by the regulations. Moreover, the Schedule also lists the following as specific indications that the agreement will be secondary:[20]

(a) promotional material is supplied directly to potential customers;

(b) persons are granted agencies without reference to existing agents in a particular area or in relation to a particular group; and

(c) customers normally select the goods for themselves and merely place their orders through the agent.

This is clearly a very complicated assessment and has unsurprisingly given rise to considerable litigation as to whether an agent's activities are properly regarded as primary (and therefore regulated) or secondary (and therefore unregulated). Indeed, in *Amb Imballagi Plastici Srl v Pacflex Ltd*[21] Waller LJ suggested that the test for ascertaining whether the agent is engaged in secondary activities was "an almost impenetrable piece of drafting".

31–004 In *Tamarind International Ltd v Eastern Natural Gas (Retail) Ltd*[22] the court had to determine whether Tamarind International, sales agents for a gas and electricity supplier, were engaged in secondary activities and not therefore not subject to the Commercial Agents Regulations

19 para.3.
20 para.4.
21 [2000] E.C.C. 381 at 383.
22 [2000] C.L.C. 1397.

1993. The agents' job here was to use Eastern Natural Gas' promotional material to persuade existing customers of competitor suppliers to sign up with Eastern for their future gas requirements. It was clear that the agents were effectively operating exclusively on behalf of Eastern Natural Gas since Tamarind's employees were devoting between 85–98 per cent of their time to Eastern Natural Gas. In finding that the activities of Tamarind were not secondary for the purpose of the regulations, Morison J stated that the proper approach in this matter was to:

> **". . .look at the nature of the commercial bargain between the principal and agent. Was it in the principal's commercial interests that this agent should be appointed to develop the market in the particular goods by the agent's expenditure of money and his own resources?"**

In adopting this test, Morison J rejected the submission of counsel that a "horizontal" approach should be preferred. The "horizontal" approach would suggest that the issue of whether the commercial agent's activities are primary or secondary is determined by assessing how much time and effort is expended in respect of that agency agreement as compared with the other activities of the commercial agent. It seems reasonably clear that the approach required through the construction of reg.2 with the guidance and indicators in the Schedule supports the conclusion and approach of Morison J. Given the complexities of reg.2 and the Schedule in determining when commercial activities are deemed secondary, it is perhaps unfortunate that the Directive did not clarify the matter by adding a definition of "secondary activity" to be adopted by the Member States.[23]

Despite the complexities shown above it is clear that there are substantial restrictions on the definition of "commercial agent" and also on the scope of the regulations. It should be made clear here that where the regulations do not apply, the rights and obligations of both agent and principal will be governed by the agreement between the two and the relevant provisions of the common law.

Obligations of a Commercial Agent to His Principal

The duties of a commercial agent to his principal are detailed in reg.3. The duties of the commercial agent are broadly similar to those dictated by the common law.[24] The obligations are that, generally, there is an obligation to "look after the interests of his principal and act dutifully and in good faith". In addition the commercial agent must:[25] 31-005

23 See further, C. Gardiner, "The EC (Commercial Agents) Directive: twenty years after its introduction, divergent approaches still emerge from Irish and UK courts" [2007] J.B.L. 412.

24 See, for example, *Cureton v Mark Insulations Ltd* [2006] EWHC 2279 where the failure of a commercial agent to disclose the practice of selling insulation as agent and windows as principal during the same home sales visits constituted a breach of both reg.3(1) and the common law.

25 reg.3(2).

(a) make proper efforts to negotiate and, where appropriate, conclude the transactions he is instructed to take care of;

(b) communicate to his principal all the necessary information available to him; and

(c) comply with reasonable instructions given by his principal.

It was noted above that the duties of the commercial agent are broadly similar to those dictated by the common law. This is true but does not take into account one crucial fact, namely that under the principles of common law, both the rights and duties of an agent can be restricted or excluded under the normal contractual rules (looked at in Chs 29 and 30). Under the Commercial Agents Regulations the duties imposed on commercial agents cannot be restricted or excluded by agreement between the parties.[26]

Obligations of a Principal to His Commercial Agent

31-006 These are covered by reg.4 which imposes a general obligation upon the principal to "act – dutifully and in good faith" and more specifically to:

(a) provide his commercial agent with the necessary documentation relating to the goods concerned; and

(b) obtain for his commercial agent the information necessary for the performance of the agency contract, and in particular notify his commercial agent within a reasonable period once he anticipates that the volume of commercial transactions will be significantly lower than that which the commercial agent could normally have expected.

A principal is also under a duty to notify his commercial agent (within a reasonable time) of the outcome of any transaction which the agent has procured on his behalf, i.e. whether the proposed transaction was accepted, rejected or not-executed. Similarly to reg.3, the obligations of a principal cannot be restricted or excluded by agreement between the parties by virtue of reg.5.

Remuneration

31-007 Part III of the regulations deal with the remuneration of commercial agents, although the parties are free to make whatever agreement they wish in respect of remuneration where there is

26 reg.5.

no remuneration through commission. Where, however, they do not make any agreement in respect of remuneration, reg.6 dictates that the amount of remuneration payable is that which would customarily be payable under such an agreement. This will obviously be determined by: the nature of the transaction; the type of goods sold; and the country of business. Where there is no customary practice to determine the remuneration payable, the courts will make an assessment of what is reasonable in all the circumstances of the transaction.[27]

Where a commercial agent is to be remunerated either wholly or in part through commission, the regulations impose certain mandatory requirements. "Commission" is defined in reg.2 as meaning "any part of the remuneration of a commercial agent which varies with the number or value of business transactions". Thus it applies not only to the standard model of commissions where the agent secures payment upon completion of a particular transaction but also to various incentive schemes such as loyalty bonuses, yearly bonuses where they are paid by virtue of achieving a predetermined number of transactions. Where a commercial agent is paid in some part by commission, the regulations entitle the agent to commission in three distinct situations where the principal and commercial agent relationship is in operation:

(i) Where the transaction has been concluded as a result of the agent's actions.[28]

(ii) Where the transaction is concluded by a customer introduced by the agent.[29]

(iii) Where the agent is appointed sole agent in a particular geographical area or to a particular group of people and a transaction is concluded with either someone from that geographical area or with a person from within that particular group.[30]

The regulations also dictate that commission is payable in certain situations even though the agency relationship has been terminated. Under reg.8 commission is payable even after termination of the agency agreement, where:

(a) the transaction is mainly attributable to the agent's efforts during the period covered by the agency contract and if the transaction was entered into within a reasonable period after that contract terminated; or

(b) the order reached the principal (or the agent) before the agency relationship was terminated and commission would be due under one of the three situations detailed in reg.7.

---

27 See, for example, *PJ Pipe & Valve Co Ltd v Audco India Ltd* [2005] EWHC 1904 (QB).

28 reg.7(1)(a).

29 reg.7(1)(b), e.g. "follow-up" sales would obviously be covered by this provision.

30 reg.7(2).

What constitutes a "reasonable time" is a question of fact to be decided on the facts of the case and the regulations offer no guidance on this issue.[31] One further question is answered by the regulations: what is the position if an order from a customer in England (a) is received by the principal before the agreement with the exclusive agent for the principal in England is terminated and a new agent appointed to replace him, and (b) is processed and concluded after the new agent is appointed? To whom will the commission be payable? This is dealt with by reg.9 which provides that, generally, the commission in such circumstances will be payable to the original commercial agent and not to the replacement.[32]

31-008 Regulation 10 deals with the issue of when commission will become payable to the commercial agent and states that as a general rule it becomes payable:

(a) when the principal has executed the transaction;

(b) when the principal should, according to his agreement with the third party, have executed the transaction; or

(c) When the third party has executed the transaction.

Once commission becomes payable by one of the above events occurring, the commission must be paid no later than the last day of the month following the quarter in which it became due.[33]

In order to ensure that the commission paid is in fact that which is owed by virtue of the regulations, the commercial agent has the right to be provided with any information necessary to confirm the amount of commission payable to him. This includes the right to inspect the principal's accounts, or an extract thereof.[34] In addition, the principal is under a duty to provide the commercial agent with a statement of commission due.[35] This statement must also demonstrate the method of calculating the sum of commission payable. Neither of these obligations may be excluded or limited by agreement between the parties.[36]

---

31 By way of illustration, in *Tigana Ltd v Decoro Ltd* [2003] E.C.C. 23 the court held that nine months was a reasonable period in respect of a year-long agency agreement.

32 reg.9(1) allows for the sharing of the commission in such circumstances where that would be the most equitable solution.

33 Any attempt to exclude or restrict this position to the detriment of the commercial agent shall automatically be rendered void, see reg.10(4).

34 reg.12(2).

35 reg.12(1).

36 reg.12(3).

Termination

Part IV of the regulations deal with the conclusion of agency agreement.[37] Somewhat curiously it begins with something which ought as a matter of good practice be done at the very start of the agency agreement: the right of both commercial agent and principal to receive a signed written document laying down the terms of the agreement, which may well include a term detailing the requirements for termination of the agency agreement.[38] 31-009

The regulations provide for the situation where the agency agreement is for a definite period of time but both the commercial agent and the principal continue to perform their obligations under that contract (e.g. the agent continues selling goods on behalf of the principal and the principal continues to pay the agent) after the expiration of that date. Regulation 14 states that in this situation the agency agreement will be converted into an agreement for an indefinite period. The significance of this becomes clear upon reading reg.15 which allows for indefinite agency agreements to be terminated by notice from either party to the other. Regulation 15(2) lays down minimum mandatory periods of notice which must be given. They are:

- one month during the first year of the contract;
- two months during the second year; and
- three months during subsequent years.

Where an agency agreement for a definite period has been converted into one for an indefinite period under reg.14, above, reg.15(5) makes it clear that (i) the above notice periods apply, and (ii) the period of the definite period of the agency agreement should be taken into account when assessing the appropriate notice period under reg.15(2).

The regulations allow for termination without notice in three distinct situations: 31-010

(i) Where the agency agreement is for a definite period of time and is not converted into an agency agreement for an indefinite period as detailed above.

(ii) Where one party fails, either in part or otherwise, to perform his obligations under the agency agreement.

(iii) Where "exceptional circumstances" apply. Sadly the regulations do not specify what would constitute "exceptional circumstances".

37 See generally, A. McGee, "Termination of a Commercial Agency: The Agent's Rights" [2011] J.B.L. 782.

38 reg.13.

Where an agency agreement is terminated reg.17 lays down the framework for either compensation or an indemnity to be payable to a commercial agent.[39] Unless the parties agree otherwise in the agency contract, the agent is entitled to compensation rather than an indemnity.[40] This is important since it will generally be the case that compensation will be financially advantageous to the agent, whereas indemnity will be a cheaper option for the principal. It is not permissible for a commercial agency agreement to include a clause to the effect that, on termination, a commercial agent will be entitled to an indemnity unless compensation would result in a smaller payment being due: *Shearman v Hunter Boot Ltd*.[41] The inclusion of such a clause, however, will not always result in compensation, rather than an indemnity, being payable. In *Brand Studio Ltd v St Johns Knits Inc*[42] the commercial agent had agreed that, on termination, an indemnity would be payable unless a lesser sum would be due if compensation was paid instead. The court held that this unenforceable clause could be severed from the agreement since what remained was still "the sort of contract entered into by the parties" because the agent had, in either case, agreed to accept an indemnity.

Regulation 17(6) states that "the commercial agent shall be entitled to compensation for the damage he suffers as a result of the termination of his relations with his principal." In particular, damage suffered includes the loss of commission which could have been earned through the proper performance of the contract.

31-011 Where the agency contract provides for the commercial agent to be indemnified rather than compensated, the approach is somewhat different and is based upon the extent to which the principal's business has benefited from the agent's activities. Regulation 17(3) provides that the agent shall be entitled to an indemnity where:

> **"(a) he has brought the principal new customers or has significantly increased the volume of business with existing customers and the principal continues to derive substantial benefits from the business with such customers; and**
>
> **(b) the payment of this indemnity is equitable having regard to all the circumstances and, in particular, the commission lost by the commercial agent on the business transacted with such customers."**

The European Court of Justice has recently considered the definition of "new customers" in this context. In *Marchon Germany GmbH v Yvonne Karaszkiewicz*[43] the court had to determine

39 Under reg.17(9) the agent must notify the principal of his intention to seek compensation or an indemnity within one year following his termination. Failure to do so has the effect of rendering the agent unable to claim either compensation or an indemnity. Consequently, ascertaining the precise date of termination can be of crucial importance, see *Claramoda Ltd v Zoomphase Ltd (t/a Jenny Packham)* [2009] EWHC 2857 (Comm).

40 See reg.17(2).

41 [2014] EWHC 47 (QB).

42 [2015] EWHC 3143 (QB).

43 Case C-315/14 (2016).

whether the term "new customers" required the agent to have introduced completely new customers to the principal or whether it could include existing customers who are nonetheless "new" in relation to the specific goods sold by the agent in question. The court held that the latter, i.e. broader, definition was correct: a customer will therefore be regarded as being "new" for the purposes of the Regulations where they are new to the specific goods being sold by the agent even if they are already customers of the principal in relation to other goods.

The amount of the indemnity is controlled by reg.17(4) which dictates that any indemnity payable shall not be more than the agent's annual remuneration as calculated by averaging the remuneration of the agent for the previous five years.[44] It now seems clear that the use of the word "termination" in reg.17 does not preclude a claim for compensation or indemnity where a commercial agency agreement has expired, rather than being "terminated" by the principal.[45]

The rationale behind both indemnity and compensation as protective measures on behalf of commercial agents was clearly stated in the recent decision of the House of Lords in *Lonsdale (trading as Lonsdale Agencies) v Howard & Hallam Ltd (Winemakers' Federation of Australia Inc intervening)*[46] where Lord Hoffman stated:[47] 31-012

> **"They are both ways of dealing with the unfairness which it was thought might arise if the termination of the agency leaves the agent worse off and the principal better off than if the agency had continued."**

Despite this seemingly straightforward aim, the failure of the Regulations (and indeed the Directive) to give any indication as to how properly to calculate the amount of compensation due to the commercial agent (in contrast to the same issue in respect of an indemnity) has caused difficulty for English courts. This difficulty is, in part, caused by the fact that compensation under the regulations is due where there is no fault on the part of the principal. As has been seen, under the traditional approach of the common law damages are only available to the agent where the principal by terminating the agency relationship was acting in breach of contract.

In *Lonsdale* the House of Lords adopted a two-part approach in assessing the proper award of damages under reg.17 following the termination (with reasonable notice) of a commercial agency relationship. Since the parties had not made any agreement as to whether to choose indemnity rather than compensation, the default position of compensation was applicable. The two-part approach was to ask:

44 Where the agency agreement has not existed for five years at the time of termination, the maximum indemnity payable shall be the yearly average over the period of the agency agreement.

45 See the purposive approach of Davies J in *Tigana Ltd v Decoro Ltd* [2003] E.E.C. 23 at [71] onwards.

46 [2007] UKHL 32.

47 [2007] UKHL 32 at [5].

1. What should the agent be compensated for?

2. How should the compensation be determined?

Lord Hoffman dealt with the first question fairly quickly in referring to the Directive:[48]

> **"On this first question the Directive is explicit. The agent is entitled to be compensated for 'the damage he suffers as a result of the termination of his relations with the principal'. In other words, the agent is treated as having lost something of value as a result of the termination and is entitled to compensation for this loss."**

The second question, however, is much more problematic. It might have been expected that, since the compensation regime in reg.17 is based on French Law whereby an agent is compensated for the deprivation of the commercial agent's business[49] the House of Lords would adopt the jurisprudence of the French courts in assessing compensation under the regulation. Indeed, this is the approach which has been adopted by the Scottish courts.[50] The approach favoured by the House of Lords was to assess the level of compensation due through a valuation of the agency business. His Lordship supported the earlier approach of Bowers J in *Barrett McKenzie & Co Ltd v Escada (UK) Ltd*[51] where it had been suggested that it was a matter of compensating for the notional value of the agency on the open market. Thus, the level of compensation payable under reg.17 is calculated by reference to the "hypothetical purchaser" and "the amount which the agent could reasonably expect to receive for the right to stand in his shoes, continue to perform the duties of the agency and receive the commission which he would have received".[52]

31–013 On that basis, the House of Lords affirmed the decision of the Court of Appeal in awarding compensation in the amount of £5000. This was considerably less than would have been awarded if the French system of valuation had been adopted, since that system values agencies at twice the gross annual commission paid to the agent over the previous three years. In the Court of Appeal, Moore-Bick LJ approved of the approach at first instance where it had been found that the net commission of the agent was around £8,000 a year, observing that:[53]

48 [2007] UKHL 32 at [8].

49 By way of contrast, the indemnity option is based heavily on the position in German Law.

50 See, for example, *King v T. Tunnock Ltd* (2000) S.L.T. 744, strongly doubted by the House of Lords in *Lonsdale*.

51 [2001] E.C.C. 50.

52 [2007] UKHL 32 at [21]. Whilst the calculation requires an assumption that there is a "hypothetical purchaser", there is no assumption that there is always a price that a purchaser would be prepared to pay, i.e. the agency could in fact be valueless. See, *Warren T/A On-Line Cartons and Print v Drukkerij Flach B.V.* [2014] EWCA Civ 993 at [14].

53 [2006] 1 W.L.R. 1281 (CA) at [56].

"[The judge at first instance] pointed out that the agency was producing a modest and falling income in a steadily deteriorating environment and doubted whether anyone in those circumstances would have been willing to pay as much as two years' gross commission based on historical figures in order to acquire it. There was no evidence that anyone would have paid anything to buy it or that Mr Lonsdale could realistically have expected to be able to sell it. In the end [the judge] assessed compensation at £5,000."

It would appear that until there is a determination at a European level on the specific method to be adopted in calculating compensation for termination of a commercial agency agreement, such difficulties and divergences of approach are likely to continue. Nonetheless, at the domestic level it is clear that the correct approach to the valuation exercise required under reg.17 is that laid down by the House of Lords in *Lonsdale*.[54]

Payment of either compensation or indemnity can be excluded only in certain situations laid down in reg.18.[55] Those situations are:

(i) the agency agreement was terminated by the principal because of a default by the commercial agent which justifies immediate termination under reg.16, discussed above;

(ii) the agency agreement is terminated by the agent; or

(iii) the commercial agent, with the agreement of his principal, assigns his rights and duties under the agency contract to another person.

In *Volvo Car Germany GmbH v Autohof Weidensdorf GmbH*[56] the European Court of Justice in its preliminary ruling stated that the use of the words "because of a default by the commercial agent" in the first alternative required a direct causal link between the agent's default and the principal's decision to terminate. Without such a direct link the indemnity or compensation is still available. Thus, where the principal is unaware of the agent's default at the time of termination, compensation or indemnity remains payable, although the court recognised that the agent's conduct can be considered when assessing the compensation due. 31-014

However, where the agency agreement is terminated by the agent, an indemnity or compensation shall remain payable where the termination is justified:

54 This may, of course, be a complex assessment. See, for example, *Alan Ramsay Sales & Marketing Ltd v Typhoo Tea Ltd* [2016] EWHC 486 (Comm) at [89]–[119].

55 There is a prohibition on the derogation from both regs 17 and 18 by virtue of reg.19.

56 (C-203/09) [2011] 1 All E.R. (Comm) 906.

(a) by circumstances attributable to the principal, or

(b) on grounds of the age, infirmity or illness of the commercial agent in consequence of which he cannot reasonably be required to continue his activities.

Restraint of Trade Agreements

31-015 Regulation 20 deals with restraint of trade agreements, i.e. an agreement which restricts the activities of the commercial agent following the termination of the agency contract.[57] It inserts various controls into the use of such an agreement:

- It must be concluded in writing.
- It must refer to the same type of goods dealt with under the agency agreement.
- It must refer to the same geographical area or group of customers as the agency agreement.[58]
- It must not be of application for a period greater than two years following the termination of the agency agreement.

General Reading

C. Gardiner, "The EC (Commercial Agents) Directive: Twenty Years After its Introduction, Divergent Approaches Still Emerge from Irish and UK Courts" [2007] J.B.L. 412.

L. MacGregor, "'100 per cent, body and soul': The Ability of an Agent to Act for a Competitor of his Principal" [2013] 17(1) Edinburgh Law Review 71.

A. McGee, "Termination of a Commercial Agency: The Agent's Rights" [2011] J.B.L. 782.

A. McGee, "Relations between a Commercial Agent and his Principal" [2013] J.B.L. 534.

S. Saintier, "The Interpretation of Directives to Suit Commercial Needs: A Further Threat to Coherence" [2012] J.B.L. 128.

S. Saintier, "New Developments in Agency Law" [1997] J.B.L. 77.

57 reg.2(1).

58 On this point, see further, *BCM Group Plc v Visualmark Ltd* [2006] EWHC 1831 (QB).

S. Saintier, "A Remarkable Understanding and Application of the Protective Stance of the Agency Regulations by the English Courts" [2001] J.B.L. 540.

S. Saintier, "The Principles Behind the Assessment of the Compensation Option under the Agency Regulations: Clarity at Last?" [2007] J.B.L. 90.

S. Saintier, "Final Guidelines on Compensation of Commercial Agents" (2008) 124 L.Q.R. 31.

S. Sasse and J. Whittaker, "An Assessment of the Impact of the UK Commercial Agents (Council Directive) Regulations 1993" [1994] I.C.C.L.R. 100.

32

Termination of Agency

Introduction

In this chapter we will examine the various means by which an agency agreement can come to an end. We will then assess some of the effects of the termination of the agency relationship. It should be recognised at this point that just as agency law generally involves the relationships between three parties, the principal, the agent and the third party, so too does the termination of an agency agreement. We must consider therefore, not only the ability of principal and agent to terminate their internal relationship, but also the impact of that termination on the external relationship, i.e. upon third parties dealing with the agent. Note that the special position of "commercial agents" under the Commercial Agents (Council Directive) Regulations 1993 in respect to termination (e.g. notice period required, etc.) has already been considered in Ch.31 and will not be repeated here. 32-001

The Termination of the Agency

Termination by Agreement

Just as an agency agreement may be created by agreement between agent and principal, so too, the agreement can similarly be terminated. In that respect an agency agreement is no different from any other contract. Where the agency agreement is non-contractual, the position is the same and either party can end the agreement at any time. Where the agency agreement 32-002 is contractual, that contract may well specify that the agreement is to take effect only for a limited time, e.g. one month, one year, etc. In such a case, the agreement will be regarded as automatically terminated upon the lapse of that period of time. Similarly, the agreement may be silent as to how long the agency agreement will continue to operate. In such a situation there are two possibilities. First, it may be possible to imply an automatic expiration date into the agreement, e.g. by trade custom.[1] Thus in *Danby v Coutt & Co*[2] the court held that the principal was not liable for the fraudulent acts of his agents which were committed after he returned from time abroad. Here the principal appointed two agents with power of attorney prior to going abroad. Although the power of attorney did not express any duration for the agreement to remain in place, it was accompanied by a recital stating that the principal was going abroad and wanted the agents to act on his behalf. The court implied from this that the power of attorney was only effective whilst the principal was abroad and so the principal was not liable.

The second, and most likely, possibility where the agency agreement has no express duration is that it may be terminated by reasonable notice. In *Staffordshire Area Health Authority v South Staffordshire Waterworks Co*[3] (not an agency case) a dispute arose between a hospital and a water company over an agreement made in 1929 concerning the cost of water supplied to the hospital. The agreement fixed a price for the supply of water and included the words "at all times hereafter". The hospital sought to rely on those words to bind the water company to the contract in perpetuity (and therefore pay for the water at the rate agreed in 1929!). The Court of Appeal held that the agreement was determinable by reasonable notice. Cumming-Bruce LJ stated that:[4]

> **". . .the words 'at all times hereafter' mean that the obligations granted and accepted by the agreement were only intended to persist during the continuance of the agreement; and the agreement, in my view, was determinable on reasonable notice at any time".**

The water company was therefore allowed to terminate the 1929 agreement in order to renegotiate a new price for the water supplied and was not to be bound by the old agreement in perpetuity.

The question of what constitutes "reasonable notice" is obviously highly fact-sensitive and will vary considerably taking into account the nature of the agency, the expenditure incurred by the agent, and the time needed to bring the business to an orderly conclusion. In *Martin-Baker Ltd v Canadian Flight Equipment Ltd*[5] a notice period of 12 months was deemed reasonable as

1 See, for example, *Seton v Slade* (1802) 7 Ves. Jr. 265 (customary for a broker's authority to expire at the end of the day).
2 (1885) L.R. 29 Ch D. 500.
3 [1978] 1 W.L.R. 1387.
4 [1978] 1 W.L.R. 1387 at 1405.
5 [1955] 2 QB 556.

reflecting the formal nature of the distribution (agency) agreement. In particular, the exclusive nature of the distribution agreement led to a longer notice period, i.e. the agent was not permitted to sell products of other suppliers that might compete with the products supplied by the principal. Conversely, in *Alpha Lettings Ltd v Neptune Research & Development Inc*[6] the court held that a notice period of four months was reasonable as offering "ample time to bring the business to an orderly conclusion", particularly since the agency agreement was not exclusive and the agents were, therefore, able to sell competing products from alternative suppliers.

Termination of Principal's Business

The courts have on many occasions been faced with claims from disgruntled agents where the agency agreement has a fixed duration but the principal's business has, for one reason or another, ceased to exist prior to the expiration of the agency agreement. The answer as to whether the agent is entitled to damages in such an event is not entirely clear since the courts have decided the issue in both ways. 32–003

In *Rhodes v Forwood*[7] the House of Lords refused to imply a condition into the agency agreement that the business itself shall continue to be carried on during the period specified. In *Rhodes* the plaintiff had been appointed as sole agent for the sale of the respondent's coal in Liverpool for a period of seven years. After around three and a half years the principal sold the colliery and thus the agent could sell no more coal in Liverpool. This obviously caused the agents to (i) lose out on future commission to be earned in the three and half years which the agreement had left to run at the time of the sale of the colliery, and (ii) lose various expenses incurred in setting up as the sole Liverpool agent in anticipation of the agreement lasting for the full seven-year period. The House of Lords found that there was no express term of the contract requiring the principal actually to send any coal to Liverpool to be sold by the agent. The plaintiffs had argued that there was an implied condition that the principal was to send coal to Liverpool for sale by the agent and that this implied condition had been breached by the principal's sale of the business. The House of Lords declined to accept this argument.

In *Turner v Goldsmith*,[8] however, the Court of Appeal arrived at the opposite conclusion by finding that an agent was entitled to maintain an action against his principal who did not resume his business when his factory burnt down two years into the five-year agency agreement. The court based this decision on the fact that the principal had agreed to employ the agent for five years and that in not resuming his business the principal had not met his obligation to supply the agent with the samples necessary for the agent to fulfil his role as agent. At first glance, it appears that the facts are remarkably similar to those in *Rhodes*. The Court of Appeal distinguished *Rhodes*, however, on the basis that in *Rhodes* there was no express agreement actually to send any coal to the agent in Liverpool. In *Turner*, the Court of Appeal

6 [2003] EWCA Civ 704.
7 (1875–76) L.R. 1 App. Cas. 256.
8 [1891] 1 Q.B. 544.

determined that there was an express agreement to employ the agent for five years, and that in order to fulfil that agreement, the principal was to send the agent a reasonable amount of samples in order to enable the agent to earn his commission.

32–004 The distinction appears to be difficult to sustain. In *Rhodes v Forwood* there was an agreement to employ Forwood as Liverpool sales agent for a period of seven years. Surely by the logic of the Court of Appeal in *Turner* in order to fulfil that agreement, the principal was to send the agent a reasonable amount of coal to enable him to earn the agreed rate of commission? This logic cannot apply however, since in *Rhodes* the agreement expressly stated that the principal was not bound actually to send any coal at all to Liverpool. If coal was sent to Liverpool, the agreement did oblige the principal to send it to Forwood as the sole agent in Liverpool. The key point therefore is the clause in the contract in *Turner* which stated that:

> **"The said A.S. Turner shall do his utmost to obtain orders for and sell the various goods manufactured or sold by the said company as shall be from time to time forwarded or submitted by sample or pattern to him at list price to good and substantial customers".**

Thus by not continuing his business following the fire, the principal was in breach of his contractual obligation to forward samples of the goods manufactured or sold by the principal. Perhaps surprisingly, there was no equivalent term in the contract between agent and principal in the *Rhodes* case.

Death of Principal or Agent

32–005 The death of either principal or agent will suffice to terminate the agency agreement. This is whether or not the surviving party has notice of the other's death. Thus, in *Campanari v Woodburn*[9] the agent was not entitled to claim a commission earned on the sale of a painting made after the death of the principal. Similarly, in *Pool v Pool*[10] a solicitor was prohibited from recovering costs incurred after the death of the client. This is a natural application of the rule that an agent cannot enter into contracts on behalf of a principal who is incapable of entering into the contract.

Insanity of Principal or Agent

32–006 In the same way as the death of either party will terminate the agency agreement, so too will the insanity of either party. In contrast to termination through death of the principal however,

9 (1854) 15 C.B. 400.

10 (1889) 58 L.J.P. 67.

where the principal becomes incapable by reason of mental illness, although the agency agreement between the principal and the agent is terminated, the agent can continue to bind his principal through apparent authority. This is so only where (i) the requirements of apparent authority have been met, and (ii) the third party is unaware of the mental illness of the principal. In *Drew v Nunn*[11] the court had to determine to what extent the authority of an agent was terminated by the insanity of the principal. Brett LJ searched for general principle within various authorities but found none before stating:[12]

> **"I think that the satisfactory principle to be adopted is that, where such a change occurs as to the principal that he can no longer act for himself, the agent whom he has appointed can no longer act for him."**

However, by virtue of the principal having made representations to the third party as to the authority of the agent to act on his behalf, the third party was entitled to enforce the contract since the agent's apparent authority was binding upon the principal.

Irrevocable Authority

Irrevocable Powers of Attorney

The Powers of Attorney Act 1971 amended the common law position regarding the ability to revoke a power of attorney. Under the common law such a power would be revoked, for example, by the death of the principal (the donor). This is now not the case by virtue of s.4 of the Act which provides: 32-007

> **"(1) Where a power of attorney is expressed to be irrevocable and is given to secure—**
> **(a) a proprietary interest of the donee of the power; or**
> **(b) the performance of an obligation owed to the donee, then, so long as the donee has that interest or the obligation remains undischarged, the power shall not be revoked—**
> **(i) by the donor without the consent of the donee; or**

11 (1878–79) 4 Q.B.D. 661.

12 (1878–79) 4 Q.B.D. 661 at 666.

> **(ii) by the death, incapacity or bankruptcy of the donor or, if the donor is a body corporate, by its winding up or dissolution."**

Thus where a power of attorney is stated to be irrevocable and is given to secure the interest of the agent (the donee) that power will be irrevocable whilst the interest remains. Moreover, it will remain despite the death, incapacity or bankruptcy of the principal (the donor).

Lasting Powers of Attorney

32–008 The Mental Capacity Act 2005 introduced a new type of irrevocable instrument, the "lasting power of attorney". The lasting power of attorney is intended to allow a nominated individual (or individuals) known as the donee, to act on behalf of an individual who no longer has legal capacity through age or infirmity. Unlike the previous system of enduring powers of attorney,[13] however, a lasting power of attorney can extend to personal welfare and health decisions, as well as to property and financial affairs. This is made clear by s.9 of the Act, which provides:

> **"(1) A lasting power of attorney is a power of attorney under which the donor ("P") confers on the donee (or donees) authority to make decisions about all or any of the following—**
>
> **(a) P's personal welfare or specified matters concerning P's personal welfare, and**
>
> **(b) P's property and affairs or specified matters concerning P's property and affairs, and which includes authority to make such decisions in circumstances where P no longer has capacity."**

Thus, provided the formalities of the Act are complied with, a lasting power of attorney will allow an agent to act on behalf of the donor, in accordance with the terms of the lasting power of attorney, where the donor lacks capacity.[14] Decisions taken on behalf of a donor must be taken in their best interests[15] and comply with the general principles set out in s.1 of the Act, e.g. the capacity of the donor is assumed unless all practicable steps have been taken without success.[16]

13 Created under the (now repealed) Enduring Powers of Attorney Act 1985. Enduring powers of attorney created under that Act remain valid, see Mental Capacity Act 2005 Sch.4.

14 s.13 and Sch.4 para.1.

15 s.4.

16 s.1(3). See *Ali v Caton* [2014] EWCA Civ 1313.

Authority Coupled With an Interest

Where the authority given to an agent is coupled with an interest, the authority is irrevocable. This is, however, an exceptional situation, something recognised by the Supreme Court in *Re D&D Wines International Ltd (In Liquidation)*[17] where the court emphasised that an irrevocable authority would be created only where the parties had agreed that the authority would be irrevocable and that the authority was intended to secure a financial interest of the agent. Since the agreement in *Re D&D Wines* did not expressly create an irrevocable authority (when it could easily have done so) and the agreement prescribed mutual rights of termination in the event of insolvency, the court concluded that the authority was revocable. 32-009

If an irrevocable agency is to be established, the financial interest of the agent secured by the grant of authority may be either a proprietary interest of the agent or a liability owed to the agent personally. In *Re D&D Wines*, the Supreme Court held that an agent's interest in recovering a debt in respect of commission already earned could be a relevant interest (although an agent's commercial interest in continuing to act in order to earn a commission would not). Therefore, the fact that by performing under the agreement the agent can earn fees or a commission is not sufficient to render the authority irrevocable.[18] In *Clerk v Laurie*[19] it was explained that:[20]

> **"What is meant by an authority coupled with an interest being irrevocable is this—that where an agreement is entered into on a sufficient consideration, whereby an authority is given for the purpose of securing some benefit to the donee of the authority, such an authority is irrevocable."**

The authority would be irrevocable, therefore, where A owes B some money and authorises B to sell goods in order to satisfy that debt.[21] The pre-existing debt which the authority is designed to protect constitutes an interest and the authority will be irrevocable until the goods have been sold and the debt paid. In *Re Hannan's Empress Gold Mining and Development Company, Ex p. Carmichael's*[22] a man by the name of Phillips promoted a company in order to buy a mine from him. Mr Carmichael agreed to buy those shares in the company which were not sold to members of the public and granted Phillips the authority to apply for those unsold shares on his behalf. In the end Mr Carmichael was contractually bound to buy 980 shares but sought (prior to the purchase going through) to revoke the authority of Phillips to purchase the shares on his behalf. The Court of Appeal upheld the decision at first instance and held that since the

17 [2016] UKSC 47.

18 [2016] UKSC 47 at [9].

19 2 H. & N. 199.

20 2 H. & N. 199 at 200.

21 See, for example, *Spooner v Sandilands* (1842) 1 Y & C 390.

22 [1896] 2 Ch. 643.

authority was designed to protect an interest of the agent it was irrevocable. The interest of the agent here was that, as the principal was aware, if the shares were not all sold, the agent would not be able to use the company to buy the mine (and therefore receive the purchase price).

Personal Liability of Agent

32-010 The principal cannot revoke the agency where the agent has incurred a personal liability through the exercise of his authority under the agency agreement. This rule is designed to protect the agent from acting under the agency agreement, incurring liability (e.g. to pay for goods, etc.) only to be left to carry the liability where the principal revokes the agent's authority. Where the agency agreement is revoked in such circumstances, therefore, it follows that the agent will be indemnified in respect of his personal liability.

In *Read v Anderson*[23] the Court of Appeal was required to decide whether a principal could revoke an agent's authority to pay losing bets. The agent in *Read* was employed as an agent to place bets on behalf of his principal. The principal therefore gave the agent the authority to pay and receive money on those bets. It was already well established that where an agent incurs a legal liability, the agent cannot revoke the agent's authority so as to avoid indemnifying the agent for his loss. At the time of *Read*, however, gambling debts were unenforceable at law, and so therefore, the agent faced no legal liability by failing to honour the bets placed (and lost). The agent however, as a professional turf commission agent (someone who places such bets for a living) would face substantial financial loss if he failed to honour the bets since he would lose his professional reputation.[24] A majority of the Court of Appeal held that the principal was not able to revoke the agent's authority to honour the debts since, although the agent had not incurred any legal liability, he would incur a financial loss if he failed to honour the bets placed on behalf of his principal.

The legal effect of *Read v Anderson* has recently been considered by the Court of Appeal in *Temple Legal Protection Ltd v QBE Insurance (Europe) Ltd.*[25] Moore-Bick LJ considered that *Read* was:[26]

> **"not concerned with revocation of the agent's authority in the sense of his power to affect the legal position of the principal but to authority in the context of the rule that the right to reimbursement and indemnity does not extend to unauthorised acts."**

23 (1884) 13 Q.B.D. 779.

24 This was irrelevant to Brett MR who in his dissenting judgment stated that "the plaintiff's business, although it may not be illegal, is directly objected to by the law", at 782.

25 [2009] EWCA Civ 453.

26 [2009] EWCA Civ 453 at [59].

Accordingly, cases such as *Read* should not be viewed as a true class of irrevocable authority but rather as cases that recognise the ability of an agent to secure reimbursement for costs incurred through the exercise of his authority, notwithstanding the subsequent revocation of that authority.

[illegible] such cases should not be viewed as cases of irrevocable authority but rather as cases that recognise the ability of an agent to secure reimbursement for costs incurred through the exercise of his authority without [illegible] the subsequent revocation of that authority.

Index

LEGAL TAXONOMY
FROM SWEET & MAXWELL

This index has been prepared using Sweet and Maxwell's Legal Taxonomy. Main index entries conform to keywords provided by the Legal Taxonomy except where references to specific documents or non-standard terms (denoted by quotation marks) have been included. These keywords provide a means of identifying similar concepts in other Sweet & Maxwell publications and online services to which keywords from the Legal Taxonomy have been applied. Readers may find some minor differences between terms used in the text and those which appear in the index. Suggestions to **sweetandmaxwell.taxonomy@tr.com**.

Also available:

Birds' Modern Insurance Law, 12th edn
Professor John Birds and Dr Katie Richards
ISBN: 9780414102743
Publication date: April 2022
Formats: Paperback and ProView eBook

Birds' Modern Insurance Law presents a concise yet analytical explanation of the fundamental principles of insurance law. Written in an accessible and straightforward manner the work covers everything from the history of insurance and regulation, through to the various forms of insurance such as life, and liability.

Birds' Modern Insurance Law is firmly established as the leading text in this area of law. It is an essential work for undergraduate and postgraduate students as well as for those undertaking a related professional course. It is also an ideal reference source for legal and insurance professionals who want a quick reference guide.

Pitt's Employment Law, 12th edn
Professor Gwyneth Pitt and Sandhya Drew
ISBN: 9780414104457
Publication date: September 2022
Formats: Paperback and ProView eBook

Set in the context of experience in the workplace as well as within the wider social and political framework, Pitt's Employment Law provides a clear and succinct account of employment law and industrial relations law. The work is written in a straightforward and engaging style, making it easy for students to understand the topic and grasp difficult concepts. The work provides a lively and thought-provoking account of key topics, explaining significant cases from the British courts, the Court of Justice of the European Union and the European Court of Human Rights, enabling the reader to grasp the subject as a whole.

New to this Edition:

- Covid-19 and its continuing effects on employment law
- Evolving case law on the equalities
- A new Employment Bill? Prospects for reform
- The impact of Brexit as the dust settles
- Case law developments on unfair dismissal, trade union rights and contracts of employment